DATA
ACQUISITION
and
PROCESS
CONTROL
USING
PERSONAL
COMPUTERS

DATA
ACQUISITION
and
PROCESS
CONTROL
USING
PERSONAL
COMPUTERS

T A R I K   O Z K U L

Teknomed Engineering
Istanbul, Turkey

Marcel Dekker, Inc.   New York • Basel • Hong Kong

Library of Congress Cataloging-in-Publication Data

Ozkul, Tarik
    Data acquisition and process control using personal computers / Tarik Ozkul.
       p. cm.
    Includes index.
    ISBN 0-8247-9710-8 (hardcover: alk. paper)
    1. Automatic data collection systems. 2. Process control--Automation. 3. Micro-
computers--Industrial applications. I. Title.
TS158.6.O96   1996
006--dc20
                                     96-6077
                                          CIP

The publisher offers discounts on this book when ordered in bulk quantities. For more information, write to Special Sales/Professional Marketing at the address below.

This book is printed on acid-free paper.

MARCEL DEKKER, INC.
270 Madison Avenue, New York, New York 10016

Current printing (last digit):
10 9 8 7 6 5 4 3 2 1

PRINTED IN THE UNITED STATES OF AMERICA

PREFACE

Data acquisition is a popular industrial application of computers. Applying computers to controlling processes has resulted in an increase in productivity and a gain in efficiency that would otherwise be almost impossible to achieve. Although computers have been used in this area for quite some time, traditional methods of data acquisition have only recently started to change. The main reason for this change is the availability of the inexpensive computational power that comes with personal computers. In the last decade, the role of the PC in heavy-duty professional engineering applications has changed dramatically. Today's PC has much more computational power than most dedicated computers used for data acquisition in the past, and their reliability has been greatly enhanced due to the reduced number of integrated circuit components, a direct result of the proliferation of application specific integrated circuit (ASIC) chips. Trends indicate that personal computers will become even more involved in professional applications in the coming years.

Data acquisition has typically relied on the turnkey approach with the whole data acquisition system designed around a dedicated computer. Modification and upgrading of the system or the software were difficult, if not impossible, because not enough software and hardware tools were available. Data acquisition has always been a very costly venture since the system needed to be custom designed for a specific application.

This book evolved from a popular course on data acquisition and interfacing. Although there are a number of good books on the market, most of them do not take advantage of the commercial products available and instead concentrate on designing data acquisition equipment from scratch. I have always regretted the fact that readers get bogged down with unnecessary details and run out of either time or steam before they can learn how to apply their knowledge in designing useful applications. I have intended to ameliorate this situation in *Data Acquisition and Process Control Using Personal Computers*. The necessary theoretical information is presented in a concise manner, avoiding detailed derivations and proofs. The reader can always acquire these from other sources. Instead, I have preferred to introduce industry standard data acquisition hardware and to focus on designing applications using off-the-shelf hardware and PC's. The fortunate thing about industry standard data acquisition equipment is that it is available from different vendors. Although there may be minor differences between different classes of hardware, basically hardware from any vendor can be used as long as some basic requirements are matched. Such wide availability makes it unnecessary to design hardware from scratch.

The applications and case studies discussed are the result of years of consultation and hands-on experience with the equipment. Over the years, I have had the chance to work with equipment from many different vendors and software packages from many different companies. I have tried to convey these experiences together with suggestions from manufacturers about different data acquisition applications.

Over the years, many colleagues from different professions have approached me with questions regarding a variety of data acquisition applications. This clearly emphasized the need for a book of this sort for interested readers who do not necessarily have a computer or electrical engineering background. Although some of the chapters are definitely intended for electrical/computer engineering literate individuals, these chapters can be omitted without causing any discontinuity in the rest of the material.

The breakdown of the chapters is as follows:

- Chapter One is an introduction to the concept of PC-based data acquisition using real-life case studies.
- Chapter Two introduces the basic components of a data acquisition and shows how they can be utilized for designing a data acquisition system through case studies.
- Chapter Three concerns analog-to-digital and digital-to-analog converters and goes into the details of different conversion techniques.
- Chapter Four focuses on sensors and transducers. Different types of sensors and interfacing considerations for these sensors are discussed, and a selection guide is provided for most types of sensors. Selected case studies show how these sensors can be utilized in real-life problems.
- Chapter Five is an overview of industry standard PC-based data acquisition equipment. It introduces what is currently available on the market and includes a selection guide.
- Chapter Six emphasizes local data acquisition using PC's, where the PC and the sensors are in close proximity. A detailed real-life case study shows how to select hardware and design a PC-based data acquisition system.
- Chapter Seven concerns local data acquisition using IEEE-488 equipment.

- Chapter Eight is a discussion of remote data acquisition, where the PC and the application are separated by a considerable distance. Different methods are explained in detail, and a selection guide is given for remote data acquisition hardware.
- Chapter Nine concerns actuators and interfacing them with the PC. Different actuators are explained, and design examples using commercial equipment are given.
- Chapter Ten deals with recent trends in data acquisition. With the advent and popularity of computer networks, data acquisition via networked computers has become feasible and advantageous in many aspects. Another noteworthy trend in industry involves networking data acquisition equipment and actuators at the lowest level. This technology, labeled Fieldbus, is beginning to affect the whole process control industry.
- Chapter Eleven deals with the software aspect of data acquisition. Valuable information about programming languages and available industry standard data acquisition software packages is given in this chapter. The examples are detailed enough to elucidate the capabilities and programming techniques of the packages. An up-to-date list of data acquisition packages with address and price information is also included in this chapter.
- The appendixes supply valuable data sheets for many different sensors and products.

The author acknowledges the support provided by the King Fahd University of Petroleum and Minerals under project no. COE/PCDATA/153. Many people have contributed to this book. I especially wish to acknowledge Professor Dr. Harold Schumny and Howard Austerlitz for their valuable comments. My thanks to the staff of Marcel Dekker, Inc., who made this project a reality. I am grateful to Linear Technology Corporation, Burr-Brown Corporation, RS Components Ltd., Smar International Corporation, and Keithly-Metrabyte Corporation for providing data sheets and application notes. And a big thank you goes to my wife and children for their patience during the writing of this book. Success is in the hands of God; I hope God Almighty makes this work a source of knowledge for many people.

Tarik Ozkul

CONTENTS

DATA
ACQUISITION
and
PROCESS
CONTROL
USING
PERSONAL
COMPUTERS

One

INTRODUCTION to DATA ACQUISITION SYSTEMS

This introductory chapter will define the basics of data acquisition systems. It is intended to define the terminology, introduce the essential components and give several real-life examples of personal computers in data acquisition and process control applications. After you read this chapter, you will appreciate the wide-scale use of personal computers in industry and see how personal computers are used even for critical, large scale applications. Since this chapter is intended to be an introductory one, examples are given without extensive technical background. In every example, however, the reader will be directed to the proper chapter which gives detailed information about the particular type of configuration used. We hope that this chapter will encourage the novice engineer to explore personal computer-based data acquisition further.

1.1 WHAT IS A DATA ACQUISITION SYSTEM?

A human being, or any living creature in this respect, is a data acquisition system. We continuously monitor our environment with all the senses that we were blessed with and continuously make decisions about our actions.

Our eyes monitor our walking path for obstacles; our ears continuously monitor the environment for cues coming from front and behind; our nose smells; and our tongue tastes. We are a perfect data acquisition system. **A data acquisition system is a system that acquires data from the outside world for a purpose, usually for the purpose of controlling a system.**

1

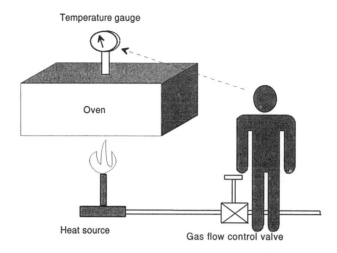

Temperature gauge

Oven

Heat source   Gas flow control valve

Figure 1.1 A manually controlled temperature control system.

The concept of a data acquisition system, as far as it is applied to industrial systems, means acquiring data from the outside world by means of sensors and turning it into useful information for the purpose of controlling a process or a system.

Sensors are special devices which turn different physical quantities available in the environment into electrical form. In general a sensor changes one form of energy into another. There exist in the environment thousands of different physical variables which are not necessarily in the electrical form. The temperature of a room, the temperature of the tea that you drink, the viscosity of oil, the velocity of the wind, the speed of a car, and the weight of an object are just a few of these millions of physical quantities that go on around us, some noticed but most unnoticed. All these variables need to be put into electrical form using sensors because this is the only form in which our computers can read something from the outside world. What is meant by the electrical parameter is the voltage or current level. In industry the information that is read from the environment (parameters) is used for the purpose of controlling a process. A typical process that we encounter everyday is controlling the temperature of an oven, which is shown in Figure 1.1. The temperature of the oven can be controlled by a human being monitoring a temperature gauge and adjusting the flow of gas feeding to the furnace. In this case the temperature variable is put into visual form by means of a temperature gauge.

In a computerized data acquisition system, we would like to convert the temperature information not into visual but electrical form to facilitate reading by our computer. We have already mentioned that the information has to be in either voltage or current form. What we did not mention then is that, in addition to being in electrical form, the data also has to be in digital format. In the coming chapters, ways of converting electrical information into digital format will be explored in detail. For the time being, let us continue with ways of converting temperature information into electrical form. There is more than one kind of device that we can use for this purpose. One of them is called a thermistor. A thermistor is a variable resistor which changes its resistance value depending on the temperature of the environment. Resistance change is still not exactly an electrical parameter, so we need to convert the resistance change further into voltage or current change. Fortunately, resistance change is one of the easiest of all parameters to convert into voltage change.

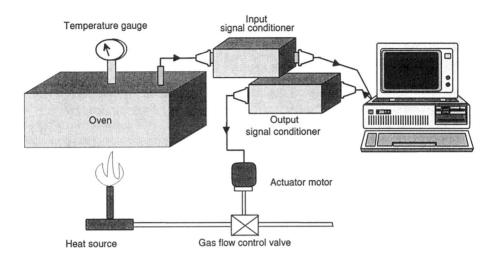

Figure 1.2 Computer controlled temperature control system.

By simply passing a constant current over a resistor or connecting the resistance in a voltage divider arrangement, we can convert the changing resistance into changing voltage.

1.2 PERSONAL COMPUTERS IN DATA ACQUISITION SYSTEMS

In the past decade we have been witnesses to a computer revolution which was brought about by personal computers. Even though computers have been with us for some time, with the introduction of personal computers, inexpensive computing power became available for the average user. Low cost made it feasible to own a personal computer or use one for applications which were not cost effective before. As a result of wide spread availability, an immense amount of software has been written for those computers and competition among the manufacturers has driven the prices down and performance up. In addition to the high performance, the reliability of the computers has also been increased due to VLSI (Very Large Scale Integration) and ASIC (Application Specific Integrated Circuit) chips used in their design. In general, the advantages of the PC's can be listed as follows:

- An enormous amount of software tools are available for designing applications for the PC.

- Due to the common availability of PC's, PC based software can be tested off-line before it goes to the factory floor.

- Due to well known hardware design, designing interface cards for PC's is simple.

- There are numerous vendors of data acquisition hardware. Because of competition the cost is reasonable.

- There are off-the-shelf data acquisition software packages for use with data acquisition hardware.

- Due to the low cost of PC's, data acquisition using computers is not costly.

Inexpensive, reliable hardware and abundant fully tested software have made personal computers an ideal choice for computers in data acquisition and interfacing with the real world. Of course there are certain physical requirements for a computer which is to operate in a harsh factory environment. One can not expect a personal computer designed for a nicely air conditioned office environment to work in a factory where extreme temperature changes and constant vibration are present. So, the inside and the outside of the personal computer should be physically conditioned for this type of environment, but no other major design change is required for the usual office personal computer. These types of computers are called industrial PC's. A typical industrial PC is shown in Figure 1.3.

As can be seen from the diagram, industrial PC's are housed in sturdy metallic cases which reduce electromagnetic noise coming from surrounding industrial machinery and enable the computer to be installed in standard industrial rack cabinets. A positive pressure fan filters air going inside the cabinet to ensure dust from the surroundings does not enter the system. Internally the industrial PC's use passive backplane for quick changing of faulty cards. What this means is that the printed circuit boards attached to the case contain only connectors and no active electronics that may fail. Even the motherboard which holds the CPU is not permanently attached to the casing. The motherboard card, just like any adapter card is plugged into the system. Thus, it is possible to upgrade the computer to a more powerful one simply by changing the CPU card. And if the CPU card ever fails it takes only couple of minutes to replace the faulty card. A hold down clamp keeps the internal adapter cards securely attached to the chassis and prevents cards from getting loose due to vibrations.

From the performance point of view, a personal computer is a significantly powerful data processing tool. The trend shows that the performance of computers doubles or triples almost every year. Nowadays the PC's have very powerful microprocessors which are much more powerful than the computers that were custom designed for data acquisition applications yesterday. It is no longer feasible to design computers from scratch for

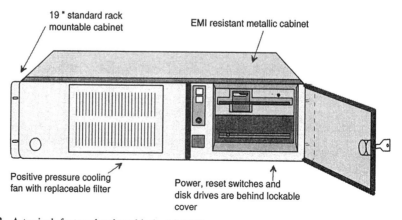

Figure 1.3 A typical, factory hardened industrial PC.

data acquisition purposes since the cost of designing, troubleshooting, programming and debugging a new computer is much more costly than buying an off-the-shelf personal computer.

With personal computers there is the added advantage of availability of spreadsheet and statistical packages which can analyze the trend of the data and can log the data automatically on to the available data base.

1.3 CASE STUDIES OF DATA ACQUISITION SYSTEMS

The following cases are all real life data acquisition examples. In all cases, personal computers and personal computer-based data acquisition products were used for collecting and processing the data. In these cases the personal computer not only processed the data but it actually took corrective action and controlled the system through the actuators connected to the system. In the following section, a brief synopsis about each one of these applications will be given.* Some of the cases will be looked at in more detail in the following chapters. In the coming chapters you will learn how to design these systems in detail.

1.3.1 Collection of Subduction Data from the Ocean Using a PC as a Data Acquisition System

In a three-year experiment designed by a major oceanographic research institution, Woods Hole Oceanographic Institute, MA, U.S.A. oceanographic and meteorological data were collected in an area of more than one million square kilometers to study the effect of the Gulf Stream currents on the weather. The term "subduction" is used by earth scientists to describe the phenomenon of earth plates sliding on top of each other. In this study the term "subduction" refers to one ocean current sliding beneath other currents. To study these effects researchers collect data from the following four sources:

- fixed location surface buoys which report the weather and sea conditions on the surface;
- free moving buoys which drift with oceanic currents and report the currents (these buoys are tracked by satellite to record their positions);
- subsurface buoys which report the conditions at depths of 300 meters; and
- towed subsurface immersed unmanned submarines.

These devices utilize a wide range of sensors for sensing temperature and the movement of current in three-dimensional space. The unmanned submarine, in particular, presents design challenges. Other than oceanic data, data for controlling the vessel is also needed.

Copyright Keithley Instruments. Some of the case studies are reprinted in part, with the permission of Keithley Instruments.

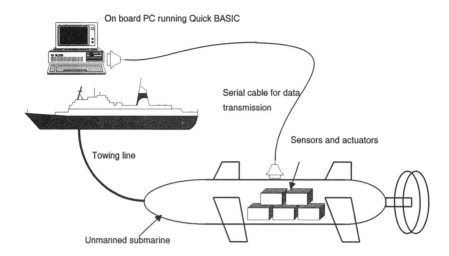

Figure 1.4 Submarine contains sensors and signal conditioners for acquiring the data.

The vessel has a pressure sensor for sensing outside pressure; inclinometers for measuring yaw and pitch angles of the vessel; position sensors for sensing wing angle; and a speed sensor for sensing the impeller blade rotation speed (see Figure 1.4). All these data are amassed by sensors without being analyzed are sent back to the research vessel towing the submarine. The two vessels are linked by a serial communication cable. The data are received through the serial port of a PC on the ship-side and analyzed by a program written in Quick BASIC language. The system involves appropriate sensors, signal conditioners on the submarine, a personal computer and a program written in Quick BASIC.

This is a typical example of a remote, non-intelligent data acquisition system. It is explained in detail in Chapter Eight which deals with remote data acquisition systems.
CUSTOMER: Woods Hole Oceanographic Institute, MA, U.S.A.
HARDWARE: Remote data acquisition crate with serial communication card, A/D converter card, Digital I/O card.
SOFTWARE: Custom software written using Quick BASIC™.
COMPUTER: IBM PC Compatible.

1.3.2 Controlling Automatic Window Glass Cutter

A five by six meter X-Y table used for cutting window glass is modernized by retrofitting the old design with a PC. The original design utilized a programmable logic controller (PLC) and a paper tape reader for loading programs. The PLC and the paper tape reader is replaced with a PC to control the movement of the cutting head. Data acquisition hardware controlled the on-board high-power DC motors and kept track of the position of the cutting head continuously through the use of position sensors. Apart from controlling the movement of the head, the PC is also used for optimizing the location of the shapes to be cut from the window glass.

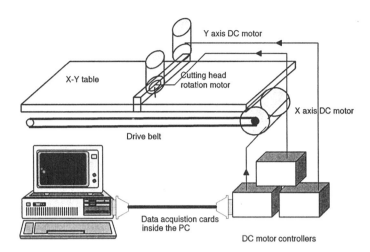

Figure 1.5 Hardware used for glass cutting application.

 The operator simply enters the shapes and the dimensions of the pieces to be cut; then the PC will arrange the shapes in such a way that the wastage will be minimized. The design with the PC is easier to maintain and saves money by reducing wastage.

The design is a typical local data acquisition system with all data acquisition hardware located inside the PC. This type of design is featured in detail in Chapter six.

CUSTOMER: Glass Works, Dammam, Saudi Arabia.
HARDWARE: National Instruments™ A/D, D/A converter cards, Digital input/output card.
SOFTWARE: Custom software written in Visual BASIC™.
COMPUTER: IBM PC Compatible.

1.3.3 Data Acquisition System Replaces Strip Chart Recorder for Monitoring an Electron Beam Welder

An outdated strip chart recording system is replaced with a PC based data acquisition system for monitoring Electron Beam Welder (EBW) parameters for quality control purposes. Seven signals from the EBW directly related to critical weld variables (beam voltage, beam current, focus coil current, X deflection, Y deflection, filament current, and chamber vacuum) are monitored by the data acquisition system. The signals are monitored at 20 Hz per channel by a data acquisition crate located outside the PC. The PC is connnected to the crate through a special 15 foot cable. The data acquistion crate contains special purpose cards for converting electron beam output signals into digital form. Since the electron beam welder system uses high voltage level signals, signals coming from the welder are isolated from the data acquistion system in order to protect the computer system from accidental short circuits. The system is capable of monitoring 8 channels at 500 Hz/channel. All signals are measured in a differential mode with single point grounding and shielded twisted pair wires.

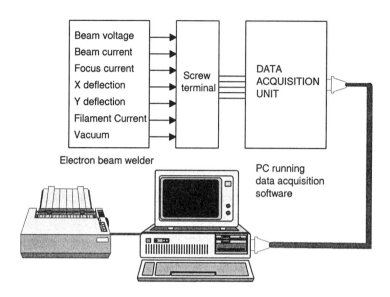

Figure 1.6 Electron beam welder connected to a PC for controlling quality of the weld.

Data is collected through a menu-driven operation and can be output as a hard copy worksheet or stored on disk. This is a typical room-local data acquistion system and explained in detail in Chapter seven. Mean and standard deviations are computed and can be compared with data obtained from a "standard weld". Deviation reports can be generated for any set of data.

CUSTOMER: Los Alamos National Laboratory, Los Alamos, NM.

HARDWARE: Keithley 500A™ data acquisiton crate connected to: 7 isolation amplifiers, AMMIA analog input card, various voltage dividers, current sensing resistors, etc.

SOFTWARE: Acquisition-Keithley Data Acquisition & Control Software Analysis-Asyst™, Lotus 1-2-3™.

COMPUTER: IBM PC.

1.3.4 Test System for Satellite Thrust Engines

Two separate PC-based systems are often used together in various aspects of testing small thrust engines used on satellites.

One system for test control uses digital I/O cards with solid state relays and a timer to operate thrust control valves. Programs written in C language control complex on/off sequences of 1 to 24 valves to simulate actual flight plans. Actuation timing to within 3 millisecond precision and aggregate on/off rates of up to 10 kHz are achieved.

A second system using an 8 channel/12 bit analog-to-digital converter board and an 8 channel/16 bit analog-to-digital converter board are used to measure eight temperatures, and eight thrust pressures. Labtech Notebook™ menu-driven software controls the acquisition in a triggered mode (triggered by the test control computer) to synchronize the acquisition of one data point near the middle of the thrust pulse of the engine.

Output data are measured in terms of the thrust multiplied by the time products. Analog data are stored on disk and later transferred to Lotus 1-2-3™ for analysis.

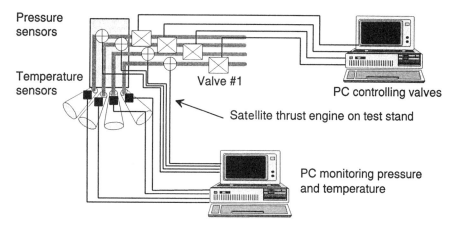

Figure 1.7 Testing and monitoring sattelite thrust engine using PC's.

Both of these are examples of local data acquisition systems without special crates. Techniques are explained in detail in Chapter Six, and the cards used for data acquisition are explained in Chapter Five. Both computers are factory hardened industrial PC's.

CUSTOMER: A California manufacturer of satellite engines.
HARDWARE: Test Controller-MetraBus™ MSSR-32 digital I/O card, MetraBus™ CTM-05-Timer Output Analyzer-MetraByte™ DAS-16 A/D converter card.
SOFTWARE: C language program for test controller Labtech Notebook™, plus Lotus 1-2-3™ for output analyzer.
COMPUTER: Both systems use industrial grade IBM compatible PC's.

1.3.5 Data Acquisition for Wind Tunnel Research

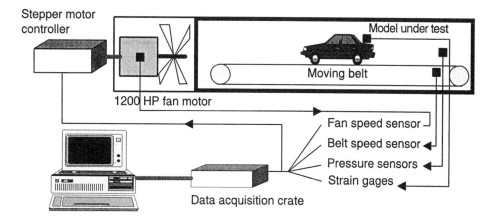

Figure 1.8 Wind tunnel setup.

A low-speed wind tunnel has been developed for aerodynamic research on a variety of models including high lift airfoil propellers, vehicles, and racing cars. To provide a fully automated testing capability, a PC-based data acquisition and control system has been developed for the facility to control the tunnel test conditions and also acquire, analyze, and present the experimental data.

The setup is a typical room-local data acquisition system which is described in detail in Chapter Six. A data acquisition crate is used for both testing control conditions and acquisition of test data. The test condition control system consists of several pressure and temperature transducers, a fan speed tachometer, a fan speed control potentiometer, as well as a tachometer and speed control for a moving ground belt (required for accurate simulation of wheeled vehicles). The tachometer outputs are monitored by digital I/O ports in the crate. The speed control potentiometers are controlled by stepper motors controlled by the stepper motor controller cards in the crate. A stepper motor/potentiometer control is an effective technique for controlling the 1200 HP motor needed to generate airspeeds up to 180 km/h.

Experimental data sensors vary depending on the application. A typical application such as a racing car involves multiple pressure transducers, strain gauge balances, and often a stepper motor is used to control the position of the model in the tunnel. To provide a single environment for data acquisition, facility speed control, data reduction, and data presentation, Asyst™ software is utilized.

CUSTOMER: Department of Aeronautics and Astronautics, South Hampton University.
HARDWARE: Keithley™ Series 500A-PS2 AMM2.
SOFTWARE: Asyst™.
COMPUTER: IBM PS/2™.

1.3.6 Pulmonary Function Testing

Pulmonary function testing for pediatric and infant care is being performed by a PC-based system. Analog inputs from a variety of sensors and conditioners are digitized and analyzed via a PC-based room-local type data acquisition system.

Inputs include 0-5 V signals from pneumatic airflow sensors, pressure transducers, a gas analyzer, and oxygen content, heart rate, and blood pressure analyzers. Typically up to 10 analog inputs and one digital input (for start/stop of system) are connected to the system. In most applications only three analog inputs are monitored at one time and typically two are plotted in real time, usually in an X-Y plot and with some calculations performed prior to plotting to the screen. Three digital outputs are used for control of various valves used to control the tests. Speeds of 100 samples/second on each of two channels, including calculation, real time display and storage to memory are achieved by a PC. Much higher rates of acquisition and display are possible but only if displayed without calculation.

HARDWARE: Keithley™ Model 575 data acquisition crate connected to outputs of various sensors /analyzers.
SOFTWARE: Microsoft Quick BASIC™, Keithley™ Data Acquisition Software.
COMPUTER: 386/16MHz IBM PC compatible with a co-processor.

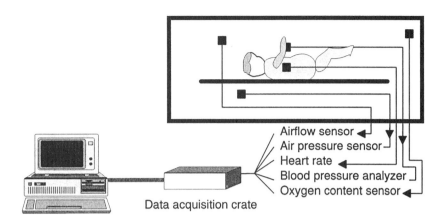

Figure 1.9   Pulmonary function test setup.

1.3.7 Computer Controlled Mechanical Testing of Materials

A PC based data acquisition and control crate configured for local data acquisition is used to control pneumatic pressure in a fatigue testing fixture to apply stress to samples of material being tested.

The PC measures the output of a load cell to monitor the pressure applied to the sample, and the output of an LVDT (linear variable differential transformer) to monitor the displacement of the sample. An analog output from the data acquisition crate is used to control the pneumatic pressure applied through an electric-to-pneumatic transducer. In addition, digital inputs are used to monitor limit switches; a digital output controls an air valve to release pressure, and a thermocouple is used to monitor the temperature of the sample when testing at elevated temperatures.

Because of the multiple channel capacity of all the modules in the system, one PC can operate several test fixtures.

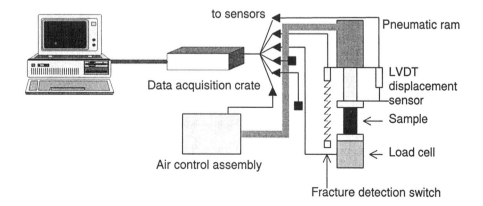

Figure 1.10   Mechanical test setup.

CUSTOMER: Department of Ceramic Engineering, University of Illinois at Urbana-Champaign.
HARDWARE: Keithley™ 500A data acquisition crate, A/D, D/A conversion cards, 1 load cell connected to 1 LVDT, 1 Electric-to-pneumatic transducer, 1 thermocouple.
SOFTWARE: Keithley™ Data Acquisition & Control Software.
COMPUTER: IBM PC compatible.

1.3.8 PC-Based Control of a Lead Flash Smelting Pilot Plant

A PC-based system is used to monitor 60 analog inputs (inside/outside reactor temperatures, gas concentrations, lead and oxygen feed rates, etc.) to investigate and develop a more energy efficient and less polluting method of producing lead. Additionally, sensors for pressure, temperature and other critical system parameters are used to determine the need for system shutdown.

Data is acquired from 60 channels and displayed on a video screen and stored in a data file at one minute intervals. Other critical parameters are monitored and additional hard wired safety interlocks to the computer are used.

The system is a partly local and partly remote data acquisition system since some of the parts are controlled via RS-232 link. Remote data acquisition techniques used for this type of setups are explained in detail in Chapter Eight which is devoted to remote data acquisition.

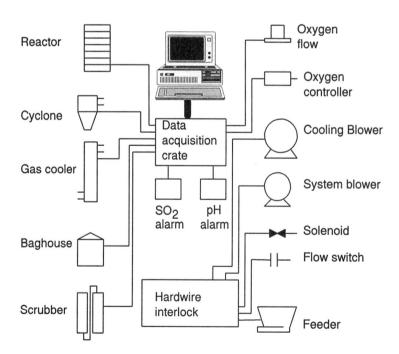

Figure 1.11 Pilot plant control setup.

CUSTOMER: University of British Columbia, Vancouver, BC, Canada.
HARDWARE: Keithley™ 500A data acquisition system, 5 pressure transducers, 16 bit A/D card with multiplexer connected to 48 thermocouples, 16 bit A/D card connected to 1 oxygen mass flowmeter, 1 sulphur dioxide detector, 4-20 mA output cards, 1 pH meter, 1-32 Digital I/O card. Also a stand-alone microprocessor based concentrate feeder is connected to the PC via an RS-232 link.
SOFTWARE: Entire system program is written in Asyst™ including control of the concentrate feeder via RS-232.
COMPUTER: IBM PC compatible.

1.3.9 Standby Generator Remote Test System

A PC-based data acquisition system is used to monitor all critical operating parameters of a 2.5 megawatt emergency standby generating system during frequent and extensive readiness exercises.

The generator system is outfitted with a remote monitoring and control system consisting of a data acquisition system and a rack mounted, industrial PC.

The system serves as a data logger and is also capable of executing a variety of exercises which can be programmed in advance by the maintenance staff. In addition to the industrial PC located at the site, a second PC is located in the maintenance office 300 meters from the generator and is connected to the on-site PC via a direct hard wired serial link operating at 9600 baud. All keyboard input for menu selection, generator system control, programming of exercises, or file maintenance can be performed at either computer location.

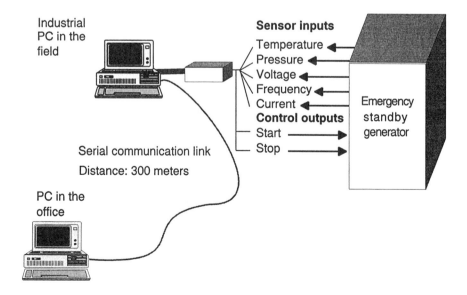

Figure 1.12 Emergency standby generator monitored and controlled by PC.

Temperatures and pressures of various engine operating systems are sensed by 4-20 mA temperature and pressure transducers and directly read by the data acquisition crate connected to the field PC. Operating power levels, voltage, frequency, and current are monitored by power system transducers and are also read by the data acquisition system. The engine/generator basic controller is an industrial process controller that includes a TTL level digital I/O card. This I/O card is connected to the digital I/O on the data acquisition crate which allows control and status information to be passed between the PC data acquisition system and the engine/generator system.

This is a typical remote, intelligent data acquisition system which is actually a combination of local and remote data acquisition systems. These types of systems are discussed in detail in Chapters Six and Eight respectively.

HARDWARE: Keithley™ 575 data acquisition system connected to 4 three phase watt transducers, 4 one phase volt. transducers, 4 one phase current transducers, 8 thermocouples and transmitters, 2 pressure transducers, 32 digital I/O from process control board.
SOFTWARE: Menu-driven selection of operating sequence and displays, written in Microsoft Quick BASIC™ and Keithley™ Data Acquisition & Control Software.
COMPUTER: In field: industrial IBM PC compatible computer. Remote: desktop IBM PC compatible.

1.3.10 Vehicle Road Simulator Test System

To provide testing capability to meet EPA (Enviromental Protection Agency, U.S.A.) requirements for vehicle durability, economy, and performance, a PC-based test system was designed.

One critical requirement of the test system was that it must assure that the road simulator dynamo meter accurately duplicated the steady state and automated conditions recorded in the test vehicle during the defined EPA drive schedule. To accomplish this, two PC based systems were developed. A laboratory PC data acquisition system was used to control the vehicle road simulator dynamometer. In addition, a portable data acquisition system using a laptop PC was used to collect data in the test vehicle during the drive schedule. The data acquired during the actual drive was then transferred to a floppy diskette where it was brought back to the road simulator lab to provide the required automation to drive and control the dynamo meter.

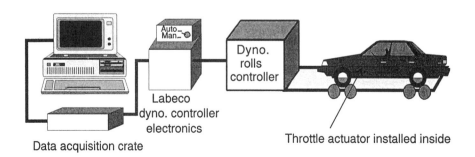

Figure 1.13 Vehicle road simulator setup.

The road simulator system consists of an industrial PC connected to a data acquisition crate which uses an analog-to-digital, digital-to-analog, and digital I/O cards to drive the physical dynamo meter. The previously recorded control parameters then provide scaled throttle position data that drive a throttle servo, fifth wheel pulses (mph) that drive the dynamo meter, and rpm for engine performance and observation. Other control and monitoring such as safety aborts, the dynamometer absorber, the throttle feedback potentiometer, and parking brake are provided to the dynamo meter.

When a vehicle is placed on the dynamo meter, the throttle actuator, the throttle feedback potentiometer, the parking brake actuator and safety switches are installed. A menu-driven system allows the operator to scale the throttle and dynamo meter so that it provides the same percent of throttle and dynamo meter values that were recorded in the EPA drive schedule.

This is a typical local data acquisition and control system which is described in detail in Chapter Six.

HARDWARE: Keithley™ 500A data acquisition crate connected to dynamometer through an A/D converter card to throttle actuator, analog output card to throttle potentiometer, and digital input/output card to various limit and safety switches.
SOFTWARE: Menu-driven routines written by system designer at Asyst™ for acquisition and control. Additionally, Lotus™, DADISP™, Asystant™, Labtech Notebook™ for general analysis applications.
COMPUTER: IBM Industrial PC.

1.3.11 Automated Growth of Semiconductor Compounds by Chemical Vapor Deposition

A PC controlled system is used to adjust the flow of various gases (e.g., trimethylgallium and arsine) across a hot substrate where they react to form a semiconductor layer on the substrate.

By adjusting the ratio of the flow rates of the gases, layers of differing compositions are grown. By changing the relative flow rates, the composition of succeeding layers are changed resulting in varying semiconductor characteristics including electrical carrier type and carrier concentration. The quality and uniformity of the semiconductor layer that is formed depends critically on the precise control of the flow of the gases, the temperature of the substrate, the precision with which the gases are switched and the time of the growth steps. In addition to control, the system provides real time process information.

Mass flow, pressure, and temperature controllers with analog set point inputs are used so that the analog outputs from the PC control system can accurately control the process with precise timing.

The system uses a data acquisition crate used in local acquisition configuration to monitor and control 15 flow and pressure controllers, 5 temperature controllers, 32 solenoids for controlling air operated flow valves, and several digital inputs to monitor safety circuits. A digital input/output board is used to synchronize a separate residual gas analyzer for monitoring the process. Semiconductor layer thickness and composition depend on

- Flow rates

- Gas components
- Pressure
- Temperature
- Time of growth

Process steps ranging from several seconds to hours are precisely controlled as background tasks by the software. The minimum resolution of system timing is 50 milliseconds. In addition to control, the system provides real time plotting of any of 12 variables (of which any 4 are observable simultaneously).

CUSTOMER: Corporate Research Laboratory-Eastman Kodak Company.
HARDWARE: Keithley™ 500A data acquisition system with A/D, analog output and digital output cards connected to 15 flow controllers; 5 temperature. controllers; 32 flow, pressure and temperature sensors; 32 solenoids; various safety interlocks; and digital output card connected to a residual gas analyzer.
SOFTWARE: Asyst™
COMPUTER: IBM PC compatible.

1.3.12 Multitasking Lung Function Characterization System

A biomedical research team uses a PC, a data acquisition card and off-the-shelf data acquisition software in a local data acquisition configuration to simultaneously acquire and analyze data for a study of lung function under the stress of exercise. Custom front panels make system control easy, freeing the operator from the details of low-level implementation.

In this experiment the subject rides a stationary bicycle ergometer which is subjected to varying work loads. The subject wears a mask which channels inhalation and exhalation through a tube to which a turbine and a gas chromatograph are attached. Built into the turbine is an infrared measuring system which detects the motions of the blades. The signal from this is converted via a ventilation measurement module (Interface Associates, Laguna Miguel, CA) into two analog volume signals: expiration and inspiration. The gas chromatograph provides readings on carbon dioxide, oxygen, and nitrogen concentrations. All 5 channels are logged to disk at rates of about 50 Hz each.

The two volume signals are used to detect the onsets of inspiration and expiration. Calculations performed on the five signals are used to derive over 30 parameters, such as oxygen consumption, carbon dioxide production, respiratory exchange ratio, and minute ventilation. These reflect the patient responses to exercise exertion on a breath-by-breath basis. Calculations are based on the differentiation of the volume signals and integration of the products of flow and gas concentration over each breath cycle. The system is a multitasking one because the parameters are calculated in real time, and displayed simultaneously with the acquisition.

Operators can also adjust the work load of the bicycle ergometer by entering watt values interactively, which the software is designed to convert to appropriate analog outputs for controlling the ergometer.

CUSTOMER: A U.S. West Coast biomedical research facility.

HARDWARE: 16 bit A/D card connected to 1 gas chromatograph, 1 ventilation measurement module.
SOFTWARE: VIEWDAC™.
COMPUTER: IBM PC compatible.

1.3.13 High Speed Package Handler

Several virtual test and measurement instrument cards for PC as well as control hardware comprise an automatic test station managed via a personal computer. The PC acts as both the host and controller for the test and analysis of functions within the unit under test (U U T).

Functions of the U U T include sorting of 30,000 packages per hour; reading and stamping bar codes; detecting the presence of stamps; and reading address lines for zip codes.

A waveform generator card is used to generate a square wave input signal to the U U T ranging from 5 kHz-30 kHz. The output return frequency signal derived from the U U T is then measured by a counter card for PC. Various voltage and resistance points are multiplexed into a multiplexer card which are later measured and recorded by the voltage measurement card. Control and sensing of AC power including three phases, is accomplished by using an isolated digital input card. Additionally, approximately 300 digital (TTL) input/output levels are monitored and controlled by several digital I/O boards. Further sensing, measurement and control hardware are provided by a relay matrix board and analog/digital I/O boards.

HARDWARE: PCIP-DMM (Multimeter board)
                         PCIP-SCAN (16 channel multiplexer/scanner)
                         PCIP-CNTR (Counter)
                         PCIP-SST (Function generator)
                         PDIS0-8 (Relay input/output)
                         PI0-96 (3 Digital interface)

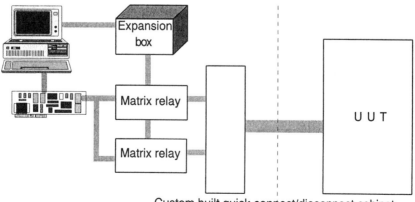

Figure 1.14   Automatic test station setup.

MID-64 (Driver card)
MCPT-8X8 (Crosspoint matrix relay board)
MBEXP-12AT (Expansion chassis)
SOFTWARE: Proprietary program written in C language.
COMPUTER: IBM PC 386SX compatible.

1.3.14 Automated Radio-Pharmaceutical Accelerator Control System

A data acquisition system is being used to control a compact, fully automated accelerator facility for the production of radio pharmaceuticals for positron emission tomography (PET). The system comprises a Tandem Cascade Accelerator (TCA) developed at Science Research Laboratory, Somerville, Massachusetts and a robotic delivery system for the on-demand synthesis of radioisotope labeled compounds in a hospital environment.

The TCA is a low cost, reliable and easy to operate alternative to a cyclotron for PET. Recent technological advances in high voltage solid state circuit components and in high current negative ion sources developed at Science Research Laboratory make possible the design of an accelerator which is compact and lightweight and which can deliver ample particle current to the target chamber for PET applications.

Capital and operating costs for the TCA system will be significantly less than for a small PET cyclotron system. It is anticipated that the availability of such an automated radio-pharmaceutical delivery system will promote the more widespread use of PET in clinical applications.

The system is a typical remote data acquisition system which has the data acquisition crate located near the accelerator and the PC located in the office a safe distance away from the radiation sources. The PC is also connected remotely to the robot controller system which handles samples. Such systems are discussed in detail in Chapter Eight of this book.

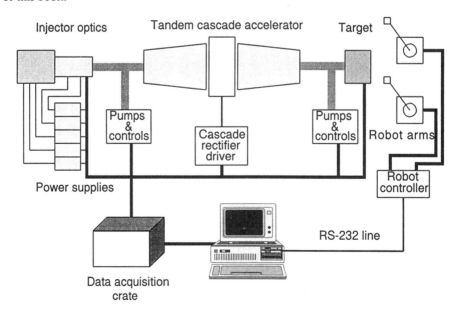

Figure 1.15 TC Accelerator setup.

CUSTOMER: Science Research Laboratory, Somerville, Massachusetts.
HARDWARE: Relay control board, analog output card, analog input card, thermocouple input card, serial interface card (data acquisition cards).
SOFTWARE: PARAGON™.
COMPUTER: IBM PS/2™ Model 60.

1.3.15 Monitoring System for Oil Drilling Head

A PC based data acquisition system is used to monitor the drill head of an oil rig. Typical parameters monitored include head pressure, fluid slurry flow (from a Doppler flow meter), thumper frequency. The system also controls the test pressure pump through a PID algorithm based on the torque feedback.

This is a typical example of a remote data acquisition and process control system with crate in the field and PC in the control room. All power controls to the pump and alarm panel (digital outputs) are handled via the data acquisition crate in the field.

Since the test environment is normally wet and subject to splash from the slurry, the data acquisition crate is mounted in a Nema 12 watertight enclosure. Communications with the remotely located control PC is done via a serial interface card located in the crate. The PC is located in the control room which is 500 meters away.

The parameters monitored are connected to the data acquisition crate through the user selected I/O cards in the following manner: The control portions of the system are handled in two ways. First, the analog output boards are used to control voltage-input controllers.

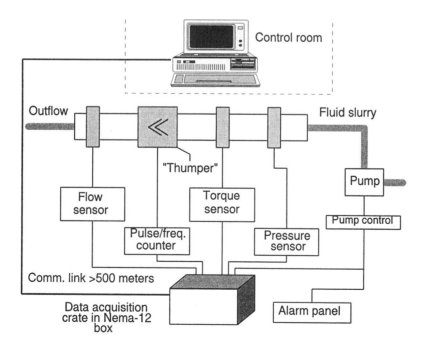

Figure 1.16 Drill head monitor setup.

These include power and motor controls whose output (power, RPM) are proportional to the control voltage input. Second, the relay boards are used to switch various relays around the machine. These relays in turn control valve-positioning, motor direction, flow, etc.

CUSTOMER: A major oil producer company.
HARDWARE: WH-AO-8 analog output card, WH-PCDB-PAR parallel interface card, WH-EM-16 relay controller card.
SOFTWARE: Keithley Data Acquisition and Control Software.
COMPUTER: IBM PC compatible.

1.3.16 Rocket Booster Test Stand

A manufacturer of solid booster fuel required a portable (rolling) test stand configuration that would not only interface to the required sensors, but also be both durable and quickly field-repairable.

The test setup consists of up to 16 thermocouples embedded in the casing and fuel partitions to monitor temperatures at various burn stages. Though destroyed during test, the thermocouples monitor events of fuel burn, case hot-spots, and completeness of burn. All thermocouples are interfaced to the crate through an intelligent thermocouple interface card, which provides all CJC compensation in less than ideal outdoor ambients. The onboard processor provides all linearization over the test range of ambient to over 4,000 degrees F.

A connector containing a DC volt battery and trigger signals is connected to the analog input card and covers the range of 100 mV to +10 V.

A third cable, from a clamp-on type induction probe, measures a pulse train from a rear mounted vane to gauge gas flow and connects to a counter board.

An Industrial grade IBM PC compatible computer and rugged panel printer provide the interface and report generation for test personnel.

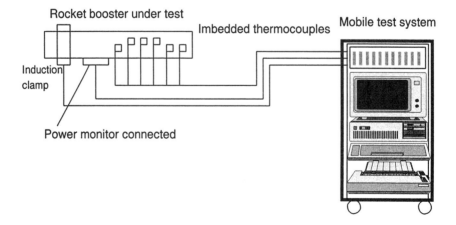

Figure 1.17   Rocket booster test setup.

CUSTOMER: A solid rocket booster manufacturer.
HARDWARE: Workhorse data acquisition crate, WH-AIN-16 analog input card, WH-CNTT-5 counter card, WH-TC-16 thermocouple interface card.
SOFTWARE: Custom written using C language.
COMPUTER: Industrial IBM PC compatible.

REFERENCES

1. Jordan, E. C. (ed.) , *Reference Data for Engineers: Radio, Electronics, Computer, and Communications,* SAMS A Division of Macmillan Computer Publishing, Sixth Edition, 1991.

2. *Keithley Data Acquisition & Control Catalog*, Keithley Instruments, Volume 24 1991.

3. Smith, B. , *Data from the Depths*, BYTE, July 1993. pp. 69-78.

Two

SIGNAL CONDITIONING for PC-BASED DATA ACQUISITION SYSTEMS

The purpose of this chapter is to introduce the basic configuration of data acquisition systems and explore the signal conditioning part in detail. The first part of the chapter explains basic signal conditioning components at the integrated circuit level and shows how to put these components together to perform signal conditioning. Several design examples are given at this stage to show the process. The first part is general purpose and has no specific reference to personal computer-based data acquisition. It is intended to teach principles of signal conditioning only.

The second part of the chapter introduces off-the-shelf, standard signal conditioning hardware designed specifically for data acquisition applications. Various components available, how to use them and how to set up custom signal conditioning circuits using these components are covered with a few design examples. The chapter also indicates commercial sources for signal conditioning hardware and gives further references for the interested reader who wants to know more about the subject of signal conditioning.

2.1 INTRODUCTION

Any data acquisition system, regardless of its type and what kind of variables it acquires from the real world, has some basic components. A specific data acquisition system may be required to take pressure and temperature readings from an oil well, whereas another system may be required to take humidity and temperature readings in a greenhouse. Even though the specific components to make these measurements may differ from system to system, the general basic categories of building blocks are common to all of them. These basic building blocks for data acquisition systems include the following:

- Sensor
- Signal conditioner
- Data acquisition hardware
- Computer

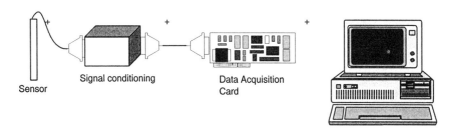

Figure 2.1 Parts of a typical data acquisition system.

1. Sensor (transducer): The sensor is the component of the system which changes the physical variable that needs to be monitored into electrical form. The physical variable that needs to be monitored or acquired from the real world can be of different types. Normally, there exists literally thousands of variables in the real world that are continuously changing around us. Depending on the process at hand, we may be interested in only a few of these parameters like temperature, pressure, weight, rate of flow etc. The function of the sensor is to change these physical parameters, temperature, pressure, weight, etc., into electrical form. The main reason behind this conversion is to enable the next block of the data acquisition system to recognize the variable. Different types of sensors and the way they work will be analyzed in the coming sections.

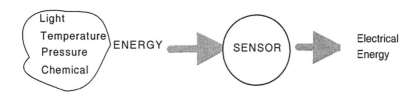

Figure 2.2 Sensor converts one form of energy into another.

2. Signal conditioning: The signal that comes from the previous building block, namely the sensor, is in electrical form but may not necessarily be in the suitable form for the next block of the data acquisition system. Most of the time the signal that is produced by the sensor is very weak in power; because of this, it is very susceptible to electromagnetic noise coming from the surrounding environment. Thus the signal needs to be properly conditioned before it travels to the next block of the data acquisition system. The most common signal conditioning operations can be summarized as follows:

- Voltage to current conversion
- Current to voltage conversion
- Voltage to frequency conversion
- Frequency to voltage conversion
- Signal amplification
- Isolation
- Filtering (low pass, high pass)
- Integration
- Differentiation

These operations will be discussed in detail in the coming sections.

3. Analog-to-digital converter: The signal generated by the signal conditioning block is in the analog form. Any continuous real time variable is called an analog variable. All real life parameters that exist in the universe are analog parameters; they change continuously. For example, temperature is a continuous real time analog parameter. The reason we call it continuous is because when it changes, it changes continuously, smoothly without any jumps. Yes, it is possible to have temperature change abruptly, but if you monitor closely enough, it is possible to see that change is still continuous. You may dip a thermometer in icy water, and then afterwards pour plenty of boiling water in the container. In this case, temperature change will be very sudden and abrupt, but it still will be continuous. Analog variables are not suitable for use in our computers even if they are electrical parameters.

Figure 2.3 Functional block diagram of an A/D converter.

What is suitable for our computers is binary logic and discrete time. Inside the computer, register values change in accordance with the master clock. This means that change is not continuous but occurs at discrete times. A computer can only read binary values from the outside world and send its output in binary form. Any time we want the computer to read an analog variable, we need to first convert this analog variable into digital form using an analog-to-digital converter. An analog-to-digital (A/D) converter is a crucial part of any data acquisition system.

4. Computer: The last element in a data acquisition system is a computer. Basically, the duty of the computer is to read the output of the A/D converter which converts analog information into digital form. The raw data which is read from the analog to digital converter have to be processed by the computer in order for it to make any sense. Processing is done by the software, which is also a very important part of the data acquisition system.

2.2 BUILDING BLOCKS OF SIGNAL CONDITIONING SYSTEMS

In the previous section, the major components of data acquisition systems were given as block diagrams without discussing the internal details of each block. In the following sections we will be discussing these building blocks individually. The major part of any data acquisition project is designing the signal conditioning part of the system. Once the signal conditioner has been designed, usually the rest of the system can be completed very easily and quickly. In terms of effort spent on design, we can say that 60% of any data acquisition project involves designing the signal conditioning part of the circuit. As a data acquisition engineer, it is of interest for us to know how those blocks are designed so that we can design any signal conditioning system needed for the application. The signal conditioning components that will be discussed all have a common very important property which makes design process very simple.

All these signal conditioning components have high input impedance and low output impedance. This may not appear significantly noteworthy at first sight, but what it means is that, the components in the system do not load each other so that the input/output characteristics of the components are not altered. Due to this important feature, all signal conditioning components can be cascaded without any loading consideration. The knowledge of these components is very useful because virtually any electronic system can be designed by cascading a number of these components. The main advantage of these is that you only need to know simple basic electrical laws to design systems using them. An in-depth knowledge of electronics is not required to use these components.

Most of these simple building blocks are available in integrated circuit form from different vendors. Dealing with these components is quite different from dealing with transistors and resistors because there is no loading effect from one component to the other. Designs can be made without regard to any loading effects. After reviewing the function of each component, a commercially available component will be reviewed briefly to further familiarize ourselves with the real world design components.

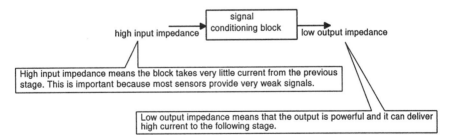

2.2.1 Operational Amplifiers

An operational amplifier is the most basic building block of data acquisition systems. A number of other signal conditioning components that will be reviewed in this section can be constructed using operational amplifiers. An operational amplifier is a high gain amplifier with differential inputs and a single ended output.

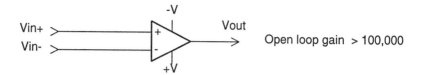

Figure 2.4 A typical operational amplifier.

The open loop gain of an operational amplifier is so high that it is accepted as infinity. Of course this does not mean that if you connect one volt to the input of the operational amplifier you will get infinite voltage at the output! The output voltage of the operational amplifier will be limited by the power supply voltage of the op-amp which is approximately 12 V to 15 V. Operational amplifiers use dual, balanced power supply voltages like +12 V, -12 V or +15 V, -15 V, etc. Usually the amplification of the op-amp is reduced to several thousands by using external components. Since as a data acquisition engineer we are only interested in using op-amps and not designing them, we will only concentrate on well known configurations utilizing op-amps. Several different configurations and amplification factors for each configuration are given below.

2.2.2 Inverting Amplifiers

The gain for the configuration, given in Figure 2.5, is as follows:

$$Vout = -\frac{R_f}{R_1} V_{in}$$

Here the negative sign indicates inversion. The load impedance for this arrangement, and the resistance seen by the Vin is R_1.

Another inverting configuration which has better noise characteristics is given in Figure 2.6. This arrangement has a better slew rate than the previous one. The slew rate is defined as the change of output per unit time.

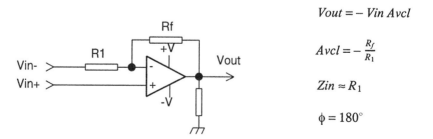

$$Vout = -\ Vin\ Avcl$$

$$Avcl = -\frac{R_f}{R_1}$$

$$Zin \approx R_1$$

$$\phi = 180°$$

Figure 2.5 Inverting configuration with feedback loop.

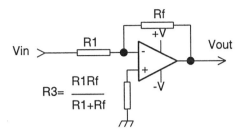

Figure 2.6 Another inverting configuration.

2.2.3 Noninverting Amplifiers

Noninverting amplifiers are used mostly as buffer amplifiers in order to avoid loading weak signal sources. The configuration for a noninverting amplifier and its amplification and input impedance are as follows:

$Vout= Vin. Avcl \qquad Avcl=(R1+R2)/R1 \qquad Zin>100 \; megaohm.$

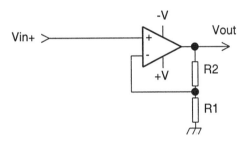

Figure 2.7 A typical noninverting combination.

2.2.4 Differential Amplifier

A differential amplifier is a configuration of op-amp which amplifies the difference of the signals that are connected to its V1 and V2 inputs. To give a numerical example assume that we connect 1.255 V to V1 input of the amplifier and 1.258 V to the V2 input of the amplifier. The differential amplifier will only amplify the voltage difference between the two inputs. (In this case the voltage difference of 1.258 - 1.255 = 0.003 V will be amplified.) The voltage that is common to both inputs will not be amplified. In this case 1.255 V is called "common voltage" in contrast to the differential voltage. The common voltage is not amplified. (This feature of the differential amplifier is called common mode rejection.) The configuration and the amplification factors are as in Figure 2.8.

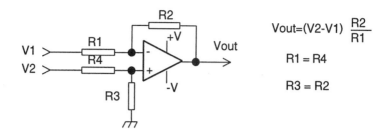

Figure 2.8 Differential amplifier configuration.

2.2.5 Operational Amplifiers Glossary

This section contains definitions of common terms used in data sheets of operational amplifiers.

COMMON-MODE INPUT IMPEDANCE
> *Effective impedance (resistance in parallel with capacitance) between either input of an amplifier and its common or ground terminal.*

COMMON-MODE REJECTION (CMR)
> *When both inputs of a differential amplifier experience the same common-mode voltage (CMV), the output should, ideally, be unaffected. CMR is the ratio of the common-mode input voltage change to the differential input voltage (error voltage) which produces the same output change.*
> *CMR (in dB) = 20 log CMV/Error Voltage*
> *Thus a CMR of 80 dB means that 1 V of common-mode voltage will cause an error of 100 μV (referred to input).*

COMMON-MODE VOLTAGE (CMV)
> *That portion of an input signal common to both inputs of a differential amplifier. Mathematically it is defined as the average of the signals at the two inputs: CMV = (e1 + e2)/2.*

COMMON-MODE VOLTAGE GAIN
> *Ratio of the output signal voltage (ideally zero) to the common-mode input signal voltage.*

COMMON-MODE VOLTAGE RANGE
> *Range of input voltage for linear, nonsaturated operation.*

DIFFERENTIAL INPUT IMPEDANCE
> *Apparent impedance, resistance in parallel with capacitance, between the two input terminals.*

FULL POWER FREQUENCY RESPONSE
> *Maximum frequency at which a device can supply its peak-to-peak rated output voltage and current, without introducing significant distortion.*

GAIN-BANDWIDTH PRODUCT
> *Product of small signal open-loop gain and frequency at that gain.*

INPUT BIAS CURRENT

DC input current required at each input of an amplifier to provide zero output voltage when the input signal and input offset voltage are zero. The specified maximum is for each input.

INPUT BIAS CURRENT vs SUPPLY VOLTAGE

Sensitivity of input bias current to power supply voltages.

INPUT BIAS CURRENT vs TEMPERATURE

Sensitivity of input bias current to temperature.

INPUT CURRENT NOISE

Input current that would produce, at the output of a noiseless amplifier, the same output as that produced by the inherent noise generated internally in the amplifier when the source resistances are large.

INPUT OFFSET CURRENT

Difference of the two input bias currents of a differential amplifier.

INPUT OFFSET VOLTAGE

DC input voltage required to provide zero voltage at the output of an amplifier when the input signal and input bias currents are zero.

INPUT OFFSET VOLTAGE vs SUPPLY VOLTAGE

Sensitivity of input offset voltage to the power supply voltages. Both power supply voltages are changed in the same direction and magnitude over the operating voltage range.

INPUT OFFSET VOLTAGE vs TEMPERATURE (DRIFT)

Rate of change of input offset voltage with temperature. This is the change in input offset voltage from +25°C to the maximum specification temperature, plus the change in input offset voltage from +25°C to the minimum specification temperature, this quantity is divided by the specified temperature range.

INPUT OFFSET VOLTAGE vs TIME

The sensitivity of input offset voltage to time.

INPUT VOLTAGE NOISE

Differential input voltage that would produce, at the output of a noiseless amplifier, the same output as that produced by the inherent noise generated internally in the amplifier when the source resistances are small.

MAXIMUM SAFE INPUT VOLTAGE

Maximum voltage that may be applied at, or between, the input without damage.

OPEN-LOOP GAIN

Ratio of the output signal voltage to the differential input signal voltage.

OPERATING TEMPERATURE RANGE

Temperature range over which the amplifier may be safely operated.

OUTPUT RESISTANCE

Open-loop output source resistance with respect to ground.

POWER SUPPLY RATED VOLTAGE

Normal value of power supply voltage at which the amplifier is designed to operate.

POWER SUPPLY VOLTAGE RANGE

Range of power supply voltage over which the amplifier may be safely operated.

QUIESCENT CURRENT

Current required from the power supply to operate the amplifier with no load and with the output at zero volts.

RATED OUTPUT

Peak output voltage and current that can be continuously, simultaneously supplied.

SETTLING TIME

Time required, after application of a step input signal, for the output voltage to settle and remain within a specified error band around the final value.

SLEW RATE

Maximum rate of change of the output voltage when supplying rated output current.

SPECIFICATION TEMPERATURE RANGE

Temperature range over which "versus temperature" specifications are specified.

STORAGE TEMPERATURE RANGE

Temperature range over which the amplifier may be safely stored, unpowered.

UNITY-GAIN FREQUENCY RESPONSE

Frequency at which the open-loop gain becomes unity.

The following pages give the full data sheet of a popular op-amp from Linear Technology Corporation. It is included in order to give the readers a sense of the capabilities and parameters of a typical op-amp. The data sheet in the following pages is reproduced in full with the permission of Linear Technology Corporation. Copyright Linear Technology Corporation.

LT1001

Precision Operational
Amplifier

FEATURES

- *Guaranteed* Low Offset Voltage
  - LT1001AM   15μV max
  - LT1001C   60μV max
- *Guaranteed* Low Drift
  - LT1001AM   0.6μV/°C max
  - LT1001C   1.0μV/°C max
- *Guaranteed* Low Bias Current
  - LT1001AM   2nA max
  - LT1001C   4nA max
- *Guaranteed* CMRR
  - LT1001AM   114dB min
  - LT1001C   110dB min
- *Guaranteed* PSRR
  - LT1001AM   110dB min
  - LT1001C   106dB min
- Low Power Dissipation
  - LT1001AM   75mW max
  - LT1001C   80mW max
- Low Noise 0.3μV$_{p-p}$

APPLICATIONS

- Thermocouple amplifiers
- Strain gauge amplifiers
- Low level signal processing
- High accuracy data acquisition

DESCRIPTION

The LT1001 significantly advances the state-of-the-art of precision operational amplifiers. In the design, processing, and testing of the device, particular attention has been paid to the optimization of the entire distribution of several key parameters. Consequently, the specifications of the lowest cost, commercial temperature device, the LT1001C, have been dramatically improved when compared to equivalent grades of competing precision amplifiers.

Essentially, the input offset voltage of all units is less than 50μV (see distribution plot below). This allows the LT1001AM/883 to be specified at 15μV. Input bias and offset currents, common-mode and power supply rejection of the LT1001C offer guaranteed performance which were previously attainable only with expensive, selected grades of other devices. Power dissipation is nearly halved compared to the most popular precision op amps, without adversely affecting noise or speed performance. A beneficial by-product of lower dissipation is decreased warm-up drift. Output drive capability of the LT1001 is also enhanced with voltage gain guaranteed at 10 mA of load current. For similar performance in a dual precision op amp, with guaranteed matching specifications, see the LT1002. Shown below is a platinum resistance thermometer application.

Linearized Platinum Resistance Thermometer
with ±0.025°C Accuracy Over 0 to 100°C

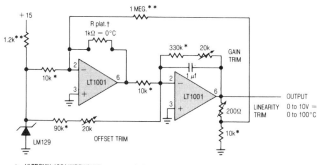

* ULTRONIX 105A WIREWOUND
** 1% FILM
† PLATINUM RTD
   118MF (ROSEMOUNT, INC.)

‡ Trim sequence: trim offset (0°C = 1000.0Ω),
  trim linearity (35°C = 1138.7Ω), trim gain
  (100°C = 1392.6Ω). Repeat until all three
  points are fixed with ±.025°C.

Typical Distribution
of Offset Voltage
V$_S$ = ±15V, T$_A$ = 25°C

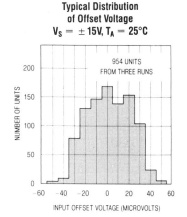

LT1001

ABSOLUTE MAXIMUM RATINGS

Supply Voltage . . . . ±22V
Differential Input Voltage . . . . ±30V
Input Voltage . . . . ±22V
Output Short Circuit Duration . . . . Indefinite
Operating Temperature Range
    LT1001AM/LT1001M . . . . −55°C to 150°C
    LT1001AC/LT1001C . . . . 0°C to 125°C
    Storage: All Devices . . . . −65°C to 150°C
Lead Temperature (Soldering, 10 sec.) . . . . . . 300°C

PACKAGE/ORDER INFORMATION

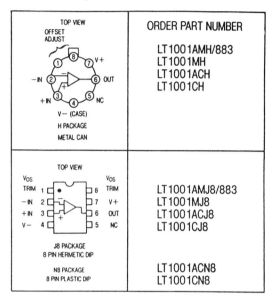

	ORDER PART NUMBER
TOP VIEW — H PACKAGE METAL CAN	LT1001AMH/883 LT1001MH LT1001ACH LT1001CH
TOP VIEW — J8 PACKAGE 8 PIN HERMETIC DIP	LT1001AMJ8/883 LT1001MJ8 LT1001ACJ8 LT1001CJ8
N8 PACKAGE 8 PIN PLASTIC DIP	LT1001ACN8 LT1001CN8

ELECTRICAL CHARACTERISTICS $V_S = ±15V$, $T_A = 25°C$, unless otherwise noted

SYMBOL	PARAMETER	CONDITIONS	LT1001AM/883 LT1001AC MIN	TYP	MAX	LT1001M/LT1001C MIN	TYP	MAX	UNITS
V_{OS}	Input Offset Voltage	Note 1 LT1001AM/883		7	15		18	60	μV
		LT1001AC		10	25				
$\frac{\Delta V_{OS}}{\Delta\,Time}$	Long Term Input Offset Voltage Stability	Notes 2 and 3		0.2	1.0		0.3	1.5	μV/month
I_{OS}	Input Offset Current			0.3	2.0		0.4	3.8	nA
I_b	Input Bias Current			±0.5	±2.0		±0.7	±4.0	nA
e_n	Input Noise Voltage	0.1Hz to 10Hz (Note 2)		0.3	0.6		0.3	0.6	$μV_{P\text{-}P}$
e_n	Input Noise Voltage Density	$f_o = 10Hz$ (Note 5)		10.3	18.0		10.5	18.0	$nV\sqrt{Hz}$
		$f_o = 1000Hz$ (Note 2)		9.6	11.0		9.8	11.0	
A_{VOL}	Large Signal Voltage Gain	$R_L \geq 2k\Omega$, $V_o = ±12V$	450	800		400	800		V/mV
		$R_L \geq 1k\Omega$, $V_o = ±10V$	300	500		250	500		
CMRR	Common Mode Rejection Ratio	$V_{CM} = ±13V$	114	126		110	126		dB
PSRR	Power Supply Rejection Ratio	$V_S = ±3V$ to ±18V	110	123		106	123		dB
R_{in}	Input Resistance Differential Mode	(Note 4)	30	100		15	80		MΩ
	Input Voltage Range		±13	±14		±13	±14		V
V_{OUT}	Maximum Output Voltage Swing	$R_L \geq 2k\Omega$	±13	±14		±13	±14		V
		$R_L \geq 1k\Omega$	±12	±13.5		±12	±13.5		
S_R	Slew Rate	$R_L \geq 2k\Omega$ (Note 4)	0.1	0.25		0.1	0.25		V/μs
GBW	Gain-Bandwidth Product	(Note 4)	0.4	0.8		0.4	0.8		MHz
P_d	Power Dissipation	No load		46	75		48	80	mW
		No load, $V_s = ±3V$		4	6		4	8	

See Notes on page 3.

LT1001

ELECTRICAL CHARACTERISTICS $V_S = \pm 15V$, $-55°C \leqslant T_A \leqslant 125°C$, unless otherwise noted

SYMBOL	PARAMETER	CONDITIONS		LT1001AM/883 MIN	TYP	MAX	LT1001M MIN	TYP	MAX	UNITS
V_{OS}	Input Offset Voltage		●		30	60		45	160	μV
$\frac{\Delta V_{OS}}{\Delta \text{Temp}}$	Average Offset Voltage Drift		●		0.2	0.6		0.3	1.0	$\mu V/°C$
I_{OS}	Input Offset Current		●		0.8	4.0		1.2	7.6	nA
I_B	Input Bias Current		●		± 1.0	± 4.0		± 1.5	± 8.0	nA
A_{VOL}	Large Signal Voltage Gain	$R_L \geqslant 2k\Omega$, $V_0 = \pm 10V$	●	300	700		200	700		V/mV
CMRR	Common Mode Rejection Ratio	$V_{CM} = \pm 13V$	●	110	122		106	120		dB
PSRR	Power Supply Rejection Ratio	$V_S = \pm 3$ to $\pm 18V$	●	104	117		100	117		dB
	Input Voltage Range		●	± 13	± 14		± 13	± 14		V
V_{OUT}	Output Voltage Swing	$R_L \geqslant 2k\Omega$	●	± 12.5	± 13.5		± 12.0	± 13.5		V
P_d	Power Dissipation	No load	●		55	90		60	100	mW

$V_S = \pm 15V$, $0°C \leqslant T_A \leqslant 70°C$, unless otherwise noted

SYMBOL	PARAMETER	CONDITIONS		LT1001AC MIN	TYP	MAX	LT1001C MIN	TYP	MAX	UNITS
V_{OS}	Input Offset Voltage		●		20	60		30	110	μV
$\frac{\Delta V_{OS}}{\Delta \text{Temp}}$	Average Offset Voltage Drift		●		0.2	0.6		0.3	1.0	$\mu V/°C$
I_{OS}	Input Offset Current		●		0.5	3.5		0.6	5.3	nA
I_B	Input Bias Current		●		± 0.7	± 3.5		± 1.0	± 5.5	nA
A_{VOL}	Large Signal Voltage Gain	$R_L \geqslant 2k\Omega$, $V_0 = \pm 10V$	●	350	750		250	750		V/mV
CMRR	Common Mode Rejection Ratio	$V_{CM} = \pm 13V$	●	110	124		106	123		dB
PSRR	Power Supply Rejection Ratio	$V_S = \pm 3V$ to $\pm 18V$	●	106	120		103	120		dB
	Input Voltage Range		●	± 13	± 14		± 13	± 14		V
V_{OUT}	Output Voltage Swing	$R_L \geqslant 2k\Omega$	●	± 12.5	± 13.8		± 12.5	± 13.8		V
P_d	Power Dissipation	No load	●		50	85		55	90	mW

The ● denotes the specifications which apply over the full operating temperature range.

Note 1: Offset voltage for the LT1001AM/883 and LT1001AC are measured after power is applied and the device is fully warmed up. All other grades are measured with high speed test equipment, approximately 1 second after power is applied. The LT1001AM/883 receives 168 hr. burn-in at 125°C. or equivalent.

Note 2: This parameter is tested on a sample basis only.

Note 3: Long Term Input Offset Voltage Stability refers to the averaged trend line of V_{os} versus Time over extended periods after the first 30 days of operation. Excluding the initial hour of operation, changes in V_{os} during the first 30 days are typically 2.5μV.

Note 4: Parameter is guaranteed by design.

Note 5: 10Hz noise voltage density is sample tested on every lot. Devices 100% tested at 10Hz are available on request.

LT1001

TYPICAL PERFORMANCE CHARACTERISTICS

Small Signal Transient Response

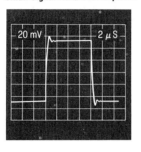

$A_V = +1$, $C_L = 50pF$

Voltage Follower Overshoot vs Capacitive Load

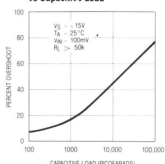

CAPACITIVE LOAD (PICOFARADS)

Small Signal Transient Response

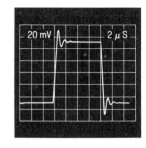

$A_V = +1$, $C_L = 1000pF$

Large Signal Transient Response

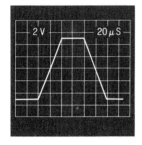

Maximum Undistorted Output vs. Frequency

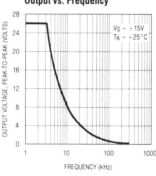

FREQUENCY (kHz)

Closed Loop Output Impedance

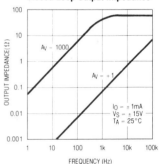

FREQUENCY (Hz)

APPLICATIONS INFORMATION

Application Notes and Test Circuits

The LT1001 series units may be inserted directly into OP-07, OP-05, 725, 108A or 101A sockets with or without removal of external frequency compensation or nulling components. The LT1001 can also be used in 741, LF156 or OP-15 applications provided that the nulling circuitry is removed.

The LT1001 is specified over a wide range of power supply voltages from ±3V to ±18V. Operation with lower supplies is possible down to ±1.2V (two Ni-Cad batteries). However, with ±1.2V supplies, the device is stable only in closed loop gains of +2 or higher (or inverting gain of one or higher).

Unless proper care is exercised, thermocouple effects caused by temperature gradients across dissimilar metals at the contacts to the input terminals, can exceed the inherent drift of the amplifier. Air currents over device leads should be minimized, package leads should be short, and the two input leads should be as close together as possible and maintained at the same temperature.

Test Circuit for Offset Voltage and its Drift with Temperature

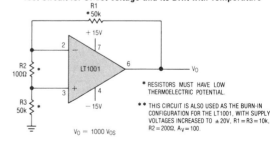

$V_O = 1000 V_{OS}$

* RESISTORS MUST HAVE LOW THERMOELECTRIC POTENTIAL.

** THIS CIRCUIT IS ALSO USED AS THE BURN-IN CONFIGURATION FOR THE LT1001, WITH SUPPLY VOLTAGES INCREASED TO ±20V, R1 = R3 = 10k, R2 = 200Ω, A_V = 100.

Offset Voltage Adjustment

The input offset voltage of the LT1001, and its drift with temperature, are permanently trimmed at wafer test to a low level. However, if further adjustment of Vos is necessary, nulling with a 10k or 20k potentiometer will not degrade drift with temperature. Trimming to a value other than zero creates a drift of (Vos/300) μV/°C, e.g. if Vos is adjusted to 300 μV, the change in drift will be 1 μV/°C. The adjustment range with a 10k or 20k pot is approximately ± 2.5mV. If less adjustment range is needed, the sensitivity and resolution of the nulling can be improved by using a smaller pot in conjunction with fixed resistors. The example below has an approximate null range of ± 100 μV.

Improved Sensitivity Adjustment

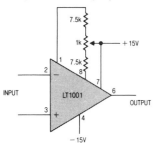

0.1Hz to 10Hz Noise Test Circuit

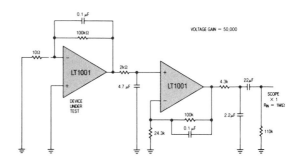

(Peak to Peak noise measured in 10 Sec interval)

The device under test should be warmed up for three minutes and shielded from air currents.

DC Stabilized
1000v/μsec Op Amp

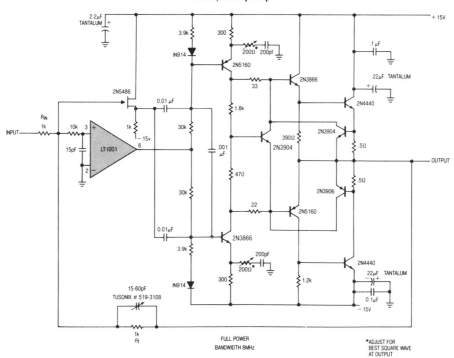

LT1001

TYPICAL APPLICATIONS

Microvolt Comparator with TTL Output

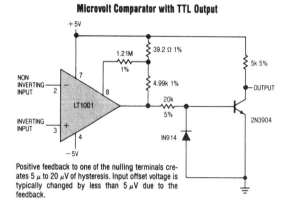

Positive feedback to one of the nulling terminals creates 5 μ to 20 μV of hysteresis. Input offset voltage is typically changed by less than 5 μV due to the feedback.

Photodiode Amplifier

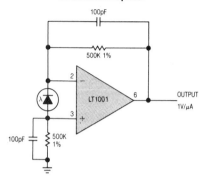

Precision Current Source

Precision Current Sink

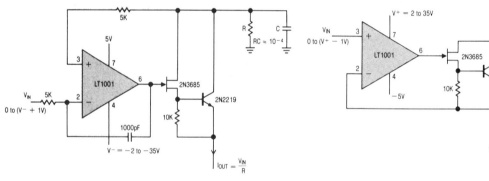

Strain Gauge Signal Conditioner with Bridge Excitation

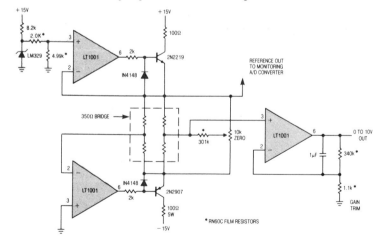

Large Signal Voltage Follower With 0.001% Worst-Case Accuracy

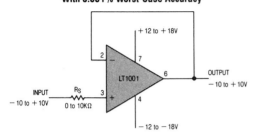

The voltage follower is an ideal example illustrating the overall excellence of the LT1001. The contributing error terms are due to offset voltage, input bias current, voltage gain, common-mode and power-supply rejections. Worst-case summation of guaranteed specifications is tabulated below.

	OUTPUT ACCURACY			
	LT1001AM /883	LT1001C	LT1001AM /883	LT1001C
	25°C	25°C	−55 to 125°C	0 to 70°C
Error	Max.	Max.	Max.	Max.
Offset Voltage	15μV	60μV	60μV	110μV
Bias Current	20μV	40μV	40μV	55μV
Common-Mode Rejection	20μV	30μV	30μV	50μV
Power Supply Rejection	18μV	30μV	36μV	42μV
Voltage Gain	22μV	25μV	33μV	40μV
Worst-case Sum	95μV	185μV	199μV	297μV
Percent of Full Scale (=20V)	0.0005%	0.0009%	0.0010%	0.0015%

Thermally Controlled Nicad Charger

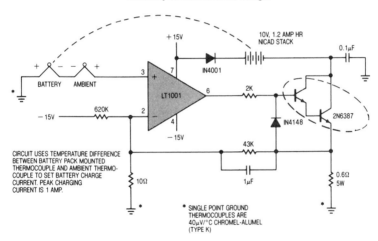

CIRCUIT USES TEMPERATURE DIFFERENCE BETWEEN BATTERY PACK MOUNTED THERMOCOUPLE AND AMBIENT THERMO-COUPLE TO SET BATTERY CHARGE CURRENT. PEAK CHARGING CURRENT IS 1 AMP.

* SINGLE POINT GROUND
THERMOCOUPLES ARE
40μV/°C CHROMEL-ALUMEL
(TYPE K)

Precision Absolute Value Circuit

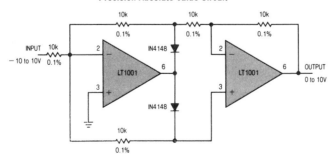

2.2.6 Comparator

A comparator is a modified version of a differential amplifier. You can think of a comparator as a differential amplifier with very high gain. The gain is so high that if one of the inputs is slightly higher than the other one, the output of the comparator will saturate at one end of the power supply voltages. If the input voltage is slightly less than the voltage on the other input, the output will saturate at the other power supply level. Usually the inverting input of the differential amplifier is called "reference input" where the non-inverting input is connected to the unknown input. If the unknown voltage is more than the reference voltage, the output will swing in the positive direction and if the unknown voltage is less than the reference voltage output will swing in the negative direction. So the comparator works in a so-called bang-bang mode. Is positive input of the comparator high? BANG! Output will saturate at the highest possible positive voltage. Is negative input high? BANG! Output will saturate at the lowest possible output voltage. A comparator configuration is given in Figure 2.9. There is no amplification factor for a comparator. There are no feedback resistors, so the gain is set to infinity.

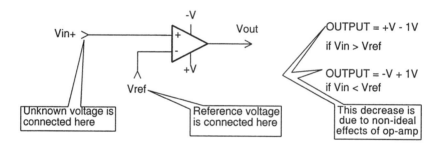

Figure 2.9 Voltage comparator.

2.2.7 Comparator with Hysteresis

A comparator, even though it is a very simple device, is one of the most commonly used configurations of op-amps. For most control operations we prefer to work with a modified version of a comparator: a comparator with hysteresis. A comparator with hysteresis is more stable and has a more preferred arrangement than the plain comparator for everyday usage. The difference between the two is that in the case of a comparator with hysteresis, input change will induce a change at the output within a band of tolerance rather than a single reference level. If the input crosses the upper limit of the band, output will swing; if the input crosses the lower limit of the band, then the output will swing in the reverse direction. Your home air conditioning system and the oven in your kitchen are examples of comparators with hysteresis. An air conditioner without hysteresis would probably destroy itself in several days due to excessive frequency of on-off cycles. The design shown in Figure 2.10 uses feedback from the output to oppose the input. If the output is already high and the input voltage falls below the reference voltage, then negative voltage is added to the reference voltage to oppose the change.

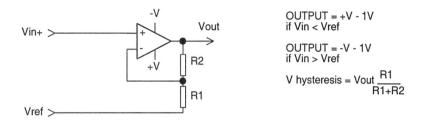

Figure 2.10 Comparator with hysteresis.

If the output is already low and the input voltage increases to cross the reference voltage level, then the feedback arrangement will add to the reference voltage to oppose the change. In short, comparator with hysteresis always opposes the change of output condition by playing with reference voltage level.

2.2.8 Adder

An adder is an arrangement of op-amps which enables one to add two or more voltage levels. An adder is also known as mixer where it mixes two or more voltage levels. The configuration for an adder is given in Figure 2.11.

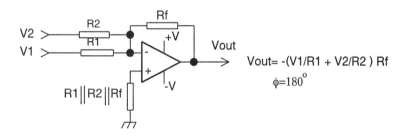

Figure 2.11 Voltage adder.

2.2.9 Integrator

An op-amp can be very easily configured as an integrator with the addition of a capacitor. When configured as an integrator, this arrangement will integrate the input signal and the output will give the integration up to that moment.

$$V_{out} = -\tfrac{1}{RC} \int Vin.dt$$

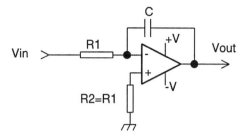

Figure 2.12 Integrator.

2.2.10 Differentiator

An op-amp can be configured as a differentiator where the output is proportional to the input change. This arrangement will give 0 V output for DC signals and a differential of the input signal for every signal.

$$V_{out} = -R1 \; C\frac{dv}{dt}$$

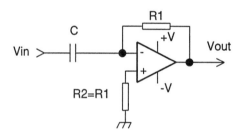

Figure 2.13 Differentiator.

2.2.11 Instrumentation Amplifier

An instrumentation amplifier is basically nothing more than a differential amplifier with very high input impedance. The reason it is called an instrumentation amplifier is that it is mostly used for amplifying very small differential signals used for instrumentation. As shown in Figure 2.14, an instrumentation amplifier is basically made up of three op-amps. The last op-amp is in differential amplifier configuration. The other two op-amps are both in non-inverting amplifier (voltage follower) configuration. Noninverting amplifier configuration has very high input impedance since the external voltage is connected to the Vin+ input directly. As a result a differential amplifier has very high input impedance which does not load the signal.

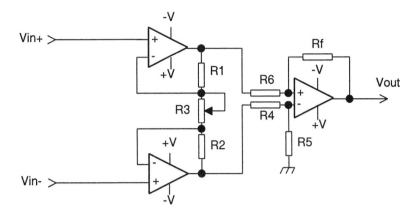

Figure 2.14 Instrumentation amplifier.

$$Vout = (V_{in+} - V_{in-})\left(\frac{R1+R2+R3}{R3}\right)\left(\frac{Rf}{R6}\right)$$

2.2.12 Peak Detector

A peak detector arrangement is used for determining the highest level of the input voltage. The diode seen in the arrangement will charge the output capacitor to the highest value and it prevents the charge from decaying. Consequently, the output will show the highest voltage in a given period of time.

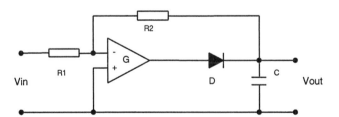

Figure 2.15 Peak detector.

2.2.13 Analog Multiplier

The following op-amp arrangement can be used as a current multiplier. The output current for this case is given by the following formula:

I4 = A * I1 * I2 * I3.

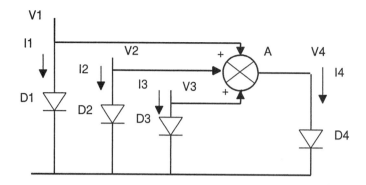

Figure 2.16 Current multiplier.

2.2.14 Sample and Hold

The duty of the sample and hold circuit is to sample the input at a requested time and then hold this level at the output for a predetermined duration. Sample and hold circuits are mostly used in conjunction with the analog-to-digital converters. Most analog-to-digital converters require the input voltage to be constant throughout the conversion process. By passing the input signal through a sample and hold circuit before coming to the A/D converter, one can make sure that during the conversion process the input voltage stays constant.

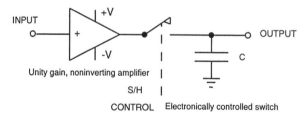

Figure 2.17 Sample and hold.

The switch shown in Figure 2.17 is an electronic version of a mechanical switch. Being electronic, the speed of an electronic switch is much faster than a mechanical one. As soon as the switch closes, the capacitor gets charged to the current voltage level at the output of the op-amp and will hold the signal until the next switch closure.

2.2.15 Analog Multiplexer

An analog multiplexer is functionally very similar to a digital multiplexer in having an input channel and several output channels. By using select lines of the multiplexer, one can direct the input signal to any one of the output channels at any given time. The only difference in the analog version is that the input signal does not necessarily have to be a digital signal. In this respect, an analog multiplexer is analogous to a rotary switch, whereby turning a knob you can establish electrical contact between the input channel and one of the output channels.

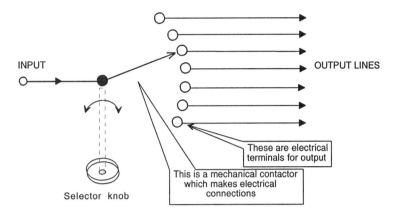

Figure 2.18 A simple rotary switch.

An analog multiplexer is a very handy component in data acquisition since it enables sharing expensive resources like A/D converters.

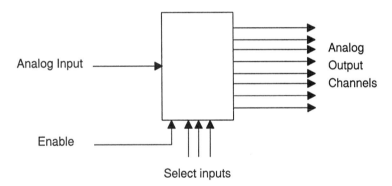

Figure 2.19 An analog multiplexer.

2.2.16 Digital-to-analog Converters

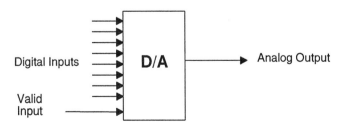

Figure 2.20 A Digital-to-analog converter.

Digital-to-analog converters are devices which convert binary information supplied into analog voltage levels. The magnitude of the voltage output is dependent on the magnitude of the binary number. A binary number can be signed or unsigned. Digital-to-analog converters are one of the most important elements of the data acquisition system; because of this, they will be discussed separately in Chapter Three.

2.2.17 Analog-to-digital Converter

An analog-to-digital converter is a device which converts analog voltage levels into digital form. The relation between the input magnitude and the output magnitude has to be linear. Analog-to-digital converters, or A/D converters, are also one of the most important of the data acquisition components. Because of their importance, analog-to-digital converters will be discussed in detail in the next chapter.

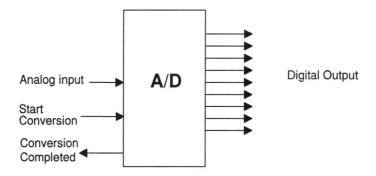

Figure 2.21 Analog-to-digital Converter.

2.2.18 Wheatstone Bridge Configuration

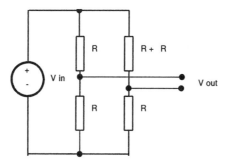

Figure 2.22 Bridge configuration for measuring small resistive changes.

Some of the sensors used in the field of data acquisition provide their output in the form of change in resistance. Even though the resistance change can be easily converted into voltage or current change by the addition of a resistor, for small resistance changes the

Wheatstone bridge structure is very suitable because of its high sensitivity. In a typical Wheatstone bridge arrangement, four resistors with equal values are placed in each part of the bridge. Anytime the resistance in one of the branches changes, the balance will be upset and the effect of the resistance change is amplified. Figure 2.22 shows a typical bridge configuration. The effect of resistance change on the output is given by the following formula:

Vout = R   Vin / 4R

2.2.19 Voltage-to-current Conversion

Voltage-to-current conversion is a technique that is used very frequently in data acquisition systems. Transmitting analog voltage signals causes many problems because the amplitude of the signal on the receiving end depends on many factors, including the impedance of the wire that is used, the quality of the connections, and in addition to that, voltage signals, especially small signals, are very susceptible to noise. Converting voltage signals to current signals gets rid of these problems very easily. Once the signal is in current form, the impedance of the wire, the distance, and connection resistance do not change the current value.

One very easy way to convert voltage signals to current signals is by connecting a shunt resistor across the voltage source. Although this looks like an ideal solution in reality it does not work because the signal source usually has a high output impedance so it can not supply much current.

In order to overcome the problem of high output impedance, an active circuit utilizing op-amps should be used. An op-amp will buffer the output of the signal source so that the current drained from the signal source will be negligible and the op-amp will provide the necessary current.

Depending on whether the signal source is floating or referenced to the ground, different circuit configurations can be used. Figure 2.23 shows a simple current to voltage converter configuration.

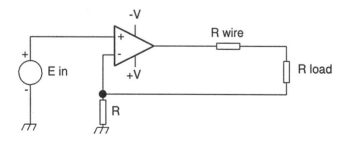

Figure 2.23 Voltage-to-current converter.

2.2.20 Isolation Amplifiers

In general signal conditioner is a buffer circuit between the sensor and the data acquisition hardware. Devices like instrumentation amplifiers have very high input impedance and low output impedance, which amplifies the output of the sensor. In some applications, hovever, not only amplification but also galvanic isolation between the application side and the data acquisition hardware side is desired. Medical applications which require getting a signal from a patient are a good example of these sorts of applications. According to the regulations any device connected to a patient should be galvanically isolated from the data acquisition hardware so that in case something goes wrong, the patient is protected from possible lethal ground currents.

Many industrial applications also require galvanic isolation, not to protect application from ground faults but to protect the data acquisition hardware and the computer from potential high voltage on the application side. In case something catastrophic goes wrong on the application side, such as short circuit of input signal or high voltage jolt, the isolation amplifier takes the burden. Isolation amplifiers can typically withstand high common-mode voltages (500 V or more). Even if the common voltage is higher than the rating of the isolation amplifier, the amplifier burns but the rest of the circuit survives the catastrophe.

Isolation amplifiers are typically either an optically or magnetically coupled type. Optical coupling is often used with digital signal isolation, whereas magnetic coupling can be used both for analog and digital signal isolation. A magnetically coupled isolation amplifier uses a transformer to galvanically isolate input side and the output side. Since it is not possible to transmit DC level signal through the transformer, a modulater at the input side converts voltage signal into frequency. The output side of the isolation amplifier has a demodulater which converts the frequency modulated signal back into the original form.

2.3 SIGNAL CONDITIONING CASE STUDIES

In this section we will be reviewing cases involving signal conditioners. All cases are real life applications of signal conditioners being used for different applications.

2.3.1 Design Example 1: Converting Pulse Width Modulated Signal into Amplitude Modulated Form

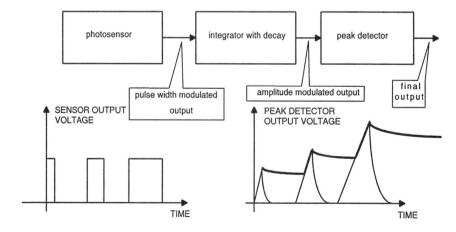

Figure 2.24 Block diagram of the system.

A sensor provides its output in the form of pulse width modulated waveform. Duty cycle of the pulse changes from 0-80% and the frequency is 200 Hz. The output of the subsystem is supposed to be connected to the input of the A/D converter which requires signal amplitude from 0-5 V. Since A/D converters can not read pulse modulated signals, the signal is to be converted into amplitude modulated form which is suitable for A/D converter.

An integrator and a peak detector cascaded together are used as a signal conditioner to convert pulse width modulated signal to amplitude modulated signal. The block diagram of the system is shown in Figure 2.24.

The sensor output is supposed to be linearly proportional to the signal conditioner output. The amplitude should increase with the increasing pulse width. An integrator is an ideal component to do this.

The integrator would integrate the pulse width modulated signal and convert it into amplitude modulation. (The wider the pulse, the higher the amplitude will be.) To ensure that the output of the integrator does not saturate at the highest possible level, a shunt resistor is placed across the capacitor of integrator for decaying the charge inside the capacitor. This arrangement ensures that the amplitude is continuously adjusted to the width of the pulses. A peak detector will join the peaks of the integrator and convert the wavefrom into a continuous form.

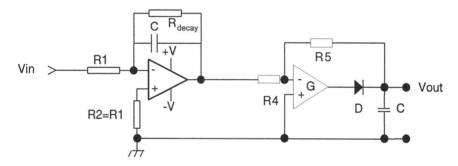

Figure 2.25 The design of the signal conditioner.

In the above design, the integrator constant $\frac{1}{RC}$ should be selected in such a way that the maximum width pulse will make the integrator output go up to +5 V but not above. Since maximum duty cycle is 80% and the frequency is 200 Hz, this means maximum pulse width will be

$$\frac{1}{200} \times 80\% = 0.004 \text{ sec, or 4 msec}$$
$$5 = \frac{1}{RC}\int_0^4 5dx \text{ or } RC = 0.004$$

If C is selected as 1μF, R will be 4 kΩ. A 1 kΩ resistor across the capacitor of integrator gives sufficient decay to the output of the integrator. R3 and R4 of the peak detector are selected equal to give unity amplification.

2.3.2 Design Example 2: One Supply Powers Precision Bridge Circuit

The following case study is reprinted with the permission of Burr-Brown Corporation. Copyright 1989-1992 Burr-Brown Corporation.

Precise amplification and a high common-mode rejection ratio make an instrumentation amplifier well suited to the task of monitoring the output of a resistive transducer bridge. For systems with only one power supply, Figure 2.26 shows how you can connect the bridge, the instrumentation amp, and an op-amp to provide a buffered reference for the instrumentation amplifier's output.

For linear operation, the amplifier inputs (and outputs) must come within no more than several volts of either ground or V+. Accordingly, the bridge properly biases both amplifier inputs, and the instrumentation amp's high common-mode rejection ratio ensures little error from this large offset.

The OPA111AM buffers the reference node of the bridge and applies that voltage to the instrumentation amp's reference terminal. (Most instrumentation amplifiers include a reference terminal, which may be biased to offset the output.) You measure between the amplifier outputs to exclude the fixed output offset.

The op-amp output can serve as a reference common for all connections following the instrumentation amplifier. This output provides low impedance over a frequency range well beyond that of the bridge signal. To handle higher frequency currents, connect capacitance between the op-amp output and ground; if necessary, decouple this capacitance with a small resistor within the op-amp's feedback loop.

The error introduced by the additional op-amp is small. The input bias current I_B of the op-amp creates a bridge error of $I_B \times R/2$, where R is the resistance of one leg of the bridge. Input offset voltage has no effect on the output voltage; it adds to the output offset with respect to ground, which is excluded from the measurement.

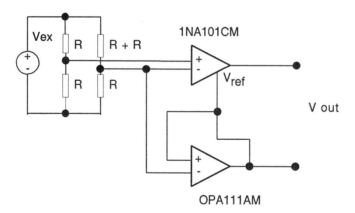

Figure 2.26 In this precision circuit, one power supply is used to excite the bridge and to develop a buffered output signal .

2.4 STANDARD SIGNAL CONDITIONING HARDWARE FOR PERSONAL COMPUTERS

The previous sections introduced op-amps, op-amp derivative signal conditioning hardware, and signal conditioning fundamentals. Fortunately, you do not have to start with op-amps and design your own signal conditioner every time you need one for your data acquisition application. Most of the signal conditioners that you will ever need are available as off-the-shelf hardware from various vendors. Using them is as simple as connecting these blocks between your sensor and A/D converter hardware. The coming sections review available hardware from different vendors and show how to configure them for your specific application.

2.4.1 Modular Signal Conditioning Hardware for PC-Based Data Acquisition

These are matchbox size modules which contain necessary electronics for a particular signal conditioning operation. They are designed to accept special input signals, such as strain, RTD, pressure, and flow, that come from sensors and output the signal to the host data acquisition system. Many data acquisition hardware is designed to accept relatively large analog input ranges like 0 to +5 V or -5 V to +5 V. In this case minimum analog voltage will correspond to minimum digital output and maximum analog input voltage will correspond to maximum digital output. The signals that come from sensors have much smaller range, typically 0 to 100 mV. If the sensor signal is connected directly to the analog-to-digital converter hardware, most of the input range of the A/D converter will be wasted and the resolution of the signal will be low. Signal conditioner modules come in between the sensor and the A/D converter to match the output range of sensor to the input range of A/D converter.

Signal conditioner modules are also useful in applications that have to deal with problems like common-mode voltage, ground loops, and isolation. The input signal of the modules are isolated from the output signals that go to the data acquisition hardware of the computer so that in case a catastrophic event damages the module, the damage is contained to the module and the rest of equipment is not affected. So signal conditioning modules provide an economical way to protect data acquisition hardware.

Signal conditioning modules have a standardized connector pin arrangement which makes it possible to use standard mounting racks. A typical module is shown in Figure 2.27. Since sensor outputs are connected to the mounting rack and not to the signal conditioner module directly, testing and replacing modules can be done without disturbing the field wiring.

The modules are filled with a potting compound which makes them mechanically resistant to vibration and harsh handling. Another nice feature of signal conditioning modules and mounting racks is the ability to multiplex many sensor outputs to a single analog-to-digital converter input.

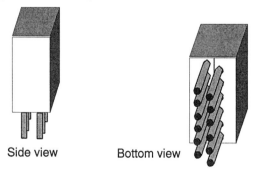

Side view   Bottom view

Figure 2.27 A typical signal conditioning module.

Data acquisition hardware vendors cited below have mounting racks which can multiplex 16 signal conditioner outputs to a A/D converter input. Special connector arrangement provided enables the user to cascade 4 mounting racks together which multiplexes a total of 64 signal conditioner modules to a single A/D converter input. This ability provides a very economical way to connect many sensors to data acquisition hardware.

All modules are designed and calibrated for a particular range, so it is not possible to change the operational parameters like gain or offset. There are wide varieties of modular signal conditioners available. Hopefully one of them will serve the purpose. These modules and mounting racks are available from vendors like Omega, Keithley, National Instruments, Advantech, and Quatech.

Typical signal conditioning modules are as follows:

The modules in this category work as simple amplifiers with preset gain. They can amplify low frequency signals up to 4 Hz.

Function	**Input**	**Output**
low frequency amplification	± 10 mV	± 5 V
low frequency amplification	± 50 mV	± 5 V
low frequency amplification	± 100 mV	± 5 V
low frequency amplification	± 10 mV	0 to +5 V
low frequency amplification	± 50 mV	0 to +5 V
low frequency amplification	± 100 mV	0 to +5 V
low frequency amplification	± 1 V	± 5 V
low frequency amplification	± 5 V	± 5 V
low frequency amplification	± 10 V	± 5 V
low frequency amplification	± 1 V	0 to +5 V
low frequency amplification	± 5 V	0 to +5 V
low frequency amplification	± 10 V	0 to +5 V

The modules in this category accept resistive temperature detector (RTD) signals and generate 0 to +5 V signal output.

Function	**Input**	**Output**
RTD sensor input	-100° C to +100° C	0 to +5 V
RTD sensor input	0° C to +100° C	0 to +5 V
RTD sensor input	0° C to +200° C	0 to +5 V
RTD sensor input	0° C to +600° C	0 to +5 V

The modules in this category are used in order to convert current output signal from process control sensors to 0 to +5 V signal.

Function	**Input**	**Output**
current to voltage	4-20 mA	0 to +5 V
current to voltage	0-20 mA	0 to +5 V

The modules in this category accept thermocouple inputs which are used for sensing high level temperatures.

Function	**Input**	**Output**
J type thermocouple input	-100° C to +760° C	0 to +5 V
K type thermocouple input	-100° C to +1350° C	0 to +5 V
B type thermocouple input	0° C to +1800° C	0 to +5 V

R type thermocouple input	0° C to +1750° C	0 to +5 V
T type thermocouple input	-100° C to +400° C	0 to +5 V
E type thermocouple input	0° C to +900° C	0 to +5 V
S type thermocouple input	0° C to +1750° C	0 to +5 V

The modules in this category amplify strain gauge signals which are used for measuring stress and strain.

Function	**Input**	**Output**
full bridge strain gauge	300 to 10 kΩ	-5 to +5 V
half bridge strain gauge	300 to 10 kΩ	-5 to +5 V

These modules are used for converting voltage signals into current signals. Some of the process control actuators accept current signals in standard 4-20 mA range. These modules can be used for converting D/A converter voltage output into current form.

Function	**Input**	**Output**
current output	0 to +5 V	4 -20 mA
current output	-5 to +5 V	4 -20 mA
current output	0 to +5 V	0 -20 mA
current output	-5 to +5 V	4 -20 mA

These modules are high frequency amplifiers with preset gain. They can amplify signals up to 10 kHz.

Function	**Input**	**Output**
high frequency amplification	± 10 mV	± 5 V
high frequency amplification	± 50 mV	± 5 V
high frequency amplification	± 100 mV	± 5 V
high frequency amplification	± 10 mV	0 to +5 V
high frequency amplification	± 50 mV	0 to +5 V
high frequency amplification	± 100 mV	0 to +5 V
high frequency amplification	± 1 V	± 5 V
high frequency amplification	± 5 V	± 5 V
high frequency amplification	± 10 V	± 5 V
high frequency amplification	± 1 V	0 to +5 V
high frequency amplification	± 5 V	0 to +5 V
high frequency amplification	± 10 V	0 to +5 V

These modules are high quality low pass filters with various corner frequencies. They are available in Butterworth or Bessel type arrangements.

Function	**Input**	**Output**
low pass filter (1 kHz c. freq.)	± 10 V	± 10 V
low pass filter (2 kHz c. freq.)	± 10 V	± 10 V
low pass filter (5 kHz c. freq.)	± 10 V	± 10 V
low pass filter (10 kHz c. freq.)	± 10 V	± 10 V
low pass filter (20 kHz c. freq.)	± 10 V	± 10 V
low pass filter (50 kHz c. freq.)	± 10 V	± 10 V

These modules are used for converting digital process control signals to level acceptable by data acquisition hardware.

Function	Input	Output
digital input	90-140 Vac/dc	TTL level
digital input	180-280 Vac/dc	TTL level
digital input	4-16 Vdc	TTL level
digital input	10-32 Vac/dc	TTL level

These modules convert digital output signals of data acquisition hardware to process control level signals

Function	Input	Output
digital output	TTL level	12-280 Vac
digital output	TTL level	5-60 Vdc

Industrial grade applications which require a large number of I/O points and unlimited expansion capability may be more suitable for DIN rail mounted signal conditioning modules. DIN rail is standardized guiderail fixture which allows quick connection and disconnection of field devices. Using DIN rail it is possible to pack many loose devices together in a neat and compact manner. There are several companies which manufacture DIN rail mountable signal conditioning modules. A typical example of this kind is presented in Figure 2.28.

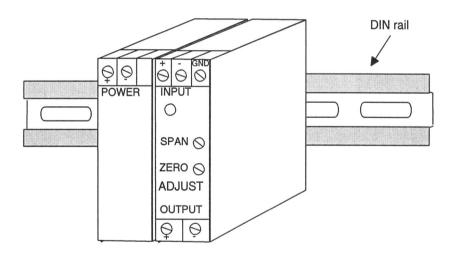

Figure 2.28 A typical DIN rail mounted signal conditioning module.

2.4.2 Signal Conditoner Design Example: Measuring Braking Force of a Bicycle

On a bicycle, brake friction, combined with the wheels' rotation, imposes a force on the brake assembly. A strain gauge is used to measure the force by sensing the opposing amount of force required to restrain the brake. The torque equals the force divided by the radius at which it is applied.

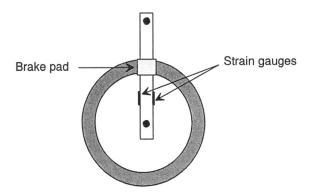

Figure 2.29 Brake force measurement arrangement.

The strain gauge is composed of a thin-film resistor pair; mechanical stress causes one resistor's value to rise while the other's falls. The gauge teams with two fixed precision resistors to form a bridge. Since there are only two active strain gages in this arrangement, as opposed to four active gages, this arrangement is called half bridge.

The strain gauge arrangement needs to be excited by a very stable reference voltage source since the output is very sensitive to reference voltage variations. A half bridge strain gauge input module is used both for exciting the bridge and amplifying the output. The module has a very stable 10 V output which is designed for this purpose.

With the brake exerting a full-scale force of 20 kg on the strain gauge, the bridge puts out a mere 20 mV and thus needs amplification. The module amplifies this signal and also rejects the bridge's 5.0 V common-mode output voltage. Internal amplification ratio of the signal conditioner module is set for 250 which maps $\pm$20 mV input voltage to $\pm$5 V output voltage range.

A small mounting rack which can accommodate four signal conditioning modules is used for field wiring the strain gages to the module.

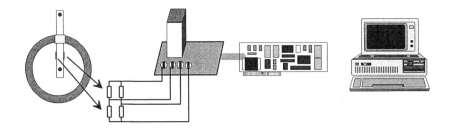

Figure 2.30 Overall connection of the system.

2.4.3 Vendor Specific Signal Conditioning Hardware

The other alternative to signal conditioning for PC-based data acquisition is to use signal conditioning crates supplied by data acquisition hardware suppliers. Unlike the signal conditioning modules explained in the previous section, the specifications for these crates can be quite different. Almost all data acquisition vendors have their own equipment for signal conditioning.

These signal conditioning crates practically perform the same function as the signal conditioning modules. The crate and the cards are more sturdy and suitable for industrial environments. National Instruments' SCXI crates, and Keithley's Series 500 crates are good examples of such hardware. Another advantage provided by these crates is the possibility of designing custom signal conditioner for a given application. If a suitable signal conditioning module is not available for a very specific data acquisition application, the user can design a custom signal conditioner on prototyping boards provided by the vendor.

REFERENCES

1. *Handbook of Linear IC Applications,* Burr-Brown, 1987.

2. Hall, Douglas V., *Microprocessors and Interfacing,* McGraw-Hill International Editions, 1986.

3. Jacob, J. M., *Industrial Control Electronics,* Prentice Hall International Edition, 1989.

4. *Linear Applications Handbook,* Linear Technology, 1990.

5. Van Putten, Anton F. P., *Electronic Measurement Systems,* Prentice Hall, 1988.

6. *Product Handbook,* Quatech, 1994.

7. *Data Acquisition Catalog and Reference Guide,* Keithley Metrabyte, Vol. 25, 1992.

8. *IEEE-488 and VXI Control, Data Acquisition and Analyses Catalog,* National Instruments, 1993.

9. *The Data Acquisition System Handbook,* Omega, 1991.

10. Hordeski, M., *Control Technology and Personal Computers: System Design and Implementation*, Van Nostrand Reinhold, New York, 1992.

SIGNAL CONDITIONING HARDWARE VENDORS

Omega Engineering, Inc., P.O. Box 4047, Stamford, CT 06907-0047 U.S.A.
Tel: 1-800-82-66342, Fax: (203) 359-7700

Keithley Metrabyte, 440 Myles Standish Blvd., Taunton, MA 02780 U.S.A.
Tel: (508) 880-3000, Fax: (508) 880-0179

National Instruments, 6504 Bridge Point Parkway, Austin, TX 78730-5039 U.S.A.
Tel: (512) 794-0100, Fax: (512) 794-8411

Advantech, Integrated Measurement Systems Ltd., 306 Solent Business Center, Millbrook Road West, Southampton SO1 0HW, England
Tel: (0703) 771-143, Fax: (0703) 704-301

Quatech, 662 Wolf Ledges Parkway, Akron, OH 44311 U.S.A.
Tel: (216) 434-3154, Fax: (216) 434-2481

Action Instruments, 8601 Aero Drive, San Diego, CA 92123 U.S.A.
Tel: (800) 767-5726, Fax: (619) 279-5726

Three

D/A and A/D CONVERTERS

This chapter is devoted to D/A and A/D converters. The first part of the chapter concentrates on D/A converter principles and different D/A converter integrated circuits available in the market. The purpose behind this section is to give the reader an idea about the different levels of complexity involved with different generations of D/A converters available in the market.

The second part of the chapter focuses on A/D converters. After reviewing the related terminology and A/D conversion principles, we will have a brief look at the integrated circuits available in the market. Just as in the case of D/A converters, integrated circuits of different generations are available with A/D converters. Choosing the wrong type of IC can make the design process considerably more difficult and costly.

Readers who are interested in learning more about the subject of A/D and D/A converters are recommended to read *Analog-Digital Conversion Handbook,* written by the engineering staff of Analog Devices, Inc., which is a comprehensive text on the subject.

3.1 INTRODUCTION

This chapter is totally devoted to the component which can be considered the heart of any data acquisition system. This component is the analog-to-digital converter. In the real world, almost all parameters that we want to measure exist in analog form; i.e. they are continuous with respect to time. These analog parameters should be converted into digital form in order for them to be processed by the personal computer. In the previous chapter, we have seen the signal conditioning circuitry which is supposed to convert sensor output into voltage form which is suitable to be read by the analog-to-digital converter. Until reaching the analog-to-digital converter, our signal is in analog form. The analog-to-digital converter converts the signal into digital form which is processable by a personal computer. Once the signal has been processed by the computer, the necessary action has then to be taken by the computer. Not all data acquisition systems generate a physical action; in most cases data are sampled and stored or sent to another unit for necessary action. But in some cases the personal computer has to activate an actuator mechanism to do necessary corrections in the real world. Personal computers generate their output in digital form. If this output is needed to be converted into analog form, a digital-to-analog converter should be used. Selection of the A/D and D/A converter is an engineering decision which often determines the performance and the cost of the data acquisition system. Due to the importance of the subject, we have felt that it is necessary to devote a chapter solely to these components. In order to understand the data sheets and conceive the capabilities of these components, it is necessary to familiarize ourselves with the terminology used in this field.

3.2 DIGITAL-to-ANALOG CONVERTER TERMINOLOGY

Digital-to-analog converters are available in integrated circuit forms. Any time a data sheet of a digital-to-analog converter is reviewed, you are likely to encounter the following terms.

Unipolar/Bipolar Output: The output of a D/A converter will be of one polarity in the case of unipolar D/A's, either positive or negative. In the case of bipolar D/A converters, the output can change polarity and swing from positive to negative or vice versa.

Multiplying D/A Converter: A D/A converter is naturally a multiplier which multiplies the reference voltage level of the D/A with the digital input code. (For the highest digital input code the output almost reaches the reference voltage level.) To give a numerical example to clarify this point, assume you have an 8 bit D/A straight binary with a reference voltage of +10 volts. The highest code "11111111" (99% full scale) will generate an analog output of +10 volts. Code "10000000" (50% full scale) will generate +5 volts. If only reference voltage or binary input code is allowed to change polarity, then this type of D/A is called a two quadrant multiplier. If both binary input and the reference voltage are allowed to change polarity, then this type is called a four quadrant multiplier.

LSB: The least significant bit of the digital code is sometimes used for defining the amount of voltage change induced at the output by changing the least significant bit value. It is either stated as voltage level or percentage of the full-scale voltage output value divided by the number of levels. To give a numerical example, consider an 8 bit D/A converter with a +10 volt reference voltage. In this case, 1 LSB is equal to $\frac{10}{2^8} = 0.0392$ volts.

ppm: Parts per million (directly related to % FS). This is a way of representing very small quantities. As a numerical example, 0.005% full scale is equal to $\frac{0.005 \times 10^4}{100} = 50$ ppm.

Offset Error: The amount of deviation of the output from true zero is when the digital input calls for 0 output. (When all bits are "off", D/A is supposed to generate 0 volts, but due to non-ideal conditions output deviates form zero. This is called offset error.)

Linearity Error (Nonlinearity): In the case of a D/A converter, consider a plot of monotonically increasing input code versus output. Ideally, this plot should be a straight line. However, due to nonlinearity, this line will not be straight. The maximum deviation of the line from a straight line is called nonlinearity or linearity error.

Differential Linearity: This is the difference between each level. (If the difference is one LSB, the differential linearity will be zero.)

Monotonicity: A converter gives an increasing analog value for an increasing code.

Absolute Accuracy: This is the difference between the expected voltage when a certain digital input is applied and the actual measured output.

Settling Time: After a data change, the time required for the output of a DAC to reach and remain within a given fraction is known as settling time. This is often $\pm1/2$ LSB.

Resolution: A DAC with n bits will provide 2^n levels of conversion. This DAC is said to have n bit resolution.

Slew Rate: The maximum rate of change of output is referred to as slew rate.

3.2.1 Digital-to-Analog Converters

A digital-to-analog converter converts digital information into analog voltage or current level. Digital-to-analog converters can be constructed very easily by using an op-amp configured as a summation amplifier. In binary logic, the most significant bit has the highest value compared to the other bits. As we move toward less and less significant bits, the importance or the value of the bit also decreases. To illustrate this concept let us consider number 1011. In this example, the most significant bit is the 4 th one, which is the leftmost digit. The value of this bit is $2^3=8$. The least significant bit is located at the rightmost digit and its value is $2^0=1$. Accordingly each digit has a certain predefined value. To convert digital information to analog, a summation amplifier with different gain set for each bit can be used.

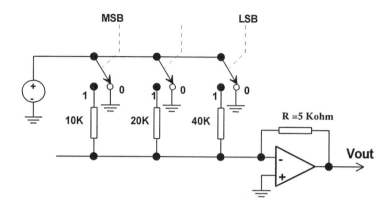

Figure 3.1 Simple weighted resistor method of building D/A converter.

Gain of the individual branches can be adjusted in such a way that a contribution from a most significant bit is more than the contribution from the total of lesser significant bits.

As far as physical implementation is concerned, there are basically two different approaches of realization. In the first approach, the resistance of each branch is unique and the branch which is connected to the most significant bit has the least resistance. All inputs are connected to a reference voltage source over switches which can be closed or opened depending on the binary value ("1" switch closed, "0" switch open). The main disadvantage of this approach is the required precision and the range of the resistor values. The resistors used in the design should be high quality precision resistors with small tolerance. Since each bit uses a different resistor value considerably higher than the value of the previous bit, the tolerance of the LSB resistor becomes comparable to the overall resistor value of the MSB. This effect becomes more and more pronounced as the number of bits increase.

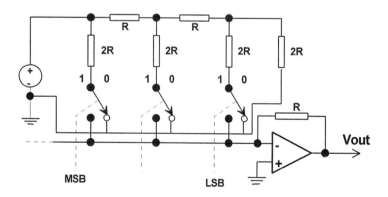

Figure 3.2 Ladder arrangement of weighted resistors.

Another approach uses a ladder network to get the necessary resistance values for the various bits. In this approach the same basic ladder pattern is repeated throughout the design. The overall resistance of the network is exactly the same as the previous arrangement. However, since the only resistors needed in the arrangement are R and 2R values, only two different values of precision resistors are needed.

In the previous arrangement, the resistor values are widely different. Especially because of this, the tolerance of the high resistor values should be extremely small to ensure the linearity of the D/A converter.

Fortunately one does not need to construct D/A converters from scratch using resistors and op-amps. There are plenty of D/A integrated circuits available on the market which could be used in designs. Several of these components are reviewed below. The integrated circuit D/A converter products on the market can basically be mentioned in three categories with respect to their difficulty of usage.

3.2.2 Digital-to-Analog Converter Selection Guide

In general, there are three different categories of commercially available D/A converters.

- **General Purpose Instrumentation D/A Converters:** This category of D/A converters usually has resolutions ranging from 12 to 18 bits. Some of these components are called "industry standard" which means that various manufacturers supply the same design chips which are pin compatible with similar specifications. If a component is industry standard, it means that one can safely buy the components from different vendors and they all work without any performance difference.

- **Pulse Code Modulation D/A Converters** are a new category of D/A converters with high dynamic performance. This category of components generally has resolutions of 16 to 18 bits, and they are utilized for high quality digital audio equipment like compact disk players, digital frequency synthesis, telecommunication systems and multimedia equipment.

- **High Speed D/A Converters** offer very fast settling current outputs. These products are used for high frequency synthesis and control systems.

The following table shows the technical specifications of some of the general purpose D/A converters manufactured by Burr-Brown Corporation. Material presented is reprinted in part, with the permission of Burr-Brown Corporation. Copyright Burr-Brown corporation,1989-1992.

In the table, the error column indicates the quantization error due to the bit size of the D/A converter in terms of percentage full-scale range. The settling time is the time it takes for the D/A converter output to reach a stable level. The range column in the table indicates the voltage or the current range of the output. In some cases the output can be unipolar or bipolar. Temperature range indicates the classification of the integrated circuit.

GENERAL PURPOSE INSTRUMENTATION D/A CONVERTERS

Description	Model	Resolution (Bits)	Error (±%FSR)	Settling Time(µs)	Range (V)	Temp. Range
V. high resolution.	DAC729	18	0.00075	5	5,10,20 U/B	Com
High resolution	DAC700	16	0.0015	1	-2 mA U	Com, Ind, Mil
	DAC701	16	0.0015	8	10 U	Com, Ind, Mil
	DAC70Z	16	0.0015	1	+/-1 mAB	Com,lnd,Mil
	DAC703	16	0.0015	8	+/- 10 B	Com,lnd,Mil
High resolution	DAC70BH	16	0.003	1	+/-1 mA,	Ind
	DAC71	16	0.003	8	+/-1 mA	Com
	DAC72BH	16	0.003	1	+/-1 mA	Ind
Bus interface, high resolution	DAC705	16	0.003	8	+/-5 V	Com, Ind, Mil
	DAC706	16	0.003	1	+/-1 mA	Com, Ind, Mi
	DAC707	16	0.003	8	+/-10 B	Com, Ind, Mil
	DAC708	16	0.003	1	+/-1 mA,	Com,Ind,Mil
	DAC709	16	0.003	8	+/-5,10,10	Com, Ind, Mil
Dual bus interface, high resolution	DAC725	16	0.003	8	+5,+10,10	Com, Ind
Low cost,	DAC710	16	+0.003	8 typ	+1 mA	Com
	DAC711	16	+0.003	8 typ	+10	Com
	DAC1600	16	+0.003	8 typ	+10 B	Com
Low cost,	DAC811	12	+0.006	4	+5,+10,10	Com,lnd,Mil
Bus interface	DAC1201	12	+0.018	4 typ	+5,+10,10	U/B Com
CMOS,	7541A	12	+0.012	1	Multiplying	Com, Ind, Mil
Industry std	DAC7545	12	+0.012	2	Multiplying	Com, Ind, Mil

NOTES: (1) Temperature range: Com = 0°C to +70°C,

Ind = -25°C to +85°C,

Mil = -55°C to +125°C .

Currently there are numerous D/A converters on the market manufactured by different vendors. Although they all function as D/A converters satisfactorily, some of the old designs are more difficult to use than the newer ones because of the extra components the designer has to use. Most manufacturers have slowly phased out the old components from the market, but one can still find some in the market. These components, which we call first generation D/A converters require additional components to become operational. The second generation D/A converters can work stand-alone and do not require additional components.

3.2.3 How to Make D/A Converter System Design Less Painful

Regardless of the different categories of D/A converters cited above, D/A converters in the market can be grouped as first generation (old) or second generation (new) D/A converters in terms of difficulty of usage. D/A and A/D converters are among the most favorite components of the chip manufacturers because of their heavy usage in industry. As a result, literally hundreds of manufacturers all around the world have been manufacturing D/A converters for years. These companies, as the current technology allows, continuously come up with faster, better and easier to use models to get a better share of the market. As a result of this, the D/A converter market is almost flooded with different types of components. For the beginner it is puzzling to decide which component to select for an application. There is one subtle point which one needs to be careful about when attempting to choose a component. Even though the technical specifications in terms of number of bits and linearity may be the same, usually the older components are more difficult to use because of the extra integrated circuits one has to use to make the design functional. In the following section old generation and new generation D/A converters will be reviewed to highlight the differences. As a user, one should select second generation components to simplify the design process.

3.2.4 First Generation Digital-to-Analog Converters

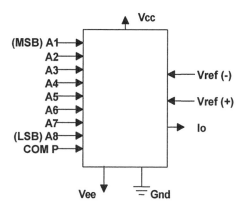

Figure 3.3 Block diagram of a typical first generation D/A converter.

First generation D/A converters are basically an array of resistors and electronic switches which are produced by bipolar technology. This type of component is low in accuracy, low in resolution in terms of the number of bits, and difficult to interface and to make operational. The components require an external voltage reference source and an external current-to-voltage converter in the case that voltage output is needed. Almost all manufacturers have first generation components which they are trying to phase out. But because of the maintainability of the old systems designed with these components, they may have to keep a stock of them. Consequently some of these components are still available.

In order to make a typical first generation D/A converter operational, it is necessary to add a reference voltage source and a current to voltage converter. If the application requires current output, then the current to voltage converter is not necessary. Since the data inputs to the first generation D/A converters are not buffered, external latches are needed to ensure that all inputs are received by converter at the same time. The addition of all these components make the design of the system complicated and reduce the reliability.

3.2.5 Second Generation D/A Converters

Second generation D/A converters have a better refined design and usually have benefitted from more recent manufacturing technologies. As a result, the second generation D/A converters on the market now have higher resolution, faster settling times, reduced power consumption and fewer required peripheral components. For most second generation D/A converters, 12 to 18 bit resolution is common. The voltage reference device which is an external component in the first generation designs become internal in the second generation. These designs also feature latches added to the input to ensure simultaneous changing of the inputs to get steady output. Some of the designs provide output both in voltage and current form. By strapping designated pins of the D/A converter together, the user can select voltage output, current output and the output range. However, there are some designs which provide both current and voltage outputs simultaneously. The following section contains full unabridged data sheets for several second generation D/A converters and several applications notes about using D/A converters. Even though there are dozens of manufacturers making D/A converters, their specifications and labeling terminology are more or less the same. The reader should read the following data sheets carefully for realistic design examples.

There are many different kinds of D/A converters available in the market. A few of these components are listed in the following pages in order to point out the differences between these components.

DAC700/702
DAC701/703

AVAILABLE IN DIE

Monolithic 16-Bit
DIGITAL-TO-ANALOG CONVERTERS

FEATURES

● **MONOLITHIC CONSTRUCTION**

● **V$_{OUT}$ AND I$_{OUT}$ MODELS**

● **HIGH ACCURACY:**
Linearity Error ±0.0015% of FSR max
Differential Linearity Error ±0.003% of FSR max

● **MONOTONIC (at 15 bits) OVER FULL SPECIFICATION TEMPERATURE RANGE**

● **PIN-COMPATIBLE WITH DAC70, DAC71, DAC72**

● **LOW COST**

● **DUAL-IN-LINE PLASTIC AND HERMETIC CERAMIC AND SOIC**

● **/QM ENVIRONMENTAL SCREENING AVAILABLE**

● **BURN-IN PROGRAM AVAILABLE (-BI)**

DESCRIPTION

This is another industry first from Burr-Brown—a complete 16-bit digital-to-analog converter that includes a precision buried-zener voltage reference and a low-noise, fast-settling output operational amplifier (voltage output models), all on one small monolithic chip. A combination of current-switch design techniques accomplishes not only 15-bit monotonicity over the entire specified temperature range, but also a maximum end-point linearity error of ±0.0015% of full-scale range. Total full-scale gain drift is limited to ±10ppm/°C maximum (LH and CH grades).

Digital inputs are complementary binary coded and are TTL-, LSTTL-, 54/74C- and 54/74HC-compatible over the entire temperature range. Outputs of 0 to +10V, ±10V, 0 to –2mA, and ±1mA are available.

These D/A converters are packaged in hermetic 24-pin ceramic side-brazed or molded plastic. The DIP-packaged parts are pin-compatible with the voltage and current output DAC71 and DAC72 model families. The DAC700 and DAC702 are also pin-compatible with the DAC70 model family. In addition, the DAC703 is offered in a 24-pin SOIC package for surface mount applications.

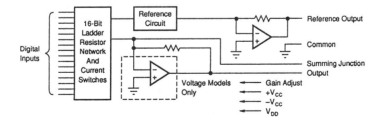

SPECIFICATIONS

ELECTRICAL

At +25°C and rated power supplies unless otherwise noted.

MODEL / PARAMETER	DAC702/703J, D MIN	TYP	MAX	DAC700/701/702/703K MIN	TYP	MAX	DAC700/701/702/703B, S MIN	TYP	MAX	DAC700/701/702/703L, C MIN	TYP	MAX	UNITS
INPUT													
DIGITAL INPUT													
Resolution			16			•			•			•	Bits
Digital Inputs [1]													
V_{IH}	+2.4	+Vcc		•		•	•		•	•		•	V
V_{IL}	−1.0		+0.8	•		•	•		•	•		•	V
I_{IH}, V_I = +2.7V			+40			•			•			•	µA
I_{IL}, V_I = +0.4V		−0.35	−0.5	•		•	•		•	•		•	mA
TRANSFER CHARACTERISTICS													
ACCURACY [2]													
Linearity Error [4]		±0.0015	±0.006		°	±0.003		°	•		±0.00075	±0.0015	% of FSR [3]
Differential Linearity Error [4]		±0.003	±0.012		°	±0.006		°	•		±0.0015	±0.003	% of FSR
Differential Linearity Error at Bipolar Zero (DAC702/703) [4]					±0.003	±0.006		±0.0015	±0.003		•	•	% of FSR
Gain Error [5]		±0.07	±0.30		•	±0.15		±0.05	±0.10		•	•	%
Zero Error [5,6]		±0.05	±0.10		•	•		•	•		•	•	% of FSR
Monotonicity Over Spec. Temp Range	13			14			°			15			Bits
DRIFT (over specification temperature range)													
Total Error Over Temperature Range (all models) [7]		±0.08			°	±0.15		±0.05	±0.10		•	•	% of FSR
Total Full Scale Drift:													
DAC700/701		±10			°	±30		±8.5	±18		±6	±13	ppm of FSR/°C
DAC702/703		±10			°	±25		±7	±15		•	•	ppm of FSR/°C
Gain Drift (all models)		±10	±30		°	±25		±7	±15		±5	±10	ppm/°C
Zero Drift:													
DAC700/701					±2.5	±5		±1.5	±3		•	•	ppm of FSR/°C
DAC702/703		±5	±15		°	±12		±4	±10		±2.5	±5	ppm of FSR/°C
Differential Linearity Over Temp. [4]			±0.012			+0.009, −0.006			•			+0.006, −0.003	% of FSR
Linearity Error Over Temp. [4]			±0.012			±0.006			•			±0.003	% of FSR
SETTLING TIME (to ±0.003% of FSR) [8]													
DAC701/703 (V_out Models)													
Full Scale Step, 2kΩ Load		4			•	8		•	•		•	•	µs
1LSB Step at Worst-Case Code [9]		2.5			°			•			•		µs
Slew Rate		10			°			•			•		V/µs
DAC700/702 (I_out Models)													
Full Scale Step (2mA), 10 to 100Ω Load		350			°	1000		°	•		•	•	ns
1kΩ Load		1			•	3		•	•		•	•	µs
OUTPUT													
VOLTAGE OUTPUT MODELS													
DAC701 (CSB Code)					0 to +10			•			•		V
DAC703 (COB Code)		±10			°			°			•		V
Output Current	±5			°			•			•			mA
Output Impedance		0.15			°			°			•		Ω
Short Circuit to Common Duration		Indefinite			°			•			•		
CURRENT OUTPUT MODELS													
DAC700 (CSB Code) [10]					0 to −2			•			•		mA
Output Impedance [10]					4			•			•		kΩ
DAC702 (COB Code) [10]		±1			°			•			•		mA
Output Impedance [10]		2.45			°			•			•		kΩ
Compliance Voltage		±2.5			°			•			•		V

PCM56P
PCM56U

DESIGNED FOR AUDIO

Serial Input 16-Bit Monolithic
DIGITAL-TO-ANALOG CONVERTER

FEATURES

● SERIAL INPUT
● LOW COST
● NO EXTERNAL COMPONENTS REQUIRED
● 16-BIT RESOLUTION
● 15-BIT MONOTONICITY, TYP
● 0.001% OF FSR TYP DIFFERENTIAL LINEARITY ERROR
● 0.0025% MAX THD: FS Input, K Grade, 16 Bits
● 0.02% MAX THD: –20dB Input, K Grade, 16 Bits
● 1.5µs SETTLING TIME, TYP: Voltage Out
● 96dB DYNAMIC RANGE
● ±3V OR ±1mA AUDIO OUTPUT
● EIAJ STC-007-COMPATIBLE
● OPERATES ON ±5V TO ±12V SUPPLIES
● PINOUT ALLOWS I_{OUT} OPTION
● PLASTIC DIP OR SOIC PACKAGE

DESCRIPTION

The PCM56 is a state-of-the-art, fully monotonic, digital-to-analog converter that is designed and specified for digital audio applications. This device employs ultra-stable nichrome (NiCr) thin-film resistors to provide monotonicity, low distortion, and low differential linearity error (especially around bipolar zero) over long periods of time and over the full operating temperature.

This converter is completely self-contained with a stable, low noise, internal zener voltage reference; high speed current switches; a resistor ladder network; and a fast settling, low noise output operational amplifier all on a single monolithic chip. The converters are operated using two power supplies that can range from ±5V to ±12V. Power dissipation with ±5V supplies is typically less than 200mW. Also included is a provision for external adjustment of the MSB error (differential linearity error at bipolar zero) to further improve total harmonic distortion (THD) specifications if desired. Few external components are necessary for operation, and all critical specifications are 100% tested. This helps assure the user of high system reliability and outstanding overall system performance.

The PCM56 is packaged in a high-quality 16-pin molded plastic DIP package or SOIC and has passed operating life tests under simultaneous high-pressure, high-temperature, and high-humidity conditions.

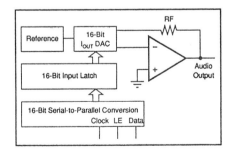

DAC7800
DAC7801
DAC7802

AVAILABLE IN DIE

Dual Monolithic CMOS 12-Bit Multiplying
DIGITAL-TO-ANALOG CONVERTERS

FEATURES

● **TWO D/As IN A 0.3" WIDE PACKAGE**
● **SINGLE +5V SUPPLY**
● **HIGH SPEED DIGITAL INTERFACE:**
  Serial—DAC7800
  8 + 4-Bit Parallel—DAC7801
  12-Bit Parallel—DAC7802
● **MONOTONIC OVER TEMPERATURE**
● **LOW CROSSTALK: –94dB min**
● **FULLY SPECIFIED OVER –40ºC TO +85ºC**

APPLICATIONS

● **PROCESS CONTROL OUTPUTS**
● **ATE PIN ELECTRONICS LEVEL SETTING**
● **PROGRAMMABLE FILTERS**
● **PROGRAMMABLE GAIN CIRCUITS**
● **AUTO-CALIBRATION CIRCUITS**

DESCRIPTION

The DAC7800, DAC7801 and DAC7802 are members of a new family of monolithic dual 12-bit CMOS multiplying digital-to-analog converters. The digital interface speed and the AC multiplying performance are achieved by using an advanced CMOS process optimized for data conversion circuits. High stability on-chip resistors provide true 12-bit integral and differential linearity over the wide industrial temperature range of –40ºC to +85ºC.

DAC7800 features a serial interface capable of clocking-in data at a rate of at least 10MHz. Serial data is clocked (edge triggered) MSB first into a 24-bit shift register and then latched into each D/A separately or simultaneously as required by the application. An asynchronous CLEAR control is provided for power-on reset or system calibration functions. It is packaged in a 16-pin 0.3" wide plastic DIP.

DAC7801 has a 2-byte (8 + 4) double-buffered interface. Data is first loaded (level transferred) into the input registers in two steps for each D/A. Then both D/As are updated simultaneously. DAC7801 features an asynchronous CLEAR control. DAC7801 is packaged in a 24-pin 0.3" wide plastic DIP.

DAC7802 has a single-buffered 12-bit data word interface. Parallel data is loaded (edge triggered) into the single D/A register for each D/A. DAC7802 is packaged in a 24-pin 0.3" wide plastic DIP.

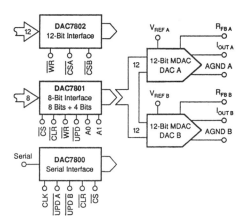

  **DAC813**

Microprocessor-Compatible
12-BIT DIGITAL-TO-ANALOG CONVERTER

FEATURES

● ±1/2LSB NONLINEARITY OVER TEMPERATURE

● GUARANTEED MONOTONIC OVER TEMPERATURE

● LOW POWER: 270mW typ

● DIGITAL INTERFACE DOUBLE BUFFERED: 12 AND 8 + 4 BITS

● SPECIFIED AT ±12V AND ±15V POWER SUPPLIES

● RESET FUNCTION TO BIPOLAR ZERO

● 0.3" WIDE DIP AND SO PACKAGES

DESCRIPTION

The DAC813 is a complete monolithic 12-bit digital-to-analog converter with a flexible digital interface. It includes a precision +10V reference, interface control logic, double-buffered latch and a 12-bit D/A con-verter with voltage output operational amplifier. Fast current switches and laser-trimmed thin-film resistors provide a highly accurate, fast D/A converter.

Digital interfacing is facilitated by a double buffered latch. The input latch consists of one 8-bit byte and one 4-bit nibble to allow interfacing to 8-bit (right justified format) or 16-bit data buses. Input gating logic is designed so that the last nibble or byte to be loaded can be loaded simultaneously with the transfer of data to the D/A latch saving computer instructions.

A reset control allows the DAC813 D/A latch to asynchronously reset the D/A output to bipolar zero, a feature useful for power-up reset, recalibration, or for system re-initialization upon system failure.

The DAC813 is specified to ±1/2LSB maximum linearity error (J, A grades) and ±1/4LSB (K, B grades). It is packaged in a 28-pin 0.3" wide ceramic DIP (–40°C to +85°C specification temperature range), 28-pin 0.3" wide plastic DIP and 28-lead plastic SO (0°C to +70°C).

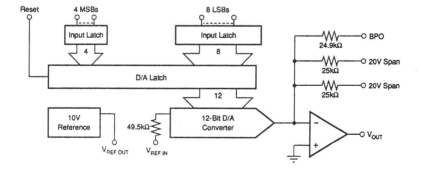

3.3 DESIGN EXAMPLES USING D/A CONVERTERS

3.3.1 Design Example 1: Interfacing D/A Converters to a Microcomputer Bus

Most second generation D/A converters are designed to be interfaced to microprocessor buses. In this example a 12 bit D/A converter, DAC811, is interfaced to a microprocessor bus. The first part of the design interfaces DAC811 to a 4 bit microprocessor. The second part of the example interfaces the same converter to an 8 bit data bus.

The DAC811 interface logic allows easy interface microcomputer bus structures. The control signal $\overline{WR}$ is derived from external device select logic and the I/O write or memory write (depending upon the system design) signals from the microcomputer.

The latch-enable lines N_A, N_B, Nc and LDAC determine which of the latches are enabled. It is permissible to enable two or more latches simultaneously as shown in some of the following examples.

The double buffered latch permits data to be loaded into the input latches of several DAC811's and later strobed into the D/A latch of all D/A's simultaneously, updating all analog outputs. All the interface schemes shown below use a base address decoder. If blocks of memory are unused, the base address decoder can be simplified or eliminated altogether. For instance, if half the memory space is unused, address line A5 of the microcomputer can be used as the chip select control.

4 BIT INTERFACE

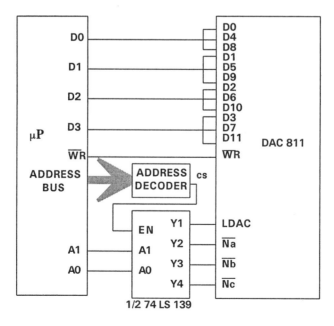

Figure 3.5 Interfacing a 12 bit D/A converter to a 4 bit microprocessor.

An interface to a 4-bit microcomputer is shown in Figure 3.5. Each DAC811 occupies four address locations. A 74LS139 provides the two to four decoder and selects these with the base address. Memory write (WR) of the microcomputer is connected directly to the WR pin of the DAC811.

8 BIT INTERFACE

The control logic of DAC811 permits interfacing to right or left justified data formats. When a 12 bit D/A converter is loaded from an 8 bit bus, two bytes of data are required. As shown in the design, this is achieved by connecting data lines D0 and D8, D1 and D9, D2 and D10, and D3 and D11 together. The base address is decoded from the high order address bits and A_0, A_1 address the appropriate latches. For the right justified case, address $X10_{16}$ loads the 8 LSB's, and address $X01_{16}$ loads the 4 MSB's and simultaneously transfers input latch data to the D/A latch. Addresses $X00_{16}$ and $X11_{16}$ are not used.

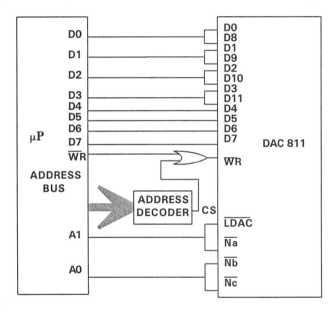

Figure 3.6 Interfacing a 12 bit D/A converter to an 8 bit microprocessor.

3.3.2 Design Example 2: Connecting Multiple Dac707S to a 16-Bit Microprocessor Bus

Most of the second generation D/A converters are designed to be interfaced to microprocessor address and data buses easily. In this design example, two DAC707 D/A converters are interfaced to a 16 bit microprocessor bus. The circuit shown has two DAC707's and uses only one address line to select either the input register or the D/A register. An external address decoder selects the desired converter.

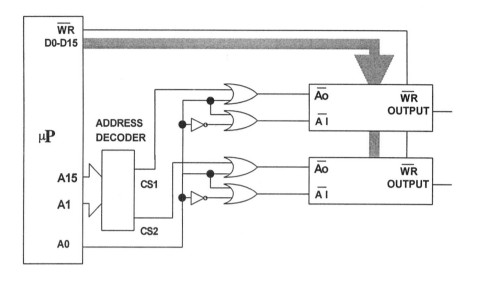

Figure 3.7 Connecting multiple DAC707s to a 16 bit microprocessor.

3.3.3 Design Example 3: Applications of a High Speed DAC Receiving Data Transmitted From a Remote Location

In some applications it may be necessary to place the D/A converter away from the microprocessor. Any time a requirement dictates that digital data be transmitted with the use of cable, especially at high speeds, line drivers and receivers are needed to preserve the bandwidth or data rate. Sending the signals from the microprocessor to the remote location as TTL level signals is not recommended since due to the low noise immunity of the TTL level signals maximum distance is limited to only a few meters. The technique chosen to transmit high speed data, both analog and digital, will determine the success of such systems. A good way to determine if it is necessary to use terminated coaxial cable is when the rise time or pulse width that is necessary to be maintained is low compared with the delay between the sending and receiving circuits.

Figure 3.8 shows a block diagram of a system that is capable of preserving a high data rate from a remote location and generate a clean analog signal. In this example, the TTL level signals are translated into differential signals on the sender side by MC10124 and translated back into TTL form on the receiving side by MC10115. Using such a technique, the distance between the sender and the receiver can be increased to more than a kilometer easily.

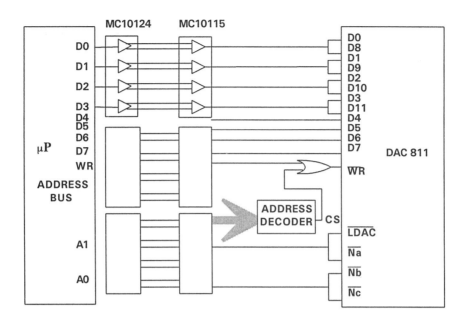

Figure 3.8 High speed DAC receiving data from a remote location.

3.3.4 Design Example 4: Precise Amplitude and Phase Synthesis of an Analog Waveform

Another use of a high speed digital-to-analog converters, such as the DAC63, occurs when the application calls for precise generation of amplitude and phase for an analog waveform. While there are many ways to accomplish this with lower frequency circuitry, the use of a high speed DAC is an attractive alternative. A high frequency D/A converter, is capable of being updated at a 50M Hz rate in the small signal mode which will substantially ease the subsequent analog filtering requirements.

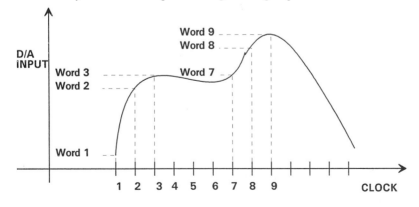

Figure 3.9 Arbitrary waveform to be synthesized.

Figure 3.9 shows an arbitrary analog waveform that needs to be synthesized. If the waveform were sampled at periodic intervals, the synthesized waveform would result. This synthesize procedure would consist of mathematically computing the closest 12 bit approximation at each sample point which would be used to generate the encoding table for the ROM. The sample points would correspond to the ROM address while the ROM output would be the associated code at each one of these addresses.

3.3.5 Design Example 5: Design of a Simple D/A Converter

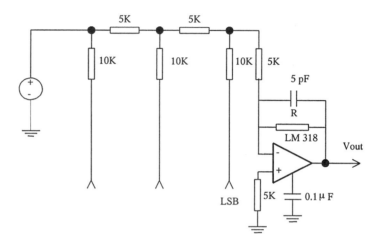

Figure 3.10 Simple D/A converter design.

The design in Figure 3.10 uses a widely available op-amp for realizing a D/A converter. Resolution can be increased by adding as many 10 KΩ stages as needed.

3.4 ANALOG-to-DIGITAL CONVERTERS

A/D converters are probably the most important part of any data acquisition system. All parameters of interest in the real world are naturally in analog form, so somehow these analog parameters need to be converted into digital form in order to be processed by the digital computer. The block diagram of a typical A/D converters is given in Figure 3.11.

The analog input is where the external analog input signal is connected to the A/D converter package. This input can be either in single ended or differential form. If the signal is referenced to the ground, then it is called a single ended signal. In case of differential input, the signal is provided on a pair of lines and the signal amplitude is the voltage difference between the two wires. A/D converters with differential input have two analog input lines which are marked with (+) and (-).

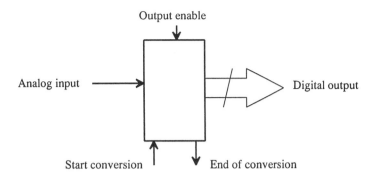

Figure 3.11 Functional block diagram of an A/D converter.

The analog-to-digital conversion process takes a finite amount of time and the conversion process is initiated by sending a start-conversion pulse into the A/D converter. When the A/D converter finishes the conversion process, it informs the peripheral components outside by giving an end-of-conversion pulse. After this, by activating the output enable line we can receive the digital data at digital output terminals. The time it takes for converting the analog signal into digital is a crucially important parameter, called conversion time.

The digital output of the A/D converter can be of different sizes depending on the quality of the A/D converter. Typical values for resolution of the A/D converters are 8 bit, 12 bit, 14 bit, 16 bit and 18 bits.

The list below shows the A/D converter chips manufactured by Burr-Brown Corporation. It is a representative table in the sense that it shows what is available in the A/D converter market as of today. Most other manufacturers have either the same or compatible components on the market. The A/D converters on the market can be divided into two categories.

1. Instrumentation analog-to-digital converters

2. Audio, communications, and DSP analog-to-digital converters

Instrumentation analog-to-digital converters have a range of resolutions ranging from 12 to 16 bits. The conversion speed in this category is around 5 to 50 microseconds. There is always a trade-off between the speed and the resolution in A/D converters. Higher resolution always requires longer conversion time. For lower resolution models, the conversion time can be around 8 microseconds.

The following table shows some of the general purpose instrumentation class A/D converters manufactured by Burr-Brown Corporation.

Description	Model	Resolution (Bits)	Linearity Error (%FSR)	Input Range (V)	Conv Time (μs)	NMC Reso-lution	Temp Range[1]	Pkg[2]	Q, BI[3] Screen	Page
Serial Output	ADC804	12	±0.012	5,10,20 U/B[4]	17	12	Mil,Ind,Com	HCD	Q, BI	9.1-78
Low Cost Data-Bus Interface	ADC574A	12	±0.012	10, 20 U/B	25	12	Mil,Ind,Com	HCD, PDIP	Q, BI	9.1-52
	ADC674	12	±0.012	10, 20 U/B	15	12	Mil,Ind,Com	HCD, PDIP	Q, BI	9.1-62
	ADC774	12	±0.012	10, 20 U/B	8	12	Mil,Ind,Com	HCD, PDIP	Q, BI	9.1-75
Sampling Data-Bus Interface	ADS807	12	±0.012	10, 20 U/B	10	12	Mil,Ind,Com	HCD	Q, BI	9.1-86
	ADS808	12	±0.012	10, 20 U/B	10	12	Mil,Ind,Com	HCD	Q, BI	9.1-86
Low Cost	ADC80AG	12	±0.012	5, 10, 20 U/B	25	12	Ind	HCD	Q, BI	9.1-20
	ADC80MAH	12	±0.012	5, 10, 20 U/B	25	12	Ind	HCD	Q, BI	9.1-36
Medium Speed, Low Cost	ADC84KG	12	±0.012	5, 10, 20 U/B	10	12	Ind	HCD	Q, BI	9.1-44
	ADC85H	12	±0.012	5, 10, 20 U/B	10	12	Com	HCD	Q, BI	9.1-44
Medium Speed, Low Cost, Mil Temp	ADC87H	12	±0.012	5, 10, 20 U/B	10	12	Mil	HCD	Q, BI	9.1-44
High-Resolution Data-Bus Interface	ADC700	16	±0.003	5, 10, 20 U/B	17	14	Mil, Ind, Com	HCD	BI	9.1-72
High Resolution	ADC71	16	±0.003	5, 10, 20 U/B	50	14	Ind, Com	CD	Q, BI	9.1-4
	ADC72	16	±0.003	5, 10, 20 U/B	50	14	Ind, Com	MC	Q, BI	9.1-4
	ADC76	16	±0.003	5, 10, 20 U/B	17	14	Ind, Com	CD, MC	Q, BI	9.1-12

NOTES: (1) Temperature Range: Com = 0°C to +70°C, Ind = −25°C to +85°C, Mil = −55°C to +125°C. (2) HCD = Hermetic Ceramic DIP, PDIP = Plastic DIP, CD = Ceramic DIP, MC = Metal Can. (3) Q indicates optional reliability screening is available for this model. BI indicates that an optional 160 hour burn-in is available for this model. (4) U/B indicates the input voltage range for the model: U = unipolar, B = bipolar.

Audio, communications, and DSP analog-to-digital converters are a category of high performance A/D converters. The resolution of this class is similar to the instrumentation class and it ranges from 12 to 16 bits. What distinguishes this class from the previous class of A/D converters is its speed of conversion. In this category, the speed of conversion is much faster and ranges from 0.1 microsecond to 1.5 microseconds.

The following table shows some of the audio and communication class A/D converters manufactured by Burr-Brown Corporation.

AUDIO, COMMUNICATIONS, DSP ANALOG-TO-DIGITAL CONVERTERS   Boldface = NEW

Description	Model	Resolution (Bits)	Linearity Error (%FSR)	Input Range (V)	Conv Time (μs)	THD+N (Typ dB)	Temp Range[1]	Pkg[2]	Q[3] Screen	Page
Ultra-High Speed	ADC600	12	±0.012	±1.25	0.1	68	Com, Ind	Module		9.2-89
	ADC603	12	±0.012	±1.25	0.1	68	Com, Mil	Special HDIP		9.2-110
High Speed	ADC803	12	±0.012	10V/20V	1.5	NA	Ind, Mil	HMD	Q	9.2-124
	ADC601	12	±0.012	10V/20V	1.0	70	Ind, Mil	HCD		9.2-107
Very High Accuracy, High Speed	ADC701	16	±0.0035	10V/20V	1.5	94	Com	40-p DIP	—	9.2-118

	Model	Resolution (Bits)	Typical Linearity	Input Range (V)	Conv Time (μs)	Max THD+N ($V_{in} = \pm FS$)	Output Format	Pkg	Page
High Performance	PCM75	16	15-Bit 14-Bit	±2.5, ±5 ±10	17	−84dB (JG) −88dB (KG)	Parallel or Serial	32-p DIP	9.2-136
Low Cost	PCM78	16	14-Bit	±1.25	4	68	Serial	28-p DIP	9.2-145

NOTES: (1) Temperature Range: Com = 0°C to +70°C, Ind = −25°C to +85°C, Mil = −55°C to +125°C. (2) HCD = Hermetic Ceramic DIP, HMD = Hermetic Metal DIP. (3) Q indicates optional reliability screening is available for this model.

3.4.1 Analog-to-Digital Converter Terminology

In the following sections we will be dealing with data sheets of A/D converters quite extensively. Some of the terminology used in the data sheets may differ slightly from one manufacturer to another, but the majority of the terms used in data sheets is widely accepted and conveys the same concept. In this section we would like to review the terminology used in the data sheets of A/D converters. Some of the terms used for A/D converters are exactly the same terms used for D/A converters.

Absolute Accuracy: The error of an A/D converter is the difference between the theoretical and the actual analog input values required to produce that code. The digital output code actually corresponds to a range of input voltages rather than a single precise input voltage. Theoretically the input voltage to produce a digital output code is defined as the midpoint of the range of input values that will produce that code.

Relative Accuracy: The relative accuracy error (expressed in %, in ppm **or** as fractions of an LSB) is the deviation of the analog value at any code from its theoretical value.

Conversion Time: The time required for a complete measurement by an analog-to-digital converter is called the conversion time. Conversion time is mainly dependent on the technology, bit size, and the conversion technique used in the A/D converter. It ranges from 0.1 microsecond for fast 8 bit converters to 400 microseconds for 16 bit. A typical figure for a general purpose A/D converter is around 25 microseconds.

Least Significant Bit (LSB): This is the smallest change of analog input value that can be resolved by the converter and expressed by the digital output code.

Resolution: This represents how many quantum levels the analog input value can be converted into. For example, an n bit resolution A/D converter can generate 2^n distinct codes for the input voltage range.

Linearity: Linearity is the deviation of the analog values from a straight line in a plot of the measured conversion relationship. Linearity is expressed either as percentage of full scale input range, in parts per million, or as a fraction of LSB.

Differential Linearity: Each digital output code in an A/D converter corresponds to a range of analog input values. Any deviation of this range from the ideal range is called differential nonlinearity.

Power Supply Sensitivity: The sensitivity of the converter digital output code to power supply variations is expressed in terms of a percentage change in analog input value (or fractions of the analog equivalent of 1 LSB).

Quantizing Error: All A/D converters have inherent quantizing error which can not be avoided. This is due to the fact that any input voltage within a given range is given the same code, expressed as +/-1/2 LSB.

Stability: Stability is insensitivity of the parameters of the converter with respect to time, temperature, etc.

Tempco: This is the temperature coefficient for different parameters of the converter, expressed as ppm/°C or %FS/°C or fractions of LSB/°C.

3.5 A/D CONVERSION METHODS

Even though all A/D converters have similar block diagrams, inside the device the actual analog-to-digital conversion can be done in a variety of different ways. Basically the conversion technique will determine the speed of the A/D converter. Some of the well known conversion techniques are as follows:

- Successive approximations
- Ramp
- Integration
- Flash
- Sigma-delta
- Voltage-to-frequency conversion

3.5.1 Successive Approximation A/D Converters

Successive approximation is a direct conversion method where an A/D converter tries to guess the level of the input voltage in a methodical way. The process of conversion is very similar to the Hi-Low game played by children. But rather than guessing the input voltage randomly by trying a collection of unrelated numbers, a systematic, foolproof method which guarantees finding the unknown level at a well-defined number of steps is utilized. This technique starts by guessing half of the given full range; then depending on whether the actual input is above or below this level, the guess is corrected by going up or down by one quarter of the full range. This process is continued until the guessed number comes sufficiently close to the input level which is dictated by the resolution of the A/D converter. A formal flowchart of the procedure is given in Figure 3.11.

The hardware of this type of A/D converter basically consists of control logic which essentially initiates the guessing process and performs it according to the way it is given in the flowchart. A D/A converter converts the digital value generated by the control logic into analog, and a comparator compares the analog input level and the guessed level that comes from the D/A converter. The comparator has a crucial role in the hardware as a judge to decide whether the generated value is above or below the input level. Successive approximation is a fast conversion method with high resolution.

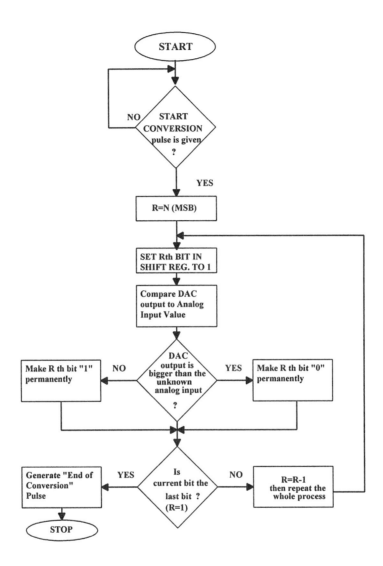

Figure 3. 11 The flow chart of the successive approximation process

Another big advantage of the successive approximation technique is its fixed time of conversion. The conversion time is independent of the analog input value. There is a large number of commercial A/D converter chips that use this technique of conversion.

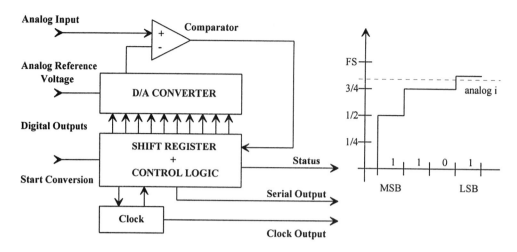

Figure 3.12 The block diagram of a 3 bit successive approximation A/D converter.

3.5.2 Ramp A/D Converter

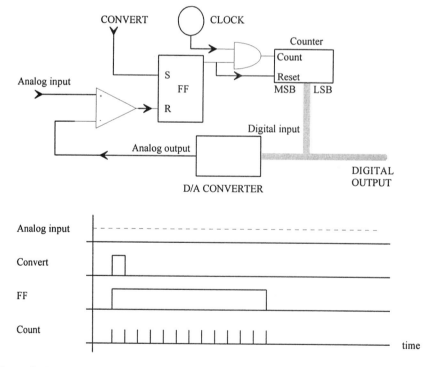

Figure 3.13 Block diagram of a ramp type A/D converter.

A ramp type A/D converter is basically made up of a counter, a D/A converter, a comparator and some logic gates to patch up the connections between the components. The principle of operation is very straightforward. A counter starts counting from zero in every conversion cycle. The output of the counter is continuously being converted into analog by a D/A converter. A comparator compares the output of the D/A with the external unknown input voltage. As soon as the output of D/A converter exceeds the unknown input level, the comparator will sense the change and the logic gates will stop the clock immediately. The frequency of the clock can be adjusted in such a way that the count of the counter corresponds to the unknown input voltage. The block diagram of the converter is given in Figure 3.13

A ramp type A/D converter has a simple design and a very straightforward conversion procedure. Because of this, it is relatively very simple to set up a Ramp type A/D converter. The disadvantage of Ramp type conversion is that the conversion speed is dependent on the unknown input voltage. If the unknown input voltage is small, the counter will catch up with the input voltage quickly and the conversion process will end quickly. If the unknown input voltage is high and close to the full-scale value, the counter will have to count all the way up to the maximum count values to reach the unknown input value. In such a case, the conversion time will be much longer.

Since the conversion time is uncertain, the user has to take the worst case values for timing calculations. Because of this, the speed is assumed to be very slow.

3.5.3 Single Slope Integrating A/D Converter

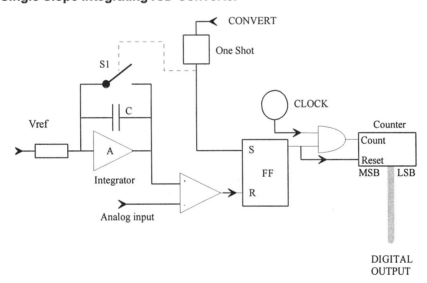

Figure 3.14 Block diagram of a single slope integrator type A/D converter.

The idea behind a single slope integrating A/D converter is very similar to the ramp type A/D converter. A single slope can be considered an analog realization of the ramp type A/D converter. A single slope integrating A/D converter uses an integrator to integrate a given reference voltage source, and a comparator compares the output of integrator with the unknown input level. Since the integrator is integrating a constant reference voltage source, the output of the integrator is a constant slope ramp signal where the slope is dependent on the reference voltage level and the value of the capacitor. While the ramp signal is climbing, in the meantime a counter counts clock pulses from a clock generator. As soon as the comparator output changes, the clock is stopped and the counter reflects the level of the unknown input voltage. By adjusting the slope of the ramp signal and the clock frequency, the counter output can be made to reflect the unknown analog input level. One shot and the controlled switch in the diagram is used for resetting the integrator and the counter and starting the ramp signal again.

This design has the same disadvantage of the ramp type A/D converter, namely the conversion time is dependent on the level of the input signal. Higher values of the input signal require more conversion time than the lower values.

This type of A/D converter can be realized at a very low cost since the design does not use any D/A converters. (The D/A converter is one of the most expensive components used in the design of an A/D converter.) The accuracy of the design heavily depends on the linearity of the integrator used. Even though the integrator output is theoretically supposed to be linear, due to non-ideal effects, the output of the integrator may not be linear at all. That would be the limiting factor of the accuracy of this type of A/D converter. If the integrator is designed using high quality components to achieve better accuracy, then the design becomes costwise comparable to designs utilizing D/A converters.

3.5.4 Dual Slope Integrating A/D Converters

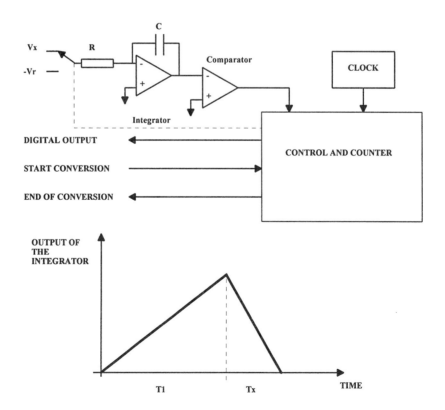

Figure 3.15 Block diagram of dual slope integrating A/D converter.

A dual slope integrating A/D converter is a refinement of the single slope integrating type A/D converter. The dual slope design uses an integrator as a ramp signal generator and a counter for counting pulses of a clock generator during the conversion process. The hardware used is very similar to the hardware used for the single slope A/D converter.

A dual slope technique corrects the linearity problem of the single slope design. In this case, the unknown input signal (Vx) is applied to the input of the integrator for a predetermined amount of time (T1) and integrated. Since the unknown input voltage is a constant (or slow enough to be assumed to be constant), the output of the integrator will be a ramp signal. After this phase, the input of the integrator is disconnected from the unknown voltage source and connected to a known negative reference voltage (Vr). Using the negative reference voltage, the output of the integrator is brought back to zero level. A comparator will sense the moment the output of the integrator is reduced to zero. The counter in the meantime will be counting and measuring the discharge time (Tx). Since Tx/T1 is proportional to the Vx/Vr, the counter output is proportional to the unknown voltage. By adjusting the clock frequency, the reference signal level, and the integrator constants, the counter can be made to reflect the unknown voltage.

The idea behind integrating and then discharging is to get rid of the nonlinearity introduced by the integrator. Sine the same nonlinearity is present during integration and disintegration, the effects will cancel and the result will be unaffected by the nonlinearity.

The dual slope technique still suffers from the problem of variable conversion time and since the conversion process involves both charging and discharging, it is slower than the other techniques of conversion. But because of its excellent noise rejection capability which emanates from integrating the unknown signal, the technique is used in equipment which does not require fast conversion time.

3.5.5 Sigma-Delta Converters

Another A/D converter which is suitable for high resolution data conversion is the sigma-delta converter. Due to the analog operations and number of iterations involved inside a sigma-delta converter, the speed of conversion is relatively low. The conversion principle of sigma-delta is considerably different than the other converters. Internal design of a sigma-delta converter is indicated in Figure 3.16.

Sigma-delta converters work on the principle of averaging the input signal. Input signal which is latched by the sample and hold device goes through a summation amplifier to be added to a comparator output. Output of the summation amplifier is first integrated by using an analog integrator and then digitized by a comparator. The operation is repeated over and over again until the cycle starts repeating itself. Once the cycle starts repeating, the conversion process is over. The output of the comparator, which is received by a digital filter, is converted into digital numbers. One drawback of the sigma-delta converter comes from the fact that the conversion time is dependent on the analog input level. Higher voltage level means longer conversion process.

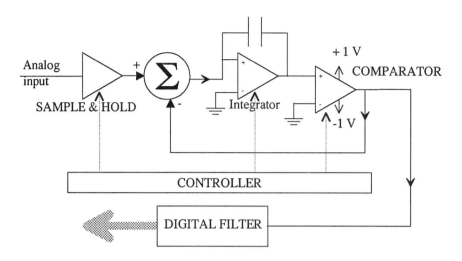

Figure 3.16 Internal architecture of a sigma-delta converter.

3.5.6 Flash A/D Converter

A flash converter is the fastest kind of all A/D converters in the market, but its resolution is lower compared to the other types of A/D converters. In a typical flash converter there are numerous voltage comparators inside the chip to compare the unknown input voltage level with preset voltage levels. Each comparator has a preset comparison level which is slightly larger than the previous comparator. Inside the chip there are as many comparators as the number of output codes produced. According to this, for a three bit flash converter, there should be eight comparators inside, one for every possible output code.

The principle of operation of flash converters is quite simple. Every comparator compares the output with the preset level and a combinatorial logic circuit looks at the output of the comparators and assigns the output of the comparator which corresponds to the input level as the digital output of the converter. Since the design of the flash converter utilizes many comparators, it is physically difficult to construct very large size A/D converters using the flash conversion technique. Currently, there are up to 12 bit size flash converters available in the market. This may increase as the VLSI fabrication techniques allow smaller geometries.

Flash A/D converters are very fast since there is internally no procedure for conversion. The whole conversion process uses only comparators and takes only one step. Because of this, the conversion speed of a flash type A/D converter is similar to the speed of D/A converters. But since the design is rather expensive, the flash type of A/D converters is the most expensive kind on the market. Flash A/D converters find applications in digitizing analog video signals generated by cameras. In this case, the signal is too fast to be digitized by any other type of converter.

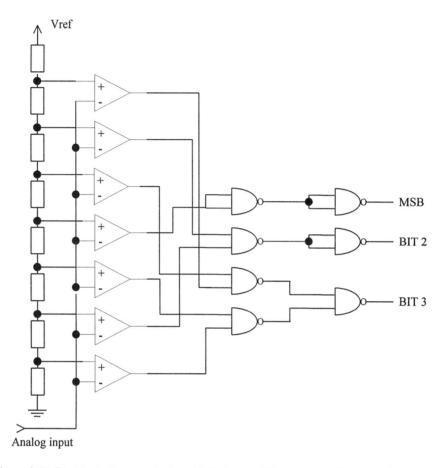

Figure 3.16 The block diagram of a three bit flash type A/D converter with gray code output.

3.5.7 Voltage-to-Frequency Converter

A voltage-to-frequency (V/F) converter can be used as a low resolution, low cost A/D converter. The V/F converter output is a pulse train where the frequency of the pulses is dependent on the input voltage. As the input voltage changes, the frequency of the output changes in a way proportional to the change of the input signal. By simply connecting the frequency output to a counter, an ordinary V/F converter can be used as an A/D converter. The apparent resolution of V/F type A/D converters is not very high; it should be expected to be around 8 to 10 bits. One major advantage of this type of converter is the ability to place the converter far away from the counter and send the information in serial form as frequency. Since the signal is in frequency form it will not be affected by additive noise as in the case of analog voltage. Their low cost also makes this type of A/D converter attractive for low resolution data conversion applications.

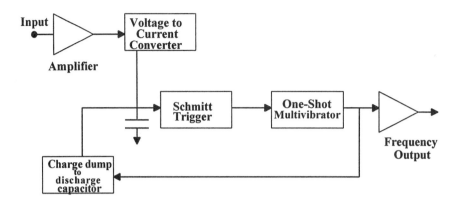

Figure 3.17 Block diagram of a V/F converter.

In the following sections there are application notes to elaborate on this type of data conversion technique.

3.6 DESIGN EXAMPLES USING A/D CONVERTERS

This section contains detailed information about designing typical chip level data acquisition systems. Often, the data sheets of A/D converter chips alone are not enough to get a design engineer to start designing with a new A/D converter in the market. In order to facilitate the design process, component manufacturers publish "application notes" to show the design engineers how they can utilize the new component in their designs. The application notes are usually very detailed and have very valuable suggestions regarding the design process that should be followed.

In this section we have included some of the applications notes published by components manufacturers. The material is not absolutely necessary for logical continuity of the coming sections so it can be skipped, however we strongly encourage the reader to study the application notes given here to get a good idea about the design process.

3.6.1 Design Example 1: A Remote Data Acquisition System*

As board space and semiconductor package pins become more valuable, serial data transfer methods between microprocessors (MPUs) and their peripherals become more and more attractive. Not only does this save lines in the transmission medium, but, because of the savings in package pins, more function can be packed into both the MPU and the peripheral. Users are increasingly able to take advantage of these savings as more MPU manufacturers develop serial ports for their products. However, peripherals which are able to communicate with these MPUs must be available in order for users to take full advantage. Also, MPU serial formats are not standardized so not all peripherals can talk to all MPUs.

Copyright Linear Technology, Reprinted in part with the permission of Linear Technology Inc.

THE LTC1090 FAMILY

A new family of 10 bit data acquisition circuits has been developed to communicate over just 4 wires to the recently developed MPU synchronous serial formats as well as to MPUs which do not have serial ports. These circuits feature software configurable analog circuitry including analog multiplexers, sample and holds, and bipolar and unipolar conversion modes. They also have serial ports which can be software configured to communicate with virtually any MPU. Even the lowest grade device features guaranteed + 0.5LSB linearity over the full operating temperature range. Reduced span operation (down to 200 mV), accuracy over a wide temperature range, and low power single supply operation make it possible to locate these circuits near remote sensors and transmit digital data back through noisy media to the MPU. Figure 3.18 shows a typical hookup of the LTC1090, the first member of this data acquisition family. For more detail, refer to the LTC1090 data sheet.

Included are eight analog inputs which can common mode to both supply rails. Each can be configured for unipolar or bipolar conversions and for single ended or differential inputs by sending a data input (DIN) word from the MPU to the LTC1090 (Figure 3.18).

Both the power supplies are bypassed to analog ground. The - V supply allows the device to operate with inputs which swing below ground. In single supply applications it can be tied to ground.

The span of the A/D converter is set by the reference inputs which, in this case, are driven by a 2.5 V LT1009 which gives an LSB step size of 2.5 mV. However, any reference voltage within the power supply range can be used.

The 4 wire serial interface consists of an active low chip select pin (CS), a shift clock (SCLK) for synchronizing the data bits, a data input (DIN), and a data output (DOUT). Data is transmitted and received simultaneously (full duplex), minimizing the transfer time required.

The external ACLK input controls the conversion rate and can be tied to SCLK as in Figure 3.18. Alternatively, it can be derived from the MPU system clock (e.g., the 8051 ALE pin) or run asynchronously. When the ACLK pin is driven at 2 MHz, the conversion time is 22 µS.

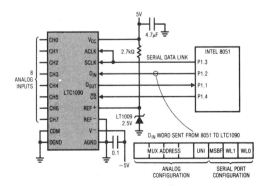

Figure 3.18 A typical hookup of the LTC1090.

Advantages of Serial Communications

The LTC1090 can be located near the sensors, and serial data can be transmitted back from remote locations through isolation barriers or through noisy media.

Several LTC1090s can share the serial interface and many channels of analog data can be digitized and sent over just a few digital lines (see Figure 3.19). Using fewer pins for communication makes it possible to pack more function into a smaller package. LTC1090 family members are complete systems being offered in packages ranging from 20 pins to 8 pins (e.g., LTC1091).

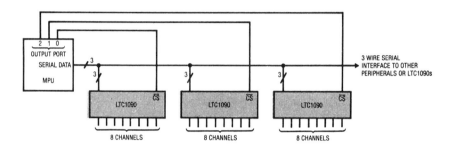

Figure 3.19 Several LTC1090s sharing one 3 wire interface.

Speed Is Usually Limited by the MPU

A perceived disadvantage of the serial approach is speed. However, the LTC1090 can transfer a 10 bit A/D result in 10 μs when clocked at its maximum rate of 1 MHz. With the minimum conversion time of 22 μs, throughput rates of 30 kHz are possible. In practice, the serial transfer rate is usually limited by the MPU not the LTC1090. Even so, throughput rates of 20 kHz are not uncommon when serial port MPUs are used. For MPUs without serial ports, the transfer time is somewhat longer because the serial signals are generated with software. For example, with the Intel 8051 running at 12MHz, a complete transfer takes 80 ms. This makes possible throughput rates of approximately 10 kHz.

Talking to Serial Port MPUs

By accommodating a wide variety of transfer protocols, the LTC1090 is able to talk directly to almost all synchronous serial formats. The last 3 bits of the LTC1090 data input (DIN) word define the serial format. The MSBF bit determines the sequence in which the AID conversion result is sent to the processor (MSB or LSB first). The two bits WL1 and WLO define the word length of the LTC1090 data output word. Figure 3.20 shows several popular serial formats and the appropriate DIN word for each. Typically a complete data transfer cycle takes only about 15 lines of processor code.

Talking to MPUs Without Serial Ports

The LTC1090 talks to serial port processors but works equally well with MPUs which do not have serial ports. In these cases, CS, SCLK and DIN are generated with software on 3 port lines. DOUT is read on a fourth. Figure 3.20 shows the appropriate DIN word for communicating with MPU parallel ports. The Figure 3.20 shows a 4 wire interface to the popular Intel 8051. A complete transfer takes only 33 lines of code.

Conclusions

The LTC1090 family provides data acquisition systems that communicate via a simple 4 wire serial interface to virtually any microprocessor. By eliminating the parallel data bus they are able to provide more function in smaller packages, right down to 8 pin DIPS. Because of the serial approach, remote location of the AID circuitry is possible and digital transmission through noisy media or isolation boundaries is made easier without a great loss in speed.

Hardware and software is available from the factory to interface the LTC1090 to most popular MPUs. The LTC1090 data sheet contains source code for several microprocessors. Further applications assistance is available by calling the factory.

LTC1090 D_{IN} Word

Type of Interface	LTC1090 Data Format	Analog Configuration					MSBF	WL1	WL0
All Parallel Port MPUs	MSB First 10 Bits	X	X	X	X	X	1	0	1
National MICROWIRE* MICROWIRE/PLUS*	MSB First 12 Bits	X	X	X	X	X	1	1	0
Motorola SPI	MSB First 16 Bits	X	X	X	X	X	1	1	1
Hitachi Synchronous SCI TI TMS7000 Serial Port	LSB First 16 Bits	X	X	X	X	X	0	1	1

Figure 3.20 The LTCO90 accommodates both parallel and serial ports.

3.6.2 Design Example 2: A Two Wire Isolated and Powered 10 Bit Data Acquisition System*

INTRODUCTION

For reasons of safety or to eliminate error producing ground loops, it is often necessary to provide electrical isolation between measurement points and the microprocessor. Unfortunately, the isolated side of this measurement system must still be provided with power. One alternative is to power the isolated side of the circuit with batteries. This solution works if power consumption is low, environmental conditions are mild and the batteries are easily accessible.

* *By Guy Hoover and William Rempferd, Copyright Linear Technology Corp. Reprinted with permission.*

If these conditions are not met, a separate isolated supply may be constructed. This can be both difficult and expensive. This design note describes a transformer isolated system in which one small pulse transformer provides both power and a data path.

The circuit of Figure 3.21 is a 10 bit data acquisition system with 700 V of isolation. The circuit takes advantage of the serial architecture of the LTC1092 which allows data and power to be transmitted using only one transformer. A 10 bit conversion can be completed and the data transferred to the microprocessor in 100 μs. Using standard ribbon cable the isolated side of this circuit has been remotely located as much as 50 feet from the transformer without affecting circuit performance.

CIRCUIT DESCRIPTION

In Figure 3.21, a 4 μs wide CS pulse clears the 74HC164 shift registers which will hold the DOUT word of the LTC1092. Additionally, the CS signal sends a 15 V pulse through the transformer which charges the 1 μF capacitor. The CS pulse width must be in the 2-6 μs range for the transformer shown, a small pulse engineering model. A pulse more than 6 μs will saturate the transformer while a pulse width of less than 2 μs will not transfer enough energy through the transformer to keep the isolated supply from drooping during the conversion. The CS pulse can be generated with software or hardware. The LT1021-5 produces a regulated 5 V at its output once the 1 μF capacitor is charged to approximately 7.2 V. The LT1021-5 regulated output powers the isolated side of the circuit. Initially several CS pulses may be required to charge the 1 μF capacitor to 7.2 V. Once charged however, only one CS pulse per cycle is required to keep the isolated supply from drooping as long as the cycle is repeated every 100 μs. The 15 V CS signal is also attenuated and delayed. This signal is used to reset the clock circuit and begin the conversion of the LTC1092. The delay is required to allow the transformer fly back to die out before transmitting the DOUT word of the LTC1092 across it.

The clock circuit is a simple oscillator that is gated by a combination of the CS signal and the 74HC161 counter so that for each CS signal the clock circuit generates 12 pulses and then is gated off. These 12 pulses are used to perform the A/D conversion and shift the DOUT word of the LTC1092 into the 74HC164 shift registers where the data can be acquired by the microprocessor.

The DOUT serial data of the LTC1092 is encoded with the clock, differentiated and sent across the transformer. The encoding circuitry pulse width modulates the LTC1092 output. The encoding circuitry uses two one shots to combine the data and the clock. For each negative going clock edge, a positive pulse is produced at the output of the encoding circuitry. A wide pulse at the output of the encoding circuitry represents a logical 1 and a narrow pulse represents a logical 0 as shown in the timing diagram of Figure 3.22. The schottky diodes on the output of the 74HC04 capacitor driver are to protect the driver from damage caused by the initial 15 V pulse and the resulting fly back.

The differentiated spikes from the transformer are "integrated" by the Schmitt inverters and the 74HC74. Again, schottky diodes as well as current limiting resistors are used to protect the gates from transformer excursions beyond the supplies at their inputs. The encoded data is decoded by one-half of the 74HC221 which reconstructs the clock. The 74HC164s convert the data to parallel format.

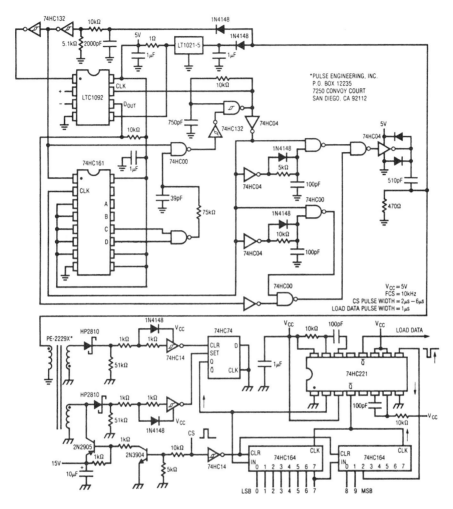

Figure 3. 21 Power and 10-bit A/D result transmitted over two isolated lines.

The 10 kohm pull-up resistor forces the output of the LTC1092 high when the A/D is in the high impedance state. When the A/D output becomes active a start bit (logic 0) is clocked out.

When this initial high to low transition is clocked into bit two of the second 74HC64, it triggers the one shot in the second half of the 74HC221 which provides a load data pulse for the microprocessor.

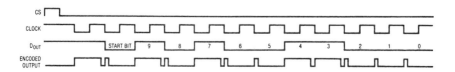

Figure 3.22 Timing diagram shows pulse width coding technique.

SUMMARY

The LTC1092 with its simple serial interface is ideally suited for this transformer isolation application. It requires only two isolated lines to transmit 10 bits of data. Additionally, during the time when data is not being transmitted, power for the A/D can be sent through these lines. The circuit provides 700 V of isolation and can perform a conversion and shift the data in 100 μs. The isolated portion of the circuit can be remotely located up to 50 feet away using ordinary ribbon cable. Possible applications for this circuit are PC based measurement systems, medical instrumentation, automotive or industrial control loops and other areas where ground loops or large common mode voltages are present.

REFERENCES

1. *1990 Linear Applications Handbook*, Linear Technology Corporation, 1990.

2. *The Handbook of Linear IC Applications*, Burr-Brown Corporation, 1987.

3. *Burr-Brown Integrated Circuits Data Book*, Volume 33, Burr-Brown Corporation, 1989.

4. Sheingold, Daniel H., ed., *Analog-Digital Conversion Handbook*, Prentice-Hall, 1986.

5. Collins T. H., *Analog Electronics Handbook*, Prentice Hall, 1989.

6. Van Putten, A., *Electronic Measurement Systems*, Prentice Hall, 1988.

Four

TRANSDUCERS and SENSORS

4.1 INTRODUCTION

The transducer is the part of the data acquisition system which provides *perception* to the system. What is meant by *perception* here is acquiring data from the external environment. The ultimate purpose of any data acquisition system is to monitor some of the real world parameters in the environment to either record the data or take corrective action according to it. The parameter of interest that is acquired from the external world can be various things; it may be the temperature in case of an oven, the force in case of weighing an object, the humidity in case of climatic control, or the acidity in case of chemical analyses. In all these cases a real world parameter is to be *sensed* by the data acquisition system.

A sensor is defined as a device which responds to a physical stimulus. Another common term used for sensor is *transducer*. Even though these two terms are often used interchangeably, a slight shade of difference exists between the two. Usually the term *transducer* is used for devices that are in raw form, whereas the term *sensor* is used for a transducer in finished form which is more suitable for connecting to the data acquisition system. An example to this is a piezoelectric crystal. The crystal itself is a *transducer* because it has the ability to convert mechanical energy into electrical energy. However when the piezoelectric crystal is housed in a suitable container with necessary signal conditioning circuitry, then it is usually called a *sensor*. The reader should be cautioned that this distinction is not very clear and the two terms are often used interchangeably. A transducer or sensor is literally defined as a device which converts one form of energy into another form. There is a growing tendency in the industry to use the term sensor and abolish the term transducer altogether. Readers who are interested in learning more about transducers and sensors are referred to *Process Control Instrumentation Technology* by Curtis Johnson which contains an up-to-date survey of sensors used in industry together with theoretical information about operational principles.

As we have seen in the previous chapters, the tool that we have for converting external analog variables into digital form is the analog-to-digital converter. One major requirement of an A/D converter is that the input to the analog-to-digital converter has to be in electrical form (either voltage or current) in order for the information to be converted into digital form. Because of this, any sensor that we are going to use in a data acquisition system has to convert the input energy into electrical energy.

Figure 4.1 Transducer converts one form of energy to the other.

The selection of a sensor is an important decision when designing a data acquisition system. For one thing, it should always be kept in mind that the sensor is the tool of perception for the data acquisition system and the sensitivity of the system will be only as good as the sensitivity of the sensor. Selection of the sensor should be the first step in designing a data acquisition system. This chapter will introduce various different sensors available and explore ways of interfacing them to data acquisition systems. In order to be in touch with reality, actual data sheets of manufacturers will be used whenever possible to review the parameters and specifications of sensors.

4.2 SENSOR SPECIFICATIONS

In this section, common terms that one may see in a typical manufacturers data sheet will be described. The terminology used for sensors is more or less similar to that used for A/D and D/A converters in Chapter 3.

Usually a manufacturer provides the data about the sensor in two categories.

- *Static specifications* usually refer to the steady-state specifications of the sensor. These may be the range, accuracy, resolution, repeatability, linearity, hysterisis and the form of the output.

- *Dynamic specifications* about the sensor usually refer to how fast the sensor responds to change of the input under the operational conditions. The parameters that describe this behavior are called rise time, time constant, dead time and frequency response.

4.2.1 Static Specifications

Accuracy is defined as the percentage error, where error is defined as the difference of actual output to the desired output. Accuracy can be stated as percent of the full-scale output, as percent of the reading, or in absolute terms of the input.

Resolution is the smallest change at the input of the sensor that will result in a change in the output. Resolution gives an indication of how small a change of input energy can be sensed by the sensor.

Repeatability is a measure of how well the output returns to a given value when the same precise input is applied several times. However, there is disagreement regarding how repeatability is defined mathematically. The two different definitions of are as follows:

$$\text{Repeatability} = \frac{\text{maximum} - \text{minimum}}{\text{full scale}} \times 100$$

$$\text{Repeatability} = \frac{\text{largest deviation} - \text{average}}{\text{full scale}} \times 100$$

Linearity may be specified in several different ways. Some of the popular techniques of specifying linearity are endpoint linearity, straight line linearity and least square linearity. Endpoint linearity is a straightforward way of describing the linearity. A straight line is drawn connecting the end points of the calibration curve which plots output versus input.

4.2.2 Dynamic Specifications

Dynamic specifications of a sensor describe the behavior of the sensor under changing input conditions. These parameters tell us whether or not the sensor that we have is fast enough to respond to the changing input signal.

Even though the static parameters of a sensor are very important for us, dynamic parameters are even more important since a sensor is rarely used to measure static input signal which is not changing. Most of the time, the input signal changes, and it is desired that the sensor senses this change and generate electrical output as soon as possible. In this context, the external input signal can be considered as *disturbance*. Using the terminology used by control engineers, the response of a typical sensor can be either a first order type or second order type response. Even though this distinction is not important for static parameters, it becomes important for dynamic parameters since it affects the way we specify the dynamic parameters. First order and second order behavior basically describe the time varying behavior of the system due to a disturbance. First order systems respond to a step input change by giving an exponential output which eventually merges to a final level. A second or higher order system may respond to a step input change either by overshooting the final level and settling after oscillations or approaching the final level from below without overshoots like a first order system. Basically the behavior of the second order system is controlled by a damping coefficient which controls the behavior. Dynamic behavior of a first order system is described by *rise time, time constant* and *dead time*. If the sensor is a second order one, the dynamic behavior is described by *damping coefficient, resonant frequency* and *settling time*. It is also possible to communicate these parameters by means of frequency response plots.

Rise time is a parameter that is used to describe dynamic behavior of a sensor and it is defined as the time it takes for the output to reach from 10% to 90% of the final output level. The input applied in this case is supposed to be a step input.

Time constant is defined as the time it takes for the output to reach 63% of the final output level. By definition, the input is supposed to be a step input in this case as well. The nice thing about the time constant is that it lets us predict the behavior of the system. After three time constants, the output will be within 5% of the final output level. After four time constants, the response of the system will be within 2% of the final output level. After five time constants, the output can practically be considered settled.

Dead time is the delay time of the sensor where the input is applied to the sensor yet there is no response from the output. The time lag between the application of the input and the first appearance of the output is called the dead time.

Settling time directly gives you the time required by the sensor to give an acceptable output. For example, 2% settling time means it takes this amount of time for the output of the sensor to be within 2% of the final desired output level.

A *damping coefficient* is a parameter which describes whether the sensor is overdamped, critically damped or underdamped.

The frequency response of a sensor indicates the behavior of the sensor to a sinusoidal input change. As the frequency of the input sinusoid is varied, the output frequency also varies accordingly. Even though the frequency of the output remains the same as the input frequency, the phase difference and the gain between the input and the output changes with changing frequency. These changes are best communicated to the user by means of frequency plots. Often the gain of the sensor is given in decibels (dB) is defined as

$$dB = 20 \log \frac{output}{input}$$

A *high frequency cutoff* is defined as the frequency where the transducer gain has fallen to 0.707 of the stable value it had at lower frequencies. Speaking in terms of decibels, this means a decrease of 3 dB from the steady state value. There is a relationship between the high frequency cutoff and the rise time which allows us to figure out one if the other is given. This relationship is given as

$$t_r = \frac{0.35}{f_h}$$

where t_r is the rise time and f_h is the high frequency cutoff.

4.3 SENSORS for DATA ACQUISITION APPLICATIONS

In the following sections several different types of transducers will be reviewed. We do not intend to review all transducers in the market since the number is quite extensive. Here we are going to review a few categories of transducers which are used most frequently for data acquisition applications. These categories include

- Temperature sensors
- Force transducers
- Level transducers
- Motion transducers
- Fluid transducers
- Position transducers
- Humidity sensors

4.3.1 Temperature Sensors

A temperature sensor is probably the most widely used type of sensor in industry. Almost all processes require the temperature of the process to be monitored at some point. As data acquisition engineers, we are supposed to determine the range of temperature to be monitored and, depending on the these data and other environmental conditions, select a suitable sensor for the job. There are different types of sensors available in the market for temperature measurement. Each one of these types of temperature sensors have certain characteristics which should be considered carefully before a sensor is selected. Selection of a wrong type would cause premature sensor failure or require frequent sensor calibrations.

The main categories of temperature sensors that are available include

- Thermocouple
- RTD (resistive temperature detector)
- Thermistor
- Integrated circuit temperature detector

Each one of those categories are reviewed in the coming sections.

THERMOCOUPLE

The basic operational principle of the thermocouple was discovered by Thomas Seebeck in the 19th century. According to this principle, any time two dissimilar materials come in contact with each other, a potential difference between the two conductors is generated. The magnitude of this potential difference is a function of the temperature. According to this principle, a thermocouple can be very easily constructed by taking two different materials and twisting them around each other.

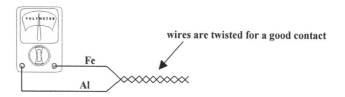

Figure 4.2 A simple thermocouple.

The magnitude of the potential difference between the wires will change with temperature, but the magnitude is also a function of the type of the materials. Some pairs of metals generate more voltage than others when they come into contact. Commercial thermocouples make use of this fact to manufacture thermocouples with relatively high voltage outputs. The voltage generated by the thermocouple is very small, at the order of a fraction of millivolts, so caution should be exercised to prevent noise from corrupting the signal. One advantage of the thermocouple is its robust and simple nature which makes it withstand and measure very high temperatures that can destroy other types of sensors. The simple operational principle of the thermocouple unfortunately becomes a problem when we connect the thermocouple to a measurement device. Being two dissimilar materials, the contact between the measurement device leads and the leads of the thermocouple creates another voltage source, but this time an undesired one. It is undesired since the voltage output of this junction is also a function of the temperature. This undesired effect is shown in Figure 4.3.

To get rid of this undesired measurement of the junction, one method used is the ice bath method in which the undesired junction is placed in an ice bath. The significance of the ice bath comes from the fact that its temperature is stable and very well known. The voltage of the undesired junction will not become zero in the ice bath, but if we know the voltage level of the junction we can simply subtract the voltage level from the overall measurement to find the actual level of the hot junction.

Another technique is measuring the temperature of the undesired junction by using a thermistor. Once we know the temperature of the undesired junction we can eliminate the voltage contributed to the overall measurement.

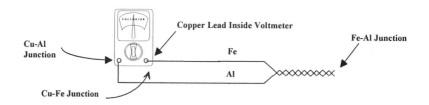

Figure 4.3 Undesired junctions in a thermocouple.

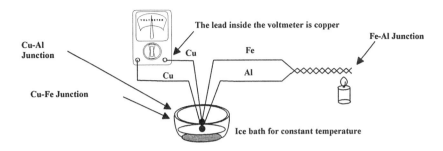

Figure 4.4 Ice bath compensation of undesired junctions.

Yet another technique is to use electronic ice point compensation integrated circuits. These integrated circuits will compensate for the voltage of the undesired junction automatically so that the measured voltage will be the actual voltage of the hot junction. This technique is shown in Figure 4.5.

There are several different kinds of industry standard thermocouples in the market. These thermocouples are made up of different materials and their temperature ranges are different. Some of the standard thermocouple types are given in Figure 4.6.

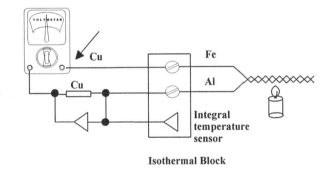

Figure 4.5 Electronic ice bath compensation circuit.

Since each thermocouple is made up of different materials, their output voltages with respect to temperature are also completely different. Figure 4.6 shows the voltage response of different thermocouples for temperature.

Since each thermocouple has different materials used in its construction, undesired junction voltages are also different. Because of this, every kind of thermocouple should be compensated accordingly. For electronic ice bath compensation, a different compensation IC should be used for each different type of thermocouple. Another problem with the thermocouple is that the voltage-temperature curve is not linear. It shows nonlinearities which are peculiar to the type of metals used in the thermocouple.

In order to convert the voltage reading of the thermocouple into temperature, the user has several choices including the following.

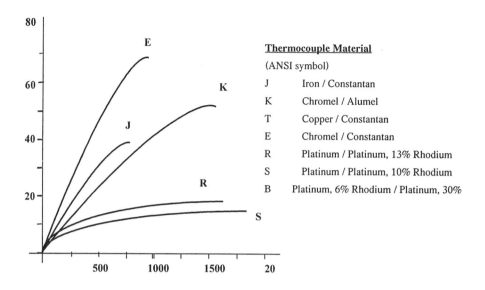

Figure 4.6 Voltage response of industry standard thermocouples.

- *Using a table:* The voltage-temperature curve for a given thermocouples are published by international standard organizations. By using these tables the user can find the corresponding temperature easily. A portion of a typical table for a K type thermocouple is given below.

THERMOELECTRIC VOLTAGE IN ABSOLUTE MILLIVOLTS

DEG F	0	1	2	3	4	5	6	7	8	9	10
50	0.397	0.419	0.441	0.464	0.486	0.508	0.530	0.553	0.575	0.597	0.619
70	0.643	0.965	0.886	0.910	0.933	0.955	0.976	1.000	1.023	1.045	1.066
80	1.068	1.090	1.113	1.13	1.158	1.181	1.203	1.226	1.208	1.271	1 294
90	1.294	1.316	1.339	1.362	1.384	1.407	1.430	1.52	1.475	1.498	1 520
100	1.520	1.543	1.566	1.589	1.611	1.634	1.657	1.680	1.703	1.725	1.748
110	1.78	1.771	1.794	1.17	2.00	2 091	2 114	2 137	2 160	2 183	2 206
130	2.206	2.229	2.22	2.275	2.298	2.321	2.344	2.367	2.390	2.13	2.436
140	2.436	2.459	2.482	2.50	2.28	2.1	2.574	2.597	2.620	2.643	2.666
150	2.666	2.689	2.712	2.735	2.78	2.781	2.804	2.827	2.850	2.673	2.896
160	2.096	2.920	2.943	2.966	2.989	3.012	3.03	3.08	3.081	3.104	3.127

- Another method of voltage to temperature conversion is made possible by using the *approximation polynomials* given by the National Bureau of Standards. For a given type of thermocouple, the voltage-temperature curve is very well defined and reproducible. So the National Bureau of Standards has published parameters to describe a polynomial for curve fitting. Those parameters are reproduced in table below.

TYPE E	TYPE J	TYPE K	TYPE R	TYPE S	TYPE T
100°C to 1000°C'	0°C to 760°C-	0°C to 1370° C-	0°C to 1000°C'	0°C to 1750°C-	-160°C to 400°C-
± 0 5°C	± 0 1 °C	± 0 7°C	± 0 5°C	± 1 °C	± 0 5°C
9th order	5th order	8th order	8th order	9th order	7th order
0 104967248	-0 048868252	0 226584602	0.263632917	0 927763167	0 100860910
17189.45282	19873 14503	24152 10900	179075 491	169526 5150	25727 94369
- 282639 0850	- 218614 5353	67233 4248	- 48840341 37	- 31568363 94	- 767345.8295
12695339 5	11569199 78	2210340 682	1 90002E + 10	8990730663	78025595.81
-448703084 6	- 264917531 4	- 860963914 9	-4 82704E + 12	-1 63565E + 12	-947486589
1 .10866E + 10	2018441314	4 83506E + 10	7 62091E + 14	1 88027E + 14	6 97688E + 11
-1 76807E + 11		-1 18452E + 12	-7 20026E + 16	-1 37241E + 16	-2.66192E + 13
1 71842E + 12		1 38690E + 13	3. 71496E + 18	6 17501E + 17	3 94078E + 14
-9 19278E + 12		-6 33708E + 13	-8 03104E + 19	-1.56105E + 19	
2 06132E + 13				1 69535E + 20	

TEMPERATURE CONVERSION EQUATION: $T = a_0 + a_1x + a_2x^2 + ... + a_nx^n$

NESTED POLYNOMIAL FORM: $T = a_0 + x(a_1 + x(a_2 + x(a_3 + x(a_4 + a_5x))))$ (5th order)

In the above formulas

T = temperature

x = thermocouple voltage

a = polynomial coefficients for a given thermocouple

n = maximum order of the polynomial

As n increases the accuracy of the polynomial increases. For a 9 th order system the accuracy is around $\pm 1°C$

Example: A K type thermocouple output is measured as 2.279 millivolts. Find the temperature that corresponds to that voltage. Assume that the thermocouple is compensated for ice bath electronically.

Solution: From the table we find the closest value to 2.279 millivolts, which is 2.275 millivolts for temperature 133 °F.

Example: For a K type thermocouple the limit of error is given as

2.2°C, or 0.75% above 0°C, or

2.2°C, or 2.00% below 0°C (whichever one is greater)

According to this, find the probable error with the above measurement.

Solution: Since the figures are given for Celsius scale we better convert 133°F to Celsius first. 133°F corresponds to 56°C. Since we are measuring above 0°C, the error will be either 2.2°C or 0.75% x 56 = 0.12°C. since we are supposed to take the greater value the error in our calculation is expected to be 56 ± 2.2°C.

Self Adhesive (Type K)

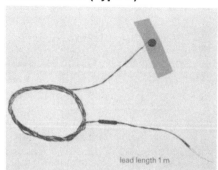

lead length 1 m

A fine wire thermocouple brazed onto a metal disc of 7 mm diameter supplied with adhesive tape to attach to any clean surface for semi-permanent temperature measurement.
The disc makes this thermocouple more robust than traditional 'patch' type self adhesive thermocouples although care must still be exercised when handling the junction.
The thermocouple is supplied with 5 further adhesive tapes to enable the device to be re-used. These strips can also be used to secure the lead.
Additional tape is available in roll form **RS** adhesive tape 512-250.

technical specification

Temperature range	0°C to +200°C
Lead	1/0·2 twisted pair P.T.F.E. insulated 1 m long

Welded Tip PTFE Insulated (Type N)

A pack of 5 type N thermocouples with each conductor insulated with P.T.F.E. Twisted pair construction with no overall insulation. Length 1 m.

technical specification

Conductor size	1/0·2 mm
Wire length	1 m
Wire diameter (with insulation)	0·6 mm
Insulation	Polytetrafluoroethylene (P.T.F.E.)
Operating temp. range	-50°C to +200°C

Figure 4.7 Shortened data sheet for thermocouple.

Thermocouples come in different sizes and forms. It is possible to find a thermocouple in a disk shape or as a hyperbolic needle or self stick type. A detailed data sheet about different forms of thermocouples is included in Appendix A. A shortened data sheet is given in Figure 4.7. The data sheets show some of the available thermocouple configurations (Courtesy RS Components).

RESISTIVE TEMPERATURE DETECTOR (RTD)

The resistivity of all metals changes with temperature in a positive way. Temperature increase will cause the resistance of the metal to increase. Since metals in general are very good conductors, the resistivity of the metal is very small and the change of resistivity due to temperature is even smaller. In order to have a practical use, a metal with a relatively high resistivity should be used so that the resistivity change due to temperature change is reasonably large to read. The ideal metal that fits the above description is platinum. Although there are metals with high resistance like tungsten available, they are brittle and physically not very suitable to be used as a detector. Most common RTDs are made of either platinum, nickel, or nickel alloys.

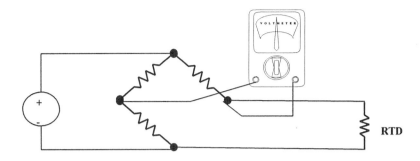

Figure 4.8 Two wire bridge arrangement for an RTD.

The resistance of RTD depends on the physical configuration, but the most common value for RTDs is around 100 ohms at 0°C. The change of resistivity for platinum RTD between temperatures 0 to 100 is about +0.00385 ohms/ohm/°C. The output of the RTD is not linear; because of this, the coefficient given above is only an approximation for the specific temperature range of 0-100°C. In other ranges the coefficient differs.

The resistance change of the RTD is quite minute. Consequently, a special bridge arrangement should be used for measuring the change of resistivity. Some RTDs are particularly designed to facilitate bridge measurement providing separate excitation and sense wires for accurate measurement.

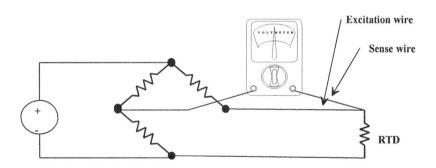

Figure 4.9 Three wire bridge measurement with RTD.

Output of an RTD is quite linear. But if high precision is required, correction is still needed. The formula used for converting an RTD reading to temperature is as follows.

$$R_T = R_0 + R_0\alpha\left[T - \delta\left(\frac{T}{100} - 1\right)\left(\frac{T}{100}\right) - \beta\left(\frac{T}{100} - 1\right)\left(\frac{T^3}{100}\right)\right]$$

where

R_T = Resistance at temperature T $\delta = 1.49$

R_0 = Resistance at T = 0°C $\beta = 0$ T>0°C

α = temperature coefficient $\beta = 11$ T<0°C

If precision is not required, then the RTD can be accepted as linear and calculations can be made based on that. Shown below are typical RTDs. (Courtesy RS Components.)

Platinum Resistance Thermometer Inserts

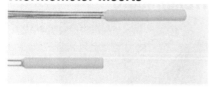

Two tubular ceramic encased Pt 100 elements to B.S. 1904:1984 (Class B), 4·8 mm diameter and 35 mm long. The inserts are supplied with either 4 strain relieved 0·5 mm diameter, hard drawn, straight nickel wires 450 mm long; or with 2 strain relieved wires 10 mm long.
The 4-wire element has fibreglass sleeves for insulation purposes, and two wires are 10 mm shorter than the others in order to identify one end of the element. This element is ideally suited for incorporation into the **RS** Thermopocket kit.
These elements are high quality units offering excellent tolerance values, and an operating temperature range of -50°C to +450°C.

Platinum Resistance Probes
Platinum Film Probe (Pt 100)

L. (overall) 150 Dia. 4
Sensing part L. 25 nom.
W. 6 nom.
Lead length 1 m mounting hole dia. 11

A platinum film element mounted in a waterproof stainless steel sheath, intended for precise measurement of temperature under adverse conditions. The probe is fitted with a ⅛ in BSPF brass compression fitting, which allows adjustment of probe insertion depth and provides simple fixing to tank, duct or oven wall, etc. The last 25 mm of the sheath (the sensing part) is flattened to give improved response time. Attached to the probe are two 7/0·2 tinned copper P.V.C. insulated leads 1 m long.

technical specification

Detector material: platinum film.
Resistance at 0°C: 100 ±0·1 Ω.
Resistance/temperature relationship and tolerance:
B.S. 1904 Grade II (DIN 43760).
Temperature range -50°C to +250°C (first 100 mm of sheath only, remainder limited to 70°C).
Time constant: Typically less than 2 secs to 63% (in water at 1 m/sec.).

Platinum Resistance Thermometry
Platinum Film Detectors
Standard and Sleeved Elements (Pt 100)

standard element   L. 30   W. 4   H. 0·82   End Pads 2 × 4

sheathed element   Body L. 36   W. 6   H. 2
Flanges 15 × 6 (0·15 thk)   Lead L. 1 m

Platinum film sensors for economical precise resistance temperature detection. Consists of a specially formulated platinum ink deposited on an alumina substrate, laser trimmed to form a highly stable metal resistance element to B.S. 1904 Grade II and DIN 43760. Rated between -50°C and +500°C, the element characteristic conforms to the temperature/
resistance relationship defined by the International Practical Temperature Scale 1968, and as such is a derivative of resistance temperature standards. Two packages are offered:
Type **158-238** is a standard platinum film element protected by a ceramic coating (temperature range as above), which incorporates gold-covered end pads for ease of connection. Its small physical size and simple (discrete resistor type) construction will render it cost-effective in a variety of temperature recording applications including accuracy and stability in reference conditions.
Type **158-244** comprises a standard element sheathed in thin stainless steel, which affords a substantial anchorage for the 1 m (length) integral leads (19/0·15 silver clad copper wire P.T.F.E. insulated). Flanges extend from the base of the sheath at each end for mounting by wrapping or clamping. May be usefully employed in monitoring and detecting absolute temperatures in heat sinks and equipments, etc. Working temperature range: -50°C to +260°C. These devices are easily installed by constructing simple bridge circuits, which will generate an output voltage characteristic equivalent to the temperature change. Excitation current can be varied, providing an adjustable output voltage characteristic. This effect may be accomplished in conjunction with the **RS** programmable current source i.c. 334Z, stock no. 308-540, refer to the Semiconductors section.
Resistance value (100 Ω ±0·1 at 0°C). Temp. coeff. (positive) 0·385 Ω per °C. Self-heating coeff. in still air (element sheathed) 0·2°C per mW. Self-heating coeff. with infinite heat sink 0·005°C per mW.
Insulation resistance for sheathed type (between leads and sheath) > 10 MΩ at 240 V a.c.

Example: An RTD film detector shown in the previous page is used in a temperature detection application. The application does not require high precision. The resistance of RTD is measured as 122.5 Ω. If the RTD resistance is measured as 100.1 Ω at 0°C, find the temperature of the application.

Solution: From the data sheet given we read that the temperature coefficient for that specific RTD is 0.385 Ω/°C positive. According to this, 122.5-100.1 = 20.15 Ω. To find temperature, 20.15/0.385 = 52.33°C

A detailed unabridged data sheet and application information of RTDs are included in Appendix A.

THERMISTOR

A thermistor, as the name implies, is a temperature sensitive resistor. Like the other kinds of temperature detectors that have been mentioned so far, its resistance changes with temperature. Thermistors, compared to the other types of detectors mentioned so far, are very sensitive components. Its temperature range is very limited to temperatures around room temperature, but its resistance change with temperature is much higher than the others. Another difference of a thermistor from the other resistors is that the temperature coefficient of the thermistor is negative whereas the thermocouple and RTD have positive temperature coefficients. This means that as the temperature increases the resistivity of RTD and thermocouple increases but the resistivity of the thermistor decreases.

Figure 4.10 shows the temperature-resistance curve for the thermistor, RTD and thermocouple. (Since the thermocouple generates voltage output, what is shown in the curve is voltage for the thermocouple.)

A thermistor is a silicon device with negative temperature characteristics. Since the coefficient is negative, any increase in temperature will cause the resistance of the device to decrease.

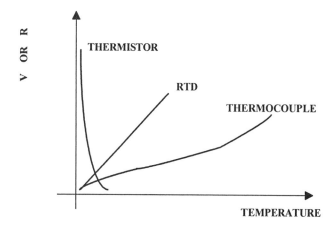

Figure 4.10 V&R versus temperature for different temperature sensors.

The output of the thermistor is quite nonlinear but well behaved. The output curve can be approximated by the so-called Steinhart-Hart curve.

$$R_2 = R_1 e^{\left(\frac{B}{t_1} - \frac{B}{t_2}\right)}$$

where

B = characteristic temperature constant (K)

T = bead temperature (K)

R1 = resistance of the thermistor at temperature t_1

R2 = resistance of the thermistor at temperature t_2

e = 2.7183

(Temperature in K = °C + 273)

The curve fit given by this equation is quite accurate. The error in the 0-100°C range is +/- 0.02°C.

Given below are short data sheets for some common types of thermistors on the market. Unabridged data sheets for thermistors are included in Appendix A.

Negative Temperature Coefficient (n.t.c.)
R-T Curve Matched Thermistors

Bead dia. 2·4 max.
Lead length 76
lead dia. 0·2

The **RS** R-T curve (Resistance-Temperature) matched thermistors are small, high quality, epoxy encapsulated, precision devices. They offer true interchangeability over wide temperature ranges. This permits the circuit designer to standardise on circuitry, eliminating the need to individually adjust circuits and allowing the thermistors to be easily replaced without the need for re-calibration. Four types are available with resistances at 25°C of **3 k, 5 k, 10 k** and **100 k**. Temperature range: -80°C to +150°C. Tolerance over temperature range: 0°C to +70°C; ±0·2°C.

Rod Thermistors (n.t.c.)

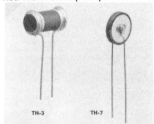

TH-3   TH-7

General-purpose current-limiting types for circuit protection.

Type	Equivalent	Typ. Res. at 25°C	Typ. Res. Hot	Dimensions
TH-3	VA1026	380 Ω	28 Ω	L. 22
	CZ13		at 0·3 A	Dia. 12
TH-7	VA1104	25 Ω	1 Ω (max.)	H. 10
	OD10	(15 Ω min.)	at 2·2 A	Dia. 16

Miniature Bead

L. 5   Dia. 1·5

Miniature glass-encapsulated thermistors for temperature measurement and control applications. Selection tolerance ±20% at 20 °C. Recommended temperature range gives a bead resistance variation from 20 kΩ to 1 kΩ.

Example: A bead thermistor 256-051 type is being used in a temperature measurement application. If the resistance of the thermistor is found to be 10K, what is the temperature of the application?

Solution: From the unabridged data sheet given in the appendix the constant B for this type of thermistor is given as 4145. Putting the data into the formula,

$$10000 = 220,000 \ e^{\frac{4145}{t_2} - \frac{4145}{25+273}} \quad \text{So } t_2 = 383.14 \text{ K which corresponds to } 110.14°C$$

INTEGRATED CIRCUIT TEMPERATURE SENSOR

All the temperature sensors reviewed so far have been passive sensors. Being passive means that the user does not have to supply power to these components to make them work. (The resistance of the component changes all by itself, but we do need to supply power to read this change.) The integrated circuit temperature sensor, unlike the other temperature sensors, is an active sensor. Being an integrated circuit device, it has to be supplied with power just like any other IC component. Since this is an active component, it is very sensitive to temperature change, and the output voltage with respect to temperature is very linear.

Integrated circuit temperature sensors have a rather limited temperature range which confines them to operation near room temperature, namely 0 to 150°C. In the operational range, the output is very high due to the active nature of the component which makes signal conditioning unnecessary.

590kH

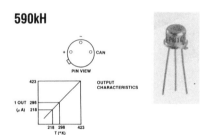

The **RS** 590kH is functionally a two-terminal integrated circuit temperature transducer which produces an output current proportional to absolute temperature. The device acts as a high impedance, constant current regulator passing 1 µA per °C. Laser trimming of the chip is used to calibrate the device to 298·2 ± 2·5 µA at 298·2K (+ 25°C). Since the **RS** 590 is a current sourcing device it is ideally suited for remote sensing applications where the output can easily be transmitted over an inexpensive two-wire twisted pair line without degradation of performance due to line resistance, connector resistance or noise.

technical specification

Operating voltage range 4 V to 30 V d.c.
Nominal current output 298·2µA at + 25 °C
Nominal temp. coeff. 1µA/°C
Calibration error at 25 °C ± 2·5 °C max.
Operating temperature range -55 °C to + 150 °C

Temperature Sensor IC
LM35

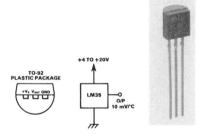

Supplied to RS by National Semiconductors

The LM35 is a three-terminal integrated circuit temperature sensor giving a linear voltage output of 10 mV per degree centigrade. Available in two versions, one operating from 0°C to 100°C (DZ version) the other from -40°C to + 110°C (CZ version). These devices are housed in TO-92 plastic packages and provide a low cost solution to temperature measurement.
Ideally suited for ambient temperature measurement such as providing cold junction compensation for thermocouples.

technical specification

Temperature range	
LM35 DZ	0°C to 100°C
LM35 CZ	-40°C to + 110°C
Absolute max. voltage	+ 35 V to -0·2 V
Operating voltage range	+ 30 V to + 4 V
Quiescent current at 5 V	91 µA typical
Accuracy at 25°C	
LM35 CZ	± 0·4°C typical
LM35 DZ	± 0·9°C typical

The output voltage is usually high enough, and output impedance low enough to be interfaced directly to the A/D conversion hardware. Some of the integrated circuit temperature sensors provide current output, whereas most others provide voltage output. The one that produces current output is very suitable for remote operation so that the output signal will not be affected by the impedance of the long wire and the noise. You will find the data sheets of some of the popular temperature sensor ICs below. Unabridged versions of the data sheets are included in Appendix A. Manufacturer data sheets are excellent sources of technical information, so browsing through them to see possible applications and limitations of the chip is strongly advised.

Example: LM35DZ is being used for a temperature measurement application. If the output is measured as 86 mV, find the temperature of the application.

Solution: Since the output of the LM35DZ increases to 10mV/°C, the temperature will be 86/10 = 8.6°C

Example: We would like to interface LM35CZ to an A/D converter. Find the bit resolution of the A/D converter needed.

Solution: The range of the LM35CZ is -40°C to 110°C and the accuracy is +/-0.4°C so the resolution of the chip output is (40+110)/0.4 = 375, which is slightly better than 8 bit resolution. Anything more than a 9 bit resolution A/D converter would be a waste for this design.

4.3.2 Temperature Sensor Selection Guide

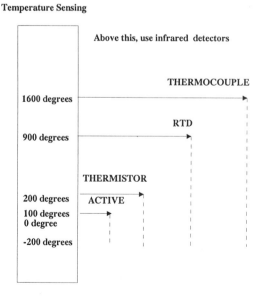

Active type temperature sensors are easy to use sensors which provide linear output. This type of temperature detectors can be used up to 100 °C, above which the detector

will be destroyed. For low temperature applications active temperature detectors are definetely the most appropriate selection. Higher temperature applications up to 200°C can use thermistors. Thermistors can provide high level signal output, but linearization of output is necessary. Applications which require measurements above 200°C can not use thermistors since they can not withstand high temperatures. RTD type sensors provide relatively high signal level, linear output and can withstand temperatures up to 900 °C. Applications which require measurements above 900°C up to 1600 °C can utilize thermocouples. Despite all problems associated with thermocouples like linearization, small signal output, and compensation, in some situations they are the only choice available for the designer. Above 1600°C the only choice available for temperature measurement is to use non-contact type infrared detectors and make measurements remotely without contacting the heat source.

4.3.3 Force Transducers

Force transducers in general are used for measuring the amount of force exerted on an object. There are basically two different laws of physics that we can utilize for the purpose of force sensing. The first law is the law which states that force is proportional to acceleration. According to the well-known formula $F = ma$, the force is proportional to mass times the acceleration. If the mass is known, by measuring the acceleration it is possible to determine the force. This type of measurement is limited to cases where the mass of the object is very well known and the object is free to move under the act of the force.

The other law of physics used for force measurement is the law stating that the deformation of a spring under force is proportional to the force and the spring constant. The formula for this is given as $F = kx$, where k is the spring constant and x the deformation of the spring. This law is more frequently used for measuring the force, and it is the basis for load cell and accelerometer designs. In all these sensors, a tiny spring exists whose deformation can be measured by various means.

The above law about springs is widely applicable to forms other than the spring. For example, an ordinary beam when subjected to force will elongate and deform. In general deformation is called strain and represented by the symbol ε. The formula for strain is given as $\varepsilon = \frac{\Delta L}{L}$, where L is the length of the beam and ΔL is the deformation of the beam.

In most engineering applications we are interested in the force applied per unit area of the beam, rather than the total force acting on the object. Force acting on per unit area is called stress and is represented by the formula $\sigma = \frac{F}{A}$, where A is the area and F is the force acting on the object.

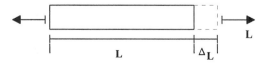

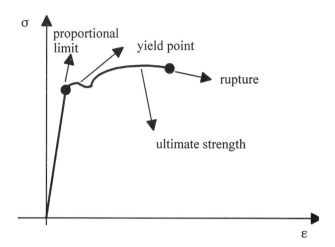

Figure 4.11 Stress-Strain diagram for mild steel.

According to material science, all materials including metals behave like springs at microscopic level. This relationship is given by the formula $\sigma = E \times \varepsilon$ where E is the modulus of elasticity, which is roughly equivalent to the spring constant in the famous law $F = kx$. This parameter, called Young's modulus of elasticity, is dependent on the particular material and for all practical purposes can be considered a constant. In reality, if the relationship between stress and strain is plotted, it resembles the schema shown in Figure 4.11.

This stress-strain relationship shows that below the proportional limit, the material behaves elasticly and its length will change proportionally to the stress (force). For measurement of force we use this relationship and somehow measure the elongation of the object. Since the modulus of elasticity is very well known for a given material, the stress-strain formula will give us the force exerted on the object.

The difficulty with this technique comes from measuring elongation. For most metals the elongation is very small and is thus very difficult to measure. Fortunately a useful tool, the strain gauge, is available to measure tiny displacements.

STRAIN GAUGE

The most widely used sensor for sensing force is the *strain gauge*. A strain gauge is a very versatile component and it is used in sensors as varied as weight sensors, load cells, pressure sensors, vibration sensors, and accelerometers. The versatility of the strain gauge comes from the fact that it is a very sensitive sensor, and by designing an appropriate mechanical enclosure it can be used for weighing very light as well as very heavy objects like trucks, railway cars, and even municipal water towers.

A strain gauge is essentially nothing more than a grid of very thin wire which is produced to very close manufacturing tolerances. The wire, which is basically a metal foil, is sandwiched between polyester backing materials. Any lateral stretching force applied to the sensor will cause the sensor to elongate, which will in turn cause the foil to become thinner. Since the resistance of any metal wire is inversely proportional to the cross section of the wire, the resistivity will change. Of course the resistance change is very small compared to the overall resistance, but it is quite linear. The sensitivity of the strain gauge is expressed by a figure called a gauge factor. A gauge factor is a dimensionless quantity which gives the ratio of change in the resistance value to the change in the length of the gauge. The higher the gauge factor, the more sensitive the gauge is.

$$GF = \frac{\Delta R/R}{\Delta L/L} = \frac{\Delta R/R}{\varepsilon}$$

A condensed version of a data sheet for a typical strain gauge is given below. A full unabridged version of the data sheet with application information and attachment procedure is given in Appendix A.

Foil Strain Gauges

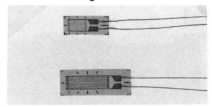

2 mm gauge L. 6   W. 2·5
2 mm rosette L. 7·5   W. 7·5
5 mm gauge L. 11   W. 4
5 mm rosette L. 12   W. 12

A range of foil strain gauges for general engineering stress and strain analysis.
These gauges have a negligible effect on the test object but allow measuremant of both static and dynamic strain. Both surfaces of these gauges are laminated thus fully protecting the copper nickel alloy foil grid.
All gauges are complete with integral wires for simple installation. Available in single or rosette styles with temperature compensation for use with either aluminium or mild steel.
For applications where point measurements or instrumentation of small components is required use the 2 mm length gauges, while for general purpose measurement the 5 mm gauges are ideal.
Suitable amplifier stock no. 308-815 also available (see this section).

technical specification

Gauge length	2 or 5 mm
Measurable strain	2 to 4% max.
Temperature range	-30 °C to + 180 °C
Gauge resistance	120 ± 0·5%
Gauge factor	2·00 (nominal)
Gauge factor temperature coefficient	± 0·015%/°C
Thermal induced output	-30 °C to 20 °C not specified
	20 °C to 160 °C + 2 micro strain/°C*
	160 °C to 180 °C ± 5 micro strain/°C*
Fatigue Life	10⁶ reversals at 1000 micro strain
Foil material	copper nickel alloy
Base material	polyimide

Temperature compensation	
Material	*linear expansion factor*
Mild steel	10·8 × 10⁻⁶/°C
Aluminium	23·4 × 10⁻⁶/°C

* 1 micro strain is equal to an extension of 0·0001%

Strain Gauge
Single

General purpose foil type, polyester backed strain gauges. Available with temperature compensation for steel (**type 11**) or aluminium (**type 23**). Each gauge has integral 30 mm flying leads. Supplied complete with two self-adhesive terminal pads to facilitate connection to the gauge, without risk of damage by applying undue heat or mechanical stress whilst connecting sensing leads to the device.

technical specification

Gauge length 8 mm
Measurable strain 3 to 4% max.
Temperature range -30°C to + 80°C
Gauge resistance 120 Ω ± 0·5%
Gauge factor 2·1 ± 1% (temp. coeff. <5%/100°C)
Fatigue life > 10⁶ reversals at 1000 μ Strain
Foil material copper-nickel alloy
Base material Polyester
Compensation Type 11 Mild steel. Linear
       Expansion factor 10·8 × 10⁻⁶/°C
       Type 23 Aluminium. Linear
       Expansion factor 23·4 × 10⁻⁶/°C

Data sheet 8155 November 87 available.

L. 13
W. 4

If one examines the data sheet for the specific strain gauge, one will notice that they come already compensated for a certain type of material (e.g. type 11, type 23, etc.) This refers to the material the strain gauge is supposed to be attached to. Temperature compensation is an important aspect of engineering strain gauges since the expansion due to heat is usually much more than the expansion due to the stress on the material. In order to sense the stress accurately and for the measurements to be independent of temperature, only the most suitable type of strain gauge should be used for the material in hand.

Example: The strain gauge with the data sheet given above is bonded to a mild steel beam for stress measurement. The beam is 20 cm long and the cross section of the beam is 5 cm^2. When force is applied, the resistance changes (decreases) by 0.02 ohms. Find the force acting on the beam. (Young's Modulus of Elasticity for Mild Steel is 20.7 10^{10} N/m^2.)

Solution: The nominal resistance of the strain gauge is given as 120 ohms. Since the resistance is decreasing, we can say that the force acting on the beam is tension because tension will cause the resistance to decrease by making the cross section of the strain gauge thinner. Using the gauge factor formula, $2.00 = (0.02/120)/(\Delta L/0.2)$. So

$\Delta L = 0.00001666$ m $= 16.66 \ 10^{-6}$m

The force acting on the beam (by using Young's modulus of elasticity), since $\sigma = E\varepsilon$, $\varepsilon = \Delta L/L$ and $\sigma = 20.7 \ 10^{10}$, is $(16.66 \ 10^{-6}/0.2) = 1724310$ N/m^2.

Also $\sigma = F/A$; from this $F = 1724310 * 0.0005 = 8621.55$ N.

Example: Assume that the above measurements will always be done in an indoor environment where the temperature varies form 18°C to 28°C. According to this, what is the resolution of this system?

Solution: Temperature compensation of the strain gauge becomes the limiting factor in these specific circumstances. One notices that all other uncertainties can be compensated for, like nominal resistance, by balancing the bridge circuit. But the gauge factor temperature compensation is due to the mismatch of mild steel and the gauge material. Manufacturers would like to get rid of this error but unfortunately they can not. This figure is given as +- 0.015%/°C.

Since temperature varies 10 °C in the environment, the maximum change of this factor will be $0.015 * 10 * (2.00/100) = 0.003$. So according to this figure, the gauge factor can be 2.00 +/- 0.003. For simplicity, assume the gauge factor is 2.003.

This will change the calculations to

$GF = (\Delta R/R)/(\Delta L/L)$ $2.003 = (0.02/120)/(\Delta L/0.2)$

$\Delta L = 0.00001664$ m $= 16.64 \ 10^{-6}$ m

From this, we will find the force acting on the beam by using Young's modulus of elasticity.

$\sigma = E\varepsilon$

$\varepsilon = \Delta L/L$

$\sigma = 20.7 \ 10^{10}$ $(16.64 \ 10^{-6}/0.2) = 1724163$ N/m^2

Also σ= F/A;   from this F = 1724163 * 0.0005 = 8611.2 N whereas the previous calculation gave 8621.55 N . There is a difference of 10 N.

This gives us a resolution of 8621/10 = 862, which is roughly better than 9 bit resolution (2^9 = 512).

Strain gauges are available in a single gauge form or in a rosette form. A single gauge can be used for measuring force only in one direction, whereas in a rosette configuration more than one gauge is placed in close proximity in a suitable geometry. Each one measures force in a certain direction, so forces in multiple directions can be sensed.

Temperature Compensation of Strain Gauges

In order to appreciate the importance of the temperature compensation for a strain gauge let us work out an example.

Example: Calculate the resistance change caused by increasing the temperature of the environment on a strain gauge.

Solution: As we have previously discussed, in temperature sensors all metals can be used as temperature sensors, some being more efficient then others. The resistance of the metal increases the temperature increases. For most metals the coefficient of change is 0.00395 Ω/°C. The resistance change for the strain gauge = 120 x 0.00395 = 0.474 Ω.

If you examine the first example that we have solved above, a force of 8000 N was changing the resistance only 0.02 Ω. So, according to this, the resistance change caused by temperature is much more than the resistance change caused by stress. From this example we can appreciate the importance of temperature compensation for strain gauges.

Temperature compensation for the strain gauge is made by using another dummy strain gauge which is exposed to the same temperature as the active gauge but not subjected to the force acting on the workpiece.

In order to see the effect of this combination, let us first take a look at the ordinary bridge configuration with no temperature compensation.

The single active strain gauge bridge configuration given in Figure 4.12 is not temperature compensated. The output voltage for this case is presented in the following formula:

$$V_{out} = \frac{\Delta R_{strain\ gage}\ V}{4R}$$

where

V = Excitation voltage

R = Resistance equal to R strain gauge

DR = Change of resistance due to force

The derivation of the formula is simple and left as a self-study exercise.

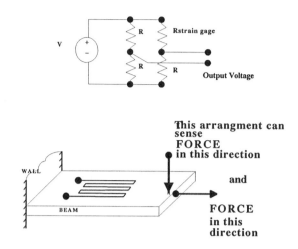

Figure 4.12 Bridge configuration for single active strain gauge which is not temperature compensated.

Temperature Compensated Single Active Strain Gauge Configuration

The single active strain gauge bridge configuration given in Figure 4.13 is temperature compensated. The output voltage for this case is given by the following formula:

$$V_{out} = \frac{\Delta R_{strain\ gage}\ V}{4R}$$

where

V is excitation voltage

R is resistance equal to R strain gauge and R dummy

ΔR is the change of resistance due to force

As you can notice the formula is exactly same as the uncompensated form. Since active and the dummy strain gauges are placed opposite to each other in the bridge, as long as they change in equal amount due to temperature, the balance of the bridge is not disturbed.

The placement of the strain gauge is very important since strain gauge is a position sensitive component. If the strain gauge is placed in an orientation where the expansion of the work piece does not affect the strain gauge, then the gauge will only respond to temperature and not to force. By placing the active and the dummy strain gauges in close proximity to each other on the same workpiece we can be reasonably sure that both gauges will be subjected to the same temperature.

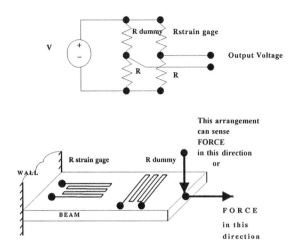

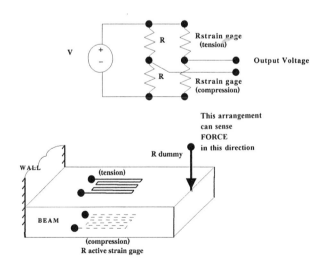

Figure 4.13 Bridge configuration for single active strain gauge which is temperature compensated.

Temperature Compensated Dual Active Strain Gauge Configuration

Figure 4.14 Dual active strain gauge, temperature compensated bridge.

In this configuration we have two strain gauges that are actively involved in force measurement. The way they are connected to the bridge will also make sure that the temperature effects caused by one of them will be canceled by the other gauge. This type of arrangement is more sensitive to force.

Formula for this type is

$$V_{out} = \frac{\Delta R_{strain\ gage}\ V}{2R}$$

Temperature Compensated Four Active Strain Gauge Configuration

In this configuration we have four strain gauges that are actively involved in force measurement. The way they are connected to the bridge will also make sure that the temperature effects caused by one of them will be canceled by the other gauge. This type of arrangement is the most sensitive arrangement for measurement of force.

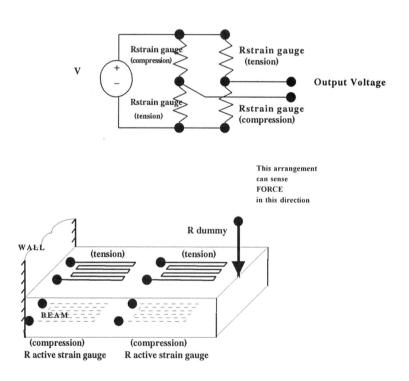

Figure 4.15 Four active strain gauge, temperature compensated bridge.

$$V_{out} = \frac{\Delta R_{strain\ gage}\ V}{R}$$

LOAD CELLS

Strain gauges are very versatile devices but they are quite painful to work with due to their extreme sensitivity. The strain gauge has to match the application in terms of heat expansion coefficient and should be mounted carefully. None of these processes is extremely difficult, but they require a certain amount of dexterity from the user. For those who do not want to go through this experiment, there are strain gauges on the market which are already installed on a beam compensated for temperature and signal-conditioned. These devices are called *load cells*. All load cells have a sturdy frame made of either steel or aluminum and strain gauges are already installed either in two or four active gauge configuration. In all cases, the bending of the frame due to the exerted force is detected. Since the deflection of the frame is also dependent on the strength of the frame, it is possible to make load cells that can measure very light or very heavy objects by changing the thickness of the frame.

Example: You are asked to design a weight balance for household use. Using the short data sheets provided for load cells given on the following page, determine the maximum resolution that you can get from the load cells.

Solution: Since the balance is designed for household use, it is better to select a load cell with 100 kg range. Recommended excitation voltage is 10 volts. In the data sheet the total error is listed as 0.025%. Since we selected the 100 kg cell, the error will be

Error = 0.025 x 1000 = 25 gm

In terms of bit resolution, 100,000/25 = 4000 equals to 12 bit resolution.

Example: In the above example, the temperature of the environment changes 50°C. Find out how this will effect the output of the load cell in terms of weight.

Solution: The temperature effect on span is given as 0.025% per 25 °C. According to this, 50 degrees will effect the span as 0.050% of the full load. Since the full load is 100 kg, the change is 0.050 x 1000 = 50 grams. So the output will change 50 grams by changing the temperature 50°C.

An unabridged data sheet for load cells is given in Appendix A.

4.3.4 Pressure Sensor

A pressure sensor is a modified form of load cell. In this case the strain gauges are mounted on the diaphragm of a pressure gauge. As the pressure increases, the diaphragm will bulge and stretch. The strain gauges are sensitive enough to sense these changes. These gauges are used in a configuration with temperature compensation in order to minimize the temperature effects.

Given below are the data sheets for pressure sensors. An unabridged version of the data sheet is given in Appendix A.

Not all the pressure sensors use strain gauge for measuring force. Another versatile sensor that can be used for this purpose is one mode of piezoelectric crystals which converts force into electrical energy directly. Piezoelectric crystals are very sensitive to temperature as well as pressure. Because of this temperature, compensation of the sensor should be made carefully.

Strain Sensors
Load Cells
2, 20 and 100kg

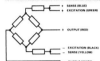

electrical connections

Three single point load cells primarily intended for use in weighing scales although they may be used in many other applications.

2 kg, 20 kg and 100 kg versions are available.

The force applied to the load face of the cell causes a deflection of the body which is measured by a bridge of four strain gauges.

All cells are 100% tested and have humidity protection to ensure long term accuracy.

A screened lead, 6-wire system is used for best accuracy. When used for weighing scales the load cell can be fitted with a platform up to the maximum size given below. The output of the cell is independent of the point through which the load acts.

The 2 kg cell has built in under and over-load protection while the larger cells are designed to give overload protection when mounted on any flat and rigid surface.

The 2 kg and 20 kg cells have mounting and platform fixing by M6 × 1·0 set screws in 10 mm deep tapped holes. The 100 kg cell has M8 × 1·25 fixings. Supplied with an instruction leaflet.

Suitable amplifiers are strain gauge amp. 308-815 (see this section) precision instrumentation amp. 302-463 (see Semiconductors - Analogue/Linear ICs).

Technical Specification

General

Recommmended excitation	10 V d.c.
Max. excitation	15 V d.c.
Output at rated load	2 mV/V ± 10%
Zero balance	± 5% of rated load
Input impedance	415 ± 15 Ω
Output impedance	350 ± 3 Ω
Insulation	5 × 10⁹ Ω
Compensated temp. range	-10°C to 50°C
Safe temp. range	-30°C to 70°C
Safe over load	150% of rated load
Ultimate overload	300% of rated load
Deflection	0·5 mm at rated load
Cable	6 core screen 7/0·2
Max. platform size 2 Kg	200 × 200 mm
20 kg	400 × 400 mm
100 kg	600 × 600 mm

Accuracy	% of rated load
Total error	0·025%
Hysteresis	0·025%
Non-repeatability	0·01%
30 minute creep (and zero return)	0·025%
Eccentricity (for normal platform size)	0·015%
Temperature effect on zero/5°C (9°F)	0·02%
Temperature effect on span/25°C (45°F)	0·025%

Tension/Compression Load Cell
250kg

A general purpose load cell for force measurement with loads up to 250 kg (500 lbsor 2·5 kN approx.) Mechanical connections are by M12 × 1·75 tapped holes in the body of the device and electrical connections are by an integral 4-core screened cable of 3 meters length.

This cell can be used for weighing but is ideally suited for the measurement of tensile of compressive forces by using the cell to replace the structural member under investigation.

Other applications include, for example, determining the power output of a motor by replacing the mounting with this cell and measuring the torque reaction produced.

technical specification

Total error	0·025%	
Non-repeatability	0·01%	of
Zero return	0·025%	rated
Temp. effect on zero 10°C	0·03%	load
Temp. effect on span 10°C	0·015%	
Recommended excitation	10 V d.c.	
Maximum excitation	15 V d.c.	
Output at rated load	2 mV/V ± 10%	
Zero balance	± 5% of rated load	
Barometric effect	None	
Input impedance	415 ± 15 Ω	
Output impedance	350 ± 3 Ω	
Insulation	> 10⁹ Ω	
Compensated temp. range	-10°C to + 50°C	
Safe temp. range	-30°C to + 70°C	
Safe overload	150% of rated load	
Ultimate overload (for failure)	300% of rated load	

Technical Specification

Deflection	0·3 mm at rated load
Sealing	IP65
Cable	4-core screened 7/0·2

Wet/Wet Differential and Gauge

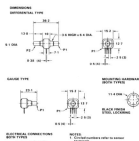

Two styles of pressure transducer each available in three pressure ranges. The differential style features wet/wet capability which allows most media types to be introduced on the active (P1) and passive (P2) sides of the device. Both styles incorporate laser trimmed bridge resistors to enable close tolerance on null/sensitivity and they also feature temperature compensation. Each sensor utilises a 0·1in square silicon chip with integral sensing diaphragm and four piezo resistors. Pressure applied to the diaphragm causes it to flex, changing the resistance which results in a low level output voltage proportional to pressure. The sensing resistors are connected as a four active element bridge for best linearity and sensitivity.

These transducers are ideal for applications requiring exact pressure measurement where repeatability, low hysterisis and long term stability are important. These transducers also benefit from advance manufacturing techniques which enhance their reliability whilst reducing unit cost.

The product is supplied complete with instruction leaflet and steel lock ring for fixing.

technical specification

(all figures are typical unless otherwise stated)

	0-5p.s.i	0-15p.s.i.	0-30p.s.i.
Full scale output	50mV	100mV	80mV
Sensitivity/p.s.i.	9·98mV	6·66mV	2·66mV
Overpressure (max.)	20p.s.i.	45p.s.i.	60p.s.i.
Recommended excitation	10V d.c.	10V d.c.	10V d.c.
Input resistance	10kΩ	10kΩ	10kΩ
Media compatibility	Limited to those which will not attack polyester, silicon, or fluorosilicone		

Pressure Sensors
250m Bar to 400 Bar

BASEEFA Apperatus Certificate No, Ex892251x Approval category EEx ia IIc T4

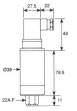

Supplied to RS by Druck Ltd.

This range of 2 wire, 4-20mA gauge style pressure sensors is intended for continuous monitoring of pressure in various hazardous applications including gas/petrochemical production and process environments.

The units utilise silicon technology for the pressure sensing element and incorporate surface mount electronic components in construction. This enables high accuracy and stability from a very compact unit. All products are housed in a robust stainless steel body with the electronics fully encapsulated which enables them to withstand high levels of shock and vibration.

The pressure port is G ¼in. female and all units are supplied complete with a DIN 43650 electrical connector.

Environmental protection rating is IP65.

The units are BASEEFA approved for use in zone 'O' gas group IIC, temperature class T4. A suitable barrier for use with these products is **RS** stock no. 256-916 available elsewhere in this section.

The BASEEFA certificate reference no. for the sensors is given above. The sensor and barrier (when used together) also carry a BASEEFA systems certificate. Both certificates and instruction leaflet are supplied with the product.

Technical Specification

Maximum overpressure	
250m bar	2 bar
1·6 bar to 25 bar	3 x pressure
60 bar to 400 bar	2 x pressure
Supply voltage	9-30V d.c.
Output current	4-20mA
Combined non-linearity hysteresis and repeatability	±0·15% FS
Zero offset and span	±5% site adjustable
Long term stability	0·1% FS p/yr
Ambient operating temperature range	-20°C to +80°C
Process media temp. range	-30°C to +120°C
Temperature effects	±0·5% FS over -10°C to +50°C
RFI protection	conforms with IT 8839 requirements from 10KHz to 500MHz
Pressure connection	G ¼ in. BSP, parallel thread)
Electrical connection	D43650 connector (supplied)
Environmental protection	IP65
Suitable barrier for use with sensors - **RS** stock no. 256-916	
BASEEFA systems certificate no.	Pending

4.3.5 Position Sensors

A position sensor, as the name implies, is used for sensing the position of an object. These kinds of sensors are used very frequently in industrial robotics applications as well as automated machinery. The position information to be sensed can be either angular or linear. The angular position sensors are often called shaft encoders. There are many different kinds of position sensors available, both angular and linear, which are based on different methods and technologies. These methods can be classified as follows

- Potentiometer type position sensors
- LVDT type position sensors
- Optical position sensors
- Ultrasonic position sensors
- Syncro resolvers
- Optical shaft encoders

POTENTIOMETER TYPE POSITION SENSORS

A potentiometer is a variable resistor which is usually shown schematically as follows

Here the middle contact is the wiping contact of the variable resistors. As the position of the wiping contact changes, the resistance between B and C changes. So the resistance gives the indication of the position. Commonly used potentiometers in electronics applications include carbon deposit type potentiometers whose lifetime is not long enough for them to be used for position sensing purposes. Most of the potentiometers used for position sensing applications are conductive plastic potentiometers, which are more reliable and durable. Resistive type potentiometers can be both linear and angular in form. Information about this kind of potentiometer with brief technical information is given below. Courtesy RS Components.

Example: What is the maximum output resolution you can get from the angular type potentiometer given in the short data sheet below?

Solution: For the potentiometer, "output smoothness" is specified as 0.1 %. This will be the limiting factor for the resolution of the device. Maximum resolution = 1 part in 1000, which means a resolution of almost 10 bits.

Precision Linear Position Transducers
50, 100 and 200mm Stroke

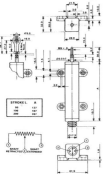

H. 28
W. (body only) 28
Mounting centres (using feet) 44

STROKE L	A
50	137
100	187
200	287

SHAFT RETRACTED / SHAFT EXTENDED

A range of precision linear position transducers with strokes of 50, 100 or 200 mm. The almost infinite resolution, output smoothness and excellent linearity make these transducers ideal not only for feedback control functions but also for use in calibration and testing of mechanical systems. Output is via an integral socket and the transducers are supplied complete with a mating plug, mounting feet and a spherical bearing (with an M5 clearance hole) for the end of the rod. The feet engage into slots in the side of the extruded aluminium body of the units thus allowing the feet to be placed in any position along the length of the devices.
These transducers should be used as potentiometers and not as variable resistors. For best results buffer the output using a high impedance amplifier.

Servo Mount Potentiometers
Conductive Plastic

Body dia. 22·22
Spigot dia. 19·05 (⅜in)
H. 13·1 (excl. terminals)
Shaft dia. 3·17 (⅛ in)
L. 12·7

A range of high quality precision servo mount potentiometers, particularly suitable for use with **RS** precision d.c. motor systems as position transducers (refer to the Motors section). The screened conductive plastic element is trimmed to a close tolerance linearity and multifinger wipers provide a high degree of output smoothness with virtually infinite resolution. Two servo bearings afford lowshaft torque and long life. As standard with many servo potentiometers the shaft dia. is ⅛ in, set inside a rugged anodised aluminium housing machined to give accurate location of the shaft (with minimal runouts) directly into drive systems. A mounting kit*consisting of three clamps, nuts, screws and mounting instructions is supplied with each potentiometer.

Technical Specification

Resistance tolerance	±20%
Linearity (independent)	±0·5%
Output smoothness (max.)	0·1%
Power rating	1 W at 40°C
Derate power to	zero at 125°C
Wiper current (max.)	10 mA
Insulation resistance	10^9 R at 500 V d.c.
Dielectric strength	1000 V r.m.s.
Electrical rotation	340° ±4°
Temperature range	-55°C to +125°C
Temperature coeff.	±400 ppm/°C
Rotational life‡	> 10^7 shaft revolutions
Mechanical rotation	360° continuous
Starting torque (max)	28×10^{-4} Nm
Running torque (max)	21×10^{-4} Nm
Shaft runout (eccentricity)	0·05 max
Pilot runout (eccentricity)	0·05 max
Lateral runout	0·05 max
Shaft end play	0·13 max
Shaft radial play	0·05 max

* Note this mounting kit is not required when the potentiometer is used with **RS** servo pot mounting kit 336-214 (refer to the motors section).
‡ Note this condition is for reciprocating revolutions, i.e. the wiper does not exceed the maximum electrical rotation. In application, it is not recommended that the wiper passes through 360° repeatedly, although the condition is allowed to a limited extent for safety considerations.

LVDT TYPE POSITION SENSORS

LVDT stands for linearly variable differential transformer. These types of sensors are mostly available in linear form. LVDT is actually nothing more than a transformer with a movable core. As the core moves, the magnetic coupling between the coils changes. One of the coils is steadily excited by a constant amplitude sinusoidal voltage source. Because of the coupling, voltage gets induced in the secondary coils. The amplitude of the voltage gives an indication of the position of the core

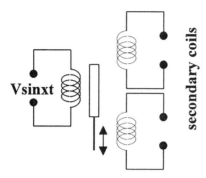

Figure 4.14 Internal construction of an LVDT.

Most LVDTs are produced with no electronics inside. For these types one can either design the electronics oneself or buy ready-to-use modules or cards for interfacing to the LVDT. You can also find LVDTs with integrated electronics. The user only needs to supply a DC voltage and read DC output from the LVDT. A data sheet for these components is given below. Courtesy RS Components.

Miniature d.c. Energised LVDT's

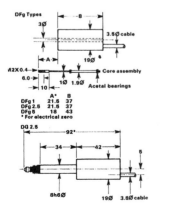

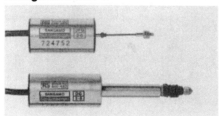

A range of four L.V.D.T.'s with electronic oscillator and demodulator built in, giving a d.c. output proportional to core position.
The DFg series have separate coil/electronic assemblies with a free core fitted with a polyacetal homopolymer bearing which can be allowed to rub on the inside of the coil assembly thus easing the guiding requirements.
The DG 2·5 has a non-rotating spring-loaded armature running in precision linear ball bearings.

Technical Specification	
Stroke DFg 1	±1 mm
DFg 2·5	±2·5 mm
DFg 5	±5.0 mm
DG 2·5	±2·5 mm
Sensitivity at 10 V energisation	780 mV
	560 mV (DFg 5)
Current consumption at 10 V energisation	10-15 mA
Input voltage	10-24 V d.c.
Output ripple	<1% f.s.d.
Response time constant	1·5 ms
Frequency response	-3 dB at 100 Hz
Temperature range	-20°C to +80°C
Temperature coefficients	
DFg 1	<0·010%/°C
others	<0·005%/°C
Sensitivity	<0·01%/°C
Non-linearity	0·3%
Cable	3 m, 5-core P.V.C. screened
Electrical connections	
Red	+ve supply
Blue	0 V supply
White	+ve output
Green	0 V output
Yellow	N/C

All % are of total stroke

Miniature a.c. Energised LVDT's Types SM1 and SM3

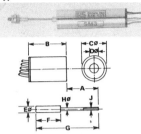

2 Channel Eurocard LVDT Oscillator/ Demodulator

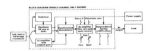

L. 160   H. 100   D. 18

A*	B	C	D	E	F	G	H	J
SM1	12.5	15	9.52	3.5	2.5	9.9	25	1	M2X.6
SM3	15	35	9.52	3.5	2.5	20.6	42.5	1	M2X.6

* For electrical zero.

Two miniature L.V.D.T.'s with ranges of ±1 and ±3 mm. Both devices offer low cost solutions to displacement measurement with all the advantages of L.V.D.T. technology.
The large radial clearance between the coil assembly and core allows friction-free operation and reduces the accuracy of guidance required.
Equivalent to Sangamo types SM1 (±1 mm) and SM3 (±3 mm).

Technical Specification

Mechanical

Stroke SM1	±1 mm
SM3	±3 mm
Non-linearity	0·5% of stroke
Body material	400 series stainless steel
Push rod material	300 series stainless steel

Electrical

Energising voltage	1 V d.c. to 10 V d.c.
Energising frequency	1 kHz to 20 kHz
Calibration load	100 kΩ
Primary resistance SM1	102 Ω
SM3	69 Ω
Secondary resistance SM1	204 Ω
SM3	200 Ω
Residual voltage at zero (typical)	0·3% f.s.d.

Electrical connections

Red and blue	Energisation
White and green	Output
Yellow	Secondary centre tap

Note: Red and white are in phase for inward displacement.

Supplied to RS by Schlumberger Industries

A standard-sized single eurocard containing oscillator and demodulation circuitry to drive 2 L.V.D.T.'s of the a.c. type.
Span and zero for both channels are by a 10-turn potentiometer on the front edge of the board.
Connections to the board are by a DIN 41612 A.C. indirect edge connector.
The drive and output signal can be adjusted via on-board jumper, over wide ranges enabling this card not only to work with all **RS** a.c. L.V.D.T.'s but most other transducers of this type as well.

Technical Specification

Power supply	±15 V d.c. ±0·6 V, 1% regulation or better. + 20 mA -40 mA no load. + 40 mA -60 mA max. load.
Supply protection	Reverse polarity protected
Transducer drive	5 V r.m.s. at 5 kHz sinusoid max. rated 50 mA
Oscillator protection	Open and short circuit protected
Transducer sensitivity ·range	0·5 to 692 mV/V in 9 coarse gain positions
Range of gain control	460 to 1 switched, 3 to ·, adjustable
Range of zero control	±20% and ±100% switched
Output voltage	±5 V into 10 kΩ min. Linear overrage to ±10 V
Output impedance	<1 Ω
Output protection	Open and short circuit protected
Output ripple	<10 mV pk-pk at 10 kHz
Output filter	Cut off frequency -3 dB at 500 Hz second order
Non-linearity	<0·1%
Temperature range	0°C to +70°C
Temperature coefficient	Zero, better than 0·01% fro/°C Gain, better than 0·01% fro/°C

OPTICAL POSITION SENSORS

Optical position sensors utilize optical reflection properties of materials. In some cases the light source and light detector is housed in the same enclosure in a certain geometry so that the beam emitted by the light source gets reflected from the target material and sensed by the light detector. The geometry is adjusted in such a way that whenever the object is at a certain distance the presence or absence of the target object is sensed. The light source may be either infrared or visible light. Other types of optical position sensors may have the light source and the light detector separately facing each other. In this case the target object passes between the emitter-detector couple and breaks the beam.

This type of detector does not really give the user the position of the object but simply informs whether the object is present or not within a specified distance. Even though these devices are not very sophisticated, they are used heavily in industry. Short data sheets of several different kinds of optical sensors are given below. Courtesy RS Components.

Diffuse and Retroreflective M12

L. 65   Dia. 12

A plug-in, optical proximity switch contained in a nickel-plated brass housing and available in 2 versions : diffuse scan and retroreflective scan. The switch has a PNP output, wired for N/O, and the rear of the unit has an LED indication of the switch status. Other features include :

● Short-circuit protected output
● Housing sealed to IP67
● Protection against polarity reversal
● Low current consumption

For a range of suitable plug-in leads see 'proximity switch accessories', elsewhere in this section. For a suitable reflector disc see 347-084, also in this section.

Technical Specification

Supply voltage	10-30 V d.c.
Load current	200 mA
Output current limit	300 mA
Sensing ranges	Diffuse scan - 100 mm
	Retroreflective scan - 2000 mm
Sensing rate	100 Hz

5m Range - Through Scan

RECEIVER OUTPUT CIRCUIT

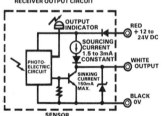

This miniature through scan system is ideal for applications where a compact, rugged product is required. The zinc diecast housings of the two near identical units are sealed to IP65. Both **transmitter** and **receiver** will operate from 12 to 24 V d.c. supplies and each unit is supplied with 2 m of cable fitted. An L.E.D. on top of the transmitter gives power-on indication. On the receiver an L.E.D. is lit to indicate an unblocked beam from the transmitter. If flickering, this L.E.D. shows that a state of marginal beam alignment exists, and further adjustment is recommended. The receiver is 'dark operate' (switch closed when light path broken) and will sink up to a maximum of 150 mA. (**Note:** there is no overcurrent protection.) Range of operation is up to 5 m. Supply inputs are reverse polarity protected. Both units are complete with a plastic mounting bracket and fixing bolts. The bracket has slotted holes to allow for fine angular adjustment once mounted.

Technical Specification

Full operating voltage range	10·8-26·4 V d.c. (max. 10% ripple)
Supply current (excluding o/p)	Transmitter 25 mA typ., receiver 25 mA typ.
Output current	Leakage 1·5-3 mA
	Sinking 150 mA max.
Range	Up to 5 m
Response time	5 ms max. (ON or OFF)
Max. switching frequency	100 Hz
Operating temperature range	-25°C to +55°C

ULTRASONIC POSITION SENSORS

Ultrasonic position sensors work on the principle of detecting ultrasound waves to be reflected by the target object. Ultrasound position sensors house both an ultrasound emitter and a detector inside the unit. By emitting an ultrasonic pulse and then measuring the delay time for the pulse to come back, ultrasound detectors can sense the distance of the target object. Given below are some ultrasound position sensors with brief data sheets. Courtesy RS Components.

Ultrasonic
M30 Diffuse Scan

L. Overall = 130 mm
L. Thread = 90 mm
L. Cable = 2 metres
Thread = M30 × 1·5 mm

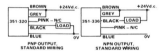

PNP OUTPUT,
STANDARD WIRING

NPN OUTPUT,
STANDARD WIRING

Two M30 proximity switches in plated brass using ultrasonic sensing techniques to detect a target. The carrier frequency of 215 kHz prevents the units responding to most false signals generated by various machinery. A 'target sensed' L.E.D. is incorporated which glows in proportion to the signal echo strength.

Available in both NPN and PNP N/O output versions, these units operate on 24 V d.c. and are environmentally protected to IP65. Almost any target can be detected with these units at distances of between 100 mm and 800 mm (adjustable). Switching frequency varies between 20 Hz at close range to 8 Hz at maximum range.

Supplied complete with instruction leaflet

Through Scan.

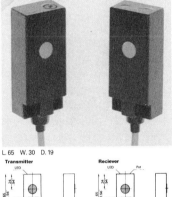

L. 65   W. 30   D. 19

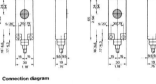

Connection diagram

An ultrasonic proximity switch which operates in the through scan mode by means of a separate sonic **transmitter** and **receiver**. The device will work with the two units situated up to 500 mm apart. When the receiver detects a break in the beam linking it to the transmitter the transistor output is switched, while a green LED on the receiver indicates when this occurs. The compact transmitter and receiver are housed in identical plastic cases, and are sealed to IP65.

- Available in both PNP and NPN versions
- High carrier frequency to make the unit immune to most industrial noise
- Sensitivity adjustment on receiver, with LED indication
- Flashing LED - warning of low power received
- Complementary outputs, enabling both states to be monitored
- Separate 'power on' LED (transmitter only)
- Reverse polarity protection on both units
- Full instructions included

technical specification	
Operating voltage	15-30 V d.c.
Carrier frequency	220 kHz
Operating range	50-500 mm
Sonic beam angle	10°
Load current	200 mA
Switching frequency	100 Hz
Hysterisis (typ.)	5 mm
Minimum object size	20 × 20 mm
Operating temperature	0-60°C
Repeatability	< 2 mm

OPTICAL SHAFT ENCODERS

Optical shaft encoders are the most popular type of position sensors for reading angular position information. The popularity comes form the fact that the output of the optical shaft encoder is digital which makes A/D conversion unnecessary. Optical shaft encoders have a wheel connected to the shift which has a code painted on it. Optical emitter-detector pairs arranged on both sides of the code wheel will read the information on the code wheel in digital form.

Optical shaft encoders provide the digital output in two different forms:

- **Absolute position output** is presented digitally in parallel form. Depending on the type of the encoder, this may be 8 bits, 10 bits or 12 bits. The digital information is presented in Gray code most of the time but there are absolute shaft encoders which provide the output in straight binary form as well.

- **Incremental output** provides the output in quadrature form with three wires. Instead of giving an absolute position, this type simply provides pulses as the shaft rotates. External counters keep track of the count. Since the signal is provided in quadrature form, the direction of rotation can be sensed and accordingly the counters can be increased or decreased. A shortened data sheet for shaft encoders which is included in the following pages gives information about this type of sensor. Courtesy RS Components.

Speed and Position Transducers
Shaft Encoders
Standard

Mechanical outline

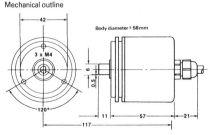

This range of enclosed optical shaft encoders, sealed to IP65, are suitable for use in many industrial applications under adverse conditions. The TTL compatible outputs remain stable across the supply voltage range of 5 V to 30 V. Channel A output is phase shifted by 90° in relation to channel B output. Channel C output is the synchronisation pulse, one per revolution and set in phase with channel A. These signals enable determination of shaft rotation, direction and position. The encoders are of precision manufacture to give high mechanical and electrical performance. Units are available with 1000, 1250, 2000 and 2500 p.p.r. resolution.

Data sheet 10748 March 92 available.

Technical Specification	
Supply voltage	5 V-30 V d.c. ± 5%
Operating temperature range	0°C to + 75°C
Storage temperature range	-30°C to + 75°C
Phase angle (output A to B)	90°
Output voltage high level (min.)	2·4 V
low level (max.)	0·4 V
Max. rotation speed:	
1000 ppr	6000 rpm
1250 ppr	4800 rpm
2000 ppr	3000 rpm
2500 ppr	2400 rpm
Typ. current consumption	70 mA (no load)
Environmental protection	IP65

MAGNETIC PICKUP SENSORS

Magnetic pickup sensors are simple proximity switches which can sense the existence of ferromagnetic objects close by. Even though they are simple sensors, they are used in many applications in industry and automotive engineering because of their ruggedness and noise immunity. The most popular application of the magnetic pickup is as a counter, counting gear teeth passing in front of the sensor. There are some versions of this sensor available which can provide the output signal in digital form. Shortened data sheets of the sensor indicate possible uses. Courtesy RS Components.

Magnetic Pick-Ups

Miniature magnetic 'pick-up' transducers suitable for use in a very wide range of sensing applications. Each device responds to movement of ferrous parts past the pole-piece on the end of the unit. Used extensively in areas such as speed regulation of motors, when sensing, for example, the teeth on a gear wheel. However, **RS** magnetic pick-ups may be used to implement feedback and control functions in many fields. Automotive applications include crank angle sensing, ignition timing, anti-skid systems and diagnostics. Applications in the computer peripherals area encompass disc drives, line printers, card punches/readers and printer terminals. The diagrams indicate the two basic modes of using these components. Note especially their small size, enabling their deployment where many conventional sensors cannot be fitted. Fully encapsulated construction for reliable operation, but **not** intended for immersion in liquids.

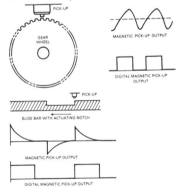

Standard

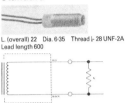

L. (overall) 22   Dia. 6·35   Thread ⅜- 28 UNF-2A
Lead length 600

This small transducer offers an inexpensive solution where a simple alternating waveform, corresponding to movement past the pole-piece, can be utilised. This pick-up is a 'passive' device requring no external power and produces a voltage across its terminations in response to variations in its magnetic field induced by proximity to **moving** ferrous parts. Encased in a steel body and supplied with two fixing nuts. Interfaces directly with **RS** tachometer i.c. 302-047

technical specification

Resistance: 130 Ω ± 10%
Inductance: 12 mH ± 10%
Output: 10 V pk-pk
Polarity: voltage on red wire positive with respect to black wire with the approach of ferrous metal.
Temperature range: -40°C to + 105°C.
Note: Output is defined for a load of 100 kΩ with the pick-up of 0·13 mm from a 38 mm dia. gear wheel with 30 teeth revolving at 13,000 r.p.m. The output will be different with other conditions and is best determined by experiment. As a general guide the following points should prove helpful:
● use the pick-up with a high impedance load
● position the pick-up as close as is safe to the moving parts - normal clearances with these devices are up to approx. 2·5 mm max.
● in a geared system use the pick-up with the **gear** wheel with the highest speed.

INDUCTIVE PROXIMITY SENSORS

Inductive proximity sensors are devices which can sense the existence of conductive objects that are situated close by. The sensing distance for the sensor is adjustable by adjusting the controls on the sensor, but it can not be more than 10 cm. The sensing distance also depends on the type of the target material. Different metals have different sensing distances.

The principle of operation of the inductive proximity sensor is sensing the eddy current losses induced in a conductor. Inside the sensor there is a coil which is continuously driven by a sinusoidal AC signal. Any time there is a conductor around the emitting coil, eddy current will be generated inside the conductor. (Eddy currents are considered losses and one tries to reduce them normally.) The eddy current losses will cause loading in the coil and the current drawn from the AC voltage source will increase. By monitoring the current drawn by the coil we can sense the existence of the conductive substances around the sensor.

Proximity Switches
Inductive

A range of inductive detectors which will sense the presence of metals, for use in many applications, including batch counting, limit switching and alarm systems. The detectors incorporate built-in amplifiers giving on-off outputs, and will detect ferrous and non-ferrous metals.

Limit Switch Style
a.c. and d.c. Powered

L. 117(overall) W. 40 H. 40

Inductive proximity switches, protected to IP67, designed to be interchangeable with **RS heavy-duty limit switches** (e.g. 337-469 and 337-475) in many applications. Available in **20 to 250V a.c.** and **10 to 30V d.c.** powered versions. By removing two screws the sense head cube may be set in any one of five positions. An LED shows when material is sensed. The d.c. version is protected against continuous short-circuit of the NPN, normally open output and against polarity reversal of the supply. This d.c. version has a red LED indicating material sensed and a green LED showing the supply is connected.
The plug-in facility of the main body into the black connection base allows easy installation and maintenance. A key-way pin prevents the connection of a d.c. unit into an a.c. wired base. Flush mounting of the unit is permissible. To avoid interaction between adjacent detectors it is advisable to allow 40 mm clearance. Cable entry is via a Pg 13·5 tapped hole (**Note:** Pg 13·5 to M20 × 1·5 cable gland adaptor 547-420, is available in the Conduit/Trunking section). Connections are via screw terminals. Performance to C.E.E. EN 50 010 (BS5271).
Max. switching currents 500mA (a.c. version) and 200mA (d.c. version). The max. surge current on the a.c. version is 4A (t ≤ 10 ms, f ≤ 5 Hz) and the max. off state leakage current is 2·5 mA. A switch mounting bracket 549-347 is available to facilitate mounting these units. For operating parameters see additional data table.

2 Wire - d.c.

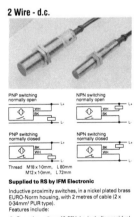

PNP switching normally open   NPN switching normally open

PNP switching normally closed   NPN switching normally closed

Thread   M18 x 1·0mm, L 80mm
M12 x 1·0mm, L 72mm

Supplied to RS by IFM Electronic

Inductive proximity switches, in a nickel plated brass EURO-Norm housing, with 2 metres of cable (2 x 0·34mm² PUR type).
Features include:

● Operating voltage 10-55V d.c. including residual ripple
● 2-wire units/4 output functions; the sensors can be connected in any of 4 combinations (see drawing - connections). The outputs are both over-load and short-circuit protected
● M18 or M12 versions available. Each type is enviromentally protected to IP67 and is flush mountable
● LED indication of switching status
● Nominal sensing range 5mm - M18 type, 2mm - M12 type. Variation +/- 10%

Technical Specification		
Max. current load		
Continuous and peak		400mA short-circuit and overload protected
Voltage drop		<4·6V
Leakage current		<0·6mA
Minimum load current		4mA
Maximum permissible transient mains voltage		1kV for 10ms at a source impedance of 5k ohm
Switching frequency		
M18 type		700Hz max.
M12 type		1100Hz max.
Correction factors for sensing distances		mild steel: 1 brass: 0·5 aluminium: 0·4 copper: 0·3 stainless steel: 0·7
Switching hysteresis		3% to 15% of sensing range
Ambient temperature range		-25°C to +80°C working

CAPACITIVE PROXIMITY SENSORS

Capacitive sensors are very similar to inductive proximity sensors in shape and function. The difference is that the capacitive sensor can sense not only conductors but also non-conductors. Capacitive sensors are sensitive virtually to all materials. Just like an ultra-sonic sensor that is used as a limit switch, it can sense any substance, metallic or nonmetallic, close by. The sensing distance is dependent on the material but at best it should not be expected to be more than 10 cm.

Capacitive

A range of proximity detectors with built-in amplifiers and switching output stages making them extremely versatile sensors. Will sense the presence of non-conducting materials such as wood, P.V.C., glass, etc., as well as ferrous and non-ferrous metals. All types have built-in potentiometers for sensitivity adjustment and L.E.D. indicators. Applications include batch counting, alarm systems, limit switching, etc. Supplied complete with adjusting screwdriver.

a.c. Powered High Sensitivity

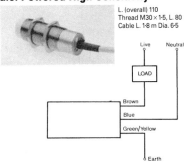

L. (overall) 110
Thread M30 × 1·5, L. 80
Cable L. 1·8 m Dia. 6·5

A capacitive proximity detector capable of sensing wooden targets at approximately 25 mm range as well as metal targets up to 65 mm range. The L.E.D. illuminates when material is sensed. The unit will directly drive **RS** mains impulse and predetermining counters, octal and 11-pin relays. Refer to the Relays/Solenoids section 28. The threaded stainless steel housing is waterproof (protection to IP65) and incorporates a 3-core cable. Supplied with two fixing nuts and operating instructions.
For operating parameters see additional data table.

a.c. Powered - Delay

L. 132
Dia. 33

P.G. 36
Mounting gland
Hole size 47 mm ø

Adjustable delay facility greatly extends the wide area of application for capacitive switching. When power is first connected (with no material sensed) the relay remains inactive for the duration of the delay period and the LED flashes. At the end of the delay period the relay changes over. When material is sensed the relay contacts change over and the LED switches off. When material is removed the delay period is initiated, the relay contacts remain in positon and the LED flashes. Once the delay period has expired the relay contacts change over and the LED switches on. The period during the 2 sec to 10 min delay may be used to prevent immediate motor start up in many hopper filling and material flow situations to aid smooth process control. High hysteresis is incorporated, together with relatively low sensitivity to allow operation in dusty environments. Protection to IP67. Case material: A.B.S. Supplied complete with Pg 36 mounting and sealing gland and full instructions. For operating parameters see addtional data table.

Additional Data – Capacitive Proximity Switches

	a.c. powered		d.c. powered		
			256-770	256-764	
	307-395	341-474	304-194	341-468	
Supply voltage	80 to	220 to	8 to	8 to	
	250 V a.c.	240 V a.c.	30 V d.c.	30 V d.c.	
Max. output current	200 mA	5 A	250 mA	250 mA	* Sense distance given for
Max. sensing rate	10 Hz	–	250 Hz	400 Hz	all items are approximate
Ambient temperature	0 °C	-55 °C to	-25 °C to	-30 °C to	and depend on target area
range	+60 °C	+75 °C	+85 °C	+100 °C	and material
Off state current	5 mA max.	–	8 mA max.	6 mA max.	
Sensing dist.*:					
Earthed Cu/Al	65 mm		–	10 mm	
Cu/Al	35 mm		20 mm	–	
Cardboard	25 mm	15 mm max.	4 mm	–	
Wood	25 mm		4 mm	from 2 mm	
P.V.C.	20 mm		10 mm	9 mm	
Mild steel	–		–	10 mm	

More than a meter   **Less than a meter**

<u>Environment dust</u>   <u>Target object metal</u>
  Use ultrasonic proximity sensor   Use the inductive proximity sensor

<u>Distance very large</u>   <u>Target non-conductor</u>
  Use through the beam optical type   Use capacitive sensor

<u>Hazardous environment</u>   <u>Distance very small</u>
  Both ultrasonic and optical suitable   Use optical proximity sensor

Figure 4.17 Proximity sensor selection guide.

The principle of operation for the capacitive sensor is sensing the change of the dielectric constant of the capacitor. Just like the inductive proximity sensor, this sensor also has a sinusoidal AC voltage source driving a capacitor. Any substance close by will change the dielectric constant of the capacitor which in turn will cause the capacitance to change. Changing capacitance gives the indication of target material in the vicinity.

Capacitive sensors are widely used in industry for sensing non-conductive materials like cardboard boxes, wrapped packages or granules of different materials.

HUMIDITY SENSORS

Humidity sensors are especially used in air-conditioned environments and green houses for sensing the humidity level. A short data sheet for a typical humidity sensor is given on the following page.

GAS SENSORS

Gas sensors are transducers which are designed to sense a specific kind of gas. Since the sensors are specifically made for a certain kind of gas, it is not possible to find gas sensors for every kind of gas available. The only kinds of gas sensors available in the market are for sensing carbon monoxide or explosive gases like methane. The sensor can be either a switch type which gives an indication only if the concentration is higher than a preset value, or the proportional output type which gives output proportional to the concentration of the gas. Courtesy RS Components.

Methane

BASEEFA Certificate No.
Ex 91Y 2343
Approval catagory
EEx ias IIc T4

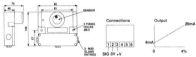

Supplied to RS by Trolex Ltd

This intrinsically safe, explosive gas sensor is intended for continuous monitoring of methane levels in sewage systems, process plants or any other areas where personal safety may be compromised.

The measuring range is 0-4% methane and will output a 4-20mA signal proportional to the gas detected. The unit has a working temperature of −10°C to +55°C and has an accuracy of ±0·1% of CH₄ (over 0 to 1·25% CH₄) and ±8% of full scale (over 1·25% to 4% CH₄). The electronics are contained in a GRP housing to which the stainless steel housed sensor module is attached.

The unit is BASEEFA approved for use in zone '0' gas group IIC, temperature class T4. Suitable barriers for use with this device are stock nos. 256-972 (supply) and 256-994 (return), available elsewhere in this section. The BASEEFA certificate reference no. for the sensor is given in the technical specification below. The sensor and barrier (when used together) also carry a BASEEFA systems certificate. Both certificates and an instruction leaflet are supplied with the product.

Technical Specification

Ambient Temperature Limits	−10 to 55°C
Humidity	95% non condensing
Protection Classification	IP52
Housing Material	Glass reinforced Polycarbonate/Stainless Steel
Sensing Principle	Catalytic Combustion
Overall Accuracy	±0·1% of CH₄. Over 0 to 1·25% CH₄ ±8% of range. Over 1·25% to 4% CH₄
Maximum Drift	±0·1% in 2 weeks
Repeatability	±0·1%
Response Time	10 seconds
Cell Operating Life	2 years
Electrical Connections	4mm Barrier Terminals (or 3 pin Plug and Socket connection)
Supply Voltage	24V d.c. via Safety Barrier (Sensor terminal voltage 10V to 15V)
Current Consumption	55mA nominal
Analogue Output	4 to 20mA to BS5863
Maximum Load Impedance	600 ohms
BASEEFA apparatus certificate no.	Ex91C2343 EExia IIC T4
Recommended barrier types	stock nos. 256-972 and 256-994
BASEEFA systems certificate	Ex 91Y 2515

Industrially Housed Humidity/ Temperature Sensors

Electronics Module

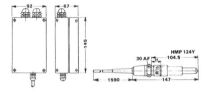

Supplied to RS by Vaisala

A humidity/temperature sensor with the electronics housed in a tough ABS case and remote mounting probe. Covers a wide range of applications but is primarily is intended for use in pressurised environments. Senses temperature as well as humidity, simultaneous using a ⅓ tolerance Pt 100 element to DIN 43760 and a Humicap® as the active sensors

selection guide

Operating temp. (electronics)	-40° to +50°C
Input voltage	240/110/24V a.c. 50/60Hz.
Measuring range RH&T	0 to 100% RH -40°C to 115°C Factory setting -20°C to +80°C
Output	4 to 20mA or 0 to 20mA
Accuracy at 20°C	±2% RH (0 to 80% RH) ±3% RH (0 to 100% RH) ±0·3°C

technical specification

Input voltage	240/110/24 V a.c.
Power consumption	5 W
Output humidity and temperature	4 to 20 mA or 0 to 20 mA
Max. external load	400 Ω
Accuracy at 20 °C	
Humidity.	±2%, 0% to 80% ±3%, 80% to 100%
Temperature	±0·3 °C
Case material	A.B.S.
Sealing	IP65
Electrical connection	Terminal block
Max. operating pressure, high pressure (HMP 124B) version only	10 MPa (1450 p.s.i)

FLOW SENSORS

Flow sensors are used for sensing the flow of liquids through the plumbing. In industry two versions of flow sensors are widely used. There are flow switches that simply indicate if there is flow through the sensor or not. These sensors are used to verify the operation of pumps and the status of the pipes whether they are clogged or not. The second kind is the true flow sensor which can actually measure the rate of flow and provide an analog output signal to indicate the rate of flow. An example of this is given below.

Combined Liquid Flow Transducer/Transmitter

L.196
W.42
H.100

1. Set system to zero flow and connect a multimeter between terminals 1 (+20 mA) and ↓ (0 mA).
2. Adjust zero pot to read 4 mA on meter.
3. Set system to full flow with multi meter still connected as 1. above.
4. Adjust span pot to read pot to read 20 mA on meter.

An instruction leaflet is supplied with this product.

- Supplied factory calibrated 4-100 l/min, can be field calibrated
- For use with most liquids
- Easy to install
- Works in any plane and accepts reverse flow

Technical Specification

Construction	
Body	Polyester
Glasstube	Borasilicate
Seals	Nitrile
Washers and shaft	Stainless steel
Rotor and locator	Acetal
Rotor tips	Stainless steel
Calibration	4-100 l/min on water
	4 mA-0 l/min.
	20 mA-100 l/min.
Max. working pressure	10bar oil/water
Max. flow rate	150 l/min.
Min. flow indication	2 l/m (max. 150 l/m)
Temperature range	5 to 80°C oil
	5 to 60°C water
Accuracy	±2%
Connections	1 in BSP parallel threads
Electrical details	Input 24 V d.c., output 4-20 mA

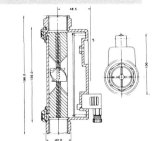

A sturdy flow transmitter designed to operate with most liquids. The fluid passes through internal flow straightners, to stabilize turbulence, before impacting on the vaned turbine rotor, which rotates at a speed proportional to the flow rate. Each rotor blade has a stainless steel tip which is detected by a sensor mounted externally to the glass tube. The detected pulses are converted via the internal circuitry to a 4 to 20 mA output signal, proportional to the flow rate. This can then be displayed on a loop powered flow indicator (see Panel Meters section, **RS** stock no. 260-151). The unit is supplied factory calibrated to 4-100 l/minute, but may be recalibrated to a maximum of 150 l/min. Recalibration is very easily achieved as follows :

VIBRATION SENSORS

Vibration sensors, or accelerometers, are used for measuring acceleration levels. These sensors use strain gauges or piezoelectric crystals. By using the formula F = m a, they first measure the force and then convert it into acceleration. Accelerometers are often used in industry for sensing vibrations and measuring acceleration of missiles, vehicles, etc. Illustrated below is a typical accelerometer with additional technical data. Courtesy RS Components.

Vibration Sensors

BASEEFA Certificate No:
Ex88B2050
Approval Catagory:
EEx ia IIc T4,

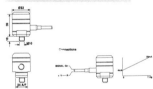

Technical Specification	
Frequency response	10Hz to 10kHz
Acceleration range	0 to 7g rms
Linearity	Better than 1%
Repeatability	±2%
Ambient temperature limits	–10 to 70°C
Temperature stability	Better than 5%
Housing material	Stainless Steel
Protection classification	Dust and Waterproof to IP67
Peak impact	20 NM
Electrical connections	Flexible braided cable 1m long
Mounting	M10x10 Stud
Tightening torque	5 NM
Supply voltage	20 to 30V d.c.
Analogue output	4 to 20mA to BS5751
Maximum load impedance	600 ohms
Recommended barrier type	Stock no. 256-944
BASEEFA systems certificate	Ex91C2340

Supplied to RS by Trolex Ltd

This high performance I.S. sensor is intended for use in general or hazardous plant environments in order to monitor vibration in the range of 0 to 7g rms. Using piezo electric as the sensing principle, it has a frequency response of 10Hz to 10kHz and will output a signal of 4 to 20mA, proportional to acceleration. The unit has a working temperature range of –10°C to + 70°C and has a temperature stability of better than 5%. Unit construction is of stainless steel and mounting is via an M10x10mm stud. The unit is BASEEFA approved for use in zone 0 areas, group IIC, temperature class T4. A suitable barrier for use with this device is **RS** stock no. 256-944 available elsewhere in this section. The sensor and barrier, (when used in conjunction with each other) carry a BASEEFA systems certificate. Both certificates and an instruction leaflet are supplied with the product.

4.4 CASE STUDIES INVOLVING SENSOR APPLICATIONS

4.4.1 Case Study 1: Inductive Loop Detector for Traffic Control Applications

Application: Traffic lights mounted on a 4-way road junction need to be turned on and off selectively depending on traffic.

Problem: Design a vehicle detector to detect any vehicles waiting at the red light.

Traffic control engineering is a branch of engineering which specializes in controlling traffic flow. Most traffic flow control applications demand vehicle detectors for sensing the position of vehicles on a multilane traffic light or for counting vehicles. The detector to be used for such applications needs to be a sturdy detector which could take harsh temperature conditions and rough treatment. One such detector is an inductive loop detector which is nothing but a loop of wire laid out on the road. A small AC current of 20-150 kHz frequency flows through the wire loop producing an alternating magnetic field. When a conductive object like a car or a truck is situated above the coil, eddy currents will be induced in the metal parts of the vehicle which in turn changes the inductance of the coil. Inductance change of the coil due to a car passing over the loop is indicated in Figure 4.18.

An LC oscillator with a fixed capacitor value resonating at its resonant frequency is used for detecting the inductance change due to the vehicle above the loop. The change is given by the formula $\Delta f \approx -0.5 f_0 \Delta L / L$ where L is inductance of the loop and f_0 is resonant frequency.

For example, if the LC oscillator is oscillating at 100 kHz and the car causes a 10% change of inductance of the loop, the frequency of the oscillation will change by -5 kHz. The change in frequency has to be detected by electronics, and an output signal should be generated indicating the presence of the vehicle. A block diagram of the vehicle sensor is given in Figure 4.19.

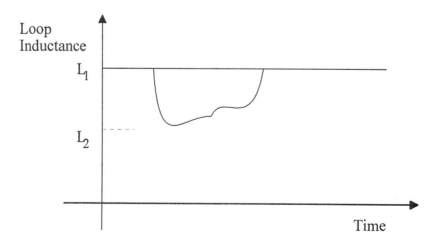

Figure 4.18 Loop inductance changes as car passes over it.

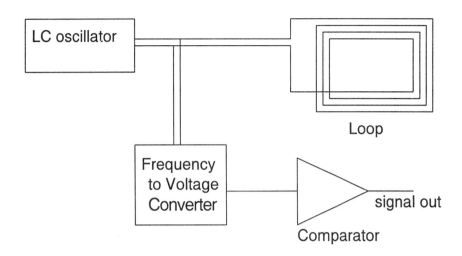

Figure 4.19 Block diagram of the vehicle sensor.

4.4.2 Case Study 2: Sewage Level Control

Application: Regulation of sewage pumps to maintain tank level in unattended treatment stations.

Problem: Sewage is held in agitated holding tanks. Its liquid level is maintained between predetermined points by a sensor which turns a high volume pump "on" (high level) or "off" (low level).

Sewage will foul, clog or corrode conventional level sensors. It may also contain solid objects as large as cinder blocks or 2 x 4's. Because of its composition, there is always the risk that the pump may be damaged or the line clogged, and sewage may not actually move from the tank in spite of control commands. A positive indication of movement is necessary to insure system and equipment safety. A pressure measurement in the lines to and from the pump is used to detect fluid movement.

As a consequence of the pump's operation, transient high pressure pulses (or spikes) are generated at its discharge side. These can be eight or ten times the normal running pressure and, while lasting only several milliseconds, could damage an unprotected sensor.

When the pump is turned off, a check valve within the pump will close. As sewage falls back to this valve, a "water hammer" (short duration pressure pulses or shock generated by a rapid change in flow rate) effect occurs.

In short, this application has two difficult measurements--the first being one of level and the second being one of pump discharge pressure. Both measurements involve difficult media.

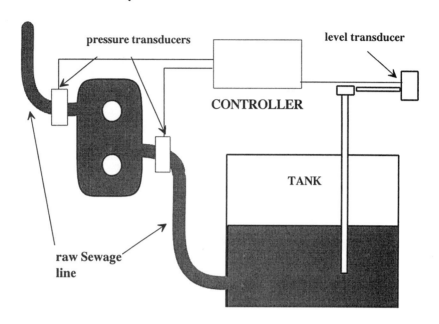

Figure 4.20 General outline of the system.

Solution: The measurement of liquid level is accomplished by mounting a 15 psi pressure sensor on the discharge side of a highly reliable commercial aquarium air pump. The pressure required to bubble air through an immersed pipe is directly related to liquid level. By using a large pipe, the possibility of clogging is reduced and the system is made relatively self cleaning. This method also safeguards the sensor since it need not be immersed while sensing liquid level. A nylon adapter with a "T" threaded into its front is used to mount the sensor.

Normal pump discharge pressure was rated at 20 psi. In view of the eight to ten times greater than normal pressure spikes, a 0-100 psi sensor was used to sense flow from the pump. Since it could be overranged to 200 psi without damage (10 times normal working pressure), it was determined that this gave maximum reliability coupled with maximum practical sensitivity of flow detection. The ability of the sensor to withstand vacuum "under pressures" is also important because falling heads after the pump is turned off can create partial vacuums at the sensor on the inlet side.

The discharge sensor is mounted in "drain" position. (Pressure "snubbers" cannot be used to dampen pressure spikes over prolonged periods of time due to the clogging nature of the media.)

Environments: Both level and discharge transducers are mounted in enclosures and do not see weather extremes. Atmospheres are mildly corrosive, generally humid, and, on occasion, explosive.

Pressure Characteristics: Level sensor: pressure constantly changes from 2-12 psi with random ripple resulting from surging sewage. Pump transducers: pressure ranges from partial vacuum to 20 psi with random spikes to 200 psi.

4.4.3 Case Study 3: Detection of Seams of a Workpiece for Welding Application

Application: A Unimation robot arm is being used for welding application where the workpiece is carried to the work cell of the robot over a conveyor belt. A photocell switch turns the conveyor belt off as soon as the workpiece is in front of the robot, but the orientation of the object can vary. The location of the seam on the workpiece should be detected for a precision welding job.

Solution: The exact position of the seam with respect to the workpiece is well known. However, since the orientation of the object can vary, the orientation has to be determined. The tools available for this application are either machine vision or sensitive proximity sensors. Machine vision is the costlier alternative of the two, for this reason, a proximity switch will be used for detecting the precise orientation of the workpiece.

An inductive proximity sensor mounted on the end effector of the robot is used for detecting the orientation of the workpiece. A robot raster scans the location where the workpiece resides as shown in Figure 4.22. Scan operation is done by starting from the top and moving from left to right. After repeating the process twice, the robot can calculate the angle AB of the workpiece with respect to the work environment which will enable it to pinpoint the exact location of the seam.

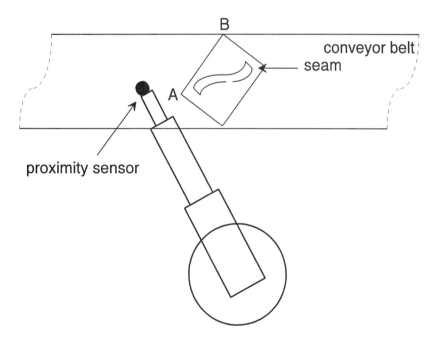

Figure 4.21 General outlook of the system.

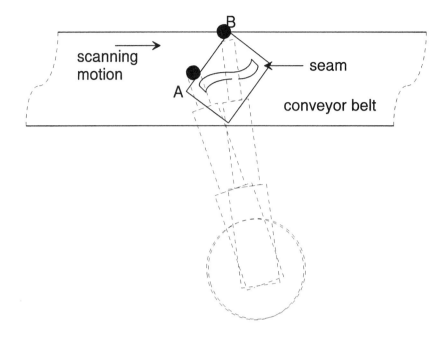

Figure 4.22 Scanning motion of the robot determines the edges of the workpiece at two different locations

4.4.4 Case Study 4: Water Level Control

Application: To monitor and control water level in water towers.

Problem: Municipal and private water towers must have a control system to govern the turn-on/turn-off function of their supply pumps. Often these towers are in remote unmanned locations. The task is to maintain a constant safe volume of water in the tank without manually monitoring the water level.

Solution: A pressure sensor monitors the water pressure at the base of the tank. The sensor signal is processed and then transmitted to a control center kilometers away. The control decisions are made here based on the status information provided by the pressure sensor. The control is automatically or manually done to retain a constant safe water level in the tank.

Pressure Characteristics: Pressure ranges are dependent upon height of water storage tank. Typically the water pressure is 35 psi. Often it is lower. For smaller tanks, it is under 10 psi. Pressure changes are gradual; however, there are large pressure spikes due to "water hammer" (short duration pressure pulses or shocks generated by a rapid change in flow rate). General outlook of this system is shown in Figure 4.23.

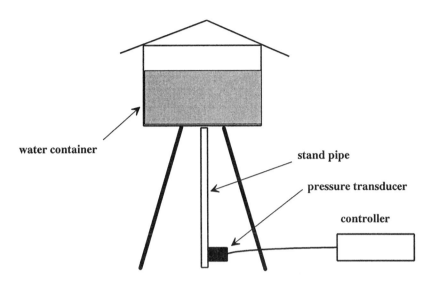

Figure 4.23 General outlook of the system.

4.4.5 Case Study 5: Oil Tanker Pumps

Application: Monitoring of loading and unloading pumps mounted on deck of ocean-going tanker.

Problem: Remote measurement of discharge pressure in loading and unloading operations provides crew with positive and centralized indication of pump performance.

Signal must be transmitted through potentially explosive environment for long distances and the sensor should be able to indicate negative pressure which sometimes occurs due to rapid emptying of the tanks.

Solution: A two wire pressure transmitter is mounted in pipe "T"s on the discharge side of the pump. The transmitter is wired back to the bridge in a deck conduit where they are powered through an isolation barrier. A readout on the bridge reads pump pressures.

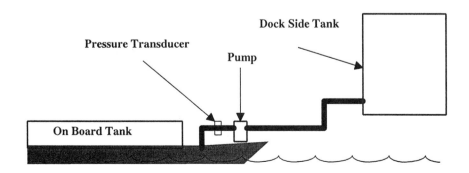

Figure 4.24 Oil tanker pump system.

4.4.6 Case Study 6: Beverage Can Coating

Application: Control of paint spraying operation to insure uniform coating of inside of steel beverage cans.

Problem: Part of the steel beverage can making operation includes spraying a lacquer coating inside of cans to prevent rusting and flavor change. Present visual method of inspection is inadequate because the coating is performed at the rate of 12,000 cans per hour. By the time a problem is observed, many cans have been miscoated. Two spraying problems occur: a clogged nozzle which stops spray altogether or sprays in blobs, and a worn nozzle which causes overcoating. With the present system, an additional bank of spraying machines is necessary to insure that every can is coated. This second coating adds time and expense to the operation.

Solution: A pressure sensor is inserted near the tip of a spray gun nozzle to monitor spraying pressures. Sensor output is fed into a multichannel data acquisition controller with one channel per spray head. (Typically five spray machines operate simultaneously.) The controller provides adjustable upper and lower set points with the upper limit set to indicate a clogged nozzle and the lower limit set to indicate a worn nozzle. When limits are exceeded, the system is immediately shut down.

Pressure Characteristics: 0 to 1000 psi range. Upper control limit set at approximately 650 psi and lower limit at 550 psi.

Paint system is of the constant flow type with spray occurring when an electrical solenoid opens the nozzle. Because pressure in the nozzle drops after every spray pulse, the lower limit is constantly tripped. A microprocessor controls the system and permits shutdown only if limits are exceeded during actual spraying time (35 milliseconds).

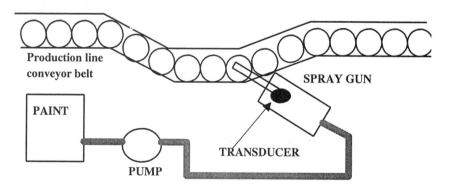

Figure 4.25 Beverage can coating system.

REFERENCES

1. *Sensor Data Book*, Omega Instruments, 1989.

2. *RS Components Catalogue*, RS Components, 1995.

3. Anton, F.P. Putten, *Electronic Measurement Systems*, Prentice Hall International, 1988.

4. Collins, T. H., *Analog Electronics Handbook*, Prentice Hall International, 1989.

5. Curtis, Johnson, *Process Control Instrumentation Technology*, Regents/Prentice Hall, 1993.

6. Austerlitz, H., *Data Acquistion Techniques Using Personal Computers*, Academic Press, 1991.

7. Derenzo, S., *Interacing,* Prentice Hall, 1990.

8. Mazda, F., (ed.), *Electronic Engineer's Reference Book*, Butterworth & Co., 1986.

9. Khrisna, K., *Microprocessor Based Data Acquistion System Design*, McGraw-Hill, 1987.

Five

INDUSTRY STANDARD DATA ACQUISITION EQUIPMENT for the PC

5.1 INTRODUCTION

In the previous chapters, we have looked at the components which make up a data acquisition system. We have looked at sensors with which we acquire data from the outside world and signal conditioners which shape the output of the sensor to make it suitable for the computer to read the signal. Starting with this chapter we will start looking at the data acquisition system as a whole and review common PC based data acquisition configurations and data acquisition equipment specifically designed for personal computers.

A book written by Howard Austerlitz titled *Data Acquisition Techniques Using Personal Computers* introduces several PC based data acqustion systems and is recommended for readers who are interested in learning more about PC based applications.

5.2 PC BASED DATA ACQUISITION SYSTEM CONFIGURATIONS

There are basically three PC based data acquisition configurations which cover almost all applications. These configurations are listed below.

140

1. Local data acquisition configuration. (application is in the immediate vicinity)

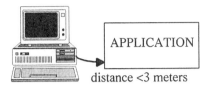

distance <3 meters

Features of immediate vicinity local configurations are as follows:

- Application is within the immediate vicinity of the computer.
- All or most of the data acquisition hardware is within the PC.
- Signal conditioning hardware is in the vicinity or in the PC.
- Distance between the PC and the application is very close, typically less than 3 meters.

This is the case where the application is in close proximity of the PC and the PC contains all data acquisition cards necessary for the application. Data acquisition speed (number of samples to be taken in a second) can be quite high in this configuration.

2. Room-local data acquisition configuration. (application is in close proximity)

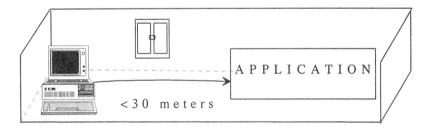

Distinctive features of this configuration are as follows:

- Application is in the vicinity but not necessarily in the immediate vicinity of the computer.
- Most data acquisition hardware including signal conditioners are located outside the PC, typically inside a crate.
- Distance between the PC and the application is less than 30 meters.

In this case, the application is in the same environment with the PC but not necessarily in very close proximity. Data acquisition cards necessary for the application are mostly located inside a crate outside the PC. There are several ways of handling such cases. Data acquisition speed can be high with this configuration but usually not as high as the previous case.

3. Remote data acquisition configuration.

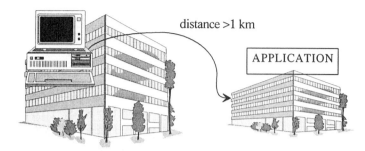

Distinctive features of this configuration are as follows:

- Most of the data acquisition hardware including the signal conditioners are outside the PC.

- Distance between the PC and the application can be from 100's of meters to 100's of kilometers.

In this case the application is far away from the PC. There are several ways of handling such cases. Usually the speed of data acquisition is slow.

5.2.1 Local Data Acquisition Configuration (Immediate Vicinity)

This is the most common and the most economical data acquisition configuration using PC's. In this case, the data acquisition application is in the immediate vicinity of the PC, so that sensors and signal conditioners are also in the immediate vicinity of the PC available for connection. In this configuration almost all of the data acquisition hardware is plugged directly into the expansion bus of the PC. Since the data acquisition hardware is in the immediate vicinity, the computer has to be in the same environment and close proximity to the data acquisition application. This proves to be the weak point of this configuration since in some cases the environment of the application is not suitable for the PC. It may not be wise to place a computer right near a furnace or a rocket test stand due to the heat and vibration generated by the application setup which is harmful for the computer. It is still possible to use computers in harsh environments by using specially designed, so-called factory hardened industrial PCs which are designed to tolerate excessive heat and vibration but that will add to the cost of the system. There are two common configurations for immediate-local data acquisition systems:

- Data acquisition hardware plugged into an industrial PC

- Data acquisition hardware plugged into an expansion chassis of a PC

Hardware available for immediate local data acquisition system are described in the following sections.

INDUSTRIAL PERSONAL COMPUTERS

Personal computers --as the name implies-- are designed primarily for personal use in an office environment. Such an environment is considered ideal for PC's since the temperature inside the room is well regulated and there are no vibrations or excessive dust in the environment. The office PC is designed to be used in offices and its hardware is optimized to take advantage of the mild environment there. Any PC that is intended to be used on a factory floor for data acquisition and process control better be ready to face all the challenges that come from the environment, namely a dusty atmosphere, extreme temperatures, vibrations and mechanical shocks. One should also expect plenty of electromagnetic noise and greasy hands. This does not mean that all PC's that perform data acquisition have to be on the plant floor. The computers in lab environments usually do similar things in terms of process control and data acquisition, yet they are treated with greater respect. As a system designer, one often has to look at the environment and decide about how harsh the operating environment is. It is also important to determine how mission critical the system computer should be, i.e. can one afford to interrupt the process even for a short duration once the process has started? Computers, like any other machine, do break down and cause interruptions of the work flow.

Usually industrial grade equipment is designed with the idea that if a failure occurs, the equipment should be maintained easily and repaired within a short time. Sometimes the process one is trying to control may not afford even the shortest duration of failure. All these factors will affect one's decision about what kind of computer you should select for the operation. If the PC will be residing and performing data acquisition in a mild environment, it is not at all a problem to use an office PC for handling the data. If it is not possible to place the computer in a suitable location and the PC has to work in an environment where there is vibration, high temperature or dust, then an industrial grade PC should be used. Industrial PC's architecturally are exactly similar to office PC's, but differ in some mechanical aspects. The following are the main distinguishing features of industrial PC's.

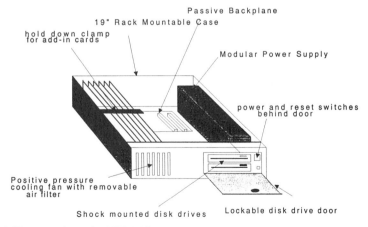

Figure 5.1 Features of a typical IBM PC compatible industrial computer.

Figure 5.2 An industrial PC.

A Rugged chassis. Chassis are made of either aluminum or steel in order to reduce electromagnetic interference from the environment and withstand environmental effects like heat, mechanical shocks and chemical spills. Most of the industrial PC's are housed in standard 19 inch rack mounts to facilitate mounting PC's on industrial equipment racks.

Shock mounted floppy and hard disks. Floppy disks and hard disks are delicate, sensitive devices which can not endure mechanical vibration for a long time. The high density drives in particular can go out of alignment quite easily if they are not adequately protected from vibration. Drives on an industrial PC are mounted on rubber shock mounts in order to minimize the effect of vibration. Disk drives are also very sensitive to dust in the environment. Since hard disks are completely sealed from the external environment they are not affected by dust, but floppy disks are easily affected by dust even by cigarette smoke. In order to reduce the effect of dust on floppy drives, industrial PC have lockable covers over the drive bays which protects the drive from dust and unauthorized people. A positive pressure cooling system also reduces the effect of dust by preventing dust from entering the cabinet.

The monitor of the industrial PC is a rack mountable type to facilitate mounting on industrial equipment racks. The screen of the monitor is protected with a Plexiglas sheet in order to prevent chemicals being spilled over the screen and to avoid accidental bumps from damaging the monitor.

Easy access. Another important feature of an industrial PC system is the easy access to internal cards in case of a failure. It is important that an industrial PC should have either a passive backplane and a modular plug-in type CPU. The advantage of the passive backplane is that the only permanent unit which is bolted inside the industrial PC is a passive backplane, all of the electronics of the PC are plugged into the passive backplane. The CPU is also on a plug-in card among the other cards that are plugged into the passive backplane. If the CPU or any other controller card fails, maintenance is as simple as opening up the system and unplugging the failed board and plugging in a working one. This feature is also important for upgradability of the processing power of the computer. The processing power of the computer can be increased by simply replacing the CPU card with a more powerful one.

Hold-down clamp for add-in cards. Industrial computers have a tie-down clamp for the add-in cards that are plugged into the passive backplane. Without a hold-down clamp, excessive vibration eventually causes the add-in cards to creep out of their slots, which in return will either cause intermittent errors or a total failure of the system. Even though all add-in cards for IBM PC® and compatibles come with a screw at the end of the card for attachment to the chassis, in a vibrating environment it is not enough to attach the card from one single point. A hold-down clamp mechanism will provide the solution to this problem.

Power supply is one of the critical components in the system. The power supply of the system is usually overrated and the cooling fan operates as positive pressure type. A positive pressure type fan blows filtered air into the system rather than sucking air out of the system. The filter is a replaceable type and is located in a handy location for quick and periodic replacement.

Keyboard. There are also special considerations for the keyboard of the industrial PC systems. Since chemical spills, dust and greasy hands are expected in the industrial environment, the keyboard is of sealed type to avoid dirt and grease getting in and sticking to the keys of the keyboard.

There are many companies which have been manufacturing industrial grade computers with qualifications listed above. Texas Micro, Keithley and Advantec are a few of these manufacturers which have good quality industrial computers.

Industrial Grade Expansion Chassis for PC's. Most industrial computers come with enough slots to accommodate necessary data acquisition cards, but in case the number of slots is not adequate, an expansion chassis can be added to the existing system. An expansion chassis has to have its own power supply in order not to load the power supply of the industrial PC system. The environmental requirements for the expansion chassis are similar to the requirements for the industrial PC system. The chassis also has to be rack mountable with a forced positive pressure type fan-cooled power supply. The connection between the expansion chassis and the main computer is achieved by a shielded ribbon connector cable which has an interface card on both ends. The maximum length of the ribbon connector cable is usually limited to less than a meter, making it impossible to place expansion chassis far from the main computer.

Figure 5.3 A typical industrial grade expansion chassis for IBM PC Compatibles (Courtesy of Keithly-Metrabyte).

5.2.2 Room-Local Data Acquisition Configuration

Room-Local Data acquisition systems are configurations where the data acquisition application is in the locality but not necessarily in the immediate vicinity of the computer. Room-local data acquisition configurations are very common for large scale data acquisition projects which require multiple cards and signal conditioners. The number of cards may be too excessive to be placed inside the computer. In such cases the cards are located inside a special crate and wired to the host computer through an interface card. The most common configurations for room-local configurations are

- GPIB networks for laboratory automation or data acquisition
- Data acquisition crate configurations

Data acquisition crates are special crates designed to hold a variety of data acquisition cards selected by the user. Data acquisition crates have expansion slots inside, just like the expansion chassis of industrial PC's but the internal expansion bus interface standard is completely different. The main difference between a data acquisition crate and the ordinary expansion chassis is that the connection cable between the crate and the host PC can be much longer than the case of an expansion chassis. The length of connection cable can be increased even further by using serial communication between the host PC and the data acquisition system.

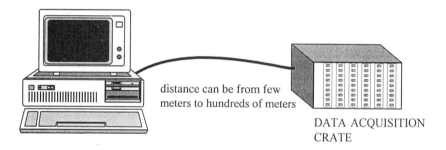

distance can be from few
meters to hundreds of meters

DATA ACQUISITION
CRATE

Figure 5.4 Room-local data acquisition configuration.

Since the interface between the host PC and the data acquisition system is not simply an extension of the PC bus, the interface inside the data acquisition crate does not have to be similar to the interface standard of the PC. This approach has some advantages and disadvantages which should be considered carefully. The disadvantage of the different interface is that you are no longer able to use the data acquisition cards that are designed for the PC ISA bus inside the data acquisition crate. Because of the different interface standards used, one will be dependent on the data acquisition cards designed by the manufacturer of the crate, or the user has to design the card for one's own application.

Although it appears to be a great disadvantage at the first sight, this approach also has some advantages. One of these is getting rid of the limitations imposed by the I/O bus of the host PC. The IBM PC® has a very crowded I/O address map which causes frequent conflicts between add-on cards.

Figure 5.5 Typical data acquisition crate (Courtesy of Keithley Instruments).

All data acquisition applications are confined to a very narrow area of the I/O map which is the only place available. Because of the limited allowable space, the number of cards that can coexist is limited and the I/O address selection has to be done very carefully. By changing the interface inside, the crate is no longer confined to the I/O address map of the host computer.

Another important advantage of this approach is the independence of the system from the host PC. The crate can be connected to any type of PC with any type interface The only part of the system that needs to be changed is the interface card of the crate which resides inside the host PC. For example, if one is using an IBM PC 486 as a host computer and one day decided to adapt a MACINTOSH as a host PC, the only part of the hardware system that would need changing would be the interface card inside the PC. It is also possible to upgrade the computational power of the system by simply using a more powerful PC as a host computer. The overall performance of this approach can be high if the crate is connected to the host computer over a fast interface like a parallel interface. If the connection from the host PC to the crate is serial, the performance will be lessened.

PRINTER PORT ATTACHED DATA ACQUISITION EQUIPMENT

The printer port of the original PC is designed as a unidirectional port only to send data to the printer. Later the design of the printer port is changed and made to operate in a bidirectional manner giving the ability to read as well as send data to the printer port.

Fortunately even with the unidirectional configuration it was possible to read from the printer port using printer port signals in an unconventional way. Furthermore, using some hardware tricks, it is even possible to design equipment which is transparent to the operation of the printer. In such cases the equipment and the printer can both be connected to the same printer port. The printer would print as usual whenever text is sent to it, and the equipment would operate without interfering with the operation of the printer. This type of operation is called "printer bypass" and is very desirable since it gives the user a "free" interface at no cost.

Recently printer port pluggable data acquisition hardware has become very popular due to the popularity of laptop and notebook computers. A notebook computer with printer port pluggable data acquisition equipment means complete freedom to operate at any location without worrying about main power and bulky equipment.

Printer port connected data acquisition equipment usually comes in crate form with fixed number of A/D and D/A outputs. Lawson Labs is a manufacturer which manufactures extra high resolution (24 bits) data acquisition equipment designed to be plugged into the parallel printer port.

REMOTE DATA ACQUISITION CONFIGURATIONS

The remote data acquisition configuration is very similar to the room-local data acquisition configuration since both methods use a stand alone data acquisition crate. In case of remote data acquisition, improved serial interface standards like RS 422, 423, 485 are frequently used to increase the communication distances to around 1.2 km. Because of the increased distances with the crate, it becomes feasible to have the host PC operating in a protected environment like an office and only the data acquisition system installed in the hostile environment.

Remote data acquisition configurations usually appear in the following formats:

- Remote acquisition using crates and serial interface standards RS-422, RS-485
- Long distance remote acquisition using modems
- Remote Data Acquisition using data acquisition modules

If the distance between the data acquisition crate and the host computer is more than 1.2 km, it is possible to use repeaters and increase the distance of communication.

distance < 1.2 km

Data acquisition crate

Figure 5.6 Remote data acquisition using crates and RS-485 communication standard.

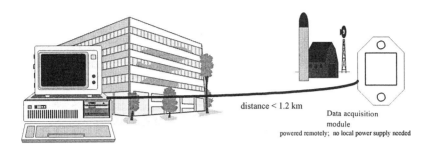

distance < 1.2 km

Data acquisition
module
powered remotely; no local power supply needed

Figure 5.7 Remote data acquisition using modules.

Up to 5 km using repeaters can be feasible. If the distance is much larger than that, modems should be used for connection to the host computer. Depending on the application and the distance, either a short haul modem or fiber optic modem or a dedicated phone line or dial-up on demand technique can be used. These configurations will be covered in detail in Chapter 8.

If the application requires sampling only a few lines at a remote location, it may not be feasible to use a crate with only a few lines to connect. In such cases, remote data acquisition modules can be used for the application. Remote data acquisition modules can be powered remotely from the host computer which eliminates the need for an additional power source. Usually the distance is around 1.2 km but it can be increased using repeaters. More information about this technique and equipment manufacturers will be given in Chapter 8.

5.3 REVIEW OF DATA ACQUISITION CARDS AVAILABLE FOR PC'S

PC based data acquisition cards are intended to be connected to the internal expansion slots of the PC. These cards are physically located inside the PC to be plugged into the expansion bus.

Recent reductions in the cost of PC's and the increases in computational power of the CPU have opened up a vast market for PC based data acquisition cards. Currently one can find data acquisition cards that can perform a wide range of data acquisition operations. Although there are literally 100's of companies that are manufacturing PC based data acquisition cards all over the world, most PC based data acquisition cards can be combined in several categories. In this section we are going to review these basic categories of data acquisition cards and explain the capabilities that one can expect in each category. Although manufacturers of these cards are totally independent and there are no published standards for them to obey, most cards in certain categories have similar capabilities. In a way this should be expected since the technical limitations imposed by the PC and data acquisition components like A/D converters are common.

In this section, representative cards from different manufacturers will be discussed to explain each category. Our intention is not to promote the data acquisition equipment from those particular manufacturers but to show the technical limitations and capabilities of each one of the categories.

All PC based data acquisition boards can be placed in one of the following categories:

1. Analog to Digital I/O boards for PC's

2. Digital Input/Output boards for the PC's

3. Analog Output boards for the PC's

4. Standard Interface boards for the PC's

5. PC based instrumentation boards

These categories, and representative commercial products from each category are discussed below in detail.

5.3.1 Analog-to-Digital Input Boards for PC's

Analog-to-digital or A/D converter cards can be combined in three subcategories:

- High performance A/D converter cards
- High resolution A/D converter cards
- General purpose A/D converter cards

HIGH PERFORMANCE A/D CONVERTER CARDS

These cards have a very high conversion rate, around 1,000,000 samples per second. (1 megasample/s). Expected resolution of the high performance A/D conversion is around 12 bits/conversion although higher resolutions like 16 or 8 bit can be found. The distinguishing feature of this category is the high speed of conversion and not the resolution. High resolution A/D converters are cited as a different category, which is discussed in the next section. Very high speed data conversion is only possible with a special kind of A/D converter chip called flash A/D converters. Currently, 12 bit is the limitation of the flash A/D converters on the market. Each card provides several input channels either in differential or in single ended mode. Differential channels are preferable due to the increased noise immunity. Especially with low level signals (millivolt level) the signal should always be read in differential form.

High speeds of conversion require special design considerations from the card designer. One of the limitations comes from the expansion bus connector which connects the data acquisition card to the host PC. For an ISA type connection standard, the maximum rate of sustained data transfer is around 250,000 sample/second. For MCA and EISA, this rate is around 1,000,000 sample/second. This is assuming that one is using fast data transfer techniques like DMA for transferring the data. With recent standards like VESA local bus and PCI, the data transfer speed can be much higher, on the order of 50 megasample/s.

If the sustained data transfer rate is not important for one's application and one only needs to sample for a brief period of time, then it is possible to use a high performance card with memory on board. Due to this available memory, the card will sample the data and temporarily put it in the buffer. Then the data can then be transferred at a lower rate through the expansion bus.

Due to the 250K data transfer limitation imposed by ISA, if the application requires a higher transfer rate, either EISA/ MCA should be used or it is necessary to have on board buffers to save the data. In this way data can be acquired at the full speed and stored in the memory of the card without worrying about transferring the data to the PC.

How much data can be stored in the on-board buffer depends on the size of the memory. With an A/D converter card that has 1 megaword of memory on board and has a conversion speed of 1 megasample/second at 12 bits, you can run the system at full speed only for 1 second. Most high performance A/D converter cards have a user adjustable speed feature. A user can thus reduce the speed of acquisition and increase the continuous sampling time. If in the specific example cited above the speed of conversion is reduced to 250,000 sample/second, the on-board memory can store 4 seconds of data without transferring them to the memory of the PC. Because of the high conversion ability, this type of card is suitable for applications that require a very high sampling rate for a very short duration of time. Short data sheet for DAS-50, a data acquisition card of this type which is made by Keithley-Metrabyte is given in the following page.

Since the conversion is supposed to be on a burst basis for a very short duration of time, there is the problem of triggering the sampling action. If the sampling is not started at the right time the internal buffer will be filled with useless data even before the time of interest is reached. Because of the high speed of conversion, one does not have time to operate on a continuous basis where one acquires samples, analyzes them, keeps them if they interest one and discards them if not. Remember, the data sits inside the on-board buffer of the A/D card and it is not even inside the PC for analysis. The only solution to this problem is to supply a hardware or software trigger signal for the start of the data acquisition. As soon as the trigger signal is given, A/D conversion should start and data should be taken at the time of interest. Later, the data can be transferred to the memory of the PC for analysis. It is advisable to have both the software and hardware trigger features available because in some cases the PC decides when the sampling should start. In this case a software trigger will be used.

In other cases, the system will be connected to a setup ready to take samples, and a hardware trigger signal will be provided externally to initiate the sampling operation. Another important feature to look for in data acquisition cards of this category is the utility software. Most data acquisition cards occupy several I/O locations in the I/O map of the PC. All data transfer and control operations have to be performed over those I/O locations. Even though it is not difficult to control the operation of the card by reading and writing into these I/O locations, it may be too difficult a task for the user who is not very familiar with the architectural features of the PC or low level languages like Assembly or C. Utility software can be used from any high level language easily and this allows the user to experiment with the features of the card rather than spending time trying to interface it.

All data acquisition cards provide switch settable base addresses. The reason for this is the limited I/O space of the PC and the possibility of installing more than one card at the same I/O address location. As a user you are supposed to locate the base location of the I/O registers to an unoccupied location. In the case of ISA architecture, this has to be done manually. Usually the manufacturer of the card recommends its card to be installed at a particular location. The location has no significance and can be changed to any location that is desired.

1 MEGASAMPLE/SEC, 4-CHANNEL ANALOG INPUT BOARD

DAS-50

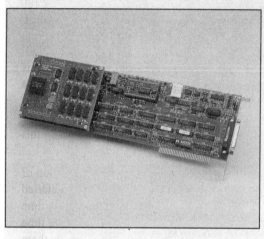

FEATURES

- 1,000,000 samples/sec
- 1 megaword memory buffer on-board
- 12-bit resolution
- Built-in track and hold
- User-adjustable conversion rate
- Triggerable via software, external or voltage level input
- 4-channel selectable input multiplexer
- Bipolar & unipolar operation

APPLICATIONS

- Laboratory automation
- Vibration/stress analysis
- Event/transient analysis
- Signal/sensor interface
- FFT

BLOCK DIAGRAM

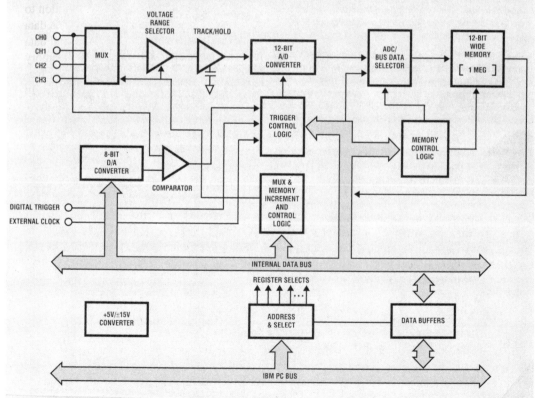

If one's PC has no data acquisition cards or prototype cards, one can go with the suggestion of the manufacturer and install the card at that particular location. VGA, serial, or parallel communication cards or disk drive cards are not of any concern to us since all these cards have their special I/O addresses which do not interfere with our cards. We are only concerned with data acquisition and prototype cards. If one is using cards from different manufacturers, one should be especially careful with the I/O base addresses. If one is not certain whether the recommended I/O location is occupied or not, then it is recommended that third party utility programs like Check-It™ or Norton Utilities™ should be used for checking the availability of the target locations.

HIGH RESOLUTION A/D CONVERTER CARDS

High resolution A/D conversion usually means A/D conversion at resolutions 16 bit or higher. For high resolution A/D conversion cards, the distinguishing factor is the high resolution and not the high speed. Actually the speed of conversion for high resolution cards can vary considerably from low speeds of a few conversion per second to 100's of K samples per second. The user is usually given the ability to trade speed for resolution. In the case of A/D converters, there is always a trade-off between high speed and high resolution; one should not expect, therefore, very high speed if one wants high resolution.

High resolution A/D converter cards are very sensitive to noise from the environment. The environment inside the PC is considered very noisy from an electromagnetic noise point of view. The noise becomes significant for high resolution A/D converter cards due to the decreased step size of the A/D converter which becomes comparable to noise levels inside the PC. In order to distinguish the input signal from the noise signal, the noise should be reduced as much as possible by shielding the card properly and always handling the signal in differential form.

In this category of cards there are usually multiple channels which are provided in differential form. However, the user can convert the differential inputs to single ended inputs if so desired. A differential form is always preferable for increased noise immunity. Especially with low level signals (millivolt level) the signal should always be read in differential form.

Since the speed of sampling is not very high in the case of high resolution A/D converter cards, direct memory access (DMA) works well with these cards. Having a DMA feature on the card is highly recommended. Utility software for driving the cards is also highly recommended since it is usually not a trivial task to program a DMA feature. Having utility software or a device driver will make the task of using the card easy in high level languages. Data sheet for a representative commercial A/D converter card of this category, DAS-HRES, is given on the following page. Courtesy Keithley Instruments.

47 KILOSAMPLE/SEC, 16-BIT ANALOG AND DIGITAL I/O BOARD

DAS-HRES

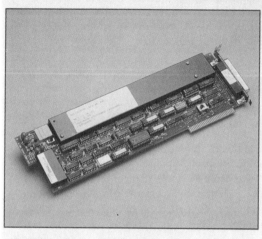

FEATURES

- 16-bit resolution
- 8 fully differential input channels
- 2 channels of 16-bit analog output
- 3 counter/timers
- Software-selectable gains 1, 2, 4 and 8
- 16 bits digital I/0
- 47 kS/s acquisition rate
- Unipolar and bipolar operation

APPLICATIONS

- Signal analysis
- Sensor interface
- Chromatography
- Process monitor/control
- Laboratory automation

BLOCK DIAGRAM

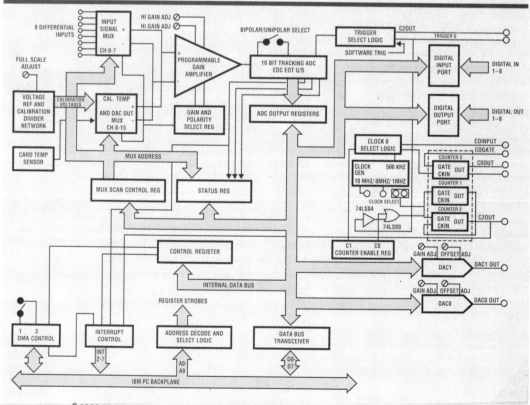

GENERAL PURPOSE A/D CONVERTER CARDS

This category contains A/D converter cards that have resolutions of 8-12 bit and a speed of 10k-100k samples per second. This category of cards is expected to have DMA capability due to their reasonable speed. Usually there are multiple channels which are user selectable. The user can select any one or all of the available channels for A/D conversion. Having multiple channels does not mean that all channels will be converted into digital simultaneously. It means that any one of the channels can be multiplexed to the A/D converter for conversion and the conversion process is sequential for selected channels. The channels are usually provided in differential form. However the user can convert the differential inputs to single ended inputs if so desires. Differential form is preferable for increased noise immunity. Especially with millivolt level signals the signal should always be read in differential form.

Most A/D cards of this category have selectable gain setting for the A/D converter chip. Gain selection can be performed either manually by toggling switches on the card, or by selection in the software. If the application requires monitoring several channels where the signal level is quite different in magnitude, software selectable gain is advisable since gain setting can be changed automatically for the particular channel. In some A/D converter cards of this category, analog-to-digital conversion can be automated by on-board timers. Timers are user programmable and every time the timer ticks, A/D conversion will start automatically for a specified period of time. Both hardware and software trigger features for starting the conversion are common in this category. Availability of utility software is again advisable in order to ease the task of programming. A representative commercial A/D converter card of this category, DAS-1400, is introduced in the following pages.

5.3.2 Digital Input/Output Boards for the PC

These data acquisition cards provide digital input and output ports for interfacing PC to peripherals or devices. There are several versions of digital I/O boards on the market:

- Low cost I/O boards
- High output current I/O boards
- High speed I/O boards
- Isolated I/O boards

100 KILOSAMPLE/SEC ANALOG INPUT BOARD

DAS-1400

FEATURES

- 100,000 sample/sec
- 12-bit resolution
- 16-channel single ended / 8-channel differential
- Software-programmable input ranges:
  - Gains of 1, 10, 100, 500 (DAS-1401)
  - Gains of 1, 2, 4, 8 (DAS-1402)
- 4 bits digital output
- 4 bits digital input
- Backward compatible with DAS-16G (without the DACs)
- Burst mode timing allows simultaneous sample & hold emulation
- Free software includes:
  - Call Driver for BASIC languages
- Pop Up Control Panel
- Complete installation & calibration routines
- Optional ASO-1400 software includes:
  - File I/O Command Driver for all languages .
  - Function Call Driver for Pascal, C, and Turbo Pascal
  - Windows 3.X compatible DLL
  - Visual Basic example program

APPLICATIONS

- Signal analysis
- Laboratory automation
- Frequency analysis
- Vibration analysis
- Product test
- Process monitoring

FUNCTIONAL DESCRIPTION

The DAS-1401 and DAS-1402 are high-speed analog and digital interface boards for IBM PC/XT/AT, 386/486 and compatible computers. The board installs directly in an expansion slot inside the computer, and turns the computer into a high-speed, high-precision data acquisition and signal analysis instrument. The boards are of multi-layer construction with integral ground plane to minimize noise and crosstalk even at high sample rates. All analog input connections are made via a 37-pin "D" connector which extends out the rear of the host computer.

The DAS-1400 offers 8 differential or 16 single-ended analog inputs with 12-bit resolution. The inputs can be set in unipolar (e.g., 0 – 10 V) or

BLOCK DIAGRAM

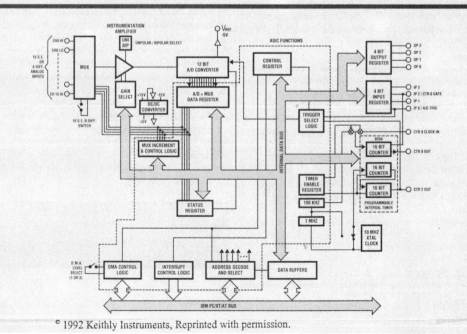

LOW COST I/O BOARDS

Low cost I/O boards generally make use of widely available programmable interface adopter (PIA) chips. Mostly the outputs are simple TTL or MOS outputs provided directly to the end connector of the card. Most of the boards in this category can generate interrupts by changes in the digital input lines. Handshaking for data transfers is also provided by latch and acknowledge signals. A representative of this category manufactured by Keithley-Metrabyte is shown below.

**24-BIT PARALLEL
DIGITAL I/O BOARD**

PIO-12

FEATURES

- 24 TTL/DTL digital I/O lines
- ±12 V, ±5 V power from IBM PC/XT
- Unidirectional, bidirectional and strobed I/O
- Interrupt handling
- Direct interface to wide range of accessory products
- Plugs into IBM PC/XT/AT bus
- Handshaking
- Compatible with ERB-24, SSIO-24, SRA-01 and ERA-01

APPLICATIONS

- Contact closure monitoring
- Digital I/O control
- Useful with A/Ds and D/As
- Communication with other computers
- Operate relays (PIO-24 recommended)
- Alarm monitoring

FUNCTIONAL DESCRIPTION

Keithley MetraByte's PIO-12 board provides 24 TTL/DTL compatible digital I/O lines. It is a flexible interface for parallel input/output devices such as instruments and displays and user constructed systems and equipment.

Twenty-four digital I/O lines are provided through an 8255-5 programmable peripheral interface (PPI) IC and consist of three ports: an 8-bit PA port, an 8-bit PB port, and an 8-bit PC port. The PC port may also be used as two half ports of 4 bits, PC upper (PC 4 – 7) and PC lower (PC 0 – 3). Each of the ports and half ports may be configured as an input or an output by software control according to the contents of a write only control register in the PPI. The ports may be both read and written. In

addition, other configurations are possible for unidirectional and bidirectional strobed I/O where the PC ports are used for control of data transfer and interrupt generation, etc. Users are referred to the Intel 8255-5 data sheet for a complete technical description and summary of the various operating modes of the PPI.

Interrupt handling is via a tristate driver with separate enable (interrupt enable — active low). This may be connected to interrupt levels 2 – 7 on the IBM PC bus by a plug-type jumper on the board. Handling of an interrupt is controlled by the 8259 interrupt controller in the IBM PC and this is set by BIOS on system initialization to respond to positive (low – high) edge triggered inputs. Users must program the 8259 to respond to their requirements and set up corresponding interrupt handlers. Interrupt input and enable lines and external connections to the PC's bus power supplies (+5V, +12 V, -12 V and -5 V) are available at the connector.

SOFTWARE

There are two software alternatives for the PIO-12. The user can either use a fully integrated data acquisition software package (e.g., VIEWDAC or EASYEST LX), or write a custom program (in BASIC, C, Pascal, etc.). Note that while not directly supported by many of the integrated software packages, virtually all packages have a direct PORT I/O function which will directly read/write data to/from the PIO-12. A guide to tradeoffs between integrated packages and writing your own program is provided in the Software Section Introduction beginning on page 12. The software section also describes a wide variety of integrated software packages.

The PIO-12 is very easy to program and most users will opt to write their own programs. No drivers are supplied with the PIO-12 since programming is simple using the I/O instructions in most programming languages. The PIO-12 uses 4 consecutive I/O locations in the computer's I/O addressing space. These are described as the BASE ADDRESS, and the BASE +1, +2 and +3. The mapping of these locations is provided below:

Base	+0	Port A
	+1	Port B
	+2	Port C
	+3	Control Register

BLOCK DIAGRAM

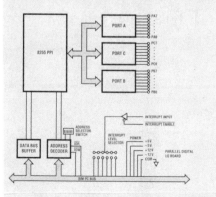

HIGH OUTPUT CURRENT I/O BOARDS

These boards are used for interfacing a computer to a device which requires high voltage and high current. A typical TTL output can only deliver current levels around 30 mA which may not be enough for driving relay coils. A high output current card can supply current levels higher than that. Other than that, all features of this category are exactly like the previous category. A representative of this category, PIO-24, is shown below.

High voltage output cards are also used for applications which require higher voltage outputs than TTL. Due to simple interface, software drivers should not be expected.

24-BIT PARALLEL DIGITAL I/O BOARD WITH HIGH CURRENT OUTPUTS

PIO-24

FUNCTIONAL DESCRIPTION

Keithley MetraByte's PIO-24 is a high current, parallel digital I/O card which allows 24 TTL/DTL-compatible digital I/O lines to be monitored or controlled by an IBM PC/XT/AT or compatible. The board provides access to the PC's interrupt input and enable lines and includes connections to the PC's power supplies (+5 V, +12 V, –12 V and –5 V). It is a flexible interface for high current parallel input/output devices such as instruments, displays and user-constructed systems and equipment.

BLOCK DIAGRAM

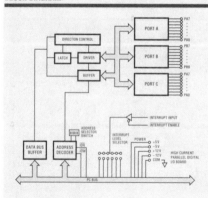

FEATURES

- 24 TTL/DTL digital I/O lines
- High current drivers 15mA (source) 64mA (sink)
- +12, –12, +5 and –5 Volt power from computer
- Emulates MODE 0 of 8255 PPI
- Interrupt input
- Direct interface to wide range of peripherals

APPLICATIONS

- Contact closure monitoring
- Alarm monitoring
- Bang-bang control
- Digital I/O control
- Relay control
- Useful with A/Ds and D/As
- Display driver
- Interface to ERB-24, SSIO-24

Twenty-four digital I/O lines are provided through buffers and drivers and consist of three ports. An 8-bit PA, and 8-bit PB port, and an 8-bit PC port. The PC port may also be used as two half-ports of 4 bits, PC upper (PC 4 – 7) and PC lower (PC 0 – 3). Each of the ports and half-ports is configured as input or output by software control according to the contents of a control register. The PA, PB, and PC ports can always be read as well as written to. After RESET (power up of IBM PC/XT), all ports are set as inputs and the contents of the write latches are zeroed.

Interrupt handling is via a tristate driver with separate enable (interrupt enable – active low). This may be connected to any of the interrupt levels 2 – 7 available on the PC bus by means of a plug-type jumper on the board. Handling of the interrupt is controlled by the 8259 interrupt controller in the IBM PC and is set by the BIOS on system initialization to respond to positive (low – high) edge-triggered inputs. Users must program the 8259 to respond to their requirements and set up the corresponding interrupt handlers.

The PIO-24 uses four I/O address locations which are fully decoded within the I/O address space of the PC. The base address is set by an 8-position dip switch and can be placed anywhere in the I/O space, but base addresses below FF hex (255 decimal) should be avoided as this address range is used by the internal I/O of the computer. The 200-3FF hex (512 – 1023) address range provides extensive unused areas of I/O space.

SOFTWARE

There are two software alternatives for the PIO-24. The user can either use a fully integrated data acquisition software package (e.g., VIEWDAC or EASYEST LX), or write a custom program (in BASIC, C, Pascal, etc.). Note that while not directly supported by many of the integrated software packages, virtually all packages have a direct PORT I/O function which will directly read/write data to/from the PIO-24. A guide to tradeoffs between integrated packages and writing your own program is provided in the Software Section beginning on page 12. The software section also describes a wide variety of integrated software packages.

The PIO-24 is very easy to program and most users will opt to write their own programs. No drivers are supplied with the PIO-24 since programming is simple using the I/O instructions in most programming languages. The PIO-24 uses 4 consecutive I/O locations in the computer's I/O

HIGH SPEED I/O BOARDS

Boards in this category usually have a large number of digital inputs and outputs and they can transfer data at a very fast pace using a DMA operation. Since programming DMA is not straightforward for most users, software drivers should be expected on this category of board. The data transfer operation can be either software initiated or externally triggered. Short data sheet for a representative of this category, PDMA-16 & 32, is shown below.

HIGH-SPEED DIGITAL I/O BOARDS
WITH DMA TRANSFER CAPABILITY

PDMA-16 & 32

FEATURES

- Transfer up to 250,000 bytes per second (PDMA-16)
- Transfer up to 400,000 bytes per second (PDMA-32)
- 8-bit (PDMA-16) or 16-bit (PDMA-32) data transfers
- Handshaking signals provided
- Internally clock driven or external triggering
- DMA, interrupt, or program controlled transfers
- Software driver simplifies programming

APPLICATIONS

- Interface to high-speed peripherals
- High-speed memory transfers from other computers
- Digital I/O control
- Printer/plotter interfaces
- Interface to external high-speed A/D and D/A converters
- Digital pattern generation

The PDMA boards are intended for applications requiring high-speed digital transfers to and/or from external computers and peripheral devices.

The PDMA boards provide two 8-bit I/O ports. Each can be set as an input or output under software control, and each of the ports are addressed as standard I/O locations. However, when operating the board in high-speed mode (under DMA control), both ports must be set to operate in the same direction.

The actual DMA transfers may be initiated by an external signal (XFER REQ), or by an internal timer. The internal timer consists of a 10-MHz precision oscillator divided by a programmable 32-bit counter (2 counters from an 8254). On receipt of a positive edge on the XFER REQ input, the XFER ACK output goes low. Completion of the transfer is signified by the XFER ACO output returning to the high state. This system allows for simple handshaking even at high speeds.

Three auxiliary output bits AUX 1 – 3 are also available for controlling or signaling external systems. All external connections are made through a 37-pin D connector that extends out the rear of the computer. Field wiring can be greatly simplified with the optional STA-U or STC-37 screw terminal accessories.

FUNCTIONAL DESCRIPTION

The PDMA-16 and PDMA-32 are high-speed 16-bit digital input/output interface boards for the IBM PC/XT/AT, 386, 486 and compatible computers. The PDMA-16 board is compatible with PC/XT and PC/AT compatible I/O slots and performs data transfers to and from memory 1 byte (8 bits) at a time. The PDMA-32 offers higher transfer rates by performing transfers to and from memory 1 word (16 bits) per transfer. However, the PDMA-32 is only compatible with 16-bit PC/AT-compatible slots. The maximum data transfer rates are 250,000 bytes per second with the PDMA-16, and 400,000 bytes per second with the PDMA-32.

Both boards perform high-speed data transfers using direct memory access (DMA). For applications not requiring full speed, the boards can be operated in an interrupt driven mode, or under direct program control.

BLOCK DIAGRAM: PDMA-16/PDMA-32

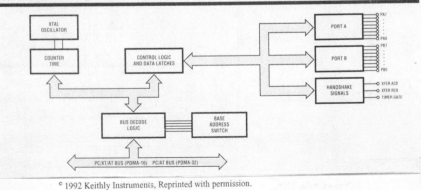

ISOLATED I/O BOARDS

These cards are similar to all other digital I/O cards. The only difference with this card is that the outputs and the inputs are optically isolated. Most industrial applications require digital input/outputs which are optically isolated. In the event of a catastrophic failure the isolation prevents the systems down the line from being affected by the catastrophe. So even if the equipment connected to the data acquisition system burns due to a lightning strike, the computer which is connected through an isolated input is not affected from the catastrophe. A represenatative of this category, PDISO-8, is shown below.

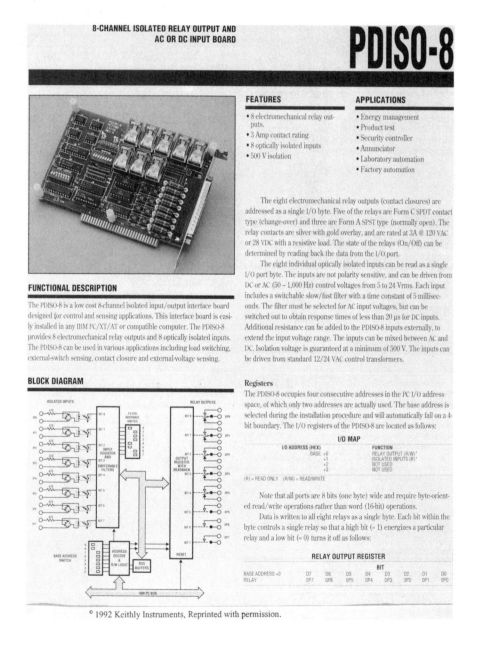

8-CHANNEL ISOLATED RELAY OUTPUT AND AC OR DC INPUT BOARD

PDISO-8

FEATURES

- 8 electromechanical relay outputs.
- 3 Amp contact rating
- 8 optically isolated inputs
- 500 V isolation

APPLICATIONS

- Energy management
- Product test
- Security controller
- Annunciator
- Laboratory automation
- Factory automation

The eight electromechanical relay outputs (contact closures) are addressed as a single I/O byte. Five of the relays are Form C SPDT contact type (change-over) and three are Form A SPST type (normally open). The relay contacts are silver with gold overlay, and are rated at 3A @ 120 VAC or 28 VDC with a resistive load. The state of the relays (On/Off) can be determined by reading back the data from the I/O port.

The eight individual optically isolated inputs can be read as a single I/O port byte. The inputs are not polarity sensitive, and can be driven from DC or AC (50 – 1,000 Hz) control voltages from 5 to 24 Vrms. Each input includes a switchable slow/fast filter with a time constant of 5 milliseconds. The filter must be selected for AC input voltages, but can be switched out to obtain response times of less than 20 μs for DC inputs. Additional resistance can be added to the PDISO-8 inputs externally, to extend the input voltage range. The inputs can be mixed between AC and DC. Isolation voltage is guaranteed at a minimum of 500 V. The inputs can be driven from standard 12/24 VAC control transformers.

FUNCTIONAL DESCRIPTION

The PDISO-8 is a low cost 8-channel isolated input/output interface board designed for control and sensing applications. This interface board is easily installed in any IBM PC/XT/AT or compatible computer. The PDISO-8 provides 8 electromechanical relay outputs and 8 optically isolated inputs. The PDISO-8 can be used in various applications including load switching, external-switch sensing, contact closure and external-voltage sensing.

BLOCK DIAGRAM

Registers

The PDISO-8 occupies four consecutive addresses in the PC I/O address space, of which only two addresses are actually used. The base address is selected during the installation procedure and will automatically fall on a 4-bit boundary. The I/O registers of the PDISO-8 are located as follows:

I/O MAP

I/O ADDRESS (HEX)	FUNCTION
BASE +0	RELAY OUTPUT (R/W)*
+1	ISOLATED INPUTS (R)*
+2	NOT USED
+3	NOT USED

(R) = READ ONLY   (R/W) = READ/WRITE

Note that all ports are 8 bits (one byte) wide and require byte-oriented read/write operations rather than word (16-bit) operations.

Data is written to all eight relays as a single byte. Each bit within the byte controls a single relay so that a high bit (= 1) energizes a particular relay and a low bit (= 0) turns it off as follows:

RELAY OUTPUT REGISTER

				BIT				
BASE ADDRESS +0 RELAY	D7 OP7	D6 OP6	D5 OP5	D4 OP4	D3 OP3	D2 OP2	D1 OP1	D0 OP0

© 1992 Keithly Instruments, Reprinted with permission.

5.3.3 Analog Output Boards for the PC

Analog output boards are digital-to-analog converter boards where the digital data that comes from the PC are converted into analog voltage levels. Usually the output voltage range is controllable either by software or by set switches on the card. Some of the D/A boards have several output channels which are individually controllable. These channels are not simply demultiplexed channels; due to the relatively low cost of D/A converters, all channels have their own D/A converter connected to them. The most common resolution for D/A boards is 12 bits, although higher and lower resolutions can be found on the market. Usually the output voltage is very precise and there are provisions for calibrating the output.

Some of the analog output cards provide analog output in voltage and current form. In reality the current output is more frequently used in industry than the voltage output. The industry standard 4-20 mA is a very well established standard which requires current signal to be sent to devices. According to this, 0 V corresponds to 4 mA and the highest output voltage corresponds to 20 mA. The advantage of the current signal over the voltage signal is due to the fact that current signal is less sensitive to noise than voltage. Although the voltage signal can be corrupted very easily in a noisy environment, the current output will not be affected much. The use of twisted pair wires will reduce the noise effect even further on the current output signal. Having an offset current of 4 mA will assure the connection to the computer is intact. If the wire breaks at some point, the current will be forced to zero which will immediately indicate a fault with the connections.

Utility software is usually provided by the manufacturer to facilitate calibration and ease of use. A representative example of analog output cards, DDA-06, is given on the following page.

5.3.4 IEEE-488 Interface Boards

IEEE-488 is a standard which is commonly used for controlling laboratory equipment. The standard allows up to 15 devices to be connected in a network fashion and by using this interface it is possible to completely automate laboratory experiments. Data to and from the devices will be transferred electronically. An IEEE-488 network requires a controller in the system to control the whole setup. Personal computers are ideally suited for this application if an IEEE-488 interface can be added. There are many manufacturers on the market producing IEEE-488 interface cards for PC's; however, compatibility seems to be a big problem among IEEE-488 cards. The main reason behind this is that the IEEE-488 standard has been revised several times. One of the most commonly followed versions is the 1987 version of IEEE-488 which is known as IEEE-488.1. So the compatibility issue is an important point in deciding which IEEE-488 card to buy.

DDA-06

6-CHANNEL, 12-BIT ANALOG OUTPUT BOARD

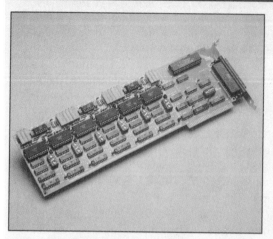

FEATURES

- 6 analog output channels
- 12-bit resolution
- +5, +10, ±2.5, ±5, ±10 V output ranges
- 4 – 20 mA current loop capability (sink)
- 24 bits of parallel digital I/O
- Simultaneous updating on all channels (switch selectable)
- Software included: setup, calibration, programming examples and demonstration programs

APPLICATIONS

- Servo control
- Programmable voltage source
- Programmable current sink
- Function generator
- Product testing
- Use with Keithley MetraByte's SSIO-24 and ERB-24 (through STA-U)

FUNCTIONAL DESCRIPTION

Keithley MetraByte's DDA-06 is an analog output and digital I/O board for the IBM PC/XT/AT and compatibles providing 6 channels of 12-bit analog output and 24 lines of digital I/O. The following functions are implemented on the DDA-06:

- 6 independent 12 bit D/A converters. Each is individually switch selectable to any of the following ranges:

    0 to +10 V, 0 to +5 V, −2.5 V to +2.5 V
    −5 V to +5 V, −10 V to +10 V, 4 – 20 mA current loop (sink)

- Each D/A has a double-buffered input for single-step update and occupies its own I/O location. By means of jumper blocks, it is possible to select any or all of the D/As to update simultaneously. Since each D/A output uses one pin of the rear 37-pin D-type connector, the D/As can be operated in either voltage output mode or current output (but not both simultaneously). In voltage mode, output settling time is typically 3 microseconds to 0.01% for a full-scale step.

- 24 bits of digital I/O are provided on the rear connector consisting of 3 ports of 8 bits. Each port can be programmed independently as an input or output and is TTL/CMOS compatible. An 8255 programmable peripheral interface chip is used for digital I/O and can be operated in the 8255 modes 0 – 2 (straight I/O, strobed I/O and bidirectional I/O).

SOFTWARE

The following utility software is included with the DDA-06.

    1) Initial setup and installation aids.
    2) Calibration program.
    3) Programming examples and demonstration programs.

No driver is supplied with the DDA-06 since programming is simple using I/O instructions in most programming languages (e.g., BASIC, QuickBASIC, C, Turbo-Pascal, etc.). Writing to a D/A converter is a simple two step procedure. The least significant 8 bits of the output word are written to the board, then the most significant four bits are written. The D/A is

BLOCK DIAGRAM

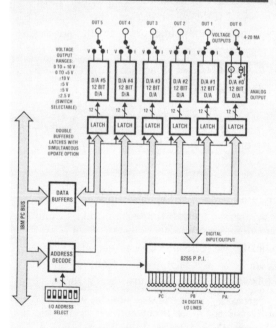

Most IEEE-488 interface cards come with utility software. Some advanced cards may even have the software in an on-board ROM. IEEE-488 software may not be very easy to write so software is an essential point to consider when purchasing IEEE-488 cards. A representative card from this category, KPC-488.2, is shown below.

KPC-488.2, KPS-488.2 & KPC-488.2AT

INTERFACES FOR THE PC/XT/AT AND PS/2

FEATURES

- Fastest data transfers
- DEBUG-488 Software Bus Analyzer
- Complete IEEE-488.2 compatibility
- Compatible software for easy upgrades
- Compatible with ASYST®, LABTECH® NOTEBOOK, LabWindows®, LabView® VIEWDAC® and HP ITG.

APPLICATIONS

- Automated production test
- Laboratory automation
- Printer/Plotter support

FUNCTIONAL DESCRIPTION

The KPC-488.2, KPS-488.2, KPC-488.2AT and KPC-488.2TM are Keithley's line of IEEE-488 interfaces for the PC/XT/AT and PS/2 computers and compatibles. The KPC-488.2 and KPS-488.2 are standard interfaces for the PC and PS/2 respectively. The KPC-488.2AT is a high speed version of the PC interface that uses the 16-bit AT bus. The TM version includes the Trigger Master™ system trigger controller with the KPC-488.2AT and is described on a separate data sheet. All boards are fully compliant with the IEEE-488.2 specifications and will operate all IEEE-488 compliant instruments including new instruments that use the Standard Commands for Programmable Instruments (SCPI). All four boards come with the same software. As a result, it is easy to upgrade from one interface to another.

DATA TRANSFER RATE

All Keithley MetraByte IEEE-488 interfaces for the PC are the fastest in their class. The KPC-488.2AT gets its speed from special accelerator logic. This interface can Read or Write data at rates up to 1.5 MBytes per second, nearly 50% faster than the industry's previous fastest GPIB-AT interface. Maximum data rates are specified for 64 Kbyte block transfers. Keithley's PC interfaces use a combination of hardware and software that provides the industry's highest data rates for both small and large blocks of data improving the performance of all configurations and applications.

BLOCK DIAGRAM

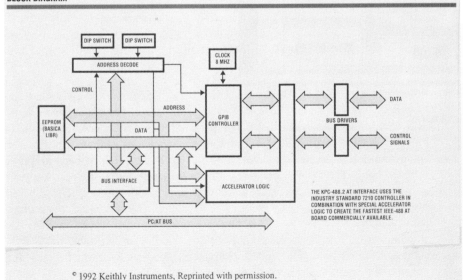

5.3.5 Standard Serial Interface Boards for the PC

The usual PC has two built in interfaces. These are the parallel printer interface and the RS-232 interface. Between these, the RS-232 is used for serial interface and the other is used as a parallel interface. Currently there are other serial and parallel interface standards that are more capable than the usually available interfaces of the PC. Serial interface standards like RS-422 and RS-485 allow longer communication distances and more capabilities.

RS-422 INTERFACE FOR PC'S

The RS-422 is a recent serial communication standard which vastly improves the distance and speed of the RS-232 and allows communication up to 1.2 km. The RS-422, like the RS-232, provides point to point communication.

RS-485 INTERFACE FOR PC'S

The RS-485 is a recently developed serial communication standard which allows the networking of computers or devices over a pair of lines. The distance of communication is 1.2 km which is much larger than what is allowed by RS-232. Unlike the RS-232 which provides point-to-point communication between two devices only, the RS-485 is a multi-drop standard which allows multiple drivers and multiple receivers to be connected to a single pair of lines. As a result of this capability several devices can be connected to the same RS-485 port of the PC. A typical representative product of this category, COM-485, is shown on the following pages.

5.3.6 Special Purpose Instrument Cards for PC

PC based instrumentation is new idea which challenges the old IEEE-488 concept of laboratory instrumentation. Instead of having all those pieces of equipment separate and then connecting them via a IEEE-488 network, this new concept suggests using PC based instrument cards which perform the same functions as those individual pieces of equipment. Since the cards are already inside the PC, there is no need to send the data for processing. The PC will get the data from the cards and process it locally. From the cost point of view, this concept is better than having individual IEEE-488 based instruments. It is very well known that instruments with a IEEE-488 interface cost much more than regular instruments with the same features, simply because handling IEEE-488 communication requires a microprocessor or a microcontroller to be included in the design of the equipment. This added intelligence increases the cost of the product. Most commonly used PC based instruments are as follows:

RS-485 INTERFACE FOR THE
IBM PC/XT/AT

COM-485

FEATURES

- Fully RS-485 compatible
- Allows networking up to 4000 feet
- 56 Kbaud maximum communications rate
- IBM asynchronous adapter card compatible
- Set up as COM1, COM2, or any other base address/ interrupt level combination
- Fully programmable serial interface characteristic

APPLICATIONS

- Simple, inexpensive PC networks
- Instrument interfaces
- 38.4 Kbaud standard broadcast industry communications
- Interface to M1000 modules

16550 UART is an enhanced upgrade to the 16450 and is 100% backwards compatible. The 16550 includes a 16-byte FIFO which can be used in both transmission and reception of data, helping to insure that no data is lost. The benefits of the FIFO are apparent even at baud rates as low as 9600 bps. A UART without a FIFO requires service every millisecond to avoid data overrun. Activities such as operating under Microsoft Windows cannot guarantee this rate.

Applications for the COM-485 include networking instruments, scanning and updating various user input and output devices (such as CRTs, keyboards, etc.), and other communication applications that require more than one device to be simply and inexpensively networked to a personal computer.

FUNCTIONAL DESCRIPTION

Keithley MetraByte's COM-485 board allows IBM PC/XT/AT and compatible computers to be networked over the RS-485 bus. Unlike the RS-422 bus, which allows multiple receivers but only a single transmitter, the RS-485 allows multiple transmitters and receivers to communicate over a 2-wire bus allowing a "party-line" network configuration. The COM-485 allows up to 32 different driver/receiver stations to communicate at 57.6 Kbaud (though standard IBM communications software limits the speed to 19.2 Kbaud, these limitations are easily overcome). COM-485 stations can be located up to 4000 feet away from each other.

The COM-485 can be set up as a COM1 or COM2 standard serial interface port, or can be set at any other Base Address/interrupt level combination. A single write to the Base Address + 7 (hex 3FF at COM1 or hex 2FF at COM2) controls the enabling/disabling of the RS-485 transmitter and receiver chip. The board is based on the 16450 UART (compatible with the 8250 UART). The

PROGRAMMING

The COM-485 is very simple to use since it is configured as a standard IBM PC/XT/AT or compatible COM1 or COM2 port. The transmitter and receiver are enabled/disabled by writing to the board's Base Address + 7 (for COM1 hex 3FF and COM2 hex 2FF). The least significant bit enables/disables the receiver and bit 1 controls the transmitter. The following diagram details the enable/disable functions.

BLOCK DIAGRAM

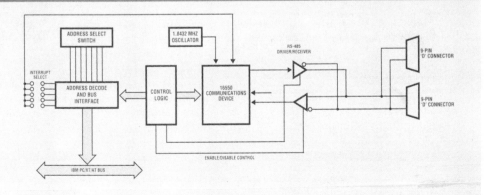

- PC based digital multimeter
- PC based channel scanner
- PC based voltage reference
- PC based oscilloscope
- PC based function generator
- PC based logic analyzer
- PC based counter
- PC based programmable resistor box
- PC based arbitrary waveform generator

Data sheet for an example of this category, PCIP-SCOPE, is shown on the following page.

5.3.7 PC Based Intelligent Data Acquisition Processors

PC based data acquisition processors are intelligent data acquisition cards which operate independently from the PC. Data acquisition processors, as the name implies, have on board microprocessors that handle data acquisition tasks. Once the processor has been programmed by the PC, it works independently and acquires samples. The card can average or perform digital processing on data and submit the results to the host PC. So, a data acquisition processor would mainly free the host PC from performing the arduous task of getting samples at predetermined times. Only in the case of extraordinary situations like data going into alarm regions, would a data acquisition processor interrupt the PC for supervisory action.

There are few commercially available products of this sort on the market. These products cost more than the simple plug-in cards for the PC because of the on-board intelligence that they have. The intelligent data acquisition cards have their own special language to program their processors. Obviously these cards are more difficult to use and more expensive than the other data acquisition products designed for the PC, but sometimes the application will dictate the need for such equipment. The applications which require very fast sampling and processing of data are good candidates for such intelligent cards. With the current technology, the maximum sustained sampling rate for a EISA or MCA type PC is 1 megasample/second. If the application demands more than that, one should consider one of these cards.

An excellent example of this category is an intelligent card manufactured by Microstar Laboratories which is called "DAQ processor."

PCIP-SCOPE

FUNCTIONAL DESCRIPTION

The PCIP-SCOPE is a two-channel digital sampling oscilloscope on a PC board, that plugs directly into any I/O slot of an IBM PC/AT/XT, IBM PS/2 model 25/30 or compatible computer. The board provides all the features you expect from a conventional oscilloscope. However, instead of using mechanical control knobs and switches, the PCIP-SCOPE uses the computer keyboard or mouse to set the various scope parameters. Instead of using a dedicated CRT, the PCIP-SCOPE uses the computer display. The display operates in a "pop up" mode. When activated, the oscilloscope screen and all the controls are displayed on the computer's screen. The computer keyboard or mouse selects the oscilloscope functions including:

BLOCK DIAGRAM

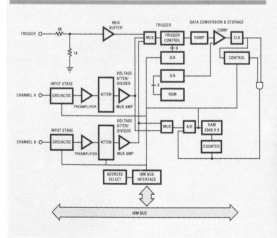

FEATURES

- Dual channel
- 2 nSec sampling for repetitive waveforms
- 10 MHz bandwidth
- 20 MHz sampling rate
- Internal, external or software triggerable
- 5 mV to 5 V input sensitivity
- Store waveforms on disk
- Acquired waveforms can be output with the PCIP-AWFG
- 2048 (single channel) or 1024 (dual channel) samples per channel

APPLICATIONS

- Engineering
- Production test
- Automated inspection
- Computer control analysis

channel selection, display mode, input coupling, vertical resolution, offset, timebase, trigger level/slope/source and mode.

The PCIP-SCOPE features two input channels and a maximum sample rate of 20 MHz. A 2048-sample memory is allocated to one channel or split evenly between the two channels. In addition, the PCIP-SCOPE provides both AC and DC input capability with Alternate or Chop modes selected automatically for dual-channel display. Either channel can be used as a trigger, or an external signal can trigger via slope, level or under computer command.

Waveforms can be stored to disk for future analysis or documentation. When used with the PCIP-AWFG, the PCIP-SCOPE creates a true storage and playback oscilloscope.

The PCIP-SCOPE can operate in two modes: manual mode and program mode, similar to the GPIB local and remote operation. In the manual mode, the front control panel of the instrument is popped up on the screen when a series of keys is pressed. This Pop Up Control Panel gives access to all functions of the PCIP-SCOPE. Since this can be activated while inside an applications package, a program can be written and debugged as measurements are being taken.

In the program mode, the PCIP-SCOPE can be fully controlled by the PC. However, unlike GPIB instruments the PCIP-SCOPE is programmed using easy to read English commands. Gone are the IEEE-488 worries of talkers versus listeners, serial and parallel polls and confusing ASCII instrument commands.

PCIP-SCOPE DISPLAY

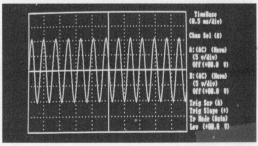

5.4 STAND ALONE INTELLIGENT DATA ACQUISITION SYSTEMS

Stand alone intelligent data acquisition systems are similar to intelligent data acquisition cards in most respects. The difference of this category from the intelligent cards is that these devices are stand alone products which can function with or without a PC connected to them. Initial programming of the system will require connection to a computer through which the program is downloaded to the data acquisition system. Once the program is downloaded, the system can function stand alone even if the connection to the PC is removed. In this mode, the unit will be functioning as a data logger. The data will be stored in the internal memory of the unit until the connection to the PC is restored and data in the buffers are downloaded to the PC.

Because of the intelligence of the system, the cost is considerably higher compared to other forms of data acquisition. Normally an intelligent system works independently and acquires data and stores them in its memory. The host PC needs to request the data from the intelligent system if it needs the information. Since the connection between the systems is usually serial and the intelligent system operates remotely, there is a considerable distance between the host PC and the stand alone data acquisition unit. Under these circumstances, transfer of data from an intelligent system to the host may take considerable time. In practice, most of the time a remote intelligent system is used in a stand alone mode and only needs to transmit compiled data intermittently, for example at the end of the day or in case of an extraordinary situation.

These stand alone intelligent data acquisition units have internal slots for accommodating different data acquisition cards. Depending on the needs of the application, suitable cards can be plugged into the unit. The internal expansion slots have different physical standards than the expansion slots of the PC so the data acquisition cards designed for PC's can not be used in these systems.

The interface to the PC can be either through a serial communication port using existing standards like RS232C, RS-485, RS-422 or by GPIB interface.

An excellent example of this category is the HP Model 48000 RTU Unit and the Model 3852 data acquisition system. (RTU stands for remote terminal unit.) In both cases the frame of the unit has internal slots which accept special purpose modules. The system has its own processor to acquire and process the data and sends only the information requested to the host computer.

The HP Model 48000 RTU unit is also an intelligent data acquisition system. The difference between the 48000 and the 3852 is that the former is designed to operate in harsh environments far from a host computer whereas the latter is designed to operate within a lab environment in close proximity to the host computer. The Model 48000 RTU can be located remotely and can communicate with the host computer over RS-232 lines, through a radio link with wireless transmission or through modem connection.

Another example to this category is the Keithley Model 576 stand alone data acquisition unit. Information about this product is given on the following page.

MODEL 576

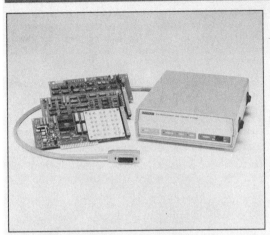

Model 576 with optional modules and 7008-3 cable.

FUNCTIONAL DESCRIPTION

The Model 576 high-speed data logging instrument contains the same basic measurement I/O features and options as the Model 575. However, due to its IEEE-488 (GPIB) interface, internal microprocessor, built-in data storage and program storage capability, the Model 576 provides radically different capabilities.

BLOCK DIAGRAM

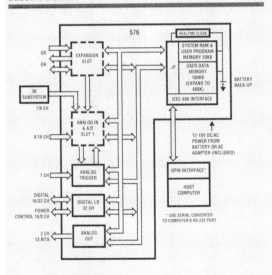

The Model 576 can operate as a standalone instrument taking and storing data and even controlling a process without any computer intervention, except to receive new instructions and to send collected data. Depending on the memory option chosen, the Model 576 can take and store over 200,000 readings over a period of seconds, minutes, hours, days, or months. With its battery-backed program and data storage, the Model 576 can be programmed, taken to a remote site, and begin taking data and/or controlling a process providing alarms, etc.

Complex data logging, monitoring and control applications may be implemented using the Model 576 built-in intelligence. Conditional triggering, subroutines, data conversion and data scaling operations are included as part of the Model 576 firmware. These routines permit the Model 576 to operate independent of the host computer in applications requiring monitoring, control and alarming.

The Model 576 is also equipped with a real-time clock. Applications may be written to trigger from the clock at a specific time-of-day with a resolution of one second. In addition, the unit provides time stamping of data at rates up to 100 channels/second.

The Model 576 can also operate in "immediate" mode in which it takes a single measurement or a single scan of channels and sends the data back to the computer as soon as it's collected. In this mode, the Model 576 operates much slower, typically <100 rdgs/sec.

The Model 576 provides a shielded, low-noise environment for sensitive measurements. The system is housed in a sturdy aluminum case drawing its operating power from a wall-mounted transformer (included) or any source supplying 12-18V (ac or dc) @ 40VA. This method also allows operation in a stand-alone configuration from a battery supply (12V) for data logging during critical power line failures.

The Model 576 may be operated with any computer with an IEEE-488 interface or an RS-232 interface (with the optional 500-SERIAL converter), see page 206 for details.

PROGRAMMING/SOFTWARE

The Model 576 is compatible with any computer and any software that supports the IEEE-488 bus. Regardless of what computer or software is used, the programming instructions to the Model 576 are a set of English-based commands that are sent over the IEEE-488 bus (Device Dependent Commands or DDCs). For more details on the Model 576 and its programmability, call us for a complete literature package.

ORDER

576/AMM1A	Model 576 with AMM1A, 12-Bit A/D, with 28 KB Program Memory and 100 KB Data Memory
576/AMM1A/MEM	Same as above except with 480 KB Data Memory
576/AMM2	Model 576 with AMM2, 16-Bit A/D with 28 KB Program Memory and 100 KB Data Memory
576/AMM2/MEM	Same as above except with 480 KB dData Memory
576-MEM	Data Memory Expansion (for field installation of MEM option)
500-SERIAL	RS-232 to IEEE-488 Converter
7008-3	GPIB Cable (3 ft)
7008-6	GPIB Cable (6 ft)

5.5 INDUSTRY STANDARD SIGNAL CONDITIONING MODULES FOR PC BASED CARDS

Any PC based data acquisition system consists of few basic parts, namely

- Computer
- Data acquisition card(s)
- Signal conditioners

Most of the time some basic signal conditioning is included on the data acquisition cards designed for the PC; so not all applications require using a separate signal conditioner. Basic signal conditioning included on the boards usually appears in different forms in different cards. For example, it appears as offset and span adjustments for A/D converter cards, or 4-20 mA current output for analog output cards, or optically isolated output for digital output cards.

For usual applications these basic signal conditionings may be satisfactory; in that case, no additional signal conditioner is required. However, most large-scale industrial applications require using separate, external signal conditioners for unusual tasks. There is also another benefit of having external separate signal conditioners. In case of a failure or an accident, only the particular signal conditioner involved will be damaged and the data acquisition card inside the PC will not be affected by the catastrophe. The cost of signal conditioning modules is negligible with respect to the cost of the data acquisition cards.

Signal conditioning modules simply transform an analog input signal into another analog signal which is more suitable for the data acquisition cards to read. Most data acquisition card manufacturers also have their line of signal conditioner modules, although as a user one can mix and match signal conditioners from different suppliers.

Typical signal conditioner modules include

- Analog input isolation modules
- Analog input amplifier modules (variety of ranges)
- Current input modules
- RTD input amplifier and lineariser modules
- Thermocouple input amplifier and compensation modules
- Strain gauge input modules
- Current output modules
- Wide bandwidth amplifier modules

Short data sheet for representative commercial product, MB-SERIES signal conditoining modules, is given on the following page.

SIGNAL CONDITIONING MODULES AND INTERFACE ACCESSORIES

MB-SERIES

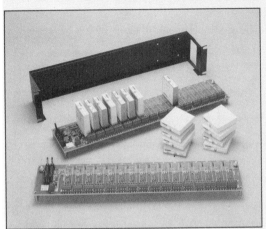

The MB01 and MB02 module mounting racks are shown with a variety of MB-Series modules and the RMT-MBBP 19-inch rack enclosure.

FEATURES

- Convert raw industrial analog inputs to high-level analog outputs
- Accepts thermocouple, RTD, strain gage, voltage, current and wide bandwidth voltage inputs
- ±5 Volt or 0 – 5 volt outputs
- 1500 Vrms transformer-based isolation
- High accuracy
- Rugged fully-potted modules
- Simple mounting in 1, 2 and 16 channel mounting racks
- Easily connected to DAS-1600, DAS-1400, DAS-20, DAS-16 and DAS-8 analog I/O boards

APPLICATIONS

- Industrial data acquisition
- Process control
- Energy management
- Production testing
- Laboratory automation

FUNCTIONAL DESCRIPTION

Keithley MetraByte's MB-Series signal conditioning modules provide a low-cost and high-performance method of interfacing real world industrial signals to an A/D conversion system. The modules convert raw sensor inputs to high-level analog outputs that are linear in engineering units. For example, the MB34-01 accepts a 100 ohm platinum RTD input and provides 0 to +5 V linearized output. Both ±5 volt and 0 to +5 volt output ranges are available for most input types. In addition a current output module is available for process control applications.

MB series modules provide 1500 Vrms transformer-based isolation, protecting your system and allowing the measurement of small transducer signals on top of large common mode voltages. All modules are identical in size (2.25 in x 2.25 in x 0.60 in) and pin connections and have been hard-potted for mechanical strength. These features, along with the modules' high (±0.05% of FS) accuracy, make MB series modules an ideal solution for industrial signal conditioning.

Up to 16 MB-Series modules can be plugged into one MB-01 or MB-02 rack. Modules can be of any type and mixed on a single mounting rack allowing the system to be tailored exactly to the application's requirements. The STA-SCM adapter board allows connection of up to 4 MB-02 racks (64 analog inputs) to a Keithley MetraByte DAS-8 or DAS-1600/1400/16 analog input board. Keithley MetraByte's DAS-20 analog I/O board can be connected to 4 MB-02s as well. The STA-MBBP board can be used to easily connect any analog I/O system to either the MB-01 or MB-02 module racks. The STA-MBBP accepts the 26-pin cable from the MB-01 or MB-02 mounting racks and provides 26 screw terminal connections. The

BLOCK DIAGRAM

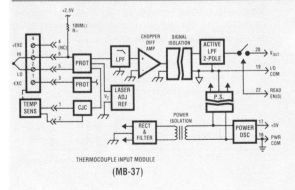

THERMOCOUPLE INPUT MODULE
(MB-37)

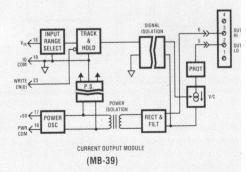

CURRENT OUTPUT MODULE
(MB-39)

5.6 ACCESSORIES FOR PC BASED DATA ACQUISITION CARDS

There are accessory cards and signal conditioner cards that are compatible with PC based data acquisition cards. These accessory cards and signal conditioners do not reside inside the PC, but they need to be in close proximity to the PC because of the short connections involved. These cards are used either for expanding or adapting the PC based data acquisition cards to the specific data acquisition application. Case studies reviewed at the end of Chapter 6 will clarify the use these cards.

5.6.1 Simultaneous Sample and Hold Accessory Board

These boards sample multiple analog input channels almost simultaneously and freeze the values at that particular instant until an A/D converter card converts the values to digital. These cards provide true simultaneous sampling of input channels. Most A/D converter cards do not sample the channels at the same time. In most cases an A/D converter card has a single A/D converter chip on board and a multiplexer on the card to multiplex several input channels into the input of the A/D converter chip. In this case, the channels are sequentially converted into digital. For most practical purposes, the conversion time of an A/D converter is fast enough to enable one to consider the channels sampled and converted simultaneously. (Most general purpose A/D converters have conversion rates of 100,000 samples per second or better.) Consider an A/D converter card with 16 input channels. The worst case time difference between the first channel and the last channel is 16 X conversion time of A/D converter.

To judge whether this is acceptable as an instantaneous sampling or not, one has to look at the specific application. (Although not foolproof, one rule of thumb for such cases is that if the sampling time is less than or equal to 1/10 of the critical time of the application, then sampling is considered practically simultaneous.) If it is not acceptable, then the solution is to use a sample and hold card to sample the channels at the same time and give the output of the sample and hold card to the A/D converter card for conversion.

Data sheet for a typical commercial product of this category, SSH-4, shown on the following page.

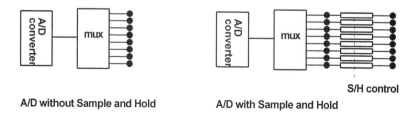

A/D without Sample and Hold   A/D with Sample and Hold

Figure 5.8 Multichannel A/D converter with and without sample and holds.

**4-CHANNEL SIMULTANEOUS SAMPLE & HOLD
ACCESSORY FOR THE DAS-20**

FUNCTIONAL DESCRIPTION

The SSH-4 is a four channel, simultaneous sample and hold accessory board for Keithley MetraByte's DAS-20 analog I/O board. The SSH-4 allows analog input data to be acquired from 2, 3 or 4 inputs with less than 40 nanoseconds of channel to channel sample time skew. Additional SSH-4s can be daisy chained into the system, allowing up to 16 channels to be sampled simultaneously. A single 50 conductor CDAS-2000 cable connects the A/D board to the SSH-4. Additional SSH-4s are connected into the system with a CACC-2000 cable.

The sample acquisition time of the SSH-4 is less than 10 microseconds. To calculate maximum sample rate, this 10 microseconds is added to the length of time the A/D converter board requires for its samples. For example, if 3 input channels were to be sampled using the DAS-20, the

BLOCK DIAGRAM

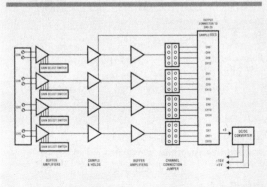

FEATURES

• Samples 4 DAS-20 channels simulataneously
• Under 40 ns aperture uncertainty between channels
• Less than 10 microseconds acquisition time
• Fully differential inputs
• 9 switch selectable input gains per channel
• Additional SSH-4s can be added to sample up to 16 channels.

sample time would be 10 μs for the SSH-4 acquisition, plus 30 μs (3 channels times the DAS-20's 10 μs conversion time) for a total of 40 μs or a 25 kS/sec, per channel. Similarly the maximum sample rate per channel for 2 channels will be 33.3 kS/s, and for 4 channels will be 20 kS/s.

CONFIGURATION GUIDE

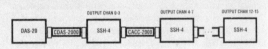

SPECIFICATIONS

Input type	Differential	
Acquisition time	< 10 μs	
Aperture time	< 250 ns typ	
Channel-to-channel aperture uncertainty	< 40 ns typ	
Output droop rate	< 10 μV per millisecond	
Input gains	1, 10, 100, 200, 300, 500, 600, 700, 800 switch selectable	
Gain errors	x1	±0.001% typ
	x10	±0.01% typ
	x100	±0.02% typ
	x500	±0.1% typ
Non-linearity	x1	±0.001% typ
	x10	±0.002% typ
	x100	±0.004% typ
	x500	±0.01% typ
Common mode rejection	90 dB	

Power supply	+5V	400 mA max
Environmental	Temp range	0 – 60 °C
	Humidity	0 – 95% non-condensing
	Dimensions with enclosure	6.687 in x 5.125 in x 2.375 in (17 cm x 13 cm x 6 cm)
	Dimensions without enclosure	6.18 in x 4.69 in x .94 in (15.7 cm x 11.9 cm x 2.4 cm)

ORDER

SSH-4	4-Channel Simultaneous Sample & Hold Accessory for the DAS-20

OPTIONS

CDAS-2000	DAS-20 to SSH-4 Cable
CACC-2000	SSH-4 to SSH-4 Cable

5.6.2 Terminal Boards

These boards provide an easy connection facility for an A/D converter or digital I/O cards. Usually these cards are totally passive, meaning that there are no electronics on them but only screw terminals for making connections to sensors and signal conditioners. Two of these products are shown below.

SCREW TERMINAL CONNECTOR	SCREW TERMINAL ACCESSORY BOARDS

FEATURES

- Provides easy-to-use screw terminals for Keithley MetraByte data acquisition boards
- Connects directly to the data acquisition board without requiring any cables
- Compatible with all boards using a 37-pin "D" connector
- Accepts wire sizes 12 – 22 AWG

FEATURES

- Provides convenient connection to Keithley MetraByte data acquisition boards
- Complete with plastic enclosure
- Screw terminals accept wire sizes 12-22 AWG
- User breadboard area for custom circuits
- Connects directly to data acquisition board with cables
- Mounts in RMT-02 enclosure

5.6.3 Analog Input Multiplexer Boards

Analog input multiplexers are used for increasing the channel capacity of a given A/D converter card. These cards are usually cascadable, meaning that one can add more cards to the same A/D converter to increase the channel capacity even further. Analog input multiplexer cards can be either isolated or non-isoltated. Isolated input channels mean that each channel is completely isolated from the other input channels. The amount of isolation voltage guaranteed is usually specified in the data sheet of the multiplexer. Another important parameter to be careful about with the analog input multiplexer boards is the settling time of channels. After the multiplexer is commanded to switch channels, it takes a finite amount of time for the multiplexer to perform the new connection between the input and the output. This time is specified as settling time. This parameter is important because during this time whatever you read from the output of the A/D converter is invalid.

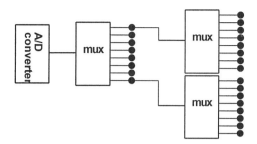

Figure 5.9 A/D converter with expansion multiplexer.

Data sheet for a typical commercial product of this category, EXP-20, is shown below.

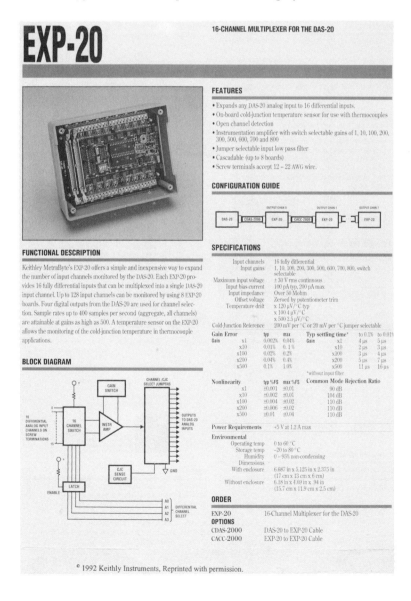

© 1992 Keithly Instruments, Reprinted with permission.

5.7 SELECTION GUIDE FOR APPROPRIATE DATA ACQUISITION PRODUCTS

IF YOUR APPLICATION REQUIRES	DO THIS	REMARKS
• Sensors are within close proximity of the PC • Environment is mild • Distance from PC is < 2 meters	Use office type PC with plug-in type data acquisition cards. If number of slots not enough, get an expansion chassis.	**Advantages:** Low cost **Disadvantages:** Low sensitivity, low reliability, low resolution
• Sensors are within close proximity • Environment is harsh • Distance from PC is < 2 meters	Use an industrial type PC with data acquisition cards. If the number of slots not enough, use an expansion chassis.	**Advantages:** Low cost **Disadvantages:** Low sensitivity, low resolution
• Distance from PC is < 2 meters • Too many measurements to take • Data has to be preprocessed before being sent to the PC	Use PC based data acquisition processors.	**Advantages:** Fast operation, frees PC from arduous tasks **Disadvantages:** Medium to high cost
• Distance from PC is <15 meters, lab environment	Select a stand alone data acquisition unit with RS232 or GPIB interface.	**Advantages:** High speed, high sensitivity, good expansion capability **Disadvantages:** Confined to lab enviroment, software more difficult, GPIB equipment expensive

Conditions	Recommendation	Advantages / Disadvantages
•Sensors are at far away location •Distance form PC is >100 meters •Only few measurements •Speed is not critical	*Use a remote data acquisition module with RS232 or RS485 interface.* *Use a stand alone data acquisition crate with RS422 interface.*	**Advantages:** Low cost, simple to control, low power **Disadvantages:** Slow process, considerable communication delay
•Sensors are at far away location •Distance from PC >100 meters •Speed is critical	*Use a stand alone crate with RS-422 interface and appropriate data acquisition cards.*	**Advantages:** High expansion capability, fast system **Disadvantages:** Costlier than modules
•Sensors are at far away location •Too many measurements to take •Distance > 100 meters •Speed is not critical	*Use a remote intelligent data acquisition system.*	**Advantages:** High speed, high resolution, local processing, less communication traffic **Disadvantages:** High cost

IF YOUR APPLICATION REQUIRES	DO THIS	REMARKS
•Distance from sensors very far (> 10 km) •Phone lines are available •Speed is not critical	*Use appropriate data acquisition modules and modem connection to PC.*	**Advantages:** High resolution, low cost **Disadvantages:** Low speed
•Distance from sensors very far (> 10 km) •Phone lines are available •Speed is not critical •Too many measurements to take	*Use intelligent remote data acquisition system with appropriate cards and use modem connection for regular downloading of data.*	**Advantages:** High resolution, high speed, local processing of data **Disadvantages:** High cost
•Distance from sensors very far (> 10 km) •Phone lines are not available •Speed is not critical •Too many measurements to take	*Use intelligent remote data acquisition cards and wireless modem.*	**Advantages:** High resolution, high speed, local processing of data **Disadvantages:** High cost
•Distance from sensors very far (> 10km) •Speed is not critical •No phone lines are available	*Use data logger with cyclic memory.*	**Advantages:** Portable, stand alone operation, low cost **Disadvantages:** Slow, manual data transfer

REFERENCES

1. Keithly Metrabyte, *Data Acquisition and Reference Guide*, Vol 25, 1992.

2. *RS Components Catalogue*, RS Components, 1995.

3. Putten, Anton F. P., *Electronic Measurement Systems*, Prentice Hall International, 1988.

4. Collins, T. H., *Analog Electronics Handbook*, Prentice Hall International, 1989.

5. Curtis, Johnson, *Process Control Instrumentation Technology*, Regents/Prentice-Hall, 1993.

6. Austerlitz, Howard, *Data Acquisition Techniques Using Personal Computers*, Academic Press, 1991.

7. Derenzo, Stephen, *Interfacing*, Prentice Hall, 1990.

8. Mazda, F., (ed.), *Electronic Engineer's Refrence Book*, Butterworth & Co., 1986.

9. Kant, Khrisna, *Microprocessor Based Data Acquisition System Design*, McGraw-Hill, 1987.

Six

LOCAL DATA ACQUISITION USING PC's

6.1 INTRODUCTION

In the previous chapter we looked at industry standard data acquisition hardware available for a data acquisition engineer who wants to set up a data acquisition system. Fortunately, with this abundant choice of equipment available, one will hardly need to develop hardware oneself for a PC based data acquisition system. The design is just a matter of selecting appropriate components necessary for the design from different vendors, interconnecting them with whatever is necessary and interfacing the whole design with a suitable software package. If a suitable software package is not available, writing the software yourself is also possible even if one is not a software engineering specialist.

In this chapter we are going to look at the design details of setting up a local data acquisition system. In the previous chapter it was explained that local data acquisition means having PC and the application being in close proximity. Due to the close proximity, the data acquisition hardware can either be placed directly inside the PC or inside a data acquisition crate which is connected to the PC through a fast connection. Usually this is the most inexpensive way to perform data acquisition. More sophisticated forms of data acquisition will be introduced in the coming chapters.

In the first part of this chapter we are going to look at the block diagram of a local data acquisition system. If the reader is not familiar with the terminology used, it is strongly advised to read Chapter 5 first before proceeding with this chapter. In the second part of the chapter a real world data acquisition case will be looked at as a case study starting with the specification sheet and guiding the reader step by step to choose necessary components for the data acquisition system. In order to give the reader a realistic flavor of the problem, the specification sheet of the client company will be given verbatim as it is specified.

Readers who are interested in learning more about noise, noise prevention techniques and filters, are recommended to read *Laboratory Automation Using the IBM PC*, an excellent book written by S. C. Gates and J. Becker. Another authoritative text in the field of noise and interference control is *Interference Control in Cable and Device Interfaces* by C. J. Georgopoulois published by Interference Control Technologies in 1988.

6.2 OVERVIEW of PC BASED LOCAL DATA ACQUISITION SYSTEM

A local data acquisition system consists of the following components:

- Computer
- Plug-in cards inside the PC
- Accessory cards like multiplexers, isolators, etc.
- Signal conditioning modules or cards

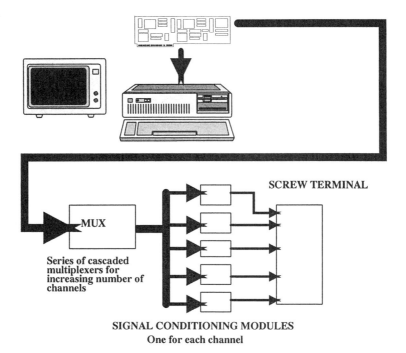

Figure 6.1 Block diagram of a local data acquisition system.

- Interconnection cables
- Software running on PC

Depending on the requirements of the application, accessory cards can be deleted from the list; otherwise, all other components are essential in a local PC based data acquisition system regardless of the size.

6.3 HOW TO CHOOSE THE APPROPRIATE DATA ACQUISITION CARD FOR YOUR APPLICATION

In order to select the appropriate cards for the system, it is necessary to look into the data acquisition system as a whole including the sensors and signal conditioners.

Special consideration should be given to the following.

The analog signals coming to the system

- Are they signal conditioned or raw output of the sensor?
- How many analog signals are coming?
- How fast should the signals be sampled?
- What is the frequency range of the signal (how fast are the signals changing)?
- Is isolation from the other channels required or not?

Signal conditioning the output of the sensors is a must in most cases. In some cases the signal may already come as signal conditioned. In such cases tackling the problem is relatively simple. One simply adjusts the gain of the A/D converter and connects the output of the signal conditioner to one of the input channels. But if the sensor output is not signal conditioned, an analog input card which accepts signal conditioner modules should be selected.

The number of input channels is also important because based on this we will decide whether we need multiplexers for expanding the system or not.

The speed of sampling, together with the number of channels will determine the speed of the A/D converter card that must be used in the system. For example, assume that we have a system with 64 input channels, and the channels should be sampled every 500 μ sec. According to this, $500 \times 10^{-6}/64 = 7.81 \times 10^{-6}$ sec. The frequency of sampling of the A/D converter card should be at least $1/7.81 \times 10^{-6} = 128,000$ Hz. So a card with a 150,000 Hz conversion rate or better should be selected for the system.

The frequency range of the signal indicates the speed of the signal. In general, signals with mainly DC components are easier to handle because they are slow changing stationary signals. Signals with AC components are fast changing signals and may require the use of filters and sample and hold circuits. According to Nyquist criteria the sampling speed should be at least twice the frequency of the input signal in order to get a healthy representation of the signal.

Isolation from the other signals is often a requirement in industrial systems to reduce interference and to protect the equipment from catastrophic events. In such cases, even if a catastrophic failure burns a channel and all the components connected to it, the other channels do not get affected because of the isolation.

For the **digital inputs**, the main considerations are

- Should the inputs be optically isolated or not?
- How many input channels are needed?
- What is the maximum frequency of sampling for these input signals?
- Are the input signals to be sensed TTL level or AC/ DC high level voltage signals?

In industrial applications most digital inputs to the system are required to be optically isolated. The reason behind this is exactly similar to the argument for having analog isolation. If a catastrophic incident were to take place, the damage should be limited only to the particular signal conditioner, but because of the optical isolation, the computer and the rest of the signal conditioners would not be affected.

For the **digital output signals**, main considerations include

- Is optical isolation needed or not?
- How many channels are needed?
- How fast is switch on needed for the output, i.e. should electromechanical relays or solid state relays be used?

All these concepts will be explored in more detail in the coming sections.

There are many factors to be considered before a data acquisition card is selected for an application. Among the most important factors to consider is the selection of the sampling rate and the resolution of the card.

6.3.1 Sampling Rates

Selection of the maximum conversion rate of the A/D converter card is a crucial decision for a succesful application. Proper selection generates a system with both optimum cost and performance. Generally speed requirement of most applications can be considered in one of the following three categories;

Slow applications: These applications require sampling rates between 1 to 10 Hz. They usually involve slow changing parameters like wheather data, slow temperature change, enviromental variables, etc. These types of applications benefit most from data acquisition cards with integrating type A/D converters. An integrating type A/D converter works slower with respect to other A/D converters, but it automatically cancels any high frequency noise in the system. Due to this no additional filtering is necessary if there is high frequency noise in the system. Non-integrating type A/D converter cards can also be used for slow data acquisition applications but filtering may be necessary. The filtering process will be elaborated more in the coming sections.

Fast applications: These applications require sampling rates around 1 Hz to 100 kHz. Most data acquisition applications can be considered in this category. Most commercially available cards can provide conversion rates up to 20 kHz. Pre-filtering of the signal is necessary with these types of cards.

Ultra-fast applications: These types of applications require conversion rates above 100 kHz. Nuclear reactions and flash photolyses are among the types of applications which require extremely high sampling rates. These types of applications require A/D converter cards equipped with flash type A/D converters. With ultra-fast applications, processing power and the memory requirements of the PC become the major bottlenecks of the system. Pre-filtering of the signal with a low pass filter is a must with this type of application.

6.3.2 Resolution

Resolution of the A/D converter card is also an important factor to consider in the selection process. Most A/D converters in the market offer resolutions around 10 to 12 bits. Cards with resolutions 16 to 20 bits are also available but cost significantly more than the 12 bit types. Ultra-fast A/D conversion cards with flash type A/D converters have lower resolutions than the other data acquisition cards. Although 8 bit is the most common resolution for flash A/D converters, 10 and 12 bits are also available at higher cost.

6.3.3 Range

Most data acquisition cards in the market accept signals in the range -10 V to +10 V. More capable data acquisition cards in the market let the user adjust the input range of the card through software. Ranges up to +/- 200 V and down to +/- 0.01 V can be selected through software.

6.3.4 Number of Channels

Another important consideration during the selection of the card is the number of channels for sampling. Most cards in the market offer at least 8 channels for sampling signals. But since the channels are multiplexed, more channels means a lower sampling rate. As an example, if a data acquisition card has a conversion rate of 100 kHz and has 8 channels and if all 8 channels need to be utilized, the conversion rate goes down to 100 kHz/8 = 12,500 Hz. Actually the individual sampling rate should be expected to be even less than 12,500 Hz due to the time lost during switching from one channel to the other.

6.4 HOW TO DETERMINE THE SAMPLING RATE FOR YOUR APPLICATION

Sampling rate of the application and the cut-off frequency of the filters are two of the most important parameters that one is supposed to figure out for a successful application. These two parameters are somewhat related to each other and very much affected by the noise in the system. For this reason all these concepts will be discussed together in this section.

Noise is generally described as any signal that interferes with the signal of interest. The sources of noise are either another interfering signal, drift noise or device noise. Drift noise refers to the changing characteristics of an electronic device due to the aging of components. Device noise is due to the random behavior of individual charge carrying electrons. These two types of noise, device and drift noise, are not a major concern to our applications. The type of noise that concerns us most is the noise which is due to other interfering signals.

In any given instant there are many active signals around the application. Although we are interested in measuring signals specific to our application, the other active signals interfere with the signal of interest and distort the signal. The most common interfering signal is due to the power lines and generated by electrical machinery drawing a large amount of current.

6.4.1 How to Seperate Noise From Primary Signal

In order to decide the sampling rate of the signal and the cutoff frequency of the filters to use, first you have to identify and separate the noise from the primary signal.

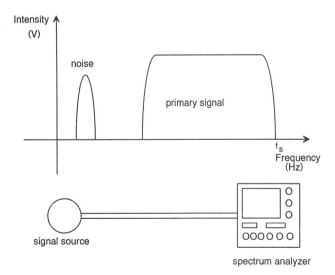

Figure 6.2 Spectrum analyzer screen displaying both primary signal and the noise.

The two variables that identify the noise signal is the amplitude, which represents the energy of the noise, and the frequency distribution of noise which identifies where in the frequency spectrum it is located.

In order to identify the noise signal an oscilloscope or a spectrum analyzer is necessary. A spectrum analyzer is an instrument which displays all the signals on the frequency domain. Once a spectrum analyzer is available, simply by looking at the display with the primary signal active and the primary signal disconnected, the amplitude and the frequency range of the noise signal can be determined very easily. Since in both cases the noise signal is available and the changes on the screen is due to the primary signal alone, the noise can be identified easily. Figures 6.2 and 6.3 indicate the spectrum analyzer screen with and without the primary signal.

Since a spectrum analyzer is an expensive equipment, it may not be available commonly. An oscilloscope, although not as usefull as a spectrum analyzer, can provide help for distinguishing noise signal from the primary signal. If the signal and the noise frequency are far apart, the primary signal appears superimposed over the noise signal and can be distinguished from the oscilloscope screen. Figure 6.4 indicates a primary signal superimposed with high frequency noise.

Yet another technique to distinguish noise from primary signal is to use a high speed data acquisition card and sample the signal as fast as possible. By using software, one can take the fast fourier transform of the signal to generate the spectrum analyzer screen on the computer. Once the fourier transform of the data is displayed, noise and the frequency content of the signal can be determined as described for the spectrum analyzer. Depending on the outcome, a more optimal data acquisition card can be utilized for sampling the data.

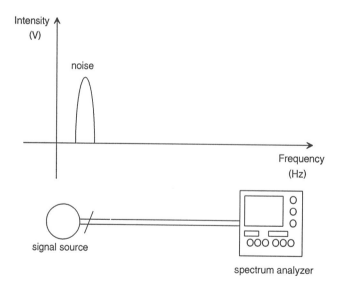

Figure 6.3 Spectrum analyzer screen after the primary signal is disconnected. Difference from the previous figure indicates the noise signal.

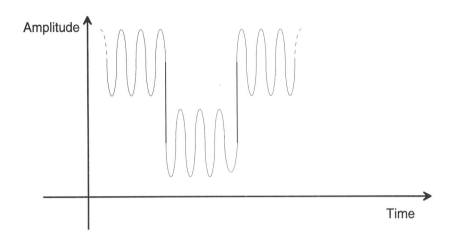

Figure 6.4 A low frequency square wave superimosed by a high frequency sinusoidal noise appears this way on an oscilloscope screen.

6.4.2 How to Decide the Appropriate Sampling Rate

Since spectrum analyzer also displays the highest frequency of the signal conveniently (marked f_s in Figure 6.2), the appropriate sampling frequency can be distinguished easily.

Theoretically, if the primary signal has the highest frequency component f_s, the signal can be properly represented if it is sampled at twice the frequency. The famous Nyquist theorem states that if the sampling rate for a signal which has highest frequency f_s should be sampled at least at $2f_s$ sampling frequency. But practically speaking, $2f_s$ is too low as sampling frequency. As a good engineering practice it is recommended that the signal is sampled at 10 times the highest frequency component. According to this, the signal should be sampled at $10f_s$ rate.

As a practical example, suppose a 1 kHz signal needs to be acquired by a PC. It is recommended that a data acquisition card with at least 10 kHz sampling rate is to be used for sampling this signal. If the data acquisition card has multiple channels, this should be taken into consideration since multiplexing channels reduces the effective sampling rate. A data acquisition card with 10 channels and 100 kHz sampling rate, effectively samples each channel around 10 kHz.

6.4.3 How to Decide the Resolution Requirement of Your Data Acquisition System

The resolution of the data acquisition system is expressed in terms of bit size of the A/D converter. An A/D converter with 10V input range and 12 bit resoution has the ability to detect $10/2^{12} = 2$ mV signals. The resolution requirement of the data acquisition system is usually dictated by the application. The noise in the system also effectively determines the maximum resolution of the system. For the above system which has 2 mV resolution, if the noise amplitude is 5 mV, the user will gain no benefit of 12 bit resolution since the least significant two bits will be corrupted by noise anyway.

The parameter which indicates the ratio of signal intensity to noise intensity is known as **signal-to-noise ratio** (SNR). SNR is defined as the ratio of signal power (P_S) to noise power (P_N). The formula for SNR is

$$SNR = 10 \log \frac{V_S}{V_N} \text{ (db)}$$

After several iterations power is expressed in terms of voltage levels where V_S and V_N are signal and noise amplitudes respectively.

As indicated by the formula, in order to measure the SNR, amplitude of the noise signal and the primary signal amplitude has to be measured. Easiest way to measure the noise amplitude is to use an oscilloscope in case noise frequency and the signal frequency are seperated enough . By adjusting the timebase of the oscilloscope to noise frequency, the noise amplitude can be measured roughly. With the same procedure the primary signal amplitude can also be measured.

6.5 HOW TO CONNECT THE SIGNAL TO YOUR DATA ACQUISITION HARDWARE

Connecting the signal to your data acquisition hardware may seem like a simple operation; however, the way connection is made has substantial effect on the overall performance of the system. As it is reviewed in the previous sections, noise has an important effect on the performance of the system. The distance between the source of the signal and the data acquisition hardware is the part where the signal is most vulnerable to external noise. In this section proper methods for connecting the signal to the data acquisition hardware will be reviewed.

6.5.1 How to Select the Cable for Connection

There are several different types of cables that can be used for transmitting signal from the source of the signal to the data acquisition hardware. Regardless of the type of cable used, it is recommended that the cable is kept as short as possible. The types of wires that can be used for transmitting small signals are as follows:

Twisted pair wire: This is the most inexpesive type of wire that can be used for transmitting differential signals. (It is recommended that small signals are always transmitted in differential form. More on this subject will be given in the coming sections.) Even millivolt level signals can be transmitted with this type of cable. A more recommended version of this type is the **shielded twisted pair wire** which has better noise rejection capability. The shield of the cable should be grounded only from one side. (More on this subject in the coming sections.)

Coaxial cable: Coaxial or triaxial cables are more expensive than twisted pair wires but their noise performance is superior. Triaxial cable is similar to regular coaxial with the difference of having a pair of wires in the core rather than a single wire core. This type of cable is ideal for transferring differrential type signals.

Ribbon or single cable: These types of wires do not offer much noise protection but they can be used with large signals of several volts in most cases. They are usable only with large signal levels with low frequencies.

6.5.2 Practices for Reducing External Noise

Other than using the proper cable for connection, there are some common practices that one can use for reducing the effects of the external noise. External noise can be either due to an electrical field or magnetic field. The noise which is due to electrical fields is generated by inducing currents on the electrical conductors of our circuit. A grounded wire mesh placed over the circuit effectively kills the electrical field and reduces the noise effect. This technique is commonly known as Faraday cup and very effective for the noise due to electrical fields.

The noise which is due to magnetic fields is generated by inducing voltage over the conducters of our circuit. Getting rid of noise due to magnetic fields is more troublesome than that of the electrical field since it requires physically isolating equipment from the magnetic field generating the noise.

Regardless of the source of noise, shielding is an effective way of reducing the noise coupled on data acquisition equipment. Shielding is done by connecting the outer conducter of the cable carrying signal to the ground. By doing this, the noise is induced in the outer shield of the wire connecting signal source to the data acquisition equipment and the signal carrying wire is not affected. One important point to keep in mind is that the shield has to be connected to ground only from one side of the connecting wire, preferably from the side of the signal source. This concept is illustrated in Figure 6.5.

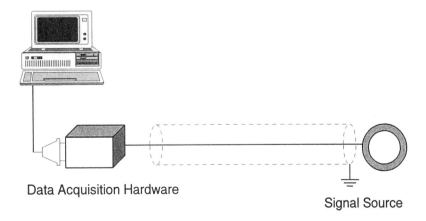

Data Acquisition Hardware

Signal Source

Figure 6.5 The wire connecting the signal source is shielded and the shield is grounded at one side.

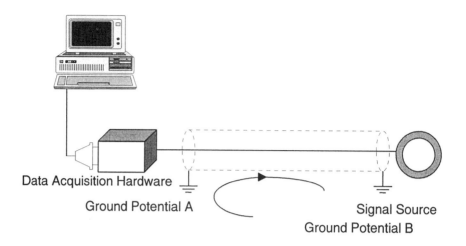

Figure 6.6 Connecting shield wire from two different points generates a ground loop which increases the noise effects.

It is important that the shield wire is connected to ground only from one side. Connecting the shield to the ground from both sides has a debilitating effect on noise. This practice actually increases the noise effects on the signal wire rather than reducing it. The reason behind this can be explained as follows. The ground potential at different locations may differ slightly due to the heavy electrical machinery connected around the particular spot. Since shield wire acts as a short circuit, heavy current flows over the shield wire from the signal source side to the the data acquisition hardware side. (Figure 6.6) This heavy current induces noise on the signal carrying wire. For this reason it should be kept in mind that the shield is to be connected to the ground only from one side.

6.5.3 Using Filters for Reducing Noise and Enhancing Signal Reading

The previous sections introduced preventive techniques for reducing noise effects on data acquisition hardware. If there is still noise in the system after all these precautions, the only way to reduce it is to use filters. Filters are not only used for reducing noise effects but also increase the quality of data acquisition by cleaning out unwanted components of the primary signal.

In this section we are going to look at different types of filters available and see which one is more suitable for which circumstance.

Filters are available as hardware and software filters. Furthermore hardware filters can be either analog or digital type. Software filters can also be analog or digital. Regardless whether analog, digital, hardware or software, filters are grouped according to their frequency response characteristics. According to this, a filter can be either

- Low pass

- High pass
- Band pass
- Band stop type

Cut-off frequency of a filter indicates the frequency at which the filtering action takes place. A low pass filter passes all frequencies below the specified cut-off frequency. A high pass filter passes all the frequencies above the cut-off frequency. Band pass filters pass all the frequencies between the start frequency and the stop frequency. Band stop filters kill all frequencies between the start frequency and the stop frequency.

The most common types of filters are as follows:

Analog filter: This type of filter is made up of capacitors and inductors. Active analog filters made up of operational amplifiers have sharper roll-off and in general better characteristics. This is the most common type of filter used for data acquisition purposes.

Digital filter: This type of filter can be realized either in hardware or in software. When realized in software form, it has excellent characteristics. However, since it is computationally intensive, it takes considerable CPU time. Digital hardware filters can also be realized in switched capacitor filter form which does not require CPU time from the PC.

As a rule of thumb, all signals should be filtered before they are connected to the data acquisition hardware. Some sensors generate not only the primary signal but also high frequency harmonics of the primary signal, which debilitates the data acquisition process. Observing the Nyquist criteria, the signal should be filtered using a filter which has cut-off frequency twice as high as the highest frequency content of the primary signal.

It is very important to know what kind of data acquisition cards, signal conditioners and filters are available in the market. For this reason, the reader is strongly urged to study the catalogs of major data acquisition hardware manufacturers to get familiar with the available components.

The table on the following page gives a listing of a brief selection of Keithley Instruments data acquisition hardware. The hardware will be referred to in the case studies given in the next section.

ANALOG & DIGITAL I/O BOARDS AND ANALOG OUTPUT BOARDS

		ANALOG INPUTS					ANALOG OUTPUTS		DIGITAL I/O			
BOARD	COMPUTER	NO. CHANNELS	BITS	MAX SAMPLE (S/S) RATE	INPUT RANGE (VOLTS)	RANGE SELECTION	CHANNELS	RESOLUTION	INPUTS/ OUTPUTS	PACER CLOCK	COUNTER/ TIMERS	PAGE
12-BIT RESOLUTION												
DAS-58	PC/XT/AT	8 SE	12	1 M	±10, ±5, ±2.5 +10, +5	Software	—	—	—	Y	0	55
DAS-50	PC/XT/AT	4 SE	12	1 M	±10, ±5, ±2.5 +10, +5	Software	—	—	—	Y	0	59
DAS-40G1	AT Only	16 SE/ 8 Diff	12	100 K	±10, ±5, ±2.5, ±1.25, ±0.625 +10, +5, +2.5, +1.25 V	Software	2	12	8 in, 8 out	Y	0	66
DAS-40G2	AT Only	16 SE/ 8 Diff	12	250 K	±10, ±1, ±0.1, ±0.02 +10, +1, +0.1, +0.02 V	Software	2	12	8 in, 8 out	Y	0	66
DAS-20	PC/XT/AT	16 SE/ 8 Diff	12	100 K	±10, ±5, ±0.5, ±0.05 +10, +1, +0.1 ±0.1 V	Software	2	12	8 in, 8 out	Y	2	70
DAS-1601	PC/XT/AT	16 SE/ 8 Diff	12	100 K	±10, ±1, ±0.1, ±0.02 +10, +1. +0.1, +0.02 V	Software	2	12	32	Y	1	74
DAS-1602	PC/XT/AT	16 SE/ 8 Diff	12	100 K	±10, ±5, ±2.5, ±1.25 +10, +5, +2.5, +1.25 V	Software	2	12	32	Y	1	74
DAS-1401	PC/XT/AT	16 SE/ 8 Diff	12	100 K	±10, ±1, ±0.1, ±0.02 +10, +1. +0.1, +0.02 V	Software	—	—	4 in, 4 out	Y	1	79
DAS-1402	PC/XT/AT	16 SE/ 8 Diff	12	100 K	±10, ±5, ±2.5, ±1.25 +10, +5, +2.5, +1.25 V	Software	—	—	4 in, 4 out	Y	1	79
DAS-16G1	PC/XT/AT	16 SE/ 8 Diff	12	70 K	±10, ±1, ±0.1, ±0.02 +10, +1. +0.1, +0.02 V	Software	2	12	4 in, 4 out	Y	1	83
DAS-16G2	PC/XT/AT	16 SE/ 8 Diff	12	70 K	±10, ±5, ±2.5, ±1.25 +10, +5, +2.5, +1.25 V	Software	2	12	4 in, 4 out	Y	1	83
DAS-16F	PC/XT/AT	16 SE/ 8 Diff	12	100 K	±10, ±5, ±2.5, ±1.25 +10, +5, +2.5, +1.25 V	Switches	2	12	4 in, 4 out	Y	1	83
DAS-16	PC/XT/AT	8 SE	12	50 K	±10, ±5, ±2.5, ±1.25 +10, +5, +2.5, +1.25 V	Switches	2	12	4 in, 4 out	Y	1	83
DAS-8	PC/XT/AT	16 SE/ 8 Diff	12	4 K	±5	Fixed	—	—	3 in, 4 out	N	3	90
DAS-8/A0	PC/XT/AT	8 Diff or SE	12	4 K	±10, ±5, ±0.5, ±0.05, ±0.01 +10, +1, +0.1, +0.02 V	Software	2	12	3 in, 4 out	Y	3	90
DAS-8PGA	PC/XT/AT	8 Diff or SE	12	4 K	±10, ±5, ±0.5, ±0.05, ±0.01 +10, +1, +0.1, +0.02	Software	—	—	3 in, 4 out	Y	3	90
DAS-8PGA/G2	PC/XT/AT	8 Diff or SE	12	4 K	±5, ±2.5, ±1.25, ±0.625 +5, +2.5, +1.25, +0.625	Software	—	—	3 in, 4 out	Y	3	90
DAS-8 LT	PC/XT/AT	8 SE	12	4 K	±5	Fixed	—	—	3 in, 4 out	Y	3	90
DAS-4	PC/XT/AT	8 SE	8	SW Limited	±5	Fixed	—	—	3 in, 4 out	N	0	97
μCDAS-16G	Micro Channel	16 SE/8 Diff	12	70 K	±10, ±1, ±0.1, ±0.02 +10, +1, +0.1, +0.02 V	Software	2	12	4 in, 4 out	Y	1	138
μCDAS-8PGA	Micro Channel	8 Diff	12	4 K	±10, ±5, ±0.5, ±0.05 ±0.01, +10, +1, +0.1, +0.02 V	Software	—	—	3 in, 4 out	Y	3	141
HIGH RESOLUTION												
DAS-HRES	PC/XT/AT	8 Diff	16	47.6 K	±10, ±5, ±2.5, ±1.25 +10, +5, +2.5, +1.25 V	Software	2	16	8 in, 8 out	Y	1	63
ADC-16	PC/XT/AT	8 Diff	16	16	±5, ±0.5, ±0.05 ±3.27, ±0.327, ±0.0327	Software	—	—	2 in, 5 out	Y	0	87
PCIP-DMM	PC/XT/AT	1	15	2.5	±200, ±20, ±2, ±0.2	Software	—	—		N	0	222
CHROM-1AT	PC/XT/AT	2 SE	14	350	+10, +5, +2, +1	Software	—	—	4 in, 4 out	N	0	104
DASCON-1	PC/XT	4 Diff	13	30	±2.047	Switches	2	12	12 I/O	N	0	94
SPECIAL PURPOSE												
PCIP-SCOPE	PC/XT/AT	2 Diff	8	20 M	±20, to ±0.02 in 10 ranges	Software	—	—		Y	0	226
DAS-TEMP	PC/XT/AT	32	0.1°	200	−25 to +105°C	Software	—	—	—	N	0	99
AT-CODAS	AT Only	16 SE/8 Diff	12	50 K	±5, ±2.5, ±1, ±0.5	Software	1	12	8 in, 8 out	Y	0	101
ANALOG OUTPUT												
DAC-02	PC/XT/AT	—	—	—	—	—	2	12	0	N	—	109
DDA-06	PC/XT/AT	—	—	—	—	—	6	12	24	N	—	106
μCDDA-04	Micro Channel	—	—	—	—	—	4	12	24	N	—	143
PCIP-AWFG	PC/XT/AT	—	—	—	—	—	1/2	12	4/8	Y	—	228
PCIP-CAL	PC/XT/AT	—	—	—	—	—	1	15	0	N	—	236

6.6 CASE STUDY OF A DATA ACQUISITION SYSTEM DESIGN

The XYZ company is a multi-million dollar petrochemical giant which produces oil based products. Like all processing industries it uses literally thousands of sensors for monitoring the state of the process. Recently they have encountered a problem in one of the chemical processes which was causing the reduction of the output quality of one of the manufactured chemicals. For some unknown reason, the output quality drops drastically even though the input parameters are not changed. They could sense the loss of the quality immediately, but even after detecting the quality loss, correcting the problem and increasing the quality was very slow. This was causing an overall reduction of the factory output. What they needed was a way to detect the sequence of events that was leading to the loss of quality so that the nature of the problem would be understood and the process control program could be corrected accordingly.

Although the problem of getting the historical data seemed like a simple one, they have quickly realized that the problem is bigger than they had thought because of the following reasons:

- The loss of quality seems to happen erratically at different times without giving any warning. Because of this, it is not possible to monitor the events leading to the phenomenon continuously 24 hours a day. The phenomenon is not repetitive so that it can be repeated and monitored.

- Once the phenomenon starts, it is necessary to look into at least 2 minutes of previous historical data to understand what is causing it.

- Although the process uses thousands of sensors, there are about 300 sensor outputs which are more likely to give a hint to the nature of the phenomenon. All these 300 outputs should be monitored continuously.

- The factory has its own process control computer, but that computer should not be used taking the above actions since this may cause the other processes to be disrupted. The actions and monitoring should be done independent of the main controller without disturbing any process parameters at any time.

The XYZ company engineers, in consultation with data acquisition engineers decided to use a PC based data acquisition system for monitoring the process parameters. The resultant system is a modified version of a common data logger. Although there are off-the-shelf data loggers available on the market, none of them has the capability for monitoring 300 inputs for a 2 minute duration. Since all signal outputs are already available in the control room, a PC placed in the control room and configured for local data acquisition seemed like the logical choice. Technical specifications of the data logger are as follows.

SPECIFICATION SHEET FOR DATA LOGGING EQUIPMENT FOR UTILITIES

General Description

The intent of this data logging device will be to capture the sequence of operation of approximately 300 inputs as shown on the readout on pages 196–202. The logging action will take place when a status change of any one of ten event triggers, noted on the readout, is detected. In addition to capturing the sequenced data that follows the event trigger, the device will also retain, in memory or on another data storage device such as a hard disk, two (2) minutes of historical data, for all monitored points, which preceded the event trigger to show the sequence of events which led to the event trigger itself.

All data, both preceding and following the event trigger, will be (1) printed out for immediate use and (2) captured internally in an MSDOS compatible format for later use. The printer should continue to print all data following an event trigger until the data logger is reset manually; however, the requirement for internal storage is limited to two (2) minutes preceding and one (1) minute following the event trigger since internal storage capacity may be limited.

The device will be mounted in an air-conditioned building and will operate in an unattended mode. It will require that signal cables from all input sources be terminated at this central location.

Paper storage for the printer shall be adequate for 1 hour of continuous logging for all monitored points and the print mechanism itself shall be of a design not requiring significant routine maintenance and which can be depended on to function properly when needed, typically after being in a standby or inactive mode for weeks or months of time.

Unit should routinely print the current date and time, at an interval to be determined by user, to indicate that it is functioning properly.

Inputs

Unit must be capable of providing millisecond resolution for up to 200 analog and 100 digital signal inputs. Approximately 1/3 would require 0.001 second resolution, 113 would require 0.1 second resolution, and 113 would require 1.0 second resolution. Analog input requirements are 4-20 mA DC and 1-5 volts DC, isolated. Digital inputs will be isolated, dry contacts. Unit should be capable of supplying necessary operating voltage to these dry contacts. The unit will provide arrangements for termination and labeling of all input wiring in a secure and easy manner.

The unit is normally expected to run in a "monitoring" mode during which it will be sampling the data. It must, at the same time, monitor up to ten (10) separate event triggers, any one of which will cause the unit to switch into the "capture" mode of operation, when it will be expected to retain at least 120 seconds of historical data for all inputs prior to the event and at least 60 seconds of subsequent data for all inputs following the event.

Output

As a minimum, the unit shall have the capability of producing a hardcopy listing of the captured information. This list will identify the time, tag number and description of the specific event trigger as well as all activities preceding and following the event trigger for the same time periods as indicated above. This printout should be initiated automatically at the time or the event. Ideally the captured data would be retained for reprinting on demand later.

Alternative, or addition, would be for the system to store the same information noted above internally, formatted either as an ASCII or a delimited LOTUS file, for later use on an IBM PC, or compatible, computer.

Power Requirements

Primary power should be 115 VAC, 60 Hertz. Unit must be capable of operating for at least a one (1) hour period during a power failure. While this ability could be an internal function of the unit itself, it could also be an external UPS system designed specifically for the data logging units requirements.

UTILITY DATALOGGER INPUTS
(SORTED BY REQUIRED RESOLUTION)

TAG	UNITS	DESC	REQ. RESOLUT (SECS)	EXIST. RESOLUT (SECS)	ON PMX	EVNT TRIG?
NEW		% POWER DIP FEEDER B	0.001		N	
NEW		DURATION OF POWER DIP FDR B	0.001		N	
NEW		% POWER DIP FEEDER A	0.001		N	
NEW		DURATION OF POWER DIP FDR A	0.001		N	
EA4511A	DIGITAL		0.001	60	Y	
EA4511B	DIGITAL		0.001	60	Y	
EA490101	AMP	42G1 FEEDER	0.001	5	Y	
EA490102	AMP	42G2 FEEDER	0.001	5	Y	
EA490103	AMP	42G3 FEEDER	0.001	5	Y	
EA490118	AMP	45-49SS TIE FEEDER	0.001	—	N	
EA49G1	AMP	42G1 EXCITATION FIELD	0.001	5	Y	
EA49G2	AMP	42G2 EXCITATION FIELD	0.001	5	Y	
EA49G3	AMP	42G3 EXCITATION FIELD	0.001	5	Y	
EB450101	DIGITAL		0.001	4	Y	
EB450102	DIGITAL		0.001	4	Y	
EB450103	DIGITAL		0.001	4	Y	
EB450104	DIGITAL		0.001	4	Y	
EB450111	DIGITAL		0.001	4	Y	
EB450201	DIGITAL		0.001	4	Y	
EB450202	DIGITAL		0.001	4	Y	
EB450203	DIGITAL		0.001	4	Y	
EB450204	DIGITAL		0.001	4	Y	
EB450301	DIGITAL		0.001	4	Y	
EB450302	DIGITAL		0.001	4	Y	
EB450401	DIGITAL		0.001	4	Y	
EB450402	DIGITAL		0.001	4	Y	
EB450501	DIGITAL		0.001	4	Y	
EB450502	DIGITAL		0.001	4	Y	
EB451101	DIGITAL		0.001	4	Y	
EB451102	DIGITAL		0.001	4	Y	
EB451103	DIGITAL		0.001	4	Y	
EB451104	DIGITAL		0.001	4	Y	
EB451105	DIGITAL		0.001	4	Y	
EB451106	DIGITAL		0.001	4	Y	
EB490101	DIGITAL	G1 BREAKER	0.001	4	Y	YES
EB490102	DIGITAL	G2 BREAKER	0.001	4	Y	YES
EB490103	DIGITAL	G3 BREAKER	0.001	4	Y	YES
EB490104	DIGITAL		0.001	4	Y	

UTILITY DATALOGGER INPUTS
(SORTED BY REQUIRED RESOLUTION)

TAG	UNITS	DESC	REQ. RESOLUT (SECS)	EXIST. RESOLUT (SECS)	ON PMX	EVNT TRIG?
EB490105	DIGITAL		0.001	4	Y	
EB490118	DIGITAL	BREAKER 18	0.001	4	Y	YES
EB560101	DIGITAL	SG1501 BUS A FEEDER	0.001	4	Y	
EB560102	DIGITAL	SG1501 BUS B FEEDER	0.001	4	Y	
EB560103	DIGITAL	SG1501 BUS A/B TIE	0.001	4	Y	
EB560104	DIGITAL	SG1501 BUS B/C TIE	0.001	4	Y	
EF4511A	HZ	45SG2701 BUS A1	0.001	60	Y	
EF4511B	HZ	45SG2701 BUS B1	0.001	60	Y	
EF490101	HZ	42G1 FEEDER	0.001	5	Y	
EF490102	HZ	42G2 FEEDER	0.001	5	Y	
EF490103	HZ	42G3 FEEDER	0.001	5	Y	
EP490101	PF	42G1 FEEDER	0.001	5	Y	
EP490102	PF	42G2 FEEDER	0.001	5	Y	
EP490103	PF	42G3 FEEDER	0.001	5	Y	
ER490101	MVAR	42G1 FEEDER	0.001	5	Y	
ER490102	MVAR	42G2 FEEDER	0.001	5	Y	
ER490103	MVAR	42G3 FEEDER	0.001	5	Y	
ER490118	MVAR	45-49SS TIE FEEDER	0.001	60	Y	
EV4511A	DIGITAL		0.001	60	Y	
EV4511B	DIGITAL		0.001	60	Y	
EV490101	KV	42G1 FEEDER	0.001	5	Y	
EV490102	KV	42G2 FEEDER	0.001	5	Y	
EV490103	KV	42G3 FEEDER	0.001	5	Y	
EV490118	KV	45-49SS TIE FEEDER	0.001	60	Y	
EV49G1	V	42G1 EXCITATION FIELD	0.001	5	Y	
EV49G2	V	42G2 EXCITATION FIELD	0.001	5	Y	
EV49G3	V	42G3 EXCITATION FIELD	0.001	5	Y	
EW490101	MW	42G1 FEEDER	0.001	5	Y	
EW490102	MW	42G2 FEEDER	0.001	5	Y	
EW490103	MW	42G3 FEEDER	0.001	5	Y	
EW490118	MW	45-49SS TIE FEEDER	0.001	60	Y	
G1DA4304	DIGITAL	G1-T/T VALVE CLOSED	0.05	?	Y	YES
G2DA4429	DIGITAL	G2-T/T VALVE CLOSED	0.05	?	Y	YES
G3DA4554	DIGITAL	G3-T/T VALVE CLOSED	0.05	?	Y	YES
	DIGITAL	G2 MANUAL TRIP - LOCAL	0.1		N	
	DIGITAL	G1 MANUAL TRIP - CONT. RM.	0.1		N	
	DIGITAL	G3 MANUAL TRIP - CONT. RM.	0.1		N	
	DIGITAL	G2 MANUAL TRIP - CONT. RM.	0.1		N	

UTILITY DATALOGGER INPUTS
(SORTED BY REQUIRED RESOLUTION)

TAG	UNITS	DESC	REQ. RESOLUT (SECS)	EXIST. RESOLUT (SECS)	ON PMX	EVNT TRIG?
	DIGITAL	G3 MANUAL TRIP – LOCAL	0.1		N	
	DIGITAL	G1 MANUAL TRIP – LOCAL	0.1		N	
G1DA1501	DIGITAL	G1 COMMON TROUBLE ALARM	0.1		Y	
G1SH4279	DIGITAL	G1 HI SPEED ALARM	0.1		Y	
G1SI4272	RPM	G1 SPEED	0.1	5	Y	
G1XA4285	DIGITAL	G1 GOV. SYS. TURB. TRIP	0.1		Y	
G1XA4360	DIGITAL	G1 AXIAL VIB SHUTDOWN	0.1		Y	
G1XH4358	DIGITAL	G1 HI AXIAL VIB ALARM	0.1		Y	
G1XH4360	DIGITAL	G1 VIB ALARM	0.1		Y	
G1XI4358	MICRON	G1 PRIM AXIAL DISPLACEMENT	0.1		Y	
G1XI4359	MICRON	G1 SEC AXIAL DISPLACEMENT	0.1		Y	
G1XI4360	MICRON	G1 BRG1 RAD VIB TURB OB	0.1		Y	
G1XI4361	MICRON	G1 BRG1 RAD VIB TURB OB	0.1		Y	
G1XI4362	MICRON	G1 BRG3 RAD VIB TURB IB	0.1		Y	
G1XI4363	MICRON	G1 BRG3 RAD VIB TURB IB	0.1		Y	
G1XI4364	MICRON	G1 BRG4 RAD VIB GEN IB	0.1		Y	
G1XI4365	MICRON	G1 BRG4 RAD VIB GEN IB	0.1		Y	
G1XI4366	MICRON	G1 BRG5 RAD VIB GEN OB	0.1		Y	
G1XI4367	MICRON	G1 BRG5 RAD VIB GEN OB	0.1		Y	
G2DA1509	DIGITAL	G2 COMMON TROUBLE ALARM	0.1		Y	
G2SH4404	DIGITAL	G2 HI SPEED ALARM	0.1		Y	
G2SI4397	RPM	G2 SPEED	0.1	5	Y	
G2XA4410	DIGITAL	G2 GOV. SYS. TURB. TRIP	0.1		Y	
G2XA4485	DIGITAL	G2 AXIAL VIB SHUTDOWN	0.1		Y	
G2XH4483	DIGITAL	G2 HI AXIAL VIB ALARM	0.1		Y	
G2XH4485	DIGITAL	G2 VIB ALARM	0.1		Y	
G2XI4483	MICRON	G2 PRIM AXIAL DISPLACEMENT	0.1		Y	
G2XI4484	MICRON	G2 SEC AXIAL DISPLACEMENT	0.1		Y	
G2XI4485	MICRON	G2 BRG1 RAD VIB TURB OB	0.1		Y	
G2XI4486	MICRON	G2 BRG1 RAD VIB TURB OB	0.1		Y	
G2XI4487	MICRON	G2 BRG3 RAD VIB TURB IB	0.1		Y	
G2XI4488	MICRON	G2 BRG3 RAD VIB TURB IB	0.1		Y	
G2XI4489	MICRON	G2 BRG4 RAD VIB GEN IB	0.1		Y	
G2XI4490	MICRON	G2 BRG4 RAD VIB GEN IB	0.1		Y	
G2XI4491	MICRON	G2 BRG5 RAD VIB GEN OB	0.1		Y	
G2XI4492	MICRON	G2 BRG5 RAD VIB GEN OB	0.1		Y	
G3DA1517	DIGITAL	G3 COMMON TROUBLE ALARM	0.1		Y	
G3SH4529	DIGITAL	G3 HI SPEED ALARM	0.1		Y	

		UTILITY DATALOGGER INPUTS (SORTED BY REQUIRED RESOLUTION)				
TAG	UNITS	DESC	REQ. RESOLUT (SECS)	EXIST. RESOLUT (SECS)	ON PMX	EVNT TRIG?
G3SI4522	RPM	G3 SPEED	0.1	5	Y	
G3XA4535	DIGITAL	G3 GOV. SYS. TURB. TRIP	0.1		Y	
G3XA4610	DIGITAL	G3 AXIAL VIB SHUTDOWN	0.1		Y	
G3XH4608	DIGITAL	G3 HI AXIAL VIB ALARM	0.1		Y	
G3XH4610	DIGITAL	G3 VIB ALARM	0.1		Y	
G3XI4608	MICRON	G3 PRIM AXIAL DISPLACEMENT	0.1		Y	
G3XI4609	MICRON	G3 SEC AXIAL DISPLACEMENT	0.1		Y	
G3XI4610	MICRON	G3 BRG1 RAD VIB TURB OB	0.1		Y	
G3XI4611	MICRON	G3 BRG1 RAD VIB TURB OB	0.1		Y	
G3XI4612	MICRON	G3 BRG3 RAD VIB TURB IB	0.1		Y	
G3XI4613	MICRON	G3 BRG3 RAD VIB TURB IB	0.1		Y	
G3XI4614	MICRON	G3 BRG4 RAD VIB GEN IB	0.1		Y	
G3XI4615	MICRON	G3 BRG4 RAD VIB GEN IB	0.1		Y	
G3XI4616	MICRON	G3 BRG5 RAD VIB GEN OB	0.1		Y	
G3XI4617	MICRON	G3 BRG5 RAD VIB GEN OB	0.1		Y	
LALL4299	DIGITAL	G1 ACCUMULATOR TANK LO LVL	0.1		N	
LALL4424	DIGITAL	G2 ACCUMULATOR TANK LO LVL	0.1		N	
LALL4549	DIGITAL	G3 ACCUMULATOR TANK LO LVL	0.1		N	
PALL4290	DIGITAL	G1 LOW LUBE OIL HDR PRESS	0.1		N	
PALL4308	DIGITAL	G1 LOW RADIAL BRG OIL PRESS	0.1		N	
PALL4415	DIGITAL	G2 LOW LUBE OIL HDR PRESS	0.1		N	
PALL4433	DIGITAL	G2 LOW RADIAL BRG OIL PRESS	0.1		N	
PALL4540	DIGITAL	G3 LOW LUBE OIL HDR PRESS	0.1		N	
PALL4558	DIGITAL	G3 LOW RADIAL BRG OIL PRESS	0.1		N	
XA1502	DIGITAL	G1 MANUAL TRIP	0.1		N	
XA1510	DIGITAL	G2 MANUAL TRIP	0.1		N	
XA1518	DIGITAL	G3 MANUAL TRIP	0.1		N	
XA4285	DIGITAL	G1 WOODWARD GOV TRIP	0.1		N	
XA4410	DIGITAL	G2 WOODWARD GOV TRIP	0.1		N	
XA4535	DIGITAL	G3 WOODWARD GOV TRIP	0.1		N	
XA4654	DIGITAL	G1 BREAKER PROT TRIP	0.1		N	
XA4655	DIGITAL	G2 BREAKER PROT TRIP	0.1		N	
XA4656	DIGITAL	G3 BREAKER PROT TRIP	0.1		N	
XAHH4358	DIGITAL	G1 TURB AXIAL DISP	0.1		N	
XAHH4483	DIGITAL	G2 TURB AXIAL DISP	0.1		N	
XAHH4608	DIGITAL	G3 TURB AXIAL DISP	0.1		N	
ZAH4661	DIGITAL	G1 MECHANICAL OVERSPEED	0.1		N	
ZAH4662	DIGITAL	G2 MECHANICAL OVERSPEED	0.1		N	

UTILITY DATALOGGER INPUTS
(SORTED BY REQUIRED RESOLUTION)

TAG	UNITS	DESC	REQ. RESOLUT (SECS)	EXIST. RESOLUT (SECS)	ON PMX	EVNT TRIG?
ZAH4663	DIGITAL	G3 MECHANICAL OVERSPEED	0.1		N	
	KPA	G3 LUBE OIL PRESSURE	1		N	
	KPA	G1 CONTROL OIL PRESSURE	1		N	
	KPA	G2 LUBE OIL PRESSURE	1		N	
	KPA	G1 LUBE OIL PRESSURE	1		N	
	KPA	G2 CONTROL OIL PRESSURE	1		N	
	DIGITAL	G2 OIL FILTER DIFF. HIGH	1		N	
	KPA	G3 CONTROL OIL PRESSURE	1		N	
	DIGITAL	G1 ACCUMULATOR LEVEL	1		N	
	DIGITAL	G1 OIL FILTER DIFF. HIGH	1		N	
	DIGITAL	G2 ACCUMULATOR LEVEL	1		N	
	DIGITAL	G3 ACCUMULATOR LEVEL	1		N	
	DIGITAL	G3 OIL FILTER DIFF. HIGH	1		N	
ARPC1013	KPA	RCVR1	1	5	Y	
ARPC1078	KPA	AIR FROM RCVR2	1	60	Y	
G1PI4290	KPA	G1-LUB OIL PRESSURE	1	5	Y	
G1TI4324	°C	G1 THRUST BRG1 TEMP	1		Y	
G1TI4325	°C	G1 THRUST BRG1 TEMP	1		Y	
G1TI4326	°C	G1 THRUST BRG1 TEMP	1		Y	
G1TI4327	°C	G1 OB TURB RAD BRG2 TEMP	1		Y	
G1TI4328	°C	G1 IB TURB RAD BRG3 TEMP	1		Y	
G1TI4329	°C	G1 IB GEN RAD BRG4 TEMP	1		Y	
G1TI4330	°C	G1 OB GEN RAD BRG4 TEMP	1		Y	
G1ZI4264	%	G1-LOW PRESS VALVE OPENING	1	5	Y	
G1ZI4265	%	G1-HIGH PRESS VALVE OPENING	1	5	Y	
G2PI4415	KPA	G2-LUB OIL PRESSURE	1	5	Y	
G2TI4449	°C	G2 THRUST BRG1 TEMP	1		Y	
G2TI4450	°C	G2 THRUST BRG1 TEMP	1		Y	
G2TI4451	°C	G2 THRUST BRG1 TEMP	1		Y	
G2TI4452	°C	G2 OB TURB RAD BRG2 TEMP	1		Y	
G2TI4453	°C	G2 IB TURB RAD BRG3 TEMP	1		Y	
G2TI4454	°C	G2 IB GEN RAD BRG4 TEMP	1		Y	
G2TI4455	°C	G2 OB GEN RAD BRG4 TEMP	1		Y	
G2ZI4389	%	G2-LOW PRESS VALVE OPENING	1	5	Y	
G2ZI4390	%	G2-HIGH PRESS VALVE OPENING	1	5	Y	
G3PI4540	KPA	G3-LUB OIL PRESSURE	1	5	Y	
G3TI4574	°C	G3 THRUST BRG1 TEMP	1		Y	
G3TI4575	°C	G3 THRUST BRG1 TEMP	1		Y	

UTILITY DATALOGGER INPUTS
(SORTED BY REQUIRED RESOLUTION)

TAG	UNITS	DESC	REQ. RESOLUT (SECS)	EXIST. RESOLUT (SECS)	ON PMX	EVNT TRIG?
G3TI4576	°C	G3 THRUST BRG1 TEMP	1		Y	
G3TI4577	°C	G3 OB TURB RAD BRG2 TEMP	1		Y	
G3TI4578	°C	G3 IB TURB RAD BRG3 TEMP	1		Y	
G3TI4579	°C	G3 IB GEN RAD BRG4 TEMP	1		Y	
G3TI4580	°C	G3 OB GEN RAD BRG4 TEMP	1		Y	
G3ZI4514	%	G3–LOW PRESS VALVE OPENING	1	5	Y	
G3ZI4515	%	G3–HIGH PRESS VALVE OPENING	1	5	Y	
STP1736A	KPA	MASTER LOADER GAIN	1	5	Y	
ARFI1022	MTPD	WET AIR FROM SEP 2	5	60	Y	
ARFI1039	MTPD	WET AIR FROM SEP 3	5	60	Y	
ARFI1056	MTPD	WET AIR FROM SEP 4	5	60	Y	
ARFI1073	MTPD	WET AIR FROM SEP 5	5	60	Y	
ARFI1080	MTPD	INST. AIR – RCVR 2	5	5	Y	
ARFI1082	MTPD	PLANT AIR FROM RCVR 2	5	5	Y	
G1FI1505	MTPD	HP STM TO GEN. 1	5	5	Y	
G1FI1506	MTPD	MP STM TO GEN. 1	5	5	Y	
G1FI1507	MTPD	LP STM TO GEN. 1	5	5	Y	
G1PI4268	KPA	EXHAUST PRESSURE	5	5	Y	
G1PI4270	KPA	EXT. PRESSURE	5	5	Y	
G1TI4287	°C	G1 LUBE OIL TEMPERATURE	5		Y	
G2FI1513	MTPD	HP STM TO GEN. 2	5	5	Y	
G2FI1514	MTPD	MP STM TO GEN. 2	5	5	Y	
G2FI1515	MTPD	LP STM TO GEN. 2	5	5	Y	
G2PI4393	KPA	EXHAUST PRESSURE	5	5	Y	
G2PI4395	KPA	EXT. PRESSURE	5	5	Y	
G2TI4412	°C	G2 LUBE OIL TEMPERATURE	5		Y	
G3FI1521	MTPD	HP STM TO GEN. 3	5	5	Y	
G3FI1522	MTPD	MP STM TO GEN. 3	5	5	Y	
G3FI1523	MTPD	LP STM TO GEN. 3	5	5	Y	
G3PI4518	KPA	EXHAUST PRESSURE	5	5	Y	
G3PI4520	KPA	EXT. PRESSURE	5	5	Y	
G3TI4537	°C	G3 LUBE OIL TEMPERATURE	5		Y	
STFI1729	MTPD	HP TO MP LETDOWN VALVES	5	5	Y	
STFI1738	MTPD	MP TO LP LETDOWN VALVES	5	5	Y	
STFI1750	MTPD	LP TO LLP LETDOWN VALVES	5	5	Y	
STFI2054	MTPD	HP STEAM TO STYRENE	5	5	Y	
STFI2066	MTPD	HP STEAM TO STYRENE	5	5	Y	
STFI2108	MTPD	MP STEAM TO EDC	5	5	Y	

			REQ. RESOLUT (SECS)	EXIST. RESOLUT (SECS)	ON PMX	EVNT TRIG?
TAG	UNITS	DESC				

UTILITY DATALOGGER INPUTS
(SORTED BY REQUIRED RESOLUTION)

TAG	UNITS	DESC	REQ. RESOLUT (SECS)	EXIST. RESOLUT (SECS)	ON PMX	EVNT TRIG?
STFI2113	MTPD	MP STEAM TO/FM UTIL STA	.5	5	Y	
STFI3405	MTPD	HP STEAM TO CIE	5	5	Y	
STFI3952	MTPD	HP STEAM TO ETHYLENE	5	5	Y	

THE RELATION BETWEEN TRIGGER POINTS IS AN [OR] RELATION.

DATA STORAGE REQUIREMENTS: 2 MINUTES BEFORE EVENT AND 1 MINUTE AFTER.

Explanation of the specifications

As shown on the specifications sheet, there are total of 300 inputs to monitor. The UNITS section in the specification sheet indicates whether the signals are digital or analog. A digital signal means one bit input indicating the status of the particular process; analog input means a 4-20 mA or 1-5 volt DC signal with a 12 bit resolution. The current inputs are marked as AMP in the units section. Anything else in the units section indicates a 1-5 volt analog output. What is written in the units section refers to the engineering unit of the parameter read by the sensor.

The breakdown of the signal outputs are as follows:

Inputs	Resolution	Sampling Interval
27 Analog inputs	12 bits	0.001 sec
7 Analog current inputs	12 bits	0.001 sec
34 Analog inputs	12 bits	0.1 sec
39 Analog inputs	12 bits	1 sec
33 Analog inputs	12 bits	5 sec
32 Digital inputs	1 bit	0.001 sec
3 Digital inputs	1 bit	0.05 sec
48 Digital inputs	1 bit	0.1 sec
6 Digital inputs	1 bit	1 sec

Basically there are three different kinds of signal outputs:

- Analog outputs with different sampling time requirements
- Analog current outputs

- Digital outputs with different sampling time requirements

According to the specifications, all analog and digital outputs coming from the system should be isolated. We will consider digital and analog outputs separately and most probably use separate data acquisition cards for sampling digital outputs and analog outputs.

To calculate the speed of the A/D converter card from the data provided, we assume that we can use signal conditioning modules for analog current inputs and all inputs can be converted by the same A/D converter card. The number of samples to be taken in one second can be calculated by multiplying the sampling rate and the number of inputs:

27 x 1000 + 7 x 1000 + 34 x 10 + 39 x 1 + 33 x 0.2 = 34,385 samples per second.

As a good engineering practice, allow at least 1/10 to 1/3 more sampling frequency capability in order to accommodate additional analog inputs in case it becomes necessary.

Since the sampling rate is not excessive, let us add a 1/3 more sampling frequency capability. 34,385 / 3 = 11,462 extra analog frequency samples capability should be added. So the minimum requirement is 45,847 samples per second.

For the digital inputs, the number of samples to take can be calculated in a similar manner: 32 x 1000 + 3 x 20 + 48 x 10 + 6 x 1 = 32,546 samples per second.

As a good engineering practice, allow at least 1/10 to 1/3 more sampling frequency capability in order to accommodate additional analog inputs in case it becomes necessary.

Since the sampling rate is not excessive let us add 1/3 more sampling capability: 32,546/3 = 10,849 additional digital sampling capability is needed, so 32,546 + 10,849 = 43,395 samples per second is the minimum sampling frequency capability requirements for the digital inputs

Looking through the catalogue we find plenty of choices for data acquisition cards which can sample at or better than this rate.

From the selection data given on page 192 we see that DAS-40G1 can sample at 45K rate with a 12 bit resolution; so this seems like an ideal choice for this case although many more options exist if we want boards with a higher capability.

For the digital inputs the sampling rate is not a problem since digital sampling, commonly known as "input" operation, takes only a negligible amount of time. In the catalog we see that some of the boards have sampling rates written as 200K, 400K, etc. whereas others are listed as "software limited." What is meant by "software limited" is that the card can go as fast as your software can. Thus, since the software becomes the bottleneck at higher speeds, your software sampling limitation is the effective limitation of the board. What is more important for digital input boards is the number of digital input channels.

Now that we have figured out which card to use, let us turn our attention to multiplexing and signal conditioning. Do not forget that there was a very important requirement on the specification sheet; all inputs, digital or analog, have to be isolated. This is quite typical of industrial equipment specifications.

We need 140 analog input channels. Referring to the technical specifications of DAS-40G1 we can determine that the board has 16 single ended channels but it offers no expansion capability. We definitely need a large expansion capability, so we now go back to the catalog and change our selection. DAS 16 offers a 70K sampling rate and has expansion capability. Therefore we revise our design to change the analog input card to DAS 16. An expansion board with an isolated input capability is marked as an ISO-4 expansion board in the catalog. So this is the only expansion board we can select because of the isolation requirement. Looking into the specification sheet of an ISO-4 carefully, we notice that it offers cascadability of boards and the number of input channels can be increased to 128 by using this technique. Since we need a total of 140 analog input channels, these boards together with an ISO-4 expansion board is not enough for the application. But since this is the only board that can be used, we will keep DAS-16 and 32 ISO-4 boards to get 128 isolated channels. The rest of the channels should be sampled by another card. From the specification sheet we know that 7 of the inputs are supposed to be current inputs. To accommodate this we will select an analog board with an additional 16 channels and an MB series signal conditioning board with 16 channel inputs. Thus, the total number of channels is 128 + 16 = 144 which is above the requirement.

Since MB boards can be used with any type of board, we are not restricted by the board type. The most inexpensive solution would be to a DAS-40 board which offers 16 channels with a 40K sampling rate. An MB board accepts 16 signals conditioning modules which are isolated; 7 out of 16 of these signal conditioning modules will be MB32-02's which convert a 4-20 mA output to a 0-5 V output, and the rest of the signal conditioning modules will be MB31-05 which converts a +/-5 volt to a 0-5 volt isolated output. By definition all signal conditioning modules are isolated electrically, which conforms to our specifications.

The overall list of the equipment for analog sampling is reproduced below.

Card	Description	Quantity
DAS-16	A/D converter card with 70K	1
DAS-40	A/D converter card with 45K	1
ISO-4	Isolation multiplexer board	32
MB-16	Signal conditioning backplane	1
MB32-02	Current-to-voltage converter	7
MB31-05	Voltage-to-voltage converter	9

As for the digital part, we are in need of 99 digital input channels. None of the boards offer 99 channel expansion capability. The next suitable choice is PIO-96 which offers 96 digital input channels. But the channels are not isolated so we have to have something else to do the isolation. The choice for this is a SSIO-24 which offers a 24 channel isolated input to any digital input board. But with this combination we are still short 3 digital input channels. For these few channels we need to use an additional card which also should be isolated. Going through the catalog again we find that the best choice for this is a PDISO-8 which is an 8 bit isolated input card for the PC. For this card you do not need any interface card other than the screw terminal connector STC-37. Compiling all the equipment needed for the digital input part, the list becomes as follows:

Card	Description	Quantity
PIO-96	96 digital input non-isolated	1
PDISO-8	8 digital input isolated	1
SSIO-24	24 channel isolated digital input	4
ADP-5037	Interface card for SSIO-24	4
STC-37	Screw terminal	1
C-1800	Interconnection cable	5

The block diagram of the design is shown in Figure 6.2.

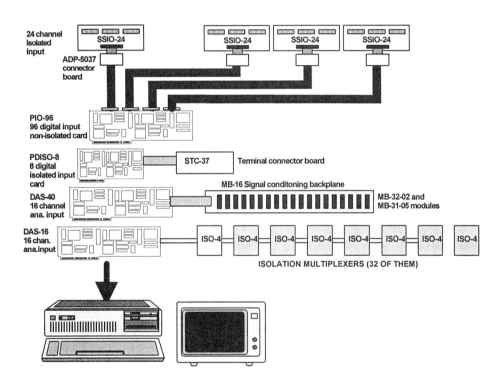

Figure 6.2 Block diagram of the data logger designed with Keithley™ equipment.

REFERENCES

1. *Keithley-Metrabyte Data Acquisition Catalog and Reference Guide*, Keithley Instruments, 1992.

2. Gates, S., Becker, J., *Laboratory Automation Using the IBM PC*, Prentice Hall, 1989.

3. Curtis, Johnson, *Process Control Instrumentation Technology*, Regents/Prentice Hall, 1993.

4. Georgopoulos, C. J., *Interference Control in Cable and Device Interfaces*, Interference Control Technologies, 1988.

Seven

LOCAL DATA ACQUISITION USING GPIB

7.1 INTRODUCTION TO THE CONCEPT OF LABORATORY AUTOMATION

Laboratory automation involves controlling laboratory equipment remotely by using a controller and reading their outputs digitally. This concept was first introduced by Hewlett Packard and implemented by a system called the general purpose interface bus (GPIB). Laboratory equipment with a GPIB interface are intelligent instruments which enable the user to perform equipment settings remotely and send the measurements digitally. The concept enabled the user to automate laboratory experiments. The system has been so popular that later it was adapted by IEEE as a standard which is also known as the IEEE-488 standard.

Laboratory equipment with a GPIB interface are usually intelligent data acquisition devices. Even equipment like a printer or plotter, although not being precisely intelligent instruments, may have a GPIB interface. In most cases GPIB equipment has the capability to take data from outside and send it to the controller digitally. For example, a frequency counter with a GPIB interface can measure the frequency and display the result on the LCD screen just like an ordinary frequency counter. The difference between this and the ordinary counter is that the equipment with a GPIB interface can send the data back automatically to the controller computer over a digital interface without any operator interference. A digital oscilloscope with a GPIB interface can measure the frequency and the peak magnitude of the signal automatically and send the result to the controller digitally. All this equipment offers the capability to change controls either locally by the switches on the faceplate, just like an ordinary equipment, or to change the controls remotely through the digital interface. Having all these features enables the researchers to automate an experiment. One sets the controls remotely to particular parameters, runs the experiment, gets the resultant data automatically, and if the results are not satisfactory, one changes the controls once again and reruns the experiment.

Readers who are more interested in the subject are recommended to read and excellent book on the subject by S. C. Gates and J. Becker titled *Laboratory Automation Using the IBM PC* published by Prentice-Hall.

7.2 HOW THE IEEE-488 SYSTEM WORKS

The general purpose interface bus, or GPIB, was developed to provide a powerful, flexible standard for the communications interface between computers and other peripheral devices, especially laboratory and test instruments. Choosing an appropriate interfacing scheme for a computer in a laboratory setup is an important decision because an inappropriate interface can hinder the future expansion of the system and also slow down the data exchange between the devices.

There have been several attempts to find a satisfactory interface which can provide flexibility and expansion capability. The earliest interfaces featured highly specialized hardware and software, usually developed for a single purpose. Often these interfaces could not be adapted to even slightly different applications, and were too inflexible to take advantage of changes in technology.

It was as a solution to this problem that the GPIB standard was developed. "GPIB" is not the only name used for this standard; HP-IB and IEEE-488 are two other frequently used terms. The name "IEEE-488" arose from the adoption of the GPIB by the Institute for Electrical and Electronic Engineers (IEEE). The IEEE published its IEEE-488 standard in 1975, adding minor revisions in 1978 and 1987. The Hewlett-Packard Company initially developed the bus and patented its handshaking scheme, hence giving the term HP-IB.

The GPIB has proved to be one of the most successful and widely accepted interfacing schemes. The advantages of GPIB over more specialized interfaces are twofold:

- First, the GPIB reduces the hardware requirements of the computer to one interface for an entire system, rather than one interface for each instrument.

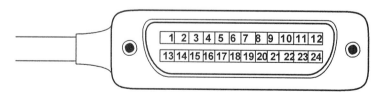

Figure 7.1 GPIB connector.

- Second, as a result of its hardware standardization, GPIB permits for generalized software packages to be used for controlling the bus.

As the name implies, the GPIB is a kind of bus. A bus is a connection scheme for communication between different pieces of hardware. A well designed bus offers

- Interfacing to a wide variety of devices
- Easy set up and reconfiguration
- High speed communication between devices
- Reliable operation

One bus you are probably already familiar with is the expansion bus of your computer where the slots which printer cards, graphics cards, and other peripherals plug into. Each expansion slot on the computer's bus offers access to all of the data, addresses, and control lines of the bus; this parallel architecture underlies the very concept of a bus.

Just as the bus in your computer allows peripheral boards to communicate with each other and with the computer, the GPIB mediates communication between your computer and GPIB instruments. Information carried by the bus is sent over a 24-pin cable which connects your computer to each device on the bus (see Figure 7.1). The connection of the GPIB bus to the computer itself is accomplished by a board which plugs into the computer's expansion bus and terminates in a GPIB connector.

As specified by the IEEE-488 standard, no more than 15 devices can be connected to any one bus. Since the computer and its GPIB interface board are considered a device, no more than fourteen other devices can be connected to your computer. The IEEE standard further specifies that the total length of the bus cabling cannot exceed 20 meters or 2 meters per device, whichever is less. The standard GPIB cable has both a male and a female connector at each end. This allows the connectors to be stacked (see Figure 7.2), which facilitates a variety of connection schemes. Figures 7.3 and 7.4 show two different connection schemes: a star configuration and a linear one. The two schemes can also be combined on the same bus.

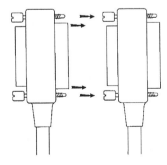

Figure 7.2 GPIB connectors can be stacked together.

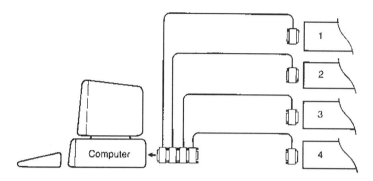

Figure 7.3 Star connection of GPIB equipment.

To facilitate communication, each device on the bus is assigned a unique GPIB address, which we refer to as the primary address of the device. Though a single bus can only accommodate fifteen devices, primary addresses can range from 0 to 30.

Primary addresses are assigned through hardware, either by DIP switches on the back panel of the device or by the controls of the front panel.

Communication between instruments on the bus is accomplished by identifying one device to send information, and one or more devices to receive the information sent. In GPIB terms, the device sending information is called a "talker" while a device receiving information is called a "listener." The device which identifies talkers and listeners is called the "controller." In most applications your computer will be the controller. The controller arbitrates the flow of information along the bus, choosing talkers and listeners and usually specifying the information which talkers are to send.

In addition to waiting until being directed to talk or listen, a device can request the controller's attention by generating a service request. To do so, it asserts another of the GPIB control lines, the SRQ (service request) line.

The IEEE standard allows multiple controller systems, but only one controller can be in charge at any one time. Controllers can pass control to one another, and a "system controller" can seize control of the bus by its own means. A bus can only have one system controller.

Commands are sent over the bus as strings (strings are sequences of ASCII characters: "TAKE DATA" is a string, "CHANNEL 7" is a string). Data are usually transferred over the bus in a string format also (i.e., as characters rather than numbers), but in some cases data can be sent in raw binary (numeric) form.

Commands sent over the bus can be of two distinct types. The first type consists of device independent commands which implement the GPIB protocol; these are the commands which identify an instrument to talk, listen, etc. All GPIB devices recognize these commands. Whenever one of these commands is sent, it is distinguished from other information sent over the bus by the assertion of one of the GPIB control lines: ATN (attention).

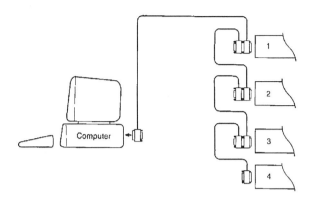

Figure 7.4 Linear connection of GPIB equipment.

All other information sent over the bus is device dependent, meaning that the response to the message sent depends on the instrument receiving it. This second type of message is sent using only the data lines of the bus; the ATN control line is not asserted.

The commands which instruct a particular instrument to do something useful, like capture a block of data, or set the output voltage to a desired level are device dependent commands. As the phrase "device-dependent" suggests, commands which instruct one instrument to perform a given task will mean something else, or nothing at all, to another instrument. This point cannot be overstressed. The user must know and use the command set for his/her particular instrument to properly control it. These commands are usually explained in the manual for the instrument.

There is a second level to the device dependent nature of most GPIB communication. The GPIB protocol allows varying schemes for signaling the end of a command, or the end of a stream of data.

In general in order to set up an IEEE-488 system, you will either use a software package or a program written in a suitable language and hardware that physically connects the GPIB bus to your personal computer. Several manufacturers offer such a connection, typically as a board which plugs into one of the expansion slots of your computer and terminates in a GPIB connector. Below is a partial list of GPIB boards manufactured by some companies.

Advantech PCL-748 *

B&C PC488A

BBS GPIB-1000

Capital Equipment PC< >488

Capital Equipment PS< >488

Contec GPIB (PC)

Hewlett-Packard HPIB *

IBM GPIB board

ICS 488-PC1 *

IO tech GP488

IO tech GP488/2

MetraByte IE-488

National Instruments GPIB-PC

National Instruments GPIB-PC2

National Instruments GPIB-PC2A

National Instruments GPIB-PCIII

National Instruments MC-GPIB

QuaTech MXI-100

Qua Tech MXI-1000

Scientific Solutions IEEE 488 LM

Scientific Solutions MC-IEEE 488

Ziatech ZT 1444

Ziatech ZT/2

Some of these boards are located in the I/O space of the personal computer, and others are located in the memory space. Those that are marked with an * occupy memory space. These devices have an on board ROM which stores assembly language subroutines for generating GPIB commands. The user has to include these subroutines in the language of his choice in order to use the board.

7.3 OVERVIEW OF IEEE-488 STANDARD

The entire IEEE-488 standard is built around four main restrictions:

- All data communications are digital.
- No more than fifteen devices can be connected together on any one bus. (Since your computer and GPIB controller card together are considered a device, this means you can connect fourteen devices to your computer.)
- The total cable length cannot exceed 20 meters or 2 meters per device, whichever is less.
- The maximum data transfer rate is 1 megabyte per second.

With these restrictions in mind the IEEE-488 standard is divided into three areas: electrical, mechanical, and functional. A fourth area, which has to do with the operational aspects of the bus, has been left undefined by the IEEE standard.

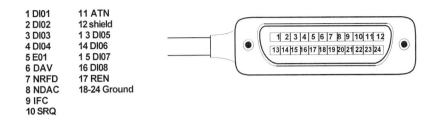

Figure 7.5 Pin functions of IEEE-488 connector.

Operational specifications limit what kind of messages can be sent and what kind of devices can be used. These specifications were intentionally left out to encourage imaginative use of the bus.

The electrical specifications of the GPIB have to do with digital voltage levels, signal timing, line termination, etc. These aspects of the GPIB are not really important to the user, but rather are intended for the designer.

Mechanically, the IEEE-488 standard is concerned mainly with connector specifications. The connector used is a 24 pin rack and panel connector. The pin functions are shown in Figure 7.5.

The standard cable has both a male and female connector on each end. This is done so that the connectors can be stacked (see Figure 7.2) to facilitate many different connection schemes. Figures 7.3 and 7.4 show two different connection schemes: star and linear. Any combination of these two schemes can be combined on your bus.

The functional specifications described by the IEEE-488 standard are quite detailed and are probably the most important for the user to understand. A good working knowledge of these specifications will help the user to realize the limitations of the GPIB.

7.3.1 Components of an IEEE-488 System

The first thing to understand about the GPIB is how the devices attached to the bus can play different roles. Any device, depending on its capabilities, can take the role of a controller, talker, listener, or none of these as an idle device. Examine the functions of these different roles.

A **talker** is a device that has been addressed to send data. There can be only one talker on the bus at any given time.

A **listener** is a device that has been addressed to receive data. There can be up to fourteen listeners on the bus at any given time.

A **controller** is a device that controls all communications on the bus. The controller is able to address the devices on the bus (including itself) as talkers or listeners. The IEEE standard allows for multiple controller systems, but only one controller can be active or in charge at any given time. The system controller is a controller that has the ability to take control of the bus at any time by its own means (a non-system controller has to have control passed to it by another controller). Only one System Controller can be used on any one bus.

7.3.2 Signal Structure of the IEEE-488 Bus

The IEEE-488 bus is divided into three basic sets of lines:

- 8 data lines: DIO1-DIO8
- 5 control lines: ATN, IFC, REN, EOI, and SRQ
- 3 handshaking lines: DAV, NRFD, and NDAC

The eight data lines are really the bus's multipurpose lines. With these lines, devices can send and receive device dependent data. In addition the controller uses the DIO lines for sending IEEE standard, device independent commands. These are referred to as multi-line or (as we will call them) GPIB commands. The controller executes these commands by placing the proper value on the DIO lines simultaneously with the assertion of the ATN control line. In this way, a device can tell the difference between a GPIB command and normal data.

The list of GPIB commands allows the controller to perform a wide variety of bus control functions. Perhaps the most important of the GPIB commands are the addressing commands. With the use of these, the controller is able to direct the flow of data on the bus by specifying which devices are talkers and which devices are listeners.

All devices must be assigned an address between 0 and 30. (We will refer to this address as the device's primary address.) Most devices come with a factory set primary address but allow you to change this address, usually by setting a bank of DIP switches on the back of the instrument. This primary address is used to calculate the talk and listen addresses of the instrument. The controller can command a device to be a talker by placing the device's talk address on the bus with the ATN line asserted.

Similarly a device can be commanded to listen by using its listen address. The diagram below shows how the talk and listen addresses are transmitted.

LISTEN ADDRESS COMMAND

NOT USED	0	1	X	X	X	X	X

ATN= 1   primary address

TALK ADDRESS COMMAND

ATN=1   primary address

NOT USED	1	0	X	X	X	X	X

As you can see, the device's primary address is put into the five low order bits of the command word to make the proper talk or listen address. Notice that 31 is not a valid primary address. This is because commands formed by using 31 are used to untalk and unlisten the devices on the bus.

Some devices require an extra byte of address information for their talk or listen functions. This type of addressing is called extended or secondary addressing. The diagram below shows the secondary addressing scheme.

SECONDARY ADDRESS COMMAND

NOT USED	1	1	X	X	X	X	X

ATN = 1   secondary address

7.3.3 Universal GPIB Commands

As we have seen before not all GPIB instruments have the same vocabulary of instructions. There are device-specific instructions that only one particular instrument can understand and execute. But on the other hand there are some GPIB instructions which should be understood by all the devices on the GPIB network. These instructions, which we call universal GPIB action commands, are understood and executed by all devices. These actions or commands send as an encoded code with ATN signal asserted.

The list below describes all of the universal GPIB action, and the succeeding table shows the encoding for these GPIB actions. Remember that all the following action commands require that the ATN line be asserted when sent.

UNIVERSAL GPIB ACTION COMMANDS

device clear--commands all devices on the bus capable of responding to go to a device dependent clear state.

group execute trigger--commands all devices addressed to listen to trigger a device dependent event.

go to local--commands all devices addressed to listen to go to local control (i.e., not GPIB control).

local lockout--commands all devices capable of responding to ignore all front panel (local) commands.

parallel poll configure--instructs all devices addressed to listen to interpret the following secondary command as either the parallel poll enable command or the parallel poll disable command, rather than a secondary address.

parallel poll enable--commands the devices that have received the parallel poll configure command to use a specific parallel poll bit and a specific level (high or low).

parallel poll disable--disables the devices that have received the parallel poll configure command from responding to a parallel poll.

parallel poll unconfigure--disables all devices from responding to a parallel poll.

selected device clear--commands all devices addressed to listen to go to a device dependent clear state. This state is the same state that the device enters on the device clear command.

serial poll disable--removes the bus from the serial poll mode.

take control--passes control of the bus to the currently addressed talker.

untalk--removes the current talker from the talker addressed state.

unlisten--removes the current listeners from the listener addressed state.

GPIB Action Command	Binary Encoding	Decimal Encoding
go to local	0000 0001	1
selected device clear	0000 0100	4
parallel poll configure	0000 0101	5
group execute trigger	0000 1000	8
take control	0000 1001	9
local lockout	0001 0001	17
device clear	0001 0100	20
parallel poll unconfigure	0001 0101	21
serial poll enable	0001 1000	24
serial poll disable	0001 1001	25
listen addresses	001p pppp	32-62
unlisten	0011 1111	63
talk addresses	010p pppp	64-94
untalk	0101 1111	95
secondary addresses	011s ssss	96-127
parallel poll enable	0110 Ibbb	96-111
parallel poll disable	0111 0000	112

KEY: ppppp = a device's primary address

sssss = a device's secondary address

I = parallel poll bit level (high or low)

bbb = parallel poll bit number (0-7)

7.3.4 Description of the Control Lines

One has now seen how the GPIB data lines are used to send data and multiline commands and messages. The five GPIB control lines are used to send what the IEEE-488 standard calls uniline messages. You have already seen how the ATN command line is used to differentiate between GPIB commands and data. The assertion of the ATN is called the *attention uniline message*. The list below shows a description of how each of the five control lines is used.

<u>GPIB CONTROL LINES</u>

ATN (attention)--The ATN line is used by the controller in charge to indicate whether the data lines are to be interpreted as data or GPIB multiline commands. When the ATN line is asserted, the data lines contain GPIB commands.

IFC (interface clear)--The IFC line can be used only by the system controller to halt all activity on the bus. All talkers and listeners are unaddressed and any serial poll is disabled.

REN (remote enable)--This line can be only used by the system controller. When asserted, remote operation of the devices on the bus is made possible. When the REN line is unasserted, all devices return to local control.

EOI (end or identify)--This line is used in conjunction with the ATN for two different messages.

> **1. End--**The End uniline message is sent by a talker to mark the end of a data transmission. The ATN line is unasserted for this message.

> **2. Identify--**The identify message is used by a controller to initiate a parallel poll. The ATN line is asserted for this command.

SRQ (service request)--The SRQ line is asserted by a device to send a message to the controller that it has encountered some device dependent state. Typical reasons for the SRQ message are error conditions or data ready conditions. Since more than one device can assert the SRQ line at one time, the controller must execute a serial or parallel poll to find out which device issued the service request.

7.3.5 GPIB Handshake Lines

The three remaining signal lines on the GPIB bus are the handshaking lines. These lines are used to insure that data are properly transmitted over the bus. Every time a byte of data or multiline command is sent over the bus, the handshaking lines are used to coordinate the transfer between the sending device and the receiving devices. The use of this handshaking procedure also removes the need for a strict data rate. There is nothing in the way of a baud rate or clock rate associated with GPIB communications.

All of the handshaking lines use an open collector, a low-true bus structure which results in a wire-OR type of operation. With this design, any device can pull the hand shaking lines low (true) at any time. For the line to be high (false), all devices on the bus must be asserting the high value.

HANDSHAKE LINES

DAV (data valid)--This line is controlled by the sending device to indicate that the data on the DIO lines are stable and valid.

NRFD (not ready for data)--This line is controlled by the receiving devices to indicate when they are ready for data. When the NRFD line is high, all the devices on the bus are ready to accept data from the DIO lines.

NDAC (not data accepted)--Receiving devices use this line to communicate that the data byte has been accepted. When the NDAC line is high, all of the receiving devices on the bus have accepted the data byte.

The handshaking sequence is initiated by the receiving devices by letting the NRFD line go high to indicate that they are ready for data. After the data on the DIO lines are stable and the sending device sees the NRFD line go high, it asserts the DAV line low. At this point, the receiving devices start to process the data on the lines and re-assert the NRFD line low. When all of the receiving devices have completed their use of the data on the DIO lines, the NDAC is allowed to go high. This signals the sending device that it no longer needs to hold the data lines valid and therefore lets the DAV line go high. When the receiving devices see the DAV line go high, the NDAC line is forced low. This completes one handshake cycle. This entire cycle is used for every data byte or multiline command sent on the GPIB. Figure 7.6 shows this sequence graphically.

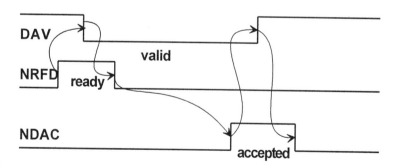

Figure 7.6 Data transfer process in IEEE-488.

7.4 HOW TO TURN YOUR PC INTO AN IEEE-488 CONTROLLER

There are basically two ways to turn your PC into an IEEE-488 controller. The first method is to put a IEEE-488 adapter card in your PC. Since there are more than a dozen companies who manufacture GPIB adapter cards, it should be no trouble to find one. But one should be warned that incompatibilities exist between devices and the controller cards due to different levels of standards. In order to be aware of such problems, it is necessary to briefly look into the history of GPIB.

GPIB was first designed by Hewlett-Packard in 1965 as a bus to connect their line of programmable instruments to HP computers. Because of the high data transfer rate, the bus quickly became popular. In 1975 it was adapted by the IEEE body as a standard (IEEE standard 488-1975). This standard later evolved into ANSI/IEEE-488.1-1987. After that this standard was improved and finally in 1990 evolved into the latest form which is known as IEEE-488.2.

Not all the cards and GPIB equipment on the market adhere to the latest standards; so, incompatibilities exist. However the latest form of the standard, namely the IEEE-488.2 is designed as a "talk precise, listen forgiving" type standard which accepts non-compatible GPIB equipment. Because of this, one is recommended to get cards which are IEEE-488.2 compatible.

GPIB cards in the market come in two varieties:

1. The first kind, the most popular one, uses I/O mapped data exchange   and driver software for IEEE-488 communication.

2. The second kind is memory-mapped and comes with onboard firmware (ROM) to store communication software. The subroutines inside the ROM can be included in the user's programming language so that no driver software is needed.

The following table offers a list of available GPIB boards on the market for IBM PC and compatibles.

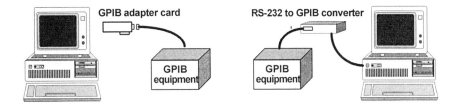

Figure 7.7 Two popular ways of converting one's PC into a GPIB controller.

BOARD NAME	FACTORY DEFAULT SETTING		
	I/O Address	IRQ	DMA#
Advantech PCL748	COOO(MEM)	NC	1
B&C PC488A	2E1	NC	NC
BBS GPIB1000	390	NC	NA
Capital Equipment PC< >488	2B8	NC	1
Capital Equipment PS< >488	2B8	3	1
Contec GPIB (PC)	2E1	7	1
HewlettPackard HPIB	DCOO (MEM)	5	2
IBM GPIB board	2E1	7	1
ICS 488PC1	COOO (MEM)	NC	1
IOtech GP488	2E1	NC	NC
IOTech GP488/2	2B0	NC	4
MetraByte IE-488	300	5	3
National Instruments GPIB-PC	2B8	7	1
National Instruments GPIB-PC2	2B8	7	1
National InstrumentsGPIB-PC2A	2E1	7	1
National Instruments GPIB-PCIII	280	7	1
National Instruments MCGPIB	EOO	3	0
QuaTech MXI-100	318	2	3
QuaTech MXI-1000	200	3	3
Scientific Solutions IEEE 488 LM	2E1	7	1
Scientific Solutions MC-IEEE 488	2B8	5	0
Ziatech ZT 1444	210	NC	NC
Ziatech ZT/2	800	NC	1

NA = feature not available on this board

NC = not configured from factory

Please note: Only Micro Channel boards can use multiple DMA channels. NonMicro Channel boards must use DMA channel number 1 except for the Hewlett Packard board which uses DMA channel 2. Also note that the Ziatech ZT/2 boards previous to revision A. 1 cannot use DMA channels 4-7.

There is yet another way to convert your computer into an IEEE-488 controller. This method involves using external converter boxes to be connected to one's RS-232 or SCSI port. Because of widescale availability, RS-232 to IEEE-488 converters are more popular than the SCSI kind.

Both methods of converting your PC into a GPIB controller will be explored in detail in the coming sections.

7.5 EXTERNAL RS-232 TO IEEE-488 CONVERTER

External RS-232 to IEEE-488 controllers are small stand alone boxes which get plugged into the serial port of your PC or any device with a RS-232 port. The devices are not exactly low cost since they pack quite a bit of intelligence inside due to their microprocessors which control the operations. They are quite versatile for control applications.

One major advantage of these devices over the plug-in cards is that these devices do not need a PC to control the applications. If one has a peripheral device with an IEEE-488 interface and one is unable to use the device because of not having an IEEE-488 interface, one can simply connect the converter device to the peripheral and the system can be used with or without the PC. The diagrams below hopefully will clarify this idea.

A stand alone RS-232 to IEEE-488 converter can be used for the following applications:

1.   Convert RS-232 to IEEE-488,   RS-232 is RECEIVE ONLY.

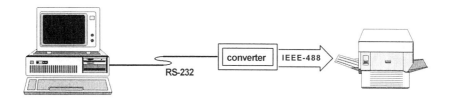

Computer communicating with an IEEE-488 peripheral.

2.   Convert IEEE-488 to RS-232,   IEEE-488 is LISTEN ALWAYS.

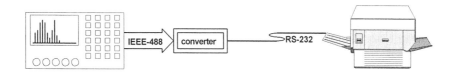

IEEE-488 peripheral dumping output on RS-232 peripheral.

3.   **IEEE-488 to RS-232,   IEEE-488 is LISTEN ONLY.**

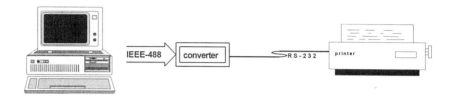

IEEE-488 controller communicating with RS-232 device.

4.   **Convert IEEE-488<>RS-232.**

5.   **Computer as a GPIB Bus Controller for IEEE-488 equipment.**

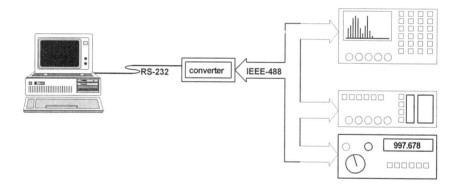

7.5.1 Case Study: Controlling IEEE-488 Devices Using an RS-232 to IEEE-488 Converter

In this section we are going to look at a typical interface converter and how to program it for controlling a laboratory instrument with an IEEE-488 interface.

Interface converters are devices which can convert a RS-232 output to IEEE-488 compatible output. Currently there are two different kinds of interface converters on the market.

- A bi-directional interface converter can convert from IEEE-488 to RS-232 or from RS-232 to IEEE-488.

- A unidirectional interface converter, is designed to convert from RS-232 to IEEE-488 only and not the other way around.

Interface Converters
IEEE488 RS-232 Bi-directional

W. 180   H. 65   D. 205

This high quality bi-directional converter/controller is a multi-function device which enables equipment fitted with serial RS-232C inputs to be used on IEEE-488 systems and vice versa. The unit can also turn any computer with an RS-232C port into an IEEE-488 bus controller for up to fourteen instruments in computer aided test and measurement applications.

Features
- Converts a PC with RS-232C to an IEEE Instrument Controller
- Supports plotters using HPGL, HP Thinkjet and Laserjet printers. No software modifications required
- 7·5 kilobyte buffer
- Comprehensive status indication
- Simple operator controls
- Xon/Xoff and DTR handshake modes
- Seven baud rates for RS-232 (110, 300, 600, 1200, 2400, 4800 and 9600 baud)
- Variable word format: 7/8 data bits, 1/2 stop bits, none/odd/even parity
- Small footprint: $180 \times 65 \times 205$ mm
- Positive retention of data cables
- Integral mains power supply with lead and BS1363 mains plug
- Supplied with comprehensive instruction manual

RS-232/IEEE488 Converter

This RS-232/IEEE488 converter allows connection of RS-232 and IEEE488 equipment operating up to 19·2Kbaud rates. DTE and DCE operation is switch selectable together with baud rate and the direction of data conversion. The unit supports DTR, RTS/CTS, DSR handshakes if required and is supplied with a power supply.

Figure 7.8 Typical unidirectional and bi-directional interface converters available on the market.

Courtesy RS Components.

Figure 7.9 TAS016 bus controller used in the case study.

A TAS016 bus controller is a typical bi-directional interface converter designed by Tastronic Controls® Ltd., Gloucester. Any programming language that can communicate with the RS-232 port can be used for controlling the TAS016. Although low level languages like assembly language certainly can be used, high level languages like BASIC, Pascal or C are more suitable because of the ease of programming.

COMMAND STRUCTURE of TAS016

The TAS016 bus controller is controlled by sending ASCII character strings to the controller. Since both the commands and the data are transmitted as ASCII strings back and forth from the interface controller, the command strings are isolated by a Bus command header string and a Bus command terminator character. The structure of any command sent to the interface controller is as resembles the scheme below.

HEADER STRING	COMMAND	TERMINATOR

A header string, as the name implies is a string of characters and the terminator is a single character. In between the header and the terminator, the command is sandwiched. (Please note that these procedures for a command message transfer are completely machine-dependent; another vendor may implement it in a totally different way.)

Figure 7.10 Back side of the TAS016 has connections for RS-232 and IEEE-488 bus.

The general form of a bus command is

ESC%GPlB xxxxxxxxxxxx %

where the Header string is ESC%GPIB, ESC represents the single ASCII character code ESCAPE (decimal 27, hexadecimal IB). The character string represented by xxxxxxx may contain one or more of the command mnemonics that describe the specific IEEE-488 operations to be performed. The trailing % is the Command terminator which indicates the end of the current command.

For example, if one would like to print the message "HELLO" on a printer with an IEEE-488 interface which is set to address "1", one would send to the interface controller

ESC%GPlB OUTPUT 1 % HELLO CR

where CR represents ASCII carriage return.

Suppose you have more than one printer with an IEEE-488 interface in the GPIB network and you want to send this message to all of them, then you would modify the text string as follows:

Assuming you have printer #1 at address 1, printer #2 at address 8, and printer #1 at address 12,

ESC%GPlB OUTPUT 1 8 12 % HELLO CR

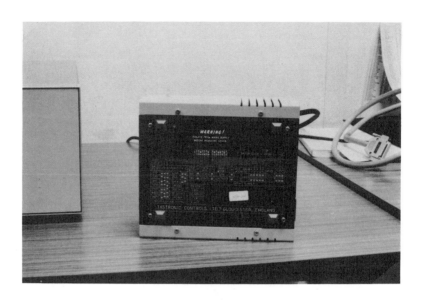

Figure 7.11 Using the DIP Switches on the back of the TAS016 one can adjust the baud rate of RS-232 connection.

The universal action commands of the IEEE-488 controller have been reviewed previously. These are the smallest set of actions which should be understood by all IEEE-488 devices. These commands are sent with an ATN line (attention) of the IEEE-488 bus asserted and command encoded on the data lines D1-8. Although an action command set is well defined, how these commands are issued to the bus controller may differ from one equipment vendor to the other. In other words, the command to issue a specific action may be vendor-dependent. In order to issue a universal action command to the TAS016 bus controller, the command has to be written in the following manner.

The Basic TAS016 Universal Action Command Set

OUTPUT	Send data to specified device(s)
ENTER	Receive data from specified device
CLEAR	Performs universal/selected device(s) clear
RESET	Performs bus reset - interface clear
LOCAL	Sets bus or specified device(s) to local control
REMOTE	Sets bus or specified device(s) to remote control
SPOLL	Conducts serial poll of specified device
TRIGGER	Executes device trigger on specified device(s)
DELIM	Sets end-of-line parameters for data from talkers
REPORT	TAS016 Error & status reports

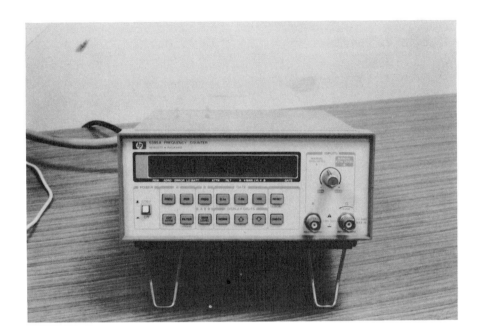

Figure 7.12 Counter used in the case study.

In order to issue these actions on the bus lines, the bus controller has to receive the command in the above syntax of strings. For example, when the controller receives the LOCAL command from the RS-232 port, it will force its bus lines into the following states:

ATN: high

D1-8: 0000 0001

The interface controller from another vendor may require a command different than LOCAL. For instance, it may be LOCALI or LOCALG, etc. Because of this, it is important to refer to the manufacturer's handbook for the convention used.

Let us use our interface controller for a simple application of reading from an intelligent counter.

The counter that we will use is an HP5385A which is designed by the Hewlett-Packard company. The equipment is a two channel frequency counter with two independent channels which can measure frequencies up to 100 MHz. It has an LCD alphanumeric screen which can display 11 digits. Because of an alphanumeric capability, the display can show numbers as well as letters. The equipment, being typical IEEE-488 equipment, will recognize and respond to universal action commands. Other than the universal action commands, it has a set of device dependent commands which is specific to itself. The GPIB address of the device is set by a DIP switch package on the back of the device.

The device dependent instructions of the HP3485A are represented below.

HP3485A Instrument Command Set

Code	Function	Description
FU1	Freq. A	Measure frequency of A-lnput
FU2	Per A	Measure period of A-lnput
FU3	Freq. B	Measure frequency of B-lnput
CK	CHECK10MHz	Check mode (10 MHz)
AT0	Attn A (X1)	Select X1 A-lnput
AT1	Attn A (X20)	Select X20 A-lnput
Fl0	FILTER A (off)	Disable A-lnput 100 kHz LPF
Fl1	FILTER A (on)	Enable A-lnput 100 kHz LPF
ML0	MAN LVL (off)	Disable manual level control
ML1	MAN LVL (on)	Enable manual level control
GA1	0.1s	Select 0.1 sec gate time
GA2	1.0s	Select 1.0 sec gate time
GA3	10s	Select 10 sec gate time
RE	Reset Gate	Reset display and restart measurement
DI	Digit Inc	Increment display digits
DD	Digit Dec	Decrement display digits
DN	Digit Norm	Display digits normal
FN11	Diag. 1	CPU self-test
FN12	Diag. 2	I/O Address
FN13	Diag. 3	Interpolator short-cal
FN14	Diag. 4	Interpolator long-cal
IN	Initialize	Reset and go to default state
WA0	Wait (off)	Wait-to-send data mode off
WA1	Wait (on)	Wait-to-send data mode on
DR<st>	Remote Display	Write to LCD "string"
DL	Local Display	Return LCD to local
ID or SI	Send ID	Send device ID
SM<num>	SRQ mask	Set service request mask = <num>
LE	Load Error	Loads data into error code register
SE	Send Error	Send error code

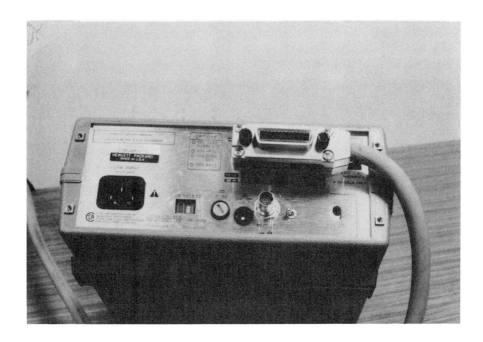

Figure 7.13 Back side of the HP5385A frequency counter.

Giving Orders Through the Interface Converter to Read Frequency

Assume that the HP3485A Frequency counter is set to respond at Device address 22. The interface converter, by default, is located at address 21. To enable the HP3485A Frequency counter to work for remote operation and to ignore the front panel controls, the TAS016 command REMOTE 22 is used.

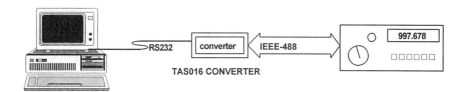

Figure 7.14 The block diagram of the setup

The TAS016 is instructed to send subsequent data to the device at address 22 by the command, OUTPUT 22.

These commands may be combined to give the command string

REMOTE 22 OUTPUT 22

Adding the Command header string and the Command terminator required to identify TAS016 commands gives the following command string:

ESC%GPIB REMOTE 22 OUTPUT 22%

This command string, when processed by the TAS016, addresses the HP3485A Frequency counter to become Remote enabled and an Active listener. Data received from the host computer can now be passed directly to the HP3485A Frequency counter via the TAS016. Once the data path to the HP3485A Frequency counter has been set in this manner, it can be commanded to select the required function and range.

For example, if the HP3485A Frequency counter requires the command FL1 to activate a low pass filter and the command AT1 to select the divide by 20 divider for input A, FL1 AT1 will select the A input with divide by 20 prescaler and connect the internal low pass filter to the A input.

The whole process therefore requires the host computer to send the character data

ESC%GPIB REMOTE 22 OUTPUT 22%FL1 AT1

A convenient method of doing this is to output the data as a literal string. In BASIC this is achieved by declaring the character data between quotation (") marks. However, the ESC character (ASCII code decimal value 27, hexadecimal 1B) is classed as a Control code and cannot be declared as a literal character and so is given special treatment. The BASIC function CHR$ forms a character with the ASCII character code declared in its numeric argument. Thus ESC can be generated by the construct CHR$(27). The data to be output by the host computer becomes

CHR$(27)+%GPIB REMOTE 22 OUTPUT 22%FL1 AT1

This would typically be directed to the Computer RS-232 serial interface opened on channel 1 using the program line

10 PRINT #1, CHR$(27)+U%GPIB REMOTE 22 OUTPUT 22%FL1AT1

If we would like the counter to make a measurement, we should issue the command FU1 to make a reading from input A. We include this code in the string as well

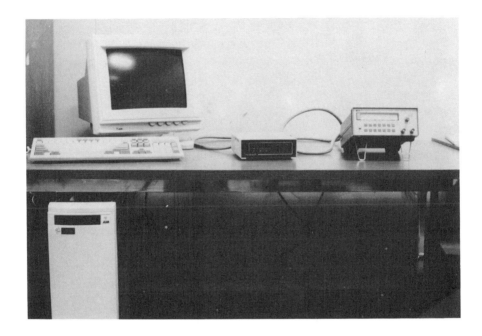

Figure 7.15 Actual arrangement of the setup.

10 PRINT #1, CHR$(27)+U%GPIB REMOTE 22 OUTPUT 22%FL1AT1FU1

When this line of code is executed the HP3485A Frequency counter would normally start to take a reading.

Reading Back the Data

While remotely controlled, the HP3485A Frequency counter is commanded to output a reading when instructed to become an Active talker on the bus. This means that the TAS016 must become an Active listener to receive the reading and transmit it to the host computer. The BASIC program line to achieve this is

20 PRINT #1, CHR$(27)+'%GPIB ENTER 22%

Since we are expecting an integer numeric value representing a frequency, we can assign the reading to the numeric variable A and display it on the computer screen with

> 30 INPUT #1,A
>
> 40 PRINT A

Putting It All Together

The whole process of setting the TAS016 and HP3485A Frequency counter to take a single frequency reading with attenuater and LPF on and display the value on the host computer screen becomes

> 10 PRINT #1, CHR$(27)+%GPIB REMOTE 22 OUTPUT 22%FL1AT1FU1
>
> 20 PRINT #1, CHR$(27)+%GPIB ENTER 22%
>
> 30 INPUT #1,A
>
> 40 PRINT A
>
> 50 END

This simple example demonstrates the basic functions required to control a typical IEEE-488 instrumentation device using the TAS016. In general the process of controlling GPIB equipment with TAS016 can be summarized this way:

1. Instruct the TAS016 to set a TRANSMIT data path to the required instrument

2. Command the instrument to perform the required function by issuing a device dependent command string

3. Instruct the TAS016 to set a RECEIVE data path from the required instrument

4. Read the function result into the host computer.

A Word of Caution!

Hewlett-Packard, being the inventor of this system, has been designing GPIB equipment and controller computers for some time. HP has a special dialect of BASIC called HPBASIC which is enriched with special commands to control GPIB equipment easily. These special commands are not available with the common BASIC compilers and interpreters. Usually the examples given in the HP IEEE-488 equipment manual are written for that special HP dialect of BASIC and they will run only by the HP-designed controller. If one would like to use HP instruments with other vendors' controllers, one has to be careful with the sample programs given in the HP equipment manual since, as they are, they run only with HPBASIC. Other vendors have other ways to implement these instructions and they are not necessarily difficult. Just read the manuals carefully.

7.6 USING A PLUG-IN TYPE GPIB CARD

The previous section showed us how to use an external RS-232 to IEEE-488 converter to convert one's PC to an IEEE-488 controller. Another easy way to convert a computer to a controller is to install a GPIB card inside the computer. Plug-in type GPIB cards for PC's come in two different forms. One type has the necessary programs stored in an on-board ROM. By calling these machine language routines from a high level language you can use the card together with the PC as a GPIB controller. The other category of cards are I/O mapped and device drivers are used for necessary low level software. Both of these kinds are fully reviewed in the coming sections.

7.6.1 Memory Mapped GPIB Cards

In this category we are going to examine a PCL 848 A/B multifunction IEEE-488 interface card designed by Advantech Co. Ltd. This card has an onboard EPROM which contains all the necessary programs. The location of the onboard EPROM can be selected by the user to avoid the possibility of conflict with other firmware available on the PC system. The card has DMA and interrupt capabilities. Since the EPROM has the routines in machine language form, any high level language that can call assembly language routines can use the card as a GPIB controller. Since all high level languages, like BASIC, Pascal and C, have this capability, any one of them is a suitable candidate for writing programs.

As an example, let us use the HP3485A frequency counter that we have used in the previous section with this card. Using the switches provided on the card, we locate the on board firmware in location HD000 hex. The HP3485 frequency counter is located at address 23.

```
10  DEF SEG=&HD000
20  OUTPUT%=3 : ENTER%=6
30  ADDR%=23         'GP-IB address of HP3485A
40  TMP$="FUl"       'HP3485A F.Counter programming code
50  CALL OUTPUT%(ADDR%,TMP$)
60  FOR I=1 TO 10
70  D$=SPACE$(80)
80  CALL ENTER%(ADDR,D$)
90  PRINT D$
100 NEXT I
110 END
```

In BASICA notation DEF SEG will define the location of the EPROM. The EPROM contains machine language routines for IEEE-488 universal action commands.

These routines are called by giving their offset location relative to the beginning location of the EPROM. For example the universal action command OUTPUT has an offset address of 3, and ENTER has an offset address of 6. A complete list of the universal action commands and their offsets is listed below.

Universal Action Commands and Firmware Offsets

COMMAND	Offset	Description
ABORT	9	abort
DEVCLR	15	Device clear
DEVICE	57	Install IEEE-488 device driver instead of printer driver
ENTER	6	Enter string
ENTERA	51	Enter long string
EOL	12	Terminator for input, output strings
INIT	0	Initialize
LLO	18	Local lockout
LOCAL	21	Go to local
OUTPUT	3	Output string
OUTPUTA	54	Output long string
PPOLL	24	Parallel poll
PPOLLC	27	Parallel poll configure
PPOLLU	30	Parallel poll unconfigure
REMOTE	33	Place a device in remote mode
SEND	36	Send device specific commands
SPOLL	39	Serial poll
STATUS	42	Status
TIMEOUT	45	Set timeout period
TRIGGER	48	Group execute trigger
ERRPTR	60	Error number

CONTROLLING GPIB CONTROLLER CARD FROM BASIC

Sample Programs

Interactive data transfer using PCL 848 A/B:

```
10  ' FILE NAME : Interactive
20  ' Program Example : INTERACTIVE DATA TRANSFER
```

```
40  ' Purpose :    This program outputs data strings entered by
50  '              users and enters data from the IEEE-488 bus.
80  ' Initialization
90
100 LIN.Y=1 : KEY OFF : CLS
110 DEF SEG=&HD000
120 ABORT%=9 : OUTPUT%=3 : ENTER%=6 : STATUS%=42
130 CALL ABORT%
140 '
150 '
160 '
170 KEY(1) ON : KEY(2) ON : KEY(3) ON : KEY(4) ON : KEY(5) OFF
180 KEY(6) OFF: KEY(7) OFF: KEY(8) OFF: KEY(9) OFF: KEY(10) OFF
190 KEY 1," CLS ":KEY 2,"OUTPUT":KEY 3,"ENTER ":KEY 4," EXIT "
200 KEY 5," ":KEY 6,"       ":KEY 7,"     ":KEY 8,"
210 KEY 9," ":KEY 10,"
220 ON KEY(1) GOSUB 390
230 ON KEY(2) GOSUB 440
240 ON KEY(3) GOSUB 560
250 ON KEY(4) GOSUB 810
260
270 GOSUB 330
280 KEY ON
290 GOTO 290       'Loop here waiting function key
300
310 ' Display message
320
330 COLOR 15,7:LOCATE 22,1,0PRINT " ";SPACE$(79):LOCATE 22,1
340 PRINT "Select function key l":COLOR 7,0:LOCATE 1,1
350 RETURN
360 '
370 'Clear Screen
380 '
390 CLS:GOSUB 330
400 RETURN
410 '
420 'OUTPUT UTILITY
430 '
```

```
440  TMP$=SPACE$(80)
450  IF 22-LIN.Y<6 THEN CLS:LIN.Y=1
460  LOCATE 22,1,0PRINT " ";SPACE$(79):LOCATE LIN.Y,1
470  PRINT
480  INPUT "To which address ? ",ADDR%
490  LINE INPUT "OUTPUT string ? ",TMP$
500  E.FG%=0 : CALL OUTPUT%(ADDR%,TMP$)
510  GOSUB 710
520  IF S%=0 THEN PRINT "Data transmitted 1"
530  PRINT : PRINT : LIN.Y=CSRLIN : GOSUB 330
540  RETURN
550  '
560  '
570  'ENTER UTILITY
580  '
590  PRINT
600  D$=SPACE$(80)
610  IF 22-LIN.Y<6 THEN CLS : LIN.Y=1
620  LOCATE 22,1,0:PRINT " ";SPC(79):LOCATE LIN.Y,1
630  INPUT "From which address ? ",ADDR%
640  CALL ENTER%(ADDR%,D$)
650  GOSUB 740              'Error check
660  IF S%<>0 THEN 690       'Error happened
670  PRINT "ENTERED STRING  :"
680  PRINT DS
690  PRINT : LIN.Y=CSRLIN : GOSUB 430
700  RETURN
720  '
730  ' TIMEOUT CHECK ROUTINE
740  '
750  CONDITION
760  CALL STATUS%(CONDITION%,S%)
770  IF S%=1 THEN PRINT "TIMEOUT 1"
780  IF S%<>0 AND S%<>1 THEN PRINT "INTERFACE ERROR 1"
790  RETURN
800  '
810  END
```

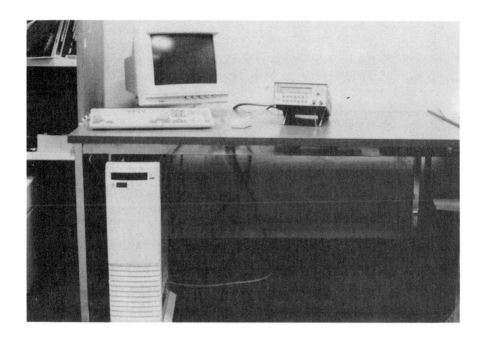

Figure 7.16 Actual arrangement of the setup.

7.6.2 I/O Mapped GPIB Cards for the PC

The other category of plug-in type GPIB cards for the PC are I/O mapped cards. Unlike the previous kind of GPIB boards which carry their own routines on the card, these cards have their software stored in a device driver. The style of calling universal action commands is very similar to the previous category. The only difference is that in this category of cards one does have to specify the offset location for the specific universal action command instructions. The example below shows typical universal action commands the way they are issued in this category of GPIB cards.

CALL SendIFC(0)   Assert interface clear signal

CALL DevClear(0, Device_Address)   Clear the device with the
                                                    specific address

CALL Send(0, Device_Address, " Device specific instructions")

CALL Receive(0,6, Reading$, STOPend)

7.7 CASE STUDY: DATA ACQUISITION WITH IEEE-488 EQUIPMENT

In this section we are going to look at a case study using a data acquisition crate which has an IEEE-488 interface. Although GPIB equipment is very often used for data acquisition purposes, there are only a few manufacturers that manufacture data acquisition equipment for GPIB networks. Most simple applications use a single digital voltmeter for making measurements or analog-to-digital conversions. Usually this approach is acceptable if the speed or the number of analog channels required for data acquisition is not very demanding. Digital voltmeters use a dual ramp method of conversion which gives excellent resolution but the conversion time is very slow.

For applications which are beyond simple DVM's, there are data acquisition crates with IEEE-488 interfaces. A typical example of this category of equipment is the HP 3497A data acquisition unit. This unit is designed to operate either stand alone or in a GPIB network. It also has a RS-232, RS-422 interface through which the device can be used with serial communication.

The unit is able to

- Measure voltage levels from microvolt to 120 volt
- Measure temperature through its thermocouple, thermistor and RTD interface
- Measure resistance using four wire bridge technique
- Measure frequency
- Measure pressure

Figure 7.17 Front side view of HP3497A.

Figure 7.18 Back side view of HP3497A

- Accommodate up to 1000 analog channels and scan them at 300 channels/sec
- Generate alarm signals
- Generate programmable current output of 4-20 mA for control purposes
- Use digital inputs
- Use an onboard real time clock

The data acquisition unit has internal slots and speciality boards; by installing these special boards, the capabilities listed above can be achieved.

The unit, being a GPIB device, understands universal action commands and has device-specific instructions. Some of the device-specific instructions of the HP3497A are reproduced below:

AC chan#, chan#   ANALOG CLOSE (Closes 1 to 4 channels of analog assemblies.)

AF chan#   ANALOG FIRST CHANNEL

AI chan#   ANALOG INPUT (Closes channel and triggers DVM to take a measurement.)

AO slot#,chan#,value ANALOG OUTPUT

AR   ANALOG RESET

AS   ANALOG STEP

7.7.1 Device Specific Instruction Set for HP3497A

Using HP 3497A is very straightforward. The analog or digital channels are opened or closed by using appropriate instructions and the output is sent to the controller. Most of these operations can be achieved by using ENTER and OUTPUT commands of the universal action commands.

We would like to use the above setup for automatically measuring the linearity of voltage to frequency converter chips. We are receiving V-F converter chips from a vendor and would like to verify the linearity of the components in the range 0 to 5 volts. The circuit is designed in such a way that as the input voltage changes from 0 to 5 volts, the output frequency of the V-F converter should change from 1 kHz to 70 kHz. We simply plug in the components to the circuit and connect it to the test setup for verification. The HP 3497A data acquisition unit is being used as a programmable voltage generator by using its analog output facilities. The HP5385A is being used for measuring the frequency output of the circuit.

The following simple program measures the input voltage and the output frequency:

HP5385A address set to 23

HP3497A address set to 24

Voltage output is taken from analog output channel number 1 of the HP3497A. Frequency output is connected to channel A of the HP5385A. No filters are connected to the output.

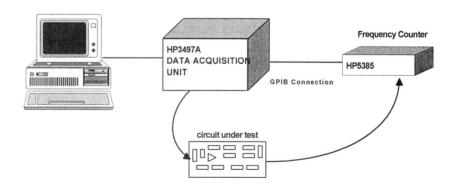

Figure 7.19 Block diagram of the experiment setup.

```
10  DEF SEG=&HD000
20  OUTPUT%=3 : ENTER%=6
30  FOR VALUE=1 TO 5000 STEP 5
35  ADDR%=24          'GP-IB address of HP3497A
40  TMP$="AO,1,1VALUE"        'HP3497A programming code
50  CALL OUTPUT%(ADDR%,TMP$)
70  D$=SPACE$(80)
75  ADDR%=23    'GPIB ADDRESS OF HP5385A
77  TMP$="FU1"       'HP5385A programming code
80  CALL ENTER%(ADDR,D$)
90  PRINT VALUE, D$
100 NEXT VALUE
110 END
```

The program given applies voltage output from slot number 1, channel number 1 of the HP3497 data acquisition unit starting from 0 to 5 volts in increments of 5 mV. The operation is repeated 1000 times and the voltage, and frequency outputs are printed. The program can be modified to store the values and perform a statistical analysis of the data to decide whether to accept or reject the component.

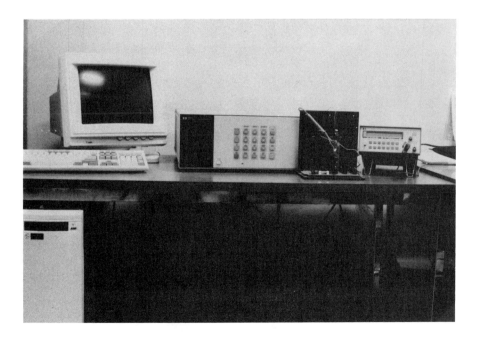

Figure 7.20 Circuit under test.

REFERENCES

1. *Multi-Function IEEE-488 Interface Card Manual*, Advantec, 1990.

2. *3497A Data Acquistion/Control Unit Operating, Programming and Configuration Manual*, Hewlett-Packard, 1987.

3. *54200A/D Digitizing Oscilloscope Operating, Programming and Configuration Manual*, Hewlett-Packard, 1987.

4. *5385A Frequency Counter Operation and Service Manual*, Hewlett-Packard, 1987.

5. *IEEE Standard Digital Interface for Programmable Instrumentation--IEEE Std. 488-1978,* The Institute of Electrical and Electronic Engineers, 1978.

6. *ASYST GPIB/IEEE-488 Module Manual*, Keithley Instruments, 1990.

7. *TAS016 IEEE-488/RS232C Converter Handbook*, Tastronic Controls, 1988.

8. *NI-488.2 Software Reference Manual*, National Instruments, 1992.

9. *Tutorial Description of the Hewlett-Packard Interface Bus*, Hewlett-Packard, 1980.

10. Austerlitz, H., *Data Acquisition Techniques Using Personal Computers*, Academic Press, 1991.

11. Gates, S. C., Becker, J., *Labaratory Automation Using the IBM PC*, Prentice Hall, 1989.

Eight

REMOTE DATA ACQUISITION USING PC's

8.1 INTRODUCTION

In the previous chapters we have looked at different ways of using PC's for data acquisition applications. In Chapter Six we concentrated on local data acquisition, where the PC actually resides in the environment of the application in close proximity to the sensors and actuators. In Chapter Seven, we enlarged the circle of data acquisition somewhat to expand to a lab environment which allowed limited distance between PC, instruments and application. In this chapter we will concentrate on remote data acquisition applications where the PC and the application are significantly distant from each other.

The concept of "remote" is a rather relative concept. In general what is meant by "remote" is having sufficient distance between the PC and the from the local environment of the application and the sensors. As a rule of thumb, anytime the distance between the PC and the application is more than 20 meters, remote data acquisition methods should be utilized. Starting from 20 meters, the distance between the PC and the application can be increased up to a kilometer very easily with almost no extra hardware. Increasing distance further is possible but requires additional specialized equipment. The distance can be increased with almost no limit.

Remote data acquisition applications constitute a very important class among data acquisition applications since most realistic applications demand considerable distance between the application and the computer. Most of the time it is physically impossible to put a PC near the application. There is hardly any room for one's PC in a wind tunnel for example.

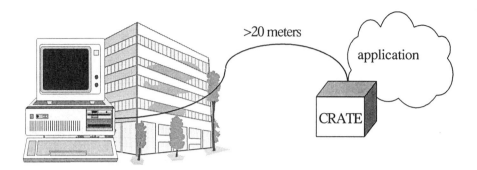

Figure 8.1 Typical remote data acquisition application.

In some other cases it may be physically possible to put the PC near the application, but because of the environmental conditions like temperature, dust or vibration present in the surrounding area, it would be wiser to put the PC away to increase the reliability of the system. High temperature ovens and blast furnaces are examples of environments which are not PC friendly. In such cases we would like to locate the PC in a more suitable climate where your floppy disks would not melt away.

Remote data acquisition is almost always associated with serial communication. Readers who would like to know more about serial communication techniques are recommended to read *C Programmers Guide to Serial Communication*, by Joe Campbell, published by Howard W. Sams & Company in 1987.

8.2 REMOTE DATA ACQUISITION TECHNIQUES

Depending on the size of the data acquisition application and the requirement of speed, there are different techniques that can be used for remote data acquisition. These methods, from the simplest to the most sophisticated can be listed as follows:

- Remote data acquisition using *data acquisition modules*
- Remote data acquisition using remote *passive data acquisition crates*
- Remote data acquisition using remote *intelligent data acquisition crates*

The main difference between the above methods is the number of channels to sample and the speed of data acquisition. The distance between the application and the PC is a function of the interface standard used. By using suitable standards, any one of the above techniques can have distance from the PC ranging from 100's of meters to 100's of kilometers.

Figure 8.2 compares these methods in terms of number of acquisition channels versus the speed of data acquisition. Each one of these methods will be reviewed in detail in the coming sections.

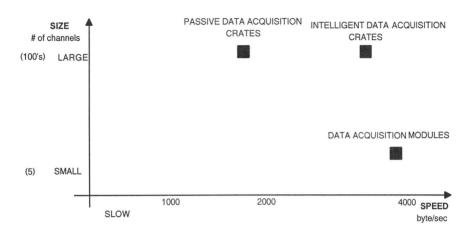

Figure 8.2 Speed vs. size plot of remote data acquisition techniques.

8.3 DISTANCE BETWEEN PC AND THE APPLICATION

The distance between the PC and the application is a function of the interface standard used. In general the distance capability of popular interface standards are as follows:

RS-232	20 meters / 20 kbaud
RS-422	1200 meters / 100 kbaud
RS-485	1200 meters / 100 kbaud

In data communication applications there is always a trade-off between the speed and the distance of communication. The distance can be increased if one is willing to reduce the speed. Or the speed can be increased if the distance is kept short. The figures given above are not absolute and should be viewed with this consideration in mind. As an example, RS-485 can communicate at 10 Mbaud if the distance is limited to 20 meters, at 100 meters the maximum speed is around 1 Mbaud, etc.

8.3.1 Using Repeaters for Increasing Distance

If the distance provided by the standard is not sufficient, then the first thing to try is to reduce the speed of communication. According to the discussion above, the distance can be increased considerably if one is willing to reduce the speed. If reducing the speed is not possible because of the speed requirement of the application, repeaters should be used for strengthening the signal without reducing the speed of communication.

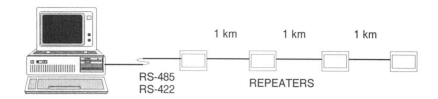

Figure 8.3 Using repeaters with RS-422 or RS-485.

Any number of repeaters can be connected in series for strengthening the signal for increasing the distance of communication. But if more than four repeaters are needed, alternative distance increase techniques should be tried. The cost of the design may become prohibitive compared to other techniques like using modems for that particular application.

8.3.2 Using Fiber Optic Modems for Increasing Distance

Another technique that will give more distance than repeaters is the use of modems. Modems can be either fiber optic or electrical types and the communication lines can be either special dedicated lines or phone lines.

Fiber optic modems are of special interest to data acquisition applications because of the following reasons:

- Fiber optic modems are virtually immune to electromagnetic noise which is a major concern in data acquisition environments.
- Fiber optic modems provide electrical (galvanic) isolation between the application and the PC naturally.
- The distance and the speed can be very high with fiber optic modems, a low cost plastic fiber optic cable and a low cost fiber optic modem connected to the RS-232 port of a PC can provide distances up to 3.5 km at speeds 19.2 kbaud. With special fiber optic communication equipment plugged into high speed communication ports the speed can be in the order of 100's of Mbaud for several kilometers without repeaters.

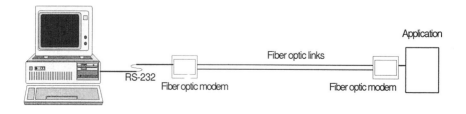

Figure 8.4 Using fiber optic modems for increasing distance between application and PC.

8.3.3 Using Short Haul Modems for Increasing Distance

Short haul modem or asynchronous line drivers require a dedicated 4-core line between the application side and the PC. This type of modem is connected to the RS-232 port of the PC directly to provide distances up to 40 km and speed up to 38,800 baud. Due to the speed/distance trade-off lower distance should be expected at high baud rates. (19.2 kbaud at 1250 meters.)

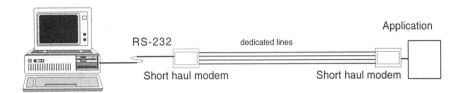

Figure 8.5 Using short haul modem for increasing distance between the PC and the application.

8.3.4 Using Analog Phone Line Modems for Increasing Distance

If the distance between the application and the PC is considerable, it may be wise to consider the option of using phone lines. This option may not always be a viable one since it depends on the availability of phone lines which may not always be the case. For applications which are not time critical nor involve large amount of data exchange, phone lines offer a cost effective alternative. They are ideal for downloading data periodically from the application, e.g. daily activities at the end of the day. If the amount of data to exchange is excessive and the line is needed to be available continuously, a leased line would be a logical choice. In either case using phone lines requires a modem to be used on both the PC side and the application side. Currently V.32bis which provides communication at 14,400 bits/sec. and V.34 which communicates at 28,800 bits/sec are top of the line standards. These standards use forward error-correction technique to allow on-the-fly error correction which is very desirable for data acquisition applications. Standards like V.42bis which offer data compression may offer effective data communication at 38,800 baud but the user should be cautious since the effective data transmission rate depends on the data itself and it may not always be possible to get the 38,800 rate all the time. The modems should be tested in the actual environment with actual data for reliability of communication.

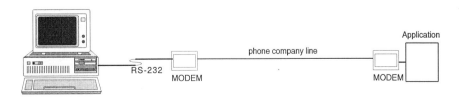

Figure 8.6 Using analog dial up modems and phone company lines for increasing the distance between the application and the PC.

The table below shows different distance increasing equipment with their distance capabilities:

EQUIPMENT	USED WITH	DESCRIPTION AND DISTANCE
Asynchronous line driver	RS-232	Requires special dedicated 4 wire link Required on both ends of PC and the application Maximum distance 1250 meters with 19.2 kbaud rate.
Fiber optic modem	RS-232	Requires two dedicated fiber optic cables Distance 3.5 km with 19.2 kbaud rate, or 1 km with 64 kbaud rate.
Short haul modem	RS-232	Requires customer owned dedicated line Requires one on both ends of the line Distance 35-40 km, with 1.5 Mb/sec.
Analog modem	RS-232	Ordinary phone lines, 14,400 baud.
Digital modem	RS-232	Requires switched 56 service from phone company Equipment required on both ends, 57.6 kbaud speed.

Short data sheet given on the next page indicates some of the equipment used for increasing distance between the application and the computer.

8.4 REMOTE DATA ACQUISITION USING DATA ACQUISITION MODULES

Remote data acquisition modules are small, intelligent, microcontroller based modules which can be powered remotely and can communicate serially with a host computer. Since the hardware of the module is very slim, it takes a relatively very small amount of power to make the module operational. This power can either be supplied locally or remotely.

The module, being intelligent, has its own vocabulary of commands. The user can simply send the command from a host computer serially in ASCII form and the module will take the necessary action accordingly. Normally the speed of execution of the command by the module is very fast, but because of the delay involved in the serial communication process the speed of data acquisition is not very high.

Remote data acquisition modules, being physically small, can not accommodate more than a few analog or digital channels. Most of the modules on the market have the signal conditioning available on the module enabling user to simply "plug in" the sensors. The hardware of the application will then be ready for data acquisition.

The remote data acquisition modules use serial communication with the host computer. Most of the units on the market use either the RS-232 or the RS-485 standard for data communication. Of these two, the modules with the RS-485 interface are preferred in applications where a multiple number of modules are needed for the application.

Line drivers
Asynchronous In-Line

W. 45
H. 17
D. 85

The **RS** Microdriver asynchronous line drivers are a low-cost method of extending the communication distance of a V24/RS-232C interface. The Microdrivers are installed at both ends of the line using a simple 4 wire link. Plugging directly into a 25 way D type RS-232C socket with a simple solderless connector at the other end for line connections.

Microdrivers are available in both in-line and wall mount versions. Wall mount versions, either single channel white plastic faced or dual channel metal clad, are ideal for use where a permanent installation is required and may be fitted into standard electrical mounting boxes (refer to electrical wiring accessories section). Line connections to the in-line version are made via a 4 way plug-in terminal block, whilst 'Krone' connectors (with supplied fixing tool) are used on the wall mount versions.

● Guaranteed speed of 19·2k bits/second at a distance of 1250m (at lower speeds much greater distances are possible).
● Uses a simple 4 wire interface suitable for most types of inexpensive cable (eg. **RS** stock no.367-987)
● Internal link options allow configuration. Pins 2 & 3 are transmit and receive respectively but may be crossed by soldering wire links. Also pins 8 and 20 may be pulled high by 1K resistors.
● Operation without external power when used on most V24/RS-232C interfaces. Maximum current taken from any pin is 6·8 mA.

Modem V32/V22bis/V22 with Autodial and Error Correction

This **RS** modem offers error-free, full duplex data communication of 9600 baud over the dial up telephone network. A speed of 19200 baud is achievable over the same network when employing V32 with MNP5 data compression/error correction. This unit can also be configured for asynchronous or synchronous data transfer over the PSTN.
Features :
● Extended AT command set
● DTE transmission speeds to 19200 baud
● V42 and MNP level5 error correction/data compression
● Fully auto sensing on originate and answer (V32/V22bis/V22)
● Data buffering with XON/XOFF and hardware flow control
● 10 entry telephone number store
● Asynchronous/synchronous operation

Technical Specification

Network Connection

Data transfer rate	Up to 19200bps with V32 & MNP5
Modulation technique :	
V32	32 point trellis
	16 point uncoded
V22bis	16 point QAM
V22	DPSK type A & B
Operational modes :	
V32	9600bps full duplex
fallback	4800bps full duplex
V22bis	2400bps full duplex
Connection	BT 600 series jack plug for PSTN
	3 wire bell tinkle suppression supported
Signal level	-9dBm
Interface	600 ohm
Equalisation	Automatic adaptive
Echo cancellation	Local and distant end cancellation

Autodial/Auto Answer

Dial method	Pulse and tone dialling
Call progress	Internal loudspeaker, extended response messages
Call control	Extended AT command set
Mode selection	Automatic configuration on transmit and receive for V32/V22bis/V22
Call disconnection	Loss of carrier, DTR, manual or by command
Signal quality action	Retrain, adaptive speed or disconnect
Telephone directory	10 stored numbers
Security	Single number call back

Data Connection

DTE interface	Compliant with V24/V28, Tx Rx RTS CTS DSR DCD TCK RCK DTR RI ETC
Protocol	Async command Async/synchronous data
Async word format	10 bit command mode 10/11 bit word data mode
DTE speed	1200, 2400, 4800, 9600, 19200bps
Error correction	V42 including lap/M & MNP4
Data compression	To MNP5
Synchronous clock	Internal, external & slave

Diagnostics

Loop tests	V54 analogue and digital loops. In-built test generator
Self tests	Automatic test on power-up. Timed loopbacks

RS-232C Fibre Optic Interface

W. 53
L. 77
D. 19

The **RS** stock no. 300-776 RS-232C transceiver is a full duplex asynchronous data link for the transmission of EIA RS-232C signals from d.c. to 64 k bits/s. The transceiver provides an effective, high performance, means of extending transmission distances up to
1 km with the additional benefits of noise immunity, data security, reduced error rate and elimination of ground loops.
The **RS** stock no. 300-776 is fitted with a 25-pin 'D'-type plug for direct connection to the RS-232 interface ports of modems, terminals, CPU's, etc. The **RS** 25-way 'D' gender changer 489-649 can be used where an adaptor with female connectors is required. Power connection is via a standard 2·5 mm jack socket allowing operation from standard mains adaptors.
Optical connection is via SMA-style connectors compatible with **RS** terminated optical fibre leads 368-564, etc.
·The units are supplied for connection to DTE equipment, but can be used with DCE equipment by selection of two internal plug-in links. An instruction leaflet is supplied with each transceiver illustrating DTE/DCE changeover and fibre optic interconnection details.

Technical Specification

absolute max. ratings

Supply voltage	9 V d.c. min. 15 V d.c. max.*
Supply current	120 mA max.
Operating temperature range	0 °C to ÷ 60 °C

electro-optical characteristics

Transmitter:

Input voltage - Mark (1)	-3 min. -25 V max.
Space (0)	+ 3 V min. + 25 V max.
Data rate	d.c. to 64 k bits/s.
Pulse width	15 μs min.
Peak emission wavelength	820 nm typ.
Power output	100 μW typ. †

Receiver:

Flux level Logic 0	3 μW min.
(at 820 nm) Logic 1	0·5 μW max.
Output voltage - Mark (1)	-4 V typ.
Space (0)	÷ 4 V typ.
Pulse width distortion	5 μs max.
Rise and fall times (10% to 90%)	1 μs typ.
Output load	300 Ω min.
Bit error rate (BER)	10⁻³ typ.

*Power jack socket - tip wired to positive.
† Into 200 μ core fibre, NA 0·27.

Figure 8.7 Remote data acquisition modules. (Courtesy Keithley-Metrabyte.)

The RS-485 interface standard has the networking ability which allows multiple modules up to 32 to be connected to a single serial port of the host computer. Modules with the RS-232 interface standard are mostly used for applications where a single module (or only a few) is needed.

The modules with the RS-232 interface standard can also be networked so that multiple modules can be connected to a single serial port of the host computer. However, there are disadvantages of this configuration. These issues will be covered in greater detail in the coming sections.

8.4.1 Commercially Available Data Acquisition Modules

In this section we will examine in detail some of the commercially available data acquisition modules.

One of the popular modules available on the market is Metrabyte® M series of Modules made by Keithley Metrabyte Corporation. We will look at these modules as examples of this category and explore how to use them.

METRABYTE M SERIES REMOTE DATA ACQUISITION MODULES

MetraByte M series modules are self contained units which can be interfaced to the sensor directly at a remote location. The modules are physically small and the power requirement is low; hence the power required can either be supplied locally or can be delivered together with the communication wires. Modules can accept large power supply variations (+10 to +30 V), which is expected due to the resistive voltage drops of the long transmission lines used for supplying power to the modules.

Figure 8.8 Inside view of a data acquisition module.

A module is equipped with an internal voltage regulator to stabilize possible voltage variations. Due to this feature, the designer does not have to worry about the voltage drop over the power lines.

The typical power requirement of the module is about 0.75 watts which can be considered very small. In extreme cases, this much power can even be supplied locally by rechargeable batteries and solar chargers.

The information transfer connection of the module with the host computer is performed either over a RS-232 or RS-485 standard serial interface. It is not possible to use a given module with both standards, so MetraByte delivers modules either with a RS-232 or RS-485 interface. The capabilities and remote connection distances are quite different for RS-232 and RS-485 standards; so a designer of the system must weigh the advantages and disadvantages of both systems and order modules accordingly. Details of connection schemes and advantages and disadvantages of these standards will be provided in the next section.

MetraByte offers a large selection of M series modules with a built-in internal signal conditioning ability. These modules, which are called M1000/2000 series, accept very specific input signals like thermocouple output, RTD input, frequency input, etc., and convert them into digital output which is transmitted serially. The communication interface of the module is either RS-232 or RS-485. The list below shows different M series modules with different signal conditioning functions built in. A M3000/4000 series of modules provides analog output voltage or current capability.

Figure 8.9 M series modules can be stacked together if more of them is required.

M1000 Series Analog Input to Serial Digital Output Modules

Analog Input Type
- Fixed voltage input
- 4-20 mA current input
- Thermocouple input
- 4 wire resistive bridge input
- Frequency input
- Pulse input
- Digital input

M2000 Series Scaled Analog Input to Serial Digital Output Modules

Analog Input Type
- Fixed voltage input
- 4-20 mA current input
- Frequency input
- Pulse input

M3000 Series Serial Digital Input to Analog Output Modules
- Fixed range output voltage type
- Current output type

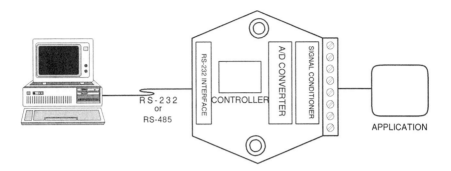

Figure 8.10 Functional block diagram of a typical M series module.

M4000 Series Serial Digital Input to Scaled Analog Output Modules
- Fixed range output voltage type
- Current output type

All the modules listed come with an RS-232 or RS-485 type interface for connection to the host.

Explanation of Technical Specifications of Remote Data Acquisition Modules

Technical specifications for M1000 series modules are given in Table 8.1. The operational environment temperature range for the module is specified as -25 to +70 degrees centigrade, which means that modules can withstand harsh operational temperatures and can be installed in the field directly. The other environmental figure mentioned in the specifications, storage, means that the device can be stored within -25 degrees to +85 degrees without any permanent damage.

The fact that storage temperature is up to +85 degrees but the operational temperature is up to +70 degrees means that beyond the +70 degree mark the internally generated heat by the module would not be dissipated adequately and eventually the rising temperature will destroy the module. Operational temperature range should be obeyed carefully in order to avoid such mishaps. Notice that the relative humidity for the module is specified as 0 to 95% noncondensing which means that the device can operate in a wide humidity range but it is not waterproof and one should take precautions for protecting the module from water in the field.

Mechanically, the module is housed in an ABS plastic case (a variety of strong, environmentally resistant plastic) with captive connectors. These connectors allow the modules to be stacked and to be attached to each other easily.

M1000 SERIES: MODEL INPUT/OUTPUT
Voltage Inputs

M1111	+/-100 mV Input/RS-232C Output
M1112	+/-100 mV Input/RS-485 Output
M1121	+/-1 V Input/RS-232C Output
M1122	+/-1 V Input/RS-485 Output
M1131	+/-5 V Input/RS-232C Output
M1132	+/-5 V Input/RS-485 Output
M1141	+/-10 V Input/RS-232C Output
M1142	+/-10 V Input/RS-485 Output
M1151	+/-100 V Input/RS-232C Output
M1152	+/-100 V Input/RS-485 Output

Current Inputs

M1211	+/-10 mA Input/RS-232C Output
M1221	+/-1 mA Input/RS-232C Output
M1231	+/-100 mA Input/RS-232C Output
M1232	+/-100 mA Input/RS-485 Output
M1251	4 – 20 mA Input/RS-232C Output
M1252	4 – 20 mA Input/RS-485 Output

Thermocouple Inputs

M1311	J-Type Input/RS-232C Output
M1312	J-Type Input/RS-485 Output
M1321	K-Type Input/RS-232C Output
M1322	K-Type Input/RS-485 Output
M1331	T-Type Input/RS-232C Output
M1332	T-Type Input/RS-485 Output
M1361	S-Type Input/RS-232C Output
M1362	S-Type Input/RS-485 Output

RTD Inputs

M1411	.00385 RTD In/RS-232C Output
M1412	.00385 RTD In/RS-485 Output
M1421	.00392 RTD In/RS-232C Output
M1422	.00392 RTD In/RS-485 Output

Bridge Inputs (E = Excitation Voltage)

M1511	+/-30 mV In, 5 V E/RS-232C Out
M1512	+/-30 mV In, 5 V E/RS-485 Out
M1521	+/-30 mV In, 10 V E/RS-232C Out
M1522	+/-30 mV In, 10 V E/RS-485 Out
M1531	+/-100 mV In, 5 V E/RS-232C Out
M1532	+/-100 mV In, 5 V E/RS-485 Out
M1541	+/-100 mV In, 10 V E/RS-232C Out
M1542	+/-100 mV In, 10 V E/RS-485 Out

Frequency and Pulse Inputs

M1601	Frequency Input/RS-232C Output
M1602	Frequency Input/RS-485 Output
M1611	Pulse Input/RS-232C Output
M1621	Event Counter/RS-232C Output
M1622	Event Counter/RS-485 Output
M1631	Frequency In/RS-232C Out
M1632	Frequency In/RS-485 Out

Digital Inputs/Outputs

M1701	7 Digital I/O/RS-232C Output
M1702	7 Digital I/O/RS-485 Output
M1711	15 Digital I/O/RS-232C Output
M1712	15 Digital I/O/RS-485 Output

M2000 SERIES: MODEL INPUT/OUTPUT
Voltage Inputs

M2111	+/-100 mV Input/RS-232C Output
M2112	+/-100 mV Input/RS-485 Output
M2121	+/-1 V Input/RS-232C Output
M2122	+/-1 V Input/RS-485 Output
M2131	+/-5 V Input/RS-232C Output
M2132	+/-5 V Input/RS-485 Output
M2141	+/-10 V Input/RS-232C Output
M2142	+/-10 V Input/RS-485 Output

Current Inputs

M2222	+/-1 mA Input/RS-485 Output
M2251	4 – 20 mA Input/RS-232C Output
M2252	4 – 20 mA Input/RS-485 Output

Bridge Inputs (E = Exitation Voltage)

M2511	+/-30 mV In, 5 V E/RS-232C Out
M2512	+/-30 mV In, 5 V E/RS-485 Out
M2521	+/-30 mV In, 10 V E/RS-232C Out
M2522	+/-30 mV In, 10 V E/RS-485 Out
M2531	+/-100 mV In, 5 V E/RS-232C Out
M2532	+/-100 mV In, 5 V E/RS-485 Out
M2541	+/-100 mV In, 10 V E/RS-232C Out

Frequency and Pulse Inputs

M2601	Frequency Input/RS-232C Output
M2602	Frequency Input/RS-485 Output
M2611	Pulse Input/RS-232C Output

MODEL 3000 SERIES: MODEL OUTPUT RANGE/INPUT
Voltage Output

M3121	±1 V Output/RS-232C Input
M3122	±1 V Output/RS-485 Input
M3131	±5 V Output/RS-232C Input
M3141	±10 V Output/RS-232C Input
M3142	±10 V Output/RS-485 Input
M3161	0 – 1 V Output/RS-232C Input
M3171	0 – 5 V Output/RS-232C Input
M3172	0 – 5 V Output/RS-485 Input
M3181	0 – 10 V Output/RS-232C Input
M3182	0 – 10 V Output/RS-485 Input

Current Output

M3251	4 – 20 mA Output/RS-232C Input
M3252	4 – 20 mA Output/RS-485 Input

M4000 SERIES: MODEL OUTPUT RANGE/INPUT
Voltage Output

M4121	±1 V Output/RS-232C Input
M4141	±10 V Output/RS-232C Input

Current Output

M4251	4 – 20 mA Output/RS-232C Input
M4252	4 – 20 mA Output/RS-485 Input

CONVERTERS/REPEATERS

M1100/115	Converter RS-232 to RS485 (115 VAC)
M1100/230	Converter RS-232 to RS485 (230 VAC)
M1300/115	Repeater RS-485 (115 VAC)
M1300/230	Repeater RS-485 (230 VAC)
PS-M1000	Plug-in power supply with screw terminals

Table 8.1 The complete list of M series modules. (Courtesy Keithley-Metrabyte.)

The communication wires and signal wires are connected to the module over a screw terminal plug that is mounted on one side or two sides of the module.

If one looks at the communication parameter specifications one will notice that the baud rate for communication with the module is user selectable and it can increase up to 38,400. All modules are individually addressable. (The address for the modules can be assigned by the user.) And it is possible to connect up to 124 modules to a single communication channel at the same time. The maximum communication distance is specified as 10,000 feet which corresponds to more than 3 kilometers. But this distance and 124 simultaneous modules are possible only by using repeaters (repeaters are signal strengthening devices which are installed on the communication lines in order to increase the distance of communication) and only in the RS-485 standard. With the RS-232 standard, modules can be connected simultaneously and the distance of communication is less. More on this subject will be given in the next sections when we discuss connection schemes in specific standards. Another important piece of information given in the technical specifications is that the communication parameters are stored in the permanent storage so that they do not need to be loaded every time the system is powered on.

REMOTE DATA ACQUISITION WITH DATA ACQUISITION MODULES THROUGH RS-232 SERIAL PORT

The M series data acquisition modules can be hooked up into the RS-232 serial port of the computer and can be used for remote data acquisition. Originally the RS-232 is designed for point to point communication so only one device can be connected to the RS-232 serial port of the computer, but it is possible to stretch the standard with a trick to accommodate more than one device connected to the port.

The RS-232 is an old but very popular communication standard which is very widely used in PC communications. All personal computers have at least one or two RS-232 ports to be used for serial communication. In case two ports are not sufficient, it is always possible to add additional ports to the computer through plug-in serial communication cards. Being an old standard, there are advantages and disadvantages of using the RS-232 for remote data acquisition. The **advantages** include the following.

- RS-232 is very popular, widely available with PC's.
- Separate transmit and receive lines can accommodate full duplex operations.
- RS-232 is the interface standard of low cost dumb terminals, so in some applications one can use a dumb terminal instead of a PC.

The **disadvantages** of RS-232 are the following:

- Low noise immunity.
- Very short communication distance: around 15-70 meters.
- The distance is dependent on the baud rate. At a distance of 20 meters the maximum baud rate is limited to 19200.

- Designed for point to point communication: multiple module connection is only possible with a daisy chain connection.
- Reduced reliability due to a daisy chain connection scheme; the chain will be broken if any of the modules is out of service.
- Delay in communication due to daisy-chained modules.
- Echo characters due to daisy-chained modules.

If only one module is connected to the host PC, then some of these disadvantages which are due to daisy chaining will disappear but the fact still remains that the distance with RS-232 is very much limited. Distance limitation is the single most important reason limiting the use of the RS-232C for remote data acquisition operations.

A single remote data acquisition module can be connected to the host PC as shown in Figure 8.11.

As mentioned before, even though a RS-232 is not designed for multiple-device connection, it is possible to connect more than one device to a single RS-232 port through a technique called "daisy chaining." If more than one data acquisition module with a RS-232 interface needed to be connected to the host PC, then the modules should be daisy chained.

Daisy chaining is done by connecting the transmit output of one module to the receive input of the other module and so on. For the daisy chain to transmit, the output of the host PC should be connected to the receive input of the first module, and then the transmit output of the first module should be connected to the receive input of the next module. The connection scheme should continue in this way. The transmit output of the last module should be connected to the receive input of the host PC. According to this connection scheme, any information that is transmitted from the PC goes through each one of the modules. Each module receives and then retransmits the message to the next module. Obviously this will delay the transmission of the messages and the reliability of the scheme is reduced since any device that is out of commission will break the chain and the devices connected to the daisy chain will not be able to communicate with the host PC. This connection scheme is shown in Figure 8.12.

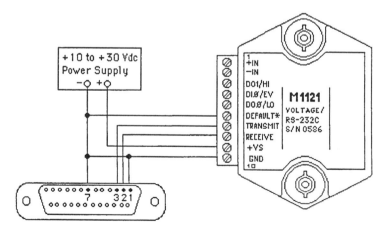

Figure 8.11 Connection of a single module to the host PC through a RS-232 port. (Courtesy Keithley Metrabyte.)

SPECIFICATIONS COMMON TO M1000/M2000

Analog
- Single channel analog input.
- Maximum CMV, 500 Vrms input to output @ 60 Hz.
- 15 bit measurement resolution.
- Leakage current, input to output @ 115 Vrms, 60 Hz: $<2\mu A$ rms.
- 8 conversions per second.
- Autozero.
- Autocalibration.
- No adjustment pots.

Digital
- 8-bit CMOS microcomputer.
- All scaling, linearization and calibration performed digitally.
- Nonvolatile memory eliminates pots and switches.

Digital Filtering
- Small and large signal with user selectable time constants from 0 to 16 seconds.

Digital Inputs
- Voltage levels: $\pm30V$ without damage.
- Switching levels: High, 3.5V min., Low, 1.0V max.
- Internal pull up resistors for direct switch input.

Digital Outputs
- Open collector to 30V, 30 mA max. load.
- **Alarm outputs**
- HI/LO limit checking by comparing input values to downloaded HI/LO limit values stored in memory.
- Alarms: latching (stays on if input returns to within limits) or momentary (turns off if input returns to within limits).

Communications
- RS-232C, RS-485.
- Up to 124 multidrop modules per host communications port.
- User selectable channel address.
- Selectable baud rates: 300, 600, 1200, 2400, 4800, 9600, 19200, 38400.
- ASCII Format command/response protocol.
- Can be used with "dumb" terminal.
- Parity options: odd, even, none.
- All communications setups (address, baud rate, parity) stored in nonvolatile memory.
- Checksum can be added to any command or response.
- Communications distance up to 10,000 feet.

Event Counter
- Up to 10 million positive transitions @ 60 Hz max., filtered for switch debounce.

Power Requirements
+10V to +30 Vdc, 0.75W max.

Mechanical
Dimensions: See dimension drawings.
Case: ABS with captive mounting hardware.
Connectors: Screw terminal plug (supplied).

Environmental
Temperature Range: Operating $-25°C$ to $+70°C$
                              Storage: $-25°C$ to $+85°C$
Relative Humidity: 0 to 95% noncondensing

Table 8.2 Technical specifications of M1000/2000 modules.

It is absolutely essential that all modules connected to the daisy chain have the same baud rate and a separate ID code. All modules must be set to echo all received characters since this is the way transmitted messages by the modules will reach the host PC. Otherwise, the message sent by the host PC will reach the modules. Since the messages are handed from one module to the other in a sequential way, it is very important that the connection between the modules are done properly. Any break of the chain at any one of the modules causes the communication link to break.

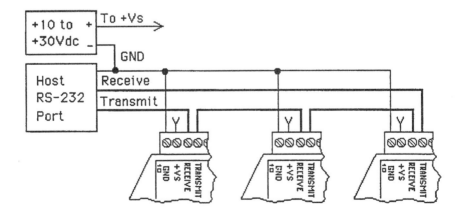

Figure 8.12 Connecting a series of modules with a RS-232 interface to a host PC. "Daisy Chaining" (Courtesy Keithley MetraByte.)

In a daisy-chained RS-232 connection with the remote data acquisition modules, the communication is always initiated by the host PC by transmitting an instruction intended for one of the modules. The information will be received by the first module on the line. Since all modules on the daisy chain are set up to "echo" received characters, the first module will echo the received character by re-transmitting it to the next module in the daisy chain. Since the module has to listen to the whole message to understand whether the message was intended for it or not, there is a communication delay which is equal to the duration of transmitting one character. Since every module in the chain will be delaying the message by a duration of one character transmit, the total delay in the chain can be calculated by multiplying the delay time by the number of modules in the chain. The delay for different baud rates is shown in the table below.

Baud rate	Delay time
300	33.30 ms
600	6.70 ms
1200	5.33 ms
2400	4.17 ms
4800	2.08 ms
9600	1.04 ms
19200	0.52 ms

The figures are calculated assuming that every character transmitted has 10 bits. The delay has to be multiplied by the number of modules in the daisy chain since each module will delay the message by that specified amount of time. In addition to that, the message sent by the host PC, or the answer from the module is much longer than one character. Since a typical message broadcast by the host has about 10 ASCII characters, the delay time with a daisy chain of several modules becomes quite excessive.

Design Problem: A daisy chain of eight data acquisition modules is connected to an RS-232 port of the PC for a remote data acquisition application. The baud rate is set at 1200 and the message is sent with 1 start bit, 1 stop bit and no parity. Calculate the maximum delay time of the system for a message that has 12 ASCII characters.

Solution: At 1200 baud the message delay for one module is 8.33 ms. Since there are eight modules and there are 12 characters in the message, the total will be

$$\text{Delay time} = 8.33 \times 8 \times 12 = 799.68 \text{ ms.}$$

Obviously 0.8 sec delay for one message is quite excessive. As we can see from the example, as a designer one should be aware of the delay factor if one considers using daisy chaining techniques with remote data acquisition modules.

REMOTE DATA ACQUISITION WITH DATA ACQUISITION MODULES
THROUGH RS-485 SERIAL PORT

A RS-485 is a recently developed serial standard which enables multiple drivers and receivers to be connected over a pair of lines. This standard specifies the signal levels for logic "1" and logic "0" as much less than that of RS-232, thus making signal transitions much faster. The signal is transmitted and received in differential form as opposed to a single ended signal of the RS-232 standard. The differential transmission feature both increases the distance of communication and noise immunity of the signals. This standard also adds a feature which was not available with the RS-232 standard: it allows networking multiple devices to be connected to the same serial port. Unlike the cumbersome daisy chain scheme of RS-232 the connection scheme with RS-485 is very simple, straightforward and true networking.

The RS-485 has major advantages over the old RS-232 standard; these advantages are

- Excellent noise immunity due to the balanced nature of the connection lines.
- High rates of communication possible. High rate can be traded off with the distance of communication.
- Multidrop connection; all modules are connected in parallel.

But there are also disadvantages working with RS-485:

- Due to unpopularity and scarcity of products one needs a RS-485 driver card for the PC.
- Half duplex operation; either transmits or receives but not both at the same time.

Since this standard is not very popular, RS-485 ports do not come as a standard issue feature on PC's yet. But there are several RS-485 card vendors on the market which sell plug-in cards for providing additional RS-485 standard serial ports for PC's. So, by installing one of these cards you can either change your existing COM1 or COM2 serial port to RS-485 standard or you can install them as additional serial ports. For example, COM1, COM2 may be RS-232 and COM3, COM4 may be RS-485. Data sheet for a representative product made by Keithley Instruments, RISCOM-8, is given in the following pages. Another alternative is to buy an external RS-232 to RS-485 converter. This equipment will convert your RS-232 serial ports to RS-485 standard externally. But day by day the RS-485 appears more as a standard port beside RS-232, especially with high end laser printers that are designed to be shared among users.

The distance and the speed characteristics of RS-485 are as follows:

Line length (max.) = 1200 meters

Frequency (max) = 10 Mbaud/15 meters

RISCOM-8

FEATURES

- 8 RS-232, RS-422, or RS-485 ports
- Reconfigure individual ports between RS-422 and RS-485 with simple jumper change
- Low-power CMOS technology
- Programmable serial characteristics
- 5-, 6-, 7- or 8-bit character length
- Even, odd or no parity
- Speeds of 300 bps to 115.2 kbps
- Supports full duplex operation up to 57.6 kbps on all ports
- Interrupt or polled operation
- Separately programmable Tx and Rx baud rates

APPLICATIONS

- Interface with modems, printers or plotters
- Instrument interface
- Network interfaces
- Interface to M1000 modules

FUNCTIONAL DESCRIPTION

The RISCOM-8 I/O expansion board for the PC/XT/AT and compatibles plugs directly into one full-size I/O slot and provides interfaces to 8 serial ports through a DB-78 connector. The RISCOM-8 is factory configured for RS-232, RS-422 or RS-485, however, it is possible to convert a RS-485 port to a RS-422 port and visa versa utilizing jumpers. An octopus cable is available to convert the DB-78 interface to individual DB-25 connectors.

The RISCOM-8 supports full duplex communications simultaneously on all channels at rates up to 57.6 Kbaud (rates to 115.2 Kbaud can be sus-tained on one or two channels) although actual throughput may be limited by the PC. The baud rate, parity (even, odd or none), number of data bits (5, 6, 7 or 8) and the number of stop bits (1, 1½ or 2) are software-selectable. All the standard RS-232 bus control lines (e.g., data set ready, clear to send, data terminal ready) are supported as well as "clear to send" and "request to send" in RS-422. The control lines supported are selected through software.

The RISCOM-8 uses the Cirrus Logic CD180 Intelligent Octal UART which off-loads the PC processor by implementing a 24-byte FIFO on each port and managing channel interrupt priorities, special character recognition and automatic flow-control functions. The low power CMOS design of the RISCOM-8 makes it ideal for applications requiring a large number of serial ports.

BLOCK DIAGRAM

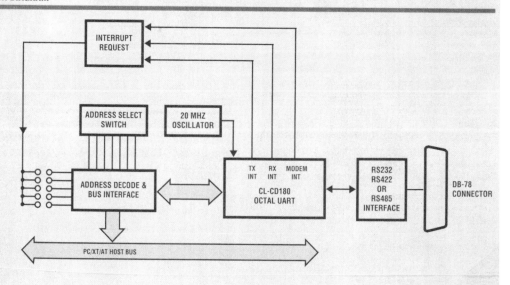

1 Mbaud/130 meters

100 kbaud/1200 meters

Mode of Operation =Differential input and output

Driver logic levels

"0" = +2 to +5V

"1" = -2 to -5V

Noise immunity = 1.8 V

Number of devices allowed on one line = 32.

Connecting remote data acquisition modules to the RS-485 serial port of the host PC is very simple and straightforward. The connection scheme for a single module is shown in Figure 8.13.

Connecting multiple modules to the port is also very straightforward. This scheme is shown in Figure 8.14.

As can also be seen from the diagrams, connection of the M series modules with an RS-485 interface is very simple and straightforward. Simple four wire twisted pair phone cables can be used for wiring. Power can also be sent from the host computer's site by a pair of additional lines. This way, the remote data acquisition module will be completely self-sufficient and no external connection other than the sensor connection will be required in the field.

Obviously due to large distances up to 1.2 km, voltage drop on the power lines due to ohmic losses are expected, but since the modules accept unregulated power input this does not usually present a problem.

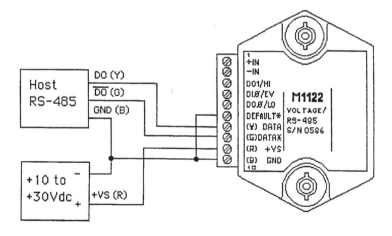

Figure 8.13 Connecting a single remote data acquisition module to the host PC over a RS-485 serial port. (Courtesy Keithley Metrabyte.)

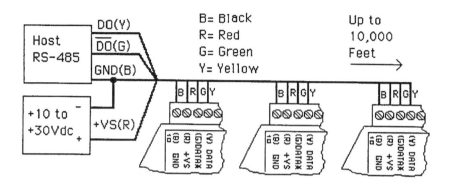

Figure 8.14 Connecting multiple remote data acquisition modules with a RS-485 serial port. (Courtesy Keithley MetraByte.)

According to the manufacturer Keithley-Metrabyte, the distance of communication is dependent on the thickness of the wire that is used for connection. For a 22 gauge wire, the maximum distance for a single module is calculated as 4000 feet. For larger diameter wires, the distance can be increased.

Wire gauge	Max. no of modules times meters distance total
22	1,300
20	2,000
18	3,500

Accordingly, if we have four modules that are connected by a 18 gauge wire and if we are trying to supply power from the host PC, then the distance should not be more than 875 meters.

Please note that these limitations are valid only if the power is supplied remotely through the host PC. If the power is locally supplied, then these limitations should be discarded. In this case, the only limitation will be due to the limitations imposed by the RS-485 standard.

8.4.2 Communication with M Series Data Acquisition Modules

M series remote data acquisition modules are microcontroller-based, intelligent data acquisition modules which are designed to be interfaced directly to the sensors in the field.

The data acquired by the module in the field will be converted into digital and sent to the host computer over the standard serial interface.

The communication between the host and the module is done through serial ports using ASCII characters. The modules have unique ID numbers so that the host can address them individually. The conversation between the modules and the host PC is always initiated by the host. In other words, the modules are never allowed to interrupt the host PC. A module will respond only if it is specifically addressed to send data.

The modules have a limited intelligence which enables them to take actions on their own even if they do not communicate with the host. For example, the M1000 series modules can generate high or low alarms depending on the input data. The host can provide the high and the low limits but even if the module is not addressed, the module can generate the alarms on its own. The M1000 series modules have a limited intelligence built in them which enables them to be programmed remotely. With this feature one can program the address of the module, baud rate for communication, and high/low alarm limits remotely without removing the modules.

M1000 series modules have a limited instruction set which they can execute. In addition to the common instructions which all M1000 modules respond to, there are also some instructions which are module dependent and not valid for all modules. When a host sends instructions to the modules, the first letter sent is always a dollar sign followed by a two number module identity number and then a two letter instruction. A module will always respond to a given instruction by sending an asterisk (*) and supplying data if there are any data to return. Data are always given in a string of nine characters consisting of sign, five digits, decimal point and then two more digits. If the host wants to make sure that data are received by the module, then when it sends the intruction, it puts a number sign (#) sign rather than a dollar ($) sign. In this case, the module will echo the whole instruction and then supply the data if there are any.

8.4.3 Instruction Set of M1000 Series Modules

Common M1000 instructions and brief explanations are given below. In all examples the ID code of the module is assumed to be 1.

Clear Alarms (CA)

    Command : $1CA

    Response: *

Action: Clears HI and LO alarms. These alarms are automatically set when the data value exceeds the limits set by the user.

Clear Events (CE)

    Command : $1CE

    Response: *

Action: Clears a register called event counter.

PROGRAMMING M1000/M2000
The command structure for programming M1000 series modules is
very simple. The command starts with either a $ (dollar sign) or a #
(pound sign), which is followed by the desired module address (up to
124), followed by a two character command. Many commands are then
followed by data to be written to the module. The command line is
ended with a carriage return.

The # command requests a long form response from the module. A
long form response begins with a * (asterisk) character, followed by the
module address, followed by the two character command received, followed by the requested data (if necessary), followed by a checksum
which can be used for error checking. The $ command requests a short
form response. The short form response is a * followed simply by the
requested data.

If an error is detected by the module, the response will return with a ?
as a first character, followed by a message describing the type of error.

The complete set of available commands are displayed for the M1000 in
the table below.

COMMAND	EXAMPLE	DESCRIPTION
DI	$1DI	Read Digital Inputs
DO	$1DOFF	Set Digital Outputs
ND	$1ND	New Data
RD	$1RD	Read Data
RE	$1RE	Read Event Counter
RL	$1RL	Read Low Alarm Value
RH	$1RH	Read High Alarm Value
RS	$1RS	Read Setup
RZ	$1RZ	Read Zero
WE	$1WE	Write Enable

—— **Write Protected Commands** ——

CA	$1CA	Clear Alarms
CE	$1CE	Clear Events
CZ	$1CZ	Clear Zero
DA	$1DA	Disable Alarms
EA	$1EA	Enable Alarms
HI	$1HI+12345.67L	Set High Alarm Limit
LO	$1LO+12345.67L	Set Low Alarm Limit
RR	$1RR	Remote Reset
SU	$1SU12345678	Setup Module
SP	$1SP+00600.00	Set Setpoint
TS	$1TS+00600.00	Trim Span
TZ	$1TZ+00000.00	Trim Zero

The following program has been written in BASICA for the IBM PC/XT/
AT or compatible computer. Similar programs can easily be written for
other computers, and in other languages. The program assumes that a
M1311 J-type thermocouple has been configured as Module #3, and
that an RS-232 serial interface board connected to the module is at
COM1:

```
10 '*** sample program ***
20 OPEN "COM1:300, N, 8, 1,
   CS, DS, RS" AS # 1              'open the communication
                                    port COM1:
30 FOR I = 1 TO 1000               'start a loop
40 PRINT # 1, "$3RD"               'tell the module to send
                                    temperature data.
50 INPUT # 1,TEMP$                 'read the temperature
60 PRINT "CURRENT TEMP IS",TEMP$   'print the result
70 NEXT I
80 CLOSE
```

Figure 8.15 M1000/2000 series instructions. (Courtesy Keithley-MetraByte.)

Clear Zero (CZ)

Command : $1CZ

Response: *

Action: This instruction clears the output offset register to zero.

Disable Alarms (DA)

Command : $1DA

Response: *

Action: Most M1000 series modules have digital outputs which can be used either as
regular digital outputs or alarm outputs. This instruction is used to disable them if they
are used as alarm outputs.

Digital Input (DI)

Command : $1DI

Response: *

Action: This command reads the status of digital inputs and alarms.

Digital Output (DO)

Command : $1DO

Response: *

Action: This command controls the digital outputs of the module.

Enable Alarms (EA)

> **Command :** $1EA
>
> **Response:**   *

Action: Opposite of disable alarms command.

High Alarm Limit (HI)

> **Command :** $1HI+00100.00M
>
> **Response:**   *

Action: The high alarm command sets the value and the type of the high alarm. The data specified by the HI command is stored in nonvolatile memory and compared with the sensor data after every A/D conversion. The high alarm is activated if the input data is greater than the value stored by the HI command. Alarm can be of two different types, either latching (L) or momentary (M) which is indicated by the last letter that is sent by the host.

Low Alarm Limit (LO)

> **Command :** $1LO+00000.00M
>
> **Response:**   *

Action: The low alarm command is similar to HI command in all respects except this one specifies low limit.

New Data Command (ND)

> **Command :** $1ND
>
> **Response:**   *

Action: New Data command will only send new data to the host. The M1000 modules perform A/D conversions repetitively even when they are not asked for the results. Since the conversion speed is low, around 8 conversions per second, it is possible for the host to read the same data several times. The ND command makes sure that only new data, not a re-read data, will be sent to the host.

Read Data (RD)

> **Command :** $1RD
>
> **Response:**   *+00076.87

Action: This command requests the data value from the module.

Read Events (RE)

> **Command :** $1RE
>
> **Response:**   *0000112

Action: This command reads the total number of events accumulated in the events counter. The module responds to that instruction with 7 decimal digits.

Read High Alarm (RH)

Command : $1RH

Response: *+00567.00L

Action: This command reads back the value and the type of the high alarm value stored previously by the HI command.

Read Low Alarm (RL)

Command : $1RL

Response: *+00000.00L

Action: This command will read the low alarm limit.

Remote Reset (RR)

Command : $1RR

Response: *

Action: This instruction is used to give a reset to the processor of the module. The RR command does not clear the event counters and values in the EEPROM. However, the data in the RAM will be lost. The module will reset and calibrate itself; the whole process takes about two seconds.

Read Setup (RS)

Command : $1RS

Response: *31070142

Action: This command will read back the setup information stored in the modules memory.

Read Zero (RZ)

Command : $1RZ

Response: *+00000.00

Action: This command will read back the value stored in the output offset register.

Setpoint (SP)

Command : $1SP+00450.00

Response: *

Action: The value specified with SP command is negated and put into offset register. This is used to null out the sensor offset.

Setup Command (SU)

Command : $1SU31070182

Response: *

Action: This command is used to store setup information on the EEPROM.

Trim Span (TS)

    Command : $1TS+00500.00

    Response: *

Action: This instruction is used for calibrating the module.

Trim Zero (TZ)

    Command : $1TZ

    Response: *

Action: This instruction is used to force the output to zero value. It is generally used for calibration purposes.

Write Enable (WE)

    Command : $1WE

    Response: *

Action: The purpose of this command is to safeguard the accidental change of EEPROM values. No EEPROM value can be changed unless a WE command is issued right before a command that requests change in the EEPROM values.

The modules have an internal EEPROM for storing parameters like ID number, baud rate and alarm limits. Since the values are permanently stored in EEPROM, there is no need to store the values. Another advantage of having an EEPROM is that it makes it possible to change parameters remotely without removing the module from the field.

The resolution of an A/D converter inside the modules is 15 bits which is considered very good. The A/D converter has autozero and autocalibrate features which are transparent to the user and thus enables the device to calibrate or autozero itself. The full scale outputs of the A/D converter can be adjusted using the Trim Span (TS) command which adjusts calibration values and stores them in the nonvolatile storage. This is intended only to compensate for long-term drifts due to the aging of the analog circuits and has +/- 10% of the original calibration values set in the factory. The output of the A/D converter then goes through either one of the digital filters which is designed to filter out noise. The selection of a small signal or large signal filter is done automatically by the module. The M1000 series modules have an additional feature which allows the user to display data either in F or C degree form. For non-temperature applications always C scale should be selected. Scaled data are added with data stored in the output offset register to obtain the final output value. The data in the output data register is continuously compared with the data stored in the high and low alarm registers. In case the output value exceeds one of these values corresponding alarm will be generated. High latch and low latch are the two latches which latch if there is an alarm condition. They stay latched even if the output value goes below the alarm levels.

8.4.4 Keithley MetraByte M2000 Series Modules

The M2000 series modules are modified versions of the M1000 series modules with more intelligence built in them. The M2000 series is similar to the M1000 series in every respect except that the M2000 series allow custom input-to-output transfer functions. As far as the technical specifications and mechanical dimensions are concerned, the two series are exactly alike. As an additional feature, the M2000 series has extra instructions which enable the user to program any input-to-output relation desired to the module. Input-output relations can be linear or nonlinear; even quite complicated input-output relations can be programmed to the module quite easily by piece-wise linearizing the function and giving the module the breakpoints. Within the given breakpoints, the module will extrapolate the values in a linear fashion. The limitation of the module for piece-wise describing a nonlinear curve is 24 pieces of straight line segments.

PROGRAMMING M2000 SERIES MODULES

The instruction set of the M2000 series modules is a super set of the M1000 series modules. The M2000 series modules have four extra instructions in addition to the instructions of the M1000 series. The M2000 series are designed to handle nonlinear input/output transformations whereas the M1000 series can only handle linear input-output relations. The new instructions of the M2000 series are basically for programming the nonlinear input/output curve of conversion. The technique used for handling non-linearity is by piece-wise describing the nonlinear curve of the input/output relation. The new instructions of the M2000 series are presented below.

Breakpoint (BP)

> **Command:** $1BP 03 +00100.00

> **Response:** *

Action: Programs the specified breakpoint (03). Up to 23 breakpoints can be specified. Breakpoints should start from the minimum value and progressively increase up to the maximum breakpoint. Breakpoints should start from 00. Not all the breakpoints should be specified.

Erase Breakpoints (EB)

> **Command:** $1EB

> **Response:** *

Action: Erases all previously entered breakpoints.

Minimum (MN)

> **Command:** $1MN -00100.00

> **Response:** *

Action: Programs the minimum point of the transfer function.

Maximum (MX)

> **Command:** $1MX +00500.00

> **Response:** *

Action: Specifies the maximum point of the transfer function

8.4.5 Keithley MetraByte M3000/4000 Series Modules

MetraByte M3000/4000 series modules are programmable output modules which convert digital data into analog form. In terms of communication techniques and technical specifications and mechanical dimensions, the M3000/4000 series is exactly like the M1000/2000 series. Of course due to the different functions performed by the M1000/2000 and M3000/4000, the instruction sets are different. The MetraByte M3000/4000 modules all have 12 bit D/A resolution which provides 4096 steps for the particular output. The basic difference between the M4000 series from the M3000 series is that the former has more intelligence built in the modules to perform fully programmable output slew rates, programmable data scaling, true analog readback of the signal, and programmable initial values. Moreover, a watchdog timer provides orderly shut down in the event of host failure. The technical specifications of the M3000/4000 series and list of modules are shown below.

SPECIFICATIONS FOR M3000/4000

Analog Output	Single-channel analog output		
Voltage	0 – 1 V, ±1 V, 0 – 5 V, ±5 V, 0 – 10 V, ±10 V	**Digital**	8-bit CMOS microcomputer
Current	0 – 20 mA, 4 – 20 mA		Digital scaling and calibration
Input isolation	500Vrms		Nonvolatile memory eliminates pots and switches
Resolution	12-bit		Programmable data scaling (M4000)
Accuracy	0.1% FS (max) accuracy over temperature		Programmable High/Low output limits
Throughput	1000 conversions per second		Programmable initial value (M4000)
Settling time to			Programmable watchdog timer provides orderly shut-down
0.1% FS	300 µs typ (1 ms max)		in the event of host failure (M4000)
Output Slewing			
Manual Mode		**Communications**	RS-232C, RS-485
(–FS to +FS)	5 s		Up to 124 multidrop modules per host communications port
Programmable			User-selectable channel address
Output Slew Rate	0.1 V/s (mA/s) to 10,000 V/s (mA/s) (M4000)	Selectable baud rates	300, 600, 1200, 2400, 4800, 9600, 19200, 38400
Autozero &			ASCII format command/response protocol
Autocalibration	no adjustment pots		Can be used with "dumb" terminal
Voltage Compliance	+12 V		Parity options: odd, even, none
Output Drive,			All communications setups (address, baud rate, parity)
Short Circuit Current	5 mA min, 10 mA max		stored in nonvolatile memory
			Checksum can be added to any command or response
Analog Output Readback (M4000)			Communications distance up to 10,000 feet
	8-bit Analog-to-Digital Converter		
Accuracy over Temp.			
(–25 to +70 °C)	2.0% FS max		

8.4.6 How to Communicate with Remote Data Acquisition Units Using Standard Computer Languages

The M series modules communicate with the host PC using ASCII characters. Since almost all languages have special provisions for communicating serially with ASCII characters using the serial ports, it is very straightforward to communicate with the modules. Testing the operation of the modules can be done interactively with any one of the modem packages which can send and receive data from modems.

In particular, C, BASIC, APL and PASCAL are suitable for communicating with remote data acquisition modules. The following BASIC program to transmit and receive ASCII strings shows how easily the program can be done.

```
390 OPEN "COM1:300,N,8,1,RS,CS,CD,DS" AS #1

400 PRINT : INPUT"Command  : ";C$

410 IF C$ = "q" OR C$ = "Q" THEN CLOSE : END ELSE GOSUB 460

420 PRINT"Response :   "; : GOSUB 560 : GOTO 400

430 '

440 ' Transmit data sub-routine

450 '

460 OUT &H3FF,2   'Enable Transmit Mode(COM1:) on some internal RS-485 Bd.'s

470 OUT &H3FC,&HB 'Turn ON RTS, Control external 232/485 Conveters

480 PRINT#1,C$    'Transmit command string

490 IF (INP(&H3FD) AND &H60) <> &H60 THEN GOTO 490  'Wait for complete Tx Data

500 OUT &H3FC, &H9 'Turn OFF RTS signal

510 OUT &H3FF,1    'Enable Receive Mode(COM1:) on some internal RS-485 Bd.'s

520 RETURN

530 '

540 ' Receive data sub-routine

550 '

560 T = TIMER : RX$ = ""

570 IF TIMER > T + .5 THEN PRINT"timeout error" : RETURN

580 IF LOC(1) = 0 THEN GOTO 570 ELSE Y$ = INPUT$(1, #1)

590 IF Y$ = "*" OR Y$ = "?" THEN RX$ = Y$ ELSE GOTO 560

600 Y$ = INPUT$(1,#1) : RX$ = RX$ + Y$

610 IF Y$ <> CHR$(13) THEN GOTO 600 ELSE PRINT RX$ : RETURN
```

The following C program shows how to use the remote data acquistion modules with C language.

```c
#include <stdio.h>;
#include <dos.h>;
#include <stdlib.h>;
#include <conio.h>;

void (interrupt far *oldvec)();

const buffersize    = 512;                    /*Define Tx & Rx buffer sizes */

unsigned int offset  = 0;      /* com1 = 3f8, com2 = 2f8   */
unsigned int intno   = 0;              /* Interrupt number       */
unsigned int rfront  = 0;      /* Begin of Rx buffer      */
unsigned int rback   = 0;              /* Max Rx chars pointer    */
unsigned int tfront  = 0;      /* Begin of Tx buffer      */
unsigned int tback   = 0;              /* Max TX char pointer     */
unsigned int rxchars = 0;              /* Current # of Rx chars   */
unsigned int txchars = 0;              /* Current # of Tx chars   */
unsigned int mstat   = 0;              /* Modem Status Storage    */
unsigned int lstat   = 0;      /* Line Status Storage     */

char    rxbuffer[512];         /* Establish receive buffer */
char    txbuffer[512];         /* Establish send buffer    */

void com485_tx()               /* COM-485 bd's to Transmit */
 {outp(offset+7, 0x02);}

void com485_rx()               /* COM-485 bd's to Receive  */
 {outp(offset+7, 0x01);}

void rts_enable()              /* Enable RTS signal       */
 {com485_tx();
  outp(offset+4, 0x0b);}

void rts_disable()             /* Disable RTS signal      */
 {com485_rx();
  outp(offset+4, 0x09);}

void enable_8259(n)            /* Enable 8259             */
```

```
{int d;
 d = (inp(0x21) & !(1 << n));
 outp(0x21, d); }


void disable_8259(n)                  /* Disable 8259        */
{int d;
 d = (inp(0x21) | (1 << n));
 outp(0x21, d); }


void txintr_enable()                  /* Enable UART Tx interrupt */
{int d;
 rts_enable();                        /* Enable RTS signal       */
 d = (inp(offset+1) | 0x0f);          /* Read Intr. Enable Reg.   */
 outp(offset+1, d);}                  /* Turn On TX Intr.         */


void txintr_disable()                 /* Disable UART Tx interrupt*/
{int d;
 d = (inp(offset+1) & 0x0d);          /* Read Intr. Enable Reg.   */
 outp(offset+1, d);}                  /* Turn OFF TX interrupt    */


void set_baud(rate)                   /* Set baud rate           */
{ int old;
 rate = (384 / (1 << (rate - 1)));
 old = inp(offset+3);
 outp(offset + 3, 0x80);
 outp(offset   , rate & 0xff);
 outp(offset + 1, rate / 256);
 outp(offset + 3, old); }


void set_communications(baud, data)   /* Set parity, data bits   */
{set_baud(baud);
 outp(offset+3, data);}


int lenrxbuf()                        /* Get Rx buffer length    */
{return (rxchars);}


int lentxbuf()                        /* Get Tx buffer length    */
{return (txchars);}
```

```
void clear_buffers()            /* Clear Rx & Tx Buf Vars  */
{ disable();
 tfront  = 0;
 tback   = 0;
 txchars = 0;
 rfront  = 0;
 rback   = 0;
 rxchars = 0;
 enable(); }


char rx_char()                  /* Get char from Rx buffer     */
{ char v = 0;
{ if (rxchars < 1)
   {return (0);}
    else
    {disable();
    v = rxbuffer[rfront];
    rfront = ((rfront+1) % buffersize);
    rxchars--;
    enable();
    return (v);}  }  }


void set_stats()
{ mstat = inp(offset);          /* Dummy read Rx register      */
 mstat = inp(offset+6);          /* Read modem status register   */
 lstat = inp(offset+1);         /* Dummy read Intr I.D. register */
 lstat = inp(offset+5); }        /* Read line status register    */


void send_char(c)               /* Place character in TX buffer  */
{ if (txchars > (buffersize - 1)) {}
   else
    {disable();
    txbuffer[tback] = c;
    tback = ((tback+1) % buffersize);
    txchars++;
    enable();}  }
```

```
void tx_char(c)                      /* Transmit Character        */
{ send_char(c);                      /* Pass Character to TX buffer   */
  txintr_enable(); }                 /* Enable TX interrupt        */


void tx_string(str,count)            /* Transmit a Character string   */
char *str;
int  count;
{ count = 0;                         /* Initialize character index   */
  while (count <= strlen(str))       /* Loop thru characters to TX    */
  {send_char(str[count]);           /* and place them in TX buffer   */
   count++;}
  send_char(0x0d);                   /* Load <CR> into TX buffer      */
  txintr_enable(); }                 /* Enable TX interrupt, TX chars */


void far interrupt int_proc()
{ t:
  outp(0x20,0x20);
  switch (inp(offset + 2)) {
  case (0):  {mstat = inp(offset+6);
             break;}
  case (2):  {disable();
             if (txchars > 0) {
                outp(offset,(txbuffer[tfront] & 0x7f));
                if ((txbuffer[tfront] == 0x0d) || (txchars <= 1))
                  {txintr_disable();
                   while ((inp(offset + 5) & 0x60) != 0x60) {};
                   rts_disable();}
                tfront = ((tfront+1) % buffersize);
                txchars--;}
             enable();
             break;}
  case (4):  {disable();
             rxbuffer[rback] = (inp(offset) & 0x7f);
             rback = ((rback+1) % buffersize);
             rxchars++;
             enable();
             break; }
  case (6):  {lstat = inp(offset+5);
```

```
                break;} }
     if ((inp(offset + 2) & 0x01) == 0)
       {goto t; }
       else
         {outp(0x20,0x20);} }


  void init_port(intno,com)              /* Initialize selected COM port    */
  { disable();
    clear_buffers();               /* Reset Rx/Tx pointers           */
    set_stats();               /* Initialize status variables     */
    rts_disable();               /* Guarantee RTS signal OFF        */
    com485_rx();               /* Guarantee COM-485 RX mode       */
    oldvec = getvect(com);          /* Save old Comm. interrupt vector */
    setvect(com, *int_proc);          /* Set comm. vector to our routine */
    outp(offset + 1, 0x0d);          /* Enable Modem, Line status, Rx intrs */
    enable_8259(intno);          /* Enable Interrupt controller     */
    enable(); }


  void close_com(comport)
  { disable();               /* Disable interrupts          */
    if (comport == 1)
      {intno = 4;}
      else
        {intno = 3;}          /* Get comm. Interrupt to disable   */
    disable_8259(intno);          /* Disable Interrupt controller    */
    setvect(0x0d-comport,oldvec);     /* Restore old interrupt vector    */
    enable(); }               /* Enable Interrupts          */


  opencom(comx,baudrate,paritytype,dbits,sbits)  /* Open Com port        */
  { if ((comx<1) || (comx>2))          /* Check for valid COM port     */
      {return(-1);}          /* Return Error condition if not   */
      else
        {if (comx == 1)
          {offset = 0x03f8;          /* Set OFFSET value for COM1:     */
           intno  = 4;}          /* Set hardware Intr # for COM1:   */
          else
            {offset = 0x02f8;          /* Set OFFSET value for COM2:     */
             intno  = 3;}          /* Set hardware intr # for COM2:   */
```

```c
        set_communications(baudrate, (dbits-1)+(4*(sbits-1))+(paritytype*8));
        init_port(intno, 0x0d-comx);
        return(0);} }


main()
{ char ch = 0;
 char c  = 0;
 int ss;
 int steps;
 printf("Terminal mode, press <ESC> to quit\n");
 if (opencom(1,7,5,3,1) == 0)       /* OPEN port,  COM1,300,M,7,1     */
  {while (ch != 27) {
   c = rx_char();              /* Get character for RX buffer     */
   if (c > 0)                  /* If received char. then display   */
    printf("%c",c);
   if (c == 0x0d)              /* If <CR> then new line on screen  */
    printf("\n");
   if (kbhit() == 0) {}        /* Test for keyborad entry          */
    else
    { ch = getchar();          /* If keyboard then display and TX  */
     if (ch = 'F')
       {printf("\n ENTER NUMBER of STEPS, DEFAULT=50");
       steps=50;
       steps=getchar();
       printf("\n STEPS =%d", steps);
       for(ss=1;ss=steps;ss++)
         { tx_char('$');
          tx_char('1');
          tx_char('D');
          tx_char('O');
          tx_char('F');
          tx_char('F');
         tx_char('$');
          tx_char('1');
          tx_char('D');
          tx_char('O');
          tx_char('0');
          tx_char('0');}
```

```
    }
    if (ch == 0x0d)
    {printf("\n");
    tx_char('$');
    tx_char('1');
    tx_char('R');
    tx_char('D'); }
  x_char(ch);} }
  close_com(1);}          /* Close communications port    */
exit(0); }
```

8.4.7 Case Studies Using M Series Modules

In the following sections, case studies show the use of remote data acquisition modules.

CASE STUDY 1: WATER LEVEL CONTROL AND MEASUREMENT IN MUNICIPAL WATER TANKS

The problem is to monitor the water level in a municipal water tower of a small community. The water tower is located on top of a hill and it is 30 meters tall. The water tower is aesthetically designed and because of the irregular shape of the tower it is difficult to guess the water content by simply observing the level. The plot of the relation between the height of water and the water contents is nonlinear and given as shown in the Figure below.

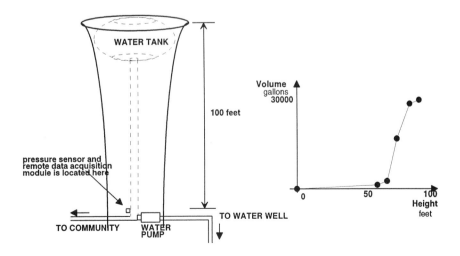

Although it is possible to figure this out mathematically, this plot is generated experimentally after the tower is designed.

The design of the controller for the pump is supposed to turn the motor on when the water level is at 80 feet (5 feet above the bottom level of the tank) and shut the motor off when the water level is at 95 feet (5 feet below the top level of the tank). Apart from the control function we would like to monitor the actual water level continuously to know the level of water consumption and to be aware of any malfunction in the piping and pump condition. (Broken pipes could easily be figured out from the steady high consumption rate. Pump burnout could be understood when the water level stays steadily below the lower threshold level.)

Design: This case is an ideal application of remote data acquisition modules. To monitor water level we will use a pressure sensor and a remote data acquisition module to turn the pump on and off and to send the actual water level data.

To figure out the technical requirements from the pressure sensor we do the following.

1 foot of water produces a pressure of 0.4335 psi. Since the tower is 100 feet, total pressure will be

$$100 \times 0.4335 = \textbf{43.35 psi}$$

So, we have to select a 0-50 psi pressure sensor. A pressure sensor which can withstand instantaneous high pressures up to 100 psi that may be generated due to water hammer is preferable. The sensor selected is shown in Figure 8.16. The sensor produces an output of 0-5 volts. The module that we select should accept this input. Going through the list of modules, we find modules M1131 and M1132 that accept input 0 to 5 volts. M1131 has a RS-232 and a M1132 has a RS-485 connection. The host computer is needed to be housed in one of the buildings adjacent to the water tower since there is no suitable air conditioned room inside the water tower.

Signal Conditioned Transducers
Stainless Steel Housing

DATA INSTRUMENTS

Connections
Supply voltage — red
Signal output — brown or white
Ground — black

L = 45 (excl cable), Dia = 39
Mounting = ½"hex, Thread = ¼"-27 NPT, Cable length = 610

Fully signal conditioned and temperature compensated transducers suitable for pressure applications that involve measurement of corrosive media in harsh environments. Rugged stainless steel housing with stainless steel isolated diaphragm, shielded connector cable. The low pressure devices, up to 50 psi, are absolute devices, the higher pressure devices are sealed gauge, ie, sealed at atmospheric pressure in manufacture.

Typical media include oil, gases, aqueous solutions, hydraulic fluids, alcohols, freon, ammonia, acids and petrol.

Reference, V_s	9V
Output	5V (span 1.0V dc—6.0V dc)
Supply voltage	9V—20V dc
Operating temp range	−55°C to +125°C
Linearity	< ±0.50% FSO (< ±1.0% FSO for SA15A, SA25A)
Hysteresis	±0.25% FSO typ
Shift with temperature	
0°C to +85°C	0.01% FSO/°C typ
−55°C to +125°C	0.02% FSO/°C typ
Zero pressure output	1.0V dc ±0.15V dc max
Stability (1 year)	±1.0% FS output

Figure 8.16 Pressure sensor specifications.

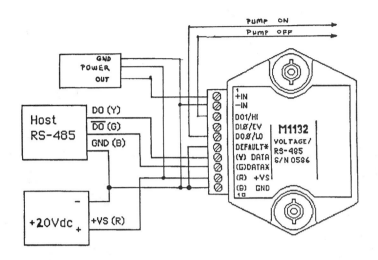

Figure 8.17 Schematic of connections to the module, sensor and the host computer.

To save the computer from environmental hazards, it has to be housed in an air conditioned room. The wiring distance from the tower to the room inside the building adjacent to the tower is measured as 650 feet. This distance is too much for the RS-232, so the only selection available is a M1132 module with a RS-485 connection to the host computer.

The host computer has an RS-485 adapter card installed which converts COM2 into the RS-485 port. Supply voltage of the sensor is connected to the supply voltage of the remote data acquisition module. But since the sensor can only accept voltage level between 9 to 20, we have to make sure that the voltage level satisfies both the module and the sensor. 20 V is selected as the supply voltage. The signal output of the sensor is connected to the voltage inputs of the module and the digital outputs DO1 and DO0 are connected to suitable relays for turning the pump motor on and off. The rest of the connections are shown in Figure 8.17.

The conversion of the actual water level to volume of water available is done in the host computer. Basically the host computer has the data from the plot entered in a piecewise linear form. The level reading is applied to the function to find out the actual volume. The portion of the program for volume conversion is not shown in this case study. The next case study has a similar problem which is explicitly analyzed.

After the connection to the module is made with the host computer, the following commands are issued to module over the host computer remotely.

- We would like to operate the module at 9600 baud rate.
- The voltage for upper threshold level of water is 4.118 volts
- The voltage for lower threshold level of water is 3.468 volts.

The following commands are issued only once during the setup phase of the system:

Figure 8.18 The pressure sensor and the module used in the case study.

Host is set to 300 baud, the module address is set to "1".

$1CA	clear alarms
$1WE	write enable
$1HI+04118.00M	upper limit is programmed with momentary value
$1WE	write enable
$1LO+03468.00M	lower limit is programmed with momentary value
$1RL	read low alarm to verify
$1RH	read high alarm to verify
$1EA	enable alarms
$1WE	
$1SU31A28140	module set up with 9600 baud, even parity with ID code "1".
$1RR	remote reset

After this instant, the host computer should be set to 9600 baud, even parity to resume the communication with the module. Connection to the default input of the remote data acquisition module should also be removed. After this

$1RD	read data

command will supply the data. High and low alarm latching will be done automatically by the module. So the module will control the pump motor without any intervention from the host computer. To check the actual water level, the host computer has to issue a $1RD command to read the pressure. Pressure information will be converted to the water contents inside the host computer by the look up table or piece-wise approximation of the formula.

CASE STUDY 2: AUTOMATED MEASUREMENT AND COMPUTERIZED BILLING BY AN OLIVE OIL PRODUCER.

An olive oil marketing firm has a small collection point set up near the farms. The company collects olives from the local farmers and presses some of them for olive oil production. The firm decided to computerize its operation in order to speed up the process. Accordingly, the olives that brought in by the farmer in baskets are weighed by a balance which has connection to the host computer. The olives are then sifted to separate the small ones from the bigger ones. The big ones are reserved for table consumption for further packing and marketing after a second weighing process. The small ones are pressed and the olive oil is produced. The payment rate for olives for table consumption and that for olive oil produced is different. The olive oil output of the press is also measured and recorded. The farmer is paid accordingly.

Design: A design based on remote modules is selected for this application since there are only two analog inputs to be measured. The weighing of the olives is done by a load cell which can measure 0 to 250 kg. The output of the load cell comes out as 0-100 mV. Measurement of the olive oil output is measured by pressure measurement as was done in case study #1. The shape of the tank is irregular; because of this, the pressure output is converted into volume output by a pressure sensor. The volume of the tank is 12,000 gallons and it is mounted in an upright position. The tank is 50 feet tall.

The pressure sensor selected has an output 0-20 psi. Since 1 foot of olive oil generates pressure of 0.3253 psi, the pressure generated by the olive oil when the tank is full is calculated as

$$50 \times 0.3253 = 16.26 \text{ psi}$$

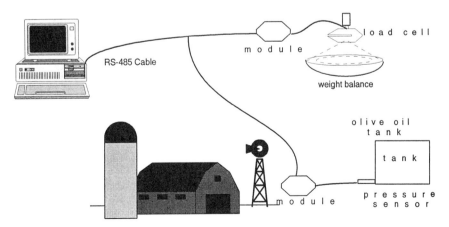

Figure 8.19 The olive oil collection farm and the arrangement of the sensors and modules.

We selected a M2131 remote data acquisition module which can accept an input of 0 to 5 volts and has a RS-232 output. The programming of the module will be done in the following way.

Start programming with the olive oil tank empty. Enter the minimum value:

Command: $1MN+00000.00

Response: *

In this example, the maximum point may be programmed by filling the olive oil tank to obtain the maximum pressure output. However, this is awkward and unnecessary. Since the olive oil tank capacity is known to be 12,000 gallons and the pressure can never reach 25 psi, we can simulate a maximum that we know can never be attained. To do this we may apply 5 V to the module input to simulate 25 psi. The 5 V source does not have to be accurate. We can set the maximum value to 15,000 gallons, which is more than what the olive oil tank can hold.

Disconnect the pressure sensor and apply 5 V to the module input:

Command: $1 MX+15000.00

Response: *

Reconnect the pressure sensor to the M2131. Starting with the olive oil tank empty, we may begin to program the breakpoints. We will set a breakpoint every 600 gallons for a total of 20 breakpoints.

To set the first breakpoint, fill the tank with 600 gallons of olive oil . Since we will be using actual volumes of olive oil to 'calibrate' the olive oil tank, the accuracy at which we can measure 600 gallons will greatly influence the final performance of the system.

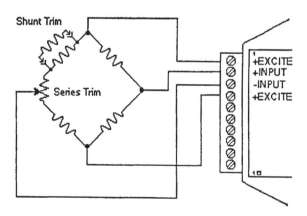

Figure 8.20 Schematic of connection with load cell.

With 600 gallons in the olive oil tank used as the input excitation, program the first breakpoint:

        Command: $1BP00+00600.00

        Response: *

Test:

        Command: $1

        Response: 00600.00

Fill the olive oil tank with an additional 600 gallons to program the second breakpoint. The olive oil tank now holds 1200 gallons of oil:

        Command: $1BP01+01200.00

        Response: *

Test:

        Command: $1

        Response: +01200.00

Figure 8.21 Actual arrangement of load cell.

Repeat these steps until the olive oil tank is full. For each step, fill the olive oil tank with an additional 1500 gallons and program the breakpoint with the accumulated amount of oil in the olive oil tank. When the breakpoint programming is complete, the M2131 will give a very accurate indication of the volume of olive oil in the olive oil tank directly in units of gallons.

In this example, the actual transfer function of the system is unknown. Instead, the function is plotted in the field by applying known inputs to the system. Note that the voltage produced by the pressure sensor does not have to be known to program the M2131. However, it is wise to record the voltages produced by the sensor at each break-point. With this information, replacement M2131's may be programmed with a voltage source to avoid repeating the tank filling exercise.

A load cell is used in weighing olives and mated to a M1521 module. The load cell is rated for 3 mV/V, which results in a maximum +30 mV with 10 V excitation. However, in this particular application, the load cell is used only in tension; so its ideal output will be from 0 to +30 mV.

The load cell is mounted in its final position with the weighing attachments. Clear any offset data that may be stored in the M1521 module:

Command:	$1 WE (CZ is write-protected)
Response:	*

Command:	$1 CZ (Clear Zero)
Response:	*

Verify that the zero trim is cleared:

Command:	$1RZ (Read Zero)
Response:	*+00000.00

Obtain an initial offset reading from the load cell with no weight attached:

Command:	$1RD (Read Data)
Response:	*+00002.34

The initial offset is +2.34 mV. The M1521 has a useful input range of +60 mV. After subtracting the offset, the "input overhead" is -62.34 mV and +57.66 mV. The expected 0 to +30 mV output of the load cell easily falls within the overhead range and no external trimming is necessary.

To trim zero:

Command:	$1WE	(TZ is write protected)
Response:	*	
Command:	$1TZ+ 00000.00	(zero is the desired output)

Now read the data output to verify the trim:

| **Command:** | $1RD | (Read Data) |
| **Response:** | *+00000.00 | |

The load cell system has been trimmed to zero.

8.4.8 Design Examples Using M2000 Series Modules

M2000 series modules have the ability to interpret nonlinear input functions. The previous case studies partly showed how to use this ability of M2000 series modules to solve difficult nonlinear problems quickly and easily. The following design examples are reprinted by permission of Keithley-Metrabyte to clarify the programming procedure even further.

LINEAR SCALING WITH M2000 MODULES

Rescaling the M2000 to a linear transfer function is the easiest and most common way to reprogram the module. The linear scale function is defined by specifying the two end points of the linear function. Any linear function within the analog input range of the module may be defined.

Custom scaling requires a calibrated analog input signal to define the end points of the linear transfer function. The signal could be a voltage, current, or frequency depending on the specific model type. The Minimum and Maximum commands are used to program the end point data into the module's memory.

PROGRAMMING PROCEDURES

1. Make sure the module has not been previously programmed with Break Point (BP) Commands. If it has, clear the break points with the erase break points (EB) command.

2. Clear any data in the output offset register with the clear zero (CZ) command.

3. Determine the end points which will be used to define the linear function. The analog input values must lie within the operating range of the module. The analog inputs used to determine the end points will also define the overload outputs of the module. Construct an output data format that is best suited for your application.

4. Apply a calibrated analog signal to the module input corresponding to the most negative input of the desired linear scale. Perform a minimum (MN) command to store the function end point into the module's memory.

5. Apply a calibrated analog signal to the module input corresponding to the most positive analog input value. Perform a maximum (MX) command to load the end point data into the module memory.

6. Verify that the transfer function has been correctly loaded into the module by applying test inputs to the module and reading out the data with the read data (RD) command.

Example 1

Reprogram a M2151, 4-20 mA module to output data in terms of percent; that is, 4 mA will read out to be 0% and 20 mA will read out as 100%.

1. If the module had been previously programmed with break points, erase the function table with the erase breakpoints (EB) command:

Command:	$1WE
Response:	*
Command:	$1 EB
Response:	*

2. Clear any offset data with the clear zero command:

Command:	$1WE
Response:	*
Command:	$1CZ
Response:	*

3. The minimum analog input in this case is 4 mA. Any current less than 4 mA will result in a negative over-range (-99999.99). The maximum positive input is 20 mA. Since the minimum value of 4 mA corresponds to 0%, the appropriate output data would be +00000.00. The output data corresponding to 20 mA is +00100.00. This data format gives us whole units of "percent" to the left of the decimal point. To get the maximum resolution from the module, set up the number of displayed digits with the setup (SU) command so that all digits are displayed.

Command:	$1WE	
Response:	*	
Command:	$1SU310701C2	(typical)

Response: *

4. Apply exactly 4 mA to the current input of the module. Program the end point with the minimum command:

Command: $1 WE
Response: *
Command: $1 MN+00000.00
Response: *

5. Apply exactly 20mA to the module input and store the maximum end point with the maximum (MX) command:

Command: $1 WE
Response: *
Command: $1 MX+00100.00
Response: *

6. Verify the module response by testing it with various inputs within its range:

Input Current	Output Data
8 mA	+00025.00
12 mA	+00050.00
16 mA	+00075.00

Rescaling is now complete.

Example 2

A paddle-wheel low sensor will be used to monitor the flow of water in a pipe. The characteristics of the sensor and the size of the pipe results in an output frequency of 10 Hz. per gallon per minute. The operating range is from 1 to 20 gallons per minute.

We would like to scale a M2000 module to output data in units of 0.1 gallons. The logical module choice in this application is the M2601 frequency input module. The frequency output of the flow sensor will range from 10 Hz to 200 Hz, easily within the 5 Hz to 20 kHz range of the M2601.

1. Erase Breakpoints:

Command:	$1WE
Response:	*
Command:	S1 EB
Response:	*

2. Clear Zero:

Command:	$1WE
Response:	*
Command:	$1CZ
Response:	*

3. The minimum end point in this case is 10 Hz corresponding to an output of +00001.00 gpm. The maximum frequency at 20 gpm is 200 Hz. The maximum output data is +00020.00. To get 0.1 gpm resolution, set up the module to display six digits:

Command:	$1WE	
Response:	*	
Command:	$1SU31070182	(typical)
Response:	*	

4. Using a calibrated frequency generator, apply 10 Hz to the module input. Set the minimum point:

Command:	$1WE
Response:	*
Command:	$1MN00001.00
Response:	*

5. Set the frequency generator to 200 Hz to program the maximum point:

Command:	$1WE
Response:	*
Command:	$1MX+00020.00
Response:	*

6. Use the frequency generator to verify a few points in the scale:

Analog Input	Data Qutput
30 Hz	+00003.00
100 Hz	+00010.00
155 Hz	+00015.50

Programming is now complete and the M2601 can be attached to the flow sensor.

Example 3

In many cases the analog calibration values may be produced directly by the sensors to be used in a system. The module may be re-ranged in the field to encompass any errors due to sensor inaccuracies.

In this example, we wish to use a pressure sensor to measure the volume of water in a cylindrical tank that is 10 feet tall with a capacity of 1500 gallons. The pressure sensor is mounted at the bottom of the tank producing an output corresponding to the height of the water in the tank. The pressure sensor chosen produces 1 V @ 0 psi and 5 V @ 10 psi. A full tank with 10 feet of water will produce 4.335 psi (1 ft = 0.4335 psi), well within the range of the pressure sensor. M2131, + 5 V input module will be used as the interface.

1. Erase breakpoints:

Command:	$1WE
Response:	*
Command:	$1 EB
Response:	*

2. Clear zero:

Command:	$1 WE
Response:	*
Command:	$1 CZ
Response:	*

3. To produce the analog Xmin and Xmax end point values, we will use the actual water levels in the tank to produce a calibration pressure. The accuracy of the pressure transducer is not important, as long as it is stable and linear. To set the minimum value, we will empty the tank and set the minimum value to +00000.00. The maximum value will be programmed with the tank full and the maximum output data will be set to 01500.00 gallons. In this case an output resolution in units of gallons is acceptable and we can set

up the module so that 5 digits are displayed. The digits to the right of the decimal point will always read out "00".

Command:	$1WE
Response:	*
Command:	$1SU31070142
Response:	*

4. With the tank empty, program the minimum point:

Command:	$1 WE
Response:	*
Command:	$1 MN +00000.00
Response:	*

5. Fill the tank with water and program the maximum point:

Command:	$1 WE
Response:	*
Command:	$1 MX +01500.00
Response:	*

6. Verify the scaling. In this case, it is difficult to verify the scaling quickly and accurately. A "ballpark" check can be made by letting water out of the full tank and checking to see if the module output readings are reasonable. A more accurate check can be made by filling the tank with known amounts of water and verifying the output readings

Example 4

M2251 4-20 mA module will be used to provide a computer interface to an existing process 4-20 mA signal. The loop transmitter produces a linear 4-20 mA signal corresponding to a sensor temperature of 0-200 degrees C. In this case, we would like to take advantage of the factory linearity correction in the M2251 for greater accuracy. To do this, we must use the same analog input minimum and maximum points as programmed at the factory. The M2251 minimum and maximum points are 0 mA and 25 mA. The 4-20 mA span of the process transmitter must be extrapolated to 0-25 mA to provide the correct data when using the MN and MX commands.

The transfer relationship of the 4-20 mA transmitter can be described by the equation:

$$T = 12.5X \text{ mA} - 50$$

Plug values of 0 mA and 25 mA into the equation to derive extrapolated values of T:

$$T = 12.5 * (0) - 50 = -50$$
$$T = 12.5 * (25) - 50 = +262.5$$

These values will be used in the MN and MX instructions.

Program the module:

1. In this case, it is assumed that the M2251 is fresh from the factory and it still contains linearity correction in the break point table. In order to take advantage of the linearity correction, the break points will not be erased.

2. Clear zero:

Command:	$1WE
Response:	*
Command:	$1CZ
Response:	*

3. The minimum endpoint has been extrapolated to be -00050.00 @ 0 mA. The maximum point is +00262.50 @ 25 mA. We'll setup the module to display temperature with 0.1 degree resolution:

Command:	$1WE	
Response:	*	
Command:	$1SU31070142	(typical)
Response:	*	

4. Apply an 0 mA (open circuit) to the current input and program the minimum point:

Command:	$1WE
Response:	*
Command:	$1 MN-00050.00
Response:	*

5. Apply exactly 25 mA to the current input to program the maximum point:

Command:	$1WE
Response:	*
Command:	$1MX+00262.50
Response:	*

6. Apply test currents to the module to verify the scaling:

Apply 4 mA to the input:

| Command: | $1 |
| Response: | +00000.00 |

Apply 20 mA to the input:

| Command: | $1 |
| Response: | +00200.00 |

Example 5

A voltage-output pressure sensor produces 0 V @ 100 psi and 5 V @ 600 psi. Its output characteristic is nonlinear and may be described by the equation:

$$P = 100 + 80 \text{ V} + 4 \text{ V}^2$$

where

  V = sensor output in volts

  P = pressure in psi

A simple linear equation may be derived by using the end point data:

$$P = 100 + 100 \text{ V}$$

Unfortunately, describing the sensor output with this equation results in a 25 psi error at V = 2.5 V. To obtain better accuracy, we may approximate the quadratic transfer function using break points. Since the sensor output range is 0 - 5 V, the M2131 with an input range of +/- 5 V is most suitable for this application. For simplicity, we will use only four evenly spaced break points to plot the function. This will result in a function approximation with a maximum error of 1 psi. For better conformity, more break points may be used.

1. First, construct the function table:

	Analog Input	Output
Minimum	0 V	+00100.00
Maximum	5 V	+00600.00
Break point 00	1 V	+00184.00
Break point 01	2 V	+00276.00
Break point 02	3 V	+00376.00
Break point 03	4 V	+00484.00

Notice that we've broken up the curve into five evenly spaced voltage segments by using four break points. The break point output values were obtained by plugging the break point voltage values into the quadratic equation that describes the sensor.

2. Prepare the M2131 by erasing any stored breakpoints. (All programming commands must be preceded by a write enable (WE) command. In the interest of simplicity, the write enable commands are not shown in this or any of the following examples.)

      Command: $1EB

      Response: *

3. Clear any data in the output off:

      Command: $1CZ

      Response: *

4. We will set up the output data to display psi with 0.1 resolution:

      Command: $1SU31070182   (typical)

      Response: *

(The SU data may vary depending on your particular module setup. See the Setup section in the M1000 manual).

5. Apply 0 volts (short) to the input of the M2131 to enter the minimum point of 100 psi:

      Command: $1 MN+00100.00

      Response: *

6. To set the maximum point, apply 5 V to the input and program the maximum point to be 600 psi:

Command: $1 MX+00600.00
Response: *

7. Program the first break point:
Apply 1 volt to the input and perform the break point command:

Command: $1BP00+00184.00
Response: *

Verify the break point data:

Command: $1
Response: *+00184.00

Repeat the procedure for the remaining breakpoints:
Apply 2 volts to the input:

Command: $1 8P01 +00276.00
Response: *
Command: $1
Response: *+00276.00

Apply 3 volts to the input:

Command: $1 BP02+00376.00
Response: *
Command: $1
Response: +00376.00

Apply 4 volts to the input:

Command: $1 BP03+00484.00
Response: *
Command: $1
Response: +00484.00

The function programming is now complete.

8. The transfer function may be verified by applying test inputs to the module and obtaining output data. The data can then be compared to the original quadratic equation to check for conformity error.

Example: Apply 0.5 volts to the M2131 input and read data:

      Command: $1
      Response: +00142.00

To check, plug 0.5 volts into the quadratic equation:

$P = 100 + 80 \, (.5) + 4 \, (.5)^2 = 141$

The conformity error at this point is +1 psi.

8.5 REMOTE DATA ACQUISITION USING DATA ACQUISITION CRATES

Remote data acquisition modules are excellent devices for small scale, applications distributed over large area. If the application needs only few analog or digital input lines and the frequency of conversion is not very demanding, then the remote data acquisition modules are the ideal equipment for such cases. Since each module is a separate entity, even if the data acquisition application is distributed in a large area with sensors at considerable distances from each other, this does not pose any problem.

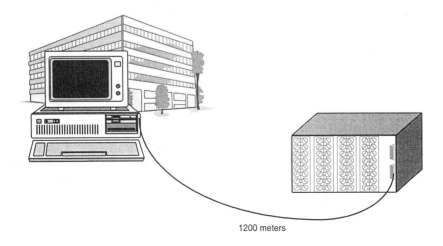

1200 meters

Figure 8.22 Remote data acquisition with crates.

Even though remote data acquisition modules are excellent devices, in cases where the number of channels is more than six, the module approach starts getting expensive. Another problem with the modules is the fact that conversion speed is slow. The modules used in the case studies have a conversion rate of 5 conversions per second. If the application demands high speed, even if one does not need many channels in your application, remote data acquisition modules can not be used. Such cases are suitable for remote data acquisition crates.

A "crate" is a sturdy box containing data acquisition equipment inside. Usually the box is rack mountable and comes in standard 19" size which is the common equipment size for the industry. The size is not as small as a remote data acquisition module and the power can not be supplied remotely. Usually the power consumption is large enough to require a separate power supply for the crate. The interface to the host computer can be one of the following:

- RS-232 serial (19K baud rate at 20 meter)
- RS-485 serial (100K baud at 1200 meter)
- Long distance Byte Parallel (500,000 byte/sec at 1200 meter)

A crate has its own communication processor which handles communication with the host PC. If serial communication is used for communicating with the crate, the speed of data acquisition will be slow due to the communication speed even though the crate can acquire data at a much faster rate. In cases where the data acquisition speed is critical, the parallel interface is the only choice that will satisfy the requirements.

Remote data acquisition crates basically have all the advantages of remote data acquisition modules and more. The **advantages** of using remote data acquisition crates can be listed as follows.

- Crates can be connected together on a string to increase capacity.
- The user can select the data acquisition cards to go inside the crate.
- A wide variety of cards is available.
- Communication speed can be very high especially in the parallel communication mode.
- Large expansion capability.
- Serial communication distance can be increased using repeaters.

The **disadvantages** are

- There are many industry standards for remote data acquisition crates. Almost all data acquisition equipment manufacturers manufacture data acquisition crates of some sort. But they are all proprietary and are not compatible with each other. This simply means one is obliged to continue using the products of whichever company one started with.

- The data acquisition crates are distributed just like remote data acquisition modules; however, the cost per node is much higher than that of remote data acquisition modules. This means that it is not feasible to put a remote data acquisition crate in an isolated location where there are only a few data acquisition signals available.

Since there is no industry standard for crates, to show the abilities of typical remote data acquisition crates, let us look at few commercially available units. Under this category, Keithley Metrabyte® corporation has

- Workhorse® system
- Metrabus®
- Series 500® Data Acquisition Instruments

Omega Instruments® has

- OM-900® series
- μmega 4000® system

Please note that although these systems qualify to be remote data acquisition crates, the distance and speed capabilities may differ widely. The figures given in the previous section are only general information and may not be applicable to all these units.

8.5.1 Workhorse Systems

Workhorse® is one of the most widely known of the remote data acquisition units. A short data sheet indicating technical specifications of Workhorse is given on the following page. Let us take a look at the capabilities of the Workhorse system.

Workhorse is a remote data acquisition crate system which can be connected to a host PC and controlled serially or in parallel from distances up to 4000 feet. The crates can accommodate up to 7 data acquisition cards which can be selected from a wide variety of cards. These cards are not compatible with a PC expansion bus. Serial communication with the host PC does not require any special card inside the PC; usual RS-232 or RS-485 output can be connected directly to the Workhorse. (In case the computer does not have RS-485 as standard, a separate card has to be installed.) If parallel connection between the host PC and Workhorse' is desired, then a special communication board has to be installed inside the host PC. With this special card installed, the two units can communicate up to a speed of 500,000 byte/sec.

If one single crate is not sufficient for the application, more units can be cascaded together to increase the size of the crate. The typical system block diagram for the Workhorse system is shown in Figure 8.23.

ADDITIONAL WORKHORSE TECHNICAL DETAILS AND FEATURES

The next section of the Workhorse introduction briefly describes some of the more salient technical details/features of the Workhorse system. This section is meant as an overview only, and for further details and specifications please refer to the specific data sheets that are included later in this chapter.

Workhorse Communications Interface

The only currently available Computer to Workhorse interface is the standard -PAR system that has been implemented on the WH-PCDB-PAR, WH-uCDB-PAR, and WH-PCDB-ISO driver boards that plug into the host computer, and their WH-CIB-PAR counter-part in the Workhorse chassis. (However, there are more interfaces in development. Please call for further information).

The standard -PAR (for PARallel) interface is a 25 wire, fully synchronous, fully differential interface. The system utilizes 12 independent, high performance RS-485 line drivers and receivers in each interface board. A full hand-shaking system has been implemented that assures that both transmitter and receiver are "In-Sync." However, this high performance interface has been made transparent to the computer. The computer simply writes an address, then reads or writes the data. All hand shaking is done in the interface board hardware. These features combine to form an extremely noise immune, and high speed (less than 2 microsecond access time) interface for the Workhorse. A diagram of the standard parallel interface cable is shown below:

DB25 PINOUT

D0+	1	14	D0–
D1+	2	15	D1–
D2+	3	16	D2–
D3+	4	17	D3–
HNIB+	5	18	HNIB–
rd.+	6	19	RD–
PF+	7	20	PF–
AS+	8	21	AS–
GND	9	22	DS–
DS+	10	23	GND
ACK+	11	24	ACK–
/LC	12	25	ATN–
ATN+	13		

I/O Boards

There are a wide variety of I/O boards currently available for the Workhorse, and there are quite a few more in development. Included in this first release are a 16-point, electro-mechanical relay output board, an 8-point DPDT electro-mechanical relay output board, a 16-point Solid State relay output, a 16-point low-level digital input board, a 16-point, low-level digital output board, a 32-point digital I/O board, a 16-channel analog input board, a 16-channel thermocouple input board and a 8-channel analog output board.

System Modularity

All Workhorse electrical and electronic components can be installed, removed or replaced without having to remove wiring, cables, or disassembling the system. In fact all Workhorse boards can be replaced without the use of any tools. This guarantees that even in the unlikely event that a Workhorse component did fail, the system can be back up and running again in a matter of minutes.

System Size and Density

It's no secret that rack space in most applications is expensive. For this reason the Workhorse chassis has been developed to offer extremely high point density. A single chassis that measures 10.25" (deep) by 12.25" (high) by 17.25" (wide) can contain 112 3-amp relay outputs, 112 analog inputs, or 224 low-level digital I/O points. This corresponds to less than 2 square inches per I/O point. Note that the chassis size also includes all field wiring connections, power supplies and communications boards. There is no sense in building a dense I/O system, and then taking up a lot of room with terminal panels, communications interfaces and power supplies.

Chassis Mounting

The WH-CH-7 chassis is easy to mount either in 19" racks, or against any flat surface (as may be found in the rear of a NEMA enclosure). The chassis is shipped standard with a set of "ears" or mounting brackets that allow the chassis to be inserted and secured in a 19" rack. However, these "ears" are simple pieces of L shape steel (angle-iron). By removing the brackets from the front of the chassis, reversing them, and then mounting them on the rear (with pre-drilled and tapped holes), the chassis is ready for mounting to any flat surface.

Software

The Workhorse system has been developed based on a very simple 6-bit address with 8-bit data. However to simplify programming, the WORKHORSE software interface has been developed to greatly simplify programming of Workhorse applications. All commands are in the form of high level, easy to read commands. For example, the command to read a voltage from an analog input board is Vin, the command to write a voltage to an analog output board is Vout.

The software is provided in the form of a DOS device driver, that is automatically loaded each time you turn yours on. Reading from or writing to the driver is as simple as reading or writing a disk. In BASIC the PRINT and INPUT commands are used. Other languages have similar commands. The following section details some of the available I/O commands. For further details please refer to the Workhorse Software data sheet late in this section.

Vin [[bb],ccc],gg	Selects input range "gg" and reads the input voltage (in Volts) of channel "ccc" on the A/D board at Board Address "bb", chan, gain. "ccc" will be 0-15 for a standard A/D board. However, if WH-AEX-16 expansion boards are used, expansion board #1 is read by simply reading channels 16-31, board #2 by reading channels 32-47 etc.
VOut [[bb],ccc],gg,d.ddd	Sets the output voltage of the D/A board at Address "bb", channel "ccc" into the "gg" output range, and then sets the output voltage to "dd.ddd" volts.
Bin [[bb],ccc]	Reads a single bit/point (0 or 1) from bit "ccc" (0-15 for 16 input boards, 0-31 for 32 input boards etc.) of the digital input board at address "bb".
BOut [[bb],ccc],d	Sets the single output relay or point of output number "ccc", of the digital output board at board address "bb" to "d" (0 or 1).
TEmp [bb],ccc],gg	Sets the Temperature measurement board at address "bb" into range "gg", and reads the input temperature (in degrees C of F).

A simple program to read and display all 16 channels of a WH-AIN-16 (analog input board) at board address 0 is shown below.

IN BASICA

```
10 OPEN "WH$" FOR OUTPUT AS #1   'Open the communications link
20 OPEN "WH$" FOR INPUT AS #2    'to the device driver
30 '
40 FOR I = 0 to 15               'Set up 16 channel loop
50 PRINT #1, "VIN,0,1"           'Request a voltage reading from
                                  channel 0 of the thermocouple
                                  board at address 0
60 INPUT #2, VOLT$               'Read the voltage data
70 PRINT "CH #",I," READS
  ",VOLTS,"V"
80 NEXT I                        'Display the output
```

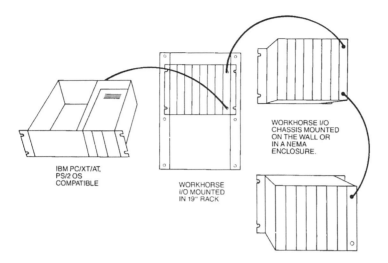

Figure 8.23 Workhorse® , typical system block diagram.

The Workhorse chassis comes in several different configurations to accommodate a connection to various mounting enclosures like NEMA or a 19" rack system. The main features of the Workhorse are highlighted below.

- Full speed operation at distances to 1200 meters.
- Fixed field wiring. No wires ever need be disconnected to remove or install a board.
- High-strength steel chassis that is easily mounted in 19-inch racks, in NEMA enclosures or directly to the wall.
- Each system includes an easy-to-use software driver that makes reading and writing data simple.
- Up to 1024 digital I/O points.
- As few as 16, or as many as 3,584 analog inputs.
- Stand alone or factory network/ distributed processing.

Applications include

- Factory automation and monitoring
- Process control, energy management
- Automated test and inspection
- Building alarm and monitoring system
- Supervisory control and data acquisition
- Machine control

The Workhorse is a rugged chassis and family of monitoring and control I/O devices designed to interface to personal computers. The Workhorse combines a low-cost I/O with the programmability of the computer to provide cost-effective solutions for one's industrial data acquisition needs.

THE WORKHORSE CONCEPT

The Workhorse concept is simple; a single parallel driver board is plugged into a personal computer. There are driver boards available for IBM PC/XT/AT and compatible computers. Interfaces for serial (RS-232, RS-422, RS-485, Current Loops) and IEEE-488 systems are also available.

The parallel driver board in the computer connects (via a cable) to one or more Workhorse chassis. Each chassis contains

- Up to 7 Workhorse I/O boards per chassis
- A chassis interface board (CIB) that is connected to the host computer (and optional chassis) by cables.
- A 100-watt power supply.

All field wiring is then connected to the chassis. The Workhorse field-wiring system assures that once the system is wired, it never needs to be disconnected or altered to install, remove or replace any board or power supply.

The following different data acquisition cards are available for Workhorse crates.

Analog I/O Boards

WHAIN16	16 Channel Analog Input (12 bit)
WHAEX16	16 Channel Analog Input Expansion
WHAEX32	32 Channel Analog Input Expansion
WHIAI8	8 Channel Isolated Analog Input (12 bit)
WHTC16	16 Channel Thermocouple Input
WHRTD8	8 Channel RTD Input
WHREX8	8 Channel RTD Input Expansion
WHAO8	8 Channel Analog Output (12 bit)
WHMBEX16	16 Channel Signal Conditioning Expansion (uses MB series modules)

Digital I/O Boards

WHEM16	16 Point Electromechanical Relay
WHEM16/S	16 Point Electromechanical Settable Relay
WHSSR16	16 Point Solid State Relay
WHDI116/AC	16 Point Isolated Digital Input

Figure 8.24 Workhorse crate. Notice the passive backplane.

WHDIO16/HC   16Point Isolated Digital Output

WHDIB32   32 Point Digital I/O

WHCNTT5   5 Channel Counter/Timer

Miscellaneous Boards

WHDIAG   Diagnostic Board

WHEXT   Extender Board

WHPROTO   Prototyping Board for custom circuitry

8.6 REMOTE DATA ACQUISITION USING INTELLIGENT DATA ACQUISITION CRATES

What makes a data acquisition crate intelligent is the embedded computer. With the embedded computer, the system looks very much like a PC with data acquisition cards inside. Although the concept is very similar to having a factory hardened PC as a front end data acquisition unit, there are some minor differences. The idea behind having intelligent remote data acquisition crates is to have the ability to preprocess the data and then send the result in processed form.

Remote intelligent data acquisition crates normally have a serial link to the host PC used for communication. In a non-intelligent remote data acquisition crate, all the data that were acquired from the application would have to be sent back to the host computer.

In some cases this causes huge data traffic from the crate to the host PC and may very easily exceed the data transmission capability of the serial link. In such cases what is needed is an intelligent front end data acquisition crate which would process the data, take necessary control actions and send the processed data back to the host PC.

A visible difference between an intelligent data acquisition crate and an industrial PC with data acquisition cards inside is in the peripherals. Data acquisition crates are not designed to be interfaced to a monitor or keyboard. Often their only link to the outside world for communication and programming is through the link to the host PC.

Different vendors have different intelligent data acquisition units available on the market. These units have their own special commands and architecture. An example of an intelligent data acquisition crate is the Workhorse data acquisition crate. This unit functions as a dumb data acquisition unit and sends every piece of data it acquires. By adding a special CPU card in one of the slots, the Workhorse system can be converted into a remote intelligent data acquisition system.

Remote intelligent data acquisition systems are often used for supervisory control purposes and given a special name "SCADA" (supervisory control and data acquisition) in industry. SCADA systems can be networked by using usual networking techniques for transferring data. The data sheet below gives the technical details of a Worksmart card which converts the Workhorse system into an intelligent system.

WORKSMART

EMBEDDED CONTROLLER ORDERING GUIDE

WORKSMART is a true PC-compatible controller designed to work in conjunction with the WORKHORSE family of I/O modules. With appropriate software, WORKSMART allows users to develop custom solutions that meet their specific application needs. Typical applicaions include:

• Batch process control
• Supervisory control and data acquisition (SCADA)
• Material handling systems
• Machine control
• Manufacturing test and measurement

The WORKSMART eliminates the need for a separate PC and takes one I/O slot of the CH-7 chassis.

ORDER

WH-WSPEC-01	WORKSMART 286
WH-WSPEC-02	WORKSMART W/ARCNET installed
WH-WSPEC-03	WORKSMART W/ETHERNET installed
WH-WSPEC-04	WORKSMART W/IEEE installed
(Optional interfaces for WORKSMART 286)	
WH-WSARC-01	ARCNET Interface
WH-WSETH-01	Ethernet Interface
WH-WSIEEE-01	IEEE Interface

IEEE-488 Interface The WH-CIB-488 allows the use of the WORKHORSE with any computer having an IEEE-488 interface. The interface card allows the WORKHORSE chassis to function as as a GPIB instrument and share the GPIB bus with other WORKHORSE chassis or instruments, or a mix of both, up to a total of 14. The interface acts as a T/L-addressed GPIB bus slave with full source/acceptor handshake capabilities. This interface does not require a PC-compatible computer.

ORDER

WH-CIB-488

COMPUTER INTERFACES When using the WORKHORSE parallel interface (WH-CIB-PAR), a driver board must be installed in the host PC. One PC-installed driver board can address multiple WORKHORSE chassis containing up to 3,584 analog or 1,024 digital I/O points.

PC/XT/AT Driver Interfaces Two versions are available for the PC/XT/AT bus: the non-isolated WH-PCDB-PAR, and the isolated driver board version WH-PCDB-ISO. The WH-PCDB-PAR transfers data/address information between the WORKHORSE and PC over a 25-pin cable at distances up to 4,000 feet. The WH-PCDB-ISO functions identically and provides bus-to-computer isolation of 500 VDC.

ORDER

WH-PCDB-PAR	Non-isolated
WH-PCDB-ISO	Isolated

8.7 REMOTE DATA ACQUISITION USING MODEMS

If the distance between the application and the host PC is more than the distance provided by a few RS-485 with repeaters (4 km), other techniques for communication need
to be used. If phone lines are available between the application and the host computer,
then we can use the phone lines for data communication. Using phone lines requires using modems. Regardless of the baud rate, modems come in several different versions.

- Modems for switched voice grade phone lines (up to 9600 baud over
  ordinary phone lines)
- Modems for wide band leased phone lines (up to 19,200 baud rate over
  leased high quality phone lines)
- Limited distance modems with dedicated lines (up to 1.5 Million bits/sec
  over dedicated customer owned lines--distance up to 50 km)
- Wireless modems (up to 9600 baud over a distance of 50-60 km)
- Fiber optic modems for noisy environments (up to 2-3 km at most)
- Line drivers for increasing the range of RS-232 signals (up to 1.2 km)

Among these modems, the limited distance modem, wireless modem, fiber optic
modem and line drivers for the RS-232 do not use the phone lines but use dedicated customer owned and laid connection lines. In the case of the fiber optic modem, the connection is done over two pairs of fiber optic cables laid between two fiber optic modems.
Figure 8.25 shows two different fiber optic modems.

Figure 8.25 Fiber optic modems.

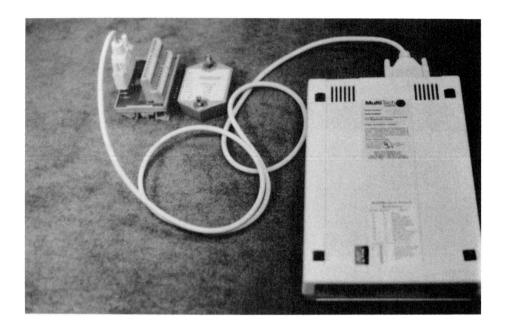

Figure 8.26 Line driver for RS-232 port.

The connection between the modems is very simple and the baud rate of the serial port is the baud rate of the fiber optic modem. This type of modem is especially suitable for environments where the electromagnetic noise is above normal. Since fiber optic modems use light pulses they are intrinsically safe for environments that present a fire or explosion hazard.

Line drivers for RS-232 ports are used for increasing the distance of communication. These devices come either in small serial port powered packages or in larger boxes which are mains-powered. A mains powered driver gives one a larger distance of communication. Usually the distance of communication is up to 1.2 km. Figure 8.26 shows typical line drivers.

The modems that are designed to be used with phone lines are of special interest to us. The data can be transmitted raw over the phone lines or they can be compressed by the modem as they being sent. There are internationally recognized data compression standards to compress the data and increase the data throughput rate. The speed of communication of the ordinary voice grade switched phone lines is limited by 9600 baud rate. With suitable compression algorithms, the data transfer rate can be increased to 14,400 baud. But be warned that the data compression ratio is dependent on the data that one is transmitting and one is not guaranteed to get 14,400 baud throughput all the time. As an example an already compressed data can not be compressed any further by the modem anymore. Detailed information about modem standards is given in Table 8.2.

Modem type	Max. Data Rate	Transmission Technique	Modulation Technique	Transmission Technique	Line Use
Bell System					
103A, E	300	asynchronous	FSK	Half, Full	Switched
103F	300	asynchronous	FSK	Half, Full	Leased
201B	2400	synchronous	PSK	Half, Full	Leased
201C	2400	synchronous	PSK	Half, Full	Switched
202C	1200	asynchronous	FSK	Half	Switched
202S	1200	asynchronous	FSK	Half	Switched
202D/R	1800	asynchronous	FSK	Half, Full	Leased
202T	1800	asynchronous	FSK	Half, Full	Leased
208A	4800	synchronous	PSK	Half, Full	Leased
208B	4800	synchronous	PSK	Half	Switched
209A	9600	synchronous	QAM	Full	Leased
212	0-300	asynchronous	FSK	Half, Full	Switched
	1200	asynch/synch	PSK	Half, Full	Switched
CCITT					
V.21	300	asynchronous	FSK	Half, Full	Switched
V.22	600	asynchronous	PSK	Half, Full	Switch/Le
	1200	asynch/synch.	PSK	Half,Full	Switc/Le
V.22 bis	2400	asynchronous	QAM	Half, Full	Switched
V.23	600	asynch/synch	FSK	Half, Full	Switched
	1200	asynch/synch	FSK	Half, Full	Switched
V.26	2400	synchronous	PSK	Half, Full	Leased
	1200	synchronous	PSK	Half	Switched
V.26 bis	2400	synchronous	PSK	Half	Switched
V.26 ter	2400	synchronous	PSK	Half, Full	Switched
V.27	4800	synchronous	PSK	Half,Full	Switc/Le
V.29	9600	synchronous	QAM	Half, Full	Leased
V.32	9600	synchronous	TCM/QAM	Half, Full	Switched
V.33	14400	synchronous	TCM	Half, Full	Leased

Table 8.2 Modem operational characteristics.

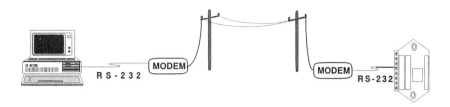

Figure 8.27 Communication with remote data acquisition modules using modem over phone lines.

If one is willing to pay for a high bandwidth phone service, with the leased phone lines, the data communication rate can be increased to 19,200 baud. If this is not enough, the data transmission rate can be increased to a 56,000 baud rate by changing analog phone service to a digital Switched 56 service. Switched 56 is a new service by phone companies which provides a 56,000 baud rate with digital modems.

Short haul (limited distance) modems operate on customer laid lines up to 1.5 Mbaud. The distance in such cases is limited to 50 km or so. This is ideal for a plant or corporate environment to facilitate speedy data transmission.

Radio modems are like short haul modems in the sense that they do not require phone company lines. The transmission speed is limited to a maximum rate of about 9600 baud and the distance is around 50 to 60 kilometers.

Most of the real world applications do not require anything more than the ordinary voice grade phone lines. The data transmission rate provided by ordinary modems in most cases is adequate although some applications require leased or dedicated phone lines.

As far as using remote data acquisition modules with modems, the procedure is the same for all remote data acquisition units. Regardless of whether one has a remote data acquisition module, a remote data acquisition crate, or an intelligent remote data acquisition crate, modems can quite easily be used with all of them the same way.

Figure 8.28 Communication with wireless modems.

To acquire data remotely from a data acquisition module you need a Hayes® compatible modem with automatic answer capability. Although it is not absolutely necessary to have the same type of modem on both host PC side and the remote data acquisition module side, it would be advisable to choose them the same to avoid any incompatibility problems that may arise. Most modems have option switches on the back or underneath the modem for selecting options. Some modems use software for selecting the parameters, but for this specific application one should select a type which can select options manually using dip switches on the back of the modem unit. The remote data acquisition module side of the modem should have its DTR signal forced high by the option switches. Carrier Detect (CD) signals of the modem on the remote data acquisition module side should be left unconnected. The "terse" mode of both modems should be selected by option switches to make it easy for the program to understand problems that occur with the modem or the line.

The example given below is for Multimodem® by Multitech® systems corporation. In the given arrangement, the remote data acquisition module can never initiate a call to the host. The conversation is always initiated by the host PC. When the host PC calls the modem on remote data acquisition, the module side answers the call automatically. This is achieved by invoking the auto answer mode of the second modem on the remote data acquisition module side. When the phone rings the modem answers automatically and expects to see a data terminal ready signal from the module. Fortunately, this signal can be forced high by the option switches on the modem. After these initial settings, the connections between the remote data acquisition module and the modem will be as shown in Figure 8.29.

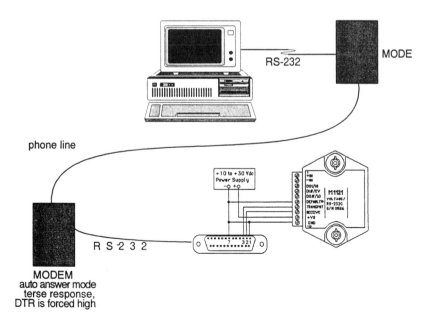

Figure 8.29 Connections between host PC, modem and remote data acquisition module.

The program given below shows how modems can be used with remote data acquisition modules. The following program runs in the host PC and communicates with the module with a 1200 baud, 8 bit, no parity format.

```
10 CLS:OPEN "COM1:1200,N,8,1,CS,CD,DS,asc" AS #1
15 PRINT#1,"+++";:INPUT#1,A$   'Enter Hayes Command Mode, get OK prompt
20 PRINT#1,"ATH1":GOSUB 230       'Hang up for a short while"
30 PRINT#1,"ATDT,8602810"         'Send Dial Command
40 PRINT#1,"ATO"
50 IF INP(&H3FE)<128 THEN GOTO 50  'Wait for Carrier before proceeding
60                     'Read any Echoed commands
70 IF (EOF(1)=0 AND LOC(1)>0) THEN IN$=INPUT$(LOC(1),#1):GOTO 70
80                     'Send 5 Read Data Commands
90 GOSUB 230
95 FOR X=1 TO 5:PRINT#1,"$1RD":PRINT "$1RD":GOSUB 160:NEXT
100 GOSUB 230
110 PRINT#1,"+++";:INPUT#1,A$   'Enter Modem Command Mode, get OK prompt
120 PRINT#1,"ATH0"            'Send Command to Hang-up the Phone
130 CLOSE#1:END             'End the session
140 '
150 ' Sub-Routine to Recieve module data
160 T=TIMER
170 IF TIMER>T+2 THEN PRINT"Device Timeout":RETURN
180 IF EOF(1) THEN 170 ELSE IN$=INPUT$(1,#1)
190 IF IN$="*" OR IN$="?" OR IN$>CHR$(0) THEN PRINT IN$;
200 IF IN$<>CHR$(13) THEN 180 ELSE RETURN
210 '
220 ' 3 Second Delay Routine
230 T=TIMER
240 IF TIMER<T+3 THEN 240 ELSE RETURN
```

If phone lines are not available, radio modems can be used for transmitting data from the module to the host PC. The following program shows how radio modems can be used with remote data acquisition modules.

Figure 8.30 Actual connection between the modem and the remote data acquistion module.

```
10 '
20 ' Initialize variables to default conditions
30 '
40 KEY OFF:FOR T = 1 TO 10 : KEY T ,"" : NEXT    'Clear all function key values
50 COMPORT  = 1         'Select COM1:
60 COMDELAY  = 2        'Communications response time-out value
70 LOOPDELAY = 1.1      'Main Loop Delay
80 NOCOMM$  = "TIMEOUT" 'Value returned if no device response detected
90 '
100 ' Initialize screen, COM port, and command
110 '
120 COLOR 15,1 : CLS : KBD$ = ""
130 LOCATE 1, 31 : PRINT"RADIO DEMO PROGRAM"; : LOCATE 25, 7
140 PRINT"<F1> Command        <F2> Loop Delay        <ESC> Quit";
150 GOSUB 500: GOSUB 750: ON ERROR GOTO 690
160 OPEN COMM$ + "1200,M,7,1,RS,CS,CD,DS" AS #1 : ON ERROR GOTO 0
170 '
180 ' Main program loop
190 '
```

```
200   WHILE KBD$ <> CHR$(27)
210   LOCATE 5, 41 : PRINT"                    ";
220   LOCATE 5, 30 : PRINT"Command  : ";CMD$;
230   GOSUB 340              'Transmit CMD$ to remote station
240   GOSUB 420              'Receive device response message
250   LOCATE 7, 41 : PRINT"                    ";
260   LOCATE 7, 30 : PRINT"Response : ";RSP$;
270   GOSUB 540              'Delay past RT3 on R.M.I.
280   GOSUB 620              'Check for keyboard characters
290   WEND
300   CLOSE : CLS : END
310   '
320   ' Output command to COMMUNICATIONS PORT
330   '
340   OUT OFFSET+4, &HB              'Turn ON RTS Signal
350   WHILE (INP(OFFSET+6) AND &H10)=&H0:WEND      'Delay for CTS HIGH
360   PRINT#1, CMD$                  'Output Command data
370   WHILE (INP(OFFSET+5) AND &H60)<>&H60:WEND  'Make sure all data sent
380   OUT OFFSET+4, &H9 : RETURN              'Turn OFF RTS signal
390   '
400   ' Input response data from COMMUNICATIONS PORT
410   '
420   RSP$ = "" : T = TIMER
430   IF TIMER > (T + COMDELAY) THEN RSP$ = NOCOMM$ : RETURN
440   IF EOF(1) THEN GOTO 430
450   IF LOC(1) > 0 THEN IN$ = INPUT$(1, #1) : RSP$ = RSP$ + IN$ ELSE GOTO
      440
460   IF IN$ = CHR$(13) THEN RETURN ELSE GOTO 450
470   '
480   ' Input command to transmit
490   '
500   LOCATE 20, 1 : INPUT "Enter Command : "; CMD$ : GOSUB 840: RETURN
510   '
520   ' Delay for modem to clear
530   '
540   T = TIMER : WHILE TIMER < (T + LOOPDELAY) : WEND : RETURN
550   '
560   ' Main program loop delay
```

```
570 '
580 LOCATE 20,1:INPUT "Enter Delay Time:";LOOPDELAY : GOSUB 840:
RETURN
590 '
600 ' Read character from keyboard
610 '
620 KBD$ = INKEY$ : IF KBD$ = "" THEN GOTO 650
630 IF KBD$ = CHR$(0) + CHR$(59) THEN GOSUB 500  '<F1> Enter Command
640 IF KBD$ = CHR$(0) + CHR$(60) THEN GOSUB 580  '<F2> Main loop delay
650 RETURN
660 '
670 ' Communications port error handler, END PROGRAM
680 '
690 LOCATE 20,1 : PRINT"Error opening communications port, press any key";
700 WHILE KBD$ = "" : KBD$ = INKEY$ : WEND
710 CLOSE : CLS : END
720 '
730 ' Get communications port
740 '
750 ON ERROR GOTO 760
760 LOCATE 20, 1 : INPUT"Enter communications port [1,2] ", COMPORT
770 IF COMPORT = 1 OR COMPORT = 2 THEN GOTO 780 ELSE GOTO 760
780 IF COMPORT = 1 THEN OFFSET = &H3F8 : COMM$ = "COM1:"
790 IF COMPORT = 2 THEN OFFSET = &H2F8 : COMM$ = "COM2:"
800 GOSUB 840: ON ERROR GOTO 0 : RETURN
810 '
820 ' Clear line where prompts are located
830 '
840 LOCATE 20, 1 : PRINT SPACE$(79); : RETURN
```

8.8 REMOTE MONITORING OF DATA ACQUISITION APPLICATIONS

In some data acquisition applications the intention is to monitor the application remotely. This is different than the remote data acquisition that we have been dealing with so far. In a remote monitoring application the PC and the data acquisition hardware is near the application. Unlike the remote data acquisition case where the data is acquired from the application and sent to a computer located at a remote location, In remote monitoring the

PC and the hardware is placed near the application but through some means operation of the computer is controlled remotely. The concept behind this is shown in Figure 8.31

The distance between the PC located in the acquisition site and the monitoring site depends on the connection method used. Since the RS-232 port of the PC's can be used for connection, hardware like the following can be used to connect the PC's:

- Fiber optic modem
- Short haul modem
- Voice grade phone lines
- Switched 56 lines

Communication software running in the background of both PC's allow the PC on the monitoring site to display all the information available on the remote PC as if it were part of the monitoring PC. Even the hard disk and the floppy disks of the remote PC can be virtually mapped to the monitoring PC so that all the data can be viewed and the PC can be controlled remotely.

These software products are categorically called remote control software and they are marketed by several companies. Some of the better known brand names are

- Reachout Remote Control
- Close-Up
- Northon PC anywhere for Windows
- Carbon Copy for Windows
- Lap Link

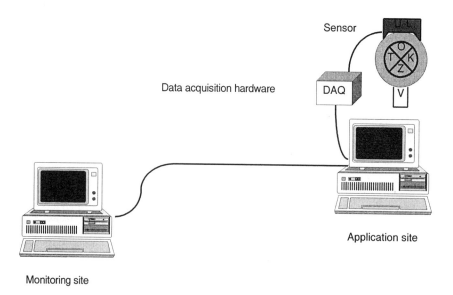

Figure 8.31 Remote monitoring of a data acquisition computer.

Another product that can be used for similar purpose is a hardware product called Extender®. Unlike the software packages listed above this device is a purely hardware device with no software involvement. Since there is no software involvement, operation of this device can be extremely fast. In this case the computer and the data acquisition hardware are placed near the application. A hardware interface box enables the user to place the monitor and the keyboard of the PC up to 300 meters away from the CPU of the computer. This concept is indicated in Figure 8.32. A company called CyberResearch manufactures and markets extender products for such applications.

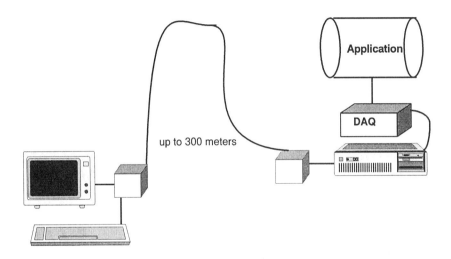

Figure 8.32 The extender hardware enables putting monitor and the keyboard away from the CPU.

8.9 SELECTION GUIDE FOR REMOTE DATA ACQUISITION APPLICATIONS

8.9.1 Distance: Near (<30 Meters)

SIZE OF THE APPLICATION: SMALL (<5 CHANNELS)

If speed of the application:

Slow: <5 conversions/sec

Use remote data acquisition modules with RS-232 or RS-485 interface.

Medium: <10K conversions/sec

Use remote data acquisition crates with RS-485 interface.

Fast: >100K conversions/sec

Use remote data acquisition crates with parallel interface. Use remote intelligent data acquisition crates.

SIZE OF THE APPLICATION: MEDIUM (5-30 CHANNELS)

If speed of the application:

Slow: <5 conversions/sec

Use remote data acquisition modules with RS-485 interface

Medium: <10K conversions/sec

Use remote data acquisition crates with RS-485 interface.

Fast: >100K conversions/sec

Use remote data acquisition crates with parallel interface. Use remote intelligent data acquisition crates.

SIZE OF THE APPLICATION: LARGE (>30 CHANNELS)

Speed of the application:

Slow: <5 conversions/sec

Use remote data acquisition crates with RS-485 or RS-232.

Medium: <10K conversions/sec

Use remote data acquisition crates with RS-485 interface.

Fast: >100K conversions /sec

Use remote data acquisition crates with parallel interface. Use remote intelligent data acquisition crates.

8.9.2 Distance: Medium (30 to 3000 meters)

SIZE OF THE APPLICATION: SMALL (<5 CHANNELS)

If speed of the application:

Slow: <5 conversions/sec

Use remote data acquisition modules with RS-485 interface.

Medium: <10K conversions/sec

Use remote data acquisition crates with RS-485 interface.

Fast: >100K conversions/sec

Use remote data acquisition crates with parallel interface. Use remote intelligent data acquisition crates.

SIZE OF THE APPLICATION: (MEDIUM 5-30 CHANNELS)

If speed of the application:

Slow: <5 conversions/sec

Use remote data acquisition modules with RS-485 interface only.

Medium: <10K conversions/sec

Use remote data acquisition crates with RS-485 interface.

Fast: >100K conversions/sec

Use remote data acquisition crates with parallel interface. Use remote intelligent data acquisition crates.

SIZE OF THE APPLICATION: LARGE (>30 CHANNELS)

If speed of the application:

Slow: <5 conversions/sec

Use remote data acquisition crates with RS-485.

Medium: <10K conversions/sec

Use remote data acquisition crates with parallel interface.

Fast: >100K conversions/sec

Use remote data acquisition crates with parallel interface. Use remote intelligent data acquisition crates.

8.9.3 Distance: Far (3 to 50 Kilometers)

SIZE OF THE APPLICATION: SMALL (<5 CHANNELS)

If speed of the application:

Slow: <5 conversions/sec

Use remote data acquisition modules with RS-232 and voice grade phone lines and modem with 1200 baud.

Medium: <10K conversions/sec

Use remote data acquisition crates with RS-232 interface,leased line with 19.2K modem and compression.

Fast: >100K conversions/sec

Use remote data acquisition crates with short haul modems.

SIZE OF THE APPLICATION: MEDIUM (5-30 CHANNELS)

If speed of the application:

Slow: <5 conversions/sec

Use remote data acquisition modules with RS-232 and voice grade phone lines and modem with 200 baud.

Medium: <10K conversions/sec

Use remote data acquisition crates with RS-232 interface, leased line with 19.2K modem and compression.

Fast: >100K conversions/sec

Use remote data acquisition crates with short haul modems.

SIZE OF THE APPLICATION: LARGE (>30 CHANNELS)

If speed of the application:

Slow: <5 conversions/sec

Use remote data acquisition modules with RS-232 and voice grade phone lines and modem with 2400 baud.

Medium: <10K conversions/sec

Use remote data acquisition crates with short haul modems.

Fast: >100K conversions/sec

Use remote data acquisition crates with short haul modems.

8.9.4 Distance: Very Far (>50 Kilometers)

SIZE OF THE APPLICATION: SMALL (<5 CHANNELS)

If speed of the application:

Slow: <5 conversions/sec

Use remote data acquisition modules with RS-232 and voice grade phone lines and modem with1200 baud.

Medium: <10K conversions/sec

Use remote data acquisition crates with RS-232 interface, leased line with 19.2K modem and compression.

Fast: >100K conversions/sec

Intelligent remote data acquisition crates with leased phone lines 19.2 modem with compression.

SIZE OF THE APPLICATION: MEDIUM: (5-30 CHANNELS)

If speed of the application:

Slow :<5 conversions/sec

Use remote data acquisition modules with RS-232 and voice grade phone lines and modem with1200 baud.

Medium: <10K conversions /sec

Use remote data acquisition crates with RS-232 interface, leased line with 19.2K modem and compression.

Fast: >100K conversions/sec

Intelligent remote data acquisition crates with leased phone lines, 19.2K modem with compression.

SIZE OF THE APPLICATION: LARGE: (>30 CHANNELS)

Speed of the application:

Slow :<5 conversions/sec

Use remote data acquisition modules with RS-232 and voice grade phone lines and modem with 2400 baud.

Medium: <10K conversions/sec

Intelligent remote data acquisition crates with leased phone lines, 19.2K modem with compression.

Fast: >100K conversions/sec

Intelligent remote data acquisition crates with leased phone lines, 19.2K modem with compression.

REFERENCES

1. *GW-Basic 3.2 Users Manual,* Microsoft, 1986.

2. *Keithley Metrabyte M1000/2000 Users Manual*, Keithley Instruments, 1987.

3. *Keithley Metrabyte Workhorse Chassis Users Manual*, Keithley Instruments, 1987.

4. *Multimodem Owners Manual*, MultiTech Systems, 1986.

5. *Omega Engineering Data Acquisition Catalog*, Omega Engineering, 1989.

6. *1994 Catalog*, RS Components, 1994.

7. Held, G., *Understanding Data Communications,* John Wiley and Sons. 1991.

8. Gates, S. C., Becker, J., *Labaratory Automation Using The IBM PC*, Prentice-Hall, 1989.

9. Campbell, Joe, *C programmers Guide to Serial Communication*, Howard W. Sams & Company, 1987.

Nine

INTERFACING ACTUATORS to the PC

9.1 INTRODUCTION

Actuators are mechanical devices which turn electrical signals provided by the PC into physical movement. So far we have looked at ways of providing data to the computer and not been interested in taking a corrective physical action by the PC. In reality, providing physical action by the PC is as important as acquiring data. This chapter is solely devoted to various actuators available for PC's and their control. We will look at different actuators and see how to control them under the command of the PC. Data acquisition, together with the actuation, makes the PC much more useful than the case where the PC is utilized only for acquiring data.

The connection of the PC with the external world is necessarily done through the input/output ports. Any peripheral device that provides input to the PC, like a keyboard or a disk drive, has to be connected to an input port of the PC. In the same way, any peripheral device that provides any sort of output, like printers, plotters and modems, has to be connected to the output ports. The usual ports of the PC that we are all familiar with, like parallel printer ports LPT1, LPT2, serial ports COM1, COM2, are all considered as output ports of the PC. Input and output ports deal with signals in digital form. Of course the ports that we have listed above are not the only input/output ports available on the PC. It is possible to increase the number of ports as needed.

Peripheral devices that are connected to the computer use the digital signals that come out of the I/O ports of the PC and convert them into a physical action to generate something useful. Actuators can be considered as peripheral devices in that sense. Actuators are devices that convert digital signals into physical movement. In the following sections of this chapter, different types of actuators and ways of interfacing them to the output ports will be discussed.

Readers who are interested in learning more about actuators are recommended to read *Electric Motor Controls*, by Rex Miller and Mark R. Miller published by Prentice-Hall.

9.2 ACTUATORS THAT CAN BE USED BY THE PC

An actuator is any device that converts electrical commands of the computer into physical action. By using actuators, we can turn valves on, move objects, open or close gates and in general generate a physical motion. Actuators are an essential part of any automatic control process since they enable the computer to take a corrective action to control the parameters of a given process.

There are several different actuators suitable for use with computers.

- Stepper motors
- DC motors
- AC motors
- Solenoids
- Solenoid valves
- Hydraulic actuators
- Pneumatic actuators

We will consider each one of these actuators and the ways of interfacing them to the computer in the coming sections.

9.3 STEPPER MOTORS

A stepper motor is a very versatile and highly reliable motor which is very suitable for computer use. What makes a stepper motor so desirable is the fact that it operates digitally with pulses. Each pulse causes the motor to rotate a predetermined amount. Since the angle of movement taken by the motor for each pulse is very well known, it is possible to know the end position of the shaft without getting feedback about the position of the shaft. Because of this fact, a stepper motor is the only motor that does not require position feedback. Later we will see that all other motors require position feedback for precision position control.

A stepper motor is made up of four energizing coils in the stator located at 90 degree angles to each other and a permanent magnet rotor that requires no brushes for electrical contact. Having no brushes makes the stepper motor a highly reliable motor. In order to rotate the stepper motor in a certain direction, the coils should be energized in a given sequence such that the rotor gets aligned with the adjacent stator coil.

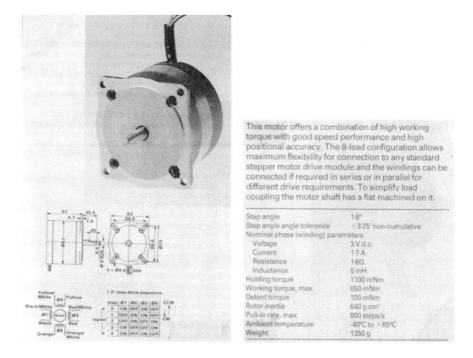

Figure 9.1 A typical stepper motor. (Courtesy RS components.)

Coils of the stepper motor are energized by passing DC current through them. The amount of current determines the power of the motor and it is dependent on the particular type of motor being used. In general it may range from 100 mA for miniature size motors and up to 5 amps for larger size ones.

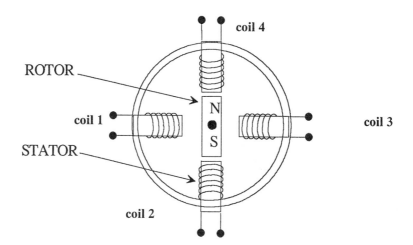

Figure 9.2 Inside view of a simple stepper motor.

There are different ways of driving a stepper motor. By using different drive techniques, the speed, the torque and the step size (resolution) of the stepper motor can be changed. In the following sections these different drive mechanisms are reviewed.

9.3.1 Wave Drive

Wave drive is the easiest of all drive techniques. Although the torque generated by this drive method is less compared to the other drive techniques, its simplicity is the advantage. In wave drive, only one coil is energized at any given time. The energizing sequence works in a round robin fashion energizing only one coil at any given time. Energizing coils in clockwise sequence will cause the motor to turn in clockwise direction and counterclockwise sequence will cause rotation in the reverse direction.

<u>Clockwise rotation</u>

The energizing sequence for clockwise rotation is shown below.

Coil 1	Coil 2	Coil 3	Coil 4
ON	OFF	OFF	OFF
OFF	ON	OFF	OFF
OFF	OFF	ON	OFF
OFF	OFF	OFF	ON

At the end of the cycle the whole process is repeated starting from the first step for sustained clockwise movement. It should be emphasized that the order of the energizing sequence is very important; any missing step in the cycle will cause the stepper motor to stop the movement and cause the motor to vibrate back and forth in the last position.

<u>Counterclockwise rotation</u>

The direction of rotation is a function of the energizing sequence and can be altered by energizing coils in the reverse order. For example, for a counterclockwise operation, the energizing sequence of the coils should be as shown in the table below.

Coil 1	Coil 2	Coil 3	Coil 4
OFF	OFF	OFF	ON
OFF	OFF	ON	OFF
OFF	ON	OFF	OFF
ON	OFF	OFF	OFF

Then the above cycle should be repeated for continuous operation.

By altering the sequence at any given time the direction of rotation can be changed, for example:

Coil 1	Coil 2	Coil 3	Coil 4	Movement
OFF	OFF	OFF	ON	Clockwise
ON	OFF	OFF	OFF	Clockwise
OFF	ON	OFF	OFF	Clockwise
ON	OFF	OFF	OFF	Counter-clockwise
OFF	OFF	OFF	ON	Counter-clockwise
OFF	OFF	OFF	ON	Clockwise
OFF	OFF	ON	OFF	Clockwise

It is very important that the coils always get energized according to the sequence, even after stopping and waiting at a location. If, for example, the motor is stopped by energizing Coil 3 as the last coil, then when it is time to resume the motion, Coil 4 should be energized for clockwise rotation (Coil 2 for counter-clockwise rotation) no matter how long the motion is paused.

9.3.2 Full Step Drive

There are different drive methods for driving a stepper motor. The one that is shown above is the system known as wave drive where there is only one coil energized at any given time. In this system, every time a coil is energized the motor advances by one full step. Another method that advances the motor by one full step size is known as full step drive. Full step drive systems energize two coils at a time as opposed to the wave drive which energizes only one coil. The energizing sequence for full step drive for clockwise and counter-clockwise direction is shown below.

Clockwise operation

Coil 1	Coil 2	Coil 3	Coil 4
ON	ON	OFF	OFF
OFF	ON	ON	OFF
OFF	OFF	ON	ON
ON	OFF	OFF	ON

Then the above cycle should be repeated from the beginning for continuous rotation in the clockwise direction.

Counterclockwise operation

Coil 1	Coil 2	Coil 3	Coil 4
OFF	OFF	ON	ON
OFF	ON	ON	OFF
ON	ON	OFF	OFF
ON	OFF	OFF	ON

Then repeat the above cycle for continuous operation.

By altering the sequence at any given time, the direction of rotation can be changed, for example:

Coil 1	Coil 2	Coil 3	Coil 4	Movement
ON	OFF	OFF	ON	Clockwise
ON	ON	OFF	OFF	Clockwise
OFF	ON	ON	OFF	Clockwise
ON	ON	OFF	OFF	Counter-clockwise
ON	OFF	OFF	ON	Counter-clockwise
OFF	OFF	ON	ON	Counter-clockwise

Full step drive generates more torque than the wave drive even though the step size is exactly the same in both cases. Higher torque means that the stepper motor can handle higher loads and the motor can be driven faster. The increase in torque can be easily be explained since there are two coils which are activated simultaneously in case of full step drive. The strength of a magnetic field generated by two coils is more than the strength of the magnetic field generated by one coil alone.

According to the above diagram, the resultant magnetic field strength will be $\sqrt{2}$ F. The torque generated by the motor is directly proportional to the strength of the magnetic field.

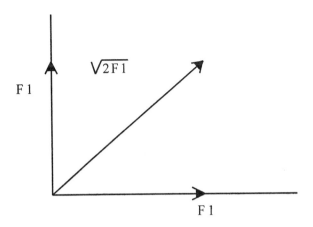

Figure 9.3 In full wave drive the resultant magnetic field is stronger than the wave drive.

9.3.3 Half Step Drive

Another stepper motor driving technique is known as half step drive. In this system with every pulse the motor will advance only half of the specified step size. The energizing sequence in this system shown below.

Clockwise movement

Coil 1	Coil 2	Coil 3	Coil 4
ON	OFF	OFF	OFF
ON	ON	OFF	OFF
OFF	ON	OFF	OFF
OFF	ON	ON	OFF
OFF	OFF	ON	OFF
OFF	OFF	ON	ON
OFF	OFF	OFF	ON
ON	OFF	OFF	ON

For counter- clockwise operation, the step sequence should be reversed.

For the simple stepper motor design that we considered in the examples given above, the step size of the stepper motor is always 90 degrees. In reality the step size for a typical stepper motor is much less than 90 degrees. In general, step sizes range from 7.5 degrees to 1.8 degrees and smaller step size always indicates better quality. Small step size is desirable since this will increase the mechanical resolution of the system. The drive techniques mentioned above and the step sequences are the same regardless of the step size of a given stepper motor.

The step size of the motor can be reduced either by increasing the number of coils in the stator or by modifying the design of the rotor. Increasing the number of coils in the stator of the stepper motor is not practical due to the space limitation inside the stator. Almost invariably, rotor design is modified to get a smaller step size from the ordinary four coil stepper motor. Using ingenious design techniques, the step size of the motor can be reduced to 1.8 degrees. The key to decreasing the step size is to increase the number of N-S poles in the rotor. By increasing the number of magnet pairs and keeping the number of them odd, we can make sure that every time we energize a coil there is a magnet pair close by which will be aligned with the coil exactly.

9.3.4 Driving Stepper Motors

Energizing the coils of a stepper motor requires a considerable amount of current. The figure below shows the technical data for several common stepper motors. The typical figures for the impedance of the coils and rated voltage and current are given for several common stepper motors in the following table and Figure 9.5

Motor	Rated Current	R. Voltage	R (Ohm)	Power Dissipation
Type 1	0.1 Amps	12 Volts	120	1.2 Watts
Type 2	0.24 Amps	12 Volts	47	3 Watts
Type 3	1 Amp	5 Volts	19	19 Watts
Type 4	1.7 Amps	3 Volts	12.3	36 Watts

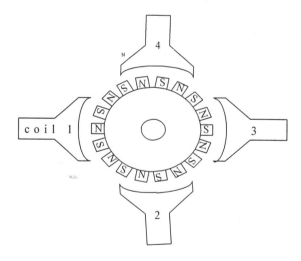

Figure 9.4 Multiple pole stepper motor.

Stepper Motors
7·5° Step Angle

Two 7·5°, 12 V bi-directional stepper motors with permanent magnet rotors and 4-phase unipolar construction. Applying the correct electrical pulse sequence (dual phase energisation) to the windings of the stepper motor results in a 7·5° step angle rotation of the spindle (i.e. 48 steps per revolution). This step angle can be halved to 3·75° if the motor is driven by a modified pulse sequence (alternate single/dual phase energisation). When correctly loaded and driven these motors will produce discrete output steps. The number of steps and speed of rotation are respectively determined by the number of pulses and frequency of the input signal. This provides an ideal method of both speed and position control.

Applications include:

● Paper and magnetic tape drive
● Teletype printers
● Camera iris control and film transport/sorting.
● Co-ordinate plotters and chart recorders.
● Medical equipment, e.g. blood samplers.
● Fuel flow control and variable speed syringe pumps
● Pulse counting - metering.
● Digital to analogue conversion.

These motors are directly compatible with the **RS** stepper motor driver i.c. SAA 1027, stock no. 300-237, refer to Semiconductors/Accessories section. Alternatively the motors can be driven by the **RS** stepper motor drive board, stock no. 332-098 and 342-051 (refer to this section) with much improved torque-speed performance. Using these boards also allows the step angle to be halved (if required) to 3·75° per step resulting in higher resolution, greater performance stability and faster stepping rates (refer to stepper motors data sheet). The **RS** stepper motors may be driven directly by the programmable stepper control board later in this section.

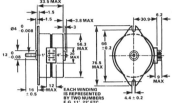

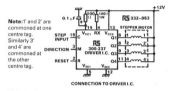

CONNECTION TO DRIVER I.C.

This 4-phase stepper motor is designed for direct drive applications requiring simple electronic interface. The working torque is approximately ten times that of the size 1 motor. Connections via six soldering tags.

technical specification	
Step angle	7·5°
Step angle tolerance	± 20′ non-cumulative
Working torque, max.	57 mNm
Holding torque	85 mNm
Pull-in rate, max.*	130 steps/s
Phase (coil) resistance at 20°C	47Ω/phase
Phase (coil) inductance	400 mH/phase
Current per coil	240 mA
Ambient temperature range	-20°C to + 70°C
Max. motor temperature	120°C
Rotor inertia	45 g cm²
Nominal voltage	12 V d.c.
Power consumption	5·3 W

* Max. pull-in rate is the maximum speed at which an unloaded motor can start without losing steps.

Figure 9.5 Technical data for stepper motors. (Courtesy RS components.)

In all cases the amount of current is much more than the current that can be supplied or drained by the output of the typical TTL gate or output buffers. Since the current is excessive, a power amplifier is needed for energizing coils under computer control. The possible choices of components for amplifying the weak power output of the PC to the power level needed by stepper motors include power transistors, Darlington pair power transistors, power MOSFETs or relays. Relays are not going to be considered at this stage since they are electromagnetic devices and they are not fast enough to drive the stepper motors at an acceptable speed. The most common solution for the power amplification is to use switching mode power transistors. A typical npn power transistor is shown in Figure 9.6.

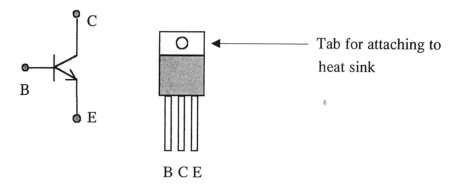

Figure 9.6 Typical power transistor, TAP 120.

By connecting the transistor in the configuration shown in Figure 9.7, the coils can be energized by TTL level output port signals. Notice the diodes connected in parallel with the coil. This component is absolutely required in order to protect the transistor from dangerously high level back EMF voltage generated by the coil. The coil of the stepper motor, being an inductor, generates high voltage as the current through the coil is switched off. (Voltage across inductor is given by $V = L(di/dt)$) The voltage generated, unless there is a diode protection, will appear across the power transistor in reverse and cause the transistor to break down very quickly. This diode is called the flywheel diode and should be used every time an inductor is interfaced to a power transistor. Since there are four coils inside the stepper motor, four power transistors and four flywheel diodes are needed for the stepper motor interface. The connections between the stepper motor coils, transistors and the output port of the PC is shown in Figure 9.7

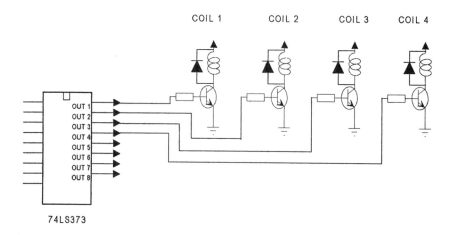

Figure 9.7 Connections between the stepper motor and the output port.

BIPOLAR Transistor Tables

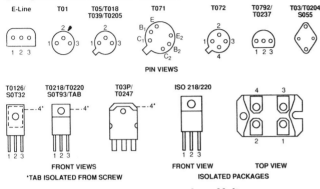

PIN VIEWS

FRONT VIEWS
*TAB ISOLATED FROM SCREW

FRONT VIEW   TOP VIEW
ISOLATED PACKAGES

BIPOLAR Transistors Pinout Data

	1	2	3	4
A	Base	Collector	Emitter	–
B	Base	Emitter	Collector	–
C	Emitter	Base	Collector	–
D	Collector	Base	Emitter	–
E	Base	Collector	Emitter	Collector
F	Emitter	Base 1	Collector	Base 2
G	Base	Emitter	Collector	Case
H	Emitter	Base	Collector	Case
I	Emitter	Collector	Base	Collector

Table 4 NPN Power Transistors - Low Voltage

type	package/pinout		I_c (max.)	P_t (max.)		V_{ceo} (max.)	V_{cbo} (max.)	hfe (min.-max.) @	I_c	V_{ce}	f_t (typ.)	complement	application
MJE340	T0126	I	0·5A	20W	Tc = 25°C	300V	–	30-240	50mA	10V	–	MJE350	General purpose high voltage
TIP47	T0220	E	1·0A	40W	Tc = 25°C	250V	350V	30-150	300mA	10V	10MHz (min.)	–	High voltage
BD135	T0126	I	1·5A	8W	Tc = 70°C	45V	45V	40-250	150mA	2V	250MHz	BD136	Audio driver
BD131	T0126	I	3·0A	15W	Tc = 60°C	45V	70V	20 (min.)	2·0A	1V	60MHz	BD132	General purpose
BD131	T0126	I	3·0A	15W	Tc = 60°C	45V	70V	20 (min.)	2·0A	1V	60MHz	BD132	Audio matched pair
TIP31A	T0220	E	3·0A	40W	Tc = 25°C	60V	100V	10-50	3·0A	4V	3MHz (min.)	TIP32A	General purpose power switch
TIP31C	T0220	E	3·0A	40W	Tc = 25°C	100V	140V	10-50	3·0A	4V	3MHz (min.)	TIP32C	General purpose power switch
BD437	T0220	E	4·0A	36W	Tc = 25°C	45V	45V	40 (min.)	2·0A	1V	7MHz (min.)	BD438	Audio power amp
D44C10	T0220	E	4·0A	30W	Tc = 25°C	80V	–	10 (min.)	1·0A	1V	50MHz	–	Linear & switch
D44Q5	T0220	E	4·0A	31W	Tc = 25°C	225V	–	20 (min.)	2·0A	10V	20MHz	–	Linear & switch
BD539A	T0220	E	5·0A	45W	Tc = 25°C	60V	60V	12 (min.)	3·0A	4V	–	BD540A	Linear & switch
BD539B	T0220	E	5·0A	45W	Tc = 25°C	80V	80V	12 (min.)	3·0A	4V	–	BD540B	Linear & switch
BD539C	T0220	E	5·0A	45W	Tc = 25°C	100V	100V	12 (min.)	3·0A	4V	–	BD540C	Linear & switch
2N6542	T03	B	5·0A	100W	Tc = 25°C	300V	–	12-60	1·5A	2V	6MHz (min.)	–	High speed inductive switch
BUP41	T0126	I	6·0A	10W	Tc = 25°C	50V	60V	100-500	2·0A	2V	120MHz	–	Very fast switching
TIP41A	T0220	E	6·0A	65W	Tc = 25°C	60V	100V	15-75	3·0A	4V	3MHz (min.)	TIP42A	General purpose power switch
TIP41C	T0220	E	6·0A	65W	Tc = 25°C	100V	140V	15-75	3·0A	4V	3MHz (min.)	TIP42C	General purpose power switch
BU407	T0220	E	7·0A	60W	Tc = 25°C	150V	330V	–	–	–	10MHz (min.)	–	High voltage horiz. def.
SM3180	T0126	I	8·0A	20W	Tc = 25°C	25V	40V	150 (min.)	5·0A	1V	150MHz (min.)	–	Low sat. high speed switch
2N6544	T03	B	8·0A	125W	Tc = 25°C	300V	–	12-60	2·5A	3V	6MHz (min.)	–	High speed inductive switch
TIP33A	SOT93	E	10·0A	80W	Tc = 25°C	60V	100V	20-100	3·0A	4V	3MHz (min.)	TIP34A	Audio power amp & power switch
2N6099	T0220	E	10·0A	75W	Tc = 25°C	60V	70V	20 (min.)	–	–	–	–	General purpose
D44H10	T0220	E	10·0A	50W	Tc = 25°C	80V	–	20 (min.)	4·0A	1V	50MHz	–	General purpose switch
2N3055E	T03	B	15·0A	115W	Tc = 25°C	60V	100V	20-70	4·0A	4V	–	MJ2955	High power epitaxial amp & switch
2N3055H	T03	B	15·0A	115W	Tc = 25°C	60V	100V	20-70	4·0A	4V	800KHz (min.)	PNP3055	High power homotaxial amp & switch
TIP3055	SOT93	E	15·0A	90W	Tc = 25°C	70V	100V	20-70	4·0A	4V	–	TIP2955	High power amp
BD743A	T0220	E	15·0A	90W	Tc = 25°C	60V	70V	20-150	5·0A	4V	5MHz (min.)	BD744A	Power amp & high speed switch
BD743B	T0220	E	15·0A	90W	Tc = 25°C	80V	90V	20-150	5·0A	4V	5MHz (min.)	BD744B	Power amp & high speed switch
BD743C	T0220	E	15·0A	90W	Tc = 25°C	100V	110V	20-150	5·0A	4V	5MHz (min.)	BD744C	Power amp & high speed switch
2N6546	T03	B	15·0A	175W	Tc = 25°C	300V	–	12-60	5·0A	2V	6MHz (min.)	–	High speed inductive switching
2N3773	T03	B	16·0A	150W	Tc = 25°C	140V	160V	15-60	8·0A	4V	–	–	High power switch
BUP30	T0220	E	20·0A	35W	Tc = 25°C	30V	60V	70-300	1·0A	2V	120MHz	–	Very fast switching
2N3772	T03	B	20·0A	150W	Tc = 25°C	60V	100V	15-60	10·0A	4V	200KHz (min.)	–	High power inductive switch
MJ15003	T03	B	20·0A	250W	Tc = 25°C	140V	140V	25-150	5·0A	2V	2MHz (min.)	MJ15004	High power linear
SM3159	T03	B	20·0A	200W	Tc = 25°C	200V	400V	10-30	15A	10V	10MHz	SM3160	High power audio
2N3771	T03	B	30·0A	150W	Tc = 25°C	40V	50V	15-60	15A	4V	200KHz (min.)	–	High power inductive switch
BUS52	T03	B	40·0A	350W	Tc = 25°C	250V	–	15 (min.)	40A	4V	–	–	Inductive switch
BUV20	T03	B	50·0A	250W	Tc = 25°C	125V	160V	10 (min.)	50A	4V	8MHz	–	Inductive switch
BUP54	T03	B	50·0A	300W	Tc = 25°C	275V	–	10 (min.)	40A	4V	–	–	Fast switching
BUP53	T03	B	60·0A	300W	Tc = 25°C	250V	–	10 (min.)	50A	4V	–	–	Fast switching
BUS50	T03	B	70·0A	350W	Tc = 25°C	125V	–	15 (min.)	50A	4V	–	–	Inductive switch
BUP52	T03	B	70·0A	300W	Tc = 25°C	200V	–	10 (min.)	70A	4V	–	–	Fast switching
BUP51	T03	B	80·0A	300W	Tc = 25°C	175V	–	10 (min.)	70A	4V	–	–	Fast switching
BUP49	T03	B	90·0A	300W	Tc = 25°C	80V	–	15 (min.)	80A	4V	–	–	Fast switching
BUP48	T03	B	100A	300W	Tc = 25°C	60V	–	10 (min.)	100A	4V	–	–	Fast switching

Figure 9.8 Popular discrete power semiconductors and the pinout data. (Courtesy RS components.)

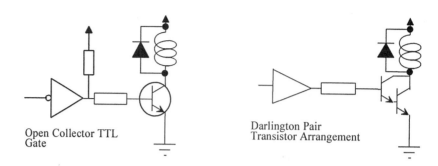

Figure 9.9 Darlington and open collector TTL arrangements for driving power transistors.

Please note that the output of the output port may need to be buffered by buffers or by open collector TTL gates if the base current requirement of the power transistor is more than what the output port can supply. As can be seen from Figure 9.8, a typical power transistor with a 1.5 A current sink capability requires a minimum of 25 mA base current. Even though the exact figure may be higher or lower than that depending on the particular type of transistor, it is easy to see that this much current is beyond the capability of an ordinary TTL output. Only special buffers like the 74373 or 74374 can supply this much current. A better approach is to use NPN Darlington pair transistors where the base current requirement can be as low as 250 µamps. Darlington pair transistors can be used with normal TTL output without any need for special buffering.

In the approaches that we looked at so far, the computer has to keep track of all the pulses that are sent to the motor as well as handle the sequence of the pulses. We know that the sequence of the pulses depends on the direction of rotation. Keeping track of the pulses (the number of pulses which have been sent to the motor) and the sequence of pulses applied are of crucial importance since this is the only way we can keep track of the present location of the shaft of the stepper motor. Since a stepper motor provides no feedback regarding the current position of the shaft, the final position has to be guessed by starting from a known 'home' position and keeping track of the number of pulses applied to the motor. This simple task of keeping track of the pulses applied and the necessary sequence of pulses may seem like a trivial task; however, it takes considerable computer time since the computer has to apply pulses at a fixed rate to keep the speed of the motor constant.

The task of the computer can be reduced to a certain extent by using simple hardware components. One such approach is to use a presettable shift register for keeping track of the sequence of pulses applied to the motor for a specific direction of rotation. In this case, all that is required from the computer is to specify the direction of rotation, and to give clock pulses to rotate the motor. The energizing sequence is taken care of by the shift register.

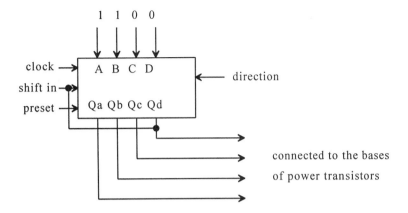

Figure 9.10 A simple shift register scheme to take care of pulse sequence.

Even if the energizing sequence is taken care of by the shift register, applying clock pulses is still time consuming for the PC since the speed of the motor and the pulses applied to the motor are much slower than the speed of the computer. Either computer has to apply pulses and wait idly dedicating itself to the control operation only, or in between the pulses it continues to operate and gets interrupted every time a stepper motor needs another pulse. For this reason, intelligent stepper motor controllers are used for applying pulses and keeping track of the end position of the motor.

Another reason to use intelligent stepper motor controllers is to increase the speed of the stepper motor. Normally the movement of the stepper motor is always in discrete steps, that is, with each pulse the rotor will accelerate then decelerate and come to a complete stop. The next pulse will cause the motor to go through the acceleration and deceleration cycle again. By applying pulses this way, the maximum pulse rate is quite limited. A typical figure for a stepper motor is around 300 pulses per second. It is possible to achieve higher pulse rate if one is willing to sacrifice the discrete movement nature of the stepper motor. If the pulse rate is increased beyond 300 pps, the rotor will not be able to come to a complete halt at the end of the pulse cycle. Due to the mechanical inertia of the rotor, however, it will continue to turn and eventually stop at a location which is not predictable. But if the travel from one point to another is well thought of it in advance, then it is possible to travel at a very fast rate. This 'travel plan' is called an acceleration curve for the stepper motor. A typical acceleration curve for the stepper motor is given in Figure 9.11.

Notice that the starting point is below the 300 pps rate which allows the motor to start and stop at each pulse. We can gradually increase the pulse rate (acceleration part of the curve) until we reach an absolute maximum beyond which the motor can not follow pulses any more, then we travel at the maximum rate for a certain amount of time and start decelerating gradually to 300 pps rate. It is not allowed to stop before the pulse rate reaches 300 pps since stopping when frequency is higher would cause the rotor to pass the desired location due to inertia of the rotor and stop at an unpredictable point. When this happens, even once, we lose track of the position of the motor.

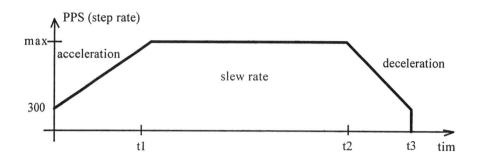

Figure 9.11 Typical acceleration curve for a stepper motor.

This method is the fastest way to drive the stepper motor from one point to another. The integral of this curve will reveal the total number of pulses applied to the motor. So, in order to find the cutoff points of this curve, the number of pulses required to go from point A to B should be known and the duration of acceleration, deceleration and the duration of high speed pulse rate should be calculated. Most of the time it is feasible to use a separate microcontroller to handle these calculations and apply pulses to the stepper motor. In this case, the only function of the PC is to supply the microcontroller with the direction of rotation and the number of pulses that should be applied. After acquiring this information, the microcontroller will take over, calculate the cutoff points and by moving according to the acceleration curve, will move the stepper motor in the fastest possible way.

There are commercial stepper motor controllers for the IBM PC which can control several motors simultaneously. One such commercial product uses three 8039 microcontrollers to control three stepper motors simultaneously. Most stepper motor controller cards for PC's on the market do not include a power interface for the stepper motors. The user is supposed to get the controller and the power amplifier separately and connect and external power supply (not the power supply of the PC) to feed the power interface. The primary reason for this approach is the power consumption of the stepper motors. Each winding of an ordinary stepper motor takes about 5 watts of power. Assuming that one uses full wave drive and several stepper motors simultaneously, the total power required becomes quite heavy for the power supply of the PC. Figure 9.12 shows several commercially available stepper motor driver boards with the supporting technical information. Figure 9.13 shows a typical stepper motor driver card designed for PC and Figure 9.14 indicates a typical configuration for controlling stepper motors with a PC.

Unipolar - 2A

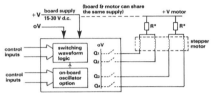

*R value and rating depends on motor voltage & current and the value of +V motor.

Board connection schematic diagram.

A standard single Eurocard complete with a 32-way DIN 41612 plug connector for plugging into any Eurocard compatible racking system. The board can also be surface mounted if required. Features include:

● Directly compatible with any of the **RS** stepper motors
● 4-phase unipolar motor drive up to 2 A/30 V d.c. per phase.
● Full step and half step drive modes (for higher resolution, greater performance stability and faster stepping rates).
● External control inputs are C-MOS and open collector TTL logic compatible.
● Pre-set control for setting predetermined motor phase excitation pattern.
● On-board 12 V, 50 mA d.c. output for external use.
● Drive board and the motor can share the same d.c. power supply.
● Provision for assembly of on-board oscillator (if external clock not available) having clock pulse output, base speed, top speed and stop/run control inputs.
Supplied with full instructions.

Board supply voltage	15-30 V d.c. (+10% max.)
Board supply current	60 mA*
Motor current per phase	2 A max.
Motor supply voltage	30 V d.c. max.
On-board d.c. output	12 V d.c., 50 mA max.
Clock (step) input frequency	25 kHz max.
	10µs min. pulse width
External control inputs	C-MOS/open collector T.T.L. compatible
	Logic '0':0 V
	Logic '1':12 V

Bipolar Choppers

A standard single eurocard complete with a 32-way DIN 41612 plug connector to suit eurocard compatible racking systems. The board employs the well established bipolar chopped constant current principle to provide a substantial increase in the torque capability of the stepper motor. This at the same time increases the efficiency of the system by eliminating the power dissipating dropper resistors required in the unipolar drive mode.

3·5A

● Drives motors up to 36 V and 3·5 A/phase.
● On board output drive current setting (0·7 to 3·5 A).
● Output overload protection.
● Synchronisation output for multi-axis systems.
● Full and half step drive modes.
● Provision for assembling on board oscillator (if external clock not available) having clock pulse output, base speed, top speed and stop/run control inputs.
● TTL and C-MOS compatible control interface.
● Output Disable input to allow manual motor rotation.
● 5 and 12 V d.c. auxiliary outputs for external device energisation
User instructions supplied.
Caution : serious damage to the output stage can occur if any of the motor connections become disconnected while the output is energised.

Technical Specification	
Supply voltage	
motor	15-36 V d.c.
logic	15-24 V d.c.
motor and logic may share the same supply.	
Auxiliary outputs	12 V, 50 m
(regulated)	5 V, 50 mA d.c.
Motor drive	0·7-3·5 A, set on board via DIL switch
	switch
Control inputs	C-MOS or open collector TTL compatible
logic 0	0-2 V d.c.
logic 1	9-30 V d.c.
Monitor outputs	open collector transistors
logic 0	1 V, 30 mA max.
logic 1	24 V d.c. max.
Clock input	20 kHz max.
	10 µs min. pulse width
Operating temperature	0°C to +40°C
Weight	700 g

Figure 9.12 Commercial stepper motor driver boards. (Courtesy RS Components.)

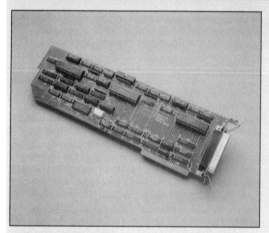

3-AXIS, HIGH-SPEED STEPPER MOTOR CONTROLLER

MSTEP-3

FEATURES

- 3-axis stepper control
- 3, 4, or 5 phase motors
- Up to 16,666 pulses per second
- Software included
- Two 8-bit I/O ports

APPLICATIONS

- X-Y table control
- High-speed motor control
- Robotics
- Mechanical positioning control

Once a command is loaded into the PPMC-103C controller chip, the host computer is no longer burdened by the execution of the particular motion but may monitor its status as needed. The associated stepper motor may be moved any number of steps up to 24 bits of resolution (0 to 16,777,216 steps) either with a controlled acceleration/deceleration profile or constant stepping rate. Associated with each motor are 5 limit switch inputs as well as a motor-enable input. The limit switches provide normal and emergency stop limits at both ends of travel, plus a home or reference point at any intermediate point. A normal stop is defined as a normal deceleration to rest without loss of the step count due to inertial effects. An emergency stop is a sudden stop that may lead to run on of the motor and hence loss of location from the step count. This would normally require recalibration by return to the reference or home point. The emergency stop amounts to an immediate cessation of step pulses regardless of what the motor is doing at the time. In addition to controlling the number of steps travelled by the motor (normal motion), the board executes the following commands:

Initialization	Determines initial parameters for each axis
Move Normal	Moves the motor the desired number of steps with a controlled rate of acceleration/deceleration.
Move Constant	Rotates motor at constant speed for a specified number of steps.
Find Limit	Rotates motor to an outer limit switch.
Find High-Speed Limit	Rotates motor to a high-speed or inner-limit switch.
Find Base Point	Rotates motor to home or reference-limit switch.
Read Status	Read PPMC-103C controller status.
Decelerating Stop	Stops motor normally.
Emergency Stop	Instantly stops motor by removing drive pulses (may lead to loss of true location from step count).
Single Step	Single step or "jog" command.

FUNCTIONAL DESCRIPTION

Keithley MetraByte's MSTEP-3 is a plug-in, 3-axis, stepper-motor controller board for the IBM PC/XT/AT and compatibles. Each independent stepper channel consists of a Sil-Walker PPMC-103C intelligent controller chip capable of executing a variety of motion control commands. The PPMC-103C contributes greatly to the boards simplicity of use. Keithley MetraByte's driver software further enhances the ease of stepper-motor control by personal computer.

All connections necessary for operation with Keithley MetraByte's accessories are made through the rear plate using a standard 50-pin connector. Keithley MetraByte offers as options a stepper-motor driver (M3-DRIVE), a compatible power supply (M3-PWR-24), a popular type of stepper motor (STEP-MOT1), and a screw-terminal adapter (STA-50) that allows the MSTEP-3 to be connected to drivers other than the M3-DRIVE.

BLOCK DIAGRAM

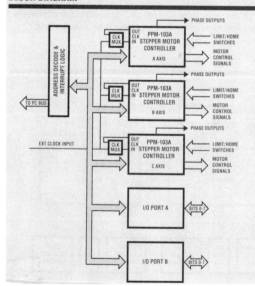

Figure 9.13 Stepper motor controller boards. (Courtesy Keithley Metrabyte.)

PC Based Stepper Motor Controller Card

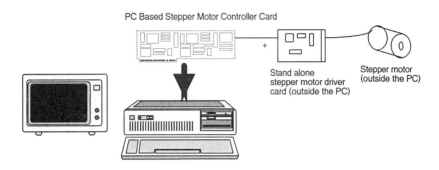

Stand alone
stepper motor driver
card (outside the PC)

Stepper motor
(outside the PC)

Figure 9.14 Essential components for controlling stepper motors with PC.

9.4 DC MOTORS

DC motors are extremely versatile and low cost actuators that are used very widely in industry. Even though this type of motor is not as suitable as a stepper motor for interfacing to the computer, its low cost and high power output make it desirable for computer controlled applications.

A DC motor is the most powerful and efficient kind of electromagnetic motor and it has the highest weight to power ratio. (Its output is stronger than the output of a comparable weight stepper motor or any other type of motor.)

Of course there are also disadvantages associated with DC motors. Their reliability is considered low because of the brushes involved for passing current to the rotor. (In the case of a DC motor, the rotor is not a permanent magnet so there has to be current passing over the rotor for continuous rotation. In order to pass current over the rotor which is continuously rotating, we need to use brushes that touch the rotor continuously. Because of the resulting friction, the brushes tend to wear out in time and reduce the reliability of the motor.) Another problem with the DC motor is the high mechanical inertia of the rotor. It takes a finite amount of time for the rotor to reach the full speed and takes a finite amount of time to stop the rotor. Because of that, it requires advanced planning and applying the brakes to the motor in advance when one wishes to stop at a precise location. Finally, the last disadvantage of the DC motor is that it can only be used in a closed loop with some position feedback devices.

DC motors come in a variety of sizes and shapes. Figure 9.15 shows light power DC motors which can be driven by 12 volts and require a current of several amps. The DC motors used in industry use industry standard higher DC voltages like 90 or 189 volts. These motors are specially designed with light rotors to decrease the inertia of the motor. There are standard off-the-shelf speed controllers available for these motors. Figure 9.16 shows industrial grade DC motors designed for heavy power applications.

Steel Geared

Medium Duty   NEW N

size 1 and 2   L. 24   size 3 and 4   L. 26
size 5   L. 29   size 6 and 7   L. 31

A range of seven high quality, geared d.c. motors. The reversible motor employs an ironless rotor giving linear speed-torque performance. The commutation system uses precious metal brushes for high efficiency and sensitivity to suit servo application as well as general purpose requirements. The gearbox construction employs a fibre wheel first stage followed by steel gears on bronze shafts. The output drive shaft has a flat machined on it to simplify load coupling.
The units are directly compatible with the **RS** peristaltic pump head system stock no. 330-812 etc. Electrical connections are via rear solder tags.

technical specification	1	2	3	4	5	6	7
r.p.m. at 12V d.c.	220	130	65	40	20	8	4
Max. power (W)	4	4	4	4	4	4	4
Max. torque (mNm)							
continuous	200	200	300	600	600	600	600
peak	600	600	900	1800	1800	1800	1800
Gearbox reduction	18:1	30:1	60:1	100:1	200:1	500:1	900:1
Nom. V (V d.c.)	12	12	12	12	12	12	12
Starting V min no load (V d.c.)	0·15	0·15	0·15	0·15	0·15	0·15	0·15
Nom. no load current (mA)	15	15	15	15	15	15	15
Max. cont op. current (mA)	493	493	493	493	493	493	493
Terminal resis. (Ω)	10	10	10	10	10	10	10
Max. rotor temp. (°C)	85	85	85	85	85	85	85
Weight (g)	247	247	252	252	257	262	262

Heavy Duty

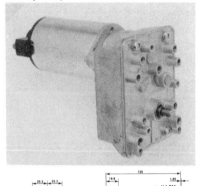

Two high powered, d.c. motor/gearboxes, supplied with two output shaft adaptors to convert the 8 mm output shaft to **a)** a 10 mm output shaft for general use or **b)** an especially tongued shaft to allow the motor/gearbox to power the type 303 peristaltic pump system stock no. 320-540 etc.

Features include:
● Quick change brush system.
● Sintered bronze bearings.
● Choice of 100 rpm or 20 rpm output.

technical specification		
Type	1	2
rpm at 12V d.c	100	20
Max. power (W mech.)	16	16
Max. torque (mNm)		
continuous	1200	1200
peak	1200	4000
Gearbox reduction	26:1	130:1
Nom. voltage (V d.c.)	12	12
Starting voltage, min. no load	3 V	3 V
Nom. no load current (mA)	590	590
Max. continuous operating current (mA)	2800	2800
Terminal resistance (Ω)	2	2
Max. rotor temperature	130°C	130°C
Weight (g)	670	670

Figure 9.15 Small size DC motors for light power applications. (Courtesy RS Components.)

Unlike the stepper motor which advances a known amount every time a pulse is given, a DC motor has no such ability. The end position of the stepper motor can be predicted since we know that every pulse will advance the motor for a known amount. But for the DC motor it is not possible to know where the end point will be when the motor is energized. For this reason, it is a must that a DC motor be used together with a feedback device which provides information regarding the position of the motor.

The most common feedback devices used with DC motors and AC motors are potentiometers--either rotary or linear type--or optical feedback devices. The DC motor can be controlled by either power transistors or relays, although the relays are not recommended because of their slow response time and low reliability. (Any mechanical device with moving parts has a lower reliability than the semiconductor counterpart with no moving parts.)

d.c. Industrial Electric Motors
Permanent Magnet Totally Enclosed Motors and Motor/Gearbox Combinations

Supplied to RS by Leroy Somer Ltd.

d.c. motor

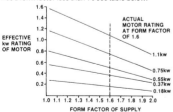

d.c. motor and gearbox combinations

A range of **foot mounted**, permanent magnet motors available with a selection of Compabloc 2000 **multi reduction** gearboxes. Suitable for applications requiring variable speeds with constant torque over a wide speed range. The 3000 rpm motors are continuously rated and protected to **IP55**. Produced to metric frame sizes which conform with IEC dimensional standards. The tubular body casings are made from rolled steel and have cast aluminium endshields. **Frame sizes 56VL, 63L and 71VL** are all **naturally cooled** i.e. heat from the motor is dissipated by natural convection and radiation.
Frame sizes 80L and **80VL** are **fan cooled**. Bearings are of the single row deep groove radial type, packed with a lithium based grease and sealed for life. The armature is insulated with class F material and rated to operate in the ambient temperature range 0 to +40°C. The motors **operate at 180 V d.c.** derived from a d.c. motor controller, suitable type **RS** stock no. 343-436, see this section.
Replacement **carbon brushes** are available. Other features include :

● High efficiency
● Top mounted terminal box with metric conduit or cable gland entries
● Direction of rotation easily changed
● Can withstand high overload currents
● All motors have milled keyways and fitted keys
● Environmentally protected to **IP55**

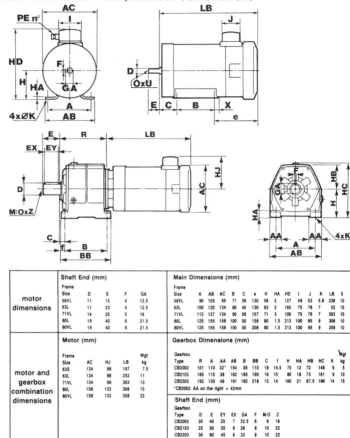

	Shaft End (mm)					Main Dimensions (mm)													
motor dimensions	Frame Size	D	E	F	GA	Frame Size	A	AB	AC	B	C	e	H	HA	HD	I	J	K	LB	X
	56VL	11	15	4	12.5	56VL	90	105	95	71	36	130	56	2	127	49	53	5.8	238	10
	63L	11	23	4	12.5	63L	100	120	134	80	40	130	63	2	165	75	78	7	52	10
	71VL	14	25	5	16	71VL	112	137	134	90	56	157	71	3	100	75	78	7	303	10
	80L	19	40	6	21.5	80L	125	155	158	100	50	158	80	1.5	213	100	95	9	306	10
	80VL	19	40	6	21.5	80VL	125	155	158	100	50	208	80	1.5	213	100	95	9	358	10

	Motor (mm)				Gearbox Dimensions (mm)													
	Frame Size	AC	HJ	LB	Wgt kg	Gearbox Type	R	A	AA	AB	B	BB	C	f	H	HA	HB	HC	K	Wgt kg
motor and gearbox combination dimensions	63S	134	98	197	7.5	CB2002	101	110	32*	154	85	110	18	14.5	75	12	72	148	9	5
	63L	134	98	252	11	CB2103	165	110	38	182	165	195	16	15	80	18	73	161	9	10
	71VL	134	98	303	13	CB2203	192	135	48	191	192	218	13	14	100	21	87.5	196	14	15
	80L	158	133	308	15	*CB2002: AA on the right = 42mm														
	80VL	158	133	358	22															

Shaft End (mm)								
Gearbox Type	D	E	EY	EX	GA	F	M:O	Z
CB2002	20	40	25	7	22.5	6	6	16
CB2103	25	50	35	6	28	8	10	22
CB2203	30	60	45	6	33	8	10	22

motor selection table						
frame size	rating kW	armature voltage	speed	nominal current	efficiency	weight kg
56VL	0·18	180	3000	1·5	0·75	5·3
63L	0·37	180	3000	2·4	0·79	11
71VL	0·55	180	3000	3·8	0·80	13
80L	0·75	180	3000	5·2	0·81	18
80VL	1·1	180	3000	7·6	0·84	22

All motors are given a kW rating at a form factor of 1·6. The rating can be uprated if the motors supply has a form factor less than 1·6 see table below.

EFFECTIVE kw RATING OF MOTOR

ACTUAL MOTOR RATING AT FORM FACTOR OF 1.6

1.1kw
0.75kw
0.55kw
0.37kw
0.18kw

FORM FACTOR OF SUPPLY

Figure 9.16 Industrial grade DC motors (Courtesy RS Components.)

The direction of rotation of the DC motor is controlled by the direction of the current passing over the rotor, and the speed of the rotor is controlled by the magnitude of the rotor current. Controlling the speed of the DC motor is not a trivial task and usually it is not a major concern when we control DC motors using computers. Speed information can be indirectly gathered through the feedback devices. A simple scheme for controlling the direction of rotation of the DC motor is shown in Figure 9.17.

In the scheme given in Figure 9.17, the current is being supplied to the motor over the resistors. This type of drive technique is called rheostat drive in industry since the current to the motor is controlled by means of a high power resistor called a rheostat. This arrangement uses only two power transistors but due to the series resistors, the torque generated by the motor is limited and there is considerable power dissipation over the resistors. However, if the speed of the motor needed to be reduced this is a method that can be used. The motor turns in one direction when T1 is turned On and it turns in the reverse direction when T2 is turned On. By turning both transistors On we can form a closed loop using resistors over the terminals of the motor which would cause dynamic braking and would stop the motor immediately after power cut off. This is very suitable since a DC motor has a high rotor inertia which causes it to free rotate for a considerable amount of time even after the power is cut off to the motor.

Yet another scheme uses both npn and pnp transistors for achieving the purpose of controlling the direction of rotation. In this case, the transistors should be turned On and Off in pairs. Turning T1 and T3 will result in turning in one direction. During this process, T2 and T4 should be Off. By turning the T2 and T4 On and the others Off, we can reverse the direction of the motor.

Like the other control scheme this method also allows dynamic braking for quick stopping of the DC motor. The second scheme is much better than the first one in many respects. There is no power dissipation over resistors as in the first method and the performance of the system is much higher. Almost all commercial DC motor controllers use the second scheme as a basis for their design. The designs which are supposed to handle very high power DC motors have the transistor replaced with triacs.

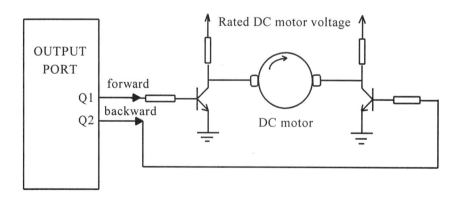

Figure 9.17 Controlling the direction of rotation of a DC motor through the output port of the PC.

9.4.1 Speed Control of DC Motors

There are basically two methods for controlling speed of a DC motor:

- Direct current regulation
- Speed control with pulse width modulation

The first method is suitable for low power applications which use light duty DC motors, whereas the second method is the only method available for high power applications which require high power DC motors.

DIRECT CURRENT REGULATION

Controlling the speed of the DC motor can be achieved by controlling the current through the motor. Power transistors can be used in the active region for controlling the amount of current through the armature of the DC motor. However, when transistors are used in the active region, there will be quite a large power dissipation over the transistors. Because of this, a direct current control method is used only with small, light duty DC motors to limit the dissipation over the transistors and should be exercised very carefully. Large heat sinks should be mounted to the transistors and D/A converters should be used for applying the base voltage. Due to a large number of components and power dissipation, this method is applicable only to small size DC motors and not recommended for speed control of large power DC motors.

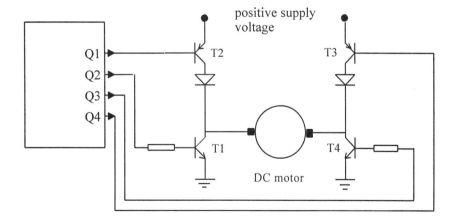

Figure 9.18 Another scheme for controlling the direction of rotation of a DC motor.

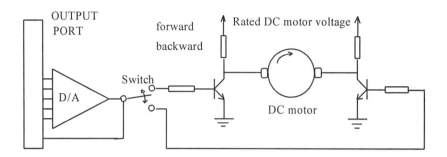

Figure 9.19 A possible way of controlling the speed of the DC motor.

SPEED CONTROL WITH PULSE WIDTH MODULATION

The second method which is more favorable for large power DC motors is to use a switching power transistor and change the duty cycle of the switching frequency of the transistor. As the duty cycle is changed, the On time of the transistor changes. This will cause the average voltage applied to the motor to change, and this in turn will cause the speed of the motor to increase or decrease. This method uses the minimum number of components and is very effective in changing the speed of the motor. The power dissipation over the switching transistor is reasonable. Almost all commercially available DC speed controllers use the PWM technique to control the speed of DC motors.

Please note that all the above schemes are for DC motors with a permanent magnet-stator. These are usually small size DC motors. There are also large DC motors with coils in the stator where the current passed through the stator causes a magnetic field inside the motor.

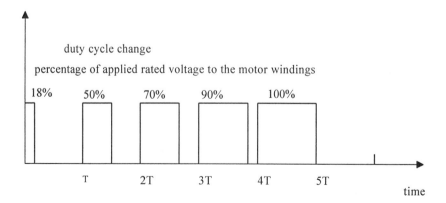

Figure 9.20 Pulse width modulation.

The speed of these types of motors can be controlled quite easily by controlling the field current in the stator. Usually the field current is much less than the armature current that goes through the rotor. The speed regulation of this type should be done through controlling the field current of the stator. It is possible to use power transistors in the active region for controlling the current through the field of the stator.

9.4.2 DC Motor Speed Control Using the PC and Commercial Equipment

Fortunately, one does not have to build a speed controller for DC motors from scratch. There are commercially available speed controllers for DC motors which supply field current and armature current to the DC motor as well as generate DC voltage needed for the motor. These speed controllers use pulse width modulation, dynamic braking and stator field current control together to get maximum performance from the DC motor. Using all these factors together, the speed of the DC motor can be changed from one RPM level to the other in milliseconds. All these commercial speed controllers require speed feedback from the DC motor through tacho generators. A tacho generator is a small precision DC motor which is directly coupled to the shaft of the main DC motor and generates a DC voltage in proportion to the speed of the main DC motor. A controller needs this feedback in order to respond to speed change demand in the quickest possible time.

The set speed of the motor can be changed on the fly to change the speed of the DC motor. The speed control input of the speed controller is an analog input which has a range from 0 to 10 volts or industry standard 4-20 mA current loop. To control the speed of an industrial grade DC motor using a PC, first one has to have an analog output card for the PC and connect the voltage output of the card to the speed control input of the speed controller. The data sheet for a typical speed controller is given on the following pages. A detailed data sheet is included in Appendix B.

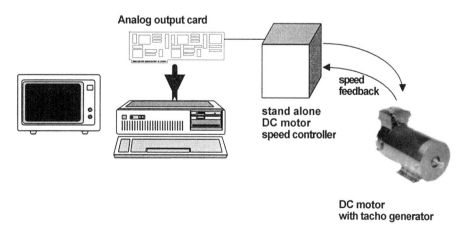

Figure 9.21 Controlling speed of industrial grade DC motors using commercially available components.

For the system shown in Figure 9.21, the user should keep in mind that, the connection between the PC and speed controller should be galvanically isolated in order to avoid catastrophic problems. Most speed controllers have speed control inputs already isolated from the rest of the circuitry in order to accommodate this design feature.

0-9kW '512' Range

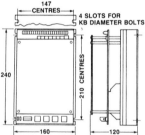

Technical Specification

Supply voltage	110/240/415 V
Supply frequency	45/65 Hz a.c.
Armature output voltage	90/180/320
Armature output current :	
0-4·5kW controller	16 A
0-9kW controller	32 A
Field output voltage	100/210/370
Field output current	2 A
Typ. full load regulation	0·1% tacho generator feedback
	2% armature voltage feedback
Control modes	Armature/Tacho generator
Max. a.c. line current :	
0-4·5kW controller	30 A
0-9kW controller	60 A
max. form factor	1·5

The 512 range of isolated d.c. motor speed controllers are suitable for use with both d.c. shunt and permanent magnet motors.

● Switch selectable current calibration
● Switch selectable Armature/Tacho generator feedback
● Buffered 0-10 V output for a speed reference meter
● Buffered 0-7·5 V output for a current meter (7·5 V = 150%)
● Independent control of speed ramp, both up and down from 0-20 secs.
● Jumper selectable single phase input voltage 110/240/415 V 45-65 Hz a.c.
● Access to control transformer enabling low voltage motor control
● Linear current feedback allowing accurate torque control
● Zero speed relay output, enabling simple reversal of drive, rated 3 A at 240 V a.c./3 A at 24 V d.c.
● Drive healthy relay output rated 3 A at 240 V a.c./3 A at 24 V d.c.
● Stall detection and trip
● High speed fuse protection
● Field bridge suitable for UK or continental voltages
● Overload capacity 150% of nominal current for 30 secs.
● Adjustable maximum current level
● Adjustable maximum and minimum speed
● Adjustable I.R. compensation (for armature voltage feedback speed control)
● Adjustable speed stability
● Indication of mains supply on; stall trip and overcurrent trip

The controllers are supplied with a comprehensive instruction manual.

Small Power 0-360W

Dimensions

	Length	Width	Height
panel mounting	226	125	80
boxed	226	134	83

This range of cost effective d.c. motor speed controllers are suitable for use with shunt wound and permanent magnet d.c. motors. Available in both boxed and panel mounting versions. The boxed version is protected to IP22. Supplied with a comprehensive instruction manual.

Features include :
● High transient overload capability
● Improved commutation
● Smoother quieter running
● Considerably increased brush life
● Adjustable maximum and minimum speeds
● Fused input supply
● IR compensation
● Adjustable overload
● Control potentiometer supplied with panel mounting version as standard

Technical Specification

Power supply	110/240 V a.c.50/60 Hz
Form factor :	
260 model	1·05
360 model	1·1 (50 V d.c.) 1·2 (200 V d.c.)
Field output current	0·25 A
Armature output voltage :	
260 W model	200 V d.c.
360 W model	50/200 V d.c.
Armature output current :	
260 W model	1·3 A at 200 V
360 W model	2·5 A at 50 V d.c. 2 A at 180 V d.c.

Figure 9.22 Commercial DC motor speed controllers. (Courtesy RS Components.)

9.5 AC MOTORS

AC motors constitute the backbone of industry. These motors, being very reliable and relatively maintenance free, are used in many industrial applications. The principle of operation of AC motors is the generation of a rotating magnetic field inside the motor. The rotor of the AC motor gets coupled to the rotating magnetic field and turns continuously with it. The rotor of the AC motor is quite simple, having no windings. Precisely because of this, there is no need for brushes in an AC motor. These features make an AC motor more reliable and maintenance free when compared to a DC motor. Figure 9.23 shows several different commercially available AC motors.

More detailed information about AC motors is included in Appendix B. AC motors are quite difficult to control using computers. The simple turning on and off can be achieved quite easily by using triacs or relays; however, the speed control of the AC motor is much more difficult than the DC motor. The speed of the AC motor is dependent on the frequency of the mains supply. If one wants to control the speed, the frequency of the AC supply voltage has to be changed.

Industrial Electric a.c. Motors
Totally Enclosed Fan Cooled (TEFC) Squirrel Cage Induction Motors

Supplied to RS by ABB Industry Ltd.

A range of single and three phase a.c. induction motors available in foot mounting (both versions) and flange mounting (three phase versions only). Ideal for a wide variety of industrial applications including pumps, fans, process and machinery drives, the motors are continuously rated and environmentally protected to IP55.
Produced to metric frame sizes as per the CENELEC Harmonisation Document HD231 and IEC publication 71; 1971 dimensional standards; the motors are totally interchangeable with similar frame sized units. The casing of the motors are manufactured from high tensile strength, pressure die cast aluminium alloy with the laminated stator wound with double insulated copper wire and impregnated with a two component polyester resin to give a class F winding insulation rating.

Other features of the motors include:

● Top mounted terminal box with metric/Pg type conduit knockouts
● Axial sealing ring located between the internal cooling fan and end shield, to prevent ingress of dirt, water or other matter
● Motors able to withstand a load of 200% full load torque at the rated voltage and frequency
● All motors have milled key ways and fitted keys
● Direction of rotation easily changeable

2 Pole and 4 Pole : Three Phase Motors

Available in both foot and flange mounting, these motors may be connected in either STAR (Y) for incoming supply voltages of 380-420/440-480 V or DELTA (Δ) for 220-240/250-280 V incoming 50/60 Hz three phase supplies (frame sizes 63 to 100).
Note: the 4 kW 112 frame size motor is supplied DELTA (Δ) connected for use on 380-420 V supplies. A range of three phase and single phase input a.c. motor speed controllers is available allowing this range of motors the ability to achieve variable speed outputs, rather than just the stated fixed speed. Similarily soft starters are available allowing motor speeds to be ramped up over a time period (see further in this section).

Figure 9.23 Commercially available AC motors. (Courtesy RS components.)

Panel Mounting Single and Three Phase Input RECENTLY INTRODUCED

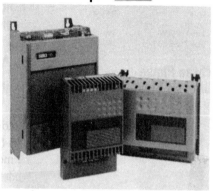

This high technology range of inverters is specifically designed to RS requirements. Using the latest microprocessor technology these drives offer the user a reliable and electrically rugged high performance product, which is adaptable to the wide variety of industrial a.c. induction motor applications. The IP20 enclosure allows installation within a wiring panel or suitable enclosure (see enclosures, accessories and fans section). These inverters have the following features and benefits.

● 16 bit microprocessor technology giving very comprehensive control of power pattern generation, voltage, frequency and current (582 and 583)
● Galvanically isolated input and output signals preventing damage to the units in the event of incorrect connection
● Speed, start, stop, direction set by remote potentiometers and switches giving flexibility in control system design
● Independently programmable acceleration and deceleration times from 0·25 - 100 seconds
● d.c. injection breaking facility for rapid stopping of the motor (582 and 583)
● Maximum and minimum speed setting potentiometer adjustments
● Selectable stop mode allowing either coast or ramp to stop (580 ramp to stop only)
● Analogue input to control the frequency of 3 phase output (0-10V)
● Low speed/frequency voltage boost giving extra

torque for high starting torque loads
● Selectable 50Hz or 60Hz operation for UK or worldwide markets
● Protection facilities for over current, Ith overload, motor stalled and d.c. link over voltage
● Overload capability at 150% for 30 seconds
● Selectable output voltage/frequency characteristic following linear to base frequency, linear to 2 × base frequency and 'fan law' outputs
● Can accept tachogenerator signal input allowing very close speed control
● Single phase have 3 phase or 3 wire 220/240V inputs on 0·75kw and above
● All units supplied with a comprehensive instruction manual

Note : A speed range of 10:1 is achievable with the motor controller/motor combinations.

technical specification	
Input voltage frequency	50/60Hz
Input supply voltage	582/583 220/240V ± 10%
	580 220/240V line a.c.
Ambient temp. range	0 to 40°C
Output frequency range	0 - 120Hz
Ventilation	natural
Atmosphere	non-flammable, non corrosive and dust free
Humidity	85% R.H. at 40°C (non-condensing)

Figure 9.24 Stand alone inverters for AC motor speed control. (Courtesy RS components.)

Since the frequency of the main supply is fixed either at 50 or 60 Hz, if we want to change the frequency, we have to first change the AC supply voltage into DC voltage. Then, DC voltage can be converted back into AC voltage with a different frequency using complicated arrangements using triacs. There are commercially available speed changers called "inverters" for controlling the speed of AC motors which utilize micro-controllers to handle the firing time of the triacs. Examples of some of these products are shown in Figure 9.24.

9.5.1 AC Motor Speed Control Using the PC

Unlike DC motors whose speed can be changed over a wide range, AC motors have a limited range of speed change with inverters. At best the speed ratio can be changed from 10 to 1. Some of the inverters available on the market are suitable for interfacing to the computer. The particular unit shown in the figure has an analog isolated speed control input of 0-10 volts. Using this input, the output frequency can be changed from 0 to 120 Hz. In order to control the speed through the computer, an analog output card has to be installed inside the computer and the output of the card should be connected to the inverter. A block diagram of this system is shown in Figure 9.25.

AC motors, unlike DC motors, can be used without speed feedback. Since the speed of the AC motor is dependent on the frequency of the supply voltage and the speed varies only very little from the no load condition to the full load condition, speed feedback is not necessary.

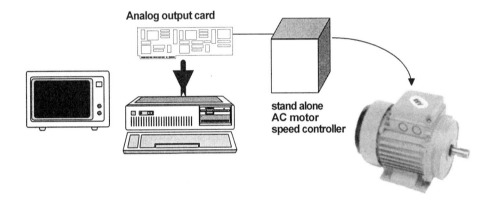

Figure 9.25 Speed control of AC motors using PC and stand alone inverters.

9.6 USING SHAPE MEMORY ALLOYS AS ACTUATORS

Shape memory alloys are a special category of metal alloys which exhibit a very interesting characteristic. These alloys undergo changes in shape or hardness when heated or cooled and do so with great force. these alloys have a characteristic called shape memory effect. This means that the crystal structure of the alloy will change into another form at a specific temperature. A shape memory alloy can be easily stretched or deformed below the transition temperature. In case of a wire, it can be stretched up to 8% of its original length. When the wire is heated to its transition temperature (which is usually below 100 °C), the wire contracts back to its original length with a much greater force than the force used for stretching the wire. In a way, shape memory alloys behave exactly like muscles, contracting whenever signaled. The cycle of deforming and contraction can be repeated for millions of cycles provided:

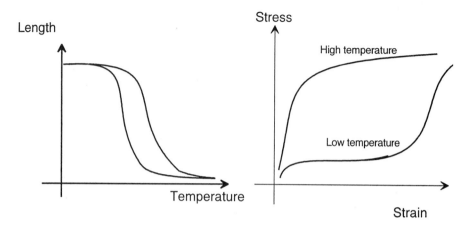

Figure 9.26 Temperature-length and Stress-strain diagrams for SMA.

- The material is not stretched beyond its elastic limit
- A mechanism (e.g. spring) always stretches the material after it is cooled

A temperature versus deformation diagram of a typical shape memory alloy is given in Figure 9.26. A typical shape memory alloy actuator is shown in Figure 9.27.

Shape memory alloys are made of elements like Ti, Mn, Fe, Ni, Cu, Zn, Al, Si, Ag, Cd, In, Sn, Pt, and Au. Among the well known alloys is an SMA (shape memory alloy) called Nitinol™ made of equal percentage of Ti and Ni. Changing the percentage about 1% causes the transition temperature to change within the range of -100°C to 100°C. Another widely known SMA is made of copper-zinc-aluminum. Specifications for Flexinol™, a nickel-titanium alloy are given below.

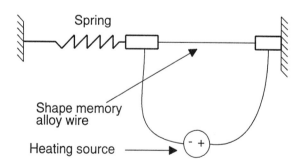

Figure 9.27 Shape memory alloy set-up.

Specification for Flexinol™ SMA wire

Wire diameter (μ meter)	Linear resistance (Ω/meter)	Activation current (milliamps)	Stretching weight (gms)	Recovery weight (gms)	Cycle rate (cycle/min)
37	860	30	4	20	68
50	510	50	8	35	67
100	150	180	28	150	50
150	50	400	62	330	30
250	20	1000	172	930	13

The contraction time for all wires is 1/1000 sec and cooling is in still air at 20°C. By using several wires in parallel, the lifting force of the wire can be increased.

Shape memory alloy wires can be used for computer controlled actuation purposes. There are many commercial products based on SMA wires like, microvalves, microrobot actuators, and tactile sensing devices.

SMA devices can be used either as simple on-off devices without feedback like solenoids or as variable displacement devices with feedback like DC motor driven actuators.

Using SMA devices as variable displacement devices requires careful monitoring of position and current through the wire. Pulse width modulated arrangements are the most suitable type of control mechanism for this purpose. A suitable scheme for computer controlled displacement scheme is indicated in Figure 9.28.

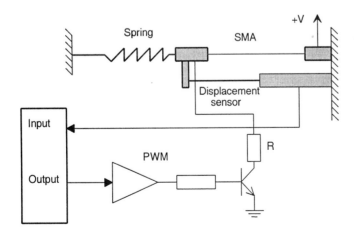

Figure 9.28 Computer controlled varable-displacement actuation of SMA wire.

9.7 SOLENOIDS

A solenoid is a simple rugged device which consists of a coil and a ferromagnetic shell to house the coil. Inside the coil there is a movable core which is called a plunger. When the coil is energized, a magnetic flux generated pulls the core inside the coil. The physical motion generated by the core is used then for doing simple push-pull type operations. The action generated by the solenoid works only one way by pulling the core in. Getting the core out of the coil has to be achieved by some external mechanical means like a spring force or mechanical lever. Even though it is possible to control the amount of movement of the plunger precisely for position control, solenoids are mainly used as on-off devices in industry. In every cycle the core goes in and out completely. Solenoids are considered reliable components because of their simple mechanical structure. The average lifetime of a tubular solenoid is about 50 to 100 million operations. Solenoids are mostly used for operations which do not require the control of the distance or the amount of force exerted on the mechanism. Typical uses are controlling the lock mechanism, pulling a lever, etc.

A solenoid can be interfaced to the computer using a single bit of the output port and a power transistor. Since a solenoid is an inductor by nature, it is absolutely essential to use a flywheel diode to protect the transistor.

There are different versions of the solenoid depending on the type of movement of the plunger. Most solenoids have a plunger that makes a linear back and forth movement. These types of solenoids are usually called tubular solenoids. Another type of solenoid is called a rotary solenoid, where the plunger rotates at a predefined angle. The angular stroke depends on the type of the solenoid and can vary from 25 to 95 degrees. Figure 9.30 shows typical solenoids and related technical data.

While using solenoids in designs, the designer has to be careful about the duty cycle and the heat generation of the solenoid. Solenoids can be operated at a higher voltage, but in such cases the duty cycle should be kept short in order to avoid an extreme rise in the temperature of the solenoid. Temperature rise can not only destroy the component but also reduce the force output of the solenoid considerably.

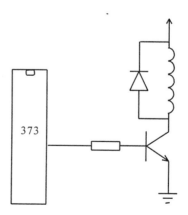

Figure 9.29 Connecting a solenoid to an output port.

General Purpose Solenoids
Standard and Large

Robust pull-action solenoids available in two basic sizes. The design offers high force/size ratios. All the coils are continuously rated (100% duty cycle) at the stated voltages though they may be operated at higher voltages (providing appropriately higher forces) if the duty cycle is reduced accordingly (see below). Connections for all types are via 200 mm long flying leads.

Note: When a.c. coils are energised the armature must be allowed to travel fully into the coil.

technical specifications - standard types

type	stock no.	coil voltage	force (kgf) at 6 mm stroke	max. stroke	coil power
1	**349-709**	12 V d.c.	0·35	18	10 W
2	**349-715**	24 V d.c.	0·35	18	10 W
3	**349-462**	240 V a.c.	0·3	12	10·5 VA
4	**349-478**	240 V a.c.	0·4	24	15 VA

All data relates to a continuous duty cycle at 20°C

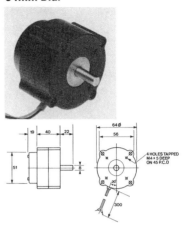

duty		10%	25%	50%	100%
349-709	V max. d.c.	38 V	24 V	17 V	12 V
349-715	V max. d.c.	77 V	48 V	34 V	24 V
349-462	V max. a.c.	565 V	424 V	314 V	240 V
349-478	V max. a.c.	536 V	412 V	311 V	240 V

technical specification - large types

stock no.	coil voltage	force (kgf) at 6 mm stroke	max stroke	coil power
346-340	12 V d.c.	0·6	18	12 W
346-356	24 V d.c.	0·6	18	12 W
346-362	240 V a.c.	0·7	18	20 VA

All data relates to continuous duty cycle at 20°C

duty		10%	25%	50%	100%
346-340	V max. d.c.	38 V	24 V	17 V	12 V
346-356	V max. d.c.	77 V	48 V	34 V	24 V
346-362	V max. a.c.	585 V	406 V	312 V	240 V

Rotary Solenoids
64mm Dia.

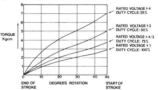

A solenoid operating from 12 V d.c. and producing a pure rotary displacement of 45° (with no axial movement). A return spring and stop are fitted at the rear end of the shaft. On energising the coil the shaft rotates clockwise (looking on to shaft) through 45° and holds. On removal of the supply, the shaft returns (under spring tension) to the rest position and rests against a mechanical stop.

Featuring robust construction and high torque output (which is at maximum at the beginning of the shaft movement) it is ideally suited to typical mechanical loads where initial resistance needs to be overcome. The stop mechanism and spring return assembly may be removed from the rear of the solenoid, in which case the shaft still rotates through 45° but will remain in the activated position after the supply has been removed. The reset torque must then be supplied by the assembly attached to the rotor shaft. Without the stop the solenoid operation is virtually silent. Applications include counting and sorting systems, material handling, indicating, shutter systems, tape/ film advance, etc.

technical specification

Max. coil temperature rise	65°C
Dielectric strength (20°C)	1000 V a.c. for 1 min
Insulation resistance (20°C)	1000 MΩ at 500 V d.c.
Coil voltage nominal	12 V d.c.
Coil resistance	11Ω
Operating current typ.	1·1 A
Max. stroke	45°
Rotor moment of inertia	$61·5 \times 10^{-3}$ gcm²
Weight	0·82 kg

Figure 9.30 Various solenoids. (Courtesy RS Components.)

9.7.1 Solenoid Valve

A solenoid valve is nothing more than a solenoid which opens and closes a valve to control either pneumatic or hydraulic pressure. For operations which require an extremely high force, the usual motors, like stepper, DC, or AC motors, can not be used. Only hydraulic machinery, hydraulic motors and actuators, can be used for applications that require a large force such as lifting trucks, opening up bridges, compacting trash, etc. Solenoid valves are used in pneumatic or hydraulic systems for actuating the machinery.

As far as the interfacing to the computer is concerned, solenoid valve interfacing is exactly like interfacing an ordinary solenoid to the computer.

Air, Gas and Fluid Solenoid Valve

A range of 2-way and 3-way direct operating normally closed solenoid valves for use with :

● Air and other non-corrosive gases
● Some industrial fluids (provided they are compatible with the materials used in the valve construction i.e. valve disc: nitrile rubber; valve seat and cover: brass; valve body; aluminium)

The valve body is aluminium alloy and the coil is fully encapsulated in nylon. The valve body is connected to 0·25 inch blade connection for earthing purposes. Electrical connection is made via a 3 pin DIN connector (suitable DIN 43650 appliance connector **RS** 488-949, refer to the Connectors - Terminals/Test Leads section). The valve should be mounted vertically with all the pipes running horizontally and an upstream filter should be fitted if there is a possibility of solids being present in the fluid. Main body ports are ¼in. BSP, 3-way exhaust port is ⅛in. BSP.

Technical Specification

Voltage supply	24V d.c., 110V a.c. 240V a.c. 50Hz
Power consumption :	
a.c.	24VA (inrush)
	14VA (constant)
d.c.	9W
Pressure	10·3 bar (150 psi)
Temp. range	-20 to +60°C (dependent on medium)
Orifice size	1·2mm dia. (3-way)
	2·4mm dia. (2-way)

2-Way PVC

A range of 2-way direct acting normally closed solenoid valves.

Featuring
● Wetted valve internals of non-metallic materials, with EPDM seals and bodies of PVC
● BSP parallel ports suitable for use with **RS** stainless compression fittings
● Epoxy encapsulated coils
● 3-pin DIN connector rated to IP65 can be positioned through 360° in 90° increments
● 8W nominal coil power
● Zero head pressure capability

These valves can be mounted in any position, but mounting with coil uppermost is preferred.

Technical Specification

Voltage supply	24V d.c., 110V a.c. or 240V a.c. (±10%)
Power consumption	
a.c.	21VA inrush
	12VA/8W (constant)
d.c.	8W
Cycling frequency	300 c.p.m.
Viscosity	37 CST
Max. fluid temp.	-30°C to +50°C
Pressure range	0-1·5 bar
Flow rate	6·7l/min
Orifice size	4·0mm
Ambient temp.	+50°C
Seal material	EPDM

Solenoid valves come in different varieties depending on how many inlets they open, close or divert. A two-way solenoid is an ordinary solenoid valve which simply opens or closes an inlet port. A three-way solenoid has an inlet and two outlets. The valve diverts the flow from one outlet to the other. Figure 9.32 illustrates different varieties of valves, their functions and schematic diagrams used in industry.

Solenoid Valve Schematic Diagram Key

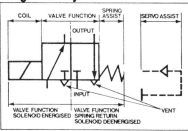

Circuit Function A

A 2-way normally closed valve. When the coil is energised the valve is open. De-energising closes the valve.

Circuit Function B

A 2-way normally open valve. When the coil is energised the valve is closed. De-energising opens the valve.

Circuit Function C

A 3/2-way outlet A normally vented valve. When the coil is energised the input port P is connected to the output port A, with the vent R closed. De-energising closes the input port P nd allows the output A to exhaust through the vent R.

Circuit Function D

A 3/2-way outlet B normally pressurised valve (i.e. vent normally closed). When the coil is energised the outlet port B is allowed to vent through the exhaust R, with the input port P closed. De-energising connects the input port P to the outlet port B with the vent R closed.

Circuit Function E

A 3/2-way mixer valve with P2 normally open. When the coil is energised the inlet P1 is connected to the output A, with inlet P2 closed. De-energising closes P1 and connects P2 to the outlet A.

Circuit Function F

A diverter valve. When the coil is energised the inlet P is connected to the outlet A. De-energising connects the inlet P to outlet B and closes outlet A.

Explanatory Notes

1. The designation 3/2-way indicates a valve that has three ports and which has two modes of operation. It is normal practice to refer to 2/2-way valves as 2-way.
2. The port designation of A, B, P, P1, P2 and R are used on the schematic diagrams and are also marked on the valve bodies. 3-way valve bodies are marked for a specific circuit function but can often be used for other functions. Reference to the schematic diagrams and technical specifications will indicate the appropriate connections and pressure capabilities should an alternative circuit function be required.

Figure 9.32 Solenoid valve schematic diagram key. (Courtesy RS Components.)

One of the most important considerations regarding solenoid valves is the chemical compatibility with the liquid or the gas that is being controlled. Valve manufacturers fine tune the valves for specific applications by using appropriate material in the body and the seals of the valve. This chemical compatibility of information should be carefully examined before a valve is used in an application. Detailed information about chemical compatibility is given in Appendix C.

It should be noted that the pressures that can be handled by solenoid valves are at most around 10 bar (150 psi). High power hydraulic machinery applications require pressures that may be up to 1000's of psi. Obviously ordinary solenoid valves can not handle such high pressures. In such cases, solenoid valves are used as pilot valves for actuating mechanical valves which are used for handling such high pressures. There are mechanical hydraulic amplifier assemblies that can control high hydraulic pressures by relatively low pressures controlled by pilot valves. Pilot valves are a special category of solenoid valves. Even though the internal arrangement is similar to ordinary valves, the external connections are designed differently. Figure 9.33 shows some typical pilot valves used for pneumatic or hydraulic control. Detailed information about pilot valves is given in Appendix C.

3 Port Direct Operated Poppet Solenoid + Pilot Valves

Main features :
- ¼in ports
- Standard DIN 43650 Electrical Connection (connectors provided)
- Push button manual override
- 24V d.c., 110V a.c., 240V a.c. options
- Surge voltage protection
- Coils may be orientated at various angles to the base
- Suitable for low pressure switching 0-9 bar

Supplied to RS by SMC Pneumatics

A selection of direct operated 3 port poppet type solenoid operated spring return valves. Selective porting can be provided from these valves for up to 6 different valve functions.

VALVE FUNCTION	3-WAY NORMALLY CLOSED	3-WAY NORMALLY OPEN	2-WAY NORMALLY CLOSED
DE-ENERGIZED			
ENERGIZED			

VALVE FUNCTION	2-WAY NORMALLY OPEN	SELECTOR	DIVERTER
DE-ENERGIZED			
ENERGIZED			

Technical Specification	
Fluid	Air, inert gas
Operating pressure range	0 ∿ 9 bar
Ambient and fluid temperature	Max. 50°C
Response time	Max. 20ms
Max. operating frequency	10Hz
Lubrication	Not required
Manual override	Non-locking push button type
Mounting orientation	Free
Cv factor	0·7
Electrical entry	DIN 43650 connector
Voltages: a.c.	110V/240V 50/60Hz
d.c.	24V
Voltage allowance	-15% ∿ 10% of rated voltage
Insulation	Class B or equivalent (130°C)
Temperature rise	Max. 45°C
Apparent power a.c.:	
inrush	12·7VA (50Hz), 10·7VA (60Hz)
holding	7·6VA (50Hz), 5·4VA (60Hz)
Power consumption d.c.	4·8W
Lamp/surge voltage protection circuit :	
a.c.	Zener
d.c.	Diode

Figure 9.33 A typical pilot solenoid valve. (Courtesy RS Components.)

9.8 CONTROLLING PNEUMATIC SYSTEMS WITH THE PC

A pneumatic system uses air pressure for controlling the movement of air cylinders called RAM's. An air cylinder is an assembly of a piston, connecting rod and cylinder body. The movement of the piston is controlled by applying air pressure to one side of the piston and venting open the other side of the piston. An air cylinder is called double acting if there are openings on both sides of the piston; it is called single acting if there is an opening on only one side. A single acting cylinder requires a spring assembly inside to provide the return of the piston to the original position. Figure 9.34 shows some typical air cylinders.

Pneumatic Cylinders
Miniature Cylinders
(10mm - 25mm bore)

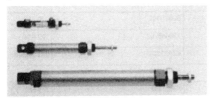

Supplied to RS by Compair Maxam

The RS range of miniature, single and double acting cylinders offer a wide choice of bore sizes and stroke lengths. The cylinders come with an integral magnetic piston and only require a sensor bracket (see miniature cylinder accessories) fitting to convert a standard miniature cylinder to a magnetic sensing miniature cylinder.

Material specification and construction is of highest order throughout, making these cylinders very durable.

The modular nature of the system allows the user to adapt or modify his miniature cylinders in line with changing automation requirements.

These cylinders conform to the requirements of ISO 6432, CETOP RP52P, BS 4862 (Part 1) and AFNOR NFE 49 030.

Material Specification

Cylinder body	Non-magnetic stainless steel
Piston rod	Non-magnetic stainless steel BS 304S11/12 SAE 304L
Seals	Nitrile
End caps	Anodised aluminium
Piston	Aluminium
Cushioning device	Polyurethane

Double acting

Technical Specification

Pressure range	0·8 to 10 bar
Temperature range	-20 to +70°C
Air condition	Filtered, regulated/lubricated or dry

Cylinder Thrusts (Newtons)

Note: An efficiency of 80% should be assumed due to frictional losses, and so the tabulated figures should be multiplied by 0·8 to give effective thrust.

Cyl bore mm	Piston rod Ømm	Area cm²	3 ●	3 ■	4 ●	4 ■	5 ●	5 ■	6 ●	6 ■
10	4	0·8	0·66	24	19	32	26	40	33	48	39
16	6	2	1·73	60	52	80	69	100	87	120	104
20	8	3·1	2·6	93	78	124	104	155	130	186	156
25	10	4·9	4·1	147	123	196	164	245	205	294	246

Cylinder bore mm	7 ●	7 ■	8 ●	8 ■	9 ●	9 ■	10 ●	10 ■
10	58	46	64	52	72	59	80	66
16	140	121	160	138	180	156	200	173
20	217	182	248	208	279	234	310	260
25	343	287	392	328	441	369	490	410

Surface of piston : ● Extending side of piston
■ Retracting side of piston

Single acting

Technical Specification

Pressure range	0·8 to 10 bar
Temperature range	-20 to +70°C
Air condition	Filtered, regulated/lubricated or dry

Cylinder Thrusts (Newtons)

Note: An efficiency of 80% should be assumed due to frictional losses, and so the tabulated figures should be multiplied by 0·8 to give effective thrust.

Cyl. bore mm	stroke	thrust at 6 bar	Spring force extended	retracted
10	10	37	10	7
10	25	34	13	7
16	10	86	31	23
16	25	75	42	22
20	25	145	37	25
25	25	245	43	30

Figure 9.34 Typical air cylinders. (Courtesy RS Components.)

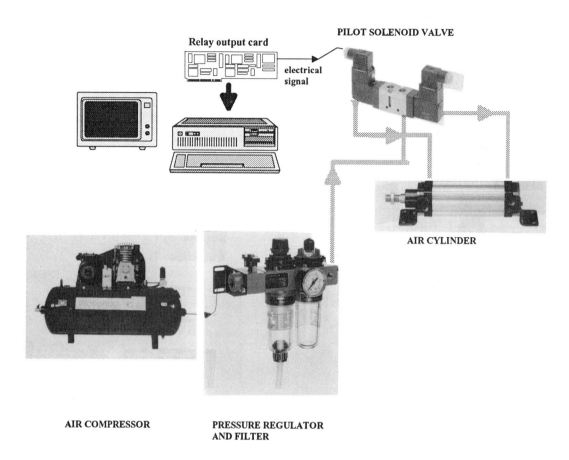

Figure 9.35 Controlling a pneumatic system with PC.

Detailed information about cylinders is given in Appendix C. Pneumatic systems can not be used for precision positioning applications since it is difficult to control the position of the piston precisely. Since air is compressible, the piston is likely to change position under load. Because of this reason, pneumatic systems are used for applications that require the piston to be fully in or out. A typical pneumatic system is shown in Figure 9.35.

9.9 CONTROLLING HYDRAULIC SYSTEMS WITH THE PC

Hydraulic systems in many respects resemble pneumatic systems. A hydraulic system uses pressurized oil for actuating the cylinder instead of air. Since oil is incompressible, it is possible to control the movement of the piston very precisely. The plumbing associated with hydraulic systems is more complicated than with pneumatic since the return oil has to be collected and vented to an oil reservoir. In contrast, in a pneumatic system we can vent the exhaust to air. As far as computer control aspect is concerned, interfacing solenoids is exactly the same as in pneumatic systems. The only difference in this case is that the end position of the piston is connected to a linear position sensor to control the position of the piston exactly.

REFERENCES

1. *Data Acquisition and Control Catalogue*, Vol. 22, Keithley Metrabyte,1990.

2. Hall, Douglas V., *Microprocessors and Interfacing.* McGraw-Hill International Editions, 1986.

3. *Solenoids Engineering Design Guide*, Lucas Ledex, 1990-1991.

4. Collins, T. H., *Analog Electronics Handbook*, Prentice Hall International, 1989.

5. Curtis, Johnson, *Process Control Instrumentation Technology*, Regents/Prentice Hall, 1993.

6. Austerlitz, Howard, *Data Acquistion Techniques Using Personal Computers*, Academic Press, 1991.

7. Derenzo, Stephen, *Interfacing,* Prentice Hall, 1990.

8. Mazda, F. F, (Ed.), *Electronic Engineer's Refrence Book*, Butterworth & Co. Ltd., 1986.

9. Miller, R., Miller, M. R., *Electric Motor Controls*, Prentice Hall, 1989.

10. Mazda, F. F., *Power Electronics Handbook*, Butterworth & Co. Ltd, 1990.

11. Barber, A., *Pneumatic Handbook*, The Trade & Technical Press Limited, 1989.

12. Pinches, M. J., Ashbey, J. G., *Power Hydraulics*, Prentice Hall International, 1989.

Ten

NETWORKED DATA
ACQUISITION and FIELDBUS

In this chapter we are going to look at several new trends in industry which started to influence the data acquisition and process control field. The force of change due to these new trends is very strong, but there is no dominant single method or standard emerged for these trends. Usually what dominates the market and becomes an industry standard is dictated by factors other than technical superiority. Often marketing and chip support, (integrated circuit chips provided by third party vendors for supporting the hardware design) become more important factors in influencing the popularity of a standard.

Since there are no firm standards available at this moment (and none are likely to emerge in the near future) this chapter is intended to introduce these new trends and main contenders contributing to the area.

These new trends in the data acquisition and process control field are

- Networked data acquisition
- Fieldbus

In the coming sections each one of these trends are explained in detail.

10.1 DATA ACQUISITION OVER A LOCAL AREA NETWORK*

As discussed in the previous chapters in detail, data acquisition is one of the major application areas of personal computers. Another popular area of personal computer usage is in local area networks. According to statistics, the number of networked personal computers is steadily increasing. Currently it is estimated that nearly 75% of the personal computers being used in the corporate environment are networked. This ratio is expected to increase even further in the near future.

These two trends are merging and the combination is promising synergetic solutions even to very difficult applications. Combining PC based data acquisition and local area network (LAN) communication technology brings about revolutionary new concepts at a very affordable cost (Figure 10.1).

Readers who would like to learn more about local area networks are recommended to read *Guide to Connectivity* by F. J. Derfler published by Ziff-Davis Press, 1995.

PC based data acquisition, as discussed in the previous chapters, has become a viable solution for problems previously tackled with special computers or dedicated equipment. The PC offers an attractive combination of upgradable processing power, flexible user interface, inexpensive storage, inexpensive application software, and wide availability. Because of this, PC's have become very popular for data acquisition system. Instrument vendors have complemented this development by introducing PC based data acquisition hardware which contributed to the popularity of PC's even further. Many vendors offer a variety of hardware and software products that allow PC's to do a wide range of data acquisition operations.

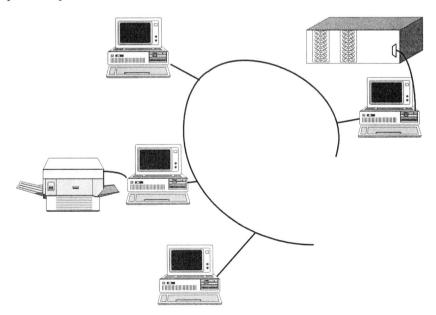

Figure 10.1 Networked data acquisition allows all PC's in the system to use the system resources.

* Adapted from Ref. 1.

LAN technology, on the other hand, has initially started for the purpose of mainframe communication and quickly became the universal technique for communication among computers of all types. There are many vendors of PC LAN hardware and software. This has caused the cost of this technology to decline to the point where it became feasible for the motherboard manufacturers to place the LAN hardware directly on the motherboard of the computer.

In reality LAN technology is not new to the process control field. Local area networks have been used by supervisory control and data acquisition (SCADA) systems for process control purposes for quite some time. But other than that, LAN has not been popular in general purpose data acquisition and logging systems.

10.1.1 An Overview of Current Local Area Network Communication Technology

A local area computer network consists of hardware (wiring, interface cards, repeaters, bridges, routers, etc.) and a software portion (drivers, protocol stacks, network operating systems, and utilities). LANs usually operate within a limited geographical area like a building or campus, as opposed to wide area networks (WANs) which can have much larger coverage. A modern LAN is usually no longer than several kilometers with data rates up to 100 million bits per second. Contrary to WAN networks, which are leased, LAN connections are usually owned by the user. A typical LAN contains a cable system (which is sometimes called a trunk) and nodes. A LAN can be characterized by

- Topology (star, ring, bus)
- Transmission medium (twisted pair wire, coaxial, fiber optic cable)
- Network access method (FDM, TDM, token)
- Transmission technology (carrierband, broadband)

Currently there are literally hundreds of network hardware and software vendors. Even though there were many hardware standards available in the beginning, due to standardization efforts, only a few popular methods have emerged that are currently in use by most PC network installations. In the following sections we will concentrate on systems which emerged as popular, industry standard LAN schemes.

10.1.2 Network Wiring Schemes

Most PC LANs in use today use one the four types of wiring schemes listed below. It is possible that a LAN uses more than one wiring scheme in an installation.

- Thick coaxial cable (Thicknet or 10Base5) typically is used for the backbone of a LAN that covers an entire building. A single segment of this type of wire can extend to a distance of up to 500 meters. Connecting a network node to a Thicknet cable requires active transceivers.

- Optical fiber can carry high speed communication and it is typically used as backbone in a LAN installation. Due to inherent noise immunity and ground isolation properties of fiber optic cable, it is often used to connect two buildings to each other. Fiber optic cable, however, is much more difficult to terminate and tap than other types of cables. It requires a repeater at each tap and expensive interface electronics and optics. On the other hand, one can use fiber optic cable over long distances, at extremely high speeds and in environments that are electromagnetically noisy which may be hostile to electronic signals on a wire.

- Thin coaxial cable (Thinnet, Cheapernet, or 10Base2) is used for covering smaller distances than thick coaxial cable. Typically distances are limited to less than 200 meters per segment. This method is used to connect together a small group of network nodes. Connection between groups of nodes is typically done by attaching the thin coax to a thick coax or optical fiber backbone via a repeater, bridge, or router device.

- Twisted pair wiring (UTP or 10BaseT) is used for connecting a single network node to a hub device. In this case the distance is limited to maximum of 100 meters. UTP wiring is a popular way of connecting nodes to a network.

PC network interface cards come with suitable connectors for attaching to one or more of the four wiring schemes mentioned above. Connection to thick coaxial wiring is done by attaching an external transceiver device to the interface card via a 15 pin AUI connector. Fiber optic cable can be connected directly to a fiber-ready interface card, or a wire to fiber optic converter which converts optical signals to electrical signals can be used. Thin coaxial and twisted pair wiring is attached directly to the PC interface card. The lowest cost interface cards have only twisted pair wiring connections. RJ11 type connectors popular with phone cable connections are also being used as alternate connectors for twisted pair wires.

10.1.3 Ethernet vs. Token Networks

There has been many networking schemes tried in the past. Out of the many communication methods used, Ethernet and Token Ring Networks have emerged as the two favorite PC LAN methods. Among the two, Ethernet is the more popular technique with the lower cost. Token Ring Networks, on the other hand, due to their reliability and repeatable timing characteristics which some system designers find valuable, are still going strong despite the cost disadvantage.

Ethernet is a bus scheme, where every node in the network is attached to every other node over a single wire. The method is indicated in Figure 10.2.

In an Ethernet connection the rules of transmission are as follows:

- Each node has similar priority when it comes to transmission
- Every node is allowed to transmit whenever it senses that the bus is idle
- Every node receives every transmitted message

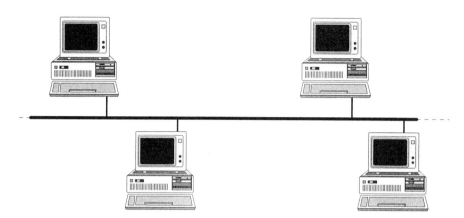

Figure 10.2 Ethernet bus arrangement.

Since every node has similar priority and each one has the freedom to transmit whenever it finds the line idle, it leads to the possibility of two or more nodes starting a transmission at about the same time (called a collision). When a Ethernet transmitter detects a collision it abandons its transmission, waits for a statistically determined brief interval, and tries again. This scheme is called CSMA/CD (Carrier Sense Multiple Access with Collision Detection). Ethernet is standardized by IEEE Standard 802.3 (ISO 8802-3).

The main disadvantage of Ethernet is due to its undeterministic nature. Since it is not a deterministic protocol, the time for a data packet to get from the transmitter node to a receiver node cannot be determined absolutely. The time depends on network loading and the number of transmit collisions that are taking place. As a result, some experts argue that Ethernet should not be used for time critical messages such as safety alarms and real-time machine control information. On the other hand some Ethernet proponents argue that this limitation in practice does not cause any problem since 95 % of messages go through without any collision. Some vendors use an alternate Ethernet connection to get time critical information to the destination node.

Ethernet is a very popular method. Due to its huge popularity it has good chip support from industry. There are many integrated circuit chip manufacturers which manufacture Ethernet chips, making hardware design of Ethernet very simple, which, in turn reduces the cost of Ethernet connection.

Token network is another popular scheme of networking. In a Token Ring Network (IEEE 802.5, ISO 8802-5), each node is attached to only two other nodes, as shown in Figure 10.3.

In a Token Ring Network transmitted packets travel from node to node around the ring. Each node in the ring receives the packets transmitted by two neighboring nodes, recognizes those that are addressed to itself, and repeats only those packets addressed to other nodes. Only the node holding the "token" is allowed to originate a transmission.

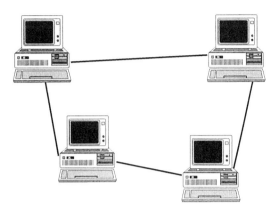

Figure 10.3 Token ring connection scheme.

The token is a software flag that's passed around the network to allow each node an equal opportunity to initiate transmissions. Packets may travel in either direction around the ring, allowing operation of the network even if the ring is broken at some point.

Token network can be either in ring form or in bus form. A Token bus (IEEE 802.4) has the same bus arrangement as an Ethernet, but uses the token passing scheme to control transmission permission.

Since, in a token network, each node gets an equal opportunity to transmit, and no collisions are possible, the amount of time needed to complete the transmission of a packet can be determined absolutely. This deterministic nature of Token Ring makes it popular in situations where time-critical messages must be sent over the network.

The main disadvantage of Token Networks is the higher cost of wiring and interfaces relative to Ethernet hardware. Token network interface cards are more expensive than Ethernet cards because of the increased logic required to perform token passing, and because they are made in lower quantities than Ethernet cards. It does not have as much chip support as Ethernet from integrated circuit manufacturers.

10.1.4 LAN Software

The software portion of a network is above the connections scheme and performs about the same functions regardless of wiring and interface scheme used. The interface card hardware isolates the network software from most of the details of the wiring scheme.

Network software is described by ISO as a series of layers. These layers start from the driver software which communicate with the interface card, and finish at the highest level that interfaces directly with the user (application software). The structures and the duty of these layers are very well defined.

Driver software which resides at the lowest level handles the hardware interfaces of the network card and presents a set of common functions to the higher layer. Currently there are three defacto standard interfaces between the driver layer and the next layer in the rank. These standards are as follows:

- Packet driver interface (oldest standard by FTP corporation)
- NDIS interface (developed jointly by IBM and Microsoft for LAN Manager network operating system)
- ODI interface (developed by Nowell for NetWare network operating system)

At the lowest level, the driver software handles the various hardware interfaces and presents a set of common functions to the higher level software. There are three somewhat standard interfaces between the driver and the next software level. These are the packet driver interface, the NDIS interface, and the ODI interface. The packet driver interface was developed by the FTP Corporation and is the oldest de facto standard. NDIS was developed mainly by IBM and Microsoft for the LAN Manager network operating system and is slowly spreading into more general use. ODI was developed by Novell for use with the Netware network operating system and is also spreading into general use. Most of the popular network operating systems allow you to use one or more of these defacto standard driver interfaces and most network interface hardware vendors supply packet, ODI, and NDIS drivers with their products.

Functions provided by the driver layer are used by the software layers above. The middle portion of the software layer which is called "Protocol Stack" uses the driver functions for orderly exchange of information between network nodes. There are currently three defacto, popular protocol standards used in protocol stacks. These protocols are TCP/IP, IPX/SPX, and NetBeui.

- The TCP/IP protocol is a popular protocol currently in use by the worldwide Internet. This is a very capable protocol that was developed through government funding, as a result it is public domain and it can be used without royalties or fees.
- The IPX/SPX protocol is developed by the Novell corporation. It is currently being used by NetWare family of network operating systems. This is a proprietary protocol which can only be used by purchasing or licensing from Novell corporation.
- NetBeui is a protocol currently being used in Microsoft LANManager and Windows for Workgroups network operating systems. This is also a proprietary protocol and must be purchased or licensed from IBM or Microsoft.

Top layers of the OSI are the network operating and utility software which provides services like network file system, printer sharing, remote session, mail services, configuration management, information archiving, and diagnostic services.

10.1.5   Client/Server vs. Peer to Peer Networks

Peer to peer networks are characterized by the ability of nodes to share resources of other nodes. All nodes of the network run the same operating system, and every node is allowed to communicate with each other.

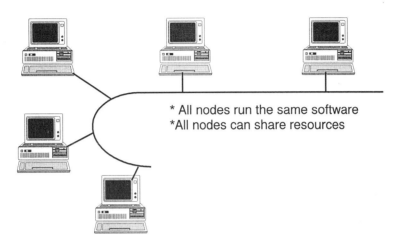

* All nodes run the same software
*All nodes can share resources

Figure 10.4 Peer to peer network

In a client/server network, one or more computers are designated as server nodes. Only servers are allowed to share their resources with other nodes on the network. This is quite different from the peer to peer network where everybody is allowed to share everybody else's resources. In the case of a client/server network, clients and servers run different software. Servers run a capable version of the network operating system whereas clients run a less capable version of the network operating system. Client nodes may use the resources (file system, printers, etc.) of one or more server, but may not use the resources of other clients directly. (Figure 10.5).

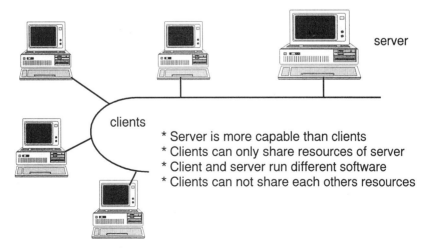

server

clients

* Server is more capable than clients
* Clients can only share resources of server
* Client and server run different software
* Clients can not share each others resources

Figure 10.5 Client/server network.

Client/server networks are the most popular network organization for PC LANs. Specific computers on the network are dedicated to the server tasks and run highly capable (and expensive) server software packages. Clients run relatively simple client software packages. Network software packages like Novell NetWare, Microsoft/IBM LANManager, and Banyan Vines are examples of client/server network softwares.

Peer networks are popular in small, workgroup oriented networks where the network security is not critical. Each node in a peer network runs a software package that is more elaborate than client software packages but less capable than server packages. Lantastic, Novell NetWare Light, and Microsoft Windows for Workgroups are examples of peer networks.

10.1.6 Mixing Data Acquisition and Network Hardware/Software

PC motherboard architecture, except for the processors, are very much similar to the way it was first designed in 1982. Keeping the motherboard design unchanged was partly necessary to keep the compatibility between the old generation PC's and new generation PC's which was one of the reasons for the spectacular success of IBM PC compatibles. But as far as the I/O map of the PC is concerned, the design of the PC is quite inadequate with only 16 levels of interrupts and 1024 I/O locations. Due to the limited I/O locations, inevitably there will be an IRQ, port address, high memory, or DMA channel overlap due to the added cards inside the PC. Because of this, most modern network and data acquisition cards are completely software programmable via vendor supplied utility software packages.

Using external data acquisition hardware will alleviate this problem of hardware interactions, but the possibility of software conflict is still possible. Software conflicts can be very subtle and may even appear like hardware problems. Microsoft regularly publishes data on software conflicts with popular software packages and suggests remedies. Problems related to video driver conflicts are sspecially often confused with hardware problems.

A more direct interaction between data acquisition and network software is in low memory usage. Most network software is loaded in the low memory space (addresses below 1 Meg.). Most DOS based data acquisition programs also require large memory space. This often causes insufficient memory problems. Fortunately new operating systems like Windows, Windows NT and OS/2 relieve insufficient memory problems and provide firm operating system ground for data acquisition packages.

10.1.7 Data Acquisition in a Client/Server Network

Although having both network and data acquisition capability causes conflicts and problems, the benefits of the arrangement outweigh the problem considerably. One immediate advantage is having almost unlimited file storage space on a large file server. Disk space on a server is relatively inexpensive, since it is shared by all the client computers. Well designed LANs offer server file system access speeds that rival or even exceed local disk speeds.

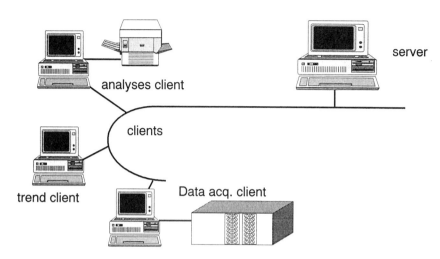

Figure 10.6 Typical data acquisition in a client/server environment.

Another advantage of the networking is the availability of the data to all nodes of the network. Once the data is available on the server it can be shared immediately with all other nodes on the LAN.

Client/server networks offer other advantages like simultaneous data acquisition and analysis. One PC may be performing data acquisition and sending the data to the server whereas another may be doing data processing which is just written to the server and yet another one may be doing trend analyses. Each one of these PC's can work on different tasks without degrading performance of each other or the performance of the network. (Figure 10.6)

10.1.8 Data Acquisition in a Peer Network

Peer to peer networks are characterized by the ability of each node to communicate directly with every other node. This feature can be very useful in data acquisition applications. A popular peer to peer network, Windows for Workgroups has a utility called "Net DDE" which takes advantage of this capability. Net DDE is an extension of the Windows Digital Data Exchange (DDE) technique that allows data transfer between applications running on different PCs.

In a stand alone PC one can utilize DDE for transferring data from one application to another. In a network environment Net DDE can be used for transferring data directly from a data acquisition program running on one PC to an application software package running on another machine. There are many analysis, presentation, and data base programs that support Net DDE, including Lotus 123, Excel, Microsoft ACCESS, Intouch WonderWare, etc. (Figure 10.7).

Since peer to peer networks allow direct communication between nodes, they can be used for sending data in files from one PC to another. Because small peer networks are simpler than client/server networks to set up and operate, they are recommended for small to medium size data acquisition networks involving few computers.

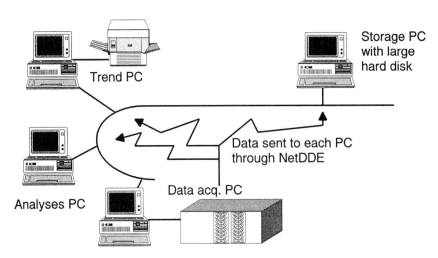

Figure 10.7 Data acquisition in a peer to peer network through NetDDE.

In a small data acquisition system where there are only a few computers, it is simpler and less costly to use a peer network and treat one of the peer nodes as a server. The "server" node in a peer network should have a large, fast disk drive and good quality printer. The data acquisition PC can send the data to the server and all the computers in the system can have access to a good quality printer at the same time.

10.1.9 Direct Network Communication with the Data Acquisition Instrument

Due to the developments in the integrated circuit field, Ethernet support chips and powerful embedded microcontrollers became available at a very reasonable cost. Large capacity RAM and EEPROMs are available as on board storage elements. Putting all these technologies together it is possible to put network capability directly on the data acquisition equipment. This way data acquisition equipment becomes a node in the system rather than the PC that it is connected to. The associated network interface software is available from the embeddable operating systems vendors. One such operating system called QNX provides the ability to be ported into different hardware platforms.

Fluke corporation has data acquisition equipment with networking ability built in. The primary host computer interface of the new NetDAQ data acquisition system from the Fluke Corporation is Ethernet. This allows data recording, processing, and analysis to be done in the most convenient place, no matter where the instrument is placed. It also minimizes sensor to instrument wiring, which is a major cost in any data acquisition installation. More and more manufacturing areas are being wired for network communication because of the use of desktop computers for production scheduling, supervisory control, and data gathering for SPC. Once an area has network wiring installed, it is inexpensive and convenient to add a network capable data acquisition instrument (Figure 10.8).

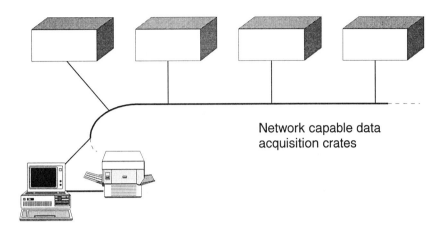

Figure 10.8 Data acquisition with network capable crates.

The major drawback of RS-232 and RS-485 serial interfaces for data acquisition is speed. Unless an expensive, special purpose interface card is added to the PC, the serial interface cannot be operated above about 38.4K baud without shutting down everything else the PC is doing. On Ethernet, data throughput rates of greater than 100,000 bytes per second are normal on inexpensive interface hardware. These kinds of rates are only challenged by IEEE-488 (expensive interfaces and inconvenient wiring) and parallel port methods (short range, inconvenient wiring).

Another benefit of network methods is the ease of switching access to the instrument between host computers. On a network, if one host is done using the instrument, another can start using it immediately without any communication cable rewiring. The only real drawback to network methods is the slight increase in complexity of installing and configuring a PC network interface. This is being addressed by the network hardware vendors who are including very intelligent setup software with their products. You can also use a parallel to LAN adapter (PLA) that simply plugs into the PC's parallel port and requires very little setup. PCMCIA LAN adapters for portable computers are also starting to become available.

10.2 CONVERTING A NETWORKED PC TO A PROCESS CONTROL WORKSTATION

In the previous section it was mentioned that networking was not new to distributed control system (DCS) environment. Proprietary DCS systems have been using Ethernet or Token Ring networks for quite some time. These systems use special (and highly priced) process control workstations for displaying information about the process.

Another utilization area for PC is in the replacement of these process control workstations. A PC with networking cards inside can work as a process control workstation.

Actually it can do the job better than proprietary terminals because of its intelligence and third party software products that it can run.

10.2.1 What Is Needed in an Engineering Workstation?*

A process control workstation needs to have several parts which are listed below.

- The process window
- The configuration window
- The maintenance window
- The historical data/analyses window

Normally a typical DCS control room has a terminal dedicated for each one of these windows.

THE PROCESS WINDOW

The process window shows the process going on inside the whole plant in an animated form. All critical parameters, tank levels, process temperatures sensor outputs are displayed on the screen in an easily understandable format. Usually process windows contain a graphical schematic of the plant and the associated parameters in an animated graphical form.

The idea behind displaying information in a graphical form is not for cosmetic reasons but rather to enable the process engineer to interpret the situation of the plant quickly in one glance. For this reason, the process window shows the most critical information preferably in animated form to enable quick interpretation.

In order to display the process information on the PC, either the data should be available on the network in a known format, e.g., like X windows using MOTIF, or the data should be accessed from a known database. There are third party software packages available form different vendors for converting proprietary DCS process window information into known formats. Having data available in proprietary format makes the conversion process difficult.

THE CONFIGURATION WINDOW

The configuration window enables the process control engineer to modify the graphical display of the process window and set up hardware in the field. The communication parameters, device types, device outputs are all handled and configured through the configuration window.

*Adapted from Ref. 2.

THE MAINTENANCE WINDOW

The maintenance window displays an up-to-date maintenance record of all devices in the plant. This window enables the process engineer to view the current state of the devices, whether they require scheduled maintenance, calibration, etc.

THE HISTORICAL DATA/ANALYSES WINDOW

This window displays a historical record of the processes and indicates trend information. The trend data are very valuable for peeking into the overall performance of the plant. As an example, trend data at some point may indicate that efficiency of a certain process is decreasing over the time. By viewing these data the process engineer may decide that it is time for the routine scheduled maintenance for a reactor or to change a sensor.

PITFALLS TO AVOID

When setting up a PC for such a task, there are several key points with which one must be careful.

- The network card and the video card should be set up in such a way that they should not conflict with each other and the memory used by them should be excluded from general use by the memory manager.
- Video resolution of the PC should be increased to 1024 X 768 with 256 colors to display the needed information with sufficient resolution on the screen.
- A graphical interface like Windows or OS/2 should be selected as the operating system.

10.2.2 Case Study of a PC Based Workstation Setup

A process control plant with DCS system installed has dedicated terminals for process window, configuration window, analyses window and maintenance window. Although the data were accessible through the control room, the management is interested in having a portable notebook type computer set up as a workstation which can be carried around the plant and can be hooked up to the network at any point desired. The notebook PC has Windows software and a network card installed. It is desired that the same PC is used for displaying configuration, maintenance, process and historical windows.

The plant in question has DECNET installed with MOTIF as the graphical standard. Process and configuration windows are displayed in the control room terminals using the MOTIF graphical standard. Maintenance information is kept on a Novell® file server and the historical data are stored in Sybase® data base and a proprietary flat database.

To make the PC compliant with MOTIF, an X emulation software from Hummingbird's eXceed® for Windows is used. The package allows use of TCP/IP.

Historical data stored in Sybase are accessed through a software package called Q&E which comes with Excel 4.0. Since Excel runs on Windows it is possible to display all necessary information in Sybase on Excel. Information in the flat database is accessed through a third party software called @Glance®. Through this package, information in the flat proprietary database is transferred to Excel.

With these additions, a normal PC attains the ability to display information once displayed only in DCS terminals.

10.3 FIELDBUS

Fieldbus is a new standard which has started a revolutionary new era in process control. With this standard, traditional analog control methods are being replaced with digital techniques which in turn use PCs as the controller. Our interest in Fieldbus, as far as this book is concerned, is due to the fact that since Fieldbus is inherently digital, a computer is needed as a controller. Due to the processing power and network capabilities, a PC is an ideal choice for a Fieldbus controller. The proliferation of the Fieldbus standards in the process industry will cause the popularity of PC control to increase even further.

The benefits provided to the end user by the Fieldbus standard is enormous. For this reason, there is a great tendency for the process industry and process instrument manufacturers to go into this field. Due to the confusion caused by the incomplete state of the standard, many manufacturers came up with their interpretation of the Fieldbus. Although there is effort on the manufacturer's side to come up with a unified standard, it seems that producing a final version of the standard will take some time. In the following sections, Fieldbus standard, as interpreted by one of the leading manufacturers of Fieldbus products, Smar International, will be looked at in detail. The coming sections are reproduced in part from Smar International's *Fieldbus: Smar Tutorials* with their permission.

10.3.1 What Is Fieldbus?

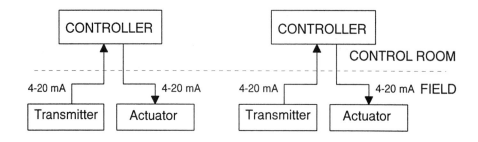

Figure 10.9 With analog signals each individual variable has a physical 4-20 mA connection.

Most processes require getting data from field instruments and sending actions to field actuators. So far industry has been using a 4-20 mA standard for controlling devices in the field. In this standard, which dates back quite some time, a current loop reaches the device in the field. Either, the current is initiated in the control room and the device interprets the current level into physical action (as in the case of an actuator), or the device in the field initiates the current and the equipment in the control room interprets the current level as data (Figure 10.9).

Fieldbus is a communication method which is set out to replace the 4-20 mA method of control. But it is not merely a digital replacement for the 4-20 mA signals. That is only a fraction of the beauty of Fieldbus, since it brings so much more capability to field devices.

10.3.2 The Reason for Fieldbus

Fieldbus is characterized by four criteria:

- Complete digital replacement of 4-20 mA
- Control, alarm, trend and other functions distributed to devices in the field
- Interoperable multivendor
- Open system; specification available without licensing agreement

Fieldbus is a complete system, with the control function distributed to equipment in the field, while still allowing operation and tuning from the control room using the digital communication. It replaces the traditional 4-20 mA (Figure 10.10) and the classic distributed control system (DCS) where the control function was centralized to one or more "control cards" (Figure 10.11).

Some manufacturers argue that their DCS has had Fieldbus for many years, but none of them meet the four criteria above.

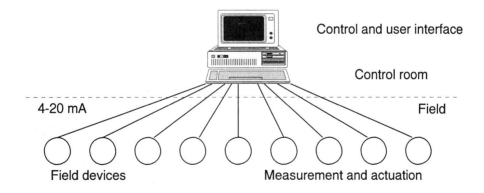

Figure 10.10 Direct digital control (DDC) system The first computerized system where control is centralized to a single computer in the control room.

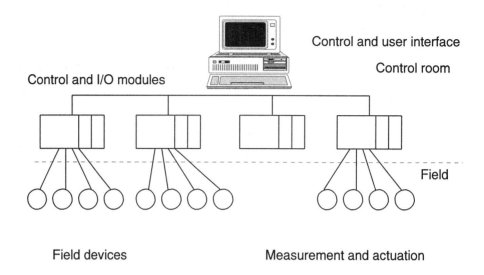

Figure 10.11 Distributed control system (DCS), with control partially distributed to a few control cards, still in the control room, each having several loops.

Fieldbus is an interoperable multivendor protocol, which started as standardization work by ISA, the Instrumentation Society of America, just like the 4-20 mA standard. Fieldbus is expected to get worldwide recognition. All major instrument manufacturers have pledged their commitment to a single Fieldbus standard. The approach was to establish the standard before commercial products were in place, as with most standards, it looks as if that will not be the case.

Some advantages of bi-directional digital communications over 4-20 mA and other good features are known from existing smart transmitter protocols. They are as follows:

- Higher accuracy and data reliability
- Multivariable access
- Remote configuration and diagnostics
- Reduction of wiring
- Use of existing analog wiring

Higher accuracy can be attributed to digital communication, since the microprocessors in, e.g., a transmitter and a controller may talk directly, rather than going through D/A and A/D conversions as in the case of 4-20 mA, of which there may be many in a closed loop. Status is passed along with measurement and control data. It is therefore possible to determine if the information is reliable or not. All data are checked and guaranteed free from distortion due to noise or an impedance mismatch that may affect analog undetected signals. Multivariable access means that more than one piece of information can be collected from a field device, e.g., a pressure transmitter is not limited to a single output for pressure, but also informs process temperature. Another example is access to set point and manipulated variable of a controller in the same device, or multiple channel inputs for a temperature transmitter.

The digital communication allows the complete configuration to be changed remotely. Calibration can be done in operation without having to apply any input or measure the output. Similarly, the status of the self diagnostics may be interrogated.

Reduction in wiring and simplification is achieved through connection of several devices on a single pair of wires, which is called multi dropping. Connection is a simple task, since everything is in parallel and terminal number matching is at a minimum. This means low cost and easy replacement of old transmitters (Figure 10.12).

There has been some attempts in the past by various manufacturers to integrate digital and analog communication on the field instruments. These devices, commonly called "smart transmitters" suffered from some problems. Some problems and disadvantages of these protocols, in comparison to 4-20 mA technology, have been

- Communication speed too slow for closed loop control

- Poor or no interoperability between devices of different type and manufacturer

- Devices must be polled for status

- No interdevice communication

The slowest option for Fieldbus is 25 times faster, and far more efficient, than the most common smart transmitter protocol, ensuring tight closed loop control. The low speed version of Fieldbus was designed to use the same type of wiring as analog and smart transmitters, being able to easily replace them. However, it should be noted that in order to use the multidrop feature, transmitters must be connected in parallel.

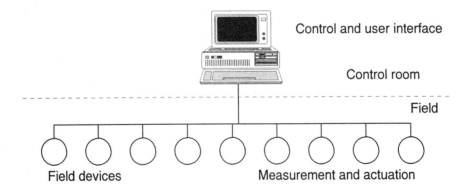

Figure 10.12 Fieldbus system where all devices connected to a single communication line.

Control totally distributed to individual devices in the field.

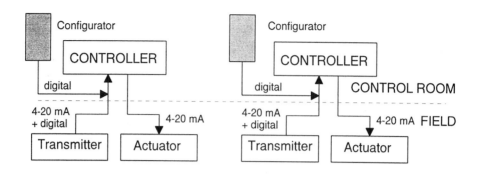

Figure 10.13 With intelligent hybrids of analog and digital signal, individual variables involved in closed loop control have a physical 4-20 mA connection. Superimposed on it is a digital signal for configuration and diagnostics.

Many smart transmitter protocols are proprietary and unique to a single manufacturer. For the user this lack of standard means being locked to a single manufacturer. If that manufacturer cannot provide an urgent replacement, or does not have a particular type of transmitter, the user's only option is to return to 4-20 mA. The user depends on a single vendor that may not provide the latest technology and features.

The ideal opposite to a proprietary system is an 'open' system. Open systems are based on off-the-shelf standards enabling multiple vendors to provide interoperable hardware and software.

The ability of 4-20 mA devices to replace any other device of the same type is called interoperability roughly meaning compatibility. Fieldbus offers the same capability. A brand Y transmitter can be replaced by a brand X transmitter of the same type at any time, without loss of functionality, and can interface to another brand Z device. Fieldbus forces interoperability between the devices, which are complying with this standard, and it is also available to all manufacturers and users without licensing agreements. It is open; it is fully disclosed; there are no secrets. The user or a third party can make their own configurations and software.

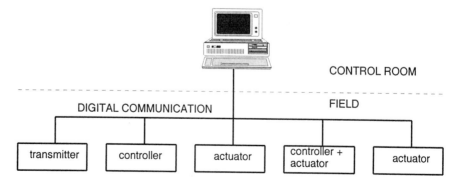

Figure 10.14 With Fieldbus pure digital communication; a single physical wire is the medium for multiple variables having logical connections.

Users may now select a device based on price, performance, quality and delivery time. They may mix and match the best of each type, just as they could with the 4-20 mA. They do not have to choose a device manufactured by a certain company just to match other devices of the same brand already installed. (Without Fieldbus, users would have been forced to develop special communication drivers in this case.) Another benefit of interoperability is that system software does not have to be upgraded when new products are introduced.

The lack of a standard means that smart features of existing intelligent field devices are largely unused. Communication is only used for calibration. For example, there are very few existing systems that have managed to make use of the multidrop capability of existing smart transmitters. Though smart devices have self-diagnostics, status is only informed when a device is polled. This is rare in most applications since communication is normally done only at calibration. One must suspect and query for a failure before one finds out about it.

The Fieldbus advantages for users are so apparent that if they were the ones to decide, Fieldbus would probably have already been chosen as the international standard. End users have had very little information and opportunity to affect the development of the standard. It appears that they are facing the problem of having to choose between one technology made available by a group of manufacturers, or another, as it emerges. Such a situation is very similar to the decision users were forced to make some years ago about which video recording technology they would buy for their homes. The users fear is to choose the "wrong" protocol in the same fashion some chose the "wrong" video technology.

Many manufacturers, on their end, also want Fieldbus to be ready. The manufacturers that really can benefit from Fieldbus are those that do not have complete control system packages, but only a good transmitter or a good valve. They do not have to venture into system design, developing a complete DCS. Field device manufacturers are relieved from man-machine interfaces such as configuration and supervisory softwares. These can be written by software companies that are specialists on that field. The later are also relieved from the neverending development of communication drivers for every new protocol they come across. Manufacturers want Fieldbus ready because they know that many users hold back purchase of new systems awaiting Fieldbus, in fear of buying the "wrong" system.

HART^{TM} is a smart transmitter protocol that has reached almost worldwide acceptance, and is strengthening its position each year that Fieldbus is delayed. Though it meets the requirement of intrinsic safety and reaches a fair amount of interoperability (more than most believe), its speed is a major limitation. PROFIBUS and FIP are other standardized open and fast protocols, but they are not intrinsically safe and the bus cannot provide power for the devices, thereby requiring four wires.

10.3.3 Turning to Fieldbus

The impact on the user, when turning to Fieldbus will be great. The main points of benefit are

- Even higher reliability operation
- Virtually unlimited flexibility

- Reduction in equipment cost

- Reduction in installation cost

- Mass of information

The simplicity of analog technology makes it easy to be understood. That is the main reason people feel so comfortable with it. 4-20 mA devices may be operated using only a screwdriver and tested with the most basic current meter. Almost anybody could configure and troubleshoot such devices.

Field devices may report failures and problems immediately, enabling maintenance personnel to pinpoint errors instantly or even before they can cause any harm. The multivariable capability of Fieldbus allows control, totalization and other signal processing in the field. Therefore, a separate controller or other signal conditioning equipment is not necessary. The host may be a simple off-the-shelf PC with man-machine interface (MMI) software. Multidropping of several devices on a single wire may drastically reduce the amount of needed cable. In many factories, a device can be a kilometer or even further away from the control room. Since every loop needs at least two pairs of wires (one for the transmitter, the other for the actuator) a refinery can have several hundreds of such loops. In all, the cabling saving for a medium or large factory is immense. Transmitters and actuators are often located next to each other, but far from the operator console, an ideal situation for multidropping. Though prices of Fieldbus devices may initially be high, the reduction in number of devices and wiring, with associated cable trays and marshaling boxes, will yield a less expensive system. Manufacturers can no longer rely on proprietary technology to keep prices high. Fieldbus will bring open competition, which will eventually reduce prices.

The multivariable access will virtually flood the control room with information. Classic recorders will not be able to handle the job. Paperless recorders and computer storage will take over. Such information may be used for statistical process control and other process management.

Fieldbus has, on top of this, software function blocks which replace many functions today performed by hardware. This provides tremendous flexibility since the control strategy may be edited without having to rewire or change any hardware. Once physically connected, logical connections between function blocks may be changed, and function blocks can be added and removed. More advanced devices may execute a virtually unlimited number of function blocks. If a system has to be expanded or improved, the need for additional hardware is minimized, just by letting existing devices execute more blocks.

10.3.4 Fieldbus Requirements

The main requirements for Fieldbus were to overcome the problems of smart transmitter protocols while maintaining the advantages of 4-20 mA standards (the main advantage of 4-20 mA is tight closed loop control).

By providing various options for communication speed and device powering, the requirements for both intrinsic safety and minimum communication delay can be met. (**intrinsic safety** is a design methodology for a circuit or an assembly of circuits in which any spark or thermal effect produced under normal operating and specified fault conditions are not capable under prescribed test conditions of causing ignition of a given explosive atmosphere). By optimization of network use, tight closed loop control can also be achieved where intrinsic safety is required.

With 4-20 mA technology it is possible to build a control loop containing only a transmitter, a controller and an actuator. Fieldbus devices must also be capable of doing so, as well as acting in a larger control system. Fieldbus must be multipurpose and as versatile as 4-20 mA. Fieldbus devices must therefore be able to operate by themselves with a simple user interface in order to be economical in small systems. The cost of a host computer with dedicated software, and certainly a DCS, cannot be justified for a small system, even though costs are going down. There would also be a logistics problem for both users and manufacturers if they were forced to keep using analog technology in small systems.

The possible complexity of a system where so many devices can be connected together (and where each device can perform the function of several conventional devices) requires a friendly user interface. The user must be freed from manual address assignment, as seen in smart transmitter protocols, and the painstaking job of tracking bits, bytes, words and memory addresses, as it is done in PLCs.

The function block model is the choice of all Fieldbus proposals. The user can easily relate to it since the device is now represented by blocks, just like blocks in ISA and SAMA control diagrams. Physical wiring will now be logical connections or soft wiring links between blocks. Though technically different, it appears very familiar, and users shall feel comfortable with it. Device address and parameter indexes are automatically assigned. Some systems, including Smar's CD600 controller, already implement a similar philosophy.

Standardization ensures interoperability, but if it is too rigid it may have adverse effects for the user. There must be room for manufacturer differentiation. If the standard forces compliance to every conceivable detail, the user would actually have nothing to choose from, because the devices from all manufactures would be exactly alike. If one manufacturer came up with a great idea, they would not be able to implement it without being forced to go through a process to have it included in the standard, whereby their competitors would learn about it.

Fieldbus specifies the basic functionality requirements, but must allow a manufacturer to add unique features to their device. These features benefit the user, and the manufacturer may use them as marketing tools. Likewise, if newer models are different from their predecessors, devices communicating with it must know that. In short Fieldbus must not hinder development and improvement of products. Fieldbus provides a mechanism that ensures that interoperability is maintained for the manufacturer-specific features as well.

The cost of shutting down a system can be very high in terms of production loss. To be able to configure the system while in operation is therefore a requirement met by Fieldbus.

The need for implementation of Fieldbus in small as well as large systems was considered when developing the entire Smar 302 line of Fieldbus devices. They have the common features of being able to act as a master on the network and be locally configured using a magnetic tool, eliminating the need for a configurator or host in many basic applications.

10.4 HOW FIELDBUS WORKS

There are two major parts to the Fieldbus system architecture: interconnection and appli-cation. Interconnection refers to the passing of data from one device to another, may it be a field device, operator console or a configurator. This is the communication protocol part of Fieldbus. The application is the automation function the system performs. By standardizing part of the application, Fieldbus has gone further than any other communi-cation standard, ensuring interoperability between conforming products.

10.4.1 Overview

The Fieldbus application architecture supports distribution of automation tasks to the de-vices in the field which are interconnected by a network. The most basic functions per-formed by a device are modeled as blocks. The blocks cooperate and are interconnected with each other, supporting the propagation parameters between devices and the operator.

The Fieldbus interconnection architecture is based on a three layer subset of the ar-chitecture from the OSI (open systems interconnect) reference model developed by ISO (International Organization for Standardization). The OSI application and system man-agement, and likewise the Fieldbus application architecture, models are based on object oriented programming (OOP) concepts. Both OSI and OOP use models to simplify un-derstanding of functionality. Both are also briefly introduced here to achieve a better un-derstanding of Fieldbus.

10.4.2 OSI Model

The OSI reference model is an internationally recognized standard for network architec-ture on which open networks are based. The standard is developed as a model for tele-communications on all levels. All the functions (facilities such as addressing, error checking and encoding/decoding) of a network have been grouped into logical sets called layers, altogether seven. The layers are piled on top of each other and are together called the protocol stack. A layer only interfaces with layers immediately above and be-low in the stack. The stack interfaces upward to the application, and downward to the transmission media. The part of the whole application performed by the system that is performed in a device is called the "application process" (AP). The AP consists of two parts, one user portion, which is the functionality, and one communication portion. In Fieldbus the user portion is the actual device function, such as measurement or control (function blocks), or the user interface.

Each layer provides services for the layer above it, and communicates with the cor-responding layer in the stack of the other station, its peer (called "peer to peer commu-nication"). The set of facilities a layer provides to the above layer is called "services."

When transmitting data from one application to another, the data is passed from the top to the bottom of the stack, being processed by each layer obtaining the physical layer frame. The frame is passed over the media.

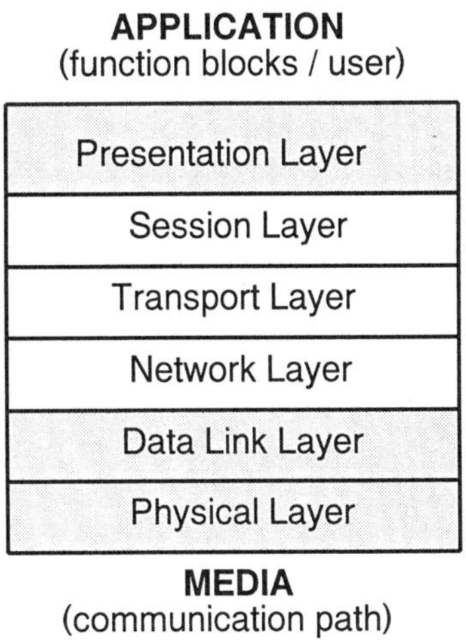

APPLICATION
(function blocks / user)

Presentation Layer
Session Layer
Transport Layer
Network Layer
Data Link Layer
Physical Layer

MEDIA
(communication path)

Figure 10.15 OSI protocol stack

On the other end, when receiving, the data are passed from the bottom to the top of the stack. The processing performed by the layers in the transmitting end is reversed by the respective layer on the receiving end, through which it obtains the original application data.

Layers 3 through 6 are not used because Fieldbus (and most other LANs) has no interconnection between networks, which is the purpose of these layers. This simplification makes Fieldbus faster and easier to implement in devices with limited processor power, such as field instruments.

The three remaining layers and functional and procedural characteristics are

1. Physical Layer (PhL): media independent activation, maintenance, and deactivation of physical links that transparently pass the bit stream for communication; it only recognizes individual bits, not characters or multicharacter frames. The standard defines types of media and signals, transmission speed and topology including number of nodes, and device power (only in Fieldbus).

2. Data Link Layer (DLL): transfers data between network entities: activation, maintenance and deactivation of data link connections, grouping of bits into characters and message frames, character and frame synchronization, error control, media access control and flow control (allowing several devices to share the network). The standard defines type of media access control, frame formats, error checking and station addressing. (Note: Addressing is actually part of the Network Layer, which is not defined in Fieldbus, where it instead is done in the Data Link Layer).

7. Application Layer (APP): gives access to a set of local and communication services for serving the distributed system interconnection between the APs and the user. Standard defines message formats and services available to the AP.

Some of the functionality of layers 3 through 6 are within the Fieldbus protocol, implemented in the application layer.

The OSI network management is an extension to the OSI layers, reaching over all the layers. System management monitors and controls operation of network resources. It is divided into system management functional areas. For Fieldbus, the most important functional area is network configuration. System management is accessed from one station to another. It is modeled as a managing system (playing the manager role), and a managed system (that plays the agent role), which has a management information base (MIB). MIB is the logical store for information and resources used to support network management

The end user is primarily concerned with the physical connection and the application. The physical layer, as previously mentioned, is already standardized and will not change. It will surely expand to include other media such as radio, but it will not change. Since all suggested Fieldbus protocols propose almost identical solutions for the user application, the Fieldbus is ready as far as the user is concerned. Users may now go ahead and learn the installation, application and operation aspects of Fieldbus without being afraid of having wasted their time. The uncertainty lies in the application and data link layers, and in the management functions. However, those are transparent to users, and only of concern to product developers.

OSI IN FIELDBUS

Only layers 1, 2 and 7 are used by Fieldbus, and the application is the functionality provided by the function blocks.

A Fieldbus device has three application processes (APs):

- Function block application
- Network management
- System management

10.4.3 Fieldbus Physical Layer

Closed loop control with performance like a 4-20 mA system and variable speed drives require high data transmission speed. Since higher speed means higher power consumption, this clashes with the need for intrinsic safety in some applications. Therefore one moderately high communication speed was selected, and other faster nonintrinsically safe options where also made available, catering to all applications. The system was designed to have a minimum of communication overhead to meet control requirements even with the low speed option.

There are several combinations for the physical layer, each with their relative merits. All devices on a bus must use the same options for media, connection and transmission rate. However, bus or nonbus powered devices may be mixed, as well as intrinsically safe or nonintrinsically safe ones.

Physical media options for Fieldbus are as follows:

- Wire
- Fiber optics (standard pending)
- Radio (standard pending)

Transmission rate options:

- 31.25 kbit/s
- 1 Mbit/s
- 2.5 Mbit/s

COMMON MEDIA CHARACTERISTICS

The data are interchanged as a synchronous serial half-duplex signal. A device transmits and receives on the same media, but not simultaneously. The signal is self-clocking, using Manchester (a.k.a. Biphase L) encoding. Since the transmission is synchronous, no start and stop bits are required. In Manchester coding, clock and data are combined so that a rising edge represents logic 0 (zero) data, and a falling edge represents logic 1 (one) data (Figure 10.16).

When transmitting, a preamble, equivalent to a telephone's 'ring' signal, is first transmitted to synchronize the receivers of other devices. The beginning and end of the message are indicated by start and end delimiters, respectively. The delimiters are not Manchester encoded, only data are, and can therefore be uniquely identified. The nonencoded bits in the delimiters are called N+ (non-data positive) and N- (non-data negative). The preamble and the delimiters added by the physical layer in the transmitting device are stripped off by the physical layer of the receiving device (Figure 10.17).

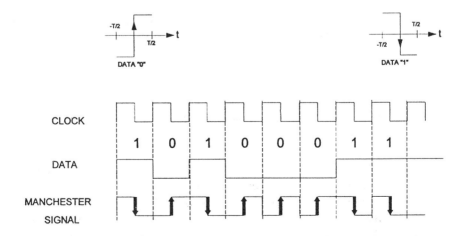

Figure 10.16 Manchester encoding.

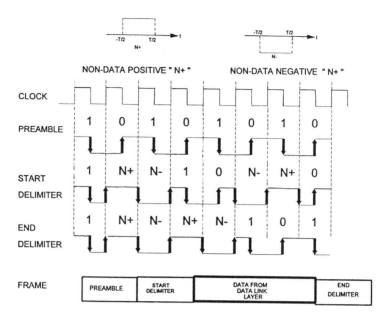

Figure 10.17 Fieldbus physical layer frame.

Redundancy may be achieved by duplication of physical layer and media. Voting (based on time-out and validity) controls which of the two media a device is using.

WIRE MEDIA CHARACTERISTICS

The wire media uses electrical signals on a normal twisted pair wire and has already been approved as an IEC/ISA standard since 1992.

The maximum distance allowed between two devices on wire media depends on the transmission rate selected.

- 31.25 kbit/s: 1,900 m
- 1 Mbit/s (voltage mode):   750 m
- 1 Mbit/s (current mode):   750 m
- 2 5 Mbit/s: 500 m

The device must isolate the communication hardware, media attachment unit (MAU), from ground to avoid electrical ground loops when devices are multidropped.

Bus topology (Figure 10.18), tree topology (Figure 10.19) and point-to-point topologies are supported. Tree topology is only supported by the low speed version. The bus has a trunk cable with two terminators. The devices are connected to the trunk via spurs. The spurs may be integrated in the device giving zero spur length. A spur may connect more than one device, depending on the length. Active couplers may be used to extend spur length. Active repeaters may be used to extend the trunk length.

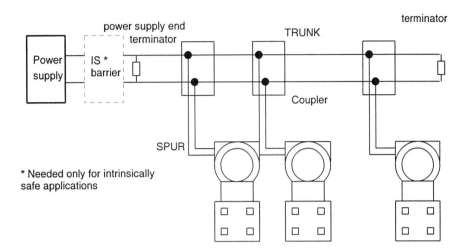

Figure 10.18 Bus topology.

The terminators are designed to have an impedance of 100 W each around the transmission frequency. A device transmits by modulating current in the network according to the Manchester encoded signal. Receiving devices sense the voltage drop generated over the two terminators as the current is modulated. The modulated current is 15 to 20 mA peak-to-peak for the low speed version, with a receiver sensitivity of 150 mV.

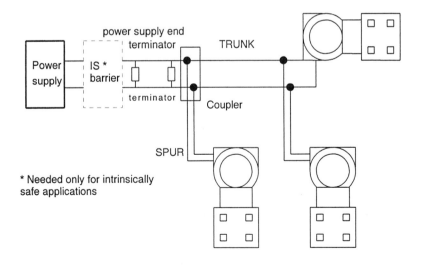

Figure 10.19 Tree topology.

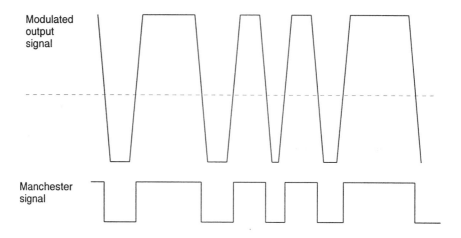

Figure 10.20 Wire media signal modulation.

10.4.4 31.25 kbit/s Wire Media Characteristics

The lowest speed wire media option, 31.25 kbit/s, is the most versatile and expected to be the most widely used type. It offers versions for intrinsic safety and device powering by bus. The number of devices is limited by this choice.

- Intrinsically safe / nonintrisically safe
- Bus powered / separately powered

The typical number of devices is indicated in the following table. The actual number varies from device type to device type.

Maximum Number of Network Nodes

	intrinsically safe	non intrinsically safe
bus powered	2-6*	2-12**
seperately powered		2-32*

* 1-4 in the hazardous area
** 1 at power supply end

In intrinsically safe systems, the safety barrier (IS) should be placed between the power supply and the power supply end terminator.

Devices may be powered by the bus, only requiring two wires for supply and communication. A single power supply, common to all devices, is connected to the network at either end of the trunk. The voltage may be in the range 9-32 VDC. The impedance of the power supply must be a minimum of 3 kW around the transmission frequency in order not to short circuit the communication signal. A Manchester coded signal has a duty cycle of exactly 50% and can be seen as an AC signal. The DC power consumption (power drain) of a device is therefore constant.

10.4.5 Fieldbus Data Link Layer FDL

The Fieldbus data link layer consists of two sublayers: the lower portion is the Fieldbus media access control (FMAC) and the upper portion is the Fieldbus data link control (FDLC). A device on the Fieldbus network is either one of two station types:

- Master station
- Slave station

A master station has the right to access the media (initiate communication). Slaves only have the right to respond to a request from a master.

10.4.6 Fieldbus Media Access Control

The Fieldbus medium access is a fusion of the token passing and polling principles. Several devices on a network may be master stations. Only the station that has the token is permitted to initiate communication. The master may poll (master requests, slave responds) the slave devices while it has the token.

The token is passed to the next master in a special frame. The devices are given individual station addresses. All frames contain the destination address (DA) and the source address (SA) for the message. The Fieldbus has services that free the user from the responsibility of assigning and keeping track of addresses.

A requirement for reliable control is reliable data. A two-byte frame check sequence (FCS) is calculated on all frame data using a polynomial in the transmitting device and added to the frame. The receiving device performs the same calculation and compares the result with the FCS, thereby detecting any error. The FCS is equivalent to the parity bits and cyclic redundancy checks of asynchronous protocols.

When the above layer requests the FDL to pass a message, the message priority is passed along with it. There are two priorities: high, e.g., alarms, and low, e.g., configuration and diagnostics data. The FDL transmits the high priority messages first.

10.4.7 Fieldbus Data Link Control

The FDLC provides various possibilities for the application layer to send data to other stations. There are two message types that can be identified in a Fieldbus system:

- Operational
- Background

Operational traffic is data transferred between devices as part of the control strategy, e.g., process variables. It is characterized as low volume, time critical and cyclic. Background traffic is data transferred between a device and the operator interface, e.g., configuration and diagnostics. It has the opposite characteristics of operational traffic: high volume, not time critical, acyclic (sporadic).

10.4.8 Object Oriented Design

When dealing with a complex system such as a Fieldbus application, the whole may appear unfathomable. By deconstructing it to parts, and even more primitive elements in a hierarchic nature to a suitable level of abstraction (recognizing essential characteristics), complex interacting parts are brought to order and the system becomes easier to grasp. That is achieved since one only needs to comprehend a few simple parts. A technique called object oriented design (OOD) was used to design the application layer and the function block application process.

There are many keywords in OOD. However, for Fieldbus study, object and class are sufficient. Objects are entities with a well-defined behavior. Systems are broken down to objects which can be said to be parts of the system. In OOD, software is based on objects that do things or change when one sends them messages or operates upon them. Therefore, OOD is not based on algorithms (execution steps). Objects often represent entities in the real world, e.g., a file. Objects may be classified according to their function and other properties they have in common. A class defines various kinds of objects. Unique properties of an object defines an instance of the class.

To order or rank abstractions, both objects and classes are organized in a hierarchy (levels of abstraction or complexity). One being built on top of the other, each level is understandable on its own. Inheritance is class hierarchy; a subclass (lower class) shares structure and behavior of a superclass (higher class). Multiple inheritance is possible, and common. Aggregation is object hierarchies: objects are built from subobjects.

For example: In a large control system one can find management system, supervisory system and field equipment, all parts of the control system. A field device may have subparts such as sensors, electronics and casing. In a system there may be a LD302, which is a kind of pressure transmitter, which is a kind of transmitter, which is a kind of field equipment. The LD302 inherits the properties and behavior of the pressure transmitter class. Therefore, an operator familiar with pressure transmitters can operate the LD302 in a matter of minutes, only having to learn the unique properties of the LD302. OOD yields smaller systems through this reuse of common mechanisms, aggregation and inheritance. Models are used extensively in Fieldbus and in all engineering because they make abstraction, deconstruction and hierarchical ordering easier.

OOD IN FIELDBUS

The Fieldbus control system has been deconstructed down to the so-called simple variables which is a suitable level of abstraction. Examples of these are float, integer and string. Simple variables are used on their own but also as parts of data structures such as the function block I/O parameters and function block links. Again these data structures are parts of the function block data type which is also a data structure.

Function blocks are part of the function block application process, which is part the field device which finally is part of the system.

Variables may be classified in many ways:

- Float
- Integer or string
- Static or dynamic
- Read or write, etc.

Variables are only one of many types of objects, but they are the most important defined in Fieldbus. Since they exist in the AP they are called application process objects (APO).

FIELDBUS APPLICATION LAYER

The distributed application processes in the system need to communicate. The Fieldbus provides logical communication paths (channels) between the application processes. Various types of connections with various combinations of characteristics are available to meet the various communication needs. Several connections may exist simultaneously, enabling multivariable access.

The Fieldbus connections are modeled in two ways:

- Client/server model
- Publisher/subscriber model

The client/server server model is used to describe acyclic data transfer. From a communication point of view, a client is an AP which is using a remote AP's functionality. The remote AP is called the server. For example, if the operator console wants to read a tuning parameter in a controller in the field, the AP in the console is the client, and the AP in the controller is the server.

The publisher/subscriber model is used to describe cyclic data transfer. From a communication point of view a subscriber *is* an AP which is using a remote AP's functionality. The remote AP is called the publisher. The publisher is actually producing (publishing) data, a subscriber is consuming (subscribing to) that data. For example, a transmitter is publishing a process variable which is consumed by a controller. The controller is publishing an output which is consumed by an actuator. Transmission is controlled by a third party, the requester, which issues a request to the publisher to publish its data. (The publisher/subscriber model is derived from the more common producer/consumer model.)

As mentioned in the OOD introduction, a Fieldbus system is broken down into variables. There is a set of services that lets an AP use the functionality of an AP in another device, such as getting the value of a variable or otherwise manipulating the object.

The primary intention of Fieldbus is to build the application using function blocks. This would be done in the function block application process (FBAP). However, within a Fieldbus device it is possible to have other types of APs, e.g., ladder logic or structured text, though no such definition has been made yet.

From a Fieldbus point of view, a device is not its hardware parts as they are to humans. For example, a pressure transmitter is not an assembly of pressure sensor, electronics and a housing, but a network node containing parameters. This network view is called the virtual field device (VFD). A device (station) contains only one FBAP. The FBAP may contain several VFDs to device a device's application into individual loops to make it easier for the operator to overview.

The VFD is the interface between protocol stack and function block AP. The VFD is the part of the real application that is visible and accessible through the network, the communication objects such as variables and blocks, etc.

Before a device can access communication objects (e.g., variables) in another device, it must first know which objects are available and their structure. Knowing the structure is important because there is no point in asking for a variable if you do not know how to interpret the answer, for example if it is a float or integer. This information may be preconfigured or obtained from the communication partner. There are two types of such services: operational services to manipulate objects and services for manipulation of their descriptive attributes.

All objects (variables, etc.) have an index for easy reference. Every parameter in the system is uniquely identified by its index plus the connection. This is the method used to request data once a Fieldbus system is up and running. The user does not have to worry about keeping track of indexes and addresses. That is done by the network and may be totally transparent to the user, depending upon the type of user interface.

A man-machine interface like a handheld terminal needs information about the object more than just for communication purposes. For example, it must know how to present the information to the user (e.g., in a menu), when it must be updated dynamically, and if there is a certain procedure involved before writing the variable. This information may be stored in the device, or may be supplied separately on magnetic media, for example.

Examples of services include

- Release connection
- Read device status
- Read device manufacturer
- Type and version
- Read entire or part of configuration
- Read variable
- Write variable
- Notify an event
- Instantiate block ("create")
- Find OD index for a parameter

- Delete block

10.4.9 System and Network Management

The purpose of network management is to provide services for central configuration and control of the network protocol stack, such as maintenance and startup of the Fieldbus system. For example, the network management manages the connections. The system management is split into two parts: a kernel which provides the basic functionality that a control application can be built upon and a part that provides optimization of operation and diagnostics of problems. It coordinates functions in all layers, controlling overall device operation and startup.

The purpose of the system management kernel is to provide functions for

- Device tag assignment
- Station address assignment
- Clock synchronization
- Scheduling of distributed APs
- Function block binding

In a system, each of the above functions can only be managed by one device (though one device may handle many of them), the others act as agents. In case a manager fails, one of the agents will assume the manager role. For the system management to perform its task, it must cooperate with the system management in other stations on the network. A simple device may implement only a part of the system management functions.

PHYSICAL DEVICE TAG ASSIGNMENT

Before a device is put on the network, the user must first assign a physical device tag to the device (i.e., it is done offline). The tag may be up to 16 characters, typically in accordance with normal instrumentation practices, e.g. PT10270.

STATION ADDRESS ASSIGNMENT

Automatically assigns and ensures that each device on the network has a unique address. An "uninitiated" device has a default address. Configuration devices detect new devices and will assign a station address, after checking for duplicate tag, bringing the device to the standby state. A temporary device such as a handheld configurator selects its own address if there is no traffic on the network.

FUNCTION BLOCK BINDING

The network automatically finds the device (station address) for a given function block. It checks for multiple tags. This function is used when resolving links between block outputs to inputs (identified by the block's tag and the parameter name) to the short address and index reference.

CLOCK SYNCHRONIZATION

For the Fieldbus system to perform scheduling and other time related functions such as time stamping of alarms and events, there is a distributed time base (clock) in each device, providing a common sense of time among all devices: system time. System management provides a mechanism for synchronization of the time in each device. This is done from a master clock which provides the correct time.

SCHEDULING

The purpose of scheduling is to minimize delays due to communication. Such delays are pure dead time which make control difficult. Scheduling also insures that variables are sampled and function blocks are executed on a precisely periodic basis, so that the delay is constant. A constant delay is a must, since a change in delay would require returning. This way, tight closed loop control is achieved with time left over for background traffic. Scheduling also insures accurate trending and predictable alarm detection.

There are three scheduled functions:

* Background traffic
* Operational traffic
* Function block execution

The synchronization is based on system time. A macro cycle *is* a period of block execution which is divided into an integer number of phases, clock units. All function blocks are executed, and all operational traffic is passed during the macro cycle (see Fig. 10.21). The function block execution starts the execution of the function blocks at the beginning of a phase by informing the FBAP at the proper time. Note that transducer blocks are not scheduled to enable special sensing techniques or measurement when a sample is available. The user may determine in what order the blocks should be executed in order to minimize delays due to parameter propagation. Background traffic is scheduled to be passed during the phases not used for function block execution or operational traffic.

In the example in Figure 10.21, a simple control loop consists of input (AI), control (PID) and output (AO), where the AI and PID are in the same physical device. No inter-device connection is necessary for the process variable. In this example, the execution period for the AO block is shorter in order to illustrate that block execution time depends on block.

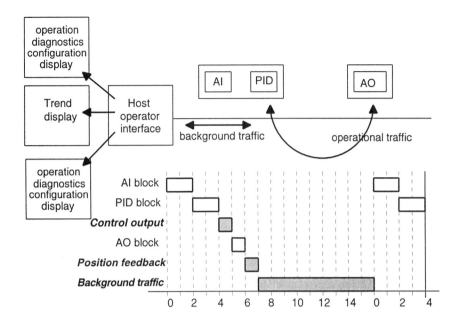

Figure 10.21 Scheduling.

Communication is scheduled in the master device which controls traffic and requests communication. Function blocks are scheduled in the individual device. Execution period/time is given by the following formula:

$$Time = 2^x \text{ seconds}$$

where x is a signed integer: -128 to 127. For example, X = -3, Time = 125 ms.

10.4.10 Function Block Application Process

The function block AP (FBAP) is where the user configures their measurement and control applications. Parts of it is distributed to the various devices in the field. It is not executed in a single control card as it is done in a DCS.

The functionality of a Fieldbus device is modeled as objects. The block object has three classes which again have subclasses under which the various blocks are grouped.

Block object

- Function block object

  · Input function block

  · Output function block

  · Control function block

  · Calculate function block

- Transducer block object
  - Input transducer block
  - Output transducer block
  - Display transducer block
- Physical block object
  - Alarm object
  - Event object
  - Trend object
  - Display list

The part of the FPAP which is standardized by Fieldbus is called the function block shell. For example, the block algorithms are not standardized. For each block there is a set of parameters that, to a certain extent, defines what minimum functionality a block will have. However, the manufacturer may implement such blocks in their own way. For example, in the PID control block there must be a GAIN parameter and therefore, the manufacturer may use this parameter as gain or proportional band.

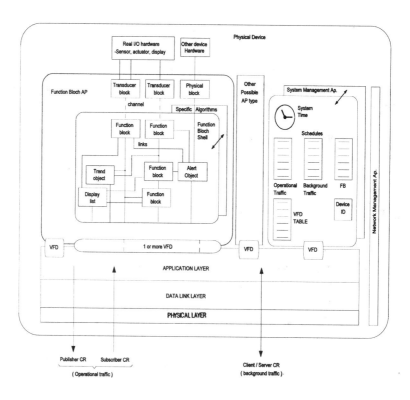

Figure 10.22 FBAP architecture

FUNCTION BLOCK

The blocks model the user configurable part of the entire application. Typically, these functionalities were previously available in individual physical devices. Now, several are included in form of software blocks in a single device. Together in a Fieldbus system, the different types of function blocks provide all the functionality necessary for most control systems. The user can build control strategies suitable for their application by linking these function blocks.

In general, function blocks can be said to use an algorithm and contain parameters in order to process input parameters, producing as results output parameters. Again, the block is just an abstraction of software and data. There are no blocks inside the device to be seen. The function block concept was designed around the PID block since it is the most complex block. The concept of local/remote set point, automatic/manual output, cascade (remote set point) and the algorithm has been carried on to other blocks, which may have appeared strange at first. A particular selection of set point and output is called the block mode. The algorithm does not refer to the PID algorithm in the PID block alone, but in general to the processing function of all blocks.

Each block is identified in the system by a tag assigned by the user. This tag must be unique in the Fieldbus system. Each parameter in a block has a name that cannot be changed. All parameters in the system are uniquely defined by the block tag plus parameter name.

Inputs from other blocks arrive asynchronously. When a block is executed a "snapshot" of the inputs is therefore taken. This also prevents input data to change during block execution. After executing the block algorithm, its outputs are updated and broadcast on the network and read by inputs of blocks using this information. This way, the output has to be communicated only once, even if it is connected to many inputs. The execution time for the block is expressed just like the execution period in equation.

Configuration is basically the assignment of tags and building of the control strategy by selecting blocks (installation), linking them and adjusting the contained parameters so as to obtain the desired operation. This may be done by a simple hand held configurator or through the use of a computer with a graphical user interface, which allows users to draw the configuration as a control diagram. Configuration may be done in advance or during operation.

Analog input blocks provide the functionality of what is known as a transmitter. They make the measurement performed by a device available to the Fieldbus system. It also optionally applies calibration, damping and a transfer function such as a square root of a measured differential pressure, enabling inferred measurements like flow (in this case) in a differential pressure transmitter. It also provides process variable alarm.

A PID control block provides the functionality of the PID controller. This enables a device to operate as a controller distributed to the field in a transmitter or valve, typically for the pressure, flow or level it measures or actuates upon. It also provides process variable and deviation alarm, UR and A/M station, override and feed-forward.

An analog output block provides the functionality of what is known as an actuator such as a valve. It makes the calculated control output available to the actuator hardware. It also optionally applies signal reversing and actual position feedback.

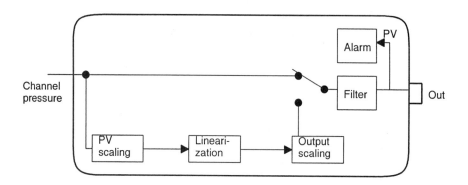

Figure 10.23 Analog input function block.

FUNCTION BLOCK LINKS

By linking function block outputs to inputs of other function blocks, control strategies can be built. When such a link is made the input "pulls" the value from the output, thereby obtaining its value. Links can be made between function blocks in the same device or in different devices (see Figure 10.23). An output may be connected to many inputs. These links are purely software, and there is basically no limitation to how many links can travel along a physical wire. Links cannot be made with contained variables. Analog values are passed as floating point in engineering unit, but are scaled to percentage (e.g., in the PID control block) to enable dimensionless tuning parameters. Digital values are passed as Boolean, 0 or 255. The analog scaling information may also be used in operator interfaces to provide a bar graph readout.

An output value is always accompanied by a status informing if, e.g., a value received from a sensor (forward path) is suitable for control or as the feedback (backward path) informing if, e.g., the output does not move the final control element. The status is determined by the source. Note that the pull system is used for backward paths as well. This way, the receiving function block can take an appropriate action.

Links are uniquely defined by the name of the output parameter and the tag of the function block it comes from. It is therefore very easy for a user to identify links. System management resolves the block tag+parameter name construct into the short reference address+index to make communication faster. Links may also be preconfigured directly using address and index. The link management automatically establishes the connections upon power on.

All function block links represent publisher/subscriber connections. The function blocks are defined to take action if communication is lost (e.g., publishing manager failure).

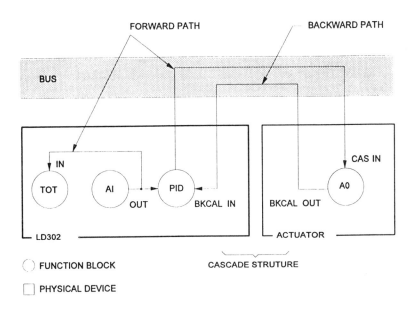

Figure 10.24 Simple control application

TRANSDUCER BLOCKS

The transducer blocks are responsible for the interface between the function blocks and the device I/O hardware. There is one transducer block for each hardware point, such as a sensor, I/O terminal or display. The standard itself does not specify any parameters for the transducer blocks, but the user group has identified parameters for various device types. Nor are the transducer blocks scheduled; the manufacturer may therefore control execution of the transducer block to, e.g., suit the sensing technique, often faster than function block execution. The interface to the function blocks (input or output class) is made device independent by the transducer blocks.

Transducer blocks cannot be linked using function block links, all their parameters are contained within. They interface to the function blocks through enumerated hardware channels, and only with blocks in the same physical device. The corresponding function block specifies the hardware channel.

- Input transducer block: Responsible for the processing of the sensor signal such as temperature characterization and trim.
- Output transducer block: Responsible for processing of the actuator and the feedback signal, such as trim.
- Display transducer block: Responsible for the local display and keyboard or equivalent.

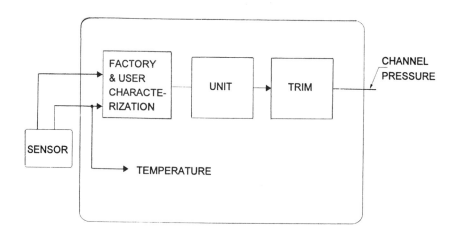

Figure 10.25 Analog input transducer block (pressure).

PHYSICAL BLOCK

There is only one physical block in a device. It is responsible for monitoring the operation of the whole device, such as self-diagnostics. It also contains device information
such as final assembly number and materials. The physical block cannot be linked using
function block links, all its parameters are contained within. The physical block may also
contain parameters that are global which may be used by any block in the device. For
example, a single set of linearization data may be used by several analog input blocks.

   The function block is not scheduled. The manufacturer may control execution to
suit device needs.

BLOCK PARAMETERS

As mentioned in the OOD section, the architecture is deconstructed down to simple variables. For variables there are two meta types:

   • Simple variable
   • Record (data structure)

For each meta type, there are many subtypes. For example, a simple variable may be a
float, integer, or string, etc. Data structures are logical groupings of related simple variable parameters. For example, the mode data structure is a collection of the target, actual
and normal modes. An alarm data structure is a collection of status/priority cause, causing value and time stamp. The block is also a type of data structure. Simple variables
may be used on their own or as elements of data structures. The advantage of data

structures is that parameters needed together can be accessed in a single request, rather than repeatedly having to request for each element.

There are many classifications of the parameters used in the blocks, and a parameter may be part of more than one classification:

- Use
- Storage
- Hierarchy
- Access

There are three classifications depending on use of the parameter in a block:

- *Input:* may be linked to a function block output to receive that value. For example, the process variable of a PID block. An input may be set by the operator if it is not linked. Input parameters consist of a value and a status.
- *Outputs:* may be linked to a function block input to propagate the value. It is calculated by the block, or may be set by the operator in certain modes, for example, the manipulated variable (output) of the PID block. Output parameters consist of a value and a status.
- *Contained:* may not be linked but is available for user interface such as configuration, operation and diagnostics. The contained parameters control the operation of the block. Depending on the block mode, it is either calculated by the block or set by the operator. For example, the tuning parameters of the PID block.

Transducer blocks and the physical block only have contained parameters. There are three classifications depending on how the parameter is stored:

- *Static:* writing to this variable increments the static revision counter. The value is remembered through a power cycle, for example, an alarm limit.
- *Nonvolatile:* writing to this variable does not increment the static revision counter. The value is remembered through a power cycle, for example, the set point of a PID block.
- *Dynamic:* the value is calculated by the function block or received as a block input. The user does not write this variable. The value does not increment the static revision counter and is not remembered through a power cycle, for example, block inputs and outputs.

There are two classifications depending on how the parameter may be accessed:

- *Write:* the variable may be both read and written.
- *Read only:* the variable may be read but not written.

There are four classifications depending on the hierarchical level of the parameter:

- *Universal:* mandatory in all function blocks. For example, all blocks have a tag and mode parameter.

- *Function:* mandatory in certain function blocks as defined by the standard. For example, an analog input block must have damping, and a PID control block must have a set point.

- *Device:* mandatory in a certain device type agreed upon by the user group. For example all pressure transmitters must have a parameter for process connection, and all temperature transmitters must have a parameter for sensor type.

- *Manufacturer:* optional and specific to the device as defined by the manufacturer. Allows a manufacturer to put in additional parameters to cover unique features of a device, for example, adjustable square root cutoff.

The inheritance of parameters plays an important role for interoperability. A conforming device will as a minimum have the parameters and associated functionality defined as device parameters.

ALERT OBJECT

Many of the function blocks have a built-in alarm function to detect high and low process variable and deviation alarms. When alarms and other critical events occur, an alert object automatically notifies the user. Thus, the operator interface does not have to perform periodic polling to determine if there is an alarm condition. The physical and transducer blocks detect failures in hardware and overall operation status.

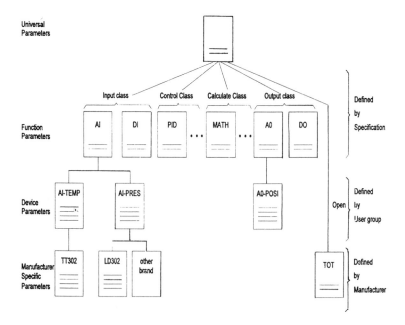

Figure 10.26 Parameter hierarchy.

The alert object alleviates the blocks from the alert handling so that its execution remains unaffected. An acknowledgment mechanism is also provided for by the alert object to know that the operator has been informed. If a reply is not received within a specified time, the alert notification is repeated. The user is also informed when an alarm condition disappears.

Examples of events are

- Mode is being forced for some reason.
- Block tag has been changed.
- Locked output/failsafe conditions.
- Feedback does not match desired output.

For the alarms, the user may configure the trip level and priority level and deadband. The alert notification to the console includes time stamp, reason, priority, present status (the alarm may already have disappeared), and the trip value.

If a change is made to the configuration an alert notification containing priority, configuration revision level, changed parameter and time stamp will be issued.

All alerts will also inform which device and block is the source of alarm, alert key for sorting by plant division and a type code identifying enumerated messages to the operator. The message may be among standard messages or others specified by the manufacturer.

For each block there is also an alarm summary of up to 16 alerts, summarizing present status, if the alarm has already been acknowledged, if it has not successfully reported to the operator, or if it is disabled.

TREND OBJECT

Trending may be done by the device itself using the trend object. This way, periodic time critical communication is not necessary. Data is collected from 20 samples and are accessed in a single communication. This reduces communication and network overhead, leaving more time for time-critical transfers.

DISPLAY LIST OBJECT

Remote operator interfaces provide monitoring and actuation of variables, such as process variable and set point. Such interfaces need access for configuration and diagnostics. These variables have been grouped into four groups, depending on usage, and may be accessed in a single communication rather than several individual ones. This reduces the number of accesses and thereby the network overhead. All operator interface data are scheduled as background traffic.

- Dynamic operation data, e.g., process variable
- Static operation data, e.g., permitted mode
- All dynamic data, all inputs and outputs
- Other static data, e.g., all alarm configurations

ACCESS RIGHTS

The operator at the console has the capability to grant or deny access to four sets of parameters in a block to a local interface or a higher level device, such as a batch program. To the function block, adjustments done from the console, locally or by a batch program will appear the same.

The four groups are:

For a higher level device:

- *Program:* mode, set point and output
- *Tune:* tuning parameters
- *Alarm:* parameters

For a handheld terminal or local interface:

- *Local*: mode, setpoint and output

OPTIMIZATION

The low speed version of Fieldbus was selected in order to meet the restrictions on processing power imposed by the need to meet intrinsic safety requirements. To meet the need of tight closed loop control restricted by the low communication bandwidth, the use of the network has been optimized in ways already described above, which are worth summarizing:

- Scheduling
- Short references
- Standard parameter definition
- Configuration change alert
- Display list object
- Alert object
- Trend object

Scheduling makes sure that the network is never idle, waiting for some parameter to arrive. The user friendly, but long, block tags and parameter names are converted to address and index. Parameters are standardized and do not have to be 'decoded' in many different ways. When a change is made in a field device, the host is automatically informed where the change was made, and needs to update only that parameter. It does not have to make continuous checks to see if the configuration has changed. The trend object and display list object reduce the number of communications necessary for access of data. Therefore, more time is left for time-critical tasks. The alert object makes sure that the host does not have to load the network by frequent polling for alarm status: when an alarm status changes, it is automatically notified.

10.5 USING FIELDBUS

For the average user an understanding of the behavior of the function blocks is the most important knowledge. A control loop (see Fig. 10.24) typically contains at least an AI block (transmitter), a PID block (controller) and an AO block (valve). The fact that these may be in three separate devices puts many requirements at the interoperation between these blocks. For example, if the operator takes over control of the valve, the controller must be informed in order to prevent windup, and to be able to make a bumpless transfer when the operator returns control of the valve. Likewise the controller must stop integration if the measurement from the transmitter is bad or nonexistent.

10.5.1 Modes

The mode has two functions: set point selection and output selection. You may compare this to the classic control modes: local/remote and automatic/manual, respectively. There are also modes for out of service and local override (safety). The number of modes implemented in a device varies from block to block. The generic block in Figure 10.27 also illustrates that input blocks have no set point selection and that output blocks have no output selection. To generalize the meaning of the operating modes:

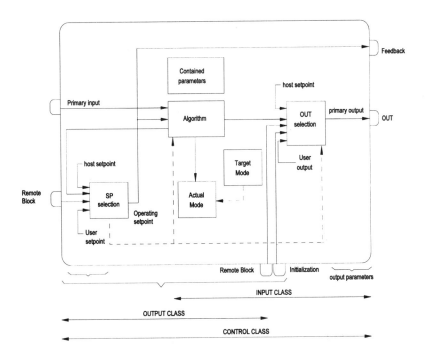

Figure 10.27 Generic block.

OUTPUT SELECTION

- *Automatic*: the block algorithm calculates the output using its inputs. This is the only mode in the output selection grouping where a set point is used.
- *Manual*: the output is set by the operator.
- *Local override*: the output follows a tracking parameter provided by another block, for example, a safety value. This mode is only set by a special block input.
- *Initialization*: the block is balancing its output, i.e., following a feedback value provided by a downstream block.
- *Remote output*: the block output is calculated and provided by a host computer.

SET POINT SELECTION

- *Local*: the block calculates the output using its inputs and the set point from the operator.
- *Cascade*: the block calculates the output using its inputs and the set point from a remote block.
- *Remote cascade*: the set point is calculated and provided by a host computer. The output is calculated by the block itself.
- *Set point tracking*: this is only valid with manual output selection. The set point is following the process variable.

In a block there are several different mode parameters, each with a particular function:

- *Target mode*: the mode requested by the operator. Only the modes allowed by the Permitted mode may be selected. The block will try to achieve this mode and may or may not succeed depending on various block and device conditions.
- *Actual mode*: the prevailing mode of the block. Depending on current conditions it may or may not be the same as the target mode. It may change not only on the user's request, but also due to other events.
- *Permitted*: defines the modes made available to the operator. It is configured by the process engineer before operation.

When a block is instantiated, brought into operation, the initial mode will be out of service. Once in operation, the last mode will remain through a power cycle. When a block is executed, the mode is first determined from the status bits of the various set point, output and feedback sources, and the overall device status.

10.5.2 Status Bits

Microprocessor-based equipment is able to detect errors in its hardware. This information is used to inform the quality of the variables passed in order to prevent integral windup in control blocks, and to provide a mechanism for blocks to shed to safety modes. All function block inputs and outputs are accompanied by statuses. For example:

- Quality: good, dubious, bad or out of service bad may be due to no communication, hardware failure, etc.

- Initialize request: force upstream block to initialize to provide bump less transfer

- Limited high, by limiter in downstream block

- Limited low, by limiter in downstream block

Statuses received with inputs from other blocks indicating discontinuities in control may cause the block to change its mode automatically. Such action is called "shedding." When the condition causing the shedding disappears, the mode will typically revert back to the previous mode. The user may configure to which mode the block is allowed to shed. The status of the output variables of a block depends on the block mode. A failure in one block may therefore lead to a chain reaction of mode shedding ensuring that all blocks are in an appropriate mode.

10.5.3 Cascade Structure

The cascade structure is an important concept in the building of control strategies. In a wider sense, cascade structure is now taken to mean that the output of one block, typically a PID block, is linked to the cascade set point of another block, not necessarily a PID block, but typically an output block. The block providing the output is said to be "upstream" in the signal path and the block receiving the cascade set point is said to be "downstream." Therefore, the cascade set point is, in a wider sense, coming from an upstream block, while the receiving block manipulates its output accordingly.

A feedback path is also provided in a cascade structure. The downstream block in the cascade structure may not always be able to accept the cascade set point from the upstream block, for example, if the cascade set point is not used because of the block's mode, or beyond the limits set for it in the block, or if the block is not able to move the actuator. If the upstream block is not informed that it may not move its output further, the integrating action of the PID controller may cause windup, or in the case of other blocks, it may think it is actuating though it is not. The status in the feedback value allows the downstream block to inform the upstream block what is going on. The PID block may also use the feedback value to balance its output.

10.5.4 Applications

Many function blocks have been defined. They may be combined to make the most simple measurement using only a single analog input block and to build classic control

strategies like single loop, cascade, ratio, cross limit, etc., or even more complex schemes. Some of which are shown in Figures 10.28 through 10.30.
The most basic input and output parameters are explained below:

- IN: process variable input
- OUT: primary output of the block
- CAS_IN: input for remote set point from another block, cascaded set point
- BKCAL_IN: Feedback input from downstream block. Value used for initialization, balancing of block output to ensure bumpless set point transfer in downstream block when it returns to local mode.
- BKCAL_ OUT: copy of selected set point to be used by upstream block for initialization of its output

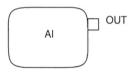

Figure 10.28 Measurement.

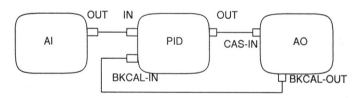

Figure 10.29 Single loop.

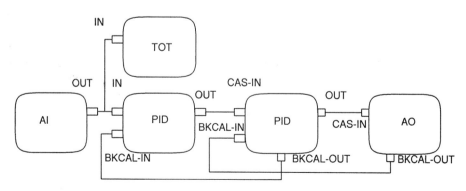

Figure 10.30 Cascade control.

- RCAS_OUT: copy of the selected set point, value identical to BKCAL_OUT, but status is based on RCAS IN communication

- RCAS_IN: input for set point from a host, selected in remote cascade mode

- ROUT_IN: input for remote output from host, selected in remote output mode

- ROUT_OUT: copy of the selected output, OUT, but with status based on ROUT IN communication

- SP (contained): set point set by operator in local mode, or set point after limitation of set point received from other block or a host

COMMERCIAL FIELDBUS PRODUCTS AND COMPONENTS

The number of users who want to implement Fieldbus has already reached a critical mass. Therefore, a number of companies decided to design and market Fieldbus products. One of these companies, Smar, is one of the first to develop a number of Fieldbus compatible products.

Smar's Fieldbus devices are based on the specification produced together with the other companies in ISP and WorldFip. Once the ISA/IEC Fieldbus is standardized, the user may upgrade the system by only changing the circuit, a memory or some software, depending on the product. Since no change will be made to the physical layer, the installation will be unaffected by such an upgrade. On a pressure transmitter the costliest part is the sensor and the mechanical parts, the price of the circuit board is low in comparison. Users' early investments in Fieldbus are largely protected, and they will not find their equipment obsolete by the time the IEC/ISA standard is ready. Likewise, today it is possible to upgrade the HART protocol intelligent pressure transmitter, LD301, by simply changing the circuit board.

Products designed by Smar can be adapted to either smart or ISP/WorldFIP Fieldbus protocol. The change only requires changing the electronics module inside the device.

10.5.5 Commercially Available Fieldbus Products

In order to provide a solution for Fieldbus now, Smar has developed a complete line of Fieldbus devices, consisting of the 302 series of transmitters and converters and a range of interfaces and configuration software:

- LD302: Fieldbus pressure transmitter with built-in PID control, totalization and alarm. For differential, gauge, absolute pressure and liquid level.

- TT302: Dual channel Fieldbus temperature transmitter with built in PID control, setpoint generator and alarm.

- IF302: Triple channel current to Fieldbus converter with built in PID control and alarm.

- Fl302: Triple channel Fieldbus to current converter with built-in PID control and alarm

- FP302: Fieldbus to pressure converter with built-in PID control and alarm.

- PCI: PC bus slot in card for interface of up to four Fieldbus channels per card. A multitude of function blocks available, enables building of complex control strategies. Function blocks are executed independently from PC.

- BC1: RS232/Fieldbus interface, plugs into DB9 connector of a PC serial port.

- PS302: Fieldbus compatible power supply.

- SB302: Fieldbus compatible safety barrier.

- Fieldbus terminator

- SYSCON: Windows-based PC software for configuration of Fieldbus systems: graphical user interface (GUI) that lets the user draw the control configuration with function blocks and links as conventional control diagram.

10.5.6 Hardware (Silicon) Support for Fieldbus

It was understood by many companies that success of the Fieldbus partly depends on cost. No matter how capable, if the price of the Fieldbus device is too high, the customers may simply decide to continue with what they have already. Reducing the cost of product partly depends on

- Development costs
- Cost of hardware

The best way to decrease both development cost and the cost of electronics is to get special purpose integrated circuits to take care of interface electronics. Thinking on this line several companies unannounced their intention to provide silicon support for Fieldbus. Smar was the first company in the world to develop an IC that implements the physical layer of Fieldbus. Smar currently has a complete line of three different ICs for Fieldbus which are available also to other companies that want to implement Fieldbus in their products. One of these ICs, the FB2050, is used in all devices in Smar's line of Fieldbus products.

REFERENCES

1. Gunderson, David, *Local Area Networking and Data Acquisition*, Instrument Society of America ISA/94, Advances in Instrumentation and Control Conference Proceedings, 1994, pp. 681-690 .

2. Coronado, Adam, *A Practical Approach to the Conversion of a PC Into an Engineer's Workstation*, Instrument Society of America ICS/94, Conference Proceedings, 1994, pp. 207-222.

3. Redman, Jim, *Client/ Server Issues in Manufacturing,* Instrument Society of America ISA/94, Advances in Instrumentation and Control, Conference Proceedings, 1994 pp. 681-690.

4. *Fieldbus*, Smar Tutorials, Smar International Corporation TX, U.S.A.

5. Derfler, F. J., *Guide to Connectivity*, Third Editon, Ziff-Davis Press, CA, U.S.A. 1995.

Eleven

INDUSTRY STANDARD SOFTWARE for PC-BASED DATA ACQUISITION

11.1 INTRODUCTION

This chapter is devoted to the other indispensable component of the data acquisition system, namely software. In the previous chapters we have examined the hardware aspects of the data acquisition system. Software is no less important than hardware in the sense that even if one has the perfect hardware setup, if the sampling rate is not adequate or if one can not sample the data periodically, the data may become totally meaningless.

In this chapter we will examine the software issues in two parts. The first part will deal with software languages. Here we will assume that one has decided to write one's own program for data acquisition. We will examine the capabilities of languages and make a comparative study of the languages suitable for data acquisition applications. In this part, one will also receive valuable hints to speed up one's programs.

The second part of the chapter concerns industry standard software packages. A wide spectrum of software packages are analyzed in terms of capabilities and programming methods. The reader will find this section especially interesting because most software packages have a unique way of programming. As the package gets more powerful, the method gets more complicated. This section will provide valuable insight into programming methods to enable one to better anticipate the operation.

11.2 COMPARATIVE STUDY OF PROGRAMMING LANGUAGES FOR DATA ACQUISITION APPLICATIONS

This section offers a comparative study of computer languages for data acquisition applications. The languages will be examined mainly from the point of view of execution speed since this is of prime interest to data acquisition applications.

11.2.1 BASIC

Basic is a popular language of software development for most people simply because of the fact that it is the first language that we learned when we learned how to use computers. There are advantages of BASIC which make it very popular among people who are not specialists in programming. For one thing, one does not have to declare variables before using them. Second, the language provides all the necessary instructions for almost any operation one wishes to perform. For those who are more computer literate, it provides ways of running assembly language programs within the BASIC language.

The advantages of using BASIC are

- Learning time is short.
- Assembly language routines can be run within the language.
- Declaration of variables is not necessary.
- An interpreter version of BASIC will execute the instruction immediately and give feedback to the programmer regarding syntax and logic errors.

The most notable disadvantage of BASIC, on the other hand, is its execution speed. In terms of speed, interpretive BASIC is very slow. Compiled version of BASIC can run faster but as a rule of thumb if one's application requires sampling speeds faster than 100 Hz, it is not recommended to use BASIC for that specific development project. New dialects of BASIC adapted for Windows enviroment, like Visual BASIC or CA-Realizer are completely different than the traditional BASIC. The similarity between these new software tools and the old BASIC is only in the name. In general the execution speed of these tools depends heavily on the video operations, e.g., screen animations etc. Heavier the animations, slower the speed of execution. With reasonable degree of video operations and a powerful processor it is possible to achieve decent speed of execution for visual programs.

In general the disadvantages of BASIC are

- Speed of execution is slow
- Internal buffer size for storage is limited.
- Because variables are not declared in the beginning, the internal buffer area gets relocated every time a new variable is used.

11.2.2 C

C is a very capable language which is preferred by most hardware and software developers. Even though C is a high level language, it has features which are only available to assembly language. Because of this, C can be used for low level hardware access operations. The routines written in the assembly language obviously run faster than any other language but for most applications, the speed provided by C is acceptable.

11.2.3 PASCAL

PASCAL is another high level language which can be used for data acquisition applications. Even though PASCAL is very capable, it has a reputation among common users as being a slow language. In reality, PASCAL can be as fast or faster than C language. Of course, one should expect some performance changes from one compiler to another. PASCAL has low level capabilities but not as many as C language.

11.2.4 APL

APL is a fourth generation language which is quite capable. Unlike the other languages, it uses a different format for the writing of programs. Those who are familiar with the method seem to like it very much whereas for others the method seems too awkward. The programs written in APL can be very compact but it is also very difficult to understand what goes on inside the program in case one needs to maintain it. Often APL programs are called "write only" programs where one can write the program but not understand it later if one needs to maintain the code. APL can run assembly language routines but it has no hardware input/output instructions. For this reason, APL is not recommended for data acquisition projects.

11.3 SELECTING A LANGUAGE

Most popular PC languages available for the average user are C, BASIC and PASCAL. Even though there are different versions of these languages from different vendors, more or less similar performance is expected from each language category. A common notion among the users is that the C language is the fastest language compared to BASIC and PASCAL; this is not necessarily true for data acquisition applications.

11.3.1 What Is Special About Data Acquisition Applications

Data acquisition applications are inherently different from other computer applications in two respects. These two distinct features, namely real time nature of the application and heavy use of input/output instructions, differentiate the data acquisition application from other applications.

Data acquisition applications and process control applications are real time applications. In general, process control applications do not require much data storage but require heavy data analyses. Data acquisition applications, on the other hand, are more data storage-oriented and involve less data analysis. This division is not very strict and it is possible to have applications of both process control and data acquisition which heavily require data analyses and data storage. These applications require precise sampling of data at regular intervals. The data need to be processed or stored in between the sampling process. As the sampling frequency is increased, the time left for processing or storing is reduced. Obviously, how frequently the data should be sampled depends on the particular application.

Another unique aspect of process control and data acquisition applications is the heavy use of external input/output processes. Even though this may not look like something that affects the program execution speed, in reality this is one of the major bottlenecks of the data acquisition process. To understand this further we have to examine the I/O process in detail. Personal computers use the system expansion bus and data acquisition cards connected to this bus for receiving data from the external world. Since the data in the real world is almost always in analog form, analog-to-digital converters are utilized for converting the analog data into digital form which is suitable for reading by the computer. The physical speed of the input/output process through the system expansion bus for IBM AT class computers with ISA configuration is quite limited. The speed limitation comes not from the speed of the processor but from the physical structure of the system expansion bus which delays the signals because of the capacitive loading and the drivers on the motherboard which buffer the signals. What this means is that even if the processor of the computer is extremely powerful, the I/O speed remains unchanged. This indeed is a major bottleneck for today's fast high end computers like 486 machines and the primary reason for the ongoing search for faster system expansion bus standards like EISA, MCA and local bus.

In summation, what is special about data acquisition applications can be summarized as follows:

- Data Acquisition applications are real time applications which necessitate real time analysis and storage of data.

- Data acquisition applications are storage-dependent applications which require large and fast data storage mechanisms.

- Data acquisition applications use input and output instructions quite frequently which are inherently slow and processor-independent instructions.

11.3.2 Testing Execution Speed of Languages

In order to test the speed of the languages for data acquisition applications accurately, a digital input/output board and a digital oscilloscope are used. The digital I/O board is used for generating an external signal to initiate, the beginning and ending of an internal data acquisition process. An external digital oscilloscope is used for measuring the duration of the pulse for determining the time it takes to execute a process. The setup is shown in Figure 11.1.

Several sample routines using input/output statements, data storage instructions, integer multiplication and floating point multiplication are written. These routines are translated into code for Turbo C, PASCAL, BASIC and Quick BASIC. Then the routines are executed in three different computers: first, in a 12 MHz 286 type machine; then in a 16 MHz 386 class machine; and lastly, in a 50 MHz 486 machine.

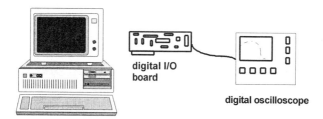

digital I/O board

digital oscilloscope

Figure 11.1 The test setup.

MEASURING THE DURATION OF INPUT/OUTPUT INSTRUCTIONS

Measuring the duration of input/output instructions requires a simple routine consisting of two consecutive output statements, sending logic "1" first and then logic "0". An infinite loop is formed using an unconditional jump statement at the bottom. Using this routine, the duration of the output instruction and the speed of the unconditional jump instruction are measured. This routine is implemented in C, BASIC and PASCAL.

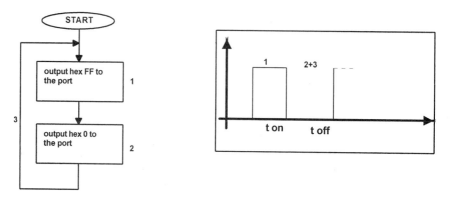

Figure 11.2 Flow chart of the first routine

Since the routine is very simple, the code written was very simple, consisting of two OUT statements and an unconditional jump statement.

The execution times are recorded as shown in the following table.

Routine #1		C	BASICA	Q. BASIC	PASCAL
286 class	On time	2.32	240	94	0.888
	Off time	3.2	320	120	2.32
386 class	On time	1.84	148	62	0.840
	Off time	2.64	204	80	2.56
486 class	On time	1.08	16	8.40	1.06
	Off time	1.04	22.0	10.4	1.08

All times in microseconds.

Comments on Test Results

As can be seen clearly from the data, the performance of input/output instructions is not very dependent on the class of the computer; 286, 386 and 486 more or less have similar performances for a given language. It may look surprising that for PASCAL language implementation of Routine 1, the performance of a 286 class computer is better than the 486 class. In reality, the reason behind this is that the performance of the input/output instructions is dependent more on the implementation of the motherboard and less on the processor. Even though a 486 processor is far more powerful than a 286 processor, because of the nature of the input/output instruction, this may not be apparent.

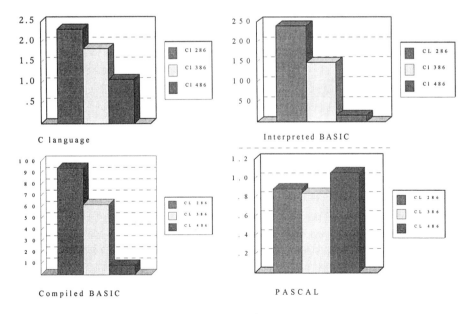

All times in microseconds.

Figure 11.3 Comparison of DOS based languages for hardware OUTPUT instruction.

MEASURING THE DURATION OF INTEGER MULTIPLICATION

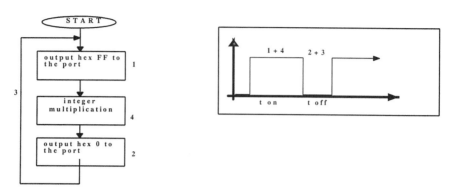

Figure 11.4 Integer multiplication test routine.

Routine two measures the duration of an integer multiplication operation. The flow chart of this operation which is shown in Fig. 11.4, is implement in four different languages, namely C, interpreted BASIC, complied BASIC and PASCAL. The duration of the routine for different classes of computers is shown in the following table and indicated graphically in Fig. 11.5.

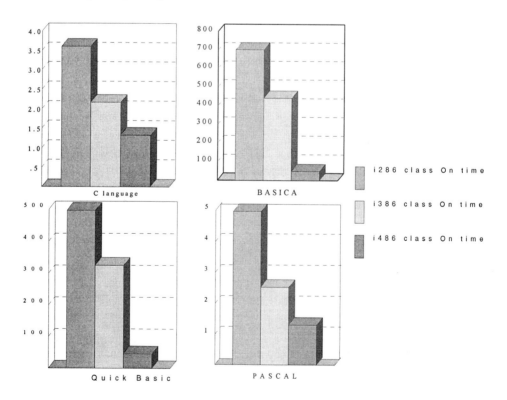

All times in microseconds.

Figure 11.5 Integer multiplication test results.

Routine #2		C	BASICA	Q. BASIC	PASCAL
i286 class	On time	3.6	700	496	4.96
	Off time	3.2	320	120	2.32
i386 class	On time	2.16	440	324	2.52
	Off time	2.64	208	80.0	2.20
i486 class	On time	1.32	48.8	45.6	1.30
	Off time	1.08	22.4	10.4	1.08

All times in microseconds.

FLOATING POINT MULTIPLICATION

In this case, a floating point multiplication operation is put in between the output statements to measure the speed of execution of the operation. The Fig. 11.6 gives the flowchart of the operation. The results are given in the following table and indicated
graphically in Fig. 11.7.

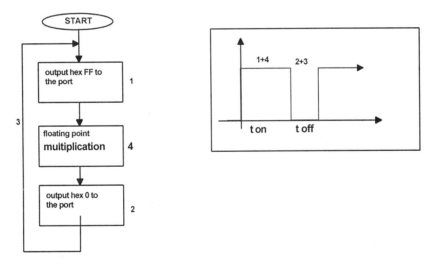

Figure 11.6 Floating point multiplication test routine.

Routine #3		C	BASICA	Q. BASIC	PASCAL
i286 class	On time	312	660	464	182
	Off time	3.2	320	120	2.32
i386 class	On time	13.8	416	304	22.8
	Off time	2.64	208	80.0	2.2
i486 class	On time	2.12	46.4	42.4	4.6
	Off time	1.08	22.4	10.4	1.08

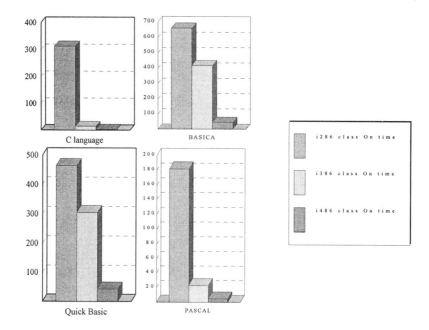

All times in microseconds

Figure 11.7 Floating point multiplication test results.

From the results it can be observed that floating point multiplication, unlike I/O instructions, is very much dependent on the class of the machine.

STORING DATA IN FILES

Most data acquisition operations require data logging which means saving data for later use. Storing data in peripheral devices like floppy disks or even hard disks is a slow process. There is uncertainty regarding the delay time associated due to the seek time of the hard disk. For slow data logging operations, this does not present any problems, but for fast data logging operations, the method is unacceptable as it is. One common technique used for fast data logging operations is making RAMDISK for storing the data. A ramdisk is a device driver provided by DOS which emulates a disk drive in the memory. Since drive is located in the solid state memory, the speed is very high and similar to the read write speed of the memory. In this routine, the data which is assumed to be coming from the data acquisition card is stored in the RAMDISK. The results for this test can be seen in the following table and in Fig. 11.9.

Data acquisition applications are different from ordinary computational applications due to the excessive input/output instructions and the large data storage requirements. Since the applications are real time applications, these processes have to be done quickly before the time for the next sample comes.

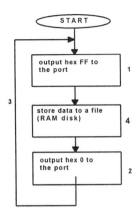

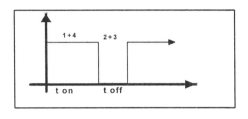

Figure 11.8 Data storage test routine.

Routine #4		C	BASICA	Quick BASIC	PASCAL
i286 class On time	232		1180	656	92 .
Off time	3.20		320	120	2.32
i386 class On time	142		760	424	61.6
Off time	2.64		208	80	2.2
i486 class On time	20		98.0	49.6	10.4
Off time	1.08		22.4	10.4	1.08

All times in microseconds

Obviously, the results show the speed of the particular compiler used and can not be generalized for all compilers in the class.

The following conclusions are derived from the tests.

- The speed of the input/output process is more or less independent of the class of the processor and typically is around 1 μ sec at best for a ISA system bus. If this does not seem adequate for the current application, the user is advised to select a computer with a different system bus architecture like MCA, EISA, etc.

- The applications which require heavy floating point arithmetic should consider higher class computers and consider C or PASCAL for the language of application.

- The applications which require fast data logging should use RAMDISK. The speed of storage in this case is dependent on the class of the processor. If the processes seem to take longer than the available time for sampling, consider using a higher class processor.

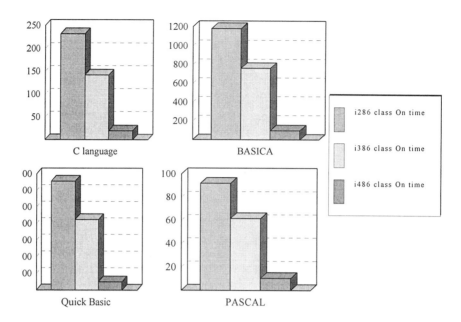

All times in microseconds.

Figure 11.9 Data storage test results.

11.4 COMMERCIAL SOFTWARE PACKAGES FOR DATA ACQUISITION

In this section we will be reviewing some of the well known commercial software packages. The capabilities of these packages range from simple to very sophisticated. Some
of the packages can be used only for simple data entry and storage while some others
can be used for data entry as well as data analysis and data presentation. Depending on
the capabilities of the package, learning these software packages may not be as easy as
learning other software packages. The primary reason for this is the fact that data acquisition software packages integrate user hardware and software together with the idiosyn-
crasies of the application, and this is clearly not an easy task. The hardware used in data
acquisition applications is not like ordinary peripheral devices; often the software package needs to have the capability to access even user designed hardware which may be totally nonstandard.

In this day and age of Windows®, software packages tend to be user friendly, enabling the user to proceed without spending too much time on learning the package. But
this may not be exactly true of the data acquisition packages. Depending on the capabilities, the learning curve for the software packages may be quite steep. Because of the
wide range of data acquisition hardware available from different manufacturers and the
inherently different nature of data acquisition problems, it is quite difficult to produce a
software package which can answer all needs. Those which can satisfy all those needs
have programming. The nature and type of programming differs significantly from

package to package. In this section we will review some of the well known software packages on the market.

In terms of capabilities, the software packages on the market can be categorized as

- Software packages without data analysis ability (data loggers), or
- Software packages that can analyze and present the data.

The first category of software packages performs simple data input/output operations without data analysis. What is expected from this category is simple I/O, data storage in files, and sequencing of events. In general these kinds of packages are called "data logger" software since mainly they are used for logging the data into hard disk or floppy disk to be analyzed later. In this category we will examine

- Labtech Acquire
- Labdas

These two packages are representative packages of this category. Although we should mention that the boundary between data logging and data analysis packages is fluid, one will find that the above data logging software all perform some sort of data presentation and analysis. Overall, however, their capability is not too significant for data analysis.

The second category of software packages are more sophisticated and offer data input/output and logging as well as data analysis. In this category we will review

- Keithly Viewdac
- Labtech Notebook
- Keithly Asyst
- KDAC500/I,
- LabWINDOWS
- LabVIEW

In addition to the above software packages, most modern spreadsheet packages can also be used for data entry, data analysis and data presentation.

11.5 SIMPLE DATA STORAGE PACKAGES WITHOUT DATA ANALYSIS ABILITY

As mentioned before, these packages are known as data loggers since their main function is to store data in a regular way. Even though they have some data analysis and data presentation capabilities, they are rather primitive.

11.5.1 Labtech ACQUIRE

Labtech ACQUIRE is a simple data acquisition software which is often included with hardware by the hardware data acquisition card vendors. The package is written in BASIC language and comes in compiled form which can fit in a 360K file space. In terms of computational hardware requirements it is not very demanding and can run with old PC-XT type computers as well as new 486 class machines. The package is simple to use and it does not require a lengthy learning time from the user.

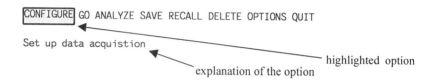

Figure 11.10 Initial screen of Labtech ACQUIRE.

In order to use ACQUIRE, the user needs to install the data acquisition hardware and then run the software. The initial startup screen of ACQUIRE is represented in Figure 11.10. Explanation of the menu functions are as follows:

CONFIGURE is used to set up the data acquisition parameters, by describing the channels the data are being acquired from and the disposition of that data.

GO calls the actual data acquisition portion of the system.

ANALYZE calls a predetermined analysis program.

SAVE allows one to save the current configuration for later use by building a library of configurations for various experiments.

RECALL lets you bring back a saved configuration from the library to make it the current configuration.

OPTIONS is used to modify the system if one was to change monitors or the analysis programs to be called by analyze.

QUIT exits from the ACQUIRE system back to DOS.

The user first needs to select the OPTIONS menu and inform the software about the computer and data acquisition hardware that is being used. The package allows only one data acquisition card to be used; multiple cards can not coexist. The user needs a device driver for the particular hardware. Nonstandard hardware is not supported by ACQUIRE and manuals do not provide any information for the user to write customdriver routines. The package does not support the use of a mouse but does support cursor arrow keys for moving around the menu. The option menu is reproduced below.

```
Current Setting    Yes

                                                 Options Menu
Display Type                               CGA (4 Colors)

Start on Key Press                                      No
Hold Display on Screen                                Yes
Hardware Interface Device                     Demo Board
Hardware Device Base Address (Hex)                   300
Analyze Drive, Path Name, File name       c:\Lotus\123
Header Lines in File?                                Yes
```

After the options have been set, the user now needs to select CONFIGURE from the main menu. The CONFIGURE menu is shown below.

```
Current Setting    1

                                                 Setup Menu

Number of Analog Channels [1..4]                        1
Number of Digital Channels                              0
Time Stamp Data?                                      Yes
Sampling Rate (Hz)                                     10
Run Duration                                          30
Starting Method                               Immediate
Trigger Channel                                        1
Trigger Threshold                                    120
Trigger Polarity                                    High

File Name                                     TUTOR.PRN
Number of Windows                                      1
Width of Windows in Seconds                           30
Window Color                                       Black
Channel Number                                         1
Channel Name                                    Sinewave
Display in Window Number                               1
Scale Factor                                         1.0
Offset                                               0.0
Minimum Displayed Value                                0
Maximum Displayed Value                               10
Trace Color                                      Magenta
```

Labtech ACQUIRE can display a total of four analog channels and one digital channel. It gives the user the option of time-stamping the data. The maximum sampling rate for the package is specified as 500 Hz, the minimum rate being about one sample every three years. The RUN duration of the sampling can be specified as any value and is restricted only by the storage space in the hard disk or floppy disks. Sampling can be started either manually or automatically by detecting a trigger condition in any one of the analog channels or the digital channel. Only one trigger source is available and multiple channels can not be used for triggering. Once the sampling is triggered, ACQUIRE will continue taking samples until the end of the RUN duration specified in the configuration menu.

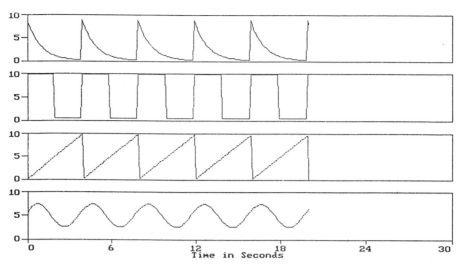

Figure 11.11 Sampling window in ACQUIRE.

In addition to the above abilities, ACQUIRE also allows the user to customize the display windows by changing the color of the trace and the window background.

If the automatic sampling mode is specified, the user can specify the voltage level and polarity that will trigger the sampling process. A sampling run is shown in Fig. 11.11.

Because ACQUIRE does not support generating digital or analog output, it is only good for sampling and not for control purposes.

A quick report card for Labtech ACQUIRE is presented below.

Hardware requirement :	PC/XT/386/486
Memory requirement:	640K
Extended memory required?	No
Mouse supported?	No
Multiple data acqusition cards supported?	No
Non-standard hardware supported?	No
Interface to other languages supported?	No
Maximum sampling rate supported:	500 Hz
Minimum sampling rate supported:	3×10^{-8} Hz
Max. number of channels can be displayed:	5 (4 ana., 1 dig.)
Triggered sampling supported?	Yes
Number of triggering sources supported:	One
Support generating output?	No

ACQUIRE can export its data in real ASCII to spreadsheet packages LOTUS 123 or Excel. Any other spreadsheet package which can import ASCII data can also be used for analyzing results.

11.5.2 LABDAS Software Package

LABDAS is basically a data logger software with some built in data analysis capability. But since the whole package is oriented more toward data logging rather than data analysis, we have preferred to mention this package in the category of data logging software packages. LABDAS is a package which is written in Qucik BASIC and comes in compiled form. The version that we tested has some bugs in the user interface which do not effect the operation of the data logging operation but are annoying for the user. The source code is also available from the manufacturer for modification by the user.

LABDAS is a sophisticated data logging software with the ability to generate output signals. This feature enables the package to be used for process control as well as for data logging. Process control applications require data monitoring, data analysis and intervention if necessary.

The package can accommodate multiple data acquisition cards in the system but nonstandard cards are not supported by the package. The device drivers for data acquisition hardware from other vendors can be provided by the software vendor but no help is provided for the user who would want to write his/her own device driver. Of course, if the source code is purchased it is always possible to modify the software to accommodate other cards but do not expect this process to be simple.

LABDAS, being a capable package with data logging and process control ability requires sophisticated programming by the user. The programming is unconventional but straight forward.

LABDAS is a menu driven package which works with function keys. It does not support a mouse but supports cursor control keys. The initial screen of the LABDAS has options for a configuration setup of the system where the user informs the package about the data acquisition hardware installed in the system. The initial screen of LABDAS is shown below.

```
PCLS-700 PC-LabDAS Data Acquisition System    Program : WELCOME
─────────────────────────────────────────────────────────────────
                    W E L C O M E     T O

            P C - L a b D A S       ( PCLS-700 )

        D A T A   A C Q U I S I T I O N   S Y S T E M


                    Copyright (Rev. 3.0) 1989

                    Advantech CO., Ltd.

            ┌──────────────────────────────────────┐
            │  DATE: 09-01-1989  TIME: 08:00:00     │
            └──────────────────────────────────────┘
─────────────────────────────────────────────────────────────────
USER HINT : Select function key !
COMMAND   :

1START  2     3     4     5CONFIG 6    7     8     9DATE  0TIME
```

The base addresses of the cards can be entered and edited in the CONFIG menu together with the address of the real time clock. The initial CONFIG screen is presented below.

```
PCLS-700 PC-LabDAS Data Acquisition System        Program : CONFIG
─────────────────────────────────────────────────────────────────

                           CONFIG MENU
                           ───────────

              DISK.C = Config. Disk Path

              I/O.C  = Config. I/O Port Address for PC-LabCards

              SCREEN = Graph screen position and TREND channel

              EXIT = Exit to WELCOME MENU

              ┌─────────────────────────────────────────┐
              │  DATE: 09-01-1989  TIME: 08:00:00        │
              └─────────────────────────────────────────┘
─────────────────────────────────────────────────────────────────
USER HINT : Select function key !
COMMAND   :

1DISK.C 2I/O.C  3SCREEN 4     5     6     7     8     9     0EXIT
```

Through CONFIG, a menu data logging path can be specified as shown below.

```
PCLS-700 PC-LabDAS Data Acquisition System        Program : CONFIG
─────────────────────────────────────────────────────────────────

                        DISK  PATH CONFIG
                        ─────────────────

    1. Disk Path for Setup Data Files ........  [B:           ]

    2. Disk Path for Logging Data Files ......  [B:           ]

    3. Disk Path for Analyz Data Files .......  [B:           ]

    4. Auto-start (Power-on) Setup File ......  [             ]

    5. Graph-display Page-1 Filename .........  [EGAPOWER.PIC  ]

    6. Graph-display Page-2 Filename .........  [EGAFLOW.PIC   ]


─────────────────────────────────────────────────────────────────
USER HINT : Function Key #10 to Exit !
COMMAND   :

1     2     3     4     5     6     7     8     9     0EXIT
```

The address of the data acquisition cards can also be specified through CONFIG.

```
PCLS-700 PC-LabDAS Data Acquisition System  Program : CONFIG.PG2
─────────────────────────────────────────────────────────────────
                    I/O ADDRESS CONFIG        ┌─────────────────────┐
                    ──────────────────        │      * NOTE *        │
     1. Real Time Clock ..... [340]H          │ Pls enter I/O Add.   │
     2. Counter/Timer (1) ... [220]H          │ in HEX format        │
     3. A/D Converter(Ch.0-15)(Card#1)[224]H  └─────────────────────┘
                     Range.[1] (0-5)       Range:  (0:10V, 1:5V
                     (Ch16-31)(Card#2)[XXX]H          2:2.5V,3:2V
                     Range.[X] (0-5)                  4:1V,5:0.5V)
     4. D/A Converter(Ch.1&2)(Card#1)[224]H
                     (Ch.3&4)(Card#2)[XXX]H
     5. Digital Output(Port 1).[22D]H  -- (Port 2).[22E]H
                     (Port 3).[XXX]H    -- (Port 4).[XXX]H
     6. Digital Input (Port 1).[226]H  -- (Port 2).[227]H
                     (Port 3).[XXX]H    -- (Port 4).[XXX]H
     7. Stepping Motor Control (PCL-738B: Ch 1/2/3)...[2E0]H
           Channel 1: Initial speed:[ 30] (1-255), Level:[ 3](0-10)
           Channel 2: Initial speed:[ 30] (1-255), Level:[ 3](0-10)
           Channel 3: Initial speed:[ 30] (1-255), Level:[ 3](0-10)
─────────────────────────────────────────────────────────────────
USER HINT : Function Key #10 to Exit !
COMMAND   :

 1    2    3    4    5    6    7    8    9    0EXIT
```

Another menu will take the user to the programming part where the user specifies the order of the data logging process. The approach used by LABDAS for doing this is by setting up a table of actions. The actions required are entered to the table by function numbers. A function number is similar to writing the desired action. In order to save space and to standardize the process, LABDAS assigns numbers to the most common data acquisition processes. The screen below shows how this data is entered into the computer.

```
PCLS-700 PC-LabDAS Data Acquisition System  Program : SETUP-EDIT
─────────────────────────────────────────────────────────────────
   Title 2 : Group Table
+--+--+-+----+----+----+--------+--+--+-+----+----+----+--------+
|Gp|Fn|Y|Pam1|Pam2|Pam3|FnRemark|Gp|Fn|Y|Pam1|Pam2|Pam3|FnRemark|
+--+--+-+----+----+----+--------+--+--+-+----+----+----+--------+
|01|26|Y|   1|2000| 400|SetMotor|14|01|Y|    |    |    |DCV     |
|02|21|Y|   1|1638|    |Set D/A |15|03|Y|    |    |    |Rd D/I  |
|03|21|Y|   2|4096|    |Set D/A |16|57|Y| $1 |  1 | $2 |If then |
|04|23|Y|   1| FFH|    |Set D/O |17|52|Y|  1 |    |    |GOTO    |
|05|23|Y|   2| FFH|    |Set D/O |18|58|Y|    |    |    |End if  |
|06|51|Y|   0|   0|   2|WAIT    |19|52|Y|  2 |    |    |GOTO    |
|07|01|Y|    |    |    |DCV     |  |  | |    |    |    |        |
|08|21|Y|   1|8192|    |Set D/A |  |  | |    |    |    |        |
|09|21|Y|   2|8192|    |Set D/A |  |  | |    |    |    |        |
|10|23|Y|   1| 55H|    |Set D/O |  |  | |    |    |    |        |
|11|23|Y|   2| 55H|    |Set D/O |  |  | |    |    |    |        |
|12|51|Y|   0|   0|   3|WAIT    |  |  | |    |    |    |        |
|13|01|Y|    |    |    |DCV     |  |  | |    |    |    |        |
+--+--+-+----+----+----+--------+--+--+-+----+----+----+--------+
─────────────────────────────────────────────────────────────────
USER HINT : Move Cursor to Edit Data.
COMMAND   :

1NEXT P 2PREV P 3INS GP 4DEL GP 5EDIT  6   7DUMP 8   9HELP 0EXIT
```

The report card for the LABDAS package is as follows.

Hardware requirement :	PC/XT/386/486
Memory requirement:	640K
Extended memory required?	No
Mouse supported?	No
Multiple data acqusition cards supported?	No
Non-standard hardware supported?	No
Interface to other languages supported?	No
Maximum sampling rate supported:	1 Hz
Minimum sampling rate supported:	3×10^{-8} Hz
Max. number of channels can be displayed:	No limit
Triggered sampling supported?	Yes
Number of triggering sources supported:	Multiple
Support generating output?	Yes
Graphic output supported?	Yes

There are also some functions provided which generate output for the purpose of process control such as D/A output generation and stepper motor activation as well as digital output generation. There are function numbers for most of the common actions required by the user in a data acquisition application. There are also some function numbers which provide IF conditions and change the sequence of actions. This is necessary for process control purposes. The user can modify the table easily by deactivating some of the functions selected before.

```
PCLS-700 PC-LabDAS Data Acquisition System  Program : CONFIG.PG3
─────────────────────────────────────────────────────────────────
                    GRAPH SCREEN POSITION
                ───────────────────────────
Display position:(Ch)(X)(Y)  Ch:Channel number,  X:1-73, Y:1-23
Page-1 :

D1:[ 0][09][ 8],D2:[ 1][26][ 8],D3:[ 2][43][ 8], D4:[ 3][58][ 8]

D5:[ 4][73][ 8],D6:[ 5][14][14],D7:[ 6][40][14], D8:[ 7][14][18]

D9:[ 8][41][18],D10:[ 9][13][22],D11:[10][40][22],D12:[11][0][0]

D13:[12][0][ 0],D14:[13][ 0][ 0],D15:[14][ 0][ 0],D16:[15][0][0]
─────────────────────────────────────────────────────────────────
USER HINT : Press ESC to edit next page !
```

The highest frequency of sampling allowed by the package is a rather slow 1 Hz. The same function can be repeated in the table more than once but the table can not be executed more frequently than 1 Hz. The data taken during the sampling can be either displayed in table form or in graphic form. If the data are to be displayed in graphic form, the screen has to be designed beforehand by any one of the graphic design software packages. After this has been done, the screen is captured by a utility program that comes with the LABDAS package. Once the screen is captured, the data can be displayed on the screen by specifying coordinates of the location of the display. The screen is assumed as a 73 X 73 matrix and the numerical data can be displayed in any location on the screen. The data itself can not be displayed in any form other than the numerical form but the background can be graphical. The graph screen positioning screen is shown above.

11.6 DATA ACQUISITION SOFTWARE PACKAGES WITH DATA ANALYSIS AND PRESENTATION CAPABILITY

The packages in this category not only log the data but also can perform sophisticated mathematical operations and present the output in graphic form. Having data presented in graphic form is a common way of presenting data in industry; by making data visual they can get attention more easily. These packages have inherent functions built in to use IEEE-488 equipment or the equipment connected to a RS-232 port. In the following sections we will review a selection of the well known packages.

11.6.1 VIEWDAC

VIEWDAC is one of the new generation data acquisition software packages which can log data as well as analyze it. The package is designed to control equipment connected to the RS-232 port and GPIB equipment connected to the GPIB controller card. Its ability to control GPIB equipment is a built in feature not offered optionally as with other software packages.

VIEWDAC is not a Windows package but its controls and interface are exactly like that of Windows version 2.0. Because of this, the users that are familiar with the Windows environment can learn to use the package in a remarkably short time. The documentation for the software is adequate and well prepared without leaving many questions for the user.

The VIEWDAC package is a graphics-oriented package with familiar Windows style dialogue boxes which enable the user to specify all the parameters easily. Sequence programming is done by means of tables which support a graphically oriented data entry.

The data analysis capability of the VIEWDAC is quite extensive. It has a library for curve fitting and popular waveform manipulation algorithms. The help system is context sensitive and well explained. Overall, VIEWDAC is a solid, easy to learn package.

In terms of computational hardware requirements, however, VIEWDAC is quite demanding. Minimum 386 system with 4 Mbyte memory is required but 6-8 megabyte is recommended by the software vendors.

The report card for the VIEWDAC is presented below.

Hardware requirement :	386/486
Memory requirement:	4 Mbyte
Extended memory required?	Yes
Mouse supported?	Yes
Multiple data acqusition cards supported?	Yes
Non-standard hardware supported?	Yes
Interface to other languages supported?	Yes
Maximum sampling rate supported:	*
Minimum sampling rate supported:	*
Max. number of channels can be displayed:	No limit
Triggered sampling supported?	Yes
Number of triggering sources supported:	Multiple
Support generating output?	Yes
Graphic output supported?	Yes

* Depends on the computer; no limit by the package

The initial screen of VIEWDAC which is shown below offers a main menu through which the user can set up the VIEWDAC environment and the equipment connected to it.

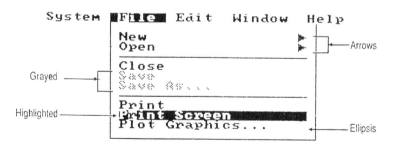

All data acquisition programs are supposed to execute a sequence of instructions in order to execute a data acquisition operation. VIEWDAC like other packages uses a sequence approach to define the steps in execution. To give some idea about sequence programming, we will look at the steps for generating a simple program.

The demo program is supposed to get data from an A/D converter input and display it on the screen. The flow chart of the operation can be examined below.

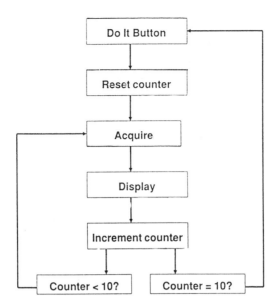

The operation starts by selecting a task from the task list. Since the operation requires executing a reading operation repeatedly, we will select the loop task and give it a name. In this example, the loop task is called loop1 and is requested to execute the loop 10 times. The screen below shows the task menu.

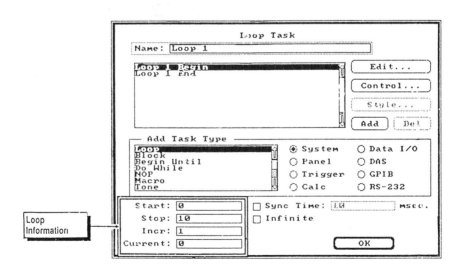

Since we would like to display the result numerically, we select a display tasks. When we select display task we are given several different options for display, like numeric display, analog display, line graph strip chart etc. We select numerical display among the given choices since we want to design a digital voltmeter. The screen below shows the associated menu screen.

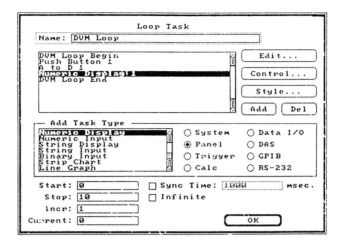

Once we select the numeric display task, VIEWDAC will automatically ask us the format of the display--the number of digits, etc. These data are entered with the numeric display task.

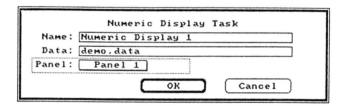

The next task is to read the A/D converter. When we select this task, VIEWDAC automatically asks us where it is going to read the information from. The details of the card, channel etc. are given in the next task shown below.

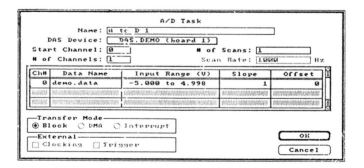

Since the process is supposed to be started manually by pressing a button, this is defined as a task. Once we select this task, VIEWDAC will ask about the font, button name, etc.

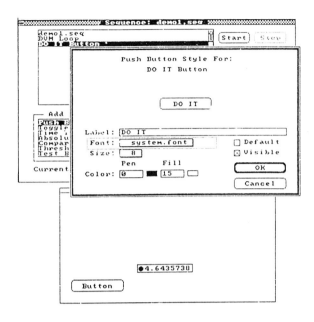

Once this is done, the application is ready to run as shown below.

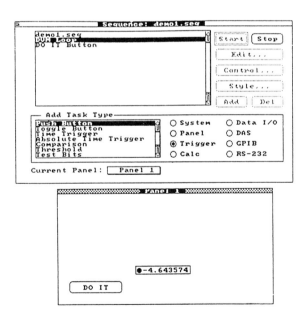

VIEWDAC has a runtime program generation capability which compiles the program generated by the user and makes it an executable code.

The program given above does not really show the data analysis capabilities of the VIEWDAC program. Listed below are the system tasks for VIEWDAC. They are ordered for the user to get a clearer picture of what VIEWDAC can do.

System tasks	Calculation Tasks	Timer/Counter functions
Loop	Expression	Frequency Measurement
Block	PID control	Event Counting
Begin Until	FFT	Pulse Output
Do While	IFFT	Time Interval
NOP	Numeric Operation	
Macro	Array Operation	**GPIB tasks**
Tone	Trig Operation	GPIB Read
Alert	Statistic Operation	GPIB Write
Fix DOS time	Bitwise Operation	Serial Poll
Lock	Logical Operation	SRQ Test
Unlock	String Operation	SRQ Wait
	Polynomial Evaluation	Reset Bus
Panel Tasks	Waveform Average	REN Off
Numeric Display	Moving Average	Device Clear
Numeric Input	Moving Median	Selected Device Clear
String Display	Moving Filter	Go To Local
String Input	Moving Peak Find	Local Lockout
Binary Input	Moving Derivative	Go To Standby
Strip Chart	Running Integral	Send Interface Clear
Line Graph		Execute Trigger
Bar Graph	**Data I/O Tasks**	REN On
Hide/Show	DOS	
Region Fill	Port I/O	**RS-232 tasks**
	Poke/Peek	RS-232 Read
Trigger Tasks		RS-232 Write
Push Button	**Data Acquisition Tasks**	RS-232 DTR/RTS
Toggle Button	A to D	RS-232 CTS/DSR
Time Trigger	A/D to file	RS-232 Flush
Absolute Time trigger	Data Acquisition	
Comparison	A to D	
Threshold	A/D to File	
Test Bits	Thermocouple	
	D to A	
	Digital Input	
	Digital Output	

11.6.2 Labtech Notebook

Labtech Notebook is a DOS-based package which is quite powerful and easy to use. It uses a graphic programming approach for developing data acquisition application programs. Since it uses a mouse for most operations, the user can program the package by simply pulling and dragging objects on the screen.

The Labtech Notebook comes with necessary additional functions for RS-232 and GPIB interfacing; so the support for equipment connected to a serial port or GPIB devices is provided.

The initial welcome screen of the Labtech is text based as can be seen below.

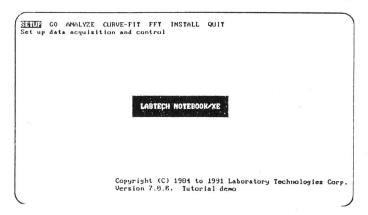

Data acquisition hardware installation is done by selecting the INSTALL option of the main menu. In many respects, the user interface reminds Labtech Acquire which is the simple data logging version of the software. So far, the graphic programming capability of the package may not be apparent until the ICON view option is selected from the SETUP menu of the package. When the ICON view is selected, the screen goes from being a text-based screen to a graphic mode to support icons and graphics. Only when Labtech Notebook requires some additional information about an icon does it go back to text mode temporarily. After getting the necessary information it returns back to graphical mode.

All necessary data acquisition functions and programming operations are available as icons on the screen. For example, the following icon symbolizes an analog input operation.

However, a filing operation looks like this.

If you would like to take data from an analog input and store it in a file, one has to put both icons on the screen and connect them by a line using a cursor as follows:

If you would like to display one channel of analog input data on the screen and save it in a file at the same time and save another analog input channel into a file, one has to do the following arrangement on the screen.

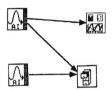

Labtech Notebook will be building up a text-based program as one drags and connects icons together. Each icon has a unique personality; for example, the two analog input icons, although they look exactly the same, in fact have different labels and sources for data. This kind of information is put into the icon by double clicking the icon. When this is done, the Labtech Notebook will go into text mode and give a screen associated with this icon to fill. A typical screen of this sort for analog input is given below.

The Labtech Notebook has a wide range of icons for display, mathematical operation and data acquisition. Some of the available icons are shown below.

File and Display Icons

Data Storage
(FILES)

Data Display
(SCREENS,
TRACES, and
ADJUST)

Time and Function Icons

 Time   Replay   Calculated

Time and Function Icons

Time   Replay   Calculated

Output Block Icons

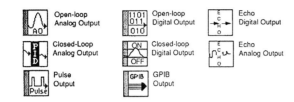

Open-loop Analog Output	Open-loop Digital Output	Echo Digital Output
Closed-Loop Analog Output	Closed-loop Digital Output	Echo Analog Output
Pulse Output	GPIB Output	

Mathematical operations (continued)

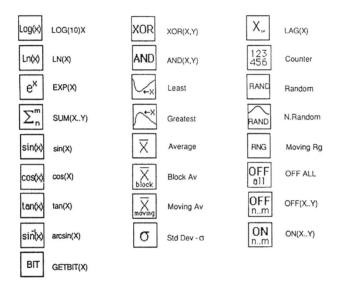

Log(x)   LOG(10)X   XOR   XOR(X,Y)   X₁.   LAG(X)

Ln(x)   LN(X)   AND   AND(X,Y)   123 456   Counter

eˣ   EXP(X)   Least   RAND   Random

Σ   SUM(X..Y)   Greatest   RAND   N.Random

sin(x)   sin(X)   X̄   Average   RNG   Moving Rg

cos(x)   cos(X)   X̄ block Block Av   OFF all   OFF ALL

tan(x)   tan(X)   X̄ moving Moving Av   OFF n..m   OFF(X..Y)

sin⁻(x)   arcsin(X)   σ   Std Dev - σ   ON n..m   ON(X..Y)

BIT   GETBIT(X)

Input Block Icons

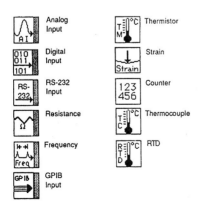

Analog Input   Thermistor

Digital Input   Strain

RS-232 Input   Counter

Resistance   Thermocouple

Frequency   RTD

GPIB Input

Mathematical Operation Icons

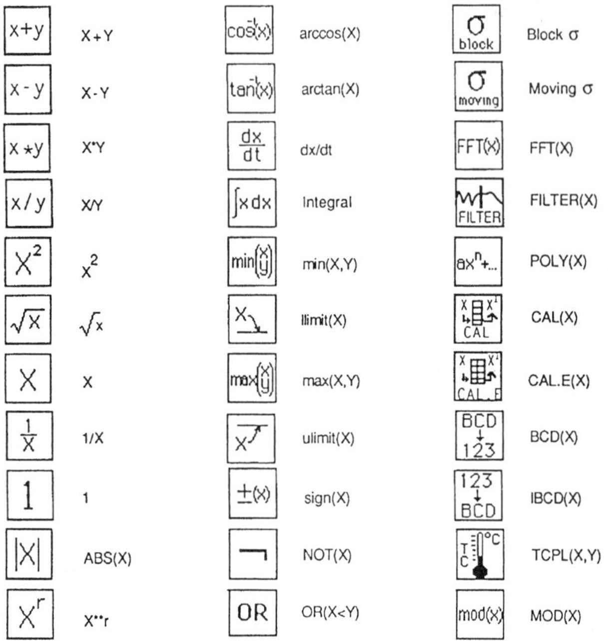

Icon	Label	Icon	Label	Icon	Label
x+y	X+Y	cos⁻¹(x)	arccos(X)	σ block	Block σ
x - y	X-Y	tan⁻¹(x)	arctan(X)	σ moving	Moving σ
x *y	X*Y	dx/dt	dx/dt	FFT(X)	FFT(X)
x / y	X/Y	∫x dx	Integral	FILTER	FILTER(X)
X²	x²	min(x/y)	min(X,Y)	ax^n+...	POLY(X)
√X	√x	X	llimit(X)	CAL	CAL(X)
X	x	max(x/y)	max(X,Y)	CAL.E	CAL.E(X)
1/X	1/X	x	ulimit(X)	BCD↓123	BCD(X)
1	1	±(x)	sign(X)	123↓BCD	IBCD(X)
|X|	ABS(X)	¬	NOT(X)	T/C °C	TCPL(X,Y)
X^r	X**r	OR	OR(X<Y)	mod(x)	MOD(X)

The report card for the Labtech Notebook is depicted below.

Hardware requirement :	XT/286/386/486
Memory requirement:	640 K
Extended memory required?	No
Mouse supported?	Yes
Multiple data acqusition cards supported?	Yes
Non-standard hardware supported?	Yes
Interface to other languages supported?	Yes
Maximum sampling rate supported:	*
Minimum sampling rate supported:	*
Max. number of channels can be displayed:	No limit
Triggered sampling supported?	Yes
Number of triggering sources supported:	Multiple
Support generating output?	Yes
Graphic output supported?	Yes

* Device specific--goes as fast as the acquisition hardware can, no limit by software.

11.6.3 ASYST

Asyst is a DOS-based data acquisition program which uses text for developing applications. The package is Forth language based and notations and the logical programming approach is also Forth-like. This is a very powerful package which runs quite fast. But the users who are not familiar with the Forth language way of programming may find the approach unusual. The package comes with a built in support for RS-232 and GPIB, so using equipment with such interfaces is quite easy. ASYST has a user interface called EASY CODER to hide the details of Forth programming from the user. But knowing the Forth approach will help the user in programming the package. The report card for ASYST is represented below.

Hardware requirement :	XT/286/386/486
Memory requirement:	640 K
Extended memory required?	No
Mouse supported?	Yes
Multiple data acquisition cards supported?	Yes
Non-standard hardware supported?	Yes
Interface to other languages supported?	Yes
Maximum sampling rate supported:	*
Minimum sampling rate supported:	*
Max. number of channels can be displayed:	No limit
Triggered sampling supported?	Yes
Number of triggering sources supported:	Multiple
Support generating output?	Yes
Graphic output supported?	Yes
Math coprocessor required?	Yes

* Device specific--goes as fast as the acquisition hardware can, no limit by software.

The programming of ASYST is done by using library functions. The user can define new functions very easily or use any function selected from hundreds of functions that come with ASYST. Some of the built-in functions are shown on the next pages.

When using the EASY CODER interface, the user can select these functions from the library and include them in the program automatically. EASY CODER will build a program as the user selects functions from the library. Some of the functions can be fine-tuned interactively by the user. The following pages give the list of functions available for the user.

Graphics

PCX Interface

PCX.PALETTE	PCX>VUP	VUP>PCX
PCX>SCR	SCR>PCX	?PCX.INFO

Plotter Operations

DEVICE.INIT	PEN.DOWN	P!
GRAPH.COMMAND	PEN.UP	P@
GRAPH.OUTPUT	PLOT.ROTATE	SLANT
HP7440	PLOTTER.DEFAULTS	?DEVICE
HP7470	PLOTTER.PENS	?DEVICES
HP7475	PLOTTER.SIZE	?PLOT.ROTATED

Standard Graphic Operations

ARRAY READOUT	DOTTED	LINE.BUFFER.ON
ARRAY.SCROLL	DRAW.LINES	LINE.BUFFER.SWITCH
AXIS	DRAW.TO	LINEAR
AXIS.COLOR	ERASE.LINES	LOGARITHMIC
AXIS.DEFAULTS	FAST.VIDEO.PLOTS.OFF	MM.
AXIS.DIVISIONS	FAST.VIDEO.PLOTS.ON	NO.LABELS
AXIS.FIT.OFF	GRAPHICS.BUFFER	NO.WINDOW
AXIS.FIT.ON	GRAPHICS.DISPLAY	NORMAL.COORDS
AXIS.ORIG	GRAPHICS.DISPLAY.MODE	NORMALIZE
AXIS.POINT	GRAPHICS.PALETTE	PIX>COORD
AXIS.SIZE	GRAPHICS.READOUT	STRIP.AUTO.CHART
AXMAX	GRID	STRIP.CHART
AXMIN	GRID.OFF	STRIP.CHART.DATA.FIT
AYMAX	GRID.ON	VUPORT.ORIG
AYMIN	HORIZONTAL	VUPORT.SIZE
CENTERED.LABEL	IBM.GRAPHICS	VUPORT>LEFT
CHAR.DIR	IN.	VUPORT>RIGHT
CHAR.JUST	KEY.DONE	WINDOW.ORIG
CHAR.SIZE	KEY.LINE	WINDOW.SIZE
CHARS.REL	KEY.ORIG	WINDOW>VUPORT
CLEAR.AXIS.DEFAULTS	KEY.OUTLINE	WORLD.COORDS
CM.	KEY.SIZE	WORLD.SET
COLOR	KEY.VAL	WXMAX
COORD>PIX	LABEL	WXMIN
CURSOR.COLOR	LABEL.COLOR	WYMAX
CURSOR.INCREMENT	LABEL.DIR	WYMIN
CURSOR.OFF	LABEL.FORMAT	X.ARRAY
CURSOR.ON	LABEL.POINTS	XY.AUTO.PLOT
DASHED	LABEL.SCALE.OFF	XY.AXIS.PLOT
DASHED&SYMBOL	LABEL.SCALE.ON	XY.DATA.FIT
DATA.ORIG	LABEL.SCALE.POINT	XY.DATA.PLOT
DATA.SIZE	LABEL.SCALE.X	XY>WORLD
DEF.PALETTE	LABEL.SCALE.Y	Y.ARRAY
DEF.VUPORT	LABEL.STRING	Y.AUTO.PLOT
DEF.WORLD	LABEL.STRING.XEQ	Y.DATA.PLOT
DENSITY	LINE.BUFFER.CLEAR	?CURSOR
DEVICE.CLEAR	LINE.BUFFER.OFF	?GRAPHICS

GPIB/IEEE-488 Interface

ASYNC.GPIB.WAIT	GPIB.SLAVE	STACK.LISTEN
ASYNCHRONOUS.GPIB	GPIB.SLAVE.RELEASE	STACK.TALK
BUFFER.LISTEN	GPIB.WRITE	STOP.ASYNC.GPIB
BUFFER.TALK	GROUP.EXECUTE.TRIGGER	SYNCHRONOUS.GPIB
BUS.INIT	LISTEN	TAKE.CONTROL
BUS#	LISTEN.LIMIT	TALK
CLEAR.ASYNC.GPIB	LISTENER	TALKER
CLEAR.GPIB.BUFFER	LOCAL.LOCKOUT	TIMEOUT
DEVICE.CLEAR	ME	TRIGGER.ASYNC.GPIB
DMA.GPIB.BUFFER	OUT>GPIB	UNLISTEN
DMA.LISTEN	PARALLEL.POLL	UNTALK
DMA.TALK	PARALLEL.POLL.BIT	?ASYNC.GPIB.ACTIVE
EOI.OFF	PARALLEL.POLL.CONFIG	?CURRENT.BUS
EOI.ON	PARALLEL.POLL.DISABLE	?GPIB.BUFFER.INDEX
EOS.CHARACTER	PARALLEL.POLL.ENABLE	?GPIB.BUSES
EOS.MASK.OFF	PARALLEL.POLL.SENSE	?GPIB.DEVICE
EOS.MASK.ON	PARALLEL.POLL.UNCONFIG	?GPIB.DEVICES
EOS.OFF	REMOTE.ENABLE.ON	?GPIB.ERROR
EOS.ON	RESET.PRIMARY.ADDRESS	?GPIB.QUEUE
GO.TO.LOCAL	SECONDARY.ADDRESS.OFF	?ME.CONTROLLER
GO.TO.STANDBY	SECONDARY.ADDRESS	?ME.LISTENER
GPIB.BUFFER.RESET	SEND.INTERFACE.CLEAR	?ME.TALKER
GPIB.DEVICE	SELECTED.DEVICE.CLEAR	?PRIMARY.ADDRESS
GPIB.DEVICE.RESTORE	SERIAL/POLL.IF..SERIAL.POLL THEN	?SERVICE.REQUEST
GPIB.DEVICE.SAVE	SERIAL.POLL	"CR.LF"
GPIB.DISPLAY	SERIAL.POLL.DISABLE	"GPIB.BUFFER
GPIB.DO...GPIB.LOOP	SERIAL.POLL.ENABLE	[]GPIB.BUFFER
GPIB.READ	SRQ.WAIT	

Overlays

CREATE.OVERLAY
FIND.WORD>
IN.OVERLAY.FILE>
INIT.OVERLAY.XEQ

LOAD.OVERLAY
OVERLAY.FILE
RELEASE.OVERLAY

RELEASE.OVERLAY.XEQ
IN.OVERLAY>
OVERLAY.SIZE

Programming Mechanics

ABORT
AND
BECOMES>
BEGIN..AGAIN
BEGIN..UNTIL
BEGIN..WHILE..REPEAT
BREAK
CALL[...]
CASE..OF..ENDOF..ENDCASE
CLEAR.CONTROL.KEYS
CLEAR.FUNCTION.KEYS
CLEAR.TOKENS
COMP
DEFER>
DO..+LOOP
DO..LOOP
ECHO.OFF
ECHO.ON
EDIT
EQUIV>
ERROR
ERROR.MESSAGE
ERROR.TRACE
ERROR.TRACE.OFF
ERROR.TRACE.ON

ESCAPE
EXIT
F*n*
FORGET
FORGET/CLR
FORGET.ALL
FUNCTION.KEY.DOES
I
IF..ELSE..THEN
IF..THEN
IMMEDIATE
INTERPRET.KEY
INTERPRET.KEYS
J
K
KEY
LEAVE
LINE.EDIT
LOAD
MYSELF
NOT
NOP
ONERROR:
ONESCAPE:
OR

PAUSE
PCKEY
QUIT
RESUME
TRACE.DOES
TRACE.OFF
TRACE.ON
TRAP.UNDERFLOW.ON
TRAP.UNDERFLOW.OFF
TURNKEY
XEQ
XOR
." ... "
: ... ;
?ERROR#
?KEY
?WORD>
?WORD>/A
?WORDS
?WORDS/A
"EXEC
"INPUT
#INPUT
[COMPILE]

RS-232 Interface

BUFFER>RS232
COM1
COM2
DSR.OFF
DSR.ON
RS232.DEVICE
RS232.EOS.CHAR
RS232.EOS.OFF
RS232.EOS.ON
RS232.IN
RS232.INT.MODE
RS232.MODE

RS232.OUT
RS232.FOL.MODE
RS232>BUFFER
SET.BAUD
SET.DATA.BITS
SET.INT.LINE
SET.PARITY
SET.STOP.BITS
?RS232.DATA
?RS232.DEVICE
?RS232.DEVICES
?RS232.DONE

?RS232.ERROR
?RS232.INDEX
?RS232.MODE
?RS232.STATUS
"RS232.OUT
'RS232.RCV.BUFFER
"RS232.RCV.RESET
"RS232.XMT.BUFFER
"RS232.XMT.RESET
[|RS232.RCV.BUFFER
[|RS232.XMT.BUFFER

Stack Operations

DEF.STACK
DEPTH
DP>SP
DROP

DUP
OVER
PICK
ROLL

ROT
SP>DP
SS.CLEAR
STACK

Comparison Operators

AND
COMP
FALSE
NOT
OR
TRUE
TRUE.INDICES

XOR
?T/F
<
<=
<>
=
>

>=
[<=]
[<>]
[<]
[=i
[>=]
[>]

Complex Number Operations

CART.FORMAT
CONJ
POLAR.FORMAT
X=*n*,Y=*m*
Z=ARG
Z=MAG

Z=O+IY
Z=POL
Z=X+IO
Z=X+IY
ZARG

ZIMAG
ZMAG
ZPOL
ZRE&IM
ZREAL

Data Acquisition: A/D, D/A, and Digital I/O

Internal and External DAS Drivers

A/D.INIT
A/D.SCALE
A/D.IN>ARRAY
A/D.GAIN
A/D.TEMPLATE
A/D.IN
ANALOG.TRIGGER-
ANALOG.TRIGGER+
ARRAY>D/A.OUT
ARRAY>DIGITAL.OUT
BOARD
CLEAR.TEMPLATE.BUFFERS

CONVERSION.DELAY
CYCLIC
D/A.TEMPLATE
D/A.SCALE
D/A.OUT
D/A.INIT
DAS.INIT
DIGITAL.IN
DIGITAL.IN>ARRAY
DIGITAL.INIT
DIGITAL.MASK
DIGITAL.OUT

DIGITAL.TEMPLATE
DIGITAL.TRIGGER
DOUBLE.TEMPLATE.BUFFERS
EXT.CLOCK
EXT.TRIG
INT.CLOCK
INT.TRIG
MASK>#
PORT.IN
PORT.OUT
PULSE.BITS
SET.BITS

11.6.4 KDAC/500

A KDAC 500 is a DOS-based program which provides an extended library of functions for BASIC or C language. This is a text based package where the user can select instructions from a rich list of functions for any operation wanted. The programming process is very similar to the BASIC language programming at the outset, but in reality a KDAC/500 gives the user the ability to run programs in the background and foreground. The background tasks are time-dependent tasks which are supposed to be executed regardless of what the processor is doing in the foreground.

The initial user welcome screen is as follows:

```
┌──────────────────────────────────────────────────────────────────────┐
│ Keithley DAC KDAC500 Installation │                                   │
│                                   ┘                                    │
│   Array Space / Maximum Size:      64K / 213K                          │
│   Clocks (Processor / Interface): 13.0MHz / 10.00MHz                   │
│   Machine Type:   IBM AT or compatible                                 │
│                                                                        │
│   Processor Type: 80286                                                │
│   RTMDS Graphics: Disabled                                             │
│                                                                        │
│   Interface Board(s):                                                  │
│   1) cff8H -*- CONFIG                    (int lev = NMI)                │
│                                          (nmi mask = 08)                │
│                                          (NMI interlock fix ON )        │
│                                                                        │
│                                                                        │
│   KDAC500 Working Directory:                                           │
│   D:\K500\                                                             │
│   Interpretive BASIC:                                                  │
│   D:\DOS\BASICA.COM                                                    │
└──────────────────────────────────────────────────────────────────────┘
```

By selecting the CONFIG menu from the initial screen, the user can install the data acquisition hardware:

```
╔════════════════════════════ HARDWARE SETUP ════════════════════════════╗
║                                                                         ║
║  AMM2: 16SE/8DI chan analog in, 16 bit A/D, global mux. Slot 1 only.    ║
║                                                                         ║
║  SLOT  CARD         SWITCH CONFIGURATION              MODULES           ║
║                                                                         ║
║    1   AMM2   Range: 10.B, Filt: 100 KHz, SING    auto AIM6 AOM3 PCM2   ║
║    2   TRG1                                        ADM1 AIM7 AOM4 PIM1   ║
║    3   NONE                                        ADM2 AIM8 AOM5 PIM2   ║
║    4   AOM5   Default Range: -10. to 10.V          AIM1 AIM9 DIM1 PROT  ║
║    5   DIO1   Port : A) IN B) IN C)OUT D)OUT       AIM2 AMM1 DIO1 STP1  ║
║    6   EXT                                         AIM3 AMM2 DOM1 STP2  ║
║                                                    AIM4 AOM1 GPIB TRG1  ║
║                                                    AIM5 AOM2 PCM1 NONE  ║
║                                                                         ║
║  F2-FILE       F3-MODULE     F4-SWITCHES    F5-CHANNELS                 ║
║  F9-LIST       F10-EXIT TO DOS                                          ║
║  Wed Jun  7 10:13   Path: D:\K500\                                      ║
╚═════════════════════════════════════════════════════════════════════════╝
```

The input signals are labeled in this screen.

```
======================   CHANNEL SETUP   ==========================

ANALOG2 : AMM2, SL 1, CH 0, 16 BIT, LOCx10, GLOx2
          , A FP 7.2
┌──────┬──────────────┬──────┬──────────┬────────────────────────────────┐
│ SLOT │   CHANNEL    │ PORT │ IONAMES  │         CHANNEL SETUP          │
├──────┼──────────────┼──────┼──────────┼────────────────────────────────┤
│  1   │  0   8       │      │ ANALOG1  │ 1) ADD IONAME      8) RESISTOR │
│  2   │  1   9       │      │ ANALOG2  │ 2) COPY IONAME     9) FILTER   │
│  3   │  2  10       │      │          │ 3) DELETE IONAME  10) OFFSET   │
│  4   │  3  11       │      │          │ 4) RENAME IONAME  11) MODE/RANGE│
│  5   │  4  12       │      │          │ 5) ACCURACY       12) CONVERSION│
│  6   │  5  13       │      │          │ 6) LOCAL GAIN     13) DISPLAY FORMAT│
│      │  6  14       │      │          │ 7) GLOBAL GAIN                 │
│      │  7  15       │      │          │                                │
└──────┴──────────────┴──────┴──────────┴────────────────────────────────┘

F2-SLOT          F3-CHAN/PORT    F4-IONAME        F5-CHANNELS
F10-RETURN
Wed Jun  7 10:13    Path: D:\K500\
```

After this, the user can simply write the program in a BASIC interpreter or C language compiler. In the beginning of the program, the KDAC/500 is called as a library of routines. The way it is performed in BASIC is now given.

10 CALL KDINIT

20 CALL ARMAKE'("sawtooth",250.,"chanout")

30 ....

In this program, statement 10 calls the KDAC/500 program as an extension to the available interpreter. Statement 20 is a function in KDAC/500 which means create an array named "sawtooth" with 250 entries with a "chanout" number of bits.

Definitions of all these functions are provided in detail. A partial list of some of the functions are reproduced below.

FOREGROUND

ANINQ	'(ARRYNM$, NUMSAMP!, IONL$, SINTV%, TM$)
ANOUTQ	'(ARRYNM$, IONL$, SINTV%, CYCLE%, TM$)
ANTRIG	'(IONS, THESHOLD#, ACTION$, MODE$)
FGREAD	'(IONL$, RANGE$, VL(), EUF$, TM$)
FGWRITE	'(IONL$, VL(), EUF$, TM$)
GETHANDLE	'(IONL$, HANDLES%())
HREAD	'(HANDLES%(), RANGE$, VL(), EUF$, TM$)
HWRITE	'(HANDLES%(), VL(), EUF$, TM$)
KDCLOCK	'(TIME%())
KDINIT	
KDPAUSE	'(TIME%, TU$)
KDTIMERRD	'(TIM#())
KDWARN	'(WARNLEVEL$)

BACKGROUND

BGCLEAR	
BGGO	'(TM$, BFN$)
BGHALT	'(BFNL$, TM$, BFN$)
BGREAD	'(ARRYNM$, NUMSAMP!, IONL$, BINTV%, RANGE$, CYCLE%, TM$, BFN$)
BGSTATUS	'(BFN$, STAT%)
BGTIME	'(TIME!)
BGWRITE	'(ARRYNM$, IONL$, BINTV%, CYCLE%, TM$, BFN$)
INTOFF	
INTON	'(IR%, TU$)
KDTIMER	'(TIM%(), TM$, BFN$)
TRIGGER	'(IONS, THRL!, THRH!, CHM$, EUF$, TM$, BFN$, CYCLE%)

TRIGGER MODES

BT	ST	WGO	NT
WBT	WST	WHT	

GRAPHICS MOVEMENTS

SCROLL	PAGEC	PAGEO	FAST
R.SCROLL	L.SCROLL		

GRAPHICS LOCATIONS

LEFT	TOP	RIGHT	CTR
BOTTOM			

GRAPHICS MODES

GRID	MAGNIFY	REDUCE	NORMAL
NOGRID			

TIME UNITS

HMIC	MIL	SEC	MIN
MIC			

STEPPER MOTOR DIRECTIONS

CCW	CW

TRIGGER DEFINITIONS

BELOW	ABOVE	BETW	NOTBETW
ON	OFF	EQUAL	PORT

PIM1/PIM2 RANGES

NONE	F.62K	F.125K	F.250K
F.500K	F.1M	F.2M	F.4M
F.8M	P1.NORMAL	P1.GATED	P2.DEFAULT
P2.READ.RESET	P2.READ.ONLY		

STEPPER

STPABSLOC	'(STP2ION$, LOC%)
STPMAXSP	'(STP2ION$, MAXSPEED%)
STPMOVEABS	'(STP2ION$, POSITION%)
STPMOVEREL	'(STP2ION$, STEPS!, DIREC$)
STPRESET	'(STP2ION$)
STPSET	'(STP2ION$, RMPRATE$)
STPSPEED	'(STP2ION$, SPEED!, DIREC$)
STPSTATUS	'(STP2ION$, MOCOMP%, LIMIT%, DIREC%, POSIT%)

The report card for the KDAC/500 is reproduced below.

Hardware requirement :	XT/286/386/486
Memory requirement:	640 K
Extended memory required?	No
Mouse supported?	No
Multiple data acquisition cards supported?	Yes up to 4
Non-standard hardware supported?	Yes
Interface to other languages supported?	Yes
Maximum sampling rate supported:	*
Minimum sampling rate supported:	*
Max. number of channels can be displayed:	No limit
Triggered sampling supported?	Yes
Number of triggering sources supported:	Multiple
Support generating output?	Yes
Graphic output supported?	Yes
Math coprocessor required?	No

* Depends on the data acquisition hardware.

11.6.5 LabWindows

LabWindows is a software package which enhances the standard C or Basic language compilers by offering an extensive set of libraries. The program gives the user the ability to work in either BASIC or C language and it also has the ability to translate codes written in one language to the other. In these respects, this package is similar to KDAC/500 and ASYST.

LabWindows providesa complete development environment for the user where the user can write the code in BASIC or in C, use the libraries provided by LabWindows, test these libraries interactively, and customize the code.

The user should keep in mind that LabWindows is not a language itself but a set of library functions for standard BASIC and C compilers. LabWindows supports Microsoft Basic, QuickBasic, Microsoft Windows Visual Basic, Microsoft C, Quick C, Borland C++ and Turbo C++ compilers. The code generated by LabWindows can either be run in the development environment or can be made an executable file using one of the above mentioned compilers.

The LabWindows development environment produces a code to be complied by the standard language compilers or it is possible to make executable files to run standalone without the LabWindows environment.

The development environment gives the user the ability to run portions of the program interactively, test the routines, and, if found satisfactory, then append the code the main program. In this way LabWindows can build a BASIC or a C program. Once the program is complete it could be run in a LabWindows environment, or any one of the specific language compilers can be used to run and make an executable file.

The report card for the LabWindows is presented below.

Hardware requirement :	PC/XT/386/486
Memory requirement:	2 Mbyte *
Extended memory required?	No
Mouse supported?	Yes
Multiple data acquisition cards supported?	Yes
Non-standard hardware supported?	Yes
Interface to other languages supported?	Yes
Maximum sampling rate supported:	**
Minimum sampling rate supported:	**
Max. number of channels can be displayed:	No limit
Triggered sampling supported?	Yes
Number of triggering sources supported:	Multiple
Support generating output?	Yes
Graphic output supported?	Yes

* Required for the development environment, not for running executable files created by compilers.

** No limit imposed by the package. Acquisition hardware dependent.

The graphics quality of the end product of LabWindows is quite good for DOS-based programs. The main advantage of the DOS based programs is that when they are compiled, they can be run on low end machines without much processing power and memory required. The screen output below shows a function generator and an oscilloscope combined. The controls of the instruments are operable by using a mouse.

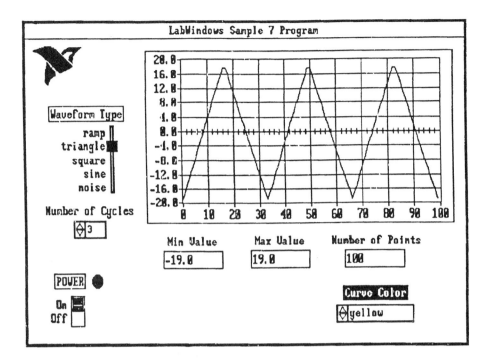

11.6.6 LabVIEW

LabVIEW is a powerful Windows-based data acquisition program which uses a graphic programming approach in developing applications. LabVIEW comes with a rich set of icons each representing particular actions. The user simply puts the necessary icons on the screen using the mouse and connects them together with lines. As the user generates the graph, LabVIEW will generate the code in the background. Apart from the usual icons for data acquisition operations, LabVIEW also comes with a library of fully developed equipment called virtual instruments. Virtual instruments are equivalent to popular models of oscilloscopes, function generators, etc. The user can simply call these equipment from the library and use them in the application much like using an icon. But at the end, when the end screen is generated, that equipment will appear fully functional. The graphic output can be manipulated by using the controls on the instrument on the screen.

LabVIEW, given all the capabilities, is a demanding software package. A minimum requirement is a 386 or 486 machine which is typical of most machines that runs Windows.

LabVIEW, being a Windows package, has all the advantages inherent of Windows based programs. The user interface is well known, and data can be exchanged with other Windows packages through DDE.

The simple program below shows how programming is done in LabVIEW.

Suppose you would like to prepare a temperature display application, where you have an A/D card and a thermistor to measure temperature. The initial screen of LabVIEW is as follows:

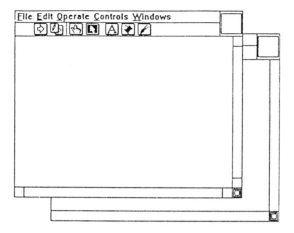

As a first step from the controls menu, select a display device for temperature. You are given choices for different types of display devices:

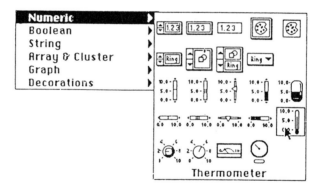

If you select a thermometer, it appears on the screen as follows:

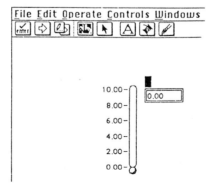

You can label and change the division on the thermometer as you wish.

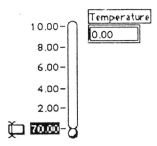

Then, select your temperature information source by selecting the appropriate channel of the A/D converter card from the Functions menu. The icon for this will appear as the following:

Suppose you would like to multiply the A/D converter reading by 100 before you display it. Then, select the multiplication icon from the arithmetic menu and put all of them on the screen. The icons would look like the following:

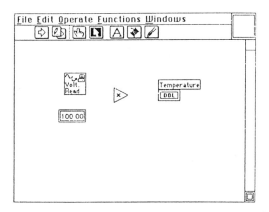

By using a mouse, the icons are connected as desired:

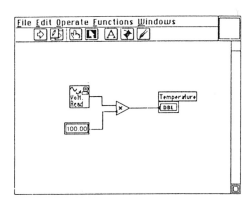

When you run the program screen, it looks like this.

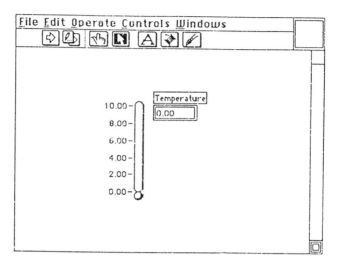

If you would like to use a digital multimeter other than a thermometer as a display device, you could do so. In that case, the final screen would be as follows:

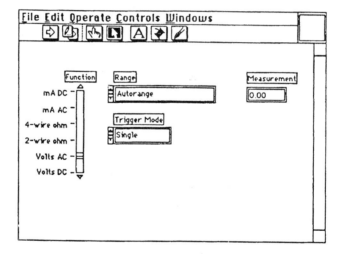

The report card for LabVIEW is represented below.

Hardware requirement :	386/486
Memory requirement:	4 Mbyte min
Extended memory required?	Yes
Mouse supported?	Yes
Multiple data acquisition cards supported?	Yes
Non-standard hardware supported?	Yes
Interface to other languages supported?	Yes
Maximum sampling rate supported:	*
Minimum sampling rate supported:	No limit
Max. number of channels can be displayed:	No limit
Triggered sampling supported?	Yes
Number of triggering sources supported:	Multiple
Support generating output?	Yes
Graphic output supported?	Yes

* Depends on the data acquisition hardware. No limit by package.

11.7 DATA ACQUISITION SOFTWARE PACKAGES

A comprehensive list of major data acquisition software packages and vendors is presented below.

GRED

CS Control Software Oy, Helsinki, Finland Tel: (358+0) 67 67 44; fax:(92+42) 571 2005

Requires: IBM PC 386 or better with 4 MB RAM and 10 MB disk space, DOS-5.0 or later.

Price: 15,150 FIM

This is as graphic based PC supervisor program which connects to most programmable logic controllers on the market. It displays trends, and includes a report generator.

CYPRIS

Cybernetic Research (PVT) Ltd., Lahore, Pakistan Tel: (92+42) 571 1004/5; fax: (92+42) 571-1003

Requires: IBM PC 386 or better with 2 MB RAM, 10 MB of disk space, DOS 5.0 or later, VGA monitor.

Price: 29,500 Pak. Rs.

This is a supervisory PC control program which can collect data from remote programmable logic controllers, log data, analyze trends, and generate reports. It can do real time control and production management. It can be interfaced to industry standard PLC and has a multilingual user interface which supports Arabic, Urdu, and Russian.

DT VEE

Data Translation Inc., Marlboro, MA, USA. Tel: 508 481-3700; fax: 508 481- 8620.

Requires: IBM PC 386 or better with 8 MB RAM, 12 MB of disk space, DOS 5.0 or later, Super VGA monitor, Windows 3.1.

Price: 1,995 US$

This is a graphic based programming language for data acquisition and control. User programs the package without writing code.

VB-EZ VISUAL BASIC PROGRAMMING TOOLS FOR WINDOWS

Data Translation Inc., Marlboro, MA USA; 508-481-3700; fax: 508-481-8620

Requires: IBM PC 386 or better with 4 MB RAM, DOS 3.3 or later, EGA or VGA monitor, Windows 3.1 or later, Visual BASIC for Windows version 2.0 or better.

Price: 195 US$

This is a package which converts visual Basic into a form which is suitable for data acquisition. Supports high speed data acquisition and analyses and display of data.

INSTA-TREND SYSTEM

Dianachart Inc., Rockaway, NJ 07886, USA. Tel: 201-625-2299; fax: 201-625-2449

Requires: IBM PC with DOS 3.2 or better, 640K RAM, 2MB disk space

Price: 755 US$

This is a real time graphics data acquisition program which is text based. The programming is done through menus without writing codes. It can receive data from programmable logic controllers and generate reports.

MET/CAL

Fluke Corp., Everett, WA, USA. Tel: 800-44-FLUKE; fax: 804-226-1934

Requires: IBM-PC 286 or better, 640K RAM, 40 MB hard disk, two IEEE-488 interface Cards.

Price: 5,950 US$

This package uses a PC as a system controller for collecting data from a wide range equipment with IEEE-488 interface. It can also be used for calibrating GPIB equipment.

SNAP-MASTER FOR WINDOWS

HEM Data Corp., Southfield, MI, USA; Tel: 313-559-5607; fax: 313-559-8008

Requires: IBM PC 386 or better with 4 MB RAM, DOS 3.1 or later, EGA or VGA monitor, Windows 3.0 or later.

Price: 995 US$

This is a fast data acquisition package which supports high speed data streaming to disk and near real time plotting of data. Text based programming.

HP-VEE GRAPHICAL PROGRAMMING LANGUAGE

Hewlett-Packard Co., VXI Instruments Div., Loveland, CO, USA. Tel: 303-679-2623 fax: 303-679-5952

Requires: IBM PC 386 or better with 12 MB RAM, 15 MB of hard disk space, DOS 3.1 or later, EGA or VGA monitor, Windows 3.1 or later.

Price: 1,995 US$

This is a graphic programming package which controls any IEEE-488, RS-232 or VXI instrument on the market. It can analyze and display data received from these instruments.

AMPS (ACQUISITION, MEASUREMENT, PROCESSING AND STORAGE)

Hyperception Inc., Dallas, TX, USA. Tel: 214-343-8525; fax: 214-343-2457

Requirements: IBM PC 386 or better, DOS 3.1 or later, Windows 3.1 or better, 2 MB of hard disk space, 4 MB RAM.

Price: 1,495 US$

This software package, together with suitable data acquisition hardware converts a PC into an intelligent instrument.

PARAGON 500

Intec Controls Corp., Walpole, MA, USA. Tel: 508-660-1221; fax. 508-660-2374

Requires: IBM PC with DOS 3.0 or better, 640K RAM, 30 MB disk space, EGA, VGA, math coprocessor.

Price: 2,200 US$ base price

This is a graphic programming package which can be used for basic Scada applications.

PARAGON 550

Intec Controls Corp., Walpole, MA, USA. Tel: 508-660-1221; fax. 508-660-2374

Requires: IBM PC with DOS 3.0 or better, 640K RAM, 30 MB disk space, EGA, VGA, math coprocessor.

Price: 3,200 US$ base price

This is an industrial automation software package which can be used for process control and monitoring.

PARAGON TNT

Intec Controls Corp., Walpole, MA, USA. Tel: 508-660-1221; fax: 508-660-2374

Requirements: IBM PC OS/2, 486DX/33 MHz, OS/2 v2.x, VGA, 120 MB of disk space, 12 MB RAM.

Price: 1050 US$ base price

This is a Client-server Scada software based on 32-bit IBM PC platform for plant floor operations.

SIGNALYZER

Intelligent Instrumentation Inc., Tucson, AZ, USA. Tel: 800-685-9911; fax: 602-573-0522

Requirements: IBM PC 386 or better, Windows 3.1 or later, intelligent data acquisition or DSP board, 2 MB of hard disk space, 2 MB of RAM.

Price: 495 US$

This is a Windows based data acquisition software package which allows sampling and storing rates of around 10 MHz.

VISUAL DESIGNER

Intelligent Instrumentation Inc., Tucson, AZ, USA. Tel: 800-685-9911; fax: 602-573-0522

Requirements: IBM PC 386DX, Windows 3.1 or later, VGA, 10 MB of hard disk, 4MB RAM.

Price: 995 US$

Application generator for data acquisition applications. Offers real time displays and user interfaces.

ASYST 4.01

Keithly Instruments Inc., Taunton, MA, USA. Tel: 508-348-0033; fax: 508-880-0 179.

Requirements: IBM PC 386 or better, 5 MB of hard disk space, 1 MB RAM, math coprocessor.

Price: 1,995 US$

Forth language based programming language designed for data acquisition applications. Text based approach to programming.

EASIEST LX

Keithly Instruments Inc., Taunton, MA, USA. Tel: 508-348-0033; fax: 508-880-0179.

Requirements: IBM PC XT/AT 386, 486, MS-DOS 3.0 or later, math coprocessor, EGA or better, 2 MB disk space, 2 MB RAM.

Price: 695 US$

Data logger software package with automatic test sequence capability.

VIEWDAC 2.1

Keithly Instruments Inc., Taunton, MA, USA. Tel: 508-348-0033; fax: 508-880-0179.

Requirements: IBM PC XT/AT 386, 486, MS-DOS 3.0 or later, math coprocessor, EGA or better, 15 MB disk space, 6 MB RAM.

Price: 1,995 US$

Graphic based data acquisition package with preemptive multitasking capability.

INTERFACE TO LAB VIEW FOR CAMAC AND VXI BUSES

Kinetic Systems., Lockport, IL, USA. Tel: 815-838-0005; fax: 815-838-4424

Requirements: IBM PC: 386 or better, Windows, Lab View 2.5.2 or newer, 8 MB of RAM.

Price:495 US$

Graphical programming link to Camac and VXI buses.

LABTECH NOTEBOOK

Laboratory Technologies Corp., Wilmington, MA, USA. Tel: 800-879-5228; fax: 508-658-9972

Requirements: IBM PC: 386 or better, Windows 3.1, 4 MB RAM.

Price: 995 US$

Graphic based programming package for data acquisition. Real time acquisition and data storage.

ORIGIN

MicroCal Software Inc., Northampton, MA, USA. Tel: 413-586-2013; fax: 508-658-9972

Requirements: IBM PC: 386 or better, Windows 3.1, 2 MB RAM, 2 MB hard disk space.

Price: 600 US$

Data acquisition and analysis package. Supports 3-D contours.

LABVIEW

National Instruments, Austin, TX, USA. Tel: 512-794-0100; fax: 512-794-8411

Requirements: IBM PC 386 or better, Windows 3.1, 387 coprocessor, 8 MB RAM, 16 MB hard disk space.

Price:1,995 US$

Graphic based data acquisition and analyses package.

LAB WINDOWS

National Instruments, Austin, TX, USA. Tel: 512-794-0100; fax: 512-794-8411

Requirements: IBM PC 286 or better, 2 MB RAM, 8 MB hard disk space.

Price: 1,495 US$

Software tools for BASIC and C language for data acquisition and control.

LAB WINDOWS/CVI

National Instruments, Austin, TX, USA. Tel: 512-794-0100; fax: 512-794-8411

Requirements: IBM PC 386/33 or better, DOS-5.0, Windows 3.1, 387 coprocessor, 8 MB RAM, 20 MB hard disk space.

Price: 1,995 US$

Software tools for C language for data acquisition and control which are designed to run under Windows.

DATASCULPTOR

NeuralWare Inc., Pittsburgh, PA, USA. Tel: 412-787-8222; fax: 412-787-8220

Requirements: PC/AT 386, 486, DOS 3.3 or later, DRDOS 6.0, Windows 3.1, 3 MB of diskspace, 4 MB of RAM.

Price: 495 US$

Data analysis package for neural network development applications.

WORKBENCH PC

Newport Electronics Inc., Santa Ana, CA, USA. Tel: 800-NEWPORT; 714-540-4914; fax: 714-546-3022

Price: 995 US$

Requirements: IBM PC, MS-DOS, Hercules, EGA or VGA, 640 kB of RAM.

Graphic based data acquisition software with RS-232 and GPIB support.

IOCALC

Newport Electronics Inc., Santa Ana, CA, USA. Tel: 800-NEWPORT; 714-540-4914; fax: 714-546-3022

Requirements: IBM PC, MS-DOS 3.0 or later, CGA, EGA or VGA, 512 kB of RAM.

Price: 550 US$

This is a spreadsheet program which can acquire and display data in real time.

TAURUS

Nivaltec SA, Buenos Aires, Argentina. Tel: (54+1) 822 9120; fax, (54+1) 821 3804

Requirements: IBM PC 386 or better, DOS 3.3 or later, VGA, 10 MB hard disk, 1MB RAM.

Price: 1,500 US$

Software package for data acquisition, supervision, and control. It supports modem, radio and satellite communications.

OMEGA TREND

Omega Engineering Inc., Stamford, CT, USA. Tel: 203-359-1660; fax: 203-359-7990

Requirements: IBM AT or better, MS-DOS 3.1 or later, 2MB hard disk space, 640 kB RAM, VGA.

Price: 349 US$

Software supports high speed data acquisition, recording and display.

WAVEFORM DSP

Omega Engineering Inc., Stamford, CT, USA. Tel: 203-359-1660; fax: 203-359-7990

Requirements: IBM 386 or better, Windows 3.1, 2 MB hard disk space, 1 MB RAM, VGA.

Price: 895 US$

This package can transfer data from a data acquisition card or from another application and perform digital signal processing on the data.

DRIVER LINX IVB

Scientific Software Tools Inc., Paoli, PA, USA. Tel: 215-889-1354, fax: 215-889-1556

Requirements: IBM 386 or better, Windows 3.0 or later, Visual Basic 1.0 or later, 4 MB RAM.

Price: 395 US$

Visual Basic based data acquisition software.

WORKBENCH PC

Strawberry Tree, Sunnyvale, CA, USA. Tel: 800-722-6004; 408-763-2620, fax: 408-736-1041

Requirements: IBM PC 386 or 486 1 MB disk space, 640 kB RAM.

Price: 995 US$

Object oriented package for data acquisition and analysis.

T.A.L. ENTERPRISES,

Philadelphia, PA, USA. Tel: 800-722-6004; 215-763-2620; fax: 215-763-9711

Requirements: IBM PC 286 or better, 1 MB RAM, 500 kB disk space.

Price: 199 US$

Mainly serial port oriented operations, can read and store data from serial port.

REFERENCES

1. *Asyst User Manual,* Keithly Instruments, 1991.

2. *KDAC/500 User Manual,* Keithly Instruments, 1991.

3. *LABDAS User Manual,* Advantech Corporation, 1990.

4. *Labtech Acquire User Manual*, Laboratory Technologies Corporation, 1988.

5. *Labtech Notebook User Manual,* Laboratory Technologies Corporation, 1988.

6. *LabVIEW User Manual*, National Instruments, November 1992.

7. *LabWindows User Manual*, National Instruments, November 1992.

8. *VIEWDAC User Manual,* Keithly Instruments, 1991.

9. *IEEE Spectrum,* November 1993 Issue, pp. 60-87.

APPENDIX A

This section contains data sheets for the following components:

- Thermocouples
- Thermistors
- Platinum resistance temperature detectors
- Semiconducter temperature sensor
- Temperature sensor IC LM35CZ and LM35DZ
- Strain gauges and load cells
- Pressure transducers

Data sheets are reprinted with the permission of RS Components.

Thermocouples

General specification for **RS** thermocouple products

	Type J	Type K	Type N	Type T	Type R	Units
Minimum continuous temperature	−40	−200	−230	−250	−50	°C
Maximum continuous temperature	+850	+1100	+1230	+400	+1350	°C
Maximum spot reading	+1100	+1300	+1320	+500	+1400	°C

Tolerances (BS4937: Part 20)

		Type J	Type K	Type N	Type T	Type R	Units
Accuracy – Class 2 (see note)		±2.5°C or 0.0075 x T	±2.5°C or 0.0075 x T	±2.5°C or 0.0075 x T	±1°C or 0.0075 x T	±2°C	°C
Temperature range – Class 2		−40 to +750	−40 to +750	−40 to +750	−40 to +350	−15 to +1760	°C
BS specification number		4937 Part 4	4937 Part 4	4937 Part 8	4937 Part 5	4937 Part 2	
+ve arm		Iron	Nickel/Chromium	Nicrosil	Copper	13% Rhodium/Platinum 87%	
Composition	Cr	none	≃10	14.2 ±0.5	unspecified		%
	Si	none	unspecified	1.4 ±0.2	unspecified		%
	Fe	100	unspecified	0-15 max	unspecified		%
	C	none	unspecified	0.05	unspecified		%
	Mg	none	unspecified	none	unspecified		%
	Ni	none	balance	balance	unspecified		%
	Cu	none	unspecified	none	balance		%
−ve arm		Nickel/Aluminium	Nickel/Aluminium	Nisil	Copper/Nickel	100% Platinum	
Composition	Cr	none	unspecified	0.02 max	unspecified		%
	Si	none	balance	4.4 ±0.2	unspecified		%
	Fe	0.3	unspecified	0.15 max	unspecified		%
	C	none	unspecified	0.05 max	unspecified		%
	Mg	none	unspecified	0.05 to 0.2	unspecified		%
	Ni	42	95	balance	40/45		%
	Cu	balance	unspecified	none	balance		%
	Mn	1.2	balance	none	unspecified		%
	Al	none	balance	none	unspecified		%

Colour codes BS1843 – 1952 (UK only)

		Type J	Type K	Type N	Type T	Type R	
Thermocouple and extension wiring	+ve arm	yellow	brown	orange	white	white	
	−ve arm	blue	blue	blue	blue	blue	
	overall	black	red	orange	blue	green	
Compensating cable and wiring and wiring	+ve arm	–	white	–	–	white	
	−ve arm	–	blue	–	–	blue	
	overall	–	red	–	–	green	

Note. T refers to measured temperature in °C.

Thermocouple basics

Thermocouples provide an economic means of measuring temperature with many practical advantages for the user, for example:

1. They can be extremely robust, by using thick wire.
2. Fine wire thermocouples respond very rapidly to temperature changes (less than 0.1 secs). For ultra fast response (10μ seconds typical), foil thermocouples are used.
3. Capable of measuring over very wide temperature ranges, from cryogenics to engine exhausts.
4. Thermocouples are easy to install and are available in many packages, from probes to bare wires or foil.

The number of free electrons in a piece of metal depends on both temperature and composition of the metal, therefore pieces of dissimilar metal in isothermal contact will exhibit a potential difference that is a repeatable function of temperature. The resulting voltage depends on the temperatures, T1 and T2, in a

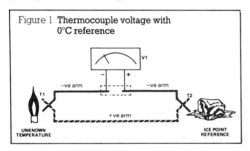

Figure 1 **Thermocouple voltage with 0°C reference**

repeatable way as shown in Figure 1.

Since the thermocouple is basically a differential rather than an absolute temperature measuring device, one junction must be at a known temperature if the temperature of the other junction is to be found from the value of the output voltage.

An alternative measurement technique is illustrated in Figure 2. This is used in most practical applications where accuracy requirements do not warrant maintenance of primary standards as shown in Figure 1. The reference junction temperature is allowed to change but it is carefully measured by some type of absolute

thermometer. A measurement of the thermocouple voltage combined with a knowledge of the reference temperature can be used to calculate the measurement junction temperature. Usual practice, however, is to use a convenient thermoelectric method to measure the reference temperature and to arrange its output voltage so that it corresponds to a thermocouple referred to 0°C. This voltage is simply added to the thermocouple voltage and the sum then corresponds to the standard voltage tabulated for an icepoint referenced thermocouple. This method is used in the circuit shown in Figure 4.

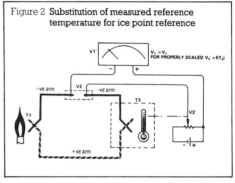

Figure 2 **Substitution of measured reference temperature for ice point reference**

Thermocouples are of specially selected materials and have been exhaustively characterised in terms of voltage versus temperature compared to primary temperature standards. The water-ice point of 0°C is normally used for tables of standard thermocouple performance eg, BS4937, Part 4 gives tables of EMF and temperature to the nearest degree for K type thermocouples. For details of EMF tables see Technical Books and Training section of current **RS** catalogue for book 904-435 (Temperature sensing with thermocouples and resistance thermometers).

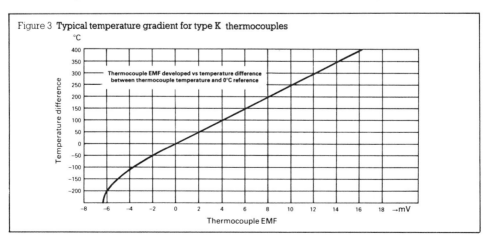

Figure 3 **Typical temperature gradient for type K thermocouples**

Typical temperature measurement circuit

The circuit shown in Figure 4 may be used in conjunction with **RS** K-type thermocouples to measure temperatures from 0 to 100°C. If the component values are changed this circuit can be used with other thermocouple types at different temperatures.

The cold junction compensation is provided by D2, the forward voltage drop of which changes approximately 2mV/°C. This voltage is reduced by a potential divider to the thermocouple output. The result, amplified by IC1 and displayed on any 100μA meter is proportional to the temperature of the measurement junction of the thermocouple.

Calibration

The zero adjustment is set by R3 and the span by R9. Calibrate as follows:

1. Place measurement junction of thermocouple in freezing water to give 0°C.
2. Adjust R3 to give a reading of zero on the meter.
3. Place the measurement junction of the thermocouple in boiling water (100°C).
4. Adjust R9 to give full scale deflection on the meter.

The circuit will then be calibrated to give a reading of 1μA per °C.

Figure 4 **Typical temperature measurement circuit**

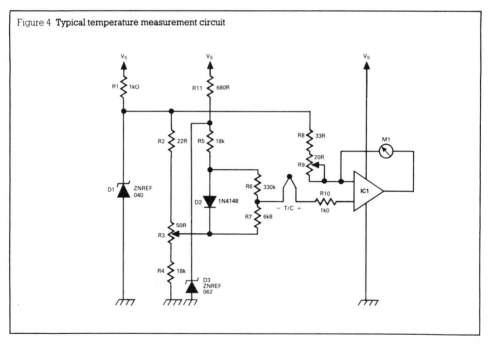

Notes:

1. The circuit is intended for use with a single supply of approximately 9V such as a PP3 battery.
2. Meter M1 should be 100μA moving coil (eg **RS** stock no. 312-561).
3. IC1 should be any op-amp of a 741 type. Final selection will depend on required accuracy, current consumption etc.

Type K and N thermocouples

Of all the base metal thermocouples used in industry today the one based on nickel, more commonly known as type K, or nickel chromium/nickel aluminium is the most widely used.

Type K thermocouples were standardised in 1916 when the science of metallurgy was less advanced than now. Type K materials are basically nickel doped with aluminium and nickel doped with chromium and in 1916 it was not possible to produce very pure nickel, consequently, many impurities are present in type K materials. In fact in recent years these impurities have had to be deliberately added to maintain calibration.

For these reasons type K thermocouples are standardised or characterised by EMF/temperature and not by alloy content. It is common to add extra elements to 'adjust' the EMF/temperature characteristics of a particular melt. Consequently, there are problems with type K thermocouples, namely:

1. The −ve arm of the thermocouple is ferromagnetic at room temperature, however, its Curie point (the temperature at which it changes from ferro to dia magnetic characteristics) is in the useful range of the thermocouple. This change causes a sudden change in EMF output. Furthermore, since the Curie point is dependent on the consistency of the alloy, which in type K is not defined, the Curie point will vary from thermocouple to thermocouple. Unknown changes in EMF at unknown temperatures are therefore experienced.

2. At high temperatures (200°C to 600°C) type K thermocouples suffer a hysteresis effect where the couple will under read when the temperature is rising and over read when the temperature is falling. The cause of this is not presently understood, however, short range ordering is suspected. The effect is dependent on the exact make-up of the alloys as well as the thermal history of the thermocouple. The net result is an unpredictable change in EMF.

3. At temperatures around 1000°C the thermocouple arms will oxidise, and because the alloys used are permeable to oxygen both internal and external oxidation will occur. The various elements used in these alloys will oxidise at different rates causing a change in constituency and hence a change in EMF.

4. The use of cobalt in the alloy for type K thermocouples causes a problem in nuclear industries, or other areas of high neutron flux. Some elements, such as cobalt, will undergo nuclear decay thus changing the make up of the alloy and its EMF output.

The type N thermocouple overcomes most if not all of these problems by optimisation of the alloys of nickel used to manufacture the thermocouple arms. Type N thermocouples are not merely an improvement over type K but are the best combination of elements giving optimum results for a thermocouple based on nickel.

The four problems encountered in type K are dealt with as follows in type N:

1. The Curie point is set well below zero by choosing a suitable combination of elements and is therefore outside the measuring range of the thermocouple.

2. The hysteresis is dependent upon the constituents of the alloy and by optimising the alloy the effect is minimised.

3. The use of silicon in the alloys results in formation of silicates on the surface of the wires, these form excellent protection against oxidisation as they are impervious to oxygen. This protection system is one of the best known and prevents internal and external oxidisation and hence change in EMF. A type K thermocouples will eventually fail mechanically when the wire is oxidised to such an extent that it is unable to withstand the thermally induced stresses placed on it and break.

4. In type N thermocouples all the elements susceptible to change due to high neutron flux are removed therefore no change of calibration is experienced.

To review the type N thermocouple is not merely an improved nickel based thermocouple but should be considered as the optimum nickel based thermocouple which, as far as possible, overcomes all of the disadvantages of not only type K but any nickel based thermocouple.

Minerally insulated type K thermocouples can suffer other problems which are shared by type N.

The sheath material for the majority of minerally insulated thermocouples is either stainless steel or inconel. Both materials can cause a loss of calibration due to alloying elements diffusing into the hot junction of the thermocouple and 'poisoning' it. These extra elements will change the EMF to temperature relationship and lead to errors. This problem is common to both types K and N but with type N a simple solution is available. The type N −ve arm is made of nisil, if the sheath is made of this material diffusion is very much reduced and the effect is no longer a problem.

Using nisil sheaths also reduces the thermal stresses generated due to the different rates of thermal expansion of steel and nickel which can lead to failure of conductors in minerally insulated thermocouples.

The specifications for type N materials define not only the EMF/temperature relationships, as in type K, but the exact quantities of components in the alloys. This means that one batch of type N from one manufacturer will be the same as another from a different source. This is not true for type K thermocouples.

Although 'half tolerance' type K thermocouples are available they are for all practical purposes a myth. The thermocouple, when calibrated, may be within half the standard tolerance of ±3°C it is not possible to guarantee this the next time the couple is heated. True half tolerance thermocouples may be available in type N.

Another advantage of type N thermocouples is the oxidisation protection system, using silica it is effective up to the melting point of the alloys, therefore the temperature range is extended to 1300°C for both the exposed junction and minerally insulated types using nisil sheaths.

Type K, N and J thermocouple products covered by this data sheet

Thermocouples	Type K RS stock no.	Type N RS stock no.	Type J RS stock no.	Instrumentation	Type K RS stock no.	Type N RS stock no.	Type J RS stock no.
Welded tip thermocouple PTFE insulated (pack of 5)	158-913	159-001		Digital temperature indicator	257-284	257-284	
Welded tip thermocouple glass fibre insulated	151-192	158-991	150-004	Recording temperature indicator	616-706		
Magnetic base thermocouple	158-597			Panel mounting digital indicators	258-108 258-186		258-186
Mineral insulated thermocouple	158-604	159-017		Thermocouple 12-way selector	332-969		
Mineral insulated thermocouples stainless steel sheath	159-023 to 159-089 & 285-453, 285-469			**Accessories**			
				Thermocouple plugs and sockets	473-127		
				Miniature	467-829 473-105 473-111	475-044 475-050 475-066	475-555 475-561 475-577 475-583 475-599 475-606
Mineral insulated thermocouples inconel sheath	159-095 to 159-152 & 285-475, 285-481			Standard	474-350 474-366 474-372		
Self adhesive thermocouple	158-626			Extension wire (solid conductor)	151-209		
Rapid response	256-130			Extension cable (stranded core)	158-979	159-168	150-010
Plug mounted air probe	256-534			Handle for plug mounted probes	159-174		
Plug mounted general purpose mineral insulated probe	256-540			Compensating cable (25m) (100m)	151-316 158-963		
Plug mounted surface band probe	256-556			Mineral insulated compression gland	158-610		
Plug mounted low insertion force	285-699			Bayonet fitting adaptor			150-032
Bayonet mounted			150-026				

Industrial style

Probes	200mm	285-728		
	400mm	285-734		
	600mm	285-740		
Melt thermocouple				285-677
Heavy duty probe				285-683

Hand-held thermocouple probes

General purpose probe	160-556
Insertion probe	256-506
Surface probe	160-540
Band probe	256-512
Air temperature probe	158-525
GP probe – high temp	256-528

Hand-held meters

LCD digital thermometer	610-067	
Peak holding thermometer	611-234	
°C/°F digital temperature indicator	612-861	
Differential temperature indicator	612-619	
Basic temperature indicator	612-855	
Fluke type 51	614-299	614-299
Fluke type 53	614-306	614-306

Type T thermocouples

Type T thermocouples have two major advantages over type K, and to a large extent over type N, namely:

1. An extended and specified low temperature range.
2. Greater accuracy (below 100°C accuracy is ±1°C).

However, there are two disadvantages:

1. The EMF/temperature characteristic is non-linear.
2. The maximum operating temperature is 400°C.

With modern electronic temperature indicators the first disadvantage will not cause a problem as its non-linearity can be taken into account.

Therefore if measurement of temperatures below 400°C is envisaged the type T is a good choice as enhanced accuracy is possible. This has resulted in the type T being used extensively in laboratories.

In industrial applications using more than one thermocouple type is avoided because of the possibility of the wrong sensor being used.

If only one thermocouple is to be selected the normal choice would be type K as this gives a good temperature range. However, for new applications consideration should be given to the use of type N due to its advantages over type K and extended temperature range. (See section on type K and N for further details.)

Type T thermocouple – food probe standard

Although the standard accuracy of type T thermocouples is ±1°C below 100°C (and stated above), these probes have been designed to comply with the requirements of the Food Hygiene (Amendment) Regulations 1990. All have a fast response time and are specially selected to have an accuracy of ±0.25°C over the working temperature range. All probes have been designed to be easily cleaned and sterilised without degrading performance and are supplied complete with 2 metres of coiled PUR type cable and a fitted miniature thermocouple connector.

Type T thermocouple products covered by this data sheet

	RS stock no.
Welded tip probe	151-259
Rapid response	256-146
PTFE insulated probe	158-907
Hypodermic probe	151-271
Panel mounting digital temperature indicator	258-186
Plug mounted air probe	285-497
Plug mounted GP probe	285-504
Plug mounted surface probe	285-510
Plug mounted low insertion force probe	285-526
Food probe, 90° surface	285-627
Food probe, standard insertion	285-548
Food probe, heavy duty insertion	285-554
Food probe, spatula	285-611
Food probe, weighted surface	285-605

Accessories

Handle for plug mounted probes	285-532
Connectors	
Miniature	475-498, 505, 511 and 470-112
Standard	475-527, 533, 549

Type K products

Thermocouples

Welded tip thermocouple
PTFE insulated RS stock no. 158-913

Features

- Supplied in packs of five
- Economic solution to temperature monitoring problems in research and development areas
- PTFE insulation for resistance to chemical attack
- Maximum working temperature +250°C
- 1/0.2mm wire for very fast response

Specification

Thermocouple wire	1/0.2mm
Overall length	1 metre
Insulation diameter	0.6mm (nom)
Insulation material	Poly tetra fluro Ethylene (PTFE)
Working temperature range	–50°C to +200°C (continuous) +250°C (spot)

Welded tip thermocouple
glass fibre insulated RS stock no. 151-192

Features

- Thermocouple junction welded in Argon, resists oxidation
- 400°C maximum working temperature
- Small welded junction minimises thermal heat sinking and provides fast thermal response
- Fibre glass insulation
- Ideal for permanent installations

Specification

Thermocouple wire	1/0.315mm
Overall length	2 metres (min)
Insulation diameter	1.5mm
Insulation	Fibre glass
Working temperature range	–50°C to +400°C

Magnetic base thermocouple **RS** stock no. 158-597

Features

- Magnetic base easily attaches to any iron or steel surface
- Rapidly installed and moved
- Can measure temperatures up to 120°C
- 2 metre PTFE lead
- Fitted with miniature thermocouple plug

Specification

Temperature range	–25°C to +120°C
Pad length	50mm
Pad width	25mm
Thickness	1mm
Lead wire	1/0.2
Insulation	PTFE
Lead length	2m

Mineral insulated thermocouples steel sheath
RS stock nos. 159-023 to 159-089 and 285-453, 285-469

Features

- For use up to 800°C
- 321 stainless steel sheath
- Available in 0.5, 1.0, 1.5, 3.0 and 6.0mm dia
- Available in 0.5, 1.0 and 2.0m lengths

Specification

Sheath material	321 stainless steel
Insulation material	Magnesium oxide (MgO)
Temperature range	0°C to +800°C
Temperature range of pot	0°C to +120°C
Lead size	7/0.2
Lead insulation	PVC
Lead length	100mm

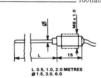

L. 0.5, 1.0, 2.0 METRES
Ø 1.5, 3.0, 6.0

Plug mounted probes, air temperature **RS** stock no. 256-534, general purpose **RS** stock no. 256-540, surface probe **RS** stock no. 256-556, low force insertion **RS** stock no. 285-699

Features

- Probes mounted directly onto a miniature thermocouple plug
- Ideal for use with **RS** hand held instruments, giving one handed operation
- General purpose probe suitable for immersion into liquid gas or flames. Maximum temperature +1000°C. Probes can be bent
- Air probe has fast response by using a low mass exposed junction
- Surface probe uses 7mm band for fast response. Maximum operating temperature +250°C

Specification

Air probe

Temperature range	0°C to 250°C
Sheath material	Stainless steel
Sheath length	100mm
Sheath diameter	3mm

General purpose probe

Temperature range	0°C to 1000°C
Probe material	mineral insulated, stainless steel outer
Probe length	150mm
Probe diameter	3mm
Response time	0.5 seconds (in water)

Surface probe

Temperature range	0°C to +250°C
Shaft material	Stainless steel
Shaft length	100mm
Response time	0.1 seconds (on clean metal)

Low force insertion

Temperature range (tip)	–50°C to +250°C
Sheath material	Stainless steel
Probe diameter	3mm
Probe length	100mm

Mineral insulated thermocouple **RS** stock no. 158-604

Features

- Can be used up to 1000°C
- Stainless steel sheath
- Compression gland available (**RS** stock no. 158-610)
- Threaded pot for easy installation (nuts supplied)
- 3mm diameter probe, 300mm long

Specification

Temperature range	0°C to +1000°C
Probe diameter	3mm
Probe length	300mm
Mounting thread	M8 x 1.0
Lead	7 x 0.2 twisted pair
Lead length	1m
Lead insulation	PTFE
Sheath material	2520 stainless steel

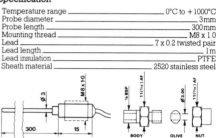

Mineral insulated thermocouples inconel sheath
RS stock nos. 159-095 to 159-152 and 285-475, 285-481

Features

- For use up to 1100°C
- Inconel 600 sheath
- Available in 0.5, 1.0, 1.5, 3.0 and 6.0mm dia
- Available in 0.5, 1.0 and 2.0m lengths

Specification

Sheath material	Inconel 600
Insulation material	Magnesium oxide (MgO)
Temperature range	0°C to +1000°C
Temperature range of pot	0°C to +120°C
Lead size	7/0.2
Lead insulation	PVC
Lead length	100mm

L. 0.5, 1.0, 2.0 METRES
Ø 1.5, 3.0, 6.0

Self adhesive thermocouple **RS** stock no. 158-626

Features

- Thermocouple junction brazed to a 7mm disc
- More robust than patch thermocouples
- Can be used up to 200°C
- Supplied with extra adhesive strips for reuse
- 1m PTFE insulated leads

Specification

Temperature range	0°C to +200°C
Disc diameter	7mm
Adhesive strip size	10 x 25mm (approx.)
Lead	1/0.2 twisted pair
Insulation	PTFE
Lead length	1m

Rapid response thermocouple **RS** stock no. 256-130

Features

● For use to +800°C
● Foil construction to ultra fast response
● Filament carrier is polyamide film – may be left in place if required

Specification

Temperature range ———————— 0°C to +800°C
Length (overall) ——————————— 170mm
Foil thickness ————————————— 0.05mm
Response time (to 63% of step change)
  grounded ——————————————— 5ms
  ungrounded ————————————— 10ms

General purpose probe – high temperature **RS** stock no. 256-528

Features

● For use up to 1100°C
● Fast response
● Probe can be shaped repeatedly

Specification

Temperature range (tip) ————— 0°C to +1100°C
Probe length ————————————— 100mm
Time constant ——————————— 0.25 (water)
Sheath material ———————— Stainless steel

Hand held thermocouple probes

Thermocouple air temperature probe **RS** stock no. 158-525

Features

● Stainless steel sheath
● 750°C maximum working temperature
● Thermocouple electrically insulated from sheath

Specification

Sheath ——————————— 9mm long, dia 5mm
Handle ————————— 76mm long, dia 13mm
Lead length ———————————————— 1mm
Sheath material ———————— Stainless steel
Handle material ————————— Nylon grade 6.6
Probe temperature range ——— –100°C to +750°C

Thermocouple surface probe **RS** stock no. 160-540

Features

● Stainless steel, splayed tripod end
● Thermocouple is attached to a thin 4mm dia metallic disc which is sprung to ensure constant pressure during measurements. The sprung action also reduces the risk of damage to the tip should excessive forces to be applied in use.
● Maximum permissible temperature of tip +750°C
● Insulated handle
  Note. Tip is not isolated from the thermocouple junction

Specification

Dimensions
Thermocuple wire ———————— 7/0.2mm dia
Sheath length ————————————— 92mm
Sheath diameter ———— 5mm widening to 7mm at tripod end
Handle length ———————————— 104mm
Sleeve length ————————————— approx. 1m

Materials
Sheath ————————————— Stainless steel
Handle ————————————— Nylon grade 6.6

General
Probe temperature range ——— –100°C to +750°C

General purpose thermocouple probe **RS** stock no. 160-556

Features

● Stainless steel sheath
● Thermocouple electrically insulated from the sheath
● Probe may be bent (once only)
● 250°C maximum working temperature
● Small contact surface area minimises heat sinking effect

Specification

General
Probe temperature range ———— –200°C to +250°C
Minimum insulation resistance
between wire and sheath ————————— <100⁴MΩ
Voltage proof ———————————— 1000V dc
Lead terminations ———————— bare wires 7/0.2mm
Dimensions
Sheath ——————————— 152mm long, dia 3.2mm
Handle ——————————— 90mm long, dia 10mm
Lead ——————————— 2m long (min), dia 3mm
Materials
Sheath ———————————— 18.8 stainless steel
Handle ———————— Hardwood sleeved in PVC
Wire insulation ———— PTFE, overall insulation PVC

Insertion probe **RS** stock no. 256-506

Features

● High quality robust probe
● Suitable for measuring subsurface temperature in solids
● Ideal for the frozen food industry
● 600°C max working temperature
● Fitted with a coiled lead of 2 metres extended length
● Terminated in a miniature thermocouple plug

Specification

General
Temperature range ——————— –100°C to +600°C
Response time ———————————— 2 sec (water)
Lead termination ————— Miniature thermocouple plug
Dimensions
Probe length ————————————— 100mm
Probe diameter ———————————— 3.3mm
Lead length coiled (approx) —————— 300mm
Lead length extended ——————————— 2m
Lead termination ————— Miniature thermocouple plug
Handle length ————————————— 90mm
Materials
Probe ———————————————— Stainless steel
Lead ———————————————————— PVC
Handle ——————————————— Polypropylene

Thermistors

NTC Thermistors

The RS range of NTC thermistors includes standard tolerance negative temperature coefficient thermistors, plus a wide range of small close tolerance R/T curve matched thermistors.

Standard tolerance thermistors

A range of 14 negative temperature coefficient bead thermistors and 4 disc thermistors constructed from a compound of nickel mangenite. Of the 14 bead thermistors, ten types are sealed in glass and three are incorporated into stainless steel probe assemblies. This range was designed primarily for temperature measurement and control, flow measurement and liquid level detection. The remaining bead type, suspended in an evacuated glass envelope, is designed for applications in amplitude control, temperature compensation and time delay circuits. The four NTC disc thermistors are intended for use in temperature compensation, measurement and control applications. Disc diameter in all cases is 10mm with a lead pitch of 5mm (nominal).

Characteristic resistance		Units	Miniature beads							Beads		
			151-136	256-045	151-142	151-158	256-051	151-164	256-067	256-118	151-029	151-013
R_{BEAD}	+20°C	Ω	–	–	–	–	–	–	–	–	2k	1M
	+25°C	Ω	1k	10k	4.7k	47k	220k	470k	1.4M	†350k	–	–
R_{MIN} (HOT)		Ω	59	130	271	338	1.3k	440	500	1.5k	115	170
R_{BEAD} TOLERANCE		%	±20	±20	±20	±20	±20	±20	±20	±20	±20	±20
T_A max ambient temp range maximum dissipation		°C	−80 to +125	−55 to +200	−80 to +125	−60 to +200	−55 to +200	−25 to +300	−25 to +300	+100 to +450	−80 to +300	−25 to +300
Maximum dissipation		mW	75	130	75	130	130	205	205	–	130	340
Derate to zero at		°C	125	200	125	200	200	300	300	450	125	300
Dissipation constant		mW/°C	0.75	0.75	0.75	0.75	0.75	0.75	0.75	1.2	1.2	1.2
Thermal time constant		s	5	5	5	5	5	5	5	20	19	19
B constant (+25 to +85°C)		°K	2910	3555	3340	3940	4145	4725*	4900*	4700*	3200	4850
B tolerance		%	±3	±3	±3	±3	±3	±3	±3	±5	±5	±5
Equivalent types			GM102 VA3400	GM103	GM472 VA3404	GM473 VA3410	GM224	GM474	GM105	MA354	GL23	GL16

* (100-200°C)
† 100°C

Characteristic resistance		Units	Probe assemblies			Evac type		Disc type			
			151-120	256-124	151-170	151-114		256-095	256-102	256-089	256-073
	R_{BEAD} +20°C	Ω	–	–	–	5k	R_{DISC}	–	–	–	
	+25°C	Ω	4.7k	35k	1.0M	–	@25°C	470	1k	4.7k	10k
	R_{MIN} (HOT)	Ω	500	600	800	79		19	35	130	260
$R_{BEAD\ DISC}$	TOLERANCE	%	±2	±2	±2	±20		±10	±10	±10	±10
T_A max ambient temp range maximum dissipation		°C	−30 to +100	−30 to +150	−30 to +250	0 to +155		−30 to +125	−18 to +125	−30 to +125	−30 to +125
Maximum dissipation		mW	50	50	50	3.0		900	900	900	900
Derate to zero at		°C	100	150	250	225		125	125	125	125
Dissipation constant		mW°C	5.0	5.0	5.0	12.5×10^{-3}			3.6		
Thermal time constant		s	180	180	180	11		30	30	30	30
B constant (+25 to +85°C)		°K	3275	4165	5000	3250		3850	4000	4300	4400
B tolerance		%	±2	±2	±2	±5		±3	±3	±3	±3
Equivalent types			JA03	JA05	JA09	RA53		KED 471	KED 102	KED 472	KED 103

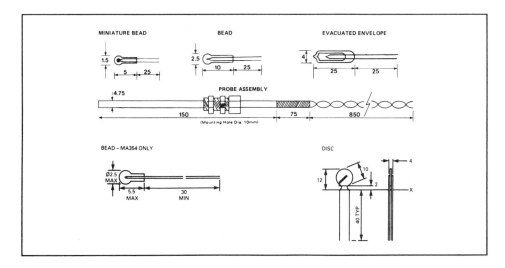

Basic formulae

The temperature coefficient ∝ at any temperature within the operating range may be obtained from the formula:

$$\propto = -\frac{B}{T^2} \text{ (per °C)}$$

To determine the resistance at any temperature within the operating range may be obtained from the formula:

$$R_2 = R_1 \cdot e^{\left(\frac{B}{t_2} - \frac{B}{t_1} \right)}$$

where

B = characteristic temperature constant (°K)
T = bead temperature in (°K)
R_1 = resistance of thermistor at temperature t_1 (Ω)
R_2 = resistance of thermistor at temperature t_2 (Ω)
e = 2.7183
(Temperature in °K = temperature in °C + 273).

Application notes

Typical applications include temperature control of ovens, deep freezers, rooms and for process control, etc. Can also be used to drive high and low temperature alarms.

In the basic circuit below, calibration should be carried out by comparison with a known standard (eg. a thermometer or thermocouple). In the case of 0°C, a mixture of ice and water can be used and for +100°C, use boiling water.

Note that non-linearity should be expected at extended temperatures.

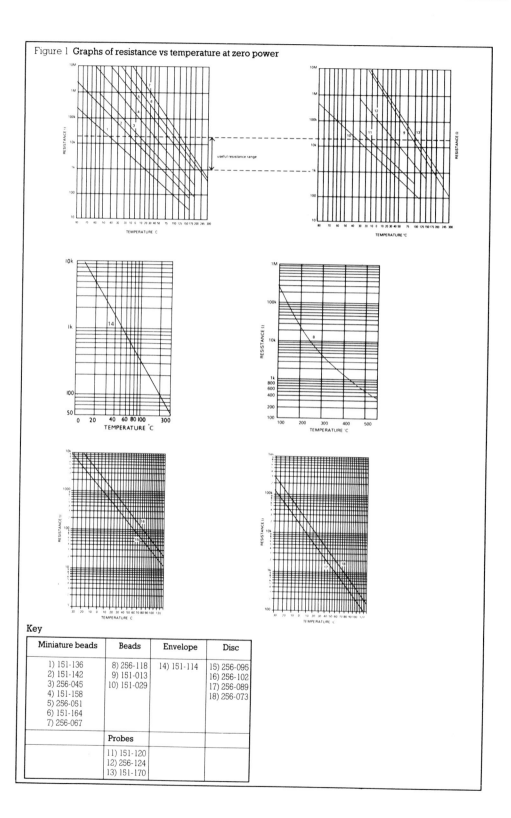

Figure 1 Graphs of resistance vs temperature at zero power

Key

Miniature beads	Beads	Envelope	Disc
1) 151-136 2) 151-142 3) 256-045 4) 151-158 5) 256-051 6) 151-164 7) 256-067	8) 256-118 9) 151-013 10) 151-029	14) 151-114	15) 256-095 16) 256-102 17) 256-089 18) 256-073
	Probes		
	11) 151-120 12) 256-124 13) 151-170		

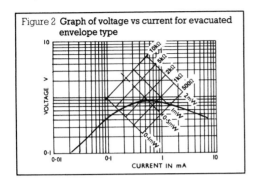

Figure 2 **Graph of voltage vs current for evacuated envelope type**

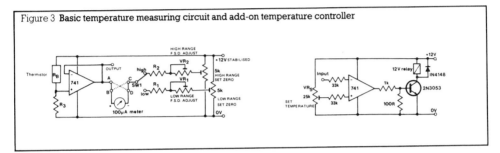

Figure 3 **Basic temperature measuring circuit and add-on temperature controller**

Table 1 **Typical resistor values for temperature measuring circuit (above)**

	Thermistor	Temperature in (°C)		Resistor values (kΩ)				
		Low	High	R_1	R_2	R_3	VR_1	VR_2
Miniature	151-136	0 to −60*	0 to +30	56	6.8	22	50	5
	151-142	0 to +30	0 to +100	18	33	22	10	20
	151-158	+50 to +100	+100 to +150	27	8.2	22	10	5
	151-164	+150 to +200	+200 to +250	12	3.9	22	5	2
Beads	151-029	0 to −30*	0 to +30	27	10	22	20	5
	151-013	+100 to +150	+150 to +200	39	8.2	22	20	5
Probe Assy.	151-120	0 to −30*	0 to +100	33	33	22	20	20

Note.
* For negative ranges reverse meter by linking A to D and B to C

R-T curve matched thermistors

A range of high quality precision curve matched thermistors, available in four characteristic resistances. The range offers true interchangeability over a wide temperature range and eliminates the need for individual circuit adjustments or padding. These thermistors provide accurate and stable temperature sensing capability for applications such as temperature measurement and compensation.

Table 2 **Resistance/Temperature characteristics**

RS stock No. 151-215		RS stock No. 151-221		RS stock No. 151-237		RS stock No. 151-243	
Temp °C	Res Ω	Temp °C	Res Ω	Temp °C	Res Ω	Temp °C	Res Ω
−80	2,210,400	−80	3,684,000	−80	7,368,000		
−70	935,250	−70	1,558,800	−70	3,117,500		
−60	421,470	−60	702,450	−60	1,404,900		
−50	201,030	−50	335,050	−50	670,100		
−40	100,950	−40	168,250	−40	336,500	−40	4,015,500
−30	53,100	−30	88,500	−30	177,000	−30	2,064,000
−20	29,121	−20	48,535	−20	97,070	−20	1,103,400
−10	16,599	−10	27,665	−10	55,330	−10	611,870
0	9,795.0	0	16,325	0	32,650	0	351,020
+10	5,970.0	+10	9,950.0	+10	19,900	+10	207,850
+20	3,747.0	+20	6,245.0	+20	12,490	+20	126,740
+25	3,000.0	+25	5,000.0	+25	10,000	+25	100,000
+30	2,417.1	+30	4,028.5	+30	8,057.0	+30	79,422
+40	1,598.1	+40	2,663.3	+40	5,327.0	+40	51,048
+50	1,080.9	+50	1,801.5	+50	3,603.0	+50	33,591
+60	746.40	+60	1,244.0	+60	2,488.0	+60	22,590
+70	525.60	+70	876.00	+70	1,752.0	+70	15,502
+80	376.50	+80	627.50	+80	1,255.0	+80	10,837
+90	274.59	+90	457.65	+90	915.30	+90	7,707.7
+100	203.49	+100	339.15	+100	678.30	+100	5,569.3
+110	153.09	+110	255.15	+110	510.30	+110	4,082.9
+120	116.79	+120	194.65	+120	389.30	+120	3,033.3
+130	90.279	+130	150.47	+130	300.93	+130	2,281.0
+140	70.581	+140	117.64	+140	235.27	+140	1,734.3
+150	55.791	+150	92.985	+150	185.97	+150	1,331.9

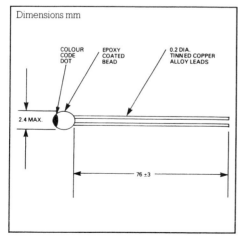

Dimensions mm

COLOUR CODE DOT
EPOXY COATED BEAD
0.2 DIA. TINNED COPPER ALLOY LEADS

2.4 MAX.

76 ±3

Table 3 **Electrical characteristics**

RS stock no.	151-215	151-221	151-237	151-243
Colour code dot	Red	Orange	Yellow	Violet
Resistance at +25°C	3kΩ	5kΩ	10kΩ	100kΩ
Temperature range	−80°C to +150°C			
Tolerance (0 to +70°C)	±0.2°C			
Dissipation constant	1mW			
Time constant	10s			

Definitions

Dissipation constant. Represents the amount of power required to raise the temperature of the thermistor 1°C above its ambient temperature, expressed in milliwatts.

Time constant. The time required for the thermistor dissipating zero power to change 63% of the difference between its initial temperature value and that of a new impressed temperature environment.

PTC thermistors

The RS range of PTC thermistors includes three types for over-temperature protection and four types for over-current protection.

Over-temperature protection

A range of three positive temperature coefficient (PTC) thermistors, manufactured from a compound of barium lead and strontium titanates. The range consists of two disc types and one stud mounted version. These devices are primarily designed for temperature sensing and protection of semiconductor devices, transformers and motors etc. As can be seen from the resistance/temperature characteristics of Figure 6, the resistance of the PTC thermistor is low and relatively constant at low temperatures. As the ambient temperature increases, the resistance rises. The rate of increase becomes very rapid at the reference temperature (Tr) of the device. Tr is also known as the threshhold, critical or switching temperature. Above Tr the characteristic becomes very steep and attains a high resistance value.

Specification		Stud	Disc
RS stock nos.		158-250	158-266 158-272
Maximum operating and storage temperature		155°C	Tr + 100°C
Minimum operating and storage temperature		−20°C	−55°C
Typical thermal resistance (embedded)	(1)	–	0.05°C/mW
Typical dissipation constant (embedded)	(1)	–	20mW/°C
Maximum power dissipation at 25°C	(2)	–	690mW
Maximum applied voltage at 25°C	(2)	–	40V
Insulation between stud and lead		500Vdc	–
Typical resistance at or below Tr −20°C			100Ω
Maximum resistance at or below Tr −20°C			250Ω
Maximum resistance at Tr −5°C	(3)		550Ω
Typical resistance at Tr	(3)		1000Ω
Minimum resistance at Tr +5°C	(3)		1330Ω
Minimum resistance at Tr +15°C	(3)		4000Ω

Notes.

(1) Dependent on method of insulation and mounting

(2) Self heating in free air

(3) Measured at 2.5Vdc

(4) Measured at 7.5Vdc.

Figure 4

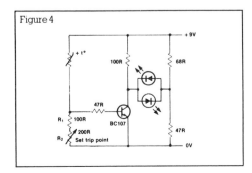

Figure 5

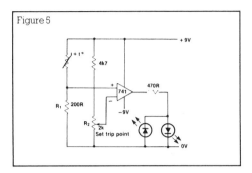

Figure 6 **Resistance/Temperature graph**

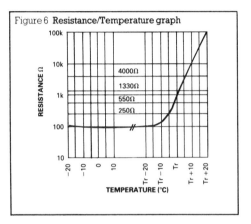

Calibration

Calibration should be carried out by heating the thermistor to the appropriate reference temperature and adjust R_2 such that the appropriate LED lights.

Series connection

In temperature sensing circuits two or more devices may be connected in series. The sensing circuit will then indicate if any of the thermistors exceeds the reference temperature. An increase in the value of R_1 may be necessary to compensate for the additional voltage drop across the thermistor.

Application notes

Basic temperature sensing circuits

Figure 4 shows a basic circuit which indicates when the temperature of the PTC thermistor is below Tr (ie. safe operation) and will also indicate when Tr is exceeded. When both LEDs are off this indicates the Tr is being approached (approx. Tr −5°C).

Figure 5 shows a circuit which has a more defined 'trip point than Figure 4 (set by R_2).

Over-current protection

Switching type Positive Temperature Coefficient (PTC) thermistors are prepared from the compounds of barium, lead and strontium titanates to give a ceramic disc. Electrical contacts are made by the metallising of the disc faces using nickel, silver, etc; the completed disc is then provided with soldered lead wires.

Specification

Ratings
Resistance tolerance at +25°C   ±25%
V_{max} 265V rms
Ambient temperature range
Operating   0-+55°C
Storage   −40 to +155°C

Definition of terms

R_{min} – Resistance of PTC at lowest point of R v T curve.

R_{25} – Resistance of PTC at +25°C.

I_{max} – Current value at turnover point of I/V curve at a specified temperature.

I_{rest} – Current value at V_{max}.

I_{peak} – Maximum allowable current through PTC.

V_{max} – Maximum voltage that may be applied to thermistor.

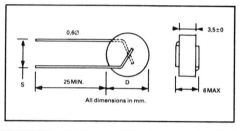

RS stock no.	Switch	I_{max} (Typ.)		I_{REST}	I_{PEAK}	RS min.	@ < 1mAdc			Dimensions (mm)	
		+25°C	+55°C				R_{25}	R_{120}	R_{155}	D	S
151-287		350	280	<11.5	1.65A	150Ω	10	< 30	> 30k	15	5
151-293	+125°C	200	155	< 8.0	815mA	300Ω	25	< 80	> 80k	10	5
151-300		110	86	< 7.0	250mA	1kΩ	70	<218	>220k	6	5
256-039	+80°C	15	8	< 4.0	58mA	3800Ω	1000	<10m	>10m	5	5

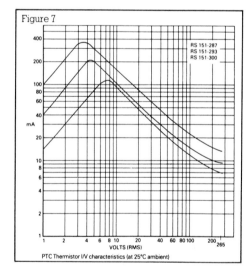

Figure 7

RS 151-287
RS 151-293
RS 151-300

PTC Thermistor I/V characteristics (at 25°C ambient)

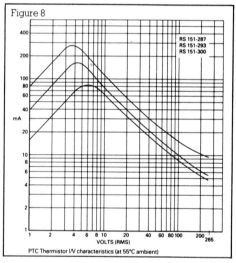

Figure 8

RS 151-287
RS 151-293
RS 151-300

PTC Thermistor I/V characteristics (at 55°C ambient)

Theory of operation

The shape of the PTC thermistor resistance vs temperature characteristics (Figure 9) can be considered in three distinct parts. The region from below 0°C to R_{min} has a negative temperature coefficient of the order of 1%/°C; the region from R_{min} to R_{max} has a positive temperature coefficient in which values as high as 100%/°C can be realised. Beyond R_{max} the TC is again negative. As a PTC thermistor is sensitive to voltage variation, R vs T curves are usually measured at a constant voltage. Figure 10 shows the characteristics of the load to be protected, together with the I/V of the thermistor on a linear scale. Region 'A' indicates the permissible load current range for normal operation.

An increase in load current beyond the I_{max} value will cause the thermistor to self-heat to a high resistance state thereby shifting its operating point to the region B. This reduces the current through and voltage across the load, effectively protecting the equipment etc.

Similarly, if the ambient temperature surrounding the thermistor should, due to a fault condition, increase, the I/V curve will depress towards the dotted position. The load attempts to consume more than I_{max} (+55°C) and the thermistor will again self-heat and shift its operating point into the low current region.

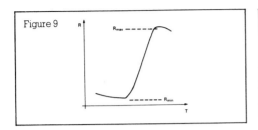

Figure 9

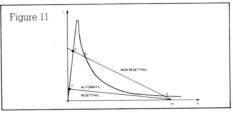

Figure 11

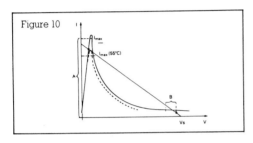

Figure 10

Selection

In order to ensure that the load is protected at the desired level and in the required reset mode, the following parameters must be taken into account;

1. Normal operating current range – Region 'A'.
2. 'Overload' current – I_{max}.
3. Operating temperature range – I/V curve shift.
4. Operating voltage range (Vs).
5. Time response – position in Region 'A'.
6. Thermistor tolerances.
7. Permissible voltage drop across device.
8. Mounting arrangement.

The reset mode required, ie. return to the 'A' region, is decided by the position of the load line in relation to the I/V curve. Figure 11 shows load line positions for the two modes, the auto-reset line intersects the I/V curve at only one point (F), thereby restricting stable operating to this point for normal load conditions. The manual or non-resetting line crosses the I/V curve at three positions, giving the possibility of operation at either point. However, point D is in an unstable region so that in practice operation only occurs at points C or E.

If response time is a particularly important factor, the position of the operating point within region 'A', for a given device (Figure 10) and the switch temperature of the PTC must be carefully considered. In circumstances where the circuit being protected is subject to short term overloads (which may be tolerated), the operating point should be the lower portion of region 'A'. Alternatively, where response time must be rapid, the operating point must be as close to the I_{max} value as practicable, not forgetting the shift in characteristic

with temperature.

Tolerances are usually quoted on the room temperature resistance (zero power), the higher values of R_{25} giving the lower I_{max}.

As a thermistor is a resistive device there will inevitably be a voltage drop across it when in circuit. The maximum permissible voltage drop for the circuit concerned will dictate the room temperature or R_{25} resistance value. It is usual to make the R_{25} value in the order of 10% of the circuit resistance (or impedance).

The thermistor should be positioned in the equipment such that the surrounding air is reasonably still and unconfined. Moving air will effectively increase the I_{max} value (at a given temperature) whilst confining the device will create a high ambient temperature, and therefore a lower I_{max}.

Modification of I/V characteristics

In certain applications it is necessary to modify the I/V curve in order to produce the necessary characteristics. To obtain an auto-resetting device with a relatively high current rating, a resistor may be connected in parallel with the thermistor to 'lift' the characteristic to the dotted position (Figure 12). This permits the load line to occupy a position in the upper 'A' region, but still crossing the combination curve at one stable point.

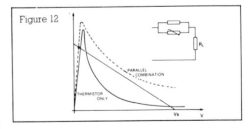

Figure 12

Parallel operation

In instances where a sufficiently high I_{max} value cannot be realised with existing devices, it is permissible to parallel connect two or more devices to achieve the required values; this may also be used to obtain lower R_{25} resistances.

RS Components Ltd. PO Box 99, Corby, Northants, NN17 9RS

△ An Electrocomponents Company

Telephone: 0536 201234
©RS Components Ltd. 1984

Data Library

Platinum resistance temperature detectors

A range of platinum film resistance temperature detectors. Three types are available as follows:
1. Basic unsheathed element (RS stock number 158-238)
2. Sheathed element (RS stock number 158-244). This comprises a platinum film element encased in a stainless steel sheath. Attached to the sheath is 1m of PTFE covered cable. The base of the sheath extends 15mm each end and may be used for mounting purposes by wrapping. If the tabs are not required, they may be cut off or folded back.
3. Sealed element (RS stock number 158-402) consists of a platinum film resistance element mounted in the end of a sealed stainless steel sheath 150mm long. The end containing the element is flattened to reduce response time. The probe is ideal for insertion into liquids and is fitted with ⅛ BSPF brass compression fitting.
The RS platinum film temperature detector lineariser (stock number 158-418) has been designed specifically for use with RS platinum film detectors and any other platinum temperature sensors which

conform to BS 1904 Grade 2. The encapsulated module is suitable for PCB mounting (0.1 in grid) and contains circuitry required to produce a linearised 1mV output per degree centigrade in the range −100°C to +500°C at the sensor.
Sensing circuitry is also incorporated in the module which will produce an output suitable to directly drive an LED to indicate low supply volts, i.e. battery 'low' indication. The module therefore provides a simple and cost effective means of accurately measuring a temperature over a wide range without the need of preliminary adjustments. Also specified is the RS platinum film 3½ digit temperature indicator (stock number 258-192) suitable for use with RS and other platinum temperature sensors.

4-wire sensor operation
This method of connection obtains maximum accuracy by compensating for any resistance introduced by connecting cables. As a platinum film sensor has a temperature coefficient of 0.385Ω/°C the cable resistance can be significant.

3-wire sensor operation
This method produces medium accuracy and some compensation for connection cable resistance but is more economical in cable costs than the 4-wire system.

2-wire sensor operation
This is a basic general purpose method of connection which will not compensate for connection cable resistance.

Dimensions (mm)

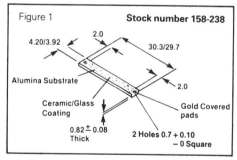

Figure 1 — Stock number 158-238

2.0
4.20/3.92
30.3/29.7
Alumina Substrate
2.0
Ceramic/Glass Coating
Gold Covered pads
0.82 ± 0.08 Thick
2 Holes 0.7 + 0.10 − 0 Square

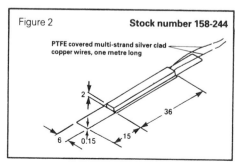

Figure 2 — Stock number 158-244

PTFE covered multi-strand silver clad copper wires, one metre long
2
36
6   0.15   15

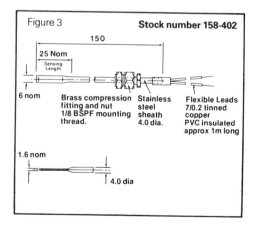

Figure 3 — Stock number 158-402

150
25 Nom
Sensing Length
6 nom
Brass compression fitting and nut 1/8 BSPF mounting thread.
Stainless steel sheath 4.0 dia.
Flexible Leads 7/0.2 tinned copper PVC insulated approx 1m long
1.6 nom
4.0 dia

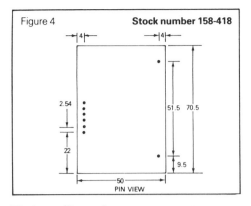

Figure 4 — **Stock number 158-418**

PIN VIEW

Platinum film resistance temperature detectors
Conforms to BS 1904 Grade 2 and DIN 43 760

Specification

Resistance at 0°C	$100 \pm 0.1\,\Omega$
Temperature coefficient	$0.385\,\Omega/°C$
Maximum temperature	500°C (156-238)
	260°C (158-244)
	250°C (158-402)
Minimum temperature	$-50°C$
Resistance tolerance $-100°C$	$\pm 0.2\,\Omega$ ($\pm 0.5°C$)
0°C	$\pm 0.1\,\Omega$ ($\pm 0.3°C$)
100°C	$\pm 0.2\,\Omega$ ($\pm 0.5°C$)
200°C	$\pm 0.35\,\Omega$ ($\pm 1.0°C$)
300°C	$\pm 0.5\,\Omega$ ($\pm 1.4°C$)
400°C	$\pm 0.65\,\Omega$ ($\pm 1.9°C$)
500°C	$\pm 0.8\,\Omega$ ($\pm 2.4°C$)

Resistance/Temperature relationship

(deg.C)	0,0	−2,0	−4,0	−6,0	−8,0
−50,00	80,31				
−40,00	84,27	83,48	82,69	81,89	81,10
−30,00	88,22	87,43	86,64	85,85	85,06
−20,00	92,16	91,37	90,59	89,80	89,01
−10,00	96,09	95,30	94,52	93,73	92,95
−0,00	100,00	99,22	98,44	97,65	96,87

(deg.C)	0,0	+2,0	+4,0	+6,0	+8,0
0,00	100,00	100,78	101,56	102,34	103,12
10,00	103,90	104,68	105,46	106,24	107,02
20,00	107,79	108,57	109,35	110,12	110,90
30,00	111,67	112,45	113,22	113,99	114,77
40,00	115,54	116,31	117,08	117,85	118,62
50,00	119,39	120,16	120,93	121,70	122,47
60,00	123,24	124,01	124,77	125,54	126,31
70,00	127,07	127,84	128,60	129,37	130,13
80,00	130,89	131,66	132,42	133,18	133,94
90,00	134,70	135,46	136,22	136,98	137,74
100,00	138,50	139,26	140,02	140,77	141,53
110,00	142,29	143,04	143,80	144,55	145,31
120,00	146,06	146,81	147,57	148,32	149,07
130,00	149,82	150,57	151,33	152,08	152,83
140,00	153,57	154,32	155,07	155,82	156,57
150,00	157,31	158,06	158,81	159,55	160,30
160,00	161,04	161,79	162,53	163,27	164,02
170,00	164,76	165,50	166,24	166,98	167,72
180,00	168,46	169,20	169,94	170,68	171,42
190,00	172,16	172,89	173,63	174,37	175,10
200,00	175,84	176,57	177,31	178,04	178,78
210,00	179,51	180,24	180,97	181,71	182,44
220,00	183,17	183,90	184,63	185,36	186,09
230,00	186,81	187,54	188,27	189,00	189,72
240,00	190,45	191,18	191,90	192,63	193,35
250,00	194,07	194,80	195,52	196,24	196,96
260,00	197,69	198,41	199,13	199,85	200,57
270,00	201,29	202,01	202,72	203,44	204,16
280,00	204,88	205,59	206,31	207,02	207,74
290,00	208,45	209,17	209,88	210,59	211,31
300,00	212,02	212,73	213,44	214,15	214,86
310,00	215,57	216,28	216,99	217,70	218,41
320,00	219,11	219,82	220,53	221,23	221,94
330,00	222,65	223,35	224,05	224,76	225,46
340,00	226,17	226,87	227,57	228,27	228,97
350,00	229,67	230,37	231,07	231,77	232,47
360,00	233,17	233,87	234,56	235,26	235,96
370,00	236,65	237,35	238,04	238,74	239,43
380,00	240,13	240,82	241,51	242,20	242,90
390,00	243,59	244,28	244,97	245,66	246,35
400,00	247,04	247,73	248,41	249,10	249,79
410,00	250,48	251,16	251,85	252,53	253,22
420,00	253,90	254,59	255,27	255,95	256,63
430,00	257,32	258,00	258,68	259,36	260,04
440,00	260,72	261,40	262,08	262,76	263,43
450,00	264,11	264,79	265,46	266,14	266,82
460,00	267,49	268,17	268,84	269,51	270,19
470,00	270,86	271,53	272,20	272,88	273,55
480,00	274,22	274,89	275,56	276,23	276,89
490,00	277,56	278,23	278,90	279,56	280,23
500,00	280,90				

Basic resistance bridge networks
Shown below are three basic resistance bridge networks. The output (V_0) for each bridge is 1mV/°C which makes it ideal for direct temperature reading when connected to a DVM or any of the RS DPM's.

Suggested values

$R_1 = R_2 = 4k$ $V_B = 12V$
$R_3 = 100R$ $V_0 = 1mV/°C$
$R_4 = R_5 = 500R$

Note: All resistors precision wirewound 0.1%, ±5ppm. (For RS precision resistors see current catalogue.)

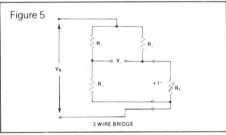

Figure 5

3 WIRE BRIDGE

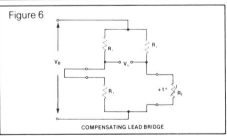

Figure 6

COMPENSATING LEAD BRIDGE

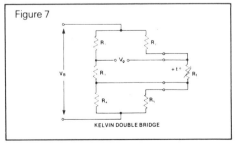

Figure 7

KELVIN DOUBLE BRIDGE

Applications

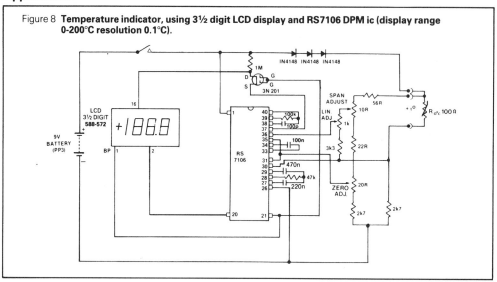

Figure 8 **Temperature indicator, using 3½ digit LCD display and RS7106 DPM ic (display range 0-200°C resolution 0.1°C).**

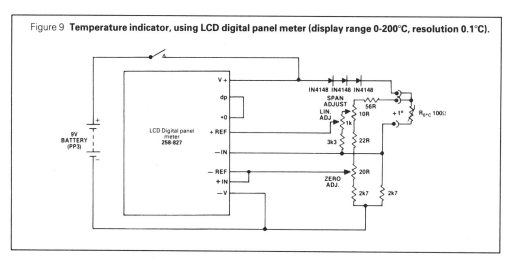

Figure 9 **Temperature indicator, using LCD digital panel meter (display range 0-200°C, resolution 0.1°C).**

Calibration

Before use, the temperature indicator circuits must be calibrated by the following procedure:

Equipment required

Resistance decade box, with a range of at least 199 ohms, resolution 0.01 ohms. (eg RS 610-297).

Calibration procedure:

1. Connect resistance decade box in place of the detector. Set decade box to 100 ohms, adjust zero potentiometer to obtain 000.0°C.
2. Set decade box to 138.50 ohms, adjust span potentiometer to obtain reading of 100.0°C (it may be necessary to alter the linearity potentiometer to obtain this reading in extreme cases).
3. Set decade box to 172.12 ohms, adjust span potentiometer to obtain reading of 190°C.
4. Set decade box to 138.50 ohms, note error reading and adjust linearity potentiometer so

the reading moves further away from the correct reading of 100.0°C by an amount similar to the error noted.

5. Set decade box to 172.12 ohms, adjust span potentiometer until a reading of 190°C is obtained.
6. Repeat (4) and (5) until correct.

Recheck:

7. Set decade box to 100.00 ohms, adjust zero potentiometer to obtain 000.0°C.
8. Set decade box to 172.12 ohms, adjust span potentiometer to obtain 190.0°C.
9. Set decade box to 138.50 ohms, check reading in 100.0°C adjust as described in (4) and (5) if incorrect.

Note to Figure 8. The remaining pins on the RS7106, except pin 32, are connected to the LCD.

Note to Figures 8 and 9. All resistors 0.5W ±2% thick film metal glaze.

Platinum film temperature detector lineariser

Specification

Power supply voltage	+7V to +15V dc
Power supply current	7mA
Low voltage warning	current limited output, suitable to drive RS LED 576-327 or similar. NB. Inaccurate readings may result if module is used when low voltage warning LED is illuminated.
Input sensor	platinum resistance thermometer element BS 1904:1964
Input temperature range	$-100°C$ to $+500°C$
Maximum measurement error	$±0.2°C$ over the range $-100°C$ to $+350°C$, $±1°C$ from $+350°C$ to $+500°C$
Ambient temperature range	$-10°C$ to $+30°C$
Output voltage	1mV per °C
Long term stability	better than 0.1°C per annum
Sensor energising current	2.1mA
Output impedance	<1 ohm

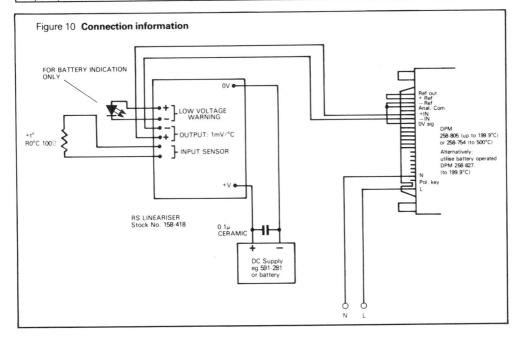

Figure 10 **Connection information**

Notes

The module has been individually calibrated, and care should be taken not to introduce significant input lead resistance error between the sensor and the module, ie avoid long, thin pcb tracks or thin connecting wires.

If the load connected to the output of the module is capacitive (ie a long length of cable) then 100 ohm resistors should be inserted in series with + and − output leads to ensure stability.

When using a lineariser with a mains powered DPM, ensure that the DPM's common mode voltage range is not exceeded. Should this occur, ensure that the lineariser is fed from an isolated supply and connect the DPM in a single ended mode. See Figure 10.

The −ve output sits nominally at 1.2V above the 0V rail, while the +ve output pin varies with temperature.

The lineariser is designed for simple installation and is suitable for remote mounting and requires no compensation loops.

Providing the remote millivolt output is read using a high input impedance instrument, such as a DPM, eg RS 258-827, there is no loss of accuracy − the cable resistance being negligible when compared with the input impedance of the DPM.

Panel mounting digital temperature indicator

A panel mounting, 3½-digit temperature indicator in a DIN size case suitable for use with RS and other platinum film sensors. The unit features automatic cold junction compensation and automatic zeroing with a 4-wire compensation system used to mini-mise the effect of lead resistance, maintaining a high overall system accuracy. This enables use with 2-, 3- or 4-wire sensors. The display is auto-ranging having a resolution of 0.1°C up to +185°C and 1°C for temperatures above. The unit is fitted with a linear analogue output which can be used to drive a chart recorder or form part of an analogue control system. Connections via a terminal strip.

Specifications

Temperature range	−150°C to +800°C
Resolution	0.1°C below +185°C
	1°C above +185°C
	(autorange change at +185°C ±5°C)
Sensor type	PT. 100Ω resistor to
	BS 1904 DIN 43760
Accuracy at 25°C	±0.2% of
	reading ±1 digit
Ambient temperature range	0°C to +45°C
Sensor operating mode	4-wire constant current
	voltage sensing
Analogue output	1mV/°C (2kΩ source)
Display type	3½-digit 11.2mm,
	7-seg. LED
Power supply requirements	220/110V,
	50 Hz, 10VA

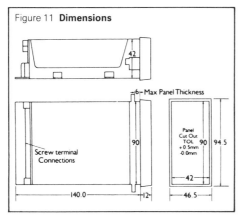

Figure 11 **Dimensions**

4-wire sensor operation

4 core copper cable should be used to connect the sensor to the input terminals as detailed in Figure 12.

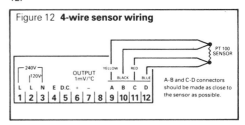

Figure 12 **4-wire sensor wiring**

3-wire sensor operation

When using a 3-wire sensor terminals 9 and 10 should be linked together and the sensor con-nected to terminals 10 (black wire), 11 (red wire) and 12 (blue wire).

2-wire sensor operation

When using a 2-wire sensor terminals 9 and 10 and terminals 11 and 12 should be linked together. The sensor should then be wired to terminals 10 (black wire) and 11 (red wire).

Semiconductor temperature sensor

Data Library

RS stock number 308-809

The RS590 semiconductor temperature sensor is functionally a two terminal I.C. which produces an output current proportional to absolute temperature. For supply voltages between +4V and +30V d.c. the device acts as a high impedance constant current regulator passing $1\mu A$ per degree Kelvin. Linearisation circuitry, precision voltage amplifiers, resistance measuring circuitry or cold junction compensation are not required for basic temperature measurement.

The RS590 is ideal in remote sensing applications. The device is virtually insensitive to voltage drops over long lines due to its high impedance current output provided the connection cable used is a twisted pair and well insulated.

Specification

Typical at +25°C (298.2K) and V_S = 5V unless otherwise stated.

Absolute maximum ratings

Forward voltage (+ to –) _____ +44V
Reverse voltage (+ to –) _____ −20V
Breakdown voltage (Case to + or –) _____ ±200V
Rated performance temperature range
                                −55°C to +150°C
Storage temperature range _____ −65°C to +175°C
Lead temperature (soldering, 10 sec) _____ +300°C

Power supply

Operating voltage range _____ +4V to +30V

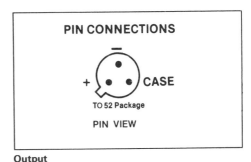

PIN CONNECTIONS

CASE

TO 52 Package

PIN VIEW

Output

Nominal current output _____ 298.2μA
Nominal temperature coefficient _____ $1\mu A$/°C
Calibration error _____ ±2.5°C max
Absolute error[2] (over rated performance temperature range)
    Without external calibration adjustment
                                        ±5.5°C max
    With + 25°C calibration error set to zero
                                        ±2.0°C max
    Nonlinearity _____ ±0.8°C max
    Repeatability _____ ±0.1°C max
    Long term drift[1] _____ ±0.1°C max
Current noise _____ 40pA/$\sqrt{Hz}$
Power supply rejection
    +4V $\leqslant$ V_S $\leqslant$ +5V_____ 0.5μA/V
    +5V $\leqslant$ V_S $\leqslant$ +15V_____ 0.2μA/V
    + 15V $\leqslant$ V_S $\leqslant$ + 30V_____ 0.1μA/V
Case isolation to either lead_____ $10^{10}\Omega$
Effective shunt capacitance _____ 100pF
Electrical Turn-on time[2] _____ 20μs
Reverse bias leakage current[3]
    (Reverse voltage = 10V) _____ 10pA

1 Conditions: constant + 5V, constant + 125°C
2 Does not include self heating effects
3 Leakage current doubles every 10°C

Operation

As previously stated the output of the RS590 is basically a proportional to absolute temperature (PTAT) current regulator i.e. the output is equal to a scale factor multiplied by the temperature of the sensor in degrees Kelvin.

Calibration error

The difference between the indicated temperature and actual temperature is called the calibration error. Since this is a scale factor error, it is relatively simple to trim out. Fig. 1 shows the most elementary way of accomplishing this.

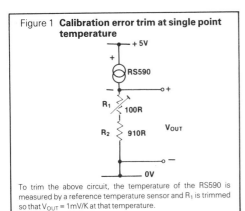

Figure 1 **Calibration error trim at single point temperature**

+ 5V

RS590

R_1 100R

R_2 910R

V_{OUT}

0V

To trim the above circuit, the temperature of the RS590 is measured by a reference temperature sensor and R_1 is trimmed so that V_{OUT} = 1mV/K at that temperature.

Each RS590 is tested for error over the temperature range with callibration error trimmed out.
This error consists of a slope error and some curvature, mostly at the temperature extremes. Fig. 2 shows a typical temperature curve before and after calibration error trimming.

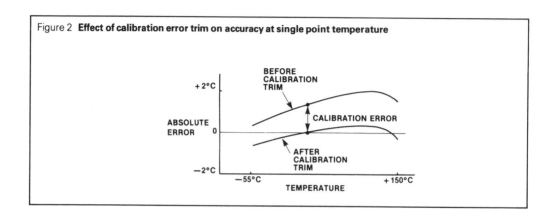

Figure 2 **Effect of calibration error trim on accuracy at single point temperature**

Nonlinearity

Nonlinearity as it applies to the RS590 is the maximum deviation of current over the entire temperature range from a best fit straight line. Fig. 3 shows the nonlinearity of the typical RS590 from Fig. 2.

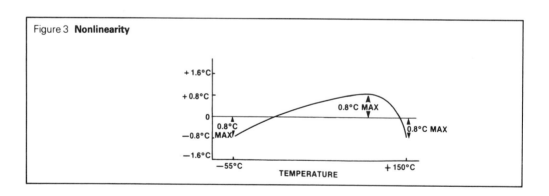

Figure 3 **Nonlinearity**

Fig 4A. shows a circuit in which nonlinearity is the major contribution to error over temperature. The circuit is trimmed by adjusting R_1 for a 0V output with RS590 at 0°C. R_2 is then adjusted for 10V out with the sensor at 100°C. Other pairs of temperatures may be used with this procedure as long as they are measured accurately by a reference sensor. Note that for +15V output (150°C) the V+ supply to the op-amp must be greater than 17V. Also note that V− should be at least −4V: if V− is ground there is no voltage applied across the device.
Note: Resistor values are typical and may need alteration depending upon magnitude of V−.

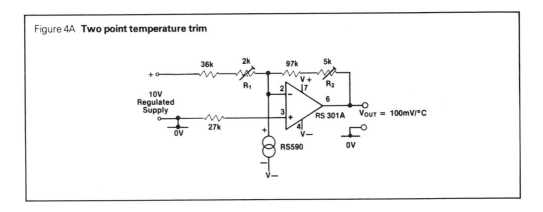

Figure 4A **Two point temperature trim**

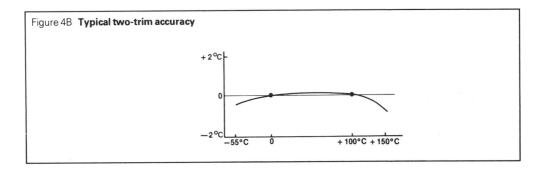

Figure 4B **Typical two-trim accuracy**

Series/Parallel connection

Several RS590 devices may be connected in series as shown in Fig. 5. This configuration allows the minimum of all the sensed temperatures to be indicated. Connecting the sensors in parallel (Fig. 6) indicates the average of the sensed temperatures.

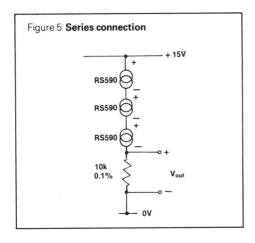

Figure 5 **Series connection**

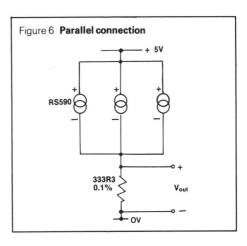

Figure 6 **Parallel connection**

Differential temperature measurement

Fig. 7 illustrates one method by which differential temperature measurements can be made.

R_1 and R_2 may be used to trim the output of the op-amp to indicate a desired temperature difference.

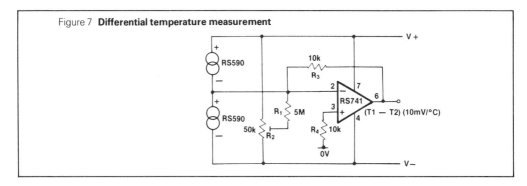

Figure 7 **Differential temperature measurement**

Temperature control

The RS590 may also be used in temperature control circuits (see Fig. 8). R_H and R_L are selected to set the high and low limits for R_{SET}. The RS590 is powered from a 12V stabilised source which isolates it from supply variations while maintaining a reasonable voltage across it. C_1 may be needed to filter extraneous noise. The value of R_B is determined by the ß of the transistor and the current requirements of the load.

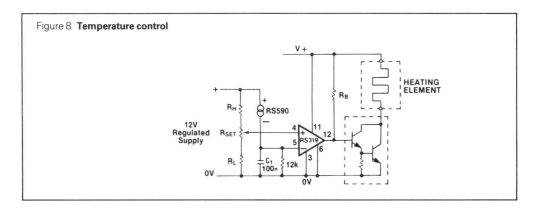

Figure 8 **Temperature control**

RS Components Ltd. PO Box 99, Corby, Northants, NN17 9RS

An Electrocomponents Company

Telephone: 0536 201234

© RS Components Ltd. 1993

Data Library

Temperature sensor ic
LM35CZ and LM35DZ

Stock numbers 317-954 and 317-960

The LM35 is a precision semi-conductor temperature sensor giving an output of 10mV per degree Centigrade. Unlike devices with outputs proportional to the absolute temperature (in degrees Kelvin) there is no large offset voltage which, in most applications, will have to be removed.

Accuracies of ¼°C at room temperature or ¾°C over the full temperature range are typical.

Absolute maximum ratings (Note 10)

Supply voltage	+35V to –0.2V
Output voltage	+6V to –1.0V
Output current	10mA
Storage temperature, TO-92 package	–60°C to +150°C
Lead temperature (soldering, 10 seconds)	260°C

Specified operating temperature range
T_{MIN} to T_{MAX} (Note 2)

LM35CZ	–40°C to +110°C
LM35DZ	0°C to +100°C

Features

● Output proportional to °C
● Wide temperature range –40°C to +110°C (CZ version)
● Accurate ¼°C at room temperature typical
● Linear output 0.2°C typical
● Low current drain (60μA typical)
● Low self heating (0.08°C typical)
● Output impedance 0.1Ω at 1mA
● Standard TO92 package.

Pin connections

**TO-92
Plastic package**

BOTTOM VIEW

Package details

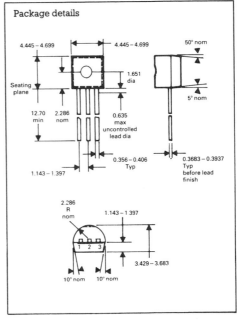

Electrical characteristics (Note 1) (Note 6)

Parameter	Conditions	LM35CZ, LM35DZ			Units (Max.)
		Typical	Tested Limit (Note 4)	Design Limit (Note 5)	
Accuracy, LM35, LM35C (Note 7)	$T_A = +25°C$ $T_A = -10°C$ $T_A = T_{MAX}$ $T_A = T_{MIN}$	±0.4 ±0.5 ±0.8 ±0.8	±1.0	 ±1.5 ±1.5 ±2.0	°C °C °C °C
Accuracy, LM35D (Note 7)	$T_A = +25°C$ $T_A = T_{MAX}$ $T_A = T_{MIN}$	±0.6 ±0.9 ±0.9	±1.5	 ±2.0 ±2.0	°C °C °C
Nonlinearity (Note 8)	$T_{MIN} \leq T_A \leq T_{MAX}$	± 0.2		±0.5	°C
Sensor gain (Average slope)	$T_{MIN} \leq T_A \leq T_{MAX}$	+ 10.0		+9.8 + 10.2	mV/°C
Load regulation (Note 3) $0 \leq I_L \leq 1mA$	$T_A = +25°C$ $T_{MIN} \leq T_A \leq T_{MAX}$	±0.4 ±0.5	±2.0	 ±5.0	mV/mA mV/mA
Line regulation (Note 3)	$T_A = +25°C$ $4V \leq V_S \leq 30V$	±0.01 ±0.02	±0.1	 ±0.2	mV/V mV/V
Quiescent current (Note 9)	$V_S = +5V, +25°C$ $V_S = +5V$ $V_S = +30V, +25°C$ $V_S = +30V$	56 **91** 56.2 **91.5**	80 82 	 **138** **141**	μA μA μA μA
Change of quiescent current (Note 3)	$4V \leq V_S \leq 30V, +25°C$ $4V \leq V_S \leq 30V$	0.2 **0.5**	2.0	 **3.0**	μA μA
Temperature coefficient of quiescent current		+ 0.39		+ 0.7	μA/°C
Minimum temperature for rated accuracy	In circuit of Figure 1, $I_L = 0$	+ 1.5		+ 2.0	°C
Long term stability	$T_J = T_{MAX}$, for 1000 hours	+ 0.08			°C

Notes.

1. Unless otherwise noted, these specifications apply: $-40° \leq T_J \leq +110°C$ for the LM35C and $0° \leq T_J \leq +100°C$ for the LM35D. $V_S = +5Vdc$ and $I_{LOAD} = 50\mu A$, in the circuit of Figure 2. These specifications also apply from $+2°C$ to T_{MAX} in the circuit of Figure 1. Specifications in **boldface** apply over the full rated temperature range.

2. Thermal resistance of the TO-92 package is 180°C/W junction to ambient.

3. Regulation is measured at constant junction temperature, using pulse testing with a low duty cycle. Changes in output due to heating effects can be computed by multiplying the internal dissipation by the thermal resistance.

4. Tested limits are guaranteed and 100% tested in production.

5. Design limits are guaranteed (but not 100% production tested) over the indicated temperature and supply voltage ranges. These limits are not used to calculate outgoing quality levels.

6. Specifications in **boldface** apply over the full rated temperature range.

7. Accuracy is defined as the error between the output voltage and 10mV/°C times the device's case temperature, at specified conditions of voltage, current, and temperature (expressed in °C).

8. Nonlinearity is defined as the deviation of the output-voltage-versus-temperature curve from the best-fit straight line, over the device's rated temperature range.

9. Quiescent current is defined in the circuit of Figure 1.

10. Absolute maximum ratings indicate limits beyond which damage to the device may occur. dc and ac electrical specifications are not ensured when operating the device at absolute maximum ratings.

Application notes

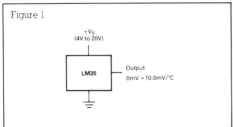

Figure 1

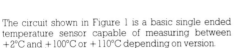

The circuit shown in Figure 1 is a basic single ended temperature sensor capable of measuring between +2°C and +100°C or +110°C depending on version.

To measure negative temperatures a negative supply is required as shown in Figure 2.

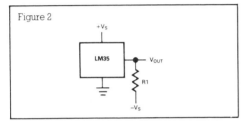

Figure 2

R1 should be selected as follows:

$$R1 = \frac{-V_S}{50 \times 10^{-6}}$$

Care must be taken when driving capacitive load, such as long cables or any load exceeding 50pF.

To remove the effect of capacitive loads the circuit shown Figure 3 should be used, however the resistor is added to the output impedance making this circuit suitable for connection to high impedance loads only.

Figure 4 shows a circuit which will overcome this problem and also give protection from radiated interference from relays or any other source of electrical noise.

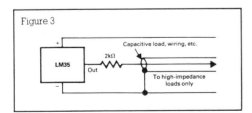

Figure 3

Figure 4

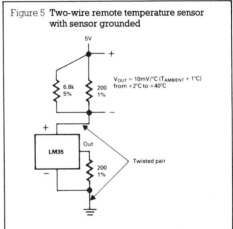

The circuits below show some typical applications of these temperature sensors.

Figure 5 **Two-wire remote temperature sensor with sensor grounded**

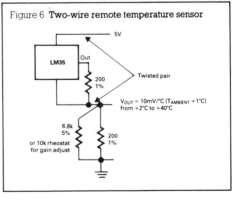

Figure 6 **Two-wire remote temperature sensor**

Figure 7 **Temperature sensor, single supply, capable of measuring negative temperatures**

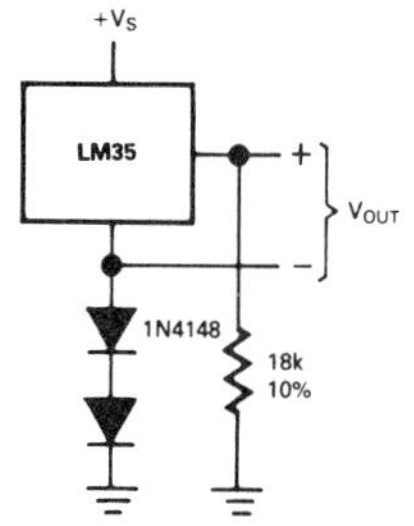

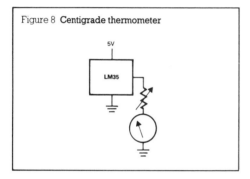

Figure 8 **Centigrade thermometer**

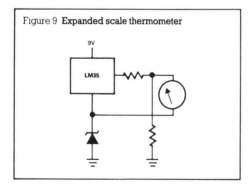

Figure 9 **Expanded scale thermometer**

RS Components Ltd. PO Box 99, Corby, Northants, NN17 9RS
An Electrocomponents Company

Telephone: 0536 201234
©RS Components Ltd. 1987

Strain gauges and load cells

Strain gauges

Two ranges of foil strain gauges to cover general engineering requirements for strain analysis. All gauges have 30mm integral leads to alleviate damage to the gauges due to excessive heat being applied during soldering and installation.

Miniature gauges can be used for precise point measurement or instrumentation of small components. The polyimide backing of the gauges can withstand temperatures up to 180°C making them ideal for higher temperature applications.

The larger size of the standard gauges will not only make these gauges suitable for larger components, but is useful to assess the average strain over the area covered by the gauge thus reducing the possibility of incorrect readings due to stress concentrations.

Gauges temperature compensated for aluminium match materials with a coefficient of thermal expansion of 23.4 x 10^{-6}/°C and are indicated by blue colour coding of the backing material.

Gauges temperature compensated for mild steel match materials with a coefficient of thermal expansion of 10.8 x 19^{-6}/°C and are indicated by red colour coding of the backing material.

Single types are intended for uniaxial strain measurements only, while rosette types can be used for biaxial measurements having two gauges at right angles to each other in the same plane. Included in the backing material are gauge lines to enable accurate alignment of gauges along principal strain.

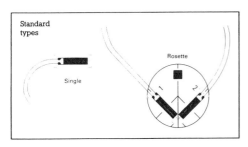

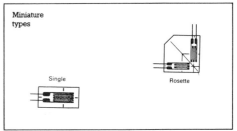

General specification (all types)

Measurable strain _____ 2 to 4% maximum
Thermal output 20 to 160°C _____ ±2 micro strain/°C*
                      160 to 180°C _____ ±5 micro strain/°C*
Gauge factor change
with temperature _____ ±0.015%/°C max
Gauge resistance _____ 120Ω
Gauge resistance tolerance _____ ±0.5%
Fatigue life _____ >10^6 reversals @ 1000 micro strain*
Foil material _____ copper nickel alloy

* 1 micro strain is equivalent to an extension of 0.0001%

Specification
(Standard polyester backed types)

Temperature range _____ –30°C to +80°C
Gauge length _____ 8mm
Gauge width _____ 2mm
Gauge factor _____ 2.1
Base length (single types)_____ 13.0mm
Base width (single types) _____ 4.0mm
Base diameter (rosettes) _____ 21.0mm

Specification
(Miniature polyimide backed type)

Temperature range_____ –30°C to +180°C
Gauge length_____ 2mm_____ 5mm
Gauge width _____ 1.6mm____ 1.8mm
Gauge factor_____ 2.0 _____ 2.1
Base length (single types)_____ 6.0mm_____ 9.0mm
Base width (single types)_____ 2.5mm____ 3.5mm
Base size (rosettes)_____ 7.5 x 7.5mm__ 12 x 12mm

Construction and principle of operation

The strain gauge measuring grid is manufactured from a copper nickel alloy which has a low and controllable temperature coefficient. The actual form of the grid is accurately produced by photo-etching techniques. Thermoplastic film is used to encapsulate the grid, which helps to protect the gauge from mechanical and environmental damage and also acts as a medium to transmit the strain from the test object to the gauge material.

The principle of operation of this device is based on the fact that the resistance of an electrical conductor changes with a ratio of $\triangle R/R$ if a stress is applied such that its length changes by a factor $\triangle L/L$. Where $\triangle R$ is change in resistance from unstressed value, and $\triangle L$ is change in length from original unstressed length.

The change in resistance is brought about mainly by the physical size of the conductor changing and an alteration of the conductivity of the material, due to changes in the materials structure.

Copper nickel alloy is commonly used in strain gauge construction because the resistance change of the foil is virtually proportional to the applied strain i.e.

$$\triangle R/R = K.E.$$

where K is a constant known as a gauge factor,

$$= \frac{\triangle R/R}{\triangle L/L}$$

And $E = strain = \triangle L/L \therefore K = \frac{\triangle R/R}{E}$

The change in resistance of the strain gauge can therefore be utilised to measure strain accurately when connected to an appropriate measuring and indicating circuit eg. RS strain gain amplifier 308-815 detailed on page 3 of this data sheet.

Application

When strain gauges are used in compressive load transducer applications, which normally require more stringent accuracy requirements, a full bridge circuit is used with active gauges in all four arms of the bridge, see Figure 1:

The load transducer shown in Figure 1 utilises four strain gauges attached to the cylinder. The gauges are connected into the bridge circuitry in such a manner as to make use of Poissons ratio i.e. the ratio between the relative expansion in the direction of force applied and the relative contraction perpendicular to the force, to increase the effective gauge factor and thus the sensitivity.

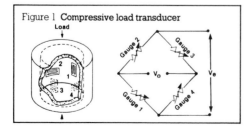

Figure 1 **Compressive load transducer**

To measure tensile loads, a ring with gauges attached as shown in Figure 2 may be used:

Under the action of a tensile load, the curvature of the ring in Figure 2 is deformed such that the inner gauges undergo tension while the outer gauges experience compressive forces.

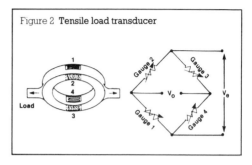

Figure 2 **Tensile load transducer**

Instructions for mounting of strain gauges

In order to obtain the best possible results from a strain gauge, it is important to thoroughly prepare the gauge and the surface of the specimen to which the gauge is to be attached, prior to bonding with the adhesives recommended in section 3 below.

1) Specimen surface preparation

An area larger than the installation should be cleared of all paint, rust etc., and finally smoothed with a fine grade emery paper or fine sand blasting to provide a sound bonding surface.

The area should now be degreased with a solvent such as RS PCB Solvent Cleaner, stock no. 555-134, and finally neutralised with a weak detergent solution. Tissues or lint free cloth should be used for this operation, wetting the surface and wiping off with clean tissues or cloth until the final tissue used is stain free. Care must be taken not to wipe grease from a surrounding area onto the prepared area or to touch the surface with the fingers.

This final cleaning should take place immediately prior to installation of the gauge.

2) Strain gauge preparation

By sticking a short length of adhesive tape along the upper face of the gauge it may be picked up from a flat clean surface. Holding both ends of the tape, orientate the gauge in the desired location and stick the end of the tape furthermost from the tags to the specimen. Bend the other end of the tape back on itself thereby exposing the back of the gauge.

3) Adhesives and strain gauge installation

Two basic types of adhesive are recommended: i) RS cyanoacrylate, ii) RS 'quick-set' epoxy. When using epoxy adhesive coat the back of the gauge with adhesive and gently push the gauge down into position, wiping excess adhesive to the two outside edges of the gauge, to leave a thin film of adhesive between gauge and sample. Stick the whole length of tape to hold the gauge in position. Care should be taken that there is an even layer of adhesive and no air bubbles are left under the grid. Cover the gauge with cellophane or polyethylene etc., and apply a light weight or clamp as required until adhesive has set. Remove tape by slowly and very carefully pulling it back over itself, starting at the end furthermost from the tags. Do not pull upwards.

If cyanoacrylate adhesive is to be used stick one end of the tape down to the specimen completely up to the gauge. Drop a fillit of adhesive in the 'hinge' point formed by the gauge and the specimen. Starting at the fixed end, with one finger push the gauge down at the same time pushing the adhesive along the gauge in a single wiping motion until the whole gauge is stuck down. Apply pressure with one finger over the whole length of the gauge for approximately one minute. Leave for a further three minutes before removing tape.

4) Wiring
The RS strain gauges are fitted with 30mm leads to enable the gauge to be soldered. The lead out wires are fragile and should be handled with care.

Installation protection
RS strain gauges are encapsulated and therefore are protected from dust and draughts etc. If however, additional protection from humidity, moisture, and mechanical damage is required RS Silicone Rubber Compound, stock no. 555-588, may be used. This should be carefully spread over the installation using a spatula.

Connecting to strain gauges
The following bridge circuits are shown with connections referring to the basic amplifier circuit, Figure 7. All resistors, precision wirewound 0.1% 5ppm. (For RS Precision Resistors see current catalogue.)

Note. The expressions are assuming that all gauges are subjected to the same strain. Some configurations produce different strain in different gauges, and allowance must be made.

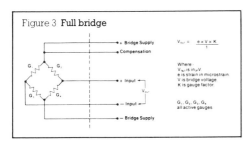

Figure 3 **Full bridge**

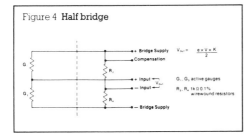

Figure 4 **Half bridge**

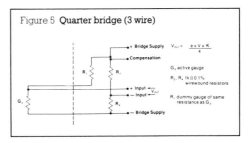

Figure 5 **Quarter bridge (3 wire)**

Strain gauge amplifier (308-815) and printed circuit board (435-692)

Description and operation
The strain gauge amplifier is a purpose designed hybrid, low noise, low drift, linear dc amplifier in a 24 pin DIL package, specifically configured for resistive bridge measurement and in particular the strain gauges detailed earlier in this data sheet.

Foil strain gauges when attached to a specimen, produce very small changes in resistance (typically $0.2m\Omega$ in 120Ω per microstrain), and are thus normally connected in a Wheatstone bridge. Overall outputs of less than 1mV on a common mode voltage of 5 volts may be encountered, requiring exceptional common mode rejection which cannot be provided by conventional means.

The strain gauge amplifier overcomes the problem of common mode rejection by removing the common mode voltages. This is achieved by controlling the negative bridge supply voltage in such a manner that the voltage at the negative input terminal is always zero. Thus for a symmetrical bridge, a negative bridge supply is generated equal and opposite to the positive bridge supply, hence zero common mode voltage.

The advantages of such a system are:
1. No floating power supply needed.
2. Bridge supply easily varied with remote sense if necessary.
3. 5 wire remote sense system.
4. Freedom from common mode effects.
5. Very high stability dc amplifier enables numerous configurations to be assembled.
6. Low noise.
7. High speed (at low gains).

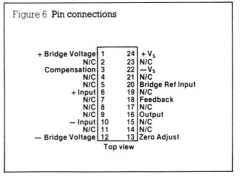

Figure 6 **Pin connections**

Specification

(At 25°C ambient and ±12V supply unless otherwise stated.)

Supply voltage	±2 to ±20V dc
Input offset voltage	1mV max
Input offset voltage/temperature	$1\mu V/°C$ max
Input offset voltage/supply	$5\mu V/V$ max
Input offset voltage/time	$1\mu V$/month max
Input impedance	$>2.5M\Omega$ min
Input noise voltage	$1\mu V$ p.p max
Band width (unity gain)	400kHz

Output current	5mA
Output voltage span	$±(V_s-3)V$
Closed loop gain (adjustable)	5 to 10,000
Open loop gain	>100dB
Common mode rejection ratio	>100dB
Bridge supply voltage/temperature	$20\mu V/°C$
Maximum bridge supply current	12mA
Power dissipation	0.5W
Warm up time	5mins
Operating temperature range	−25°C to +85°C

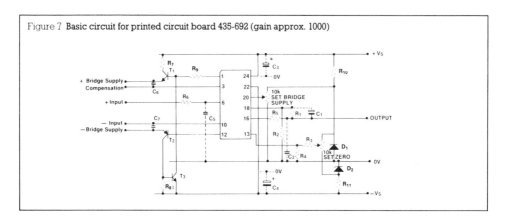

Figure 7 **Basic circuit for printed circuit board 435-692 (gain approx. 1000)**

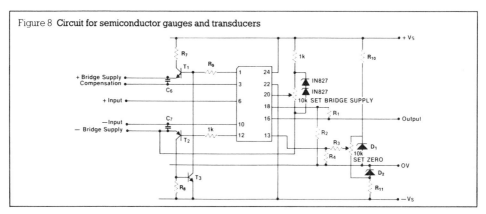

Figure 8 **Circuit for semiconductor gauges and transducers**

Component values (Figures 7 and 8)

R_1 100k	R_7 47R	C_2, C_5 10n (typ.)
R_2 100R	R_8 10R	C_3, C_4 10μ(tant.)
R_3 100k*	R_9 1k0	T_1 BD 135
R_4 68R*	R_{10} 680R	T_2 BD 136
R_5 10R	R_{11} 680R	T_3 BC 108
R_6 100R(typ.)	C_1, C_6, C_7 100n (typ.)	D_1, D_2 1N827

A glass fibre printed circuit board, stock number 435-692, is available for the basic circuit as given in Figure 7.

The board is 46 x 98mm in size and is complete with screen printed component identification and a solder mask.

Only typical values are given for certain components,

as adjustment of these values may be necessary in specific applications to obtain optimum noise reduction (see Minimisation of Noise, page 5).

*R_3 and R_4 values may be adjusted to alter the zero adjustment range when compensating for bridge imbalance.

Notes:

Gain is defined as $1 + \dfrac{R_1}{R_2}$

Zero adjustment range $±6.2 \times \dfrac{R_4}{R_3 + R_4}$ Volts

Total bridge supply = 2 × bridge ref input (pin 20)

C_5 may be omitted for input lead lengths of less than 10 metres.

T_1 and T_2 provide bridge currents up to 60mA and should be kept away from the amplifier.

T_3 and R_5 provide current limit of approx 60mA.

Where high stability power supplies are being used zero and bridge supply reference may be taken direct from the power rails.

The high output of some semiconductor strain gauges may cause large amounts of asymmetry to the bridge. In correcting for the common mode change, the negative bridge voltage will change, causing a span error. This may be calibrated out or the arrangement above used to eliminate the cause of the error. Some semiconductor strain gauge tranducers are temperature compensated by the use of series arm compensation. Thus the common mode voltage changes with temperature, and hence the arrangement above should be used. This operates by referencing the positive bridge supply to the negative supply, thus varying the common mode but not the overall bridge supply.

Minimisation of noise

1. Inherent white/flicker noise in amplifier

To keep this to a minimum use high quality (metal film) resistors and protect the amplifier from excessively high temperatures. The inherent noise level may be further reduced from its already low value by fitting C_1 and C_2 to reduce the operating bandwidth.

2. Supply frequency (or harmonics) inference.

If at 100Hz then the cause is almost likely to be from power supply rails, so use stabilized lines. If at 50Hz then it is generally caused by the location of the supply transformer and/or the wiring. Relocate the supply transformer, screen the input leads to the amplifier, and if possible reduce the operating bandwidth by fitting C_1 and C_2.

3. Power supply transient interference.

It is good practice to decouple the supply lines to the amplifier, by fitting C_3 and C_4, as close to it as possible. If a particular nuisance then fit a mains suppressor, eg. RS stock no. 238-407.

4. Electromagnetic interference

This may be picked up by input leads, output leads, supply leads or direct into the circuit. Minimisation involves a combination of screening, decoupling and reducing operating bandwidth. The shield should be connected to only one earth potential at the receiving monitoring equipment end. Try not to earth any of the dc power lines (eg. 0V). If the shield at the sensor end is earthed then earth the shield at the receiving end and if possible connect this earth potential to the strain gauge amplifier circuit shield. Decouple the power supply leads by fitting C_3 and C_4, decouple the input leads with R_6 and C_5 (note a similar action on the input is not possible). Remove any pickup from the output leads by fitting R_5 and C_2. Fit C_5 if input leads are more than 10m long and fit C_6 if remote sense is longer than 10m. Reduce the operating bandwidth by fitting C_1 and C_2.

Load cells

Introduction

Load cells are basically a beam or other shaped member arranged so that an applied load will cause a proportional strain at certain fixed points on the device. This strain can be detected in several ways, the most common being an arrangement of strain gauges. These gauges convert the strain into an electrical signal which can then be displayed, used as a control signal, etc.

Centre point load cells

The RS range of load cells is of the centre point type in which a double beam is used. They are supplied complete with a full bridge of four strain gauges fitted and calibrated ready to connect to any suitable amplifier.

Three sizes are available for weighing up to 2kg, 20kg or 100kg and, although physically different all cells are the same in method of operation and construction.

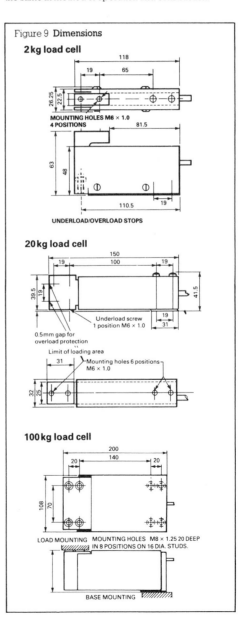

Figure 9 **Dimensions**

2kg load cell

MOUNTING HOLES M6 × 1.0
4 POSITIONS

UNDERLOAD/OVERLOAD STOPS

20kg load cell

Underload screw
1 position M6 × 1.0

0.5mm gap for
overload protection

Limit of loading area

Mounting holes 6 positions
M6 × 1.0

100kg load cell

LOAD MOUNTING   MOUNTING HOLES M8 × 1.25 20 DEEP
IN 8 POSITIONS ON 16 DIA. STUDS.

BASE MOUNTING

When used in weighing scales a platform up to the maximum size given in the specification can be used without loss of performance.

Electrical connections

The cells use a six wire full bridge system for the most accurate results. The lead to the cell is screened and the cores are colour coded as shown in Figure 10.

The RS strain gauge amplifier stock number 308-815 can be used with these load cells. Use the circuit shown in Figure 7, connecting bridge supply to excitation and compensation to sense (Figure 10). In this circuit a five wire system is employed so that the – sense wire shown in Figure 10 is not used and should be connected to the – supply.

Other amplifiers can be used but to achieve good results an accurate low drift amplifier is required.

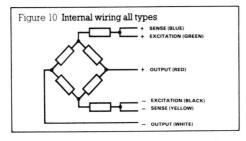

Figure 10 **Internal wiring all types**

Amplifiers such as the chopper stabilized amplifier 7650 and 7652. (stock nos. 303-854 and 630-667) and the precision instrumentation amplifier AD524 AD (stock no. 302-463) would be suitable for this application. Separate RS data sheets are available for these devices.

Mechanical fixings

Both cells are fixed by M6 x 1 set screws and the bodies of the cells are drilled and tapped to a depth of 10mm.

Care must be exercised when handling these devices – do not pull the lead or drop the device and ensure that the cell is not subjected to excessive vibration.

A platform, hopper, or any other fixture can be attached to the top or front face of these cells but it must be noted that the weight of these attachments must be taken into account. For example if a 1kg hopper is attached to the 2kg load cell for weighing out polystyrene granuals for injection moulding the cell will only weigh 1kg of the material because of the weight of the hopper.

These load cells must be mounted on a flat rigid base which is level and will not deflect under loading.

The fixing bolts must be tightened to the correct torque of 7Nm. Do not use a ratchet or 'click-stop' torque spanner on the 2kg cells as this may damage it.

Overload stops

It is vital that overload protection is provided and it is recommended that under load protection is incorporated where possible.

While these load cells can be subjected to overloads of 150% without permanent damage the use of this safety factor cannot be recommended. An overload in excess of 150% will cause permanent damage to the cell.

An underload is simply a load which raises rather than depresses the load face. The RS cells are capable of measuring these types of load.

On the 2kg load cell both over and under load stops are built into the device and therefore the cell will be protected if correctly mounted on a flat and rigid base.

With the 20kg cell the base of the beam is machined so that it will deflect and touch any flat base used at rated load. Using a flat rigid base will, therefore, automatically provide overload protection.

An extra M6 x 1 tapped hole is provided in the base for an underload stop. A mechanical stop should be provided with a no load clearance of 0.5mm so that the load face of the load cell can only be raised by 0.5mm which is equivalent to the full rated load of the unit.

Tension/Compression load cell

A general purpose load cell for force measurement with loads up to 250kg (500lb or 2.5kN approx.). Mechanical connections are by M12 x 1.75 threads in the body of the device and electrical connections via a 3m 5-core screened cable.

This cell can be used for weighing but is ideally suited for the measurement of tensile, or compressive forces by using the cell to replace the structural member under investigation.

Other applications include, for example, determining the power output of a motor by replacing the mounting with the cell and measuring the torque reaction produced.

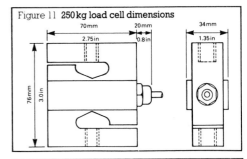

Figure 11 **250kg load cell dimensions**

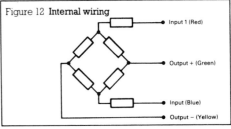

Figure 12 **Internal wiring**

Data Library

Pressure transducers

Stock numbers 303-343, 303-337,
341-913, 341-929, 341-935,
341-957, 341-963, 341-979

The RS pressure transducers are available in two ranges. Range one consists of stock nos. 303-343 and 303-337 and are both gauge types. Pressures sensed are 0-15 and 0-30 psi. This range is suitable for general purpose pressure sensing and measurement. Range two consists of stock nos. within the 341- range as shown below and are available in both gauge and differential styles. Pressures sensed are 0-5, 0-15 and 0-30 psi. This range has wet/wet capability which allows most media types to be connected to the active (P1) side of the device. Suitable applications for this type are medical instruments, barometric sensing, oxygen concentrators, engine controls etc. Advanced manufacturing techniques are used to produce this product which includes laser trimmed bridge resistors for close tolerance on null/sensitivity. For both ranges the sensing element in each transducer is a 0.1in square silicon chip with integral sensing diaphragm and four piezo resistors. When pressure is applied to the diaphragm it causes it to flex, changing the resistance, which results in an output voltage proportional to pressure when a suitable excitation voltage is applied to the device. The sensing resistors are connected as a four active element bridge for best linearity and sensitivity. The linear outputs are complementary (ie as input pressure increases, output A increases and output B decreases).

Features
- Miniature package
- Low cost
- Low null shift, high sensitivity
- Linear output proportional to pressure
- Temperature compensated
- Low hysteresis
- Wet/Wet capability (range two).

Absolute maximum ratings

Range one:

Maximum pressure:	303-343	45 psi
	303-337	60 psi
Maximum voltage		20Vdc
Operating temperature range		−55°C to +125°C
Soldering temperature, 10 secs		315°C

Range two:

Maximum pressure:	341-913	20 psi
	341-929	45 psi
	341-935	60 psi
	341-957	20 psi
	341-963	45 psi
	341-979	60 psi
Maximum voltage		16Vdc
Operating temperature range		0°C to +50°C
Soldering temperature, 10 secs		315°C

Both ranges:

Mechanical shock	tested to 150g
Vibration, 0 to 2kHz	tested to 20g

Compatibility: input media are limited to those which will not attack polyester, silicon, or silicone based adhesives.

Mechanical details

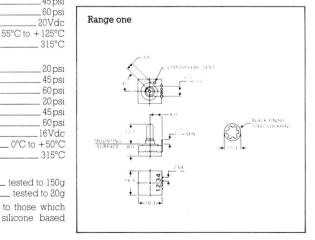

Range one

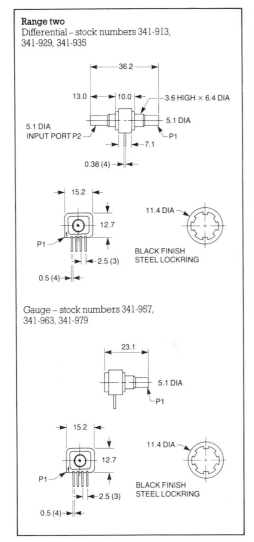

Range two
Differential – stock numbers 341-913,
341-929, 341-935

Gauge – stock numbers 341-957,
341-963, 341-979

Electrical connections

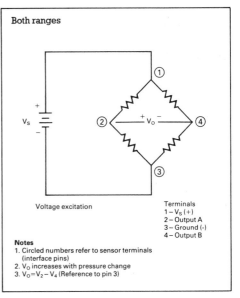

Both ranges

Voltage excitation

Terminals
1 – V_S (+)
2 – Output A
3 – Ground (-)
4 – Output B

Notes
1. Circled numbers refer to sensor terminals
   (interface pins)
2. V_O increases with pressure change
3. $V_O = V_2 - V_4$ (Reference to pin 3)

Electrical characteristics Supply voltage 10.0 ± 0.01Vdc. $T_{amb}=25°C$

Range one

Parameter	303-343			303-337			Units
	Min.	Typ.	Max.	Min.	Typ.	Max.	
Pressure range		0-15			0-30		psi
FSO (Full scale output)	98.5	100	101.5	75	79	83	mV
Null offset	−1	0	+1	−1	0	+1	mV
Sensitivity		6.67			2.63		mV/psi
Overpressure			45			60	psi
Response time			1			1	ms
Recommended excitation voltage		10	16		10	16	Vdc
Linearity (Best fit straight line) Greatest pressure at vent Greatest pressure at port		±0.5% ±1.0%			±0.3% ±0.5%		FSO FSO
Temperature error 0°C to +50°C Sensitivity shift Null shift		±1.5% ±2			±1.5% ±2		FSO mV
Repeatability and hysteresis		0.15%			0.15%		FSO
Stability over 3 years		1.5%			1.5%		FSO
Input resistance		8K			8K		ohms

Range two

Parameter		341-913			341-929			341-935			341-357			341-963			341-979			Units
		Min.	Typ.	Max.	Min.	Typ.	Max.	Min.	Typ.	Max.	Min.	Typ.	Max.	Min.	Typ.	Max.	Min.	Typ.	Max.		Units
Pressure range			0-5			0-15			0-30			0-5			0-15			0-30		psi
FSO (Full scale output)	P1>P2	47	50	53	97	100	103	77	80	83	47	50	53	97	100	103	77	80	83	mV
Null offset		−2	0	+2	−2	0	+2	−2	0	+2	−2	0	+2	−2	0	+2	−2	0	+2	mV
Sensitivity	P1>P2		10			6.67			2.67			10			6.67			2.67		mV/psi
Overpressure			20			45			60			20			45			60		psi
Response time			1.0			1.0			1.0			1.0			1.0			1.0		ms
Recommended excitation voltage			10	16		10	16		10	16		10	16		10	16		10	16	Vdc
Linearity (Best fit straight line)	P1>P2 P2>P1		±0.75 ±1.5	±1.5 ±3.0		±0.5 ±1.0	±1.5 ±2.5		±0.3 ±0.5	±1.0 ±1.5		±0.75 ±1.5	±1.5 ±3.0		±0.5 ±1.0	±1.5 ±2.5		±0.3 ±0.5	±1.0 ±1.5	%FSO %FSO
Temperature error 0°C to +50°C Sensitivity shift Null shift			±1.5 ±1.0	±3.0 ±2.0		±1.5 ±1.0	±3.0 ±2.0		±1.5 ±1.0	±3.0 ±2.0		±1.5 ±1.0	±3.0 ±2.0		±1.5 ±1.0	±3.0 ±2.0		±1.5 ±1.0	±3.0 ±2.0	%FSO mV
Repeatability and hysteresis			±0.75			±0.75			±0.75			±0.75			±0.75			±0.75		%FSO
Stability over years			±1.5			±1.5			±1.5			±1.5			±1.5			±1.5		%FSO
Input resistance			10K			10K			10K			10K			10K			10K		ohms

APPENDIX B

This section contains data sheets for the following components:

- AC industrial electric motors
- DC speed control module and accessories
- 512 DC motor controller
- Hybrid stepper motors

Data sheets are reprinted with the permission of RS Components.

ac industrial electric motors

Standards' organisations

The RS-ABB range of ac induction motors is produced to common European standards, these being IEC and CENELEC (Comité Européen de Normalisation Electrotechnique).

These two organisations work together on harmonisations of standards both worldwide and within Western Europe.

CENELEC in particular aims to remove trade obstacles in Western Europe that may occur due to differences in the regulations and standards.

New national standards are increasingly identical to or broadly based on these European standards issued by CENELEC.

Dimensional and power standards

The first edition of IEC Publication 72 was issued in 1959 and supplemented in 1970 by IEC (International Electrotechnical Commission) Publication 72A.

These contained the first recommendations and outline proposals that electric motors should be produced with similar rated powers and mounting dimensions, ie. shaft height, fixing dimensions and shaft extension dimensions.

In 1974 the joint agreement was superseded by a harmonisation document HD 231 from CENELEC. The

Features

- Manufactured to metric frame sizes
- Totally enclosed fan cooled (TEFC) construction
- Environmentally protected to IP54
- Three-phase motors available in both foot and flange mounting
- Wide voltage range on three-phase motors of 220-240V/250-280V if delta (△) connected or 380-420/440-480V if star (Y) connected
- Suitable for use on 50/60Hz supplies
- Single-phase motors available in both permanent capacitor and capacitor start-run formats
- 2-pole and 4-pole motors available.

resulting standardisation enabled a complete interchangeability between motors of different manufacture. The sizes, versions and rated outputs of 4-pole and 2-pole motors covered by the standard are shown in Table 1.

However, the European standardisation does not fully coincide with corresponding USA standards, which tend to be based on imperial dimensions rather than the corresponding metric-based European motor. Power ratings also differ between US and European motors.

Three-phase induction motor

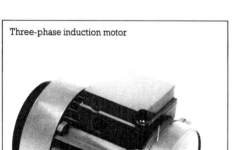

Table 1 **IEC frame sizes**

Size	Rated output, kW
Shaft height mm	Squirrel-cage motors IP54
56	0.06
56	0.09
63	0.12
63	0.18
71	0.25
71	0.37
80	0.55
80	0.75
90 S	1.1
90 L	1.5
100 L	2.2
100 L	3
112 M	4
132 S	5.5
132 M	7.5

The meaning of the standardised letters in the size designation for sizes 90-132 are S=small, M=medium long and L=long version.

Insulation classes

IEC Publication IEC85 divides insulation into classes. Each class is given a designation that corresponds to the upper temperature limit of the insulating material when used under normal operating conditions.

The correct insulation of the winding of a motor is therefore determined by both the temperature rise in the motor and the temperature of the ambient air. If a motor is subjected to an ambient temperature higher than 40°C, it must normally be derated or a higher insulation class of material used.

International standards measure temperature in degrees Celsius (°C), whilst temperature difference is stated in the unit Kelvin (K). One degree Celsius is equivalent to 1K.

The RS-ABB range of ac induction motors is manufactured to a class F insulation rating. For class F the temperature rise must not exceed 105K, provided that the ambient temperature does not exceed +40°C.

It should be noted that if the upper temperature limit of the insulation material is exceeded by 8 to 10K (see Table 2), the life of the insulation will be approximately halved.

Table 2

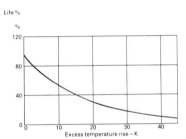

The graph illustrates the effect of exceeding the highest permitted winding temperature on winding life.

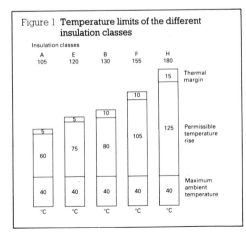

Figure 1 **Temperature limits of the different insulation classes**

General characteristics

The following is a list of general characteristics of the ac induction motors supplied by RS Components. Each one should be considered before choosing the appropriate motor for the application.

Voltage

Single-speed, three-phase motors can usually be re-connected for two voltages.

The usual way is to connect the three stator phase windings in star (Y) or delta (△). All RS-ABB motors are supplied configured in star (Y) primarily but may be converted for delta (△). This means that the three-phase input voltage range is wide. For example if the motor was connected in delta it would accept a three-phase input voltage range of 220-240V for a 50Hz supply frequency or 250-280V for 60Hz frequency.

Similarly with the motor connected in star an input voltage range of 380-420V is acceptable on 50Hz or 440-480V on a 60Hz supply system.

This wide voltage range and dual operating frequency enables the motors to be used throughout the world.

To convert the motors refer to Figure 2 where indication is given of the required link change.

Note. To use these motors in conjunction with single-phase 240V input, three-phase output ac motor speed controllers, these three-phase motors must be connected in delta (△).

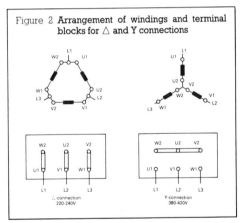

Figure 2 **Arrangement of windings and terminal blocks for △ and Y connections**

Voltage deviation

If the supply voltage at constant output power deviates from the rated voltage of the motor, the starting and maximum torques of the motor vary approximately as the square of the voltage.

The change in torque will also result in a change in the speed, efficiency and power factor (see Figure 3).

Voltage deviations also affect the temperature rise in the motor windings. If the voltage is low the temperature will rise in both large and small framed motors; if the voltage is high the temperature may drop slightly in large sized motors but rise rapidly in the small output motors.

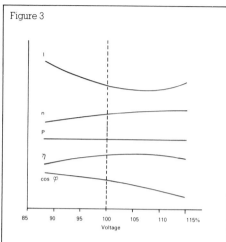

Graph showing current (I), speed (n), efficiency (η) and power factor (cos $\varnothing$) as a function of the voltage at constant output (P).

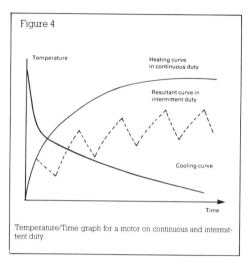

Temperature/Time graph for a motor on continuous and intermittent duty.

Power

When choosing a motor size it is essential to bear in mind that it is the power demand of the driven machine that determines the output delivered by the motor and therefore the power drawn from the supply. For example if a machine needs 4kW it will take 4kW, regardless of whether the motor is 3kW or 7.5kW.

If the smaller motor is installed it will be subjected to a continuous 25% overload that it will not be able to sustain for long periods. The protective overload device fitted should, however, protect against these types of high overloads, and disconnect the motor supply within a suitable time period.

A motor must be capable of delivering the power needed by the driven machine, and it is prudent to provide a safety margin since minor overloads that are difficult to forsee can often occur.

If a motor winding is overheated the insulation of the copper conductors may be destroyed. Given a choice between two motor sizes the larger one should always be used. However it is not a good idea to choose an unnecessarily large motor since it will be disproportionately costly to purchase and have a low power factor in service. In addition, when a squirrel cage motor is started the starting current will be excessively high, since it is proportional to the size of the motor. If a motor is loaded at full load only for short periods with periods of idling between them, known as intermittent duty, its temperature rise will be lower, and it will have a capacity to deliver a higher output than during continuous operation.

Figure 4 shows a typical temperature/time graph for a motor in both continuous and intermittent duty.

Power factor

A motor consumes not only active power (kW), which it converts into mechanical work, but also reactive power (kVAr) which is needed for magnetisation but does not perform any useful function.

The active and reactive powers are shown in Figure 5 together with the apparent power (kVA). The ratio between the active power and the apparent power is known as the power factor. The angle between P (kW) and S (kVA) is usually designated $\varnothing$. The power factor usually being referred to as cos $\varnothing$.

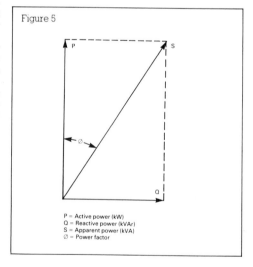

P = Active power (kW)
Q = Reactive power (kVAr)
S = Apparent power (kVA)
$\varnothing$ = Power factor

The power factor is usually between 0.7 and 0.9, however this may vary depending on the motor size and rating.

If there are many motors in an installation they will consume a lot of reactive power and will therefore have a lower power factor. Power supply authorities sometimes require the power factor of the installation to be raised. This is usually done by connecting correction capacitors to the supply: these generate reactive power and thus raise the power factor level.

Power factor correction

With phase compensation the correction capacitors are usually connected in parallel with the motor or group of motors. Capacitors must not be connected in parallel with any single phases of the winding otherwise difficulty may be experienced in starting using star/delta methods.

To calculate the value of power factor correction capacitor required the following formula should be used:

$$C = 3.2 \times 10^6 \times \frac{Q}{U}$$

where C = Capacitance, μF
  U = Capacitor voltage, V
  Q = Reactive power, kVAr.

The reactive power is obtained by using the formula

$$Q = K \times \frac{P}{\eta}$$

where K = constant from Table 2a
  P = rated power of motor, kW
  η = efficiency of motor.

Table 2a

cos ∅ without compensation	Constant K Compensation to cos ∅ =			
	0.95	0.90	0.85	0.80
0.50	1.403	1.248	1.112	0.982
0.51	1.358	1.202	1.067	0.936
0.52	1.314	1.158	1.023	0.892
0.53	1.271	1.116	0.980	0.850
0.54	1.230	1.074	0.939	0.808
0.55	1.190	1.034	0.898	0.768
0.56	1.150	0.995	0.859	0.729
0.57	1.113	0.957	0.822	0.691
0.58	1.076	0.920	0.785	0.654
0.59	1.040	0.884	0.748	0.618
0.60	1.005	0.849	0.713	0.583
0.61	0.970	0.815	0.679	0.548
0.62	0.937	0.781	0.646	0.515
0.63	0.904	0.748	0.613	0.482
0.64	0.872	0.716	0.581	0.450
0.65	0.841	0.685	0.549	0.419
0.66	0.810	0.654	0.518	0.388
0.67	0.779	0.624	0.488	0.358
0.68	0.750	0.594	0.458	0.328
0.69	0.720	0.565	0.429	0.298
0.70	0.692	0.536	0.400	0.270
0.71	0.663	0.507	0.372	0.241
0.72	0.635	0.480	0.344	0.214
0.73	0.608	0.452	0.316	0.186
0.74	0.580	0.425	0.289	0.158
0.75	0.553	0.398	0.262	0.132
0.76	0.527	0.371	0.235	0.105
0.77	0.500	0.344	0.209	0.078
0.78	0.474	0.318	0.182	0.052
0.79	0.447	0.292	0.156	0.026
0.80	0.421	0.266	0.130	
0.81	0.395	0.240	0.104	
0.82	0.369	0.214	0.078	
0.83	0.343	0.188	0.052	
0.84	0.317	0.162	0.026	
0.85	0.291	0.135		
0.86	0.265	0.109		
0.87	0.238	0.082		
0.88	0.211	0.055		
0.89	0.184	0.027		
0.90	0.156			

Efficiency

IEC Publication 34-2 describes two methods for determining the efficiency of a motor, one being the direct method the other known as indirect.

With the indirect method input power and output are each measured individually. Most motor figures quoted are determined by this method, which also includes a calculation of the losses involved.

Typical motor losses include
bearing and air friction losses
current heat losses in stator and rotor
iron losses
stray losses.

Figure 6 gives a graphic indication of the relationship between these losses.

The standards define the stray losses as 0.5% of the input power at rated duty. The standard tolerance is: 15% of $(1 - \eta)$ for motors up to 15kW where η = efficiency of motor. NEMA, the standards most widely used in the USA, permit no tolerance on the losses. Stray losses are generally calculated at 0.9% of the output.

Figure 6

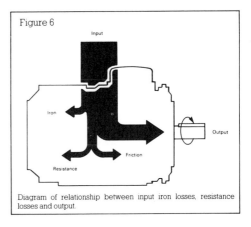

Diagram of relationship between input iron losses, resistance losses and output.

Speed

The speed of an ac motor depends on the mains frequency and the number of poles of the stator winding.

$$n = \frac{2.f.60}{P} \text{ r/min}$$

where
n = speed
f = frequency
P = number of poles.

The rule of thumb to follow for a 50Hz mains frequency is that the speed in revolutions per minute (r/min. or rpm) is 6000 divided by the number of poles.

For example a 4-pole motor will have a synchronous speed of

$$\frac{6,000}{4} = 1,500 \text{ r/min}.$$

This speed can never actually be achieved on load due to slip. On no load, however, speed is practically equal to the synchronous speed.

To calculate slip the following equation can be used

$$S = \frac{n_1 - n}{n_1} \times 100\%$$

where

S = slip %
n_1 = synchronous speed, r/min.
n = asynchronous speed, r/min.

Motor slip is proportional to the power taken from the motor.

For example

A 4-pole motor of 4kW at 415V, 50Hz, 1425 r/min.

At 4kW slip equals

$$S = \frac{1500 - 1425}{1500} \times 100 = 5\%$$

corresponding to $1500 - 1425 = 75$ r/min.

At 3kW

$$S = \frac{3}{4} \times \frac{1500 - 1425}{1500} \times 100 = 3.8\%$$

corresponding to $\frac{3}{4} \times (1500 - 1425) = 56$ r/min.

Therefore n at 3kW will be $1500 - 56 = 1444$ r/min.

The slip is inversely proportional to the square of the voltage.

For example

4-pole motor, 4kW, 415V, 50Hz, 1425 r/min.

At 380V; $S = \left(\frac{415}{380}\right)^2 \times \frac{1500 - 1425}{1500} \times 100$

$$= 5.96\%$$

corresponding to $\left(\frac{415}{380}\right)^2 \times (1500 - 1425)$

$$89 \text{ r/min}.$$

n will therefore be $1500 - 89 = 1411$ r/min.

Table 3 gives details of synchronous speed for various numbers of motor poles and operation on either 50 or 60Hz.

Table 3

	Synchronous speed at	
Poles	50Hz	60Hz
2	3000	3600
4	1500	1800
6	1000	1200
8	750	900
10	600	720
12	500	600
16	375	450
20	300	360
24	250	300
32	187.5	225
48	125	150

Operation at 60Hz

A motor wound for a given voltage at 50Hz can be used unmodified on a 60Hz supply: in such cases the motor data will change as shown below in Table 4.

Note.

1. That M/start/M and M max/M must be calculated on the basis of the 60Hz value of M.
2. The different torque figures at 60Hz. The starting torque and minimum torque figures in particular are reduced on 60Hz operation with the same supply voltage, this may lead to starting problems in certain applications.

Table 4

Motor wound for 50Hz and	Connection to 60Hz and	Data at 60Hz as % of 50Hz data				
		Output	M^1)	M_{max}/M^1	M_{start}/M^1)	Speed
220V	220V	100	83	85	70	120
	255V	115	96	98	95	120
380V	380V	100	83	85	70	120
	415V	110	91	93	85	120
	440V	115	96	98	95	120
	460V	120	100	103	100	120
415V	415V	100	83	85	70	120
	460V	110	91	94	85	120
	480V	115	96	98	95	120
500V	500V	100	83	85	70	120
	550V	110	91	94	85	120
	575V	115	96	98	95	120
	600V	120	100	103	100	120

^{1})M   Rated torque at 60Hz
M_{max}/M Maximum torque/rated torque
M_{start}/M Starting torque/rated torque

Table 5

Quantity	Data at 50Hz	Conversion factor	Data at 60Hz
Voltage	380V	–	440V
Output	11kW	1.15	12.6kW
Current	23A	1.0	23A
M_{max}/M	2.4	0.98	2.4
M_{start}/M	2	0.95	1.9
Speed	1450 r/min	1.20	1740 r/min

Example of a typical conversion of data from 50 to 60Hz operation.

Torque

The torque of a motor is the measure of its turning ability. If the power and speed are known it is easy to calculate the torque.

If we refer to Figure 7 we can see that at the periphery of a pulley there is a certain force in the belt. If this force is referred to as F and the radius of the pulley r, the product Fr is known as the torque M of the motor.

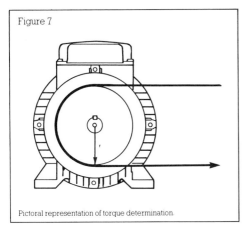

Pictoral representation of torque determination.

The power is the work performed by the motor per unit of time; work is force times distance. The force F rotates n revolutions in one minute and covers the distance n × 2 × π × r.

During motor acceleration the torque developed first drops slightly then rises to its maximum (see Figure 8). In normal motors the maximum torque occurs at 85 to 90% of full speed.

At synchronous speed torque is zero.

To calculate the rated torque of a motor the following formula can be used

$$M = \frac{30,000 \times P}{\pi \times n} \, Nm$$

Where P = output, kN
　　　　n = motor speed, r/min.

For example
A motor is rated at 1.5kW and 1400r/min. The diameter of pulley is 100mm ie. r = 0.05m. The torque and traction developed at full power will be

$$M = \frac{30,000 \times 1.5}{\pi \times 1400}$$

$$M = 10.2Nm$$

Therefore $F = \dfrac{10.2}{0.05}$

$$= 205N$$

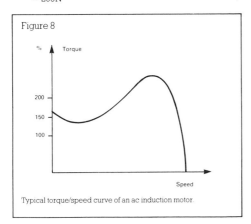

Typical torque/speed curve of an ac induction motor.

Minimum torque
IEC Publication 34-1 states certain figures for general purpose three-phase squirrel cage motors. For single-speed motors with rated output <100kW the minimum torque delivered during run up at rated voltage must not be less than 50% of the rated torque and not less than 50% of the starting torque. The figure for single-phase motors is 30% of the rated torque.

Maximum torque
The maximum torque is a measure of the overload capability of the motor. IEC Publication 34-1 lays down that general purpose motors must be capable of developing at least 160% of the rated torque for 15 seconds – without stopping or suddenly changing speed – if the rated voltage or frequency is maintained. Four-pole motors made by ABB usually have a maximum torque that is approximately 200 to 300% of the rated torque. Low speed motors usually have a slightly lower maximum torque than high speed ones.

Torque on voltage deviation
With ac induction motors, the starting current decreases slightly more than proportionately to the voltage. Thus at 90% of the rated voltage the motor draws approximately 87-89% of the starting current.

The starting torqe is proportional to the square of the current. The torque delivered at 90% of rated voltage is therefore only 75-79% of the starting torque. This factor may be of particular importance when choosing a motor for use on a weak electrical supply or when starting techniques based on current reduction methods are employed (see Figure 9).

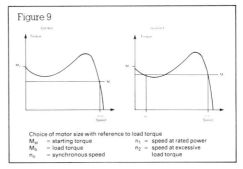

Choice of motor size with reference to load torque
M_{st} = starting torque n_1 = speed at rated power
M_b = load torque n_2 = speed at excessive
n_o = synchronous speed   load torque

Frequency of starting and reversing
When a motor is frequently started, counter-current braked or reversed, extra heat, due to the increase in losses, is produced reducing the motor's ability to perform at its rated loaded output.

The following formula can be used to obtain an approximate value.

$$P2 = P1 \times \sqrt{\frac{3600 - k_1 \times X \times ts \times \left(\frac{1st}{1}\right)^2}{3600 - X \times ts}}$$

where

P2 = permitted load
P1 = rated output of motor
X = number of starts, braking or reversals per hour
ts = starting or braking time

$\frac{1st}{1}$ = starting current/braking current

K_1 = constant: 1 for starting, 3 for braking and 4 for reversing.

The permitted value of X is determined with regards to the temperature rise within the motor.

For example

A 4-pole motor 4kW, $\frac{1st}{1} = 5.5$

starting time ts = 0.5s. X = 10 starts per hour.
Therefore

$$\frac{P2}{P1} = \sqrt{\frac{3600 - 1 \times 10 \times 0.5 \times (5.5)^2}{3600 - 10 \times 0.5}} = .979$$

If the same formula is used to calculate the required derating on 10 reversals per hour

$$\frac{P2}{P1} = \sqrt{\frac{3600 - 4 \times 10 \times 0.5 \times (5.5)^2}{3600 - 10 \times 0.5}} = .912$$

Types of duty

Various types of duty have been defined by IEC Publication 34-1 that describe how the load, and thus the motor output, varies with time. The motor must undergo a load test without exceeding the temperature limits laid down in the specification.

Actual operating conditions are often of a more irregular nature than those corresponding to any of the standard duty types. It is therefore essential that when choosing and rating a motor to decide on the type of duty that corresponds best to the thermal stresses that are expected to occur in practice.

The most standard types of duty classes are:

S1 continuous duty

Operation at a constant load, long enough for thermal equilibrium to be reached (see Figure 10).

S2 short time duty

Operation at constant load for a given time that is shorter than the time needed to reach thermal equilibrium, followed by a rest and de-energised period. De-energisation period should be long enough to allow the motor to reach a temperature that does not deviate from the temperature of the cooling medium by 2K (see Figure 11).

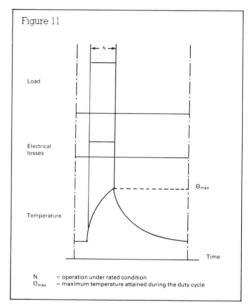

Figure 11

N = operation under rated condition
Θ_{max} = maximum temperature attained during the duty cycle

S3 intermittent duty

A sequence of identical duty cycles, where each cycle is in two parts, one at constant load and the other at rest and de-energised. In this type of duty the starting current has no significant effect on the temperature rise. The duty cycle is too short for thermal equilibrium to be reached (see Figure 12).

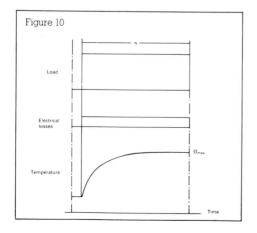

Figure 10

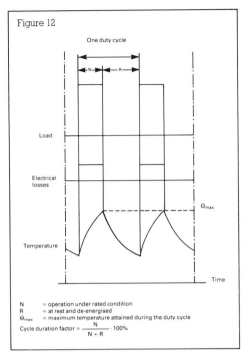

Figure 12

One duty cycle

Load

Electrical losses

Θ_{max}

Temperature

Time

N = operation under rated condition
R = at rest and de-energised
Θ_{max} = maximum temperature attained during the duty cycle

Cycle duration factor = $\dfrac{N}{N + R} \cdot 100\%$

S4 intermittent duty with starting

A sequence of individual duty cycles, where each cycle consists of a start that is sufficiently long to have a significant effect on the motor temperature, a period of constant load and a period at rest and de-energised. In this type of duty the starting current is insignificant on the temperature rise. The duty cycles are too short for thermal equilibrium to be reached (see Figure 13).

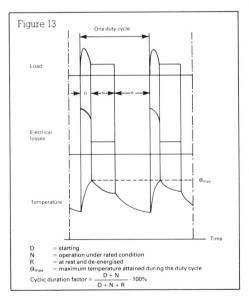

Figure 13

One duty cycle

Load

Electrical losses

Θ_{max}

Temperature

Time

D = starting
N = operation under rated condition
R = at rest and de-energised
Θ_{max} = maximum temperature attained during the duty cycle

Cyclic duration factor = $\dfrac{D + N}{D + N + R} \cdot 100\%$

S5 intermittent duty with electrical braking

A sequence of identical duty cycles, where each cycle consists of a start, a period at constant load followed by rapid electrical braking, and a rest and de-energised period. The duty cycle is too short for thermal equilibrium to be reached (see Figure 14).

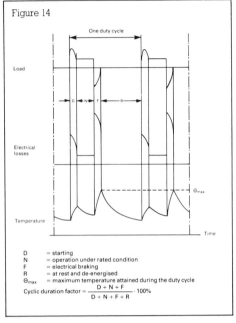

Figure 14

One duty cycle

Load

Electrical losses

Θ_{max}

Temperature

Time

D = starting
N = operation under rated condition
F = electrical braking
R = at rest and de-energised
Θ_{max} = maximum temperature attained during the duty cycle

Cyclic duration factor = $\dfrac{D + N + F}{D + N + F + R} \cdot 100\%$

S6 continuous operation
Periodic duty

A sequence of identical duty cycles, where each cycle is in in two parts, one at constant load and the other at no load, no rest and no de-energised period. The duty cycles are too short for thermal equilibrium conditions to be reached (see Figure 15).

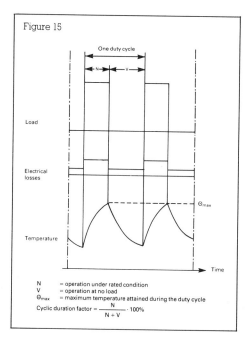

Figure 15

N = operation under rated condition
V = operation at no load
Θ_{max} = maximum temperature attained during the duty cycle

Cyclic duration factor = $\dfrac{N}{N + V} \cdot 100\%$

S7 continuous operation, periodic duty with electrical braking

A sequence of identical duty cycles, where each cycle consists of a start and a period at constant load, followed by electrical braking, no rest and de-energised period. The duty cycles are too short for thermal equilibrium conditions to be reached (see Figure 16).

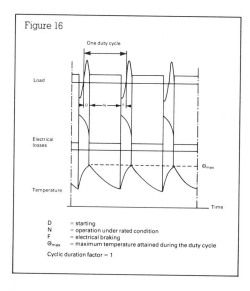

Figure 16

D = starting
N = operation under rated condition
F = electrical braking
Θ_{max} = maximum temperature attained during the duty cycle

Cyclic duration factor = 1

Uprating

Because of the lower temperature rise in a motor operated on short time or intermediate duty it is usually possible to take a higher output from the motor on these types of duty than on continuous duty S1. Table 6 gives details.

Table 6

Short-time duty, S2	Poles	Permitted output as % of rated output in S1 continuous duty for motor size:	
		63-100	112-250
30 min	4-8	110	120
60 min	2-8	100	110
Intermittent duty, S3	Poles	Permitted output as % of rated output in S1 continuous duty for motor size:	
		63-100	112-250
15%	4	140	145
25%	4	130	130
40%	4	120	110
60%	4	110	107

Changing direction

Three-phase motors

If the mains supply to the stator terminals marked U, V and W of a three-phase motor and the phase sequence of the mains is L1, L2, L3, the motor will rotate clockwise (when viewed from the drive end). To reverse direction interchange any two of the three cables connected to the starter device or the motor.

Single-phase motors

Capacitor start – capacitor run type

To reverse the direction of this type of motor the blue and yellow cables connected to terminals 3 and 12 should be interchanged (refer to Figure 17).

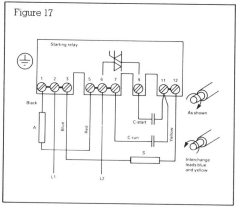

Figure 17

Permanent split capacitor type

To reverse the direction of this type of motor the connected capacitor should be moved from between terminals U1 and U5 to U1 and Z2 (refer to Figure 18).

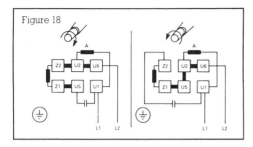

Figure 18

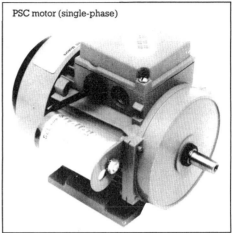

PSC motor (single-phase)

Single-phase motor variations
CSR (Capacitor start and run)
Motors are fitted with both a separate start and run capacitor. These motors are also fitted with an electronic relay which prevents any risk of damage to the starting capacitor either during heavy start or overload of the motor.

CSR motors have a starting torque of approximately 160% of full load torque, making them ideal for driving compressors, piston pumps, high pressure cleaners, etc.

CSR motor (single-phase)

PSC (permanent split capacitor)
These motors are fitted with one capacitor only that is connected in circuit both during starting and running. These motors tend to have lower starting torques typically between 25 and 50% of full load torque. PSC motors are particularly suitable for use on drives having comparatively light starting loads such as fans and centrifugal pumps.

Motor types
3-phase motor 4-pole
Foot mounted

Rating kW	(hp)	Frame size	ABB ref.	RS stock no.
.18	(.25)	63B	MK1100 15-S	320-023
.37	(.50)	71B	MK110017-S	320-039
.55	(.75)	80A	MK110018-S	320-045
.75	(1.0)	80B	MK110019-S	320-051
1.1	(1.5)	90S	MK110020-S	320-067
1.5	(2.0)	90L	MK110021-S	320-073
2.2	(3.0)	100LA	MK110022-S	320-089
3	(4.0)	100LB	MK110023-S	320-095
4	(5.5)	112M	MK14203AD	320-102

3-phase foot mounted 2-pole

Rating kW	(hp)	Frame size	ABB ref.	RS stock no.
.18	(.25)	63B	MK110004-S	266-698
.37	(.50)	71A	MK110005-S	266-705
.55	(.75)	71B	MK110006-S	266-711
.75	(1.0)	80A	MK110007-S	266-727
1.1	(1.5)	80B	MK110008-S	266-733
1.5	(2.0)	90S	MK110009-S	266-749
2.2	(3.0)	90L	MK110010-S	266-755
3	(4.0)	100L	MK110011-S	266-761
4	(5.5)	112M	MK110012-S	266-812

Flange mounted 4-pole

Rating kW	(hp)	Frame size	ABB ref.	RS stock no.
.37	(.50)	71B	MK1100 57-S	320-118
.55	(.75)	80A	MK110058-S	320-124
.75	(1.0)	80B	MK110059-S	320-130
1.1	(1.5)	90S	MK110060-S	320-146
1.5	(2.0)	90L	MK110061-S	320-152
2.2	(3.0)	100LA	MK110062-S	320-168
3	(4.0)	100LB	MK110063-S	320-174

Foot mounted motors

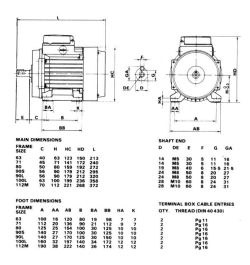

MAIN DIMENSIONS

FRAME SIZE	C	H	HC	HD	L
63	40	63	123	150	213
71	45	71	141	172	240
80	50	80	159	192	272
90S	56	90	179	212	295
90L	56	90	179	212	320
100L	63	100	199	236	358
112M	70	112	221	268	372

SHAFT END

D	DE	E	F	G	GA
14	M5	30	5	11	16
14	M5	30	5	11	16
19	M8	40	6	15.5	21.5
24	M8	50	8	20	27
24	M8	50	8	20	27
28	M10	60	8	24	31
28	M10	60	8	24	31

FOOT DIMENSIONS

FRAME SIZE	A	AA	AB	B	BA	BB	HA	K
63	100	16	120	80	19	98	7	7
71	112	20	136	90	21	112	9	7
80	125	25	154	100	30	125	10	10
90S	140	27	170	100	30	125	10	10
90L	140	27	170	125	30	150	10	10
100L	160	32	197	140	34	172	12	12
112M	190	38	222	140	36	174	12	12

TERMINAL BOX CABLE ENTRIES

QTY.	THREAD (DIN 40 430)
2	Pg 11
2	Pg 16
2	Pg 16
2	Pg 16
2	Pg 16
2	Pg 16
2	Pg 16

FLANGE MOUNTED MOTORS

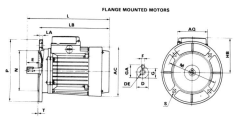

MAIN DIMENSIONS

FRAME SIZE	AC	AQ	HB	L	LB
71	140	85	102	240	210
80	158	97	112	272	232
90S	178	97	122	295	245
90L	178	97	122	320	270
100L	198	97	136	358	298

SHAFT END

D	DE	E	F	G	GA
14	M5	30	5	11	16
14	M5	30	5	11	16
19	M8	40	6	15.5	21.5
24	M8	50	8	20	27
24	M8	50	8	20	27
28	M10	60	8	24	31

FLANGE DIMENSIONS

FRAME SIZE	IEC-FLANGE	LA	M	N	P	S	T
71	F130	9	130	110	160	10	3.5
80	F165	10	165	130	200	12	3.5
90S	F165	10	165	130	200	12	3.5
90L	F165	10	165	130	200	12	3.5
100L	F215	11	215	180	250	15	4

TERMINAL BOX CABLE ENTRIES

QTY.	THREAD (DIN 40 430)
2	Pg 16
2	Pg 16
2	Pg 16
2	Pg 16
2	Pg 16

Motor selection tables: 4 pole

Size	63B	71B	80A	80B	90S	90L	100LA	100LB	112M
kW	.18	.37	.55	.75	1.1	1.5	2.2	3	4
hp	.25	.5	.75	1.0	1.5	2.0	3	4	5.5
Actual speed	1370	1400	1410	1410	1410	1420	1430	1430	1430
Power factor	.57	.60	.62	.66	.69	.71	.72	.73	.84
FLC	.8	1.25	1.65	2.1	2.9	3.7	5.2	6.9	9.1
Load torque	1.25	2.5	3.7	5	7.5	10	15	20	27
Wt.	4.5	6.5	9	10	13	16	20.5	23.5	31

2 pole

Size	63B	71A	71B	80A	80B	90S	90L	100L	112M
kW	.25	.37	.55	.75	1.1	1.5	2.2	3	4
hp	0.33	.5	.75	1.0	1.5	2.0	3	4	5.5
Actual speed	2750	2820	2820	2850	2850	2860	2870	2890	2840
Power factor	.65	.69	.73	.76	.79	.79	.82	.83	.85
FLC	0.8	1.05	1.45	1.85	2.6	3.5	4.7	6.2	7.5
Load torque	0.84	1.25	1.9	2.5	3.7	5	7.5	10	13.4
Wt.	4.5	5.5	6.5	9	10	13	16	21	30

Note. FLC is given for star connection, except for the 122m frame motors

Highest permissible no. of starts per hour at no-load

frame size	4 pole motor	2 pole motor
63B	8700	11200
71A	–	9100
71B	8000	–
80A	8000	5900
80B	8000	4900
90S	7700	4200
90L	7000	3500
100L	–	2800
100LA	5200	–
100LB	4500	–
112M	6700	3700

Max starting duration in seconds for direct-on line at rated voltage

frame size	4 pole motor	2 pole motor
63	40	25
71	20	20
80	20	15
90	20	10
100	15	10
112	15	12

**Single-phase motors
capacitor start-run 4-pole**

Rating kW	(hp)	Frame size	ABB ref.	RS stock no.
.37	(.50)	71B	MK111312-B	320-297
.55	(.75)	80A	MK111313-B	320-304
.75	(1.0)	80B	MK111314-B	320-310
1.1	(1.5)	90S	MK111315-B	320-326

Capacitor start-run 2-pole

Rating kW	(hp)	Frame size	ABB ref.	RS stock no.
.37	(.50)	71A	MK111302-B	266-777
.55	(.75)	71B	MK111303-B	266-783
.75	(1.0)	80A	MK111304-B	266-799
1.1	(1.5)	80B	MK111305-B	266-806

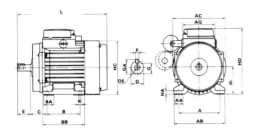

MAIN DIMENSIONS

TYPE	AC	AQ	C	H	HC	HD	L		D	DE	E	F	G	GA
								SHAFT END						
MT63	120	85	40	63	123	150	213		14	M5	30	5	11	16
MT71	140	85	45	71	141	172	240		14	M5	30	5	11	16
MT80	158	97	50	80	159	192	272		19	M8	40	6	15·5	21·5
MT90S	178	97	56	90	179	212	295		24	M8	50	8	20	27

FOOT DIMENSIONS

A	AA	AB	B	BA	BB	HA	K
100	16	120	80	19	98	7	7
112	20	136	90	21	112	9	7
125	25	154	100	30	125	10	10
140	27	170	100	30	125	10	10

Permanent split capacitor 2-pole

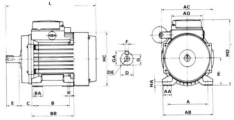

Rating kW	(hp)	Frame size	ABB ref.	RS stock no.
.18	(.25)	63B	MK111801-E	266-648
.37	(.50)	71A	MK111802-E	266-654
.55	(.75)	71B	MK111803-E	266-660
.75	(1.0)	80A	MK111804-E	266-676
1.1	(1.5)	80B	MK111805-E	266-682

MAIN DIMENSIONS

TYPE	AC	AQ	C	H	HC	HD	L		D	DE	E	F	G	GA
								SHAFT END						
MT63	120	85	40	63	123	150	213		14	M5	30	5	11	16
MT71	140	85	45	71	141	172	240		14	M5	30	5	11	16
MT80	158	97	50	80	159	192	272		19	M8	40	6	15·5	21·5
MT90S	178	97	56	90	179	212	295		24	M8	50	8	20	27

FOOT DIMENSIONS

A	AA	AB	B	BA	BB	HA	K
100	16	120	80	19	98	7	7
112	20	136	90	21	112	9	7
125	25	154	100	30	125	10	10
140	27	170	100	30	125	10	10

4 pole

Frame size	71B	80A	80B	90S
kW	.37	.55	.75	1.1
hp	.5	.75	1.0	1.5
Actual speed	1330	1400	1400	1410
Power factor	.99	.99	.99	.99
FLC	2.9	3.9	5.2	7.2
Load torque	2.5	3.7	5	7.5
Net weight	6.5	9	10	13

2 pole

Frame size	71A	71B	80A	80B
kW	.37	.55	.75	1.1
hp	.5	.75	1.0	1.5
Actual speed	2850	2850	2870	2870
Power factor	.99	.99	.99	.99
FLC	2.6	3.8	4.9	7
Load torque	1.25	1.9	2.5	3.7
Net weight	5.5	6.5	9	10

Permanent split capacitor
Foot mounted 4-pole

Rating kW	(hp)	Frame size	ABB ref.	RS stock no.
.18	(.25)	63B	MK111810-E	320-247
.37	(.50)	71B	MK111812-E	320-253
.55	(.75)	80A	MK111813-E	320-269
.75	(1.0)	80B	MK111814-E	320-275
1.1	(1.5)	90S	MK111815-E	320-281

Motor selection tables: 4 pole

Frame size	63B	71B	80A	80B	90S
kW	.18	.37	.55	.75	1.1
hp	.25	.5	.75	1.0	1.5
Actual speed	1370	1380	1400	1400	1400
Power factor	.95	.99	.99	.99	.99
FLC	1.6	2.9	3.9	5.2	7.1
Load torque	1.3	2.5	3.7	5	7.5
Net weight	4.5	6.5	9	10	13

2 pole

Frame size	63B	71A	71B	80A	80B
kW	.25	.37	.55	.75	1.1
hp	.33	.5	.75	1.0	1.5
Actual speed	2750	2850	2850	2870	2870
Power factor	.99	.97	.99	.99	.99
FLC	2	2.6	3.8	4.9	7
Load torque	.85	1.25	1.9	2.5	3.7
Net weight	4.5	5.5	6.5	9	10

RS Components Ltd. PO Box 99, Corby, Northants, NN17 9RS
An Electrocomponents Company

Telephone: 0536 201234
© RS Components Ltd. 1992

Data Library

dc speed control module and accessories

General

The RS CUBE range and associated free standing modules provide motor speed control of dc shunt wound and permanent magnet motors.

The CUBE can be simply converted into a basic speed or torque controller by the addition of an external set point reference and a run switch.

Additional functions such as motor reversal, dynamic braking and isolated drive input from both voltage and current sources can be performed using the free standing modules, that are simply connected between user controls and the CUBE input terminals.

Speed control module

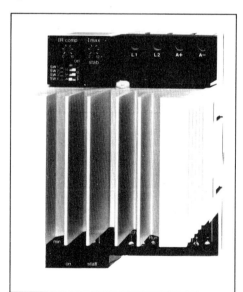

The speed of the associated dc motor is controlled by the module using a linear closed loop feedback signal based on the dc armature voltage, enabling the unit to maintain a constant motor speed through variable motor loads. Improvements in this feedback signal may be made by using a speed/voltage related signal such as that from a tachogenerator connected to the motor shaft.

Type	Rating	**RS** stock no.
Mini CUBE 503	0.5-6A	715-011
CUBE 505	1-12A	343-436
Maxi CUBE 515	2-24A	715-027
Enclosed CUBE 505/B	1-12A	715-033

A current loop within the speed feedback signal ensures that safe current levels are always applied to the armature of the motor, up to the level set by the maximum current (Imax) potentiometer, which is linearly calibrated and switchable between two ranges. Severe armature current overloads caused by motor induced faults are protected against by an instantaneous over-current trip feature.

The CUBE may also be used as a linear motor torque controller by means of an adjustable current set point. In this mode of operation over-speed limiting is a standard feature.

Features

- Fully isolated heatsink
- Adjustable ramp up and ramp down times (0-15 secs)
- Adjustable speed stability
- Adjustable motor maximum and minimum speed limits
- Adjustable armature current limit (0-100%)
- Adjustable armature IR (volt drop) compensation (for voltage feedback control)
- Switch selectable motor output current ranges
- Switch selectable speed range
- Switch selectable feedback mode either tachogenerator or armature voltage
- Motor stall timer on either faulty field circuit or excessive load
- In-built protective devices include high energy MOV suppression, high speed fuse protection of field circuit and fuseless over current protection above 200% overload
- Snap-on style mounting plate
- Torque control by regulation of motor armature current.

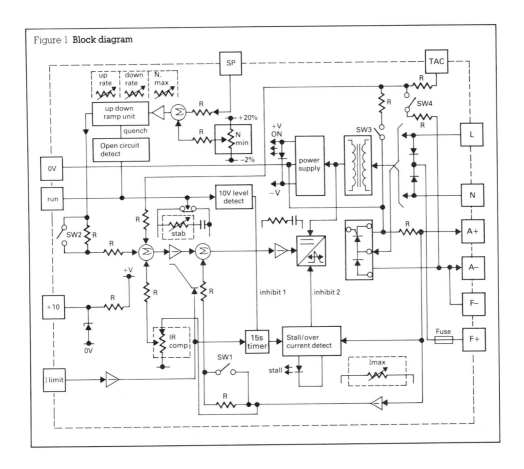

Figure 1 **Block diagram**

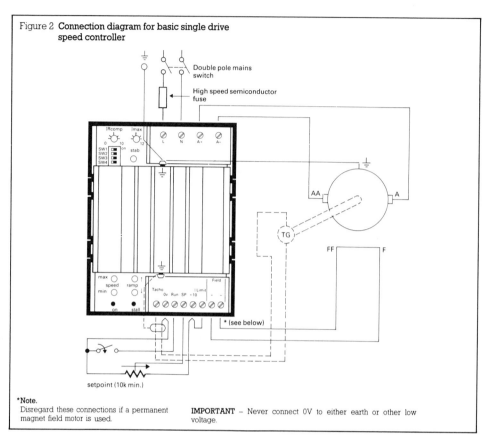

Figure 2 **Connection diagram for basic single drive speed controller**

*Note.
Disregard these connections if a permanent magnet field motor is used.

IMPORTANT – Never connect 0V to either earth or other low voltage.

Wiring

The module should be connected as per Figure 2 using the instruction leaflet supplied as a wiring guide, if basic single direction motor control is required (see later in this data sheet for other functions available using the CUBE).

If the CUBE is to be used as a single drive in an enclosure, then the following components are required as per Table 1.

Warning:

The terminals of the CUBES must not be connected to ground or other voltage under any circumstances as it is not an isolated chassis design. The unit can be controlled by other voltages using the set point isolator (**RS** stock no. 343-969).

Table 1

Qty.	Description	**RS** stock no.
1	Wall mounted IP54 enclosure for module on 6 amp range*	501-525
	OR	
1	Wall mounted IP54 enclosure for module on 12 amp range*	501-531
1	Single turn 3 watt 10k ohm pot for	173-091
1	setpoint and knob	499-078
	OR	
1	10 turn 3 watt 10k ohm pot	173-417
	and	
1	10 turn digital dial mechanism	509-721
1	2 pole 0-1 industrial rotary cam switch. Mains supply	332-133
1	Mini CUBE	715-011
	CUBE	343-436
	Maxi CUBE	715-027
1	Semiconductor mains incoming fuse	414-831
1	RUN-STOP switch	316-563
1	Mains ON or RUNNING indicator red	588-847
1	With 240V lamp block	588-819

*Note.
Additional space is available in the enclosures for other control components if required.

Setting up

The CUBE range incorporates a range of user adjustable potentiometers and switches that allows the module to be used over a wide range of output powers and speed ranges.

The module is supplied with preset values that should be adjusted when the unit is commissioned as per the instruction leaflet supplied.

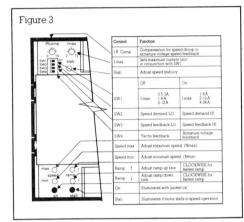

Figure 3

Control	Function		
I R Comp	Compensation for speed droop in armature voltage speed feedback		
I max	Sets maximum current limit in conjunction with SW1		
Stab	Adjust speed stability		
		Off	On
SW1	I max 0.5-3A 1-6A 2-12A	I max 1-6A 2-12A 4-24A	
SW2	Speed demand LO	Speed demand HI	
SW3	Speed feedback LO	Speed feedback HI	
SW4	Tacho feedback	Armature voltage feedback	
Speed max	Adjust maximum speed (Nmax)		
Speed min	Adjust minimum speed (Nmin)		
Ramp ↑	Adjust ramp up rate	CLOCKWISE for fastest ramp	
Ramp ↓	Adjust ramp down rate	CLOCKWISE for fastest ramp	
On	Illuminates with 'power on'		
Stall	Illuminates if motor stalls in speed operation		

Torque or current control

By using the external setpoint potentiometer as a current demand adjuster the module may be used as a torque or current controller. If this is required then the unit should be connected as shown in Figure 4.

WARNING.
Continuous operation of the motor at rated torque outside its rated speed will cause the motor to overheat.

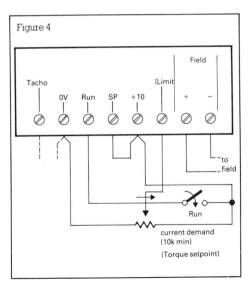

Figure 4

Specification

Voltage			220-240V ±10%
Frequency			50-60 Hz ±10%
Typical armature voltage			160-180V
Max dc armature current	Mini CUBE	3A	6A
	CUBE	6A	12A
	Maxi CUBE	12A	24A
Typical motor hp		1.25	2.5
Module power		1.1kW	2.2kW
Controller loss		20W	30W
Max ac line current rms		12A	17A
Max form factor		2	1.4
Max dc field current			2A
Feedback methods		2	1.4
0-100% load regulation		2 typ	0.1 typ
Max torque speed range (see note 1)		20:1	100:1
Ambient temperature			0 to 45°C
Ramp up/down time			1-15 secs

Note 1.
Consideration must be given to the motor as it may overheat at low speed.

Accessories

Type	RS stock no.
Reversing/Braking unit	343-947
Braking resistor pack	343-953
0-10V set point isolator	343-969
4-20mA set point isolator	343-975

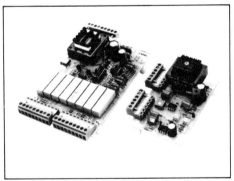

Reversing/Braking unit (RS stock no. 343-947)

Features

● Multi-functional module allows reversal of dc motors with or without dynamic braking

● Provides isolation of user controls from high voltages

● Provides facilities for user control of motor RUN FORWARD, RUN REVERSE, INCH FORWARD, INCH REVERSE, RESET and EMERGENCY STOP

● Provides no load switching of reversing contactors via drive quench circuit

● Self-powered via separate 240V ac 50 Hz supply

● May be controlled via any open collector or open drain outputs ie, will interface directly with PLC

- Lamp outputs provided to indicate drive state either forward or reverse
- Supply on LED fitted
- Push on terminal connections allow easy removal of module.

General

This multi-function module is used to control the safe reversal of dc shunt wound and permanent magnet motors by using external armature contactors. The module interfaces directly with the CUBE range providing isolation of user controls (via 24 volt supply) from high voltages.

The user has the choice of implementing either a standard 'free wheel' to stop or, if fitted with braking resistors, a dynamic (emergency) stop. Control of the braking and reversal functions are performed by remote armature contactors (not supplied) and either toggle or push type control switches.

Installation

The module should be wired as in Figure 5 using any of the various options available including a dynamic braking override to allow process resetting if stopped within a machine cycle.

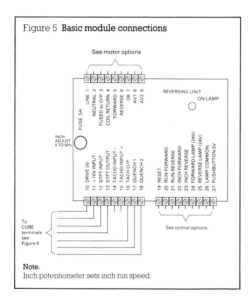

Figure 5 **Basic module connections**

Note.
Inch potentiometer sets inch run speed.

Motor options

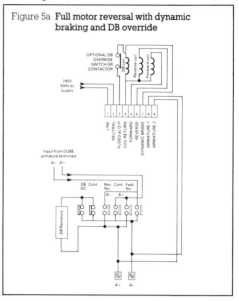

Figure 5a **Full motor reversal with dynamic braking and DB override**

Note
For dynamic braking applications **both** braking resistors must be connected in parallel. All contacts drawn at power off.

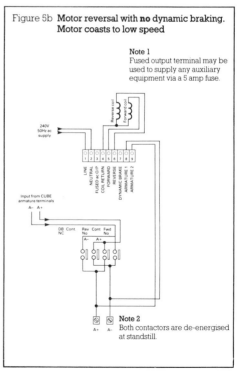

Figure 5b **Motor reversal with no dynamic braking. Motor coasts to low speed**

Note 1
Fused output terminal may be used to supply any auxiliary equipment via a 5 amp fuse.

Note 2
Both contactors are de-energised at standstill.

Control options

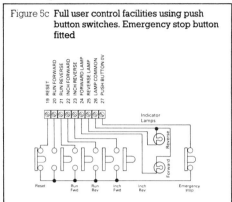

Figure 5c **Full user control facilities using push button switches. Emergency stop button fitted**

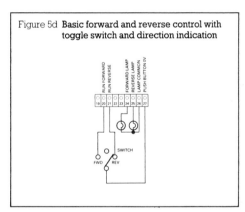

Figure 5d **Basic forward and reverse control with toggle switch and direction indication**

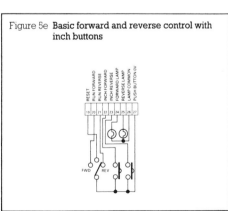

Figure 5e **Basic forward and reverse control with inch buttons**

Figure 5f **Direction control using PLC output**

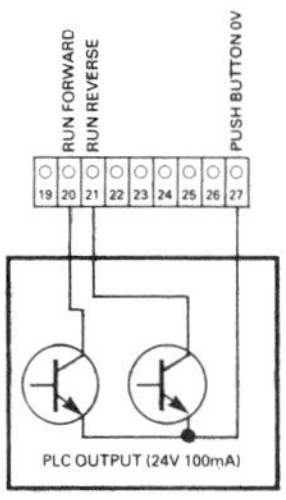

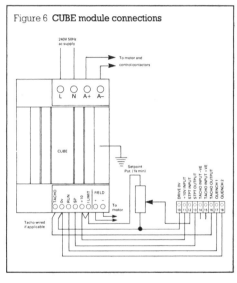

Note

Any switch with 24V 100mA minimum specification may be used. Direction is selected by an on switch, the unit performs safe interlocking.

Figure 6 **CUBE module connections**

Armature and dynamic braking contactors

One of the unique features of this module is the drive quench circuitry which is designed to 'switch off' the motor armature current before the direction changing contactors operate, ensuring that they do not operate on load.

Recommended contactors

E range standard control contactor 4kW (**RS** stock no. 345-195)
and
240 volt ac coil (**RS** stock no. 345-268)

Similarly quiet operating contactor with 240 volt ac coil (**RS** stock no. 344-158) may be used.

Set point isolators (**RS** stock nos. 343-969/975)
Features

● Current or voltage inputs available
● Self-powered via separate 110 to 240 volt ac 50/60 Hz supply

● Both units provide galvanic opto isolation of input signals
● Isolated run/stop facility available
● Push on terminal connections allow easy removal of modules
● Supply on LED fitted.

General

The input stage of these modules is self powered and may be used with any ac power source between 110 to 240 volts. It provides +10 volts reference for connection of a remote setpoint potentiometer.

The incoming setpoint is converted to a frequency by an accurate voltage controlled oscillator. The frequency pulses are then transmitted via an opto coupler to the non-isolated secondary side of the module. Here they are re-converted to a 0 to +8 volt signal by a frequency to voltage converter. The secondary is powered by the +10 volts setpoint reference of the drive and consumes 1mA, (thus limiting output range to 8 volts). Provision is made to allow the secondary side to be powered by a higher voltage eg, +15 or +24 volts and hence allow the output range to be adjusted to +10 volts maximum.

Incorporated on the modules is an isolated run/stop facility. This takes the form of a floating transistor which may be switched on by a command from the isolated side of the unit. The transistor may switch +24 volts up to 1mA, (suitable for control from a PLC output), and may be used to switch signals high or low due to its floating nature.

Installation

The modules are free standing and should be connected between user controls/reference input signal and the RS CUBE range. Similarly it can be used on any electronic device that requires an isolated input of 0-8 or 10 volts from a variable current or voltage source.

Terminal listing

1. Live input 110 to 240V ac 50/60Hz.
2. Neutral input.
3. 0V isolated (will float at same potential as incoming connection).
4. 10V isolated (will float at same potential as incoming connection).
5. I/P isolated (will float at same potential as incoming connection).
6. Switch. When connected to 0V (terminal 3) and 6 provides isolated RUN/STOP or RESET facility.
7. SW+ transistor collector. Connect to 0V on CUBE if using isolated RUN/STOP, RESET on speed control or 10V connection on CUBE if using torque control.
8. SW− transistor emitter. Connect to RUN terminal on CUBE.
9. Drive 0V.
10. Signal output.
11. 10V supply input. Consumes 1mA. If used reduces output voltage span to 0V-8V.
12. Alternative supply input. If 15 to 24V with respect to terminal 9 is inputted here. Output voltage span will be 0 to 10V.

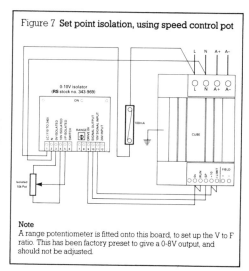

Figure 7 **Set point isolation, using speed control pot**

Note
A range potentiometer is fitted onto this board, to set up the V to F ratio. This has been factory preset to give a 0-8V output, and should not be adjusted.

Slaving

By using this module one or more cubes may be slaved off one set point speed potentiometer. The number of isolators required to control one or more drives can be easily calculated as:

Number of drives −1

ie, 3 drives require 2 isolators.

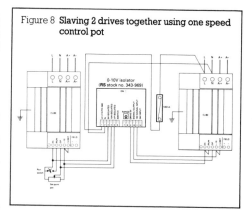

Figure 8 **Slaving 2 drives together using one speed control pot**

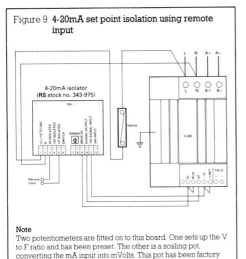

Figure 9 **4-20mA set point isolation using remote input**

Note

Two potentiometers are fitted on to this board. One sets up the V to F ratio and has been preset. The other is a scaling pot, converting the mA input into mVolts. This pot has been factory sealed.

Enclosed CUBE (**RS** stock no. 715-033)

This is a 12A CUBE (**RS** stock no. 343-436) conveniently enclosed within an IP40 enclosure. The front of the enclosure is fitted with an on/off switch and speed potentiometer. Setting up of the controller is exactly the same as for the standard CUBE.

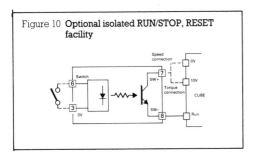

Figure 10 **Optional isolated RUN/STOP, RESET facility**

A facility exists to allow isolated operation of the CUBE run function.

Connect the switch as shown in Figure 10 connecting terminal 7 to the 0V input on the CUBE for speed control or to the 10V terminal for torque control.

Note

If torque control is required, due to the actual output voltage from the 0-10V isolator being 8 volts only 80% of the armature current is available.

512 dc motor controller

Stock numbers 512/16 320-758
512/32 320-764

General

The RS 512 controller is a compact speed and torque control module for permanent magnet and shunt wound dc motors. There are two models available.

512/16 16A dc FLC
512/32 32A dc FLC

Operational functions include 'speed/torque control mode', 'speed torque control with dynamic braking' and 'reversing with dynamic braking'. No extra free standing modules are required.

512 dc motor controller

The speed of the dc motor is controlled using a linear closed loop control with feedback signal from either armature voltage or tachogenerator enabling the motor speed to be maintained under variable load conditions. The current loop within the speed loop always assures that the safe current levels are applied to the motor, and is fully user adjustable via a current limit potentiometer and programming switches. Should the motor stall (eg. due to excessive load) then the controller will trip and remove current from the motor after approximately 15 seconds. Severe armature current overloads, caused by induced faults, are protected against by an instantaneous overcurrent trip.

Dimensions (mm)

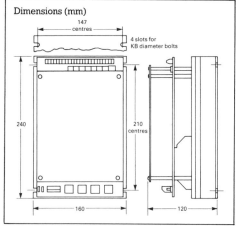

The 512 dc controller can be mounted using the fixing dimensions shown above. A suitable enclosure and additional components are listed in the table below.

Table 1

Qty.	Description		Stock No.
1	IP54 enclosure		507-270
1	Single turn 3 watt 10kΩ		173-091
1	Pot for setpoint knob		499-078
	or		
1	10 turn 3 watt 10kΩ pot		173-417
	and		
1	10 turn digital dial mechanism		509-721
1	2-pole 0.1 industrial rotary cam switch. Mains supply		332-133
1	dc motor controller	16 amp	320-758
		32amp	320-764
1	Semi conductor mains incoming fuse	16 amp	414-768
		32amp	414-780
1	Run/Stop switch		316-563
1	Mains 'on' or 'running' indicator red. With 240V lamp block		588-847 588-819

Features

- Isolated control circuitry. This allows both heatsink and/or control board to be safely connected to earth
- Adjustable ramp up and ramp down times (linear 0-20 seconds)
- Adjustable speed stability
- Adjustable motor maximum and minimum speed limits
- Switch selectable speed range
- Adjustable armature current limit (0-100%)
- Adjustable armature IR (volt drop) compensation, optimises speed regulation against load charge
- Switch selectable maximum current ranges, 2-16 amps and 4-32 amps
- Switch selectable feedback modes using tachogenerator or armature voltage control
- Overcurrent trip
- Motor stall timer (15 seconds)
- High speed fusing and over voltage protection
- Ramp output available for follower drive
- Supply 110/240/415V single phase 45/65Hz – jumper selectable
- Zero speed relay output enables simple reversing circuitry
- Field bridge suitable for UK or continental voltages.

Setting up

The 512 controller incorporates a range of user adjustable potentiometers and switches that allows the module to be used over a wide range of output powers and speed ranges.

The module is supplied with preset values that should be adjusted when the unit is commissioned as per the instruction leaflet supplied.

Control signals input/output

Control terminals **Function**

1.	Tach feedback	Positive voltage (350V max) proportional to motor speed
3.	Speed meter output	10V at 100% speed. 10mA max. Short circuit protected
4.	Minimum speed	Connect to bottom of speed demand potentiometer (approximately 30% for 10kΩ. Adjust minimum speed by P6)
5.	Run	Connect to 0V common to run
6.	Current meter output	SW8 ON: current meter output scaled for 0-5V representing 0-100% full load current. SW8 OFF: current meter output scaled for 0-5V representing 0-100% controller rated current 10mA max. Short circuit protected
7.	Torque/Auxiliary current limit	0-7.5V for 150% of full load current. No connection gives 110% full load current. I limit (P4) gives 0-100% of torque/auxiliary limit setting
8.	0V common	Signal ground for control inputs
9.	Setpoint ramp O/P	Output of ramp 0-10V for 0-100% speed setpoint
10.	Auxiliary speed demand input	0-10V for 0-100% speed. Non ramped
11.	0V Common	Signal ground for control inputs
12.	+12V	Positive power supply rail maximum load 20mA
13.	Setpoint ramp input (wiper of speed ref pot)	0-10V for 0-100%. Ramp rate adjustable by P1 and P2
14.	10V precision reference	10mA max. Short circuit protected. Temperature compensated. (Use as reference for setpoints)
15.	Stall rest	Momentarily connect to +12V (terminal 12) to reset from stall or from hold connection. Connect permanently to terminal 12 when operating in the torque control mode
16.	−12V	Negative supply rail. 20mA maximum load
18.	N/C	N/C	De-energised on stall trip
19.	Com	Relay	Contact rating 240V @ 3A ac
20.	N/O	(Volt free)	or 24V @ 3A dc
22.	N/C	Zero	De-energised at zero speed
23.	Com	Speed relay	(5% of max approximately) contact rating
24.	N/O	(Volt free)	240V @ 3A ac or 24V @ 3A dc

Terminals 2, 17 and 21 are not used.

Power terminals

Terminal **Function**

L1	Main supply terminals. M5 fixing. If a line and neutral supply is used, the neutral
L2/N	should be connected to L2/N. Supply must be correctly fused
A+	dc output from controller to motor armature M5 fixing
A−	direction of rotation.
F+	Field rectifier output to motor field winding (2A maximum). Polarity will affect
F−	direction of rotation.
FL1	Input to field rectifier. This is supplied from any ac voltage source depending on
FL2	the required field voltage.
Earth	Located in the bottom left corner of the heat fin to allow the heat fin to be earth M4 fixing.

Customer adjustment potentiometers.

P1	Ramp up rate	Rotate clockwise for faster acceleration to set speed (linear 1 to 20 seconds).
P2	Ramp down rate	Rotate clockwise for faster deceleration to lower (or zero) speed (linear 1 to 20 seconds).
P3	Speed loop stability	Optimises system stability. Rotate clockwise for faster response (excess adjustment may cause instability).
P4	I limit	Set the output current over the range 0-100% of scaled output (see table 2 for scaled current output). In cases where current scaling does not match motor current rating, scale drive for higher rating and use I limit to reduce maximum output current. Rotate clockwise to increase output current.
P5	IR comp	Optimises speed regulation against load change when using armature voltage feedback (SW3 on) rotate clockwise to increase compensation (excess adjustment may cause instability). Turn anti-clockwise when tachogenerator feedback is used (SW3 off).
P6	Min speed	Controls minimum motor speed. Rotate clockwise to increase min speed (approx 30% when using a 10kΩ speed demand potentiometer).
P7	Max speed	Controls maximum motor speed. Rotate clockwise to increase max speed (see customer option switched SW1 and SW2 for range of control. Table 1).

Customer option switches

SW3	(OFF)	TACHO GENERATOR	Drive using tachogenerator feedback for speed control.
	(OFF)	Va	Drive using armature voltage for speed control.
SW4	(OFF)	RUN	Drive ready to operate when power applied and run input terminal (5) connected to 0V common.
	(ON)	HOLD	As RUN but drive will not operate until a momentary connection is made between terminal 15 (stall reset) and terminal 12 (+12V).
SW8	(OFF)	CURRENT METER	Buffered current meter output (terminal 6) read 5V at 100% controller current eg. 16, or 32 amp=5V depending on model purchased.
	(ON)	CURRENT METER	Buffered current output (terminal 6) read 5V for 100% of full load current. ie. depends on position of SW5, SW6, SW7.

Changing between operational modes is done by altering external wiring using the wiring diagram shown below.

Connection diagram

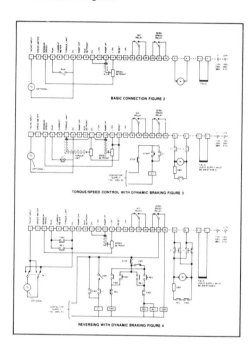

Block diagram

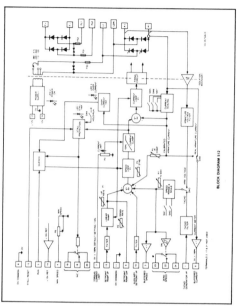

Electrical specification

Parameter	Symbol	512/16	512/32	Units
Input ratings				
Supply voltage	Vs	110/120V, 220/240V, 380/415V		Volts ac
Rated current	Is	30	60	Amps ac
Supply frequency	fs	50/60±2		Hz
Output ratings				
Nominal armature voltage	Va	90V @ 110/120Vac supply 180V @ 220/240Vac supply 320V @ 380/415Vac supply		Volts dc
Max (100%) armature current	Ia	16	32	Amps dc
Nominal motor power at 320Vdc	Pm	4.5	9	kW
Max overload		150% for 15s		
Max dc field current	If	2		Amps dc
dc field voltage	Vf	$0.9 \times Vs$		Volts dc
Max form factor		1.5		
I^2T for fusing		300		A^2S
Typical heat dissipation at maximum current		50	75	W

Hybrid stepper motors

Size	Rear shift	**RS** stock no.
17	No	440-420
17	Yes	440-436
23	No	440-442
23	Yes	440-458
34	Yes	440-464
34	No	440-470

These 4 phase hybrid stepper motors are capable of delivering much high working torques and stepping rates than permanent magnet (7.5° and 15°) types. Whilst at the same time maintaining a high detent torque even when not energised. This feature is particularly important for positional integrity. The motors are directly compatible with the **RS** stepper motor drive boards (stock numbers 332-098, 342-051 and 440-240).

Sizes 23 and 34 motors are supplied in 8-lead configuration which allows the maximum flexibility when connecting to the drive boards.

Rear extension shaft are provided on two of the motors to enable connection of other drive requirements and feedback devices.

1.8° step angle

Size 17 (**RS** stock nos. 440-420 and 440-436)

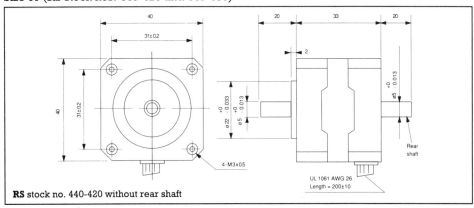

RS stock no. 440-420 without rear shaft

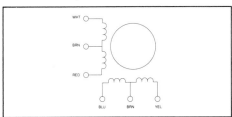

Exciting sequence and direction of rotation when facing from mounting flange end.					
Step	White	Blue	Red	Yellow	Brown	CW
1	On	On				
2		On	On		+dcV	
3			On	On		
4	On			On		

Size 23 (**RS** stock no. 440-442 and 440-458)

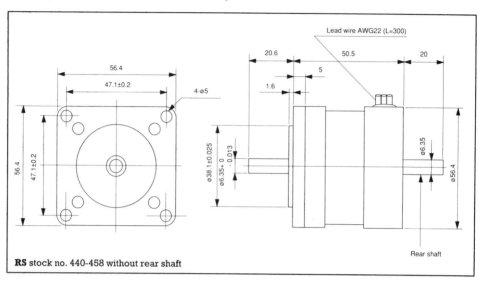

RS stock no. 440-458 without rear shaft

Size 34 (**RS** stock no. 440-464 and 440-470)

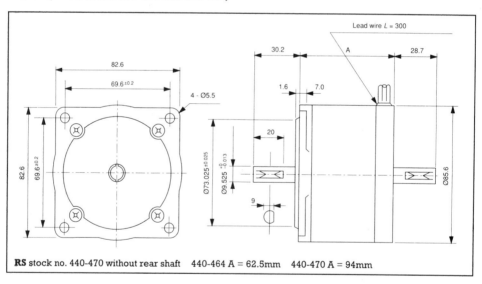

RS stock no. 440-470 without rear shaft   440-464 A = 62.5mm   440-470 A = 94mm

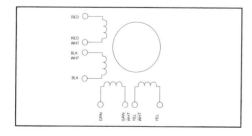

Exciting sequence and direction of rotation when facing from mounting flange end.

Step	Red	Green	Black	Yellow	Com	CW
1	On	On				
2		On	On		+dcV	
3			On	On		
4	On			On		

Technical specification

RS stock no.	440-420	440-436	440-442	440-455	440-464	440-470
Rated voltage (V)	5	12	5.1	12	3	2.5
Rated current (I)	0.5	0.16	1	0.6	2	4.5
Resistance (Ω)	10	75	5	20	1.5	0.56
Inductance(mH)	6	30	9	32	5	2.8
Detent torque (mNm)	5	4	30	30	40	100
Holding torque (mNm)	70	70	500	500	1200	2200
Step angle accuracy (%)	5	5	5	5	5	5
Step angle	1.8	1.8	1.8	1.8	1.8	1.8
Insulation class	B	B	B	B	B	B

Resonance

Certain operating frequencies cause resonance and the motor loses track of the drive input. Audible vibration may accompany resonance conditions. These frequencies should be avoided if possible. Driving the motor on the half step mode (see motor drive methods) greatly reduces the effect of resonance. Alternatively extra load inertia and external damping may be added to shift resonance regions away from the operating frequency.

Motor drive methods

The normal way of driving a 4-phase stepper motor is shown in Figure 1.

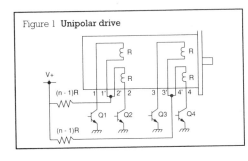

Figure 1 **Unipolar drive**

This is commonly known as the 'Unipolar L/nr drive'. Here the current in each winding, when energised, flows in one direction only. 'n', value is ≥ 1 (but not necessarily an integer) and nR is the sum of the external resistance plus the winding resistance (R). By selecting a higher value for n (ie. larger external resistance) and using a higher dc supply to maintain the rated voltage and current for each winding, improved torque speed characteristics can be obtained. Thus a 6V, 6Ω motor (1A per phase) can be driven from a 6Vdc supply without any series resistor, in the L/R mode. Alternatively it can be driven from a 24Vdc supply using 18Ω series resistance in the L/4R mode with much improved performance.

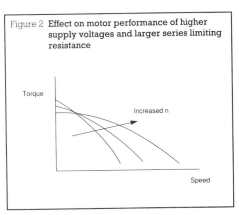

Figure 2 **Effect on motor performance of higher supply voltages and larger series limiting resistance**

Connection to RS bipolar stepper motor board

When the windings of the **RS** stepper motors are assigned ($\emptyset$1-$\emptyset$4) as shown in Figure 3, they can be connected to the board according to Figure 1.

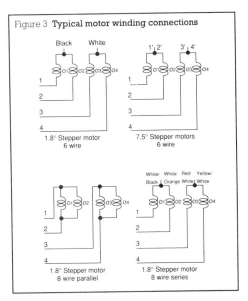

Figure 3 **Typical motor winding connections**

When using 8 lead motors with coils in parallel the motor current should be set no greater than:

$$\text{I per phase} \times \sqrt{2}$$

When using 6 lead or 8 lead motors with coils in series the motor current should be set no greater than:

$$\text{I per phase} \times \frac{1}{\sqrt{2}}$$

Motors with 4 leads have a bipolar rating and can be used according to manufacturer's specification.

To step a motor in a particular direction a specific switching sequence for the drive transistors Q1-Q4 needs to be followed. If this sequence is in Table 1 (known as the unipolar full step mode) it results in the rotor advancing through one complete step at a time.

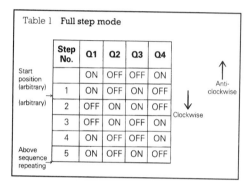

Table 1   Full step mode

	Step No.	Q1	Q2	Q3	Q4
Start position (arbitrary)		ON	OFF	OFF	ON
(arbitrary)	1	ON	OFF	ON	OFF
	2	OFF	ON	ON	OFF
	3	OFF	ON	OFF	ON
	4	ON	OFF	OFF	ON
Above sequence repeating	5	ON	OFF	ON	OFF

Anti-clockwise / Clockwise

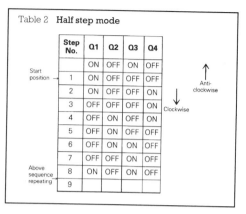

Table 2   Half step mode

	Step No.	Q1	Q2	Q3	Q4
Start position →		ON	OFF	ON	OFF
	1	ON	OFF	OFF	OFF
	2	ON	OFF	OFF	ON
	3	OFF	OFF	OFF	ON
	4	OFF	ON	OFF	ON
	5	OFF	ON	OFF	OFF
	6	OFF	ON	ON	OFF
	7	OFF	OFF	ON	OFF
Above sequence repeating	8	ON	OFF	ON	OFF
	9				

Anti-clockwise / Clockwise

Typical stepper motor control system

The operation of a stepper motor requires the presence of the following elements:

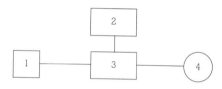

1. **A control unit**. Usually a microprocessor based unit which gives step and direction signals to the drive card. **RS** stepper motor control board (440-098) is ideally suited for this function.

2. **Power supply**. Giving the required voltage and current for the drive card.

3. **Drive card**. This converts the signals from the control unit in to the required stepper motor sequence. **RS** stock nos. 332-098, 342-051 and 440-240 are designed for the function.

4. **Stepper motor**.

Stepper motor drive boards

For control of stepper motors RS has three types of stepper drive board which are suitable to drive stepper motors of various current ranges.

Drive board	Suitable stepper motors		
Unipolar 2A (332-098) This drive is only suitable for applications where low speeds and low torques are required	440-420 440-436 440-442 440-455	Size 17 Size 17 Size 23 Size 23	
Bipolar chopper 3.5A (342-051) medium speed and torque applications	440-442 440-455 440-464 440-470	Size 23 Size 23 Size 34 Size 34	Series and parallel connection Parallel connection Series and parallel connection Series connection
Bipolar chopper 6A (440-240) and micro stepping option. High speed and torque applications	440-464 440-470	Size 34 Size 34	Parallel connection Series and parallel connection

Note: Connecting a stepper motor in series will give a good low speed high torque performance.
Connecting a stepper motor in parallel will give a good high speed lower torque performance.

Drive board connections

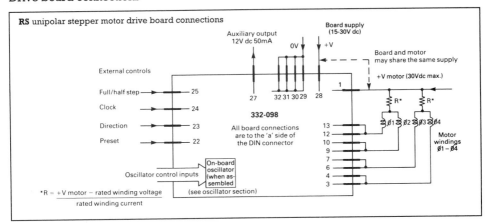

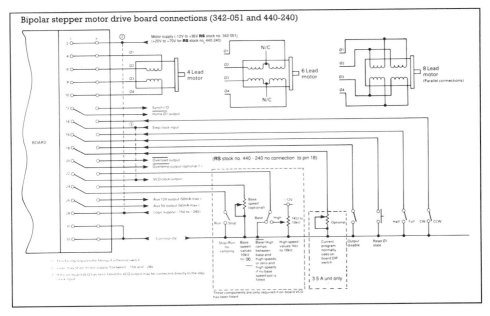

Drive motor speed torque curves

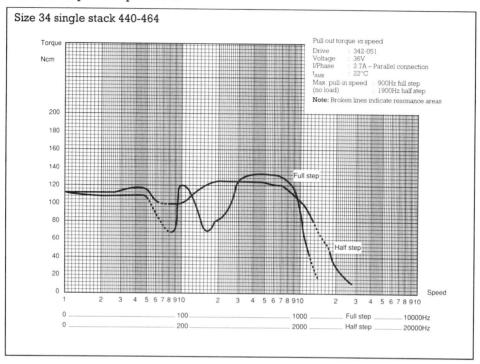

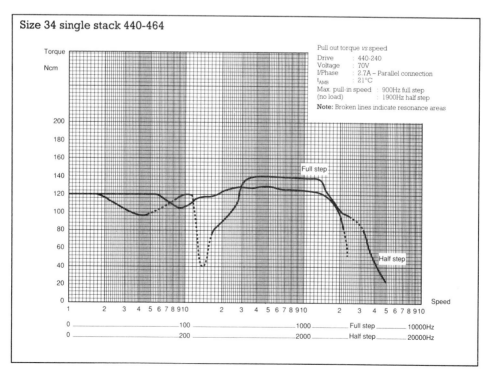

Size 34 double stack 440-470

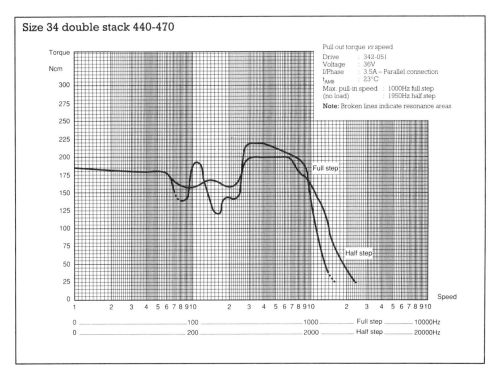

Size 34 double stack 440-470

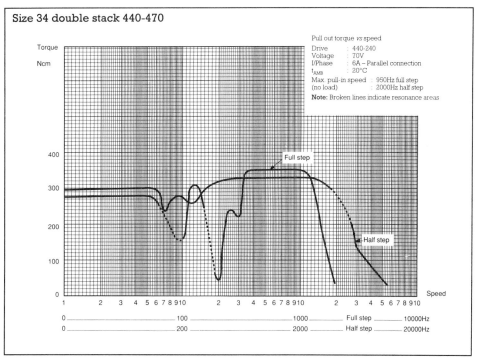

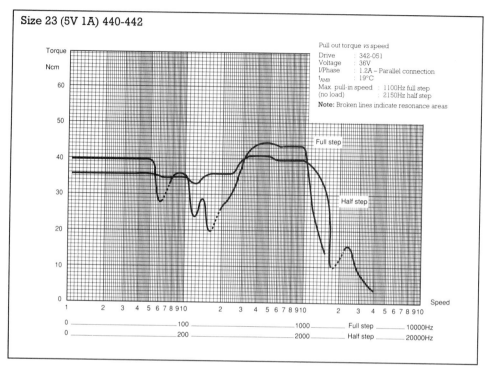

Size 23 (5V 1A) 440-442

Pull out torque *vs* speed

Drive : 342-051
Voltage : 36V
I/Phase : 1.2A – Parallel connection
t_{AMB} : 19°C
Max. pull-in speed : 1100Hz full step
(no load) : 2150Hz half step

Note: Broken lines indicate resonance areas

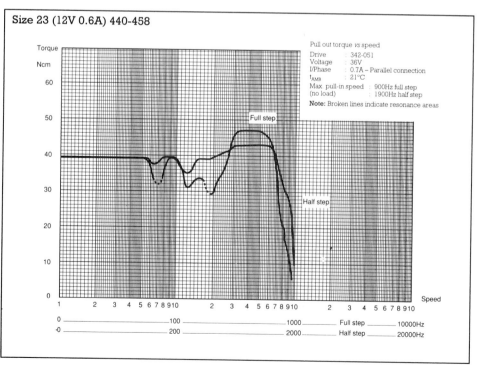

Size 23 (12V 0.6A) 440-458

Pull out torque *vs* speed

Drive : 342-051
Voltage : 36V
I/Phase : 0.7A – Parallel connection
t_{AMB} : 21°C
Max. pull-in speed : 900Hz full step
(no load) : 1900Hz half step

Note: Broken lines indicate resonance areas

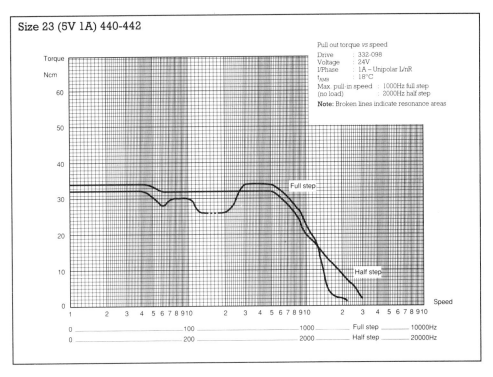

Size 23 (5V 1A) 440-442

Pull out torque *vs* speed
Drive   : 332-098
Voltage   : 24V
I/Phase   : 1A – Unipolar L/nR
t_{AMB} : 18°C
Max. pull-in speed : 1000Hz full step
(no load)   : 2000Hz half step
Note: Broken lines indicate resonance areas

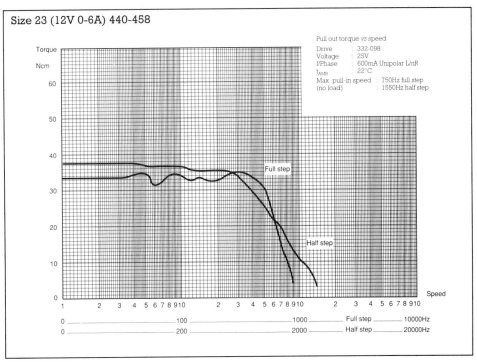

Size 23 (12V 0-6A) 440-458

Pull out torque *vs* speed
Drive   : 332-098
Voltage   : 25V
I/Phase   : 600mA Unipolar L/nR
t_{AMB} : 22°C
Max. pull-in speed : 750Hz full step
(no load)   : 1550Hz half step

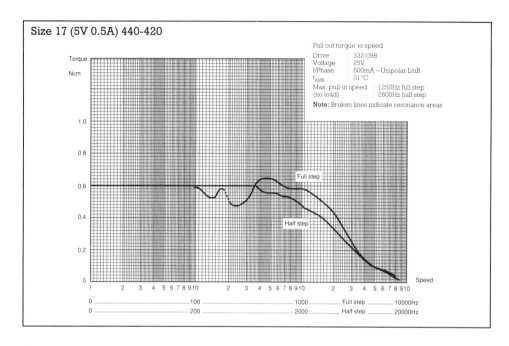

Size 17 (5V 0.5A) 440-420

Pull out torque *vs* speed
Drive   : 332-098
Voltage   : 25V
I/Phase   : 500mA – Unipolar L/nR
t_{AMB} : 21°C
Max. pull-in speed : 1250Hz full step
(no load)   : 2600Hz half step
Note: Broken lines indicate resonance areas

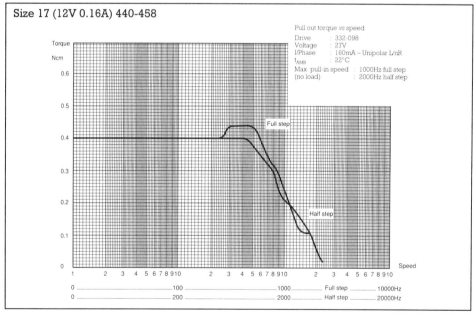

Size 17 (12V 0.16A) 440-458

Pull out torque *vs* speed
Drive   : 332-098
Voltage   : 27V
I/Phase   : 160mA – Unipolar L/nR
t_{AMB} : 22°C
Max. pull-in speed : 1000Hz full step
(no load)   : 2000Hz half step

RS Components Ltd. PO Box 99, Corby, Northants, NN17 9RS
An Electrocomponents Company

Telephone: 0536 201234
© RS Components Ltd. 1992

APPENDIX C

This section contains data sheets for the following components:

- Pneumatic cylinders and accesories
- RS/SMC solenoid and pilot valves

Data sheets are reprinted with the permission of RS Components.

Pneumatic cylinders and accessories

Miniature cylinders (10mm to 25mm bore)

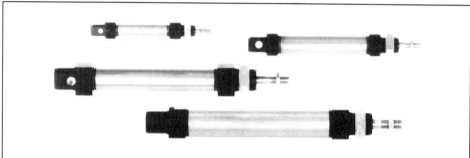

The RS range of miniature cylinders offers a wide choice of bore sizes and stroke lengths.

All cylinders automatically come with an integral magnetic piston. It only requires that a sensor kit is fitted to convert a standard miniature cylinder to a magnetic sensing miniature cylinder.

Material specification and construction is of the highest order throughout.

The modular nature of the system allows the user to adapt or modify his miniature cylinders in line with changing automation requirements.

RS cylinders conform to ISO 6432, CETOP RP52P, BS 4662 (Part 1) and AFNOR NFE 49.030.

Technical data

Pressure range _____ 0.8 to 10 bar
Temperature range _____ –20°C to +70°C
Air condition _____ Filtered, regulated
lubricated or dry

Cylinder thrusts (Newtons)

Cylinder bore mm	Piston rod Ø mm	Area cm^2 ● ■	Line Pressure (bar)															
			3		4		5		6		7		8		9		10	
			●	■	●	■	●	■	●	■	●	■	●	■	●	■	●	■
10	4	0.8 0.66	24	19	32	26	40	33	48	39	58	46	64	52	72	59	80	66
16	6	2 1.73	60	52	80	69	100	87	120	104	140	121	160	138	180	156	200	173
20	8	3.1 2.6	93	78	124	104	155	130	186	156	217	182	248	208	279	234	310	260
25	10	4.9 4.1	147	123	196	164	245	205	294	246	343	287	392	328	441	369	490	410

Surface of piston
● Extending side of piston
■ Retracting side of piston

Material specification

Cylinder body ____ Non magnetic stainless steel
Piston rod _____ Non magnetic stainless steel
                        BS 304S11/12 SAE 304L
Seals _____ Nitrile
End caps _____ Anodised aluminium
Piston _____ Aluminium
Cushioning device _____ Polyurethane

Cylinder bore mm	H (max)	ZA (max)
10	1.5	4
16	1.5	5
20	2	6.5
25	2	7

Switching characteristics. The minimum distance between two sensors is 2H maximum + 4mm.

Fitting a magnetic sensor

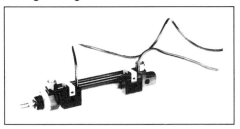

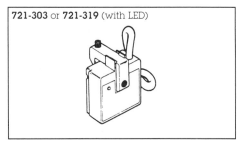

Attach the sensor onto the sensor support rail in the position sensing is required. Tighten the side screw (M5 x 12 key wrench 2.5mm). With a screwdriver tighten the top screw to prevent any possible rotation.

721-303 or **721-319** (with LED)

Purpose

The magnetic sensor detects when the piston is in close proximity. This detection is made without physical contact, the sensor operating through the non magnetic cylinder body. The sensor may also be used to obtain other positional information not necessarily associated with a cylinder.

Operation

The sensor is activated magnetically. When the sensor is subjected to the influence of a magnetic field the contacts close.

When the sensor is used in ac current, with maximum current, the switching process creates an electrical arc which results in excessive erosion of the contacts. To avoid this and to ensure longer contact life, we advise the application of a nominal current of 0.2A (the 0.5A current must be considered as the absolute maximum).

Mounting

The sensor must be positioned in contact with the cylinder body.

Technical specification for sensors

Power _____ Electrical
Mounting _____ Clamp on 6mm dia. rod
Connection _____ 2 core cable (2 x 0.75)
                                – length = 1.5m
Electrical connection __ Blue wire –/White wire +
Repetitive precision of detection _____ ±0.10mm
Operating position _____ Adjustable
Temperature range _____ –5°C to + 70°C
Mechanical protection _____ IP.67
Material specification __ Cased in thermoplastic.
                        Switch and power elements are
                        coated in polyurethane resin
Type of contact _____ Normally open
Type of current _____ ac/dc
Maximum voltage _____ ac 240V/dc 100V
Maximum at 20°C _____ ac 0.50A/dc 0.2A
Maximum power _____ 10W

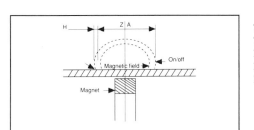

Sensor support kit

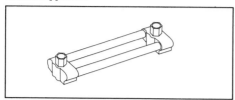

RS stock numbers

Stroke length	Cylinder bore			
	10	16	20	25
10	721-094	721-145		
15	721-101	721-151		
25	721-117	721-167	721-195	721-246
40		721-173	721-202	721-252
50		721-189	721-218	721-268
80	721-139		721-224	721-274
100			721-230	721-280
160				721-296

Cylinder mountings

Cylinder bore mm	Flange	Foot	RS stock no.		
			Rear hinge	Piston rod clevis	Spherical bearing
10	720-782	720-524	729-580	720-647	720-710
16	720-798	720-530	720-596	720-653	720-726
20	720-805	720-546	720-603	720-669	720-732
25	720-805	720-546	720-603	720-675	720-748

Dimensions
Basic cylinder

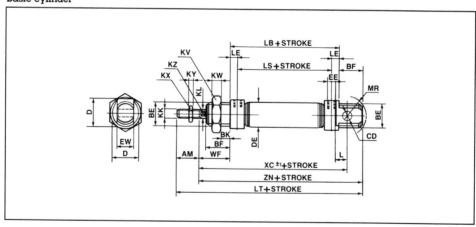

Cylinder fitted with sensor support kit

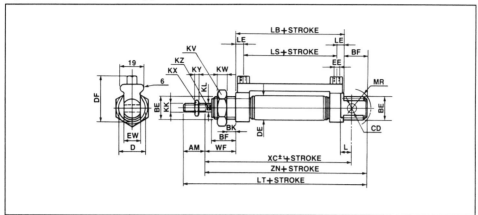

Bore size	AM	BE	BF	BK	CD	D	DE	DF	EE
10	12.5	M12 ×1.25	13	7	4	15	11.3	28.5	M5
16	16	M16 ×1.5	17	8	6	20	17.3	33.5	M5
20	20	M22 ×1.5	20	9	8	27˙	21.5	45.5	G¹/₈
25	22	M22 × 1.5	22	11	8	27˙	26.5	45.5	G¹/₈

Bore size	EW	KL	KK	KV a/f	KW	KX a/f	KY	KZ a/f	L
10	8	4	M4	19	6	7	2	/	6
16	12	6	M6	23	8	10	3	5	9
20	16	8	M8	32	11	13	4	7	12
25	16	10	M10 × 1.25	32	11	17	5	9	12

a/f Across flats

Bore size	LB	LE	LS	LT	MR	WF	XC	ZN
10	44.5	6	32.5	85.5	18	15.5	64	73
16	52.5	6	40.5	108	22	22.5	82	92
20	67.5	8	51.5	132	25	24.5	95	112
25	69.5	8	53.5	141.5	25	28	104	119.5

Flange mounting

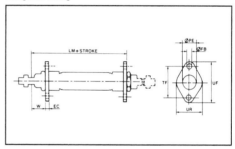

Bore size	EC	FB	LM	PE	TF	UF	UR	W
10	2.5	4.5	62.5	12.1	30	40	25	13
16	3	5.5	77.5	16.1	40	53	30	19
20	4	6.5	96	22.1	50	66	40	20.5
25	4	6.5	101.5	22.1	50	66	40	24

Foot mounting

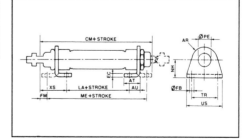

Bore size	AR	AT	AU	CM	EC	FB	FM
10	10	16	10.5	76	2.5	4.5	5
16	13	19	13	94	3	5.5	9.5
20	20	24	18	116	4	6.5	8.5
25	20	24	18	121.5	4	6.5	12.5

Bore size	LA	ME	NH	PE	TR	US	XS
10	28.5	65.5	16	12.1	25	35	23.5
16	32.5	78.5	20	16.1	32	42	32.5
20	43.5	99.5	25	22.1	40	54	36.5
25	45.5	101.5	25	22.1	40	54	40

Rear hinge mounting

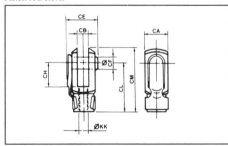

Bore size	BR	CC	EC	EV	FB	GV	NH	TB	TU	UE	UT	WK
10	5	4	2.5	8.1	4.5	79.5	24	12.5	3.5	20.5	16.5	1.5
16	7	6	3	16.1	5.5	100	27	15	5	25	22.5	2
20	10	8	4	16.1	6.5	117	30	20	6	32.5	29.5	4
25	10	8	4	16.1	6.5	125	30	20	6	32.5	29.5	4

Piston rod clevis

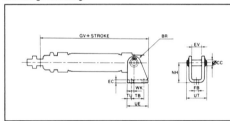

Bore size	CA	CB (B11)	CE	CF (D10)	CH	CL	CM	KK
10	8	4	11	4	8	16	21	M4
16	12	6	16	6	12	24	31	M6
20	16	8	22	8	16	32	42	M8
25	20	10	26	10	20	40	52	M10 ×1.25

Spherical bearing

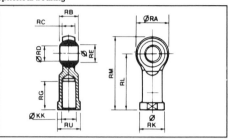

Bore size	KK	RA	RB	RC	RD	RE	RG	RK	RL	RM	RU
10	M4	16	8	6	5	7.71	14	9.5	27	35	8
12	M6	18	9	6.75	6	8.96	14	12	30	39	10
20	M8	22	12	9	8	10.4	17	16	36	47	13
25	M10 ×1.25	26	14	10.5	10	12.9	20	19	43	56	17

Sensor support kit

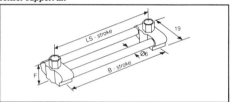

Bore size	B	F	LS
10	44.5	13.5	32.5
12	46	13.5	34
16	52.5	13.5	40.5
20	67.5	18.5	51.5
25	69.5	18.5	53.5

Magnetic sensor mounted on cylinder

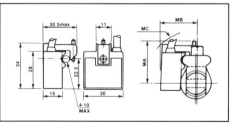

Bore size	MA	MB	MC
10	24	27	32
16	25	24	35
20	30	26	38.2
25	33	29	39

Pneumatic cylinders 32mm bore to 50mm bore

The RS range of 32-50mm bore pneumatic cylinders is built to ISO/CETOP (ISO 6431, CETOP RP43P, BS4862 Part 2) standards. The range operates on dry, non-lubricated, or lubricated air – making it the natural choice for so many varied industrial applications.

These clean-lined non tie-rod cylinders produce the most efficient transmission of thrust and offer high performance with the maximum operation and wear resistance.

Cylinder weights (kg)

Cylinder bore	Single rod cylinder	
	Zero stroke	Extra per 25mm stroke
32mm	0.41	0.05
40mm	0.68	0.07
50mm	1.05	0.11

Mounting weights (kg)

Cylinder bore	Foot (pair)	Flange	Rear hinge	Piston rod clevis	Spher. bearing
32mm	0.09	0.16	0.20	0.10	0.08
40mm	0.14	0.18	0.32	0.15	0.12
50mm	0.21	0.34	0.42	0.35	0.23

Technical data

Pressure range (air) _____ 1 bar (100kPa) to 10 bar (1000kPa)

Temperature range _____ –20°C to +70°C
In sub-zero conditions air must be water-free to prevent icing

Air condition _____ Filtered, regulated, lubricated or dry

Recommended lubricant if used _____ Mineral oils with viscosity 20-40 centistrokes

Materials

End caps _____ Aluminium LM24
Cylinder body _____ Aluminium 6063
Piston rod _____ Stainless steel 303S21
Piston _____ Aluminium
Piston rod bearing __ Sintered bronze (lubricated)
Wear ring _____ Nylon (self lubricating)
Cushion sleeves _____ Nylon (self lubricating)
Brass on high temp version
Seals _____ Nitrile rubber

Finish

End caps _____ Black epoxy powder painted
Cylinder body _____ Hard anodised

Thrust calculations

It is important that the correct bore size cylinder is used for each application. It is therefore necessary to assess accurately the load to be moved. The cylinder thrust tables given below shows the theoretical thrusts at different line pressures. They are the product of the effective piston area and the applied pressure. An efficiency of 80% should be assumed due to frictional losses, and so the tabulated figures should be multiplied by 0.8 to give effective thrust.

Cylinder Bore mm	Stroke	Piston area m²	Pressure-bar (kPa)				
			1(100)	2(200)	3(300)	4(400)	5(500)
			Thrust (Newtons)				
32	out	8.04×10^{-4}	80	160	241	321	402
	in	6.9×10^{-4}	69	138	207	276	345
40	out	1.25×10^{-3}	125	250	373	500	625
	in	1.05×10^{-3}	105	210	315	420	525
50	out	1.96×10^{-3}	196	392	588	784	980
	in	1.65×10^{-3}	165	330	495	660	825

Cylinder Bore mm	Stroke	Piston area m²	Pressure-bar (kPa)				
			6(600)	7(700)	8(800)	9(900)	10(1000)
			Thrust (Newtons)				
32	out	8.04×10^{-4}	482	562	643	723	804
	in	6.9×10^{-4}	414	483	552	621	690
40	out	1.25×10^{-3}	750	875	1000	1125	1250
	in	1.05×10^{-3}	630	735	840	945	1050
50	out	1.96×10^{-3}	1176	1372	1568	1764	1960
	in	1.65×10^{-3}	990	1155	1320	1485	1650

Maximum stroke calculations

Recommended maximum stroke lengths with respect to column loading of the piston rod.

These strokes are derived from Euler's formula

$$L = \sqrt{\frac{\pi^2 EI}{F5}}$$

L = Total column length – mm
E = Modulus of elasticity – N/mm²
I = Moment of inertia – mm⁴
F = Load N
5 = Safety factor

This formula has been used to prepare the following table of recommended maximum stroke lengths in mm with respect to bore size and working pressure. Multiply the stroke length given in the table by the appropriate mounting factor indicated below. The restrictions on stroke length apply when the piston rod is subjected to progressive loads.

Example – A 50mm bore cylinder with 6 bar working pressure, when supported with foot mountings and the load guided in both planes, has a maximum stroke of 820 x 4 = 3280mm.

When pivot mounted cylinders are mounted horizontally, side loads due to the weight of the cylinder may be more significant, both on the piston and rod but also on the mounting. This is especially so on the front pivot mounting and also on the rear pivot when the cylinder is fully extended.

Cylinder bore	Working pressure (bar)						
	4	5	6	7	8	9	10
32	570	510	460	430	400	380	360
40	810	720	660	610	570	540	510
50	1010	900	820	760	710	670	640

Mounting style	Mounting factor	Mounting style	Mounting factor
Body and rod pivot mounted at ends	1	Body rigidly supported but rod unguided (no gravitational load)	0.85
Body pivoted at mid-point and rod pivoted	1.3	Body rigidly supported. Rod guided but pivoted	2.3
Body pivoted at front end and rod pivoted	1.2	Body rigidly supported. Rod rigidly guided	4

Electrical sensors

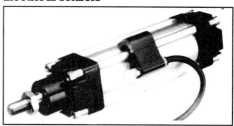

Designed for easy adjustment and simple, reliable fixing these encapsulated electrical reed switches provide electrical sensing and thus replace external limit switches. A unique encapsulated magnetic piston wear ring within the cylinder operates the switch. A choice of switch is offered, with or without LED.

Specification

Temperature range _____ –20°C to +70°C
Protection _____ IP65
Cable entry _____ PG7
Minimum stroke approx.
  fitted with two sensors _____ 10mm

Switching characteristics

Sensor type	Maximum power	Maximum switched voltage	Maximum switched current
Basic reed switch	ac 50VA dc 50W	ac 240V dc 300V	500mA
Reed switch with LED	ac 50VA dc 50W	ac 240V dc 300V	380mA* up to 25°C

*From +25°C to +70°C switched current must be linearly derated to 20mA.

Flying leads are fitted with 2m long PVC covered cable.

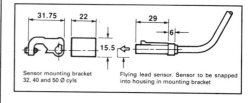

Sensor mounting bracket   Flying lead sensor. Sensor to be snapped
32, 40 and 50 Ø cyls   into housing in mounting bracket

Operation

The illustration below shows typical switching characteristics as the magnetic field passes the sensor.

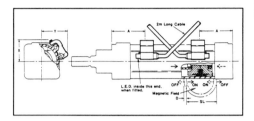

Typical switched distance and differential

Cylinder bore	Switched length SL	Differential D	Dimensions A	X	Y
32	6	2	49	28	34
40	10	2	54.5	31	38
50	12	2	55	36	43

Note. Dimension A is the distance from the end cap face to the centre of the magnetic field in the end of the stroke positions. This is where the centre of the sensor should be positioned for end of stroke sensing.

It can be seen from the illustration below left that if the sensor is not positioned to detect the end of the stroke of the cylinder, only a pulse output will be obtained. The duration of the pulse is dependent upon the speed of the piston. Subject to the condition in the note below, standard solenoid valves (not automatic or pressure differential return) can be directly operated by the sensor up to piston speeds of 0.5 metres/sec. Above this speed it is necessary to use the pulse extender switch, or alternatively a latching relay, electronic circuitry, etc in order to obtain sufficient duration of signal.

Reed switch protection

When reed switches are required to switch power to inductive loads, such as solenoids, relays, and contactors, it is often necessary to protect the reed switch contacts to prevent them welding together.

A metal oxide varistor (MOV) connected across the switch contacts provides one of the best means of protection. This reduces harmful arcing across the contacts by presenting a high resistance to the peak voltages induced at 'switch on'.

Choose an MOV with a voltage rating greater than the nominal voltage being switched (normally only two sizes are required; one for 240V and one for 110V).

When the connecting wires are long, the switches can also be damaged by surge currents caused by the capacitive effect of the wire. These currents arise in dc circuits when charge stored in the wire is allowed to discharge through the switch as the contacts are closed.

The damaging effect of the surge current can be reduced by connecting a suitable resistor in series with and close to the switch. The value of this resistor can be calculated as follows

$$\text{Series resistor } R = \frac{V \text{ (supply voltage)}}{Im} \text{ ohms}$$

where Im is the maximum current rating of the switch.

Resistor wattage $W = (\text{load current})^2 \times R$

An inrush current can also occur at 'switch on' when switching loads in ac circuits, and it is important that this current does not exceed the maximum current rating of the switch. Again the contacts can be partially protected by fitting a series resistor close to the switch.

These solutions will provide simple protection for most applications.

Cylinder bore	M	MM Ø	PJ+ stroke	TG	VD	WH	Y	ZB+ stroke	ZK+ stroke	ZM+ 2×stroke
32	24	12	64	30	18	24	41	122	122	146
40	26	16	71	36	21	28	47	137	137	165
50	31	20	76	45	26	35	52	145	145	180

Cushioned lengths (nominal)

Cylinder bore	32	40	50
Cushion length	19	21	21

Dimensions
The cylinder

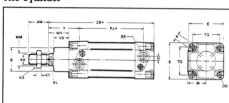

Cylinder bore	AB Ø (H13)	AH	AO	AT	SA + stroke	TR	XA + stroke
32	7	32	6	3	142	32	144
40	9	36	9	3	161	36	163
50	9	45	10	4	170	45	175

Cylinder bore	AM	B Ø	DD thread	depth	E	EE ports thread	depth	H	K α/f	KK	KY	KL a/f	KX a/f
32	22	28.00 / 27.75	M4	6.5	39	G1/8	7	5	7	M10×1.25	5	10	17
40	24	32.00 / 31.75	M5	7.5	47	G1/4	10	5	8	M12×1.25	7	13	19
50	32	38.00 / 37.75	M5	7.5	58	G1/4	10	7	8	M16×1.5	8	17	24
63	32	40.00 / 39.75	M8	12.5	72	G3/8	12	4	13	M16×1.5	8	17	24
80	40	45.00 / 44.75	M8	12.5	89	G3/8	12	12	13	M20×1.5	9	22	32
100	40	50.00 / 49.75	M10	14.0	110	G1/2	15	10	17	M20×1.5	9	22	32

Cylinder bore	M	MM Ø	PJ+ stroke	TG	VD	WH	Y	ZB+ stroke	ZK+ stroke	ZM+ 2 x stroke
32	24	12	64	30	18	24	41	122	122	146
40	26	16	71	36	21	28	47	137	137	165
50	31	20	76	45	26	35	52	145	145	180

Cushioned lengths (Nominal)			
Cylinder bore	32	40	50
Cushion length	19	21	21

Mountings
Flange mounting

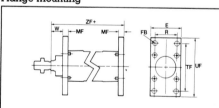

Cylinder bore	E	FB Ø (H13)	MF	R	TF	UF	W	ZF + stroke
32	45	7	8	32	64	76	16	130
40	50	9	8	36	72	86	20	145
50	60	9	10	45	90	110	25	155

Foot mounting

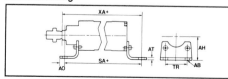

Rear hinge

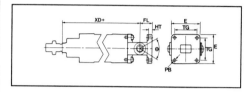

Cylinder bore	E	FL	HT	PB Ø	TG	XD + stroke	Θ
32	38	20	7	4.7	30	142	90°
40	46	23	6	5.7	36	160	90°
50	57	25	7	5.7	45	170	90°

Piston rod clevis

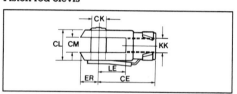

Cylinder bore	CE	CK Ø	CL	CM	ER	KK	LE
32	40	10	20	10.15 / 10.25	12	M10×1.25	20
40	48	12	24	12.15 / 12.26	14	M12×1.25	20
50	64	16	32	16.15 / 16.26	9	M16×1.5	32

Material – steel, zinc plated

Spherical bearing

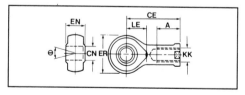

Cylinder bore	A min	CE	CNØ (H9)	EN (h12)	ER Ø	KK	LE	α°
32	20	43	10	14	28	M10×1.25	13	6
40	22	50	12	16	32	M12×1.25	15	13
50	28	64	16	21	42	M16×1.5	30	30

Material – steel, zinc plated. Bearing has an integral PTFE lining which requires no lubrication

RS/SMC solenoid and pilot valves

M5 and 1/8 in BSPT valves (SMC VZ Series)

A range of high quality pilot solenoid and pilot valves. The valves are suitable for use in areas where space is a limitation yet flow cannot be sacrificed. High flow rates are achieved by utilising a bonded spool design.

The range offered comes in M5 and 1/8 in BSPT body ported 3/2 and 5/2 solenoid and pilot

versions with integral solenoid coils of 24Vdc, 110Vac and 240Vac.

(**Note**: Valves are supplied with solenoid coils fitted, these are **not** removable.)

Five way manifolds are also available for banking a series of valves from one common air supply, and exhaust.

Technical specification

Fluid _____ Compressed air, lubricated,
non-lubricated or dry
Operating range
   internal pilot type_____ 1.5~7 bar
Flow rates
   3/2 M5 ported version _____ C_v* 0.2
   5/2 M5 ported version _____ C_v* 0.2
   3/2 1/8 in ported version _____ C_v* 0.5
   5/2 1/8 in ported version _____ C_v* 0.6
Ambient and fluid temperature _____ Max 50°C
Response time _____ 20ms or less
Max. operating
   frequency _____ 3 port 10Hz, 5 port 5Hz
Manual override _ Non-locking push-button type
Lubrication _____ Not required, (but if used
use turbine oil #1)
(ISO VG32 if lubrication is provided)
Mounting position _____ Free
Impact/Vibration
   resistance _____ 30G/5G (8.3~2000Hz)
Enclosure _____ Dust proof
Port sizes _____ M5 × 0.8 1/8 in BSP taper

*Note: C_v – The C_v rating of a valve is a flow coefficient which expresses the flow of water through the valve in US gallons per minute, for a 1psi pressure drop.

Solenoid specifications

Electrical entry _____ Shrouded, plug connector
lead with 3m of cable
Voltages ac _____ 110 $^{50}/_{60}$HZ, 240V$^{50}/_{60}$HZ
   dc _____ 24V
Allowable voltage _ −15~ +10% of rated voltage
Coil insulation _____ Class E or equivalent
Temperature rise _____ 45°C or less
Power consumption dc _____ 2.1W
Apparent power ac
   inrush _____ 4.5VA/50Hz, 4.2VA/60Hz
   holding _____ 3.5VA/50Hz, 3VA/60Hz
Surge voltage suppressor ____ dc diode, ac zener
Indicator light _____ dc LED (red), ac neon lamp

Material specification

Description	Material
Body	Aluminium die cast
Piston plate	Polyacetal
End cover	Zinc die cast/Polyacetal
Piston	Polyacetal
Spool assembly	Aluminium NBR

Pilot valves

Operating pilot pressure range

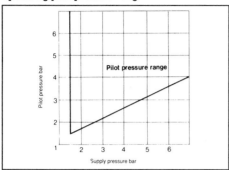

Valve selection

Function symbol V^S RS stock number

The symbols used below are to the manufacturers standards but approximate to the recommended symbols described in BS2917.

SMC part number	RS stock number
VZA312-M5	723-343
VZA512-01	723-797
VZA3120-M5	723-365
VZA5120-01	723-810
VZA3220-M5	723-359
VZA5220-01	723-832
VZ312-5MNZ-M5	723-028
VZ312-3MNZ-M5	723-034
VZ312-7MNZ-M5	723-040
VZ512-5MNZ-01	723-589
VZ512-3MNZ-01	723-595
VZ512-7MNZ-01	723-602
VZ3120-5MNZ-M5	723-084
VZ3120-3MNZ-M5	723-090
VZ3120-7MNZ-M5	723-107
VZ5120-5MNZ-01	723-618
VZ5120-3MNZ-01	723-624
VZ5120-7MNZ-01	723-630
VZ3220-5MNZ-M5	723-056
VZ3220-3MNZ-M5	723-062
VZ3220-7MNZ-M5	723-078
VZ5220-5MNZ-01	723-646
VZ5220-3MNZ-01	723-652
VZ5220-7MNZ-01	723-668

SYMBOL (Letters refer to ports marked on valves)	PORT SIZE	TYPE		RS STOCK NO
A / P R	M5	3·2 PILOT SPRING		723-343
	1/8"	3·2 PILOT SPRING		723-797
A B / R1 P R2	M5	5·2 PILOT SPRING		723-365
	1/8"	5·2 PILOT SPRING		723-810
A B / R1 P R2	M5	5·2 PILOT/PILOT		723-359
	1/8"	5·2 PILOT/PILOT		723-832
A / P R	M5	3·2 SOLENOID SPRING	24Vd.c	723-028
			110Va.c	723-034
			220Va.c	723-040
	1/8"	3·2 SOLENOID SPRING	24Vd.c	723-589
			110Va.c	723-595
			220Va.c	723-602
A B / R1 P R2	M5	5·2 SOLENOID SPRING	24Vd.c	723-084
			110Va.c	723-090
			220Va.c	723-107
	1/8"	5·2 SOLENOID SPRING	24Vd.c	723-618
			110Va.c	723-624
			220Va.c	723-630
A B / R1 P R2	M5	5·2 SOLENOID/SOLENOID	24Vd.c	723-056
			110Va.c	723-062
			220Va.c	723-078
	1/8"	5·2 SOLENOID/SOLENOID	24Vd.c	723-646
				723-652
				723-668

Dimensions (mm)

3/2 Pilot/Spring   723-343

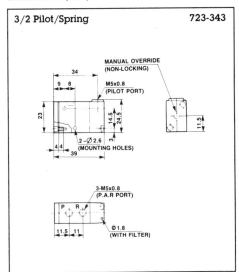

5/2 Pilot/Spring   723-365

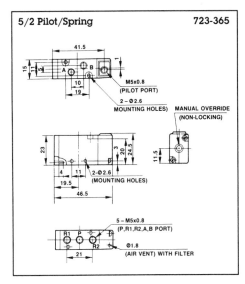

3/2 Pilot/Spring   723-797

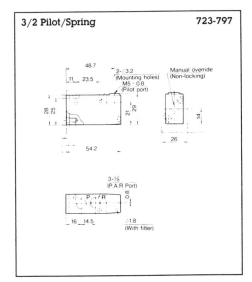

5/2 Pilot/Spring   723-810

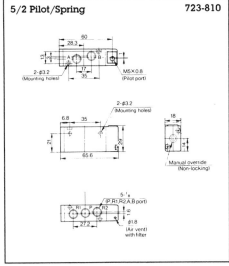

Dimensions (mm) cont.

5/2 Pilot/Pilot	723-359

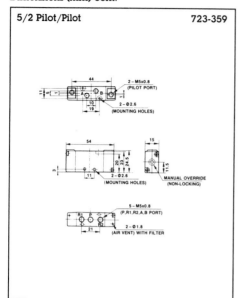

3/2 Solenoid/Spring	24Vdc 723-028
	110Vac 723-034
	240Vac 723-040

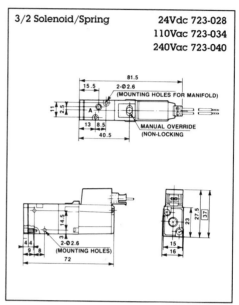

5/2 Pilot/Pilot	723-832

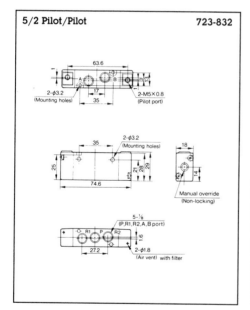

3/2 Solenoid/Spring	24Vdc 723-589
	110Vac 723-595
	240Vac 723-602

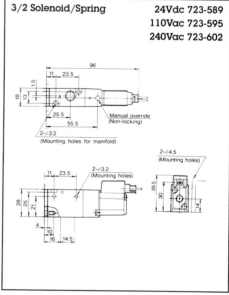

N.B. Electrical connector and leads supplied by RS, differ slightly from manufacturers shown. Leads supplied by RS have an extra outer insulation and protective shroud over the connector.

Dimensions (mm) cont.

5/2 Solenoid/Spring	24Vdc 723-084
	110Vac 723-090
	240Vac 723-107

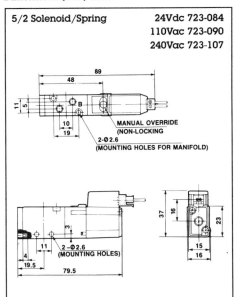

5/2 Solenoid/Solenoid	24Vdc 723-056
	110Vac 723-062
	220Vac 723-078

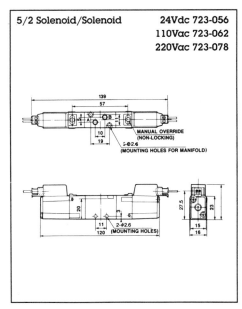

5/2 Solenoid/Spring	24Vdc 723-618
	110Vac 723-624
	240Vac 723-630

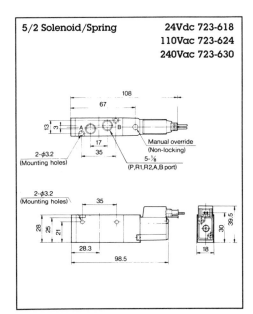

5/2 Solenoid/Solenoid	24Vdc 723-646
	110Vac 723-652
	240Vac 723-668

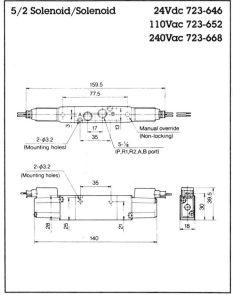

N.B. Electrical connector and leads supplied by RS, differ slightly from manufacturers shown. Leads supplied by RS have an extra outer insulation and protective shroud over the connector.

Manifolds

M5 3 port RS stock no. 723-113 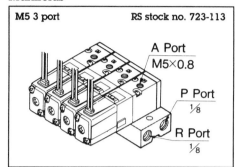 A Port M5×0.8, P Port 1/8, R Port 1/8	**M5 5 port** RS stock no. 723-129 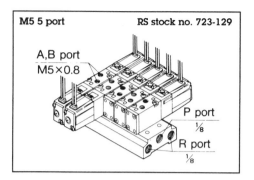 A,B port M5×0.8, P port 1/8, R port 1/8
1/8 in 3 port RS stock no. 723-854 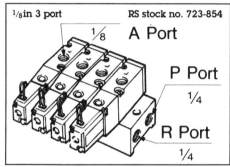 1/8 A Port, P Port 1/4, R Port 1/4	**1/8 in 5 port** RS stock no. 723-876 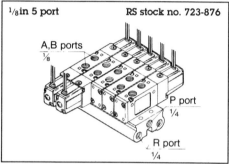 A,B ports 1/8, P port 1/4, R port 1/4

All valves shown are grommet entry and not as supplied by RS – *ie*: MNZ connector type.

1/4in 5 ported solenoid and pilot valves

A range of compact lightweight pilot solenoid and pilot power valves. Large flow capacities (C_v 0.95) are achieved by the elastomer bonded spool design of these valves.

The valves are designed to ensure low power consumption (solenoids rated at 2W have an LED indicator to show operation and have a surge voltage suppression circuit as standard.

Five-way manifolds are available for mounting a series of valves from one common air supply.

Electrical entry to the solenoid coils is made through standard DIN43650 connectors supplied on the valve.

Specifications

Fluid _____ Air
Operating pressure range
   2 position solenoid/spring _____ 1.5~9 bar
   2 position solenoid/solenoid _____ 1~9 bar
Ambient and fluid temperature _____ Max 50°C
Response time _____ 30ms or less (at 5 bar)
Max. operating cycle
   2 position single/double _____ 5Hz
Lubrication _____ Not required, will operate
            on lubricated, non-lubricated or dry air
Manual override _____ Non-locking push type
Mounting orientation _____ Free
Impact/Vibration
   resistance _____ 30G/5G (8.3~2000Hz)
Enclosure _____ Dust proof
Pilot exhaust _____ Individual

Solenoid specifications

Electrical entry _____ DIN 43650 connector
Voltages ac _____ 110, 240V $^{50}/_{60}$Hz
       dc _____ 24V
Voltage allowance _ −15~ +10% of rated voltage
Insulation _____ Class B or equivalent
Power consumption
   ac inrush _____ 5.6VA (50Hz), 5.0VA (60Hz)
     holding _____ 3.4VA (50Hz), 2.3VA (60Hz)
   dc _____ 2W (with LED)
Indicator light. Surge voltage suppressor circuit
   ac _____ Zener
   dc _____ Diode

		SMC part number	RS stock number
5/2 Solenoid/Spring	24Vdc	VF3130-5DZ-02	723-703
	110Vac	VF3130-3DZ-02	723-719
	240Vac	VF3130-7DZ-02	723-725

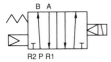

5/2 Solenoid/Solenoid	24Vdc	VF3230-5DZ-02	723-731
	110Vac	VF3230-3DZ-02	723-747
	240Vac	VF3230-7DZ-02	723-753

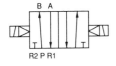

5/2 Pilot/Spring	VFA3130-02	723-826

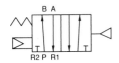

5/2 Pilot/Pilot	VFA3230-02	723-848

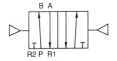

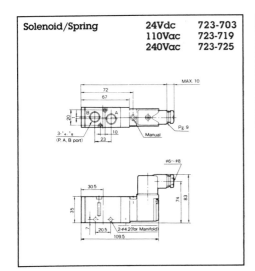

Solenoid/Spring	24Vdc	723-703
	110Vac	723-719
	240Vac	723-725

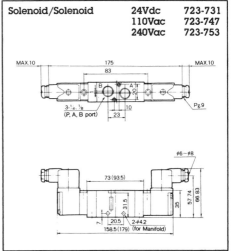

Solenoid/Solenoid	24Vdc	723-731
	110Vac	723-747
	240Vac	723-753

Pilot/Spring   **723-826**

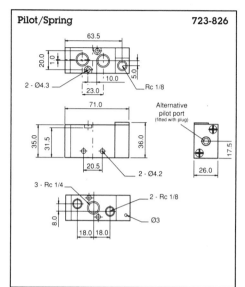

5/2 Pilot/Pilot   **723-848**

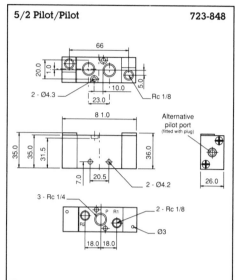

Manifold   **723-898**

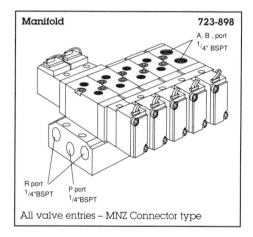

A, B , port
$^1/_4$" BSPT

R port
$^1/_4$"BSPT

P port
$^1/_4$"BSPT

All valve entries – MNZ Connector type

N.B. All valves shown are grommet entry and
not as supplied by RS – *ie*: MNZ connector type.

3 port ¹/₄in direct operated solenoid and pilot valves

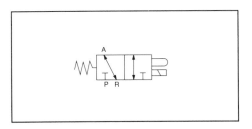

A range of direct operated 3 part balanced solenoid and pilot operated valves.

Features

- ¹/₄in BSP taper ports
- DIN43650 electrical connection
- Push-button manual override
- 24Vdc, 110Vac, 240Vac solenoid options
- Surge voltage protection
- Suitable for low pressure switching (0-9 bar)
- Coils may be oriented at any angle
- Selective porting providing six different valve functions.

Specifications

Fluid _____ Air, inert gas
Operating pressure range _____ 0~9kgf/cm²
Pilot pressure range on
   pilot/spring valve _____ 1-9 bar
Ambient and fluid temperature _____ Max 50°C
Response time _____ 30ms
Max. operating frequency _____ 10Hz
Lubrication _____ Not required
Manual override _____ Non-locking push type
   _____ Non on pilot/spring valve
Mounting orientation _____ Free
Impact/Vibration
   resistance_____ 15G/5G (40-1000Hz)
Enclosure _____ Dust proof
Effective orifice mm² (C_V factor) _____
   Sol/Spring valve _____ 12.6(0.7)
   Pilot/Spring valve _____ 7.2(0.4)
Weight of sol/spring valve _____0.3kg
Weight of pilot/spring valve _____ 0.18kg
Electrical entry _____ DIN terminal
Voltages
   ac (50/60Hz) _____ 110, 240
   dc _____ 24
Voltage allowance −15%~+10% of rated voltage
Insulation _____ Class B or equivalent (130°C)
Temperature rise _____ Max 45°C
   (when rated voltage is applied)
Apparent power ac
   Inrush _____ 19VA (50Hz), 16VA (60Hz)
   Holding _____ 11VA (50Hz), 7VA (60Hz)
Power consumption dc _____ 6W
Lamp/surge voltage protection circuit
   ac _____ Zener (Varister) neon lamp
   dc _____ Zener (Varister), LED

Material specification

Description	Material	Notes
Body	Aluminium die-cast	Metallic paint
Spool valve	Aluminium NBR	
Return spring	Stainless steel	
Moulded coil	Epoxy resin	

VALVE FUNCTION	3-WAY NORMALLY CLOSED	3-WAY NORMALLY OPEN	2-WAY NORMALLY CLOSED
DE-ENERGIZED			
ENERGIZED			

VALVE FUNCTION	2-WAY NORMALLY OPEN	SELECTOR	DIVERTER
DE-ENERGIZED			
ENERGIZED			

Dimensions (mm)

3 port solenoid/spring   24Vdc   723-674
110Vac   723-680
240Vac   723-696

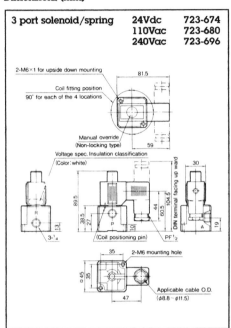

3 port pilot/spring   723-804

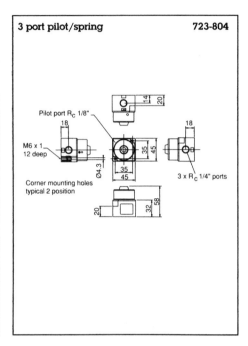

INDEX